PERSPECTIVES ON HUMANITY IN THE FINE ARTS

FIRST EDITION

by **Gary Towne**

cognella | ACADEMIC PUBLISHING

Bassim Hamadeh, CEO and Publisher
Kassie Graves, Director of Acquisitions and Sales
Jamie Giganti, Senior Managing Editor
Jess Estrella, Senior Graphic Designer
John Remington, Senior Field Acquisitions Editor
Monika Dziamka, Project Editor
Brian Fahey, Licensing Associate
Tracy Buyan, Associate Production Editor
Kat Ragudos, Interior Designer

Cover images:

Léon Bakst / Copyright in the Public Domain.
Aelbert Cuyp / Copyright in the Public Domain.
Copyright © 2012 by Michael Kranewitter, (CC BY-SA 3.0) at https://commons.wikimedia.org/wiki/File:Dresden_
    1042012_27_Frauenkirche.jpg.
Karl Friedrich Schinkel / Copyright in the Public Domain.
Copyright © 2015 by Petar Milošević, (CC BY-SA 4.0) at https://commons.wikimedia.org/wiki/File:Mosaic_of_
    Justinianus_I_-_Basilica_San_Vitale_(Ravenna).jpg.
John Singer Sargent / Copyright in the Public Domain.
Henri Rousseau / Copyright in the Public Domain.
Copyright © 2014 by LivioAndronico / Wikimedia Commons, (CC BY-SA 4.0) at https://commons.wikimedia.org/
    wiki/File:Laocoon_and_His_Sons_black.jpg.
Copyright © 2008 by Alexander Kenney / Kungliga Operan, (CC BY 3.0) at https://commons.wikimedia.org/wiki/
    File:Swan_Lake_prodution_2008_at_the_Royal_Swedish_Opera.jpg.
Copyright © 2004 by David Monniaux, (CC BY-SA 3.0) at https://commons.wikimedia.org/wiki/File:Delphi_temple_
    of_Apollo_dsc06283.jpg.

Interior image: US Public Domain

Printed in the United States of America

ISBN: 978-1-5165-1109-9 (pbk) / 978-1-5165-1110-5 (br)

cognella® | ACADEMIC PUBLISHING

CONTENTS

PREFACE

This book introduces the Fine Arts as expressions and reflections of the human condition—living conditions, religion, philosophy, aspirations and failures, politics, love, and war. The Literary Arts offer similar yet more concrete expressions, but they are mentioned in this book only as they relate to specific works of Fine Arts. Compared to literature, the Fine Arts (Visual Art, Music, Dramatic Art, and Dance) communicate something less tangible—the feelings, the psyche, the soul, the atmosphere of being human.

The human condition has changed dramatically over different periods and places. The book describes specific historical periods and geographical areas, then presents their arts, including several art forms for each, with performing arts where possible. This approach links the arts with the human situation they express more clearly than the traditional scattershot approach, but it may exclude certain examples that are traditionally part of such a course. The most important of these appear in the five introductory chapters, which include overviews followed by the structural elements of each art form.

The arts' elements underlie all later discussions. They include the basic technical concepts needed to understand the art form. In particular, the chapter on the musical elements avoids musical notation by using a simplified graphic notation. Examples like these are only graphic representations. The performing arts can never be completely represented by images alone. Their examples should be presented with appropriate audio and video recordings; the examples shared here are widely available.

Descriptions of the examples are thorough. These are more complete than most students can expect to learn, for two reasons: to demonstrate how to describe an artwork, and to encourage deeper investigation of a work. There are also a few more examples than can be easily included in a one-semester course, to allow for selection by instructors. Some figures—maps, diagrams, and the like—are included to illustrate concepts, not for memorization as artworks themselves. This leads to some final advice for the student: become familiar with each artwork by looking, listening, or watching. Let the historical background reinforce what you see and hear, as each artwork brings its historical context to life. Above all, enjoy the art and all it says about us as human beings.

DEDICATION

For my sons, Jonathan Spaulding Towne and Andrew Armstrong Towne, whose criticism, encouragement, and support have made this book possible.

Ecce quam bonum et quam jucundum habitare fratres in unum!
—Psalm 132: Vulgate

ACKNOWLEDGMENTS

My thanks to all those at Cognella who have helped (with supreme patience) to bring forth this work over a much longer period than originally envisioned: Monika Dziamka, Jamie Giganti, and Beth Riley, most excellent editors; and John Remington, who brought me to Cognella. Thanks also to Arek Arechiga, Danielle Menard, and Jennifer Levine, as well as to Jess Estrella, Chelsey Schmid, Rachel Singer, Tracy Buyan, and Dani Skeen for their careful attention to production and marketing. I must also acknowledge my colleagues at the University of North Dakota: Arthur Jones and Dorothy Keyser, for their feedback and suggestions, and Michael Wittgraf and Katherine Norman Dearden for their encouragement.

CHAPTER 1

INTRODUCTION

This book is about the arts. The arts have been a fundamental part of virtually every culture known to man. Every aboriginal culture, every historical culture, and most prehistoric cultures we know of have produced and enjoyed some sort of art. Food, clothing, and shelter are basic materials that human beings need to survive, but they are not humans' only needs. The universal presence of the arts in all human societies makes it clear that the arts nourish something that makes us human, that raises us above other beings. Some might name this the soul. Others might speak of psychological or spiritual needs. But humans seem always to create forms of art. The arts express a need for humans to alter—often to decorate—their environment or to reflect the situations of the human condition in a way that deepens understanding of them. Food, clothing, and shelter make life possible. The arts make life worth living.

What Is Art—and What Are the Arts?

Art in the grand sense is **a designed expression of attitudes as adornment of space, time, or language**. This definition is deceptively simple but nevertheless clear. Almost every word has significance. Art is **a** designed expression—not just one, but one of many different forms of artistic expression. **Designed** means that art is a product of human endeavor. If I drive a few hundred miles west of my North Dakota home, eventually I begin to see the northern Rocky Mountains rising out of the plain. This magnificent view always inspires me, but *it is not art*. The view is a natural phenomenon that exists without human intervention. However, if I take a photograph or paint a picture of it, the product of my efforts is art, because I have in some way designed or interpreted the view that I experienced.

Art is **expression**. It is impossible for a human to interact with his or her environment to produce something without having that product express something of that person's being, personality, or situation. A portrait of someone captures more than just an image. The pose and expression disclose the depth of that person as a whole being. And the externals in the picture—clothing, objects, background—reveal the person's financial, social, and even geographical situation. All art expresses something of this, however slightly.

What ultimately is expressed by art? **Attitudes**. Attitudes represent a person's responses—whether rational, emotional, psychological, or spiritual—to the environment or events. The expression a person designs automatically reflects or incorporates that person's attitudes. Arthur Miller's play *The Crucible* told the story of the Salem Witch Trials for more than historical reasons. He wrote it to denounce the paranoid Red Scare led by Senator Joseph McCarthy in the 1950s. The play expressed Miller's revulsion toward this persecution. Such attitudes can be shaped by many influences: physical surroundings, cultural conventions, political views, religion, or spirituality, to name but a few.

Adornment is a critical component of art. Art can adorn anything in the environment: flat surfaces, space, even time or the very air. Some artists, especially recent ones, would argue that adornment is an unnecessary or even negative attribute of art. This begs the question of why people produce art, collect art, patronize art, or support art in general. Even art that expresses profoundly negative ideas can adorn the life of a person, a group, or a society sympathetic to those expressions. Others might argue that the decorative function of space through the visual arts is clear, but what about music? Music adorns the very air we breathe; it uses the air as a medium for creating art using sound. It merely affects or adorns a different sense than visual art. Other art forms, like drama and dance, offer a combination of visual and auditory media through, and thus adorning, even time itself.

This brings us to the basic materials of art: **space**, **time**, and **language**. The **space arts** are those that use space in their expression. These are also sometimes known as the plastic arts or visual arts.[1] The artist manipulates space: two-dimensional in drawings or paintings, three-dimensional in sculpture, and three-dimensional in architecture and other environmental art. Space is the fundamental substance of this art; without the manipulation of space, it cannot exist.

---

1   Plastic here means art made by shaping something, not a polymer substance.

Time arts are those that, in a similar way, require time to exist. A time art must be experienced over time. The time arts are the performing arts: music, dramatic art, and dance. While in theory one can appreciate a painting or other work of space art in a momentary glance, a musical work or a play requires time for the art form and its structure to exist. Listening to one second of a musical work or watching one second of a play or ballet reveals little or nothing about the work as a whole.

The final class of art is the **language arts**. This includes both written and spoken forms: prose, poetry, plays (as written, without acting), rhetoric (speeches), and many other forms. This book may deal with an occasional work of language art if it is relevant to one of the other artworks under discussion, but since artistic expression through language is covered in so many other disciplines, we will concentrate here on visual and performing arts.

This is also the place to discuss several other terms that are often used about art that may be confusing. The term "fine art" has an old-fashioned meaning as well as a contemporary one. Up through the early twentieth century, some arts, particularly drawing, painting, and sculpture, were regarded as superior to art that was functional, like furniture, textiles, or tableware. The "superior" art forms were collectively referred to as the "fine arts" and the others as "decorative arts." The performing arts were thought of as yet another category. As the twentieth century progressed, this discrimination disappeared and the definition of art broadened. First, many designers in a wide variety of fields—from ceramics to fashion to designers of home furnishings—were recognized as artists. Then Pop Art enshrined commercial design, and performance artists devised performances that involved arts and media in revolutionary combinations. Today, if we use the term "fine art," we use it to include any manifestation of the visual and performing arts. Language (literary) arts are a separate category.

I.   The Artwork Itself—Description
II. Background
   A. Why was the work created?
   B. Who or what is depicted, if anything?
   C. What is the work's purpose?
III. Cultural Environment
   A. Location, Geography, Physical Climate
   B. Social Structures
   C. Power Structure & Politics
   D. Economic Structure & Wealth
   E. Religion or Spirituality
   F. Intellectual Climate, Ideals & Aesthetic Goals
   G. Occasions or Needs
IV. Historical Influence and/or Influence of Other Cultures

FIGURE 1.1 Understanding a Work of Art.

Understanding a Work of Art and Artistic Style

Figure 1.1 lists the things to consider for understanding a work of art. Details and examples follow.

I. The single most important factor in understanding a work of art is the work itself. This means going beyond superficial or inattentive observation or listening. The first step in understanding a work is careful description—consciously expressing the details of an artwork in thought, speech, or writing. While it is not necessary that this be written, concentrating on describing the artwork consciously will ensure that you notice subtle details that might otherwise be missed. Noticing these details will enhance your personal response to the work, and it can be positive or negative—as long as it arises from a detailed understanding. In this book, I try to give reasonably detailed expressions of nearly all the artworks presented, not only for your understanding (and mine!) but also as examples of how to approach such description.

II. Once the artwork is well described, other factors contribute depth to its understanding. The second factor to be considered for understanding an artwork is background—why was the work created, what or whom does it depict, and what was its purpose? Many factors can stimulate the creation of an artwork. An artist may be inspired just by his/her own imagination. This is often true in the performing arts: composers, playwrights, and choreographers often—even perhaps usually—bring a concept to completion and then present it to an audience. On the other hand, a work may be commissioned; this is usually true of portrait paintings. And a work may be designed with a market in mind—often true of musical collections, especially of solo works or chamber music. Depiction can play a role—obvious in a portrait or history painting, but not restricted to visual art. Composers have written musical portraits. Operas, ballets, and plays can all depict particular persons or the situations surrounding them. Any of these factors can arise as the purpose behind a work of art, and some can be more specific: a musical work to commemorate an important event—birth, death, marriage, victory; a play as a political protest; a ballet reinterpreting the art itself. These factors and more can furnish the purpose behind an artwork.

FIGURE 1.2 Aelbert Cuyp (1620–1691), *The Maas at Dordrecht*, c. 1650, oil on canvas, 115 × 170 cm, National Gallery of Art, Washington, DC.

III. The third factor for thoroughly understanding the artwork is its particular cultural environment, which has several components. For clarity and ease of understanding, examples of these here include only works of visual art, since most people find them the most immediately approachable of art forms. The same environmental factors do, of course, apply to any art.

Components of Cultural Environment

A. Location, Physical Climate, and Geography
B. Social Structures

Compare Figures 1.2 and 1.3. The seascape and flat terrain of seventeenth-century Holland in

FIGURE 1.3 Albert Bierstadt (1830–1902), *The Rocky Mountains, Lander's Peak*, 1863, oil on canvas, 87 × 307 cm, Metropolitan Museum of Art, New York.

FIGURE 1.4 Anonymous, *Augustus of Primaporta*, c. 20 BCE–37 CE, marble, perhaps copy of bronze original, 2.03 m, Vatican Museums, Rome.

FIGURE 1.5 Honoré Daumier, *The Third-Class Carriage*, 1862–64, oil on canvas, 65 × 90 cm, Metropolitan Museum of Art, New York.

Cuyp's painting (Figure 1.2) are very different from the rugged mountain valley of Bierstadt (Figure 1.3). These two paintings also reflect very different societies—Dutch merchants boarding a ship versus a camp of Native Americans. The contrast between these two works provides a dramatic example of how location, climate, geography, and social structures affect the content of the image created.

C. Power Structure and Politics
D. Economic Structure and Wealth

Compare Figures 1.4 and 1.5. Augustus was the first Roman emperor, the peak of Roman society. The statue depicts him in all his autocratic, military, and imperial glory, with symbols of his divine descent and power. The statue's very existence (among many others) and Augustus's ornate armor demonstrate his wealth within the economy of the time. Daumier's purpose, on the other hand, was to expose in his painting the gritty reality of life for the lower classes, lacking political power in the social structure of the time and ground into the poverty of the Industrial Revolution, as the painting shows them ground together in the lowest-class train seats.

E. Religion or Spirituality
F. Intellectual Climate, Ideals, and Aesthetic Goals

FIGURE 1.6 Anonymous, *Venus of Willendorf*, c. 28,000–25,000 BCE, oolitic limestone, 10.8 cm, Naturhistorisches Museum, Vienna. The finest example of this type of paleolithic statuette.

Compare Figures 1.6 and 1.7. Figure 1.6, the naked prehistoric statuette with its exaggerated breasts, hips, and vulva, along with its faceless anonymity, is of a type found throughout Europe. Although there is debate, a traditional interpretation is that these statuettes represent

FIGURE 1.7 Raphael (Raffaello Sanzio, 1483–1520), *Sistine Madonna,* 1513–1514, oil on canvas, 265 × 196 cm, Gemäldegalerie Alter Meister, Dresden. One of Raphael's last Madonnas, accompanied by Pope Sixtus IV and Saint Barbara. The Pope's face is probably that of his nephew, Pope Julius II.

a fertility symbol or mother goddess, or possibly an idealized female figure. Raphael's *Madonna* (Figure 1.7), on the other hand, presents a very different feminine and religious ideal: fully clothed, a kind but serious face, striding forward to bring the Christ child to the world and, paradoxically, virgin motherhood. The two works express dramatically different concepts of religion through equally different aesthetic ideals.

G. Occasions or Needs

Figure 1.8 shows a powerful response to important occasions and strong needs. Pablo Picasso was commissioned in January 1937 to do a painting for the Spanish Republic at the Paris Exposition of that year. After the government engaged the Nazi *Luftwaffe* to practice firebombing on the restive village of Guernica in April, Picasso abandoned his previous plan and produced this monument to the destruction and horror of war. After the exhibit, it toured the world and was then housed for safekeeping at the Museum of Modern Art in

FIGURE 1.8 Pablo Picasso (1881–1973), *Guernica*, 1937, oil on canvas, 349 × 777 cm, Museo Reina Sofia, Madrid. Picasso's monument to the horror of war and the evil of Franco's Spanish Republic.

FIGURE 1.9 Anonymous, *The Three Graces*, Roman copy of Hellenistic original, marble, Cathedral Library, Siena, Italy.

FIGURE 1.10 Raphael (1483–1520), *The Three Graces*, 1504–1505, oil on panel, 17 × 17 cm, Musée Condé, Chantilly, France.

New York until the restoration of the monarchy in Spain, where it finally arrived in 1981. This work illustrates political violence and abuse of power. Although it was commissioned for a specific occasion (the Paris Exposition), Picasso used that occasion to denounce the other occasion of the bombing and dramatically expose the brutal slaughter of the Spanish people and their need for a just and humane government.

IV.   The fourth factor is historical influence. Any artist will be influenced, positively or negatively, by earlier works (s)he is acquainted with. The ancient statue of the Three Graces found in Rome in 1460 (Figure 1.9) is believed to have been the model Raphael used for his painting of 1504–5 (Figure 1.10), but the subject was quite popular in Classical times, as the fresco from Pompeii shows (Figure 1.11, perhaps contemporary with the statue but unearthed well after Raphael's time). These three closely related images demonstrate historical influence over 1500 years.

FIGURE 1.11 Anonymous, *The Three Graces*, 1st century BCE–1st century CE, fresco from Pompeii, Museo Archeologico Nazionale, Naples, Italy.

And finally, the artist may also be influenced by the works of other cultures. Figure 1.12 shows a room decorated by James A. M. Whistler in an Oriental style, which was a fashion of his time, as Europeans and Americans began to have more direct contact with Asia. The power of the influence is evident in the room's history. Whistler was only asked to finish the room according to another artist's design. Given the authority to make a few minor changes, the impetuous Whistler, in the grip of overwhelming inspiration, completely revised the room's décor to its present appearance.

All of these factors contribute to the character of the artwork—its style.

Artistic style is a set of artistic features common to a particular period, place, or individual.

The definition above is the most compact statement of what artistic style is. Another way of looking at this is that

FIGURE 1.12 James A. M. Whistler (1834–1903), The Peacock Room, north end (1876–7), 4.22 m (height) × 6.13 × 10.26 m. Freer Gallery of Art, Washington, DC.

artworks from different places within the same time period will share some similar features. The same thing is true of works from the same place. And finally, each individual artist has his own personal touch or style, which makes his/her work different from any other artist's. Since later chapters explore artistic style in depth, I will rest content with this brief explanation and save specific examples for those.

Artistic style is related to the place and time from which it is viewed. Our American culture originates from and remains heavily influenced by the cultures of European nations, which share many common stylistic features and traditions that are different from those in the

I. Western—Culture and arts of Western Europe and places with the same cultural and artistic tradition
  A. Europe
  B. European descendant cultures, especially in the New World—the Americas, as well as Australia and New Zealand
II. Non-Western—Indigenous cultures and arts in the rest of the world
  A. Asia, Africa, Oceania
  B. Folk or Indigenous Art/Culture in Europe, the Americas, Australia and New Zealand
III. Why study the history of Western arts and culture?
  A. This is the tradition in which we live.
  B. The depth of the Western historical tradition and good documentation of it allows study of many styles and their development.
  C. Western culture has had a greater preoccupation with the written historical record than most other cultures.
    1. This makes it easier to trace the growth and development of cultures in all aspects, including the arts.
    2. It has led and continues to lead over time to more rapid change in artistic styles and greater variety of styles.
  D. In recent times, improved communication from growth of population and technology has led to increased interchange among artists (as well as everyone else). Other cultures have acquired additional relevance relating to their contact with the Western tradition in addition to their own special traits.

FIGURE 1.13 The Geography of Art & Culture.

rest of the world. Because of its Western European origins, this tradition is known as Western Art. Figure 1.13 explains the relationship of Western to non-Western Art.

Western versus Non-Western Art

As the figure demonstrates, art from non-European cultures is non-Western art. For the reasons above as well as the limited time available, non-Western art will occupy little of our attention. But one final feature of Western culture will be significant in our presentation—history. Western culture has one of the strongest historical traditions in the world, which permits us to study a greater chronological depth with precision than is possible in many other cultures. That approach will be the main focus of this book.

Getting Down to the Details—the Elements of Various Arts

The first step toward understanding a work of art is attentive observation or listening to it so that you can begin to describe it. The tools for description are the *artistic elements*. Each type of art has characteristic elements. These are components of that particular type of art, and they are universal—they can describe any artwork of that type of art, from any time or place. The metaphor of building blocks could be used to describe them, but not in the ordinary pattern of a simple single brick wall, in which there is one layer of bricks all lying in the same direction (Figure 1.14). The elements of an art form are more like the pieces of a wall in what is known as quetta bond (Figure 1.15). This is a double-thickness brick wall in which some bricks run the length of the wall (stretchers), others head into the depth of the wall (headers), and in the cavity between the two walls there are steel reinforcing bars and concrete fill. In the art form, as in the wall, some elements contribute a small localized effect (like the bricks), while others embrace long spans (like the reinforcing bars), and others glue the whole together (like the concrete fill). The elements are of many types, and they interact in many different ways.

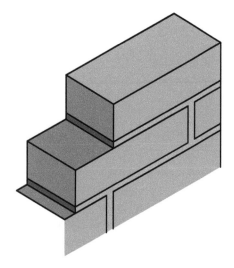

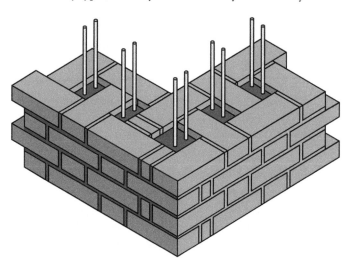

FIGURE 1.14 Single-brick wall.

FIGURE 1.15 Quetta bond.

The next four chapters will cover the essential elements of the various fine arts: visual art, music, dramatic art, and dance. The oldest art in existence is visual art. Music comes next, followed by dramatic art. Dance comes last, not because it wasn't an art in ancient times, but because no one thought to write down the steps until the fifteenth century. The remaining chapters use the artistic elements and the other tools discussed above to survey the rich tradition of Western art in the order in which they developed. Figure 1.16 gives a brief outline of the history of Western art, to be discussed in detail in those later chapters.

The necessary equipment for the study of these styles is found in the artistic elements. First, the elements of visual art.

I. Prehistoric—Varies according to when written history began in a particular place
II. Antiquity (Ancient)—The period before the Middle Ages
    A. Pre-Classical Antiquity—Before Classical Greece and Rome; includes Egypt, Ancient Near East, etc.—3500–500 BCE
    B. Classical Antiquity—Greece and Rome—500 BCE–476 CE (in Western Europe)
III. Within Classical Antiquity
    A. Classic Greece—From just before the Persian War until after Alexander the Great's conquests—500–325 BCE
    B. Hellenistic Greece—From the breakup of Alexander's empire to the conquest of Egypt by Rome—325–30 BCE
    C. Republican Rome—753 (noticeable around 500)–27 BCE
    D. Roman Empire—27 BCE–476 (500) CE
IV. Medieval (Medi = in the midst of; Aeva = ages; Medieval = of the Middle Ages)
    A. Byzantine—300–1450 CE
    B. Romanesque Period—500–1100 CE
    C. Gothic Period—1100–1400 CE
V. Renaissance (= Rebirth)—1400–1600 CE
VI. Baroque—1600–1750 CE
VII. Rococo—1725–1800 CE
VIII. Neoclassic—1750–1825 CE
IX. (Long) Nineteenth Century (Several Styles)—1789–1914 CE
    A. Romantic Style
    B. Nationalistic Style
    C. Realistic Style
    D. Impressionistic Style
    E. Postimpressionistic Style
X. 20th Century–Present—1900–Present
    A. Many Individual Styles
    B. Modernism
    C. Postmodernism

FIGURE 1.16 Periods of Western History as Related to Artistic Styles.

Image Credits

Fig. 1.2: Aelbert Cuyp / Copyright in the Public Domain.

Fig. 1.3: Albert Bierstadt / Copyright in the Public Domain.

Fig. 1.4: Photo copyright © 2007 by Till Niermann, (CC BY-SA 3.0) at http://commons.wikimedia.org/wiki/
File:Statue-Augustus.jpg.

Fig. 1.5: Honoré Daumier / Copyright in the Public Domain.

Fig. 1.6: Photo copyright © 2007 by Matthias Kabel, (CC BY-SA 3.0) at http://commons.wikimedia.org/wiki/
File:Venus_von_Willendorf_01.jpg.

Fig. 1.7: Raffaello Sanzio / Copyright in the Public Domain.

Fig. 1.8: Copyright © 1937 by Pablo Picasso.

Fig. 1.9: Copyright in the Public Domain.

Fig. 1.10: Raffaello Sanzio / Copyright in the Public Domain.

Fig. 1.11: Copyright in the Public Domain.

Fig. 1.12: James Abbott McNeill Whistler; Photo copyright © 2014 by Freer Gallery of Art and Arthur M.
Sackler Gallery, (CC BY-SA 2.0) at https://commons.wikimedia.org/wiki/File:The_Peacock_Room.jpg.

Fig. 1.14: Copyright © by Micki Prinste and Branden Warden.

Fig. 1.15: Copyright © by Micki Prinste and Branden Warden.

CHAPTER 2

ELEMENTS OF VISUAL ART

The elements of visual art are the basic structural components of works of visual art. They are universal and comprehensive; that is, they can be used to describe any form of art from any culture known to man, and they cover all aspects of the artwork. To begin with, consider the various types of visual art below.

Visual Arts—Space Arts
- Two-dimensional—Drawing, Engraving, Painting, Photography
- Three-dimensional—Sculpture
- Environmental—Architecture, Landscape
- Functional & Decorative—Cabinetry, Jewelry, Textiles

The elements of visual art to follow can be used to describe art in any of the forms listed above, although not all of the elements will necessarily be required by every artwork.

Elements of Visual Art

The first element of visual art is one that people often overlook, but it is very important. The element of medium determines what is possible in the artwork as well as its durability. You will notice that, in the captions under the figures, the medium is listed right after the artist and the name of the work. This is a customary expression of its importance.

1. MEDIUM/PHYSICAL MATERIAL
   - Two-dimensional—Pen and Ink, Charcoal/Pastel, Engraving, Etching, Lithography, Fresco, Encaustic (Wax), Tempera, Watercolor, Oil, Acrylic

- Three-dimensional—Wood, Stone, Clay, Wax, Cast (Bronze), Wrought (Copper or Bronze)
- Functional & Decorative—Wood, Metal, Fabric
- Environmental—Wood Frame, Masonry, Steel and Glass, Earth, Vegetation

The **medium** is the substance from which the artwork is made (for example, pen and ink on paper, tempera paint on wood panel, oil paint on canvas, cast bronze, marble, etc.). It is very important to identify the medium because every medium has advantages and disadvantages.

First, some of the more obvious problems. Oak-gall ink (Middle Ages and Renaissance), if made too strong and dark, can corrode the paper over time. Sulfite paper (invented in the nineteenth century) breaks down, becomes acidic, and disintegrates over time. Paintings on wood panels can mold, warp, or split. Paintings applied incorrectly to walls flake off. Certain vegetable pigments, like rose madder, fade over time. Sculptures in any medium can break, and those in wax or metal can melt. Badly engineered buildings can fall down. Such things have a negative effect on the viewer, owner, or inhabitant. Some more combinations of advantages and disadvantages are below.

Drawing—The oldest technique for making a flat image; several media are possible. Pen and ink on paper is the most permanent, but charcoal and pastels (colored chalks) are also often used. These latter two require a fixative so the powdery pigment does not fall off or blow away.

Painting—All paints have three components: pigment, solvent, and binder. The pigment is the colorant, powdered and mixed with the solvent (the carrier liquid) and the binder that holds the paint together and makes it adhere. Different combinations of these have different properties.

Fresco is one of the oldest painting techniques. Pigment is dissolved in a water-based solvent and applied to wet plaster. The advantage is permanence; the painting is there for as long as the wall lasts, although excess humidity can

FIGURE 2.1 Giotto (1266/7–1337), *The Kiss of Judas* (Arrest of Christ), c. 1305, fresco, Scrovegni (Arena) Chapel, Padua, Italy.

FIGURE 2.2 Leonardo da Vinci (1452–1519), *The Last Supper*, 1495–8, oil and tempera on gesso, pitch and mastic, 460 × 880 cm, Church of Santa Maria delle Grazie, Milan, Italy.

allow mold to grow. The main disadvantage of fresco is that the painter can only work on the portion of fresh plaster applied for that day's work, and (s)he cannot revise or improve the work. Any change requires chipping off the plaster and starting that portion again. Fresco pigments are also often transparent, so shading by overlay is difficult (see Figure 2.1). Giotto's work also shows the problem of application of pigment after the fresco dries. In this case, the blotchy dark blue of the background is azurite, a copper carbonate that reacts with wet plaster and must be applied to the dry wall. A different and well-known example of a similar problem is Leonardo da Vinci's *Last Supper* (Figure 2.2). Leonardo spent much time revising his paintings, which fresco does not allow. For the *Last Supper*, he attempted to use a mixture of oil and tempera on a double layer of dry plaster coated with gesso, pitch, and mastic (gum) that he hoped would seal the wall. Unfortunately, the experiment failed, and already within a few decades, the painting had sadly deteriorated.

With fresco, watercolor shares the problem of transparency. Painters in watercolor must proceed from the lightest to the darkest tones. These paints are also made of water and pigment, but the binder is a tree gum known as gum arabic. Watercolor is painted on paper, but special thick paper is needed to avoid rippling from the water solvent. One of the oldest painting techniques (Roman period) with consistent opacity allowing overpainting is encaustic. In encaustic painting, the binder and solvent is hot beeswax, usually painted on wood panels. The pigments can be made opaque, and revision can be done through overpainting, but when the wax cools, the paint is brittle, which is what requires the wood backing. Figure 2.3, Mummy Portrait of a Woman, is an example of the encaustic medium. The lumps on the surface illustrate a problem that arises when the wax cools too fast.

Tempera paint uses egg yolk as the binder, with water as the solvent. The paint film is somewhat rigid and usually painted on wood panels, but when carefully prepared, the binder can have some elasticity, which permits a canvas backing. Tempera is primarily opaque, although with great care, semitransparent layers can produce subtle shading, but the primary advantage of tempera is the sharp delineation between color areas and crisp detail. Figure 2.4, Botticelli's

FIGURE 2.3 Anonymous, Mummy portrait of a woman from Al-Faiyum, Egypt, Roman Period, c. 100–150 CE encaustic on cypress panel, Milwaukee Art Museum, Wisconsin. Encaustic portraits were included at the heads of late-period mummies.

Birth of Venus, demonstrates the use of tempera on canvas, which is a bit unusual. Tempera has continued to be a preferred medium for some painters up to the present day, probably because of the precision it makes possible. Figure 2.5, *Christina's World* by Andrew Wyeth, is perhaps the most famous tempera painting of recent years. It is painted on a panel, and the combination of the surface and the medium makes possible the detailed blades of grass in the hayfield as well as the sharp outlines of the buildings and Christina Olson's dress, which are critical to the painting's poignancy.

One of the greatest advances in painting was oil paint. A thin oil, like turpentine or mineral spirits, is the solvent, and the binder is a thick

FIGURE 2.4 Sandro Botticelli (c. 1445–1510), *The Birth of Venus*, c. 1486, tempera on canvas, 172 × 279 cm, Uffizi Gallery, Florence.

drying oil (linseed oil). A drying oil is one with extra chemical bonds that can attach to oxygen atoms over time, which leads to the hardening of the paint. The initial drying (of the solvent) can take a day or more, but the complete chemical oxidation reaction takes many years, and for a long time, an oil-painted surface retains some flexibility. This permits the use of stretched canvas as the base. Some have said that the oil-on-canvas technique was invented in Venice, where the humid air encouraged warping or molding of wood panels, and the nautical Venetians had plenty of canvas on hand (which permitted air circulation around the paint). Whether or not this is true, it highlights certain advantages of the oil-on-canvas technique. While Venetian painters continued to produce frescoes and occasional panel paintings after oils came into use, they produced many and very large paintings in oil on canvas. Figure 2.6, Tintoretto's *Last Supper*, demonstrates the variety of effects possible with oil paint: not only sharply defined figures but also spirit apparitions.

FIGURE 2.5 Andrew Wyeth (1917–2009), *Christina's World*, 1948, tempera on gessoed panel, 82 × 121 cm, Museum of Modern Art, New York. Wyeth preferred classic tempera technique on panel for much of his work. Note the crispness of the image.

FIGURE 2.6 Tintoretto (Jacopo Comin, 1518–1594), *The Last Supper*, 1594, oil on canvas, 3.66 cm × 5.69 m, Church of San Giorgio Maggiore, Venice. Large oil-on-canvas painting. Note the semi-transparent white of the angelic spirits (a technique called scumbling).

FIGURE 2.7 Attributed to Praxiteles (4th century BCE), *Hermes with the Infant Dionysus*, Parian marble, 2.12 m high, Archaeological Museum, Olympia, Greece, discovered in several pieces. Some are still missing, which shows the problems of stone sculpture.

FIGURE 2.8 Tilman Riemenschneider (c. 1450–1531), Holy Blood Altarpiece, before 1490, Sankt Jakobi Church, Rothenburg ob der Tauber, Germany. This late Gothic altarpiece shows the intricate detail that is possible in wood sculpture.

Oil painting was also revolutionary in other ways, since the paint could be made thick or thin, opaque or transparent, and could be altered or revised with little difficulty through overpainting (not possible with watercolor) or scraping off the half-dried area and repainting it (tempera dries too fast, and fresco must be chipped off the wall). Oil on canvas remained the primary medium for painting until the invention of acrylic and other polymer binders like latex in the twentieth century. Acrylic painting uses a liquid plastic as the binder and a water solvent. Acrylic paints have all of the properties of oils plus the advantage of not having to use volatile oil solvents, which are unhealthy to breathe over long periods of time.

Sculpture can be produced in two ways: by removing material or by building it up. The advantage of removing portions of wood or stone to create a work is that the work is solid, in a single piece. A major disadvantage is that removing too much material by error is nearly impossible to correct in stone and creates a glued imperfection in wood. Carving in this way is also laborious and slow, especially in stone. (See Figures 2.7 and 2.8.)

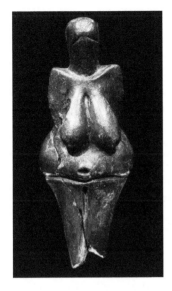

FIGURE 2.9 Anonymous, *Venus of Dolní Věstonice*, Prehistoric, terracotta (fired clay), c. 19,000–25,000 BCE, 11 cm high, Moravian Museum, Brno, Czech Republic. The earliest known piece of terracotta sculpture.

FIGURE 2.10 Edgar Degas (1834–1917), *The Little Dancer, Aged 14*, 1878–81, beeswax and textiles on metal armature, 99 cm high, National Gallery of Art, Washington, DC.

FIGURE 2.11 Frédéric Auguste Bartholdi, *Liberty Enlightening the World*, begun 1876, erected 1886, wrought (hammered) copper on iron armature (frame), 46 m high, Liberty Island, New York Harbor.

Creating sculpture by building it up is more flexible, faster, and allows the correction of errors. The usual materials are clay or wax (see Figures 2.9 and 2.10). Either substance is fragile if left untreated, and wax melts if exposed to heat. Clay sculpture is usually strengthened by firing once its water content is completely dried out (otherwise it explodes in the kiln). Fired clay is close to stone in its consistency and durability.

Because of the weight and expense of the medium, metal sculptures of any size are usually hollow. The most ancient method for creating metal sculpture is probably wrought metal using a soft metal like gold or copper on a frame. The technique is still in use today (see Figure 2.11).

More complex is the lost wax (*cire perdue*) process for producing cast bronze statues, invented in antiquity and still used today (see Figure 2.12). In this process, a central core of clay is covered with a fairly thick layer of wax, which is carefully sculpted to exactly the shape desired. This is covered with several layers of clay, beginning with a very finely ground clay to preserve the smallest detail and continuing with coarser clay for strength, leaving channels for the exit of the wax and pouring the bronze. When the core and outer mold are thoroughly dry, the whole structure is heated slowly, first to evacuate the wax (hence "lost wax") and then to fire the clay mold to a stone-like consistency. Melted bronze is then poured into the mold. After cooling, the mold is removed and imperfections are buffed off the finished sculpture. Molds can be designed

FIGURE 2.12 Donatello (c. 1386–1466), *David*, c. 1430, cast bronze (lost wax process), 158 cm high, Bargello Museum, Florence, Italy. The first large-scale nude statue since antiquity, in the classic *contrapposto* pose.

in pieces so they can be removed intact and reused. More complex or large shapes are often cast in parts that are then welded together.

Other plastic arts can use almost any material in almost any form. Fiber art includes tapestry, macramé, lace, and textiles, among many materials. Pottery can include vessels as well as sculptures. Gold- or silversmithing can include vessels, tableware, and jewelry, among other things.

Environmental arts are different from the plastic arts described above. Where those arts create objects, environmental art shapes the space around us. This can be done in three ways: architecture, gardening, and installation. Architecture is the design of structures made of various materials. The two oldest media are masonry (of stone, brick, or concrete) and wood. Stone masonry can be of cut stone (ashlar) or fieldstone (rubble). The former takes time, effort, and expense to prepare the rectangular stone blocks, while the latter uses found stone in its natural shape. Cut stone makes a more stable wall (suitable for larger structures) and requires very little mortar. Some of the oldest brick structures are made with sun-dried brick. Fortunately for their survival, they are in an area with little rainfall. Brick must be fired in a kiln, like clay statues or pottery, to be weatherproof. Masonry structures are very durable and comparatively fireproof, but they can be dangerous in earthquake-prone areas like California. In such areas, building codes require reinforcement like that in Figure 1.15.

Wood structures are less costly to build in the United States, while masonry construction is more common in much of Europe due to the scarcity and high price of wood. Wood structures are faster and less labor-intensive to build, and their lower cost permits greater space for the money spent. Wood structures are less durable than stone and more prone to damage by fire and decay. Since the late eighteenth century iron, then structural steel and various forms of concrete have combined strength and durability to allow much greater height as well as flexibility of form.

Gardening or landscaping uses vegetation and plant materials to create a living designed space. Some styles of gardening also include man-made objects, like sculptures or small architectural constructions. Small pavilions, gazebos, or artificial ruins (called follies) were fashionable in the eighteenth and nineteenth centuries (see Figure 2.13). By inserting into a landscape a man-made object whose only purpose was decorative, landscape architects paved the way for the installations that became popular in the later twentieth century.

One such installation is Robert Smithson's *Spiral Jetty* (Figure 2.14). At 460 meters long and built of large blocks of basalt and mud, it originally projected into the Great Salt Lake surrounding it so that water and salt crystals contributed to its medium according to the variable height of the lake. Unfortunately, recent drought and the drawing of excessive water

FIGURE 2.14 Robert Smithson (1938–1973), *Spiral Jetty*, 1970, installation of basalt, mud, salt crystals & water, 460 m long, Great Salt Lake, Utah. This installation is more or less permanent, depending on the level of the lake.

from the lake's inflowing rivers leave the spiral half a kilometer from the water. It is the fate of such installations to be subject to the vagaries of nature, even when they are designed to be permanent. Other installations have an intentionally brief life, like those of Christo Yavacheff and his late wife, Jeanne-Claude. One very successful one was *The Gates*, installed in New York's Central Park (see Figure 2.15): 7,503 orange steel frames, with matching fabric suspended from them, stood along the pathways of Central Park for three weeks in February 2005, splashing color over the byways of a drab, gray city in its drabbest, grayest month.

FIGURE 2.15 Christo Yavacheff (b. 1935) and Jeanne-Claude (1935–2009), *The Gates*, February 2005, Installation of steel, vinyl and fabric, 7,503 gates, Central Park, New York City.

All plastic arts in any of the above media share certain descriptive characteristics. The simplest of these is line.

2. LINE/SHAPE
- Curved, Flowing
- Straight, Angular
- Thick, Thin
- Sharp, Fuzzy

Line is the simplest of all the art elements. Line is a starting point for virtually all works of visual art, whether two-dimensional (painting, drawing, etc.) or three-dimensional (sculpture, etc., also known as plastic arts). Lines can be described in many ways: thick or thin, curved or straight, and clear or fuzzy are some of the more obvious ones. In Dürer's *Praying Hands* (Figure 2.16), the outline of the hands follows natural curves, but the thickness and clarity of the line varies to provide shading and a sense of roundness. In contrast, Duchamp's *Nude Descending a Staircase* (Figure 2.17) uses clearly defined lines, many straight and angular, to emphasize the cubist principle of the reduction of natural forms to their basic geometry.

Albrecht Dürer (1471–1528), *Praying Hands*, c. 1508, pen-and ink drawing, 29 × 20 cm, Albertina Museum, Vienna.

Marcel Duchamp (1887–1968), *Nude Descending a Staircase No. 2*, 1912, oil on canvas, 147 × 89 cm, Philadelphia Museum of Art, Philadelphia. This classic example of Cubism, caused a great stir at the 1913 Armory Show in New York, the first large exhibit of modern art in the U.S.

The third element of visual art is color.

3. COLOR
   • Hue, Saturation, Value
   • Primary, Secondary
   • Polychromatic, Monochromatic

The standard approach to color is the system published by Albert Henry Munsell (1858–1918) in 1915. Color has three components: hue or tint, saturation or chroma, and value. These three components permit a complete description of any color.

Hue is what we call the color itself, in its purest form. Munsell described five. We generally think of six, but in fact, the variety of hues is infinite, as can be seen in Figure 2.18 (the same diagram used in many computer-graphics

Standard Color Wheel.

programs for selecting color). In the physics of light, the red end of the spectrum has longer, lower-energy wavelengths, and the purple end has shorter, higher-energy wavelengths, but in color theory, the two ends of the visible spectrum are bent around to adjoin one another so that red is next to purple (which actually does reflect the interaction of pigments).

Color as it appears from pigments in paints is the focus here. Pigment mixing is *subtractive*; that is, each pigment added cuts out the reflection of certain wavelengths of light.[1] In any discussion of colors, they are divided into primary and secondary colors. For pigments, the primary colors (red, yellow, and blue) are those that, when mixed, can produce any other hue. The secondary colors (orange, green, and purple) are those resulting from mixtures of the primaries. Complementary colors are those that oppose each other on the color wheel: red against green, yellow against purple, or

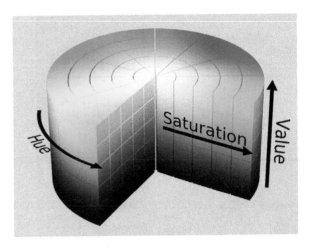

FIGURE 2.19 HSV color system, derived from that of Albert Henry Munsell (1858–1918).

orange against blue (see Figure 2.18). If all pigments are mixed together, the result is black, since all reflected colors of light are removed. Figure 2.19 enlarges on the basic color wheel.

The second component of color, saturation or chroma, measures the amount of pigment of the given color. The color circle includes an infinite variety of hues. If a hue occupies a radial line extending from the center (as in either of the Figures 2.18 or 2.19), saturation or chroma represents the particular point along that line, from transparent or no pigment at the center to the maximum amount of pigment at the circumference. But hue and saturation alone do not account for all possible variations in color. Any painter has noticed that the addition of white or black to a hue produces a color that cannot be achieved by mere addition of pigment. This component is value. Figure 2.19 shows the incorporation of value in Munsell's system, from maximum white at the top to maximum black at the bottom.

Painters use color in different ways. To begin with, natural pigments, which painters have used for millennia, rarely have pure primary or secondary colors, and painters generally use these pigments close to their naturally occurring color, with little mixing. The viewer's perception of any color is changed by the amount of it in any one place and the color(s) adjoining it. In addition, the number of colors used depends on the painter's goals and what (s)he is trying to communicate. Duchamp's *Nude Descending a Staircase* (Figure 2.17) is very nearly monochromatic; that is, having only one color. All of the colors are closely related to the same mustard yellow (probably yellow ochre pigment), presented in different values by varying additions of black and white. In contrast, Raphael's *Sistine Madonna* (Figure 1.7) is polychromatic, using mainly primary colors. Outside of flesh tones and the brown of the Madonna's veil, the only secondary color used is green for Saint Barbara's wrap and the framing curtains. Even the background of the clouds of heavenly hosts is painted in very light values of blue.

---

1   What is a primary color varies according to the way the colors are produced. Printers find that magenta (red-blue), yellow, and cyan (green-blue) give results similar to those above. Mixing colors of light itself is the opposite of adding pigments; mixing light colors is *additive*. Each color of light projected adds its wavelengths to what is present. Primary colors for the mixing of light are red, green and blue. If all these light primaries are projected to mix together, the result is white.

FIGURE 2.20 Vassily Kandinsky (1866–1944), *Improvisation 27 (Garden of Love II)*, 1912, oil on canvas, 120 × 140 cm, The Metropolitan Museum of Art, New York. Kandinsky is often credited with inventing abstract painting. This work was also exhibited at New York's 1913 Armory Show.

FIGURE 2.21 Michelangelo (1475–1564), *David*, 1501–4, Carrara marble, 517 cm high, Accademia Gallery, Florence, Italy.

In this painting, different colors clarify the different persons and objects in the work.

From the relatively simple elements of line and color, we move to the combination of these in the objects depicted. These can be representative, like the persons in Raphael's *Sistine Madonna* (Figure 1.7), completely abstract, like Kandinsky's *Improvisation 27 (Garden of Love II)* in Figure 2.20, or somewhere in between, like Duchamp's *Nude Descending a Staircase* (Figure 2.17). A representative object is the image of a real person, place, or thing as it appears to the eye. Abstract describes an image with no recognizable object. Artists can strive to make their images completely realistic, like Dürer's *Praying Hands* (Figure 2.16), but they can also go beyond realism to produce idealized images, intended to reflect the perfection of a personal or cultural ideal, like Praxiteles' *Hermes with the Infant Dionysus* (Figure 2.7), the Greek ideal of male beauty.

4. OBJECTS

- Representative, Abstract
- Realistic, Idealized
- Human—Proportions, Posture, *Contrapposto*
- Animal—Realistic, Fantastic
- Inanimate—Rocks, Vegetation, Structures
- Decorative Features—Frames, Columns, Moldings, Arabesques

The objects represented can be divided into three types: human, animal, and inanimate.

In addition to realistic portrayal of humans, proportions and accurate representations of body parts are important. In the anonymous Venus of Willendorf (Figure 1.6), bodily proportions and components are exaggerated (breasts, abdomen) or omitted (face, feet); the posture is unnaturally rigid and symmetrical. Donatello's *David* (Figure 2.12) has correct proportions and the natural resting (*contrapposto*) posture (with the weight on one leg and a tilted pelvis), but the definition of the muscles, especially in the abdomen and upper arms, is not accurate because Donatello did not have access to cadavers for anatomical dissection. Michelangelo's *David* (Figure 2.21) carries Donatello's accuracy one step further. Since Michelangelo was permitted to dissect cadavers, his anatomical accuracy is essentially perfect. The slightly exaggerated musculature is a frequent characteristic of the artist's style, and the size of the right hand has been variously ascribed to Michelangelo's discomfort with carving a block that had already been worked on, the statue's originally intended position on a buttress of the Florence cathedral dome, or an optical illusion related to the hand's position.

Depiction of animals shares many of the same considerations as that of humans, but, in addition to realistic portrayal, artists sometimes depict mythological or fantastic beasts. A well-known example is Sir John Tenniel's illustration of the Gryphon and the Mock Turtle from Lewis Carroll's *Alice in Wonderland* (see Figure 2.22). Leaving mythical creations, realistic depiction of animals and inanimate objects and their place(s) in the work needs no comment beyond the concern for accuracy discussed above with regard to humans. Decorative features may appear in most forms of art, but some are particularly relevant to furniture and architecture, like columns and moldings. Frames may appear in just about any visual art form. Arabesques, which may also appear in virtually any form of visual art, are curving designs derived from idealized vegetation. The arabesque's origins are deep in Classical Antiquity, but the decoration was retransmitted to Europe in the Middle Ages via the Byzantine Empire and Islamic culture, from which it took its name (see Figure 2.23).

Composition or organization is the visual art element that ties together all the others.

FIGURE 2.22 Sir John Tenniel (1820–1914), The Mock Turtle and Gryphon, 1865, from Lewis Carroll's *Alice in Wonderland*.

5. ORGANIZATION—COMPOSITION
- Layout, Planning, Design
- Space/Mass
- Focus—Single, Multiple
- Balance, Symmetry, Asymmetry
- Unity, Repetition, Variety, Contrast
- Depth—Overlap, Linear Perspective, Aerial Perspective

In a drawing, engraving, painting, or sculpture, the artist selects objects and features to achieve the most effective work, even if this alters the actual appearance of a scene. A photographer (at least before digital media manipulation) has fewer options. While objects in a photograph can be moved, photographers more often choose to create their desired layout with as little alteration as possible by using camera placement, focus, and lighting. In either case, the layout or design planned by the artist is critical to the success of the work. Often there is a geometric pattern underlying the work.

Consider Figure 1.7, Raphael's *Sistine Madonna*. Connecting the heads of the Madonna, the pope, and Saint Barbara, as well as the space between the two cherubs, yields a diamond. The gazes of the figures emphasize this and link them with the viewer. The pope looks at the Madonna. The cherubs also look up, more in the direction of Saint Barbara, who looks at them in an attitude that also expresses reverence to the Madonna and child, who look directly at the viewer as they stride forward, directed by the pope's hand. The gazes and the geometry create a single focus, a direct link with the viewer. The figures are balanced but asymmetrical, as each

FIGURE 2.23 Anonymous, *Tellus Mater* above arabesques, 13–9 BCE, approx. 208 × 320 cm., Ara Pacis (Altar of Peace), Rome. Tellus Mater is the allegorical Roman earth goddess, symbolizing bounty and fertility.

has its own identity and pose—unity through variety. Finally, there is a sense of depth, given by the clouds descending beneath the Madonna's approaching feet, the heavenly hosts in the background, whose light blue color contributes an atmospheric perspective, and the window drapes and cherubs lounging apparently on the windowsill. Such an extension of the picture's virtual space into the viewer's actual space is called *trompe l'œil* (trick the eye). All of the above devices and more contribute to the expressive content, the message, of the painting. It inspires reverence and thanks for the Madonna bringing the Christ child to the world, guided by the pope as intermediary, with Saint Barbara and the heavenly hosts as examples of devotion.

Beyond the elements shared by all forms of visual art, there are a few constructions whose main importance lies in architecture, although they may appear decoratively in other art forms, as noted above. These are structures whose function is to support openings, roofs, or walls. Post-and-lintel is the simplest way of supporting an opening. Posts on either side support a lintel across the top. More elaborate round posts are called columns or pillars; sometimes a building will have rectangular reinforcements carved to look like pillars but half buried in the wall. These are called pilasters. Instead of a flat ceiling, a building may have some sort of arch, called a vault. If the vaulted structure is circular, it is called a dome. Vaults and domes produce outward forces on the tops of the walls that require reinforcement. Exterior ribs on a building that serve this purpose are called buttresses. They are generally less elaborate than pilasters. These and other structures will be discussed in some detail with the relevant historical examples.

The final element of visual art (or any art) is the message.

6. EXPRESSIVE CONTENT—THE MESSAGE

Rarely—almost never—does an artist create a work of art without trying to express something. It may be the beauty and grandeur of the Rocky Mountains, as in Bierstadt's *Lander's Peak* (Figure 1.3). It may be glorifying propaganda, as in *Augustus of Primaporta* (Figure 1.4); reverse messages about oppression, as in Daumier's *Third-Class Carriage* (Figure 1.5); or war, as in Picasso's *Guernica* (Figure 1.8). It may use the image of the female as a representation of fertility, as in the Venuses of Figures 1.6 and 2.9. It may endeavor to inspire religious devotion, like the *Sistine Madonna* (Figure 1.7) and the *Holy Blood Altarpiece* (Figure 2.8). The number of possible messages is infinite—whatever the mind, psyche, soul, or spirit of the artist may conceive.

Although the elements above apply to any form of visual art, it is unlikely that any one work will contain them all. They provide a vocabulary and a way of looking at a work that permits a more detailed understanding of it. The same is true for the elements of other art forms like the performing arts, beginning with music.

Image Credits

Fig. 2.1: Giotto di Bondone / Copyright in the Public Domain.

Fig. 2.2: Leonardo da Vinci / Copyright in the Public Domain.

Fig. 2.3: Photo by Jonathunder / Wikimedia Commons / Copyright in the Public Domain.

Fig. 2.4: Sandro Botticelli / Copyright in the Public Domain.

Fig. 2.5: Copyright © 1948 by Andrew Wyeth.

Fig. 2.6: Tintoretto / Copyright in the Public Domain.

Fig. 2.7: Praxiteles; Photo copyright © 2013 by Ricardo Frantz, (CC BY-SA 2.5) at http://en.wikipedia.org/wiki/File:Hermes_di_Prassitele,_at_Olimpia,_front_2.jpg.

Fig. 2.8: Tilman Riemenschneider; Photo by Berthold Werner / Copyright in the Public Domain.

Fig. 2.9: Photo copyright © 2007 by Petr Novák / Wikimedia Commons, (CC BY-SA 2.5) at http://en.wikipedia.org/wiki/File:Vestonicka_venuse_edit.jpg.

Fig. 2.10: Edgar Degas / National Gallery of Art / Copyright in the Public Domain.

Fig. 2.11: Photo by O / Wikimedia Commons / Copyright in the Public Domain.

Fig. 2.12: Donato di Niccolò di Betto Bardi; Photo copyright © 2010 by Patrick A. Rodgers, (CC BY-SA 2.0) at http://commons.wikimedia.org/wiki/File:Donatello_-_David_-_Floren%C3%A7a.jpg.

Fig. 2.13: Daderot / Wikimedia Commons / Copyright in the Public Domain.

Fig. 2.14: Robert Smithson; Photo copyright © 2005 by Soren Harward, (CC BY-SA 2.0) at http://en.wikipedia.org/wiki/File:Spiral-jetty-from-rozel-point.png.

Fig. 2.15: Christo and Jeanne-Claude; Photo copyright © 2005 by Morris Pearl, (CC BY-SA 3.0) at http://en.wikipedia.org/wiki/File:The_Gates.jpg.

Fig. 2.16: Albrecht Dürer / Copyright in the Public Domain.

Fig. 2.17: Marcel Duchamp / Copyright in the Public Domain.

Fig. 2.18: Copyright in the Public Domain.

Fig. 2.19: Copyright © 2010 by Michael Horvath, (CC BY-SA 3.0) at https://commons.wikimedia.org/wiki/File:HSV_color_solid_cylinder_alpha_lowgamma.png.

Fig. 2.20: Wassily Kandinsky / Copyright in the Public Domain.

Fig. 2.21: Michelangelo Buonarroti; Photo copyright © 2005 by Rico Heil, (CC BY-SA 3.0) at http://en.wikipedia.org/wiki/File:David_von_Michelangelo.jpg.

Fig. 2.22: Sir John Tenniel / Copyright in the Public Domain.

Fig. 2.23: Copyright © 2014 by Miguel Hermoso Cuesta, (CC BY-SA 3.0) at http://commons.wikimedia.org/wiki/File:Ara_Pacis_Tellus_07.jpg.

CHAPTER 3

ELEMENTS OF MUSIC

Music is one of the performing arts or time arts, the other two being theater and dance. Similar to the elements of visual art, the elements of music are the basic structural components of works of music. They are universal and comprehensive; that is, they can be used to describe any kind of music from any culture known to man, and they cover all aspects of the musical work. The elements of music to follow can be used to describe music in any form, although not all of the elements will necessarily be required by every artwork. A word of caution: most people find it much easier to recognize and describe the structural elements of visual art than those of music. There is a temptation to describe music emotionally, in the way it makes one feel. There is nothing wrong about this; it recognizes the strong effect music has on our emotions. But the emphasis here is to learn to use the musical elements to describe music's structure as a path to understanding the emotional effect. In order to avoid intimidating students who do not read musical notation, as well as to make those who do read it think in new ways, I will avoid using written musical notation as much as possible.

Elements of Music

1. RHYTHM—The organization of musical events in time
   - Beat—a Rhythmic pulse of approximately uniform length
   - Accent—a stronger than usual Beat

- Metered Music—music with a repeated, regular pattern of beats or Meter
- Unmetered Music—music that may or may not have regular beats, but without a regular pattern of them
- Tempo—the speed of a piece, often described in Italian

The first musical element is rhythm. *Any* collection of sounds deliberately organized over time has rhythm. The sounds do not have to be regularly spaced. If they are, though, we call each sound pulse a beat. Most music has some underlying beat structure; that is, one can find a regular rhythmic unit that underlies what is happening in the music, even if the notes (rhythmic events) above or around the beat are longer or shorter than the beat unit, as in Figure 3.1.

There are different ways of organizing beats further. In some non-Western music, particularly that of India, different numbers of beats are added together in a repeated pattern. In Western music the repeated pattern usually involves the same regular number of beats. What defines the pattern is regularly spaced accents. Music with such a regular pattern of accented beats (called meter) is metered music. Figure 3.2 adds the accents for a duple (two-beat) meter to the beat and rhythmic event pattern above.

Meters can also be triple, quadruple, or some compound of these. Figure 3.3 is a similar example in triple meter.

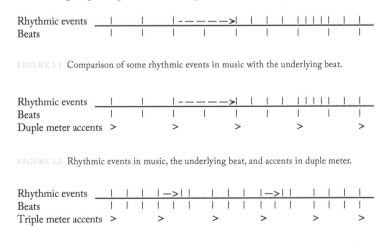

FIGURE 3.1 Comparison of some rhythmic events in music with the underlying beat.

FIGURE 3.2 Rhythmic events in music, the underlying beat, and accents in duple meter.

FIGURE 3.3 Rhythmic events in music, the underlying beat and accents in triple meter "My country 'tis of thee … ."

FIGURE 3.4 *Kyrie cunctipotens genitor*—unmetered, monophonic Gregorian chant (c. 800 CE), melismatic text setting.

Text	Translation	Melody Line
Kyrie eleison	Lord, have mercy	A
Kyrie eleison	Lord, have mercy	A
Kyrie eleison	Lord, have mercy	A
Christe eleison	Christ, have mercy	B
Christe eleison	Christ, have mercy	B
Christe eleison	Christ, have mercy	B
Kyrie eleison	Lord, have mercy	C
Kyrie eleison	Lord, have mercy	C
Kyrie eleison	Lord, have mercy	C′

Line C′ is slightly different from C; its first section is repeated to give a greater sense of ending.

Unmetered music also exists. The most extensive repertoire of unmetered Western music is Gregorian chant. In Figures 3.4 and 3.7, *Kyrie cunctipotens genitor*, the rhythm is somewhat flexible, but there is a simple underlying pulse that governs the speed of the notes.

The final component of rhythm is tempo, an Italian word. Most English-speaking musicians have an incomplete understanding of this word. Like its cognates in other Romance languages—*temps* (French) and *tiempo* (Spanish)—*tempo* (Italian) can refer to time, a period of time, a season, the weather, or a mood proceeding from these. The use of tempo indications in music indicates the desired speed, but it goes further and indicates the mood or some activity as well. *Allegro* means fast and lively, but also cheerful and happy. *Andante* comes from the verb *andare* ("to go" or "to walk"), so it indicates a walking tempo. *Largo* means large or broad, so it indicates a speed with dignity, where the beats have breadth.

2.   MELODY—A meaningful succession of musical Pitches (Tones)
   • Pitch—the audible sound of vibrations at a given speed, classified as High or Low (both in terms of their sound and their physical speed)
   • Interval—the musical distance between two Pitches
   • Step—the Interval between two adjacent pitches; two kinds: Whole Steps & Half Steps (2nds)
   • Skip—any Interval larger than a Step (3rds, 4ths, 5ths, 6ths, 7ths, & larger)
   • Octave (8th)—the interval between two pitches of the same name, called an octave because the notes are eight steps apart in the Western scale; physically, the higher note of an octave vibrates at twice the speed of the lower one.
   • Scale—the organization of one octave of adjacent pitches in rising or descending step-wise order
   • Motive—the smallest recognizable unit of a melody
   • Phrase—a larger melodic unit, comparable to a sentence in written prose
   • Contour—the shape of a melody; can be indicated precisely with musical notation or more simply as a line graph over time

The second element of music is melody. Like rhythm, the concept of melody is more general than many people are accustomed to thinking. A melody does not need to be "tuneful." By definition, a melody is any meaningful succession of musical pitches. A pitch is the sound made by vibrations of a substance at a certain speed. The pitch arising from rapid vibrations, we call

Timings (approximate)	Music
0:00–0:10	Basic motive, "da-da-da-dum," played twice by all the strings in unison, with long holds on each last note.
0:10–0:15	Motive played rapidly three times in succession over chords in strings, ending in longer note; this pattern repeated.
0:15–0:20	Motive played rapidly three times from top descending, followed by three emphatic notes, last one sustained in violins.
0:20–0:25	Motive played in unison by entire orchestra ending in long hold.
	From this point on, the rhythmic idea appears over and over, but the melody associated with it varies.
	The basic rhythmic and melodic ideas of this motive are the basic material of the entire symphony.

high; that arising from slower vibrations, we call low. In most systems of music, the pitches are separated by fixed increments. An interval is the distance between any two pitches. A step is the smallest distance—from one pitch to the next adjacent one. There are two sizes of steps, half steps and whole steps. There is also one other special interval that recognizes the distance between two notes whose frequencies of vibration are a factor of two apart. We call this distance an octave because the two notes encompass a scale of seven different pitches, with the eighth being the octave. Scale is the name for one octave of adjacent pitches in rising or descending order.

To measure the interval between two notes, count both notes plus all steps of the scale between them. For example: the interval between scale degrees 1 and 3 is 1, 2, 3—a third; between 1 and 5 is obviously a fifth; between 5 and 8 is 5, 6, 7, 8—a fourth. Three to 5 is a third; 3 to 8 (1) is a sixth; 1 to 2, 2 to 3, on to 7 to 8 is a second; 1 to 7 or 2 to 8 is a seventh, and so forth. We always count the notes according to the steps of the most common scale (the major scale), which has seven different pitches, even though there are others with five, six, eight, or twelve.

Pitches, intervals, and scales are the building blocks of melody. Using these basic materials, composers construct melodic units of various sizes and shapes. The smallest recognizable unit of melody is a motive. Probably the most famous motive in all music is the opening four-note motive of Beethoven's Fifth Symphony (three repeated notes and a fourth note lower: da-da-da-dum). Figure 3.5 is just the first twenty-three measures of the symphony, but in that short space, Beethoven uses the motive eleven times in its original form, as well as twice upside down (inverted). In fact, not only does Beethoven build this entire movement around the motive, he also derives related melodic and rhythmic patterns from it and uses them to construct the whole symphony!

Not all melodies are based on motives, but most melodies have phrases. The phrase is a larger melodic unit, comparable to a sentence in prose. See below the melody for the tune "Yankee Doodle." The tune has four short phrases (and in fact, each phrase begins with the same rhythmic motive). The structure appears in Figure 3.6.

Yan- kee Doo- dle went to town a - rid-ing on a po - - ny. He stuck a fea - ther in his hat and called it ma- ca - ro - - ni.

FIGURE 3.6 The phrases and melodic contour of the song "Yankee Doodle." The red lines are phrase dividers. The song is metered. Black barlines divide the metrical units. Text setting is syllabic.

Ky - ri - - e _____ e - - - - - - - - - le - i - son.

FIGURE 3.7 The phrases and melodic contour of the first line of *Kyrie cunctipotens genitor*, line 1, unmetered, monophonic Gregorian chant (ca. 800 CE), melismatic text setting.

Melodies can have very different characters, depending on their shapes or melodic contours. Figure 3.6 shows a melody that starts in the middle and revolves around that note until the highest note is an octave above the lowest note, then descends down to a final note between the highest and lowest notes. For contrast, Figure 3.7 shows the melody of the first line of *Kyrie cunctipotens genitor* (form described in Figure 3.4).

The melody of *Kyrie cunctipotens genitor* starts in the middle of its range. It revolves around that note and reaches up to the melody's highest point, then, over the next three unequal phrases, the melody gradually meanders down to a final note at the bottom of its range. Note that the phrases of music and text do not coincide, as well as the contrast of this melody with that of "Yankee Doodle."

3. HARMONY—the organization of simultaneously sounding Pitches
   • Chord—any group of simultaneously sounding pitches
   • Dissonance—harmony with a clashing, harsh sound (2nds & certain 4ths)
   • Consonance—harmony with a pleasing sound; two kinds:
   • Perfect—having a hollow sound (4ths, 5ths, & octaves)
   • Imperfect—having a sweeter sound (3rds & 6ths). The richest consonant harmony includes both perfect and imperfect consonances.
   • Progression—the order of successive chords. In particular, from ca. 1700–1900, Western music used almost exclusively a highly organized type of progression called:
   • Tonal Harmony—the highly organized type of progression used almost exclusively in Western music from ca. 1700–1900. This organizes the chords in such a way as to give the progression a feeling of direction. Tonal Harmony is still used, but other

styles of progression also now occur. Tonal Harmony uses three-note chords called Triads.

Harmony is the third element of music. As melody is a meaningful succession of pitches over time, harmony is the sound produced by pitches that occur at the same time—simultaneously. Like melody, which does not have to be tuneful as long as it is deliberately organized, harmony does not have to be beautiful or pleasing. Any group of simultaneously sounding pitches intentionally designed by a composer is harmony.

Harmony is organized into chords. A chord is a single group of simultaneously sounding pitches, usually of three or more notes. A two-note chord can also be regarded as a simple harmonic interval. Chords and harmonic intervals can be dissonant (dissonances), with a harsh or clashing sound, or consonant (consonances), with a pleasing sound. Consonant intervals are of two types: perfect and imperfect. Perfect consonances have a hollow, static sound. Octaves, fifths, and most fourths are perfect consonances. (Intervals like fourths and fifths are explained above under melody.) Figure 3.8, parallel organum, is a type of medieval music that uses entirely perfect consonances in its harmony.

Figure 3.9 is a medieval English *rota* (a type of round) that uses harmony in thirds and sixths—imperfect consonances. The different colored musical lines and texts show how the song's first three lines produce harmony when the canon is sung. The numbers show the intervals between adjacent notes. Three-quarters of the intervals are imperfect consonances, so this work gives a clear example of what they sound like.

Imperfect consonances can be of two sizes: major (large) or minor (small). As noted in the musical elements chart at the beginning of the chapter, the richest harmony uses both types of consonances, as you will hear in many of the subsequent examples. A great deal of the harmony you hear from day to day is tonal harmony, a complex harmonic system that grew out of musical practices used during the Middle Ages and the Renaissance. What distinguishes tonal music from all other systems is the organization of chords in progressions that have a sense of direction or propulsion. In tonal music, all of the chords based on a particular scale have their places and a subtly implied direction toward a particular harmony or harmonies.

The chords in tonal music are primarily triads: three-note chords constructed by placing two thirds (intervals) on top of one another. So, for instance, a triad built on the first scale degree

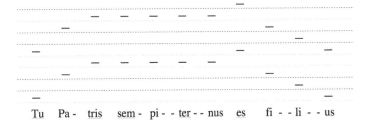

Tu   Pa - tris   sem - pi - - ter - - nus   es   fi - - li - - us

FIGURE 3.8 *Tu patris sempiternus es filius*, parallel organum, harmonized entirely in perfect consonances and having a very simple homophonic texture.

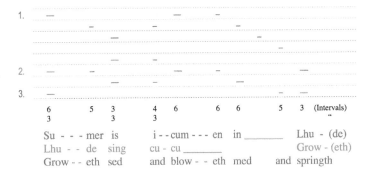

			6		5	3		4	6		6	6		5	3	(Intervals)
			3			3		3								

Su - - - mer is   i - - cum - - - en   in _____   Lhu - (de)
Lhu - - de   sing   cu - cu _____   Grow - (eth)
Grow - - eth   sed   and blow - - eth   med   and springth

FIGURE 3.9 *Sumer is icumen in* ("The Summer Canon") (thirteenth century CE), anonymous English *rota*. The harmony is nearly all imperfect consonances, polyphonic.

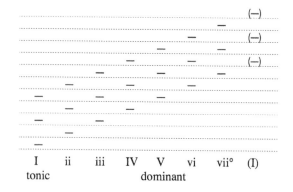

I   ii   iii   IV   V   vi   vii°   (I)
tonic   dominant

FIGURE 3.10 The triads of a major scale. Uppercase numerals indicate a major triad. The rest (lowercase) are minor except vii°, which gets into areas beyond this discussion.

will include scale degrees 1, 3, & 5. To make the chords for any scale, simply build a triad on every scale note (and name it with a Roman numeral). Those built on I (tonic), IV, and V (dominant) are the primary triads; the others are secondary (see Figure 3.10).

Every chord of this scale can have a separate key based on it. If the first triad of that scale has a chord with a major third on the bottom, it is called a major key. If the first chord has a minor third on the bottom, it is called a minor key. Beyond this level, the harmonic system of tonal music becomes quite complex. Undergraduate music majors spend one or two years studying it, so that level of complexity is beyond the scope of this book. The amount given, though, is enough to understand some basic structures of music that will appear later. The tonal system dominated all types of Western music from 1700–1900 and is still used in much music worldwide, even after other systems gained prominence in art music of the twentieth century.

4. TEXTURE—The combination of chords, melodies, or pitches. This is usually the most difficult element to hear, even for musicians.
   • Monophonic—Music with one Melody alone
   • Heterophonic—Music with one Melody played simultaneously in several different versions, some with more notes or ornaments than others, found most in non-Western music
   • Homophonic—Music with one main Melody accompanied by other notes, either in chords or simple figures, like broken chords
   • Polyphonic—Music in which the harmonies arise from several equal interlocking Melodies, or Voices, also called Counterpoint–Imitative Counterpoint if the different voices use the same motive

Texture, the fourth element of music, is probably the most difficult to hear at first, even for musicians, although the principles are simple. There are four basic musical textures. Monophonic music is music for one melody alone. Gregorian chant, like the *Kyrie cunctipotens genitor* in Figure 3.7, is the largest repertoire of Western monophonic music. Heterophonic music is an outgrowth of monophony. In heterophony, two or more versions of the same melody are performed simultaneously. One way this can occur is the intentional performing of a simple and an ornamented version of the same melody. Unintentional heterophony can occur when more than one person performs a different version of the same tune or makes mistakes. Since deliberate heterophony is primarily used in non-Western music, we will spend little time on it here. For most people, the difficulty arises in hearing the difference between homophonic and polyphonic music.

Homophony is sometimes also called melody with accompaniment. In homophony, one melody is more important than the other notes played that serve to harmonize that melody. Parallel organum, like that in Figure 3.8, is sometimes described as homophony. Another

Air (basic tune)—Simple, two-voice, homophonic, melody on top
Var. 1—Fast notes ornamenting melody on top, slow notes and chords underneath
Var. 2—Melody and chords on top, fast notes on bottom
Var. 3—Triplets and arpeggios (sweeping broken chords) on top, chords on bottom
Var. 4—Melody and chords on top, triplets and arpeggios on bottom
Var. 5—Single notes and two-note groups trading between top and bottom
Var. 6—Melody with chords mostly on top, fast notes close together on bottom; reversed in middle, with melody above bottom chords, then returns to original style
Var. 7—Fast scales on top, longer notes and chords on bottom
Var. 8—Minor key, three parts, slower, bit of imitative polyphony at beginning of each section
Var. 9—Back to major key, very short notes, imitative polyphony again, still slower
Var. 10—Longer notes, first in melody, then bass, alternating with faster three-note groups; left hand crosses over right when melody is the highest
Var. 11—Slow, begins with a little bit of imitation, later melody nicely ornamented
Var. 12—Finale, fast, triple meter, begins with melody ornamented over a very fast bass, then both hands play fast before the opening section returns with a *coda* (tail) at the end

FIGURE 3.11 Wolfgang Amadeus Mozart (1756–1791), *Twelve Variations on "Ah, vous dirai-je, Maman,"* (Twinkle, Twinkle Little Star), K 265, (1781/2), pianoforte. The basic air and some of the variations are homophonic.

example that shows the variety of melody and accompaniment that is possible is Mozart's *Variations on "Ah, vous dirai-je, Maman"* ("Twinkle, Twinkle Little Star"), Figure 3.11.[1] Air and variation sets like this one are opportunities for composers to show their ingenuity through different decorations on the same tune. In this case, the original air is a very simple, two-voice homophony. Variations 2 and 4 show how the melody can have an accompaniment that is more active than the melody itself. Variation 6 does the same, except that the melody changes place in the third strain, moving below the accompaniment, rising to its original location for the last strain. The other variations show a variety of other techniques for ornamentation and variation of melody, harmony, and texture as well.

Variation 8 actually demonstrates imitative polyphony. Variation 8 (which begins about halfway through the piece) is easy to recognize because it is the only variation in the minor key. A minor variation was one important tradition of this form. (Others included ornamenting the melody, putting it under the accompaniment, changing the meter, composing a slow lyrical setting, and ending with a fast, bombastic finale.) In Variation 8, the different harmonies arise from the interaction of several melodic lines. At the beginning, it is easy to hear how the bass line imitates what came before in the upper voice. This is imitative polyphony. In the second part of that strain, the bass drops the imitation, but the harmonies above it arise from three voices moving individually—also polyphony but not imitative. The other variations (there are twelve) show Mozart's great ingenuity in devising creative treatments of this simple tune.

---

1   This song has numerous texts. In addition to "Twinkle, Twinkle Little Star" and "The Alphabet Song" in English, there is a French folk text: *"Quand trois poules vont au champ, La première va devant, etc."* "When three hens go to the field, the first goes in front, the second follows the first, the third brings up the rear. When three hens go to the field, etc." Mozart's variations are known by the charming fourth text, *"Ah, vous dirai-je Maman, ce qui cause mon tourment, etc."* "1. Ah, let me tell you, Mama, what causes my suffering (torment). Papa wishes me to reason like a grown-up. [But] me, I know that bonbons are worth [a lot] more than reasoning. 2. Ah, let me tell you, Mama, what causes my suffering (torment). Papa wishes me to remember the verbs (words) of ancient languages. [But] me, I say that bonbons are worth [a lot] more than lessons."

FIGURE 3.12 Thomas Weelkes (1576–1623), "As Vesta Was from Latmos Hill Descending," 6-voice madrigal from *The Triumphs of Oriana* (1601). A Renaissance madrigal that illustrates text painting and different musical textures.

Text (text-painted words underlined)	Text painting in music
As Vesta was from Latmos hill descending,	Ascending lines, then descending lines, imitative polyphony
She spied a maiden Queen the same ascending,	Upward leap, then ascending lines, imitative polyphony
Attended on by all the shepherds' swain;	All voices, almost homophonic
To whom Diana's darlings, running down amain,	Descending lines, imitative polyphony
First two by two, then three by three together,	Two voices, then three voices, echoing, homophonic
Leaving their goddess all alone, hastened thither:	One voice alone, then rising fast notes
And mingling with the shepherds of her train,	Voices mingle, imitative polyphony
With mirthful tunes her presence did entertain.	Minor dorian mode, thought cheerful in the Renaissance
Then sang (all) the shepherds & nymphs of Diana:	Announcing, unanimous homophony
"Long live fair Oriana!"	Imitative polyphony, long section like cheering crowd

FIGURE 3.13 Guillaume de Machaut (c. 1300–1377), "*Kyrie*," from *Messe de Nostre Dame* (after 1360), *alternatim*, non-imitative polyphony with lines of Gregorian chant *Kyrie cunctipotens genitor* sandwiched between.

Text	Translation	Music
Kyrie eleison	Lord, have mercy	A—Elaborate non-imitative polyphony, chant hidden within
Kyrie eleison	Lord, have mercy	A—Gregorian chant *Kyrie cunctipotens genitor*
Kyrie eleison	Lord, have mercy	A—Elaborate non-imitative polyphony, chant hidden within
Christe eleison	Christ, have mercy	B—Gregorian chant *Kyrie cunctipotens genitor*
Christe eleison	Christ, have mercy	B—Elaborate non-imitative polyphony, chant hidden within
Christe eleison	Christ, have mercy	B—Gregorian chant *Kyrie cunctipotens genitor*
Kyrie eleison	Lord, have mercy	C—Elaborate non-imitative polyphony, chant hidden within
Kyrie eleison	Lord, have mercy	C—Gregorian chant *Kyrie cunctipotens genitor*
Kyrie eleison	Lord, have mercy	C'—Elaborate non-imitative polyphony, chant hidden within

Machaut based his polyphony on the *Kyrie cunctipotens genitor*, to be sung in alternation with the chant, called alternatim.

Figure 3.12, Thomas Weelkes's "As Vesta Was from Latmos Hill Descending," demonstrates imitative polyphony for much of its length. Listen for the presence of the same melody in several different voice parts in succession. This occurs frequently in the work. Polyphonic works are not necessarily imitative, though, as can be seen in Figure 3.13, the "*Kyrie*" from Machaut's *Messe de Nostre Dame*. The odd-numbered sections of this work are nonimitative polyphony, composed by Machaut. In between them, the even-numbered sections are lines from the Gregorian chant *Kyrie cunctipotens genitor* (Figure 3.4). Such alternation is called *alternatim* form.

5. TIMBRE—The quality or Tone color of a musical sound—its flavor. This is the easiest element to hear, so easy in fact that often people take it for granted and forget to mention it.
   - Instrumentation or Orchestration—the choice of instruments
   - Voicing—the distribution (high vs. low vs. mixed) of the notes of a chord
   - Dynamics—the loudness (*forte*) or softness (*piano*) of music

From texture (the most difficult musical element for most people to hear) we move to timbre, which is the most obvious and easiest. Timbre is the musical equivalent of color in visual art. Timbre is so obvious that many people forget to mention it; for example, at a symphony concert, the timbre will be mixed orchestral instruments; at a choir concert, the timbre will be mixed voices, etc. These two examples show the variation of timbre by *instrumentation*. Of course, instrumentation can also be influenced by variations in the number of instruments: string quartet, piano solo, voice and piano, etc. A more subtle influence on timbre comes from voicing. The term "voicing" refers to the way in which the notes of a chord are placed or spaced. The same chord will sound very different if all the notes are in a high register than if they are all in a low register. The first will sound brilliant, perhaps even strident. The second will sound dark and muddy. Spreading the notes out in the mid-range gives a rich, full sound, without the negative qualities of the extremes. The final component of timbre is dynamics. Dynamics are the degrees of loudness or softness of a piece. Not only does loudness affect the way in which we perceive particular sounds, but altering the loudness of one or some instruments in a group also changes the overall sound color by changing the balance of different timbres within the group. Like tempo, dynamics have Italian names. The basic ones are *piano* (soft), and *forte* (loud).[2] These can be combined or multiplied in various ways to indicate different degrees of loudness or softness. One interesting combination is in the name "pianoforte," now abbreviated to "piano," the name for an instrument that can play both softly and loudly, a "softloud."[3]

6. TEXT SETTING—the relationship of words to music, only in vocal music obviously
   - Language—The language of the text
   - Syllabic (text setting)—roughly one note per syllable
   - (Neumatic—used only for Gregorian chant)—a few notes (one neume group) per syllable
   - Melismatic—Many notes per syllable
   - Word Painting or Text Painting—expressing the words' meaning in music through certain motives, figures, harmonies, or other devices

Text setting is the sixth element of music. This is the relationship between words and music. Obviously, it applies only to vocal music. And some music that uses voices does not use words. Claude Debussy wrote an orchestral work, *Sirènes*, in which a women's chorus is used as an instrumental timbre by singing wordlessly. Clearly, text setting is not relevant here, either. The first consideration in text setting is the language of the text.

---

2   As with other Italian tempo markings, we tend to oversimplify. An Italian who tells you to "Take it easy," or "Slow down," (or "Chill") will say *"Piano, piano."* Likewise, *forte* can mean strong, as in a person, drink, or other things.

3   An old name for the instrument reverses the words, *"Fortepiano,"* a "loudsoft." This is now used to name replicas of early pianos.

Music can be sung in any known language, and the particular sounds of that language will influence the sound of the music.

Some of the unique sounds of particular languages:

Italian—pure vowels, crisp, clear consonants
German, Dutch and Russian—heavy on consonants; Russian has many diphthongs
French—nasal vowels
English—not always phonetic
Asian and African languages (some)—tonal; that is, high, low, rising, or falling pitch can make the same sound mean different things

After language, the next concern in describing text setting is to describe the distribution of syllables—their specific placement among the notes of each melodic line. The simplest text setting is syllabic (one note per syllable), as in Figure 3.6, "Yankee Doodle." The opposite of this is melismatic text setting, with many notes per syllable, as in Figure 3.4, *Kyrie cunctipotens genitor*, diagrammed in Figure 3.7. There is also an intermediate state which applies only to some Gregorian chants (and will not be further discussed here), called neumatic text setting, in which each syllable is sung to a small group of notes that are written as one cluster in medieval written chant notation.

Beyond these mechanics of text setting, it is important to consider how the music expresses the meaning of the text. Although composers have included occasional references to real sounds like bird songs or trumpet calls in melodies since the Middle Ages or before, the art of word painting, or text painting, was the greatest contribution to music of the Renaissance madrigal. In word painting, the composer illustrates in the music the meaning of specific moments in the text. Any musical element can play a part in this illustration. "As Vesta Was from Latmos Hill Descending," a madrigal by Thomas Weelkes (Figure 3.12) is a very clear example of this.

7. FORM—The total shape of a piece of music as organized through time; basic ones:
   - Strophic (vocal) or Variation (instrumental)—The same music used for different words (strophic) or played several times with changes in melody or accompaniment (variation); for instance: **A, A′, A″, A‴**, etc.
   - Binary—two-part; for instance, **AB** (more correctly ||:**A**:||:**B**:||, which equals **AABB**)
   - Ternary—three-part; for instance, **ABA**
   - Through-Composed—newly composed throughout; if portions are repeated, the repetitions are rearranged and unique. Most through-composed or other complex forms combine or expand features of the binary and ternary forms: rondo form, sonata form, etc.

Form, the seventh element of music, refers to the total construction of the work through time. Only over time is it possible to fully grasp a work's form. Musical forms range from simple ones (particularly strophic [or variation], binary, and ternary) to complex through-composed forms.

Strophic form and its instrumental equivalent, variation form, are the simplest of musical forms. In strophic form, several different verses of text are set to the same music. Most songs we hear are in strophic form. In variation form, a certain melody (or other musical unit) is set in different ways: different accompaniments, ornamentation of the melody, change from major to minor or vice versa, change of texture, etc. Mozart's "*Ah, vous dirai-je, Maman*" (Figure 3.11) is a very clear example of this. A diagram of strophic or variation form might read **A, A', A'', A'''**, etc.

The next simple musical form is two-part or binary form. In binary form, there are two distinct sections of music. While it might seem that a simple AB would suffice as a diagram, music constructed this way might not clearly define two sections. It might not be possible to hear the division between the sections, so the form would appear to be one continuous section. In order to define clearly the two sections, one or (usually) both are repeated: **||:A:||:B:||, = AABB** (the dots flanking vertical strokes indicate repeats). Each individual variation of Mozart's "*Ah, vous dirai-je, Maman*" (Figure 3.11) is a binary form.

Ternary form has three parts but usually only two sections of music: the first section is repeated at the end of the second section (**ABA**); the repeat of the A section may be altered somewhat, but its identity remains clear. By repeating the A section in this way, the limits of the B section are defined. Figure 3.14, Robert Schumann's "Important Event," from *Scenes from Childhood*, is a brief and clear example of ternary form.

More elaborate music forms are usually through-composed. A through-composed form is a continuously developing form, usually newly composed throughout, *but with repeated material*. Repetition of musical ideas (melodies, rhythms, harmonies, etc.) is essential to establish unity in a musical form, but in a through-composed form, if portions are repeated, the repetitions are usually altered or rearranged and unique. Most through-composed or other complex forms combine or expand features of the binary and ternary forms. Two of the most common through-composed forms are rondo form and sonata form.

In rondo form, the basic concept of the ternary form is extended—the first musical theme (melody) is very recognizable. After it is played (sometimes more than once to ensure recognition), a second theme enters. Then after the second theme, the first returns, followed by a third theme. After the third theme, the first returns, followed by a fourth theme, and so on, ending with a final presentation of the first theme, sometimes followed by a "tail" of additional music called a *coda*. The final movement of Joseph Haydn's Symphony no. 100, the *Military Symphony*, which will be discussed in a later chapter, is a variant rondo form called a sonata rondo, in which both the A and B themes recur.

FIGURE 3.14 Robert Schumann (1810–1856), "Important Event" *("Wichtige Begebenheit"),* from *Scenes from Childhood* (*Kinderszenen*, 1838), Op. 15, Movement 6, piano solo.

Section	Music
A	Heavy pompous descending chords, 7 in each phrase, 4 phrases
B (repeat marked)	2 phrases with heavy, faster bass line—notated just once in the music, but with directions to repeat the section
A	Same 4 phrases of heavy pompous descending chords

As written, this is ABA, ternary, although technically, when the repeat is played (as it always is), it sounds as ABBA. Even so, the ABA concept of the same outer sections with a contrasting middle section is clear.

The most common standard through-composed form is an elegant combination of binary and ternary concepts called a sonata-allegro form. The example for this, to be discussed later, is the first movement of Haydn's Symphony no. 100. A diagram of the form is in Figure 3.15 below.

The ternary aspect of the sonata-allegro form arises from the exposition and recapitulation surrounding the development. The exposition and the recapitulation contain the same thematic ideas in the same order, while the development manipulates these ideas in creative ways, not usually in the same order as they occur in the other two sections. To develop these ideas, the composer may break them into smaller units, repeat them, change their keys, mix them up, etc. Composers often see such developments as a chance to exercise their ingenuity. Thus, overall, the exposition–development–recapitulation structure is ternary in design.

But comparing the exposition and recapitulation reveals differences. Each of them is basically two parts, a variant of binary form: Theme 1–transition–Theme 2–closing. However, the harmony of the second theme changes. In the exposition, Theme 1 is in the tonic or main key of the piece; the transition changes key and Theme 2 is in the dominant key, secondary to the tonic; the closing brings the exposition to a close in the dominant key.

But the recapitulation alters this. Most musical forms end in the same key as they began, so the last part of the exposition must be changed, and Theme 2 arrives in the tonic key, which then continues through the closing of the piece. In practice, this means that most of the recapitulation is different than the exposition because, for Theme 2 to appear in a different key, the transition must also be changed, and as long as that is changed, the composer usually makes some changes in the closing as well so the movement will end conclusively. This lengthy description illustrates the complex nature of the most common through-composed form (as well as many others.)

Sonata-Allegro Form—Through-composed, combines binary and ternary

    Exposition—Two themes (melodies, ideas) in different keys

        Theme 1—Main key (tonic)

            Transition—modulates to new key

        Theme 2—New key (dominant if in a major key)

            Closing—remains in new key

    Development—Composer "plays with" Themes 1 and 2—breaks them into small units, may repeat themes or units, change keys, mix themes together, even introduce new themes or ideas. Anything goes.

    Recapitulation—Two themes—the same ones, but *this time in the same key*

        Theme 1—Tonic (main key)

            Transition—leads to *same (main) key* instead of new one

        Theme 2—*Tonic (main key)*

            Closing—remains in main key

FIGURE 3.15 Sonata-Allegro Form—Through-composed with formal structure, like two similar binary forms surrounding a freely composed section.

8. EXPRESSIVE CONTENT—The emotional (or sometimes, as in songs or opera, more concrete and specific) meaning of the work. Oddly enough, although music is usually perceived as the art form most strongly tied to emotion, analysts often shy away from assigning a definite emotional message to any given piece.

Expressive content, the final musical element, is the emotional (or sometimes, as in songs or opera, more concrete and specific) meaning of the work. The concrete image or meaning in vocal music is usually fairly clear, but for much instrumental music, there is no concrete association. Yet, oddly enough, although music is usually perceived as the most powerfully emotional art form, it is often difficult to assign a definite emotional message or feeling to any given piece. The expressive content (often inexpressible in words) is left to the performers' and listeners' private interpretations.

Musical and Stage Examples

Asterisks (*) indicate examples that appear in chapter 3.
† cited with reference to later chapter, but not played

Prehistoric
  Demonstration of bone flute. The only source for this that I know of is Werner Herzog's video, *Cave of Forgotten Dreams.*

Ancient Near Eastern
  "Hymn to Nikkal"

Ancient Greek
  "Epitaph of Seikilos"
  "First Delphic Hymn"
  Aeschylus, *The Furies (Eumenides)*, excerpts

Early Medieval, Romanesque
  * Gregorian Chant: *Kyrie cunctipotens genitor*
  * *Organum Tu patris sempiternus*
  * *Organum Rex caeli Domine*

Late Medieval, Gothic
  * English Rota: *Sumer is icumen in*
  * Guillaume de Machaut, *Messe de Nostre Dame*, 1) *"Kyrie"*
  Liturgical Drama: *The Play of Daniel*

Renaissance
  Sacred: Josquin Desprez, *Ave Maria Virgo Serena*
  Secular: Italian Madrigal—Jacob Arcadelt, *Il bianco e dolce cigno*
  * English Madrigal—Thomas Weelkes, "As Vesta Was from Latmos Hill Descending"

Baroque
  Roman—Giacomo Carissimi, *Jephthe* ("Daughter's lament"), with echoes & chorus
  German—J.S. Bach, "B Minor Mass," 4) *Gloria in excelsis* 5) *Et in terra pax*
  6) *Laudamus te* & 7) *Gratias agimus tibi*

(Neo) Classic
  * W. A. Mozart—*Twelve Variations on "Ah, vous dirai-je, Maman,"* cited above
  † Joseph Haydn—Symphony no. 100 (*The Military Symphony*), all four movements
    1. *Adagio-Allegro*
    2. *Allegretto*
    3. Menuet & Trio: *Moderato*
    4. Finale: *Presto*

Nineteenth Century
    German Romantic
        * Beethoven—"Symphony no. 5," opening twenty-three measures
                Pathétique Sonata, first movement
        Schubert—*Erlkönig*
        * Robert Schumann—"Important Event"
    Romantic Ballet
        Tchaikovsky—*Swan Lake*, Act II
    American Realism
        John Knowles Paine, *Fuga giocosa*
    French Impressionism
        Claude Debussy—*L'après-midi d'un faune*
Twentieth Century
    France
        Modernist—Igor Stravinsky, Act I of *The Rite of Spring*
    America
        Modernist—Charles Ives, *The Unanswered Question*
        Populist—Aaron Copland, *Fanfare for the Common Man* with
                popular rock arrangement by Emerson, Lake and Palmer
        Avant-Garde Experimentalist—John Cage, *Sonata V for Prepared Piano*
        Postmodern Minimalist—Terry Riley, *In C*

Image Credits

All images found in this chapter are original to the author and adapted from public domain sources.

CHAPTER 4

ELEMENTS OF DRAMATIC ART

Dramatic Art, like Music and Dance, is a Performing Art or Time Art. As with the elements of other art forms, the elements of dramatic art are its basic structural components. They are universal and comprehensive; that is, they can be used to describe any dramatic presentation from any culture known to man, and they cover all aspects of the dramatic work, although not all of the elements will necessarily be required by every artwork.

Elements of Dramatic Art

The first element of dramatic art is the play's basic structure. The idea or script is the basic creative conception of the dramatic work. Every dramatic presentation (like other art forms) arises from an idea. It is in the expression of the idea that dramatic art is unique—it involves actors impersonating characters in staged situations. This expression can take one of two forms, flexible, as in improvised theater, or planned and fixed with a written script. Some works use a combination of the two.

1. IDEA / SCRIPT
   - Improvised
   - Scripted

Having decided on a basic idea or message, the work's creator must come up with a way of using actors to communicate this to the audience. For some circumstances, improvisation can be most effective—if the location is to be informal, as in a public space, or if the creator wants the actors to have more flexibility in adapting their performance to the audience. I use the word *creator* here, because improvisation can vary widely in its structure. There may even be more than one creator. On one extreme, the idea can be thoroughly planned out, perhaps by one person, and the actors directed so that the plot moves in a specific way. On the other end are extemporaneous improvisations. In these, actors respond to each other off the cuff, and the plot, such as it is, just unfolds. Something in between is probably most common. Actors and perhaps a director may develop characters, situations and plots and come up with a rough plan from which the actors create the finished performance. This, in fact, was the way in which the Italian *commedia dell'arte* worked. Stock characters, each with an identifying mask, accent, costume and behavior, would enter a predetermined situation and improvise from there on.

A more disciplined approach to the idea for a drama is the script, almost always written by one person, with at least the actors' lines written out. Scripts did not contain much more than this until after Shakespeare. He might state the location of a scene in the script, and stage directions were limited to the essentials: enter, exit, fight, kiss, etc. Since scenery was limited, the actors' costumes had to indicate their characters, and the play's lines described the scene and situation. This is still much more structured than the improvisation, and, as time went on, it got even more so, until, by the end of the nineteenth century, a play might begin with a detailed description of the set, paragraphs long. And stage directions might indicate facial expressions, gestures and the smallest movements, even emotional states. However much detail the playwright includes, the script provides a disciplined structure that the actor must follow to bring the idea to life.

Once an idea and approach are determined, the first step toward developing it is to set to work on the second element of the dramatic art—Plot.

2. PLOT
- Episodic—Series of episodes of approximately equal weight
- Climactic—Rises to a climax, followed by a resolution, five parts;
  - Exposition—in which the characters and their types, desires, fears, and aims are introduced
  - Conflict—arising from the interaction of different characters' aims, personalities, etc.
  - Complications—further developments arising from the reactions of characters to the conflict(s).
  - Climax—the peak at which all conflicts and complications come to a head.
  - Denouement—the resolution of conflicts and conclusion

- Three genres
  - Tragedy—sad or violent ending
  - Comedy—happy or humorous ending
  - Tragicomedy—may have elements of both Tragedy and Comedy, or just be serious, without strong tragic or comedic feelings.
- Conceptual requirements; plot must clarify—
  - The Locale, or broad region, as well as the more specific Place.
  - The Period, or general historical time span, as well as the specific Time. Time is more specific than Period, but may vary in specificity, from season to minutes.
  - The Mood, or overall emotional overlay, as well as one or more specific Themes.

Most dramatic presentations follow a plot, although some plots are purposely aimless. For plots with clear structure, there are two basic types: Episodic and Climactic. An episodic plot develops through a series of episodes of approximately equal weight. A climactic plot rises to a climax in a structure with five basic parts: In the Exposition, the playwright introduces the characters and their types, desires, fears, and aims. Often there will be a reason to bring everyone onstage during this, in order to introduce that character to the audience. The details uncovered in the exposition lead to the next part, Conflict. Here, characters' goals and designs begin to create difficult interactions. These lead to Complications, the third part. In the fourth part, the Climax, all of these developments come to a head, and in the fifth stage, the Denouement, they are resolved, but by no means always happily. That depends on whether the play is comic or tragic.

Plots fall into three basic genres: Tragedy, with a sad or violent ending; Comedy, with a happy or humorous ending; and Tragicomedy (for lack of a better word), which may have elements of both Tragedy and Comedy, or may just be serious, without strong tragic or comedic feelings. Tragedy most often follows a climactic plot, since the situation must rise to a great enough emotional height to justify the sad or violent ending. Comedy and tragicomedy, on the other hand, can use either structure equally effectively.

Whatever the structure and genre, the plot must establish a framework of certain facts about the situation, which can lead to obvious effects on the plot. The first is geographical: the plot must establish the Locale, or broad region, as well as the more specific Place. For instance, a scene set in a jungle (place) in Brazil, will have very different consequences for the characters than one set on an iceberg in the arctic. The second part of the framework is temporal: the Period, or general historical time span, and the specific Time. Although Time is more specific than Period, it can vary in its degree of specificity, from season, to day, to time of day, to minutes. A fur trader in 1850 on a midwinter day will have a very different life from a commuter in downtown London during a summer afternoon rush hour. These things all contribute to the Mood, or emotional overlay of the work, which reinforces the genre, Tragedy or Comedy. The mood may also reinforce a particular Theme. Some themes have a timeless validity. Aeschylus's *The Furies*, Shakespeare's *Merchant of Venice*, Arthur Miller's *The Crucible*, and Moisés Kaufman's *Laramie Project* express in very different ways the theme of persecution. In all of them, that is both a theme and a message. Presenting the Plot, Mood and Theme as a dramatic work requires the third element of dramatic art—Characters.

3. CHARACTERS
- Impersonation—An actor or actress taking the role of another person or character. This is the distinctive feature of the dramatic arts.

- Classification by importance to the plot
  - Leading Roles—The main or most important characters
  - Supporting Roles—The characters who surround the leads and assist them in conveying the plot.
- Character types by plot genre
  - Tragedy
    - The Protagonist—a main character, focus of the action, usually good but flawed
    - The Antagonist—opposes the main character, tries to undo his/her action, often evil
  - Comedy—Stock Characters, humorous personality types, some examples—
    - The foolish (or stingy, or scheming) old man
    - The old woman busybody or gossip
    - Young lovers
    - Crafty servants, Pompous professionals, Egotistical braggarts, etc.

Mr GARRICK in the Character of HAMLET
Act I. Scene 4.th

FIGURE 4.1 David Garrick, an 18th-century English actor, as Shakespeare's Hamlet, a lead role. 18th-century English engraving.

The distinctive feature of the dramatic arts is Impersonation; that is, the actors and actresses take on the role of another person or character. It is impersonation that makes what the actor does different from the teacher in front of a class or a politician making a speech. They are themselves–the actor is someone else. Character's roles are of two types: Leading Roles, the main or most important characters, around whom the drama revolves, and Supporting Roles, those characters who support and assist the leads. The difference between these two groups is especially significant when a play is reworked (for instance from stage to film). Supporting roles may be removed or sometimes added, according to the needs of the new medium. Leading roles are rarely removed, and almost never added.

Different types of plots also have different types of characters. In tragedy, there are two opposing types: the Protagonist, a main character, usually the "good guy," in any case, the focus or mover of the action, but who may have flaws; and the Antagonist, the "bad guy," the adversary of the protagonist, who opposes the protagonist's acts. Figure 4.1 shows David Garrick, one of the most famous English actors of the eighteenth century, as Hamlet, a protagonist whose tragic flaw is indecision. In comedy, even if these two types exist, they are made humorous, treated with irony, parodied, even ridiculed. And comedy often builds on a set of Stock Characters, humorous, often exaggerated personality types, like a foolish (or stingy, or scheming) old man, an old woman busybody or gossip, young lovers, crafty servants, pompous professionals, egotistical braggarts, and many others. Figure 4.2 depicts some stock characters from the *commedia dell'arte:* Harlequin *(Arlecchino)*, a comic servant, *il dottore*, the pompous doctor, and *il capitano*, the cowardly braggart soldier.[1] All of these types are portrayed by the actors. But actors are only one group of participants in the dramatic equation.

---

1   Figure 12.7 shows porcelain figurines of *Arlecchino* and two other *commedia dell'arte* characters, *Columbina*, the tricky maidservant, and *Pantalone*, the stingy businessman.

FIGURE 4.2A *Arlecchino* (Harlequin), a supporting role (comic servant) from the improvised Italian *Commedia dell'arte*, speaks with the rustic accent of Bergamo. Maurice Sand, 19th-century print.

FIGURE 4.2B *Il dottore*, the pompous doctor from the *commedia dell'arte*, parodies graduates of the University of Bologna, whose accent he mixes with garbled Latin. Maurice Sand, 19th-century print.

FIGURE 4.2C *Il capitano*, the cowardly braggart soldier from the *commedia dell'arte*, from Spain or southern Italy—incompetent with giant sword, screams at the sight of blood. Maurice Sand, 19th-century print.

4. PARTICIPANTS—Three different levels
   - Actors and Actresses—The performers who convey the plot by impersonation; two levels of depiction:
     - Social role—position in society—policeman, queen, beggar, etc.
     - Personal role or specific personality of the character—difficult. New 20th-century approach to embracing and projecting the personal role: Method Acting. Method actors/actresses try to connect deeply to the character by drawing on their own experiences and emotions or reactions to the circumstances created in the plot.
   - Audience—Especially important in live theater. A live theater experience is an elevated form of communication that has been called a communion. Actors and audience influence each other.
     - The "dead house"—Unresponsive audience.
     - The "live house"—Happy, excited responsive audience.
     - Film or video vs. stage
       - Film production has no real audience, just various supervisory and support personnel.
       - Film actors rarely perform even a whole scene at once, and they may not know the final version of the plot.

- In film, facial expressions, gestures and delivery of lines must be as near perfect as possible, less important in live theater, where the audience is at a distance.
- Critic—More important in theater (including opera and dance) than in other art forms.

Dramatic Art involves not only actors, but participants at several (at least three) different levels:

- Actors and Actresses are (most obviously) the performers who convey the plot by impersonation. Like plot concepts, impersonation/depiction has distinct levels. First, the player must convey a social role (position in society—policeman, queen, beggar, etc.). This is the less difficult part of depiction. It can be helped by adopting a particular attitude appropriate to the character, and also by a well-designed costume and make-up. More difficult is portraying the personal role or specific personality of the character. This last is often the most difficult, and in the 20th century, a new approach to embracing and projecting the personal role was developed: Method Acting.[2] Method actors/actresses go beyond assuming the external characteristics of the role and try to connect more deeply to the character by drawing on their own experiences and emotions or reactions to the circumstances created in the plot. Developed for both stage and cinema, method acting is particularly important in film, where close-up shots expose the player's most subtle facial nuances, which must therefore perfectly reflect the character's emotions.

- The second group of participants, particularly important in live theater, is the Audience. A live theater experience is an elevated form of communication that has been called a communion. Actors and audience influence each other. If the weather is bad or the audience faces work the next day, they may be less responsive to the actors, a so-called "dead house." In this situation, the actors must work harder, even strain, to get audience reaction; they may also feel less inspired and lose some of the sparkle in their performance. On the other hand, when the audience is happy or excited, perhaps a Friday or Saturday in good weather, they are much more responsive to the players. The players sense this; it inspires their best efforts, which in turn arouse the audience more. Such a "live house" can be a scintillating theatrical experience. Of course, some concrete factors can also be involved in aiding or hindering this emotional bond, for instance language, educational level, and social standing; the actor(s) need to take these things into account to inspire the greatest communion.

  This also demonstrates one of the greatest differences and difficulties for the film or video actor. The only audience they have comprises the director, the producer, and a flock of various supporting functionaries. In addition, they rarely perform even a whole scene at once, often stopping and doing multiple "takes" of a specific line, dialog or action. Nor do they necessarily know the final version of the plot, since entire scenes may be cut in the process of editing. And, as noted above, the ability of the camera or microphone to zero in on the performer means that facial expressions, gestures and delivery of lines must be as near perfect as possible, a great challenge and a significant difference from live theater.

- The third participant is the Critic, who is more important in theater (including opera and dance) than in other art forms. Art exhibits and single night concerts are less likely to be reviewed than a theatrical production that hopes for a long run. The critic of opening night can make or break a production. Actors in large cities have been known to stay up until the first newspapers hit the streets to see how their work was received. Even now, with news, reviews, blogs and other instantaneous communication available online, the traditional opening-night party often lasts well into the early hours, since the actors need to

2   Method Acting was developed by Lee Strasburg in New York in the 1930s, partly derived from an earlier system of Konstantin Stanislavsky. Embraced by the Group Theater and later The Actor's Studio, it has been studied by many of the greatest actors of the twentieth century.

recover from a high energy level. And however or whenever it is published, a respected critic's evaluation is eagerly awaited because it is so crucial to a show's success.

5. SUPPORTING FACTORS
- Costumes & Makeup—Clarify (especially social) role, character type and emotion.
- Scenery & Properties (Props)—Establish surroundings. Hand props furnish tools.
- Special Effects, Lighting & Sound—A centuries' tradition of mechanical devices has been greatly enhanced by electronic and digital techniques.
- Music—Enhances a production, but demands more audience suspension of disbelief.

Dramatic productions may or may not use several processes to support or enhance the illusion of the characters' surroundings. Costumes can clarify the role for both audience and performer and are an important aid in projecting the social role described above. Makeup also helps in this, too, by enhancing or changing a character's (mostly facial) appearance, often dramatically. For centuries, the main components were face paint, wax and wigs, but the development in the last century of latex masks has permitted much more extreme portrayal of deformities, fantastic beasts and even alien beings. Applying this treatment is complex and time-consuming; often the actor or actresses must arrive hours before the show or filming begins. And today, characters even beyond these extended make-up capabilities can be created digitally from scratch.

Scenery helps to establish place, and Properties (Props) establish or enhance details of scenery, character or plot. Hand props are separate from the scenery but essential to rounding out a character. They are things (attributes) that are carried by the actor or actress: book, flowers, magic wand, mixing bowl, parasol, purse, spear, sword, walking stick, etc. Stage Props are rightfully part of the scenery; they are large freestanding objects—furniture, a tree stump, a ship's mast, etc. Like scenery's other parts, stage props are mostly used to establish details of place and time. The other parts of scenery are the flats. These are of two types: backdrops, which cover the entire back of the stage, and *coulisses*, narrow pieces in front of the backdrop that conceal the sides (or wings) of the stage. Figure 4.3 shows a miniature model (or mock-up) of an opera stage set, with backdrop, *coulisses* and other types of scenery flats. In most stage productions these are 2–3 centimeters thick, so they would look very much like the cardboard in this miniature. From the actor/singer's point of view, their flatness is obvious, but

FIGURE 4.3 Édouard Desplechin (1802–1871), Miniature mock-up of scenery for Act III of Gioachino Rossini's *Moïse* (Moses) (1836)—The Porch of the Temple of Isis. This side view shows how the illusion of depth is achieved.

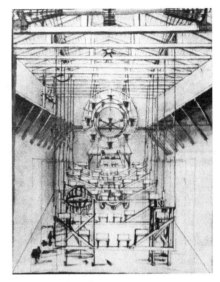

FIGURE 4.4 Giacomo Torelli (1608–1678), Set design for Act V of Pierre Corneille's *Andromède* (Andromeda) (1650). This has three machines for characters in the clouds: Left–Juno, Perseus and Cepheus, Andromeda's father; Jupiter in the center; and Right–Neptune, Andromeda and Cassiopeia, her mother.

FIGURE 4.5 Backstage machinery for Giovanni Legrenzi's *Germanico sul Reno* (Germanicus on the Rhine) at Venice's Teatro San Salvador in 1676. The giant wheel has seats for eight singers who would seem to rotate slowly around the sky on clouds. There appear to be other wheels, too, controlled by the several layers of ropes.

the picture also shows how well-painted flats give the illusion of roundness and depth when viewed from the front.

Complex stage machinery has also been part of the scenery from time to time. It was especially popular in operas and non-musical plays in the seventeenth and early eighteen centuries. *Andromeda*, by Pierre Corneille (1606–1684) used complex stage machinery in every one of its five acts. That of Act V (Figure 4.4) has three gods seated on clouds in the sky. In the course of the scene, they raise the four main characters up to themselves to become constellations.[3] The clouds may even have carried them on or off stage. Such devices were common. In fact, the other acts of this play have Venus descending from the clouds to earth, the eight winds carrying off Andromeda, Perseus arriving on a flying horse, and Juno flying across the sky in her chariot to reassure Cepheus and Cassiopeia, Andromeda's mother. Every act also uses linear perspective created by multiple rows of *coulisses*, an effect so popular it was used in almost every stage set of this era. The backstage design for a mechanism for such complex effects appears in Figure 4.5. In this scene from Giovanni Legrenzi's *Germanicus on the Rhine*, gods or spirits performed from clouds that rotated in the sky on the wheel shown here from the back.

Many effects that were done mechanically like these have been made much simpler by electronic and computer technology, but both sound and lighting effects were originally very rudimentary. The old mechanical thunder sheets, wind rollers, small doors, and actual firearms have been replaced largely by recordings which are less trouble and much more versatile. Stage lighting was originally just chandelier(s) over the stage and candle footlights, none of

---

3   Briefly, the story of the myth is that Andromeda, chained to a rock as sacrifice to a sea monster, was rescued by Perseus, who flew in on Pegasus. The key persons were rewarded by becoming constellations in the northern sky. (They *are* there.)

FIGURE 4.6 Max Bruckner (1836–1919), Set design for last scene of Richard Wagner's *Götterdämmerung* (Twilight of the Gods) (1894). The fire has finished its work on earth and is now burning Valhalla, the gods' palace.

which could be altered much. Lightning was created with gunpowder or flash powder, a significant fire hazard.[4] Theater lighting evolved from candles to oil lamps to gaslights, and finally to electric lights. This last has greatly expanded the range of lighting effects, for example: spotlighting, colored lighting, dimmers, lightning flashes, projected images and scrims. A scrim is a backdrop of a thin, net-like fabric with different scenes painted on the front and the back. The scene changes according to which side is lit. Of course, even before electric lights, designers sometimes created incredible effects. More than one work based on the last days of Pompeii (including a 2014 film) has ended with the eruption of Mount Vesuvius in the background, and the end of Wagner's opera *Twilight of the Gods* has Brünnhilde ride her horse onto a funeral pyre which sets the entire stage alight, up to the gods in Valhalla, after which the river Rhine floods and quenches the blaze (see Figure 4.6).

Wagner's work is a good example to illustrate several extremes in stage production. This scene ends a cycle of four operas (*The Ring of the Nibelung*) that takes over eighteen hours on four successive nights. They are based on Norse/Germanic myths and require many special effects for magical illusions. One of these opens the first opera. Three Rhinemaidens swim around while singing their opening ode to the magical Rhinegold. Figure 4.7a shows what the audience saw; 4.7b shows the scenery carts that moved them around behind the scrim that depicted water. Other illusions included the construction of Valhalla in the air, descent into the earth, a rainbow bridge, flying horses, a bed of fire, a dragon slaying, a talking (or singing—this is an opera) bird, and beings that rise from the earth. Quite a collection, even for opera. And Wagner's music for these works is also the extreme example of musical enhancement of the drama. Every character, every plot theme, every significant object in the works has its own signature tune. By mixing and combining them, Wagner makes it possible to hear the drama even without seeing it. Even without going to this extreme, music can greatly enhance the excitement of a production, although it may actually require a bit more suspension of disbelief on the part of the audience. How many people in real life stop to sing or dance about their emotional reactions or have an orchestral accompaniment to their daily activities? But Music is an art, and adding it to a theatrical performance is like icing on a

---

4   Even recently, between 2003 and 2015, over 850 people worldwide were killed in nightclub fires caused by pyrotechnics on stage. And Shakespeare's Globe Theater burned down because a cannon in *Henry VIII* set the roof on fire.

cake or lace on a garment—it adds an elegant final touch.

6. MEDIUM & SPACE—Varied approaches to dramatic art; each has specific space needs.

- Cinema or Video—Filmed in a Sound Stage or on Location.
- Unstaged Theater, Radio Drama.
- Puppetry (a theater surrogate)—Moveable figures replace live actors; useful for tales with fantastic effects or silly humor.
  - Traditional puppetry uses variants on the proscenium stage—four types.
    - Hand or glove puppets
    - Rod puppets
    - Marionettes
    - Shadow Puppets
  - 20th-Century innovations—
    - The *Muppets*, filmed on a sound stage
    - Nontraditional spaces; the *Bread and Puppet Theater* of Glover, Vermont, performs outdoors.
- Live Theater—The richest variety of performance spaces.
  - Environmental Theater—Wherever it happens—
  - Thrust Stages—A projecting acting area with audience on three sides.
  - Proscenium Theater—Most common modern theater style, developed after 1600.
  - Arena Theater, or Theater in the Round—Audience on all sides of the players.
  - Found Space—Improvised space wherever suitable: attic, repurposed building—

FIGURE 4.7A The Rhinemaidens in the first complete production of Richard Wagner's *Ring of the Nibelung* operas in 1876 in his custom-built theater in Bayreuth. The center figure is the famous singer Lili Lehmann, as Woglinde.

FIGURE 4.7B The Rhinemaiden machinery behind the scene.

There are several different approaches to the dramatic art, and each has specific space considerations.

Cinema or Video is often filmed in a Sound Stage, an indoor space in a large, specially constructed building. Acoustically isolated so there is no extraneous noise, it can be large or small. It usually has little or no permanent set-up other than the walls, so it can be arranged

FIGURE 4.8 Sound stage at Video Wisconsin, Brookfield, Wisconsin.

FIGURE 4.9 Location shooting in San Francisco's Chinatown. Mike Chin, director of photography, is behind the camera, which is on a dolly to assure smooth movement.

to portray any scene. Figure 4.8 is the sound stage at *Video Wisconsin*, a professional television and video production firm on the outskirts of Milwaukee. In addition to the blank floor and walls, the ceiling has racks for installation of lighting and other things needing to be suspended for a production. Film companies use sound stages for their convenience—it is not necessary to transport a lot of specialized equipment somewhere else. Sometimes, however, the complexity or size required a particular scene would be too costly to build, so the company will take what equipment it needs On Location, to a suitable site. This is rarely the actual site itself, which may not offer the desired look, or may be encumbered or otherwise difficult of access. For instance, the hundreds of so-called "spaghetti western" films made in the 1960s were filmed in Italy and Spain, and the Wyoming mountain valleys in *Brokeback Mountain* were filmed in the Alberta Rockies.[5] Figure 4.9 shows location filming in San Francisco's Chinatown.

In direct contrast to the complexity of cinema, television and video production is Unstaged Theater. Plays are sometimes read without staging in any convenient space. This was popular in the late nineteenth and early twentieth centuries. A related dramatic form that was very popular and still has followers is the Chautauqua performance, named after a summer family education retreat in upstate New York. In a Chautauqua, an actor assumes the role of a historic figure and gives a speech or lecture in that character. One of the most famous such acts was Hal Holbrook's impersonation of Mark Twain. A more structured form of reading was radio drama, popular in the early twentieth century and performed live in a radio studio with a sound effects man to provide door sounds, gunshots, horses' hooves, water dripping, and much more. The form has been revived with great popularity in Garrison Keillor's *Prairie Home Companion*. One of the most popular 1930s radio serials was *The Shadow*, starring Orson Welles (see Figure 4.10).

Puppetry is a theater surrogate, in which moveable figures in either two or three dimensions take the place of live actors. Puppetry is very ancient and dates back to the ancient Egyptians. There are four types of puppets. The simplest are hand (or glove) puppets, placed

---

5   There are sometimes humorous incongruities. For instance, Riverton, Wyoming, a prosperous community of 10,000, is represented in the film as having a tiny ramshackle post office. Not that there might not be such places in Wyoming, but Riverton is not one of them. And in the *Agony and the Ecstasy*, Michelangelo has a confrontation with Pope Julius II about the Sistine ceiling in a scene where I have counted at least four historical errors.

on the operator's hand and operated above his head. The best-known pair is Punch and Judy, illustrated in Figure 4.11a. Another offspring of the *commedia dell'arte*, Mr. Punch is a ruffian who beats other characters like Judy his wife, or the recurring policeman, with his stick. Judy is not much better, and part of their heavy-handed interaction often involves tossing their baby back and forth like a football. This is low, slapstick comedy, for which hand puppets are well suited. Rod puppets, also operated from below, are a very different case. Since they do not rely on the shape of the hand, their proportions can be much more realistic, and they can move with more grace and dignity. Figure 4.11b shows the rod puppets of the Bread and Puppet Circus. These are unusually large, but absolutely traditional in their mode of operation.

The type of puppet most often associated with serious puppetry is the marionette, suspended on strings and operated from above (see Figure 4.12a). Marionettes can be the

FIGURE 4.10 Orson Welles as *The Shadow*, title role of one of the most famous 1930s radio dramas.

most realistic of all puppets in shape, dress and proportions, as the figure shows. The standard minimum number of strings is seven, two for the head, four for the limbs and one for the back. Specialty puppets may have many more, for rolling eyes, moveable jaws, individual fingers for a pianist or toe and ankle strings for a dancer, magical effects, etc. Marionettes can do practically everything a human actor can do, with one notable exception. They cannot be convincingly rough, because they tend to sway and swing on the strings. The problem is overcome in an otherwise rudimentary variant of the marionettes—the *pupi* of Sicily and southern Italy (see Figure 4.12b).

Sicilian *pupi* lack knee joints and they have only three controlling wires, one each for the head and hands. The wires give a firmness of control that permits swordfights and battles, which, as the magnificent costumes suggest, are a large part in all of their traditional plots. The tales are drawn

FIGURE 4.11A Punch and Judy, the oldest traditional hand puppet show, here in Philadelphia. Mr. Punch is derived from *Pulcinella*, another *commedia dell'arte* character. They share the large hooked nose and costumes, but the English version is much rougher.

FIGURE 4.11B The Bread and Puppet Circus, an experimental puppetry group in Glover, Vermont, uses conventional, if enormous, rod puppets.

Marionettes on display at the Lübeck (Germany) Theater Figures Museum.

A display of traditional Sicilian pupi at the Museo etnografico eoliano (The Aeolian Ethnographic Museum), in Lipari, the largest of the Aeolian islands just north of Sicily. The characters are traditional: (L to R) Angelica, Emperor Charlemagne, Rinaldo (Renaud), Orlando (Roland), a maid (Lauretta?), Peppinninu.

from or inspired by traditional epics about the knights of Charlemagne, the characters in the figure. Charlemagne is obvious in his crown, and across from him is his nephew and greatest knight, Roland. Between them is blond Renaud, Roland's closest companion and rival in love for the beautiful Angelica, in front of Charlemagne. On the far right stand a maid and Peppinninu (aka Verticchiù), Roland's one-eyed squire. All are richly dressed; the knights' armor, all handmade and individualized, is finely detailed and polished. The figures' dignity is not hindered by their simplicity. The stiffness of the head wire permits enough control for their walk to be convincing, and their other activities are as thrilling and physical as puppets can be.

The opposite is true of the final type of puppet. Shadow puppets are especially suited for tales of mystery and magic. They can appear, disappear and change size with an ease shared by no other puppet (or human actors, for that matter). Shadow puppets are most common in East Asia, where nearly every country has its own style. They are not unknown in Europe, however, and I include Figure 4.13, described by its French performer as a tale of shadows. Shadow puppets are flat silhouettes illuminated from behind as they are pressed against a thin white screen. If the puppet is made of opaque material the shadow is black, but transparent colors will show through the screen. The puppets can be operated from below, like rod puppets, in which case the rods make visible shadows, or from behind, as these are. This latter is a bit more difficult, as the puppet must always be held and cannot be set briefly at rest. In either case, flying or acrobatic characters require no special arrangement, and for a disappearance or engorgement, just pull the puppet gradually away from the screen.

Puppetry hasn't vanished. As the figures show, it is still a vibrant and living tradition today, with some new great innovations. The giant rod puppets of the Bread and Puppet's *Domestic*

Resurrection Circus are not alone. Several groups in Europe have also built giant marionettes of about the same size. To me, they are a bit problematic, since they require cranes and thick strings that hamper the illusion more than the puppeteers below the Bread and Puppets figures. But probably the greatest innovation in puppetry was made by the late Jim Henson. By using a combination of video and puppetry techniques, the Muppets presented a variety show that used mixed glove and rod puppets side by side with full sized human guest stars and costumed monsters. The mixed media allowed all of them to mix together seamlessly in a virtual hall that even had a muppet band and a full muppet audience. And of course, there are all those impossible Hollywood puppet monsters, like Jabba the Hutt, which used three internal puppeteers and radio control. Puppetry's reservoir of theatrical creativity is far from exhausted.

FIGURE 4.13 *Théâtre d'ombres* (Theater of Shadows), by the Coppelius Company, Plélan-le-Grand, Brittany, France. France, a scene from a shadow puppet play.

Among this great variety of dramatic techniques, for the true theater lover, live theater reigns supreme. There are five basic types, determined by their performing spaces: Environmental Theater, Thrust Stage, Proscenium Stage, Arena Theater and Found Performing Space. Environmental Theater is probably the oldest kind of theater space, as it involves no special construction, like modern street theater. Even within the last century, it has existed in underdeveloped cultures. In the mid-twentieth century, Australian aborigines did at least one musical dance pantomime that depicted the different fish in the sea, and various North American native tribes have dances that

FIGURE 4.14 A street theater performance in Vancouver, British Columbia.

depict animals, and, in some cases accompanying stories. All of these are forms of environmental theater, which also survives in contemporary street theater, like that in Figure 4.14.

The earliest permanent theaters, of the ancient Greeks, were Thrust Stages, with a circular or semicircular acting area in front of a permanent architectural backdrop (the *skene*), and having the audience on three sides. Figure 4.15 shows the first of these, the Theater of Dionysus in Athens, where formal theater was invented. The first picture (4.15a) looks down from the Athenian acropolis into the theater bowl as it now exists. The thrust stage surrounded by audience is obvious, and the remnants of the *skene* building show clearly behind it. The size of the

FIGURE 4.15A Theater of Dionysus, Athens (current).

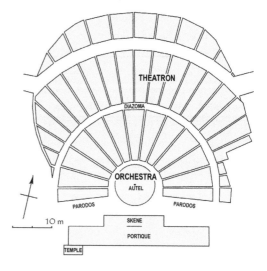

FIGURE 4.15B Theater of Dionysus, Athens (original plan, from the time of Pericles, 5th c. BCE).

humans between them also gives some idea of the theater's size; it could seat 17,000 people! Figure 4.15b shows the original design; the *orchestra* or central stage was circular, which was true of all Classic Greek theatres, like the later one at Epidaurus in Figure 4.16. Constructed between the fourth and second centuries BCE, Epidaurus' theater is the best preserved ancient Greek theatre. Although its capacity is a little less than Athens' original size (c. 14,000), the fact that its seating survives complete make Epidaurus seem larger, and it certainly is imposing when viewed from the top. One final point about Greek theaters deserves attention before moving on to Rome. Greece itself is very mountainous, and the theaters were often associated with remote shrines. For this reason, many Greek theaters are in spectacular locations, like that of Delphi (Figure 4.17).

Roman theatres, on the other hand, were often in towns and cities. They were usually smaller than those of the Greeks and slightly shallower from front to back, with a U-shaped orchestra

FIGURE 4.16 Theater of Epidaurus (fourth-second centuries BCE), capacity ca. fourteen thousand. Reported to have the best acoustics of all surviving ancient Greek theaters. Lines spoken onstage are clear even from the top.

instead of a circular one and seating around that in an arc no greater than a semicircle. In addition to the usual open-air theaters, the Romans also built smaller roofed ones called *odeons*. Due to the Roman Empire's size and the Romans' practice of duplicating the structures of their civilization wherever they settled, there are many more surviving Roman theaters than Classic Greek ones. And in some respects, they are better preserved. The theater at Sabratha (see Figure 4.18), in the northwest corner of what is now Libya, has nearly all of the decorative façade of its *skene* (Latin, *scenae frons*) preserved. Its three stories of elaborate colonnades clarify the setting for Roman comedies. The separate sections and their doorways represented houses or streets to somewhere else, as the plot required.

Another well-preserved Roman theater is that of Orange in France (see Figure 4.19). In this case, the *skene* building is complete, but most of the colonnade was looted long ago. The solid backdrop, though, retains the original acoustics and makes the theater excellent for concerts and other performances like the one pictured. The image also brings to life the crowd capacity of these ancient theaters. This one is awe-inspiring, and it is only half the size of Athens' Theater of Dionysus.

Construction of permanent theaters ceased during the Middle Ages, due to the church's condemnation as well as political instability. Beginning in the Renaissance, theaters rose again in Ferrara (1531), Rome (1545), Mantua (1549), Bologna (1550), Siena (1561), and Venice (1565).[6] Renaissance culture included a strong interest in Classical Antiquity, so it is not surprising that when the city of Vicenza commissioned a theater from its native son Andrea Palladio, he would follow that model. Figure 4.20 shows the evolution of theater design in Italy. Within the illustration, Fig. X is a general ancient (Roman) theater. Fig. XI above it is Palladio's *Teatro Olimpico* in Vicenza (1580–1585).

The *Teatro Olimpico* is indeed similar to the ancient design, but it is even more squat than Roman theaters. This is because of the space Palladio had to work with. His other innovations

FIGURE 4.17 Theater of Delphi (originally fourth century BCE, last remodeled in 67 BCE).

FIGURE 4.18 *Skene* of the Roman theater of Sabratha, Libya (North Africa, second–third century CE).

---

6   Nikolaus Pevsner, A History of Building Types. (London: Thames and Hudson, 1976): 66.

Roman theater of Orange, France (early first century CE; capacity 7,000–9,000).

include a more prominent raised stage between the orchestra and the *skene*, and an elaborate permanent Roman-style *skene* façade, that was completed by Palladio's pupil and successor Vincenzo Scamozzi (Figure 4.21a). Scamozzi took charge of construction after Palladio's death a few months into the work. He faithfully executed Palladio's plans, but the realization of the *skene* and its unique perspective views are his own. Palladio left only a sketch of the *skene*, possibly because the Academy that commissioned the theater did not yet own the land behind it. When they acquired it, Scamozzi added to Palladio's plan street views in false perspective behind every doorway off the stage. These are visible in the plan in Figure 4.20, from the side in Figure 4.21b and directly through the doors in Figure 4.21a. They represent the seven streets of the city of Thebes, for the opening performance of Sophocles' *Oedipus Rex*, and they were never dismantled. They are unique in theater design, and they anticipated the *trompe l'oeil* baroque scenery shown in Figure 4.4.

The evolution of theater design continued. The *Teatro Farnese* of Parma, built in 1618 is Fig. XII, next to the *Teatro Olimpico* in the plate of theater plans in Figure 4.20. The

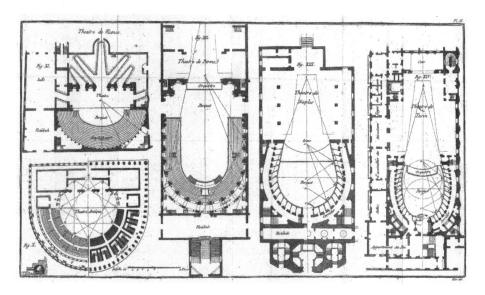

Plate II from Pierre Patte's *Essai sur l'Architecture Théatrale* (Essay on Theatrical Architecture) (1782) showing plans of five theaters. Fig. X–A Roman theater; Fig. XI–*Teatro Olimpico*, Vicenza (1585); Fig. XII–*Teatro Farnese*, Parma (1618); Fig. XIII–*Real Teatro di San Carlo*, Naples (1737); Fig. XIV–*Teatro Regio*, Turin (1740).

Farnese theatre's floor still has a semicircular end, but it is considerably longer than that of the *Teatro Olimpico*, and the galleries at the sides and rear are much steeper, giving a capacity of 4,500. The floor could serve for dancing, spectacles and, flooded, even for mock naval battles. The expense kept it from frequent use, though. The stage shows two innovations: a depth more than half that of the floor and the first proscenium arch dividing the acting and audience spaces. These two features continue with modifications in the later theaters shown.

In the north, theaters of Shakespeare's time seated the audience differently, perhaps for better protection from the colder weather, but the thrust stage remained standard. Figure 4.22 is a contemporary sketch of the Swan theater, as it existed in 1596: a partially roofed thrust stage with a "tiring house" behind for entrances, exits, and a musicians' gallery above. There is standing room around the stage for the "groundlings," and circular balcony galleries for those paying a bit more. Shakespeare's Globe (reconstructed in Figure 4.23) was similar but larger. The tiring house is more open, with spaces that can be used for acting. The fully enclosed circular space (or "wooden O" as Shakespeare described it) made it possible to restrict entrance to paying customers—a need the Greeks did not have, as their performances were free.

The form of Shakespeare's theater gave way to the new developments from Italy. As noted above, the proscenium arch developed in 1618. New theaters continued to be built, largely by noblemen.

FIGURE 4.21A Permanent stage set, Andrea Palladio & Vincenzo Scamozzi, *Teatro Olimpico* (Olympic Theater; 1585), Vicenza, Italy.

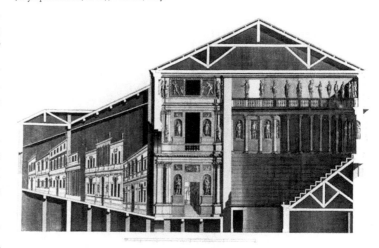

FIGURE 4.21B Side sectional view, Andrea Palladio & Vincenzo Scamozzi, *Teatro Olimpico*.

In 1637, the first public opera house, the *Teatro San Cassiano*, opened in Venice, probably similar to the somewhat later 1678 proscenium theater, the *Teatro San Giovanni Grisostomo*, built by the Grimani family (see in Figure 4.24). This design, which became standard, probably arose from the needs of opera, which was invented around 1600. The proscenium stage is the only solution that allows the audience an unobstructed view of actor/singers and dancers onstage, who themselves can see the conductor, and let all hear the orchestra, below stage level so as not to block the view.

Looking more closely at Figure 4.24 revels other significant details. The stage set is in *trompe l'oeil* perspective focused in the center. The singers stand at the front. Below them is

The Swan in 1596, a typical Elizabethan open-roof playhouse.

the orchestra pit under a double width proscenium arch that has seating boxes on its sides. There are five of these on each side, at the same levels as the balconies that extend from them to the back of the hall. Figure 4.25 shows a closer view of where the balconies and proscenium meet in the *Teatro Vendramin* of 1720, built by another noble family to essentially the same design, but without the floor-level balcony.[7] This theater also has the double proscenium arch lined with boxes, although there is now no orchestra pit. Extending back are the four levels of balconies. These are shallow, with room for one row of single seats, two at most if cramped, and there are half-partitions dividing them. The upper rear balconies might hold a couple more rows without partitions. The design was based on a cube with audience closely packed on three walls and the floor, the fourth wall being the stage. Such a design has excellent acoustics; the audience is as close to the stage as possible, and the shallow balconies provide enough angled reflection of the sound without having it get lost in the depths. Only one more feature needs comment. Figure 4.26 is a cutaway section of *La Scala* in Milan, as constructed in 1778. It has been remodeled since, but remains essentially the same. The auditorium has six rows of balconies but is otherwise similar to the preceding theaters. The

Reconstruction of Shakespeare's Globe Theater, London, showing roofed thrust stage with multiple acting areas, ground-level audience space and tiers of galleries. The stage is set for the beginning of Shakespeare's Tempest, with the rock stage props to suggest the shipwreck's isle (Bermuda).

---

7   The names of Venetian theaters can be confusing. The full name of this theater in the eighteenth century, if it were ever used, would be *Teatro Vendramin di San Luca a San Salvatore*, because the Vendramin family owned it, it was dedicated to St. Luke, and it is in the neighborhood of San Salvatore. It could be called by any one of these; it has since been renamed the *Teatro Goldoni* in honor of Venice's great comic playwright.

stage, on the other hand, has reached a depth equal to that of the auditorium, which gives room for opera's grand spectacles but is not always recognized by the audience. These design features became standard for Italian opera houses for centuries.

Despite its persistence on the European continent, the design changed as it moved to England. The Theatre Royal, Drury Lane, London, first built in the 1640s, was twice replaced, leading to the one pictured in Figure 4.27, built in 1794. The balconies have changed; they are higher and deeper all around, especially in the rear galleries, and there are no partitions. These trends continued in New York's second theater, the Park Theater, pictured in 1822 in Figure 4.28. There are only three balconies, none at floor level, and close inspection shows that they get deeper as they move toward the back. The proscenium is also wider in proportion to its height. These trends continued into the twentieth century, with a reduction in the number of balconies, an increase in their depth, and an increase in the floor's length from the stage, with unfortunate acoustical results. Only in recent years have architects begun to rediscover the virtues of early opera house design.

Although it unfortunately possesses some of the acoustical problems described above, one modernist opera house/theater is of such beauty that it demands recognition of the genius of its external design. The opera house of Sydney, Australia (Figure 4.29), designed by Jørn Utson and opened in 1973, is perhaps the most beautiful building of the last century. Situated on a point jutting into the harbor, its multiple curved shells echo the sails of ships. The shape embodies the dignity, grace and excitement of the greatest operatic and dramatic works.

The final two types of theatrical venues are simpler than the complex evolution of the proscenium theater. The first, in Figure 4.30, is the Cockpit Theatre in London, an Arena Theater, or Theater in the Round. In a theater of such a plan, developed in the second half of the twentieth century, the audience sits on all sides of the performers. Arena theaters are usually small, like this one. This gives the form its main advantage, which is closeness between the patrons and actors, who enter and exit through the audience. The disadvantage is that some part of the audience is always behind the actor's back, no matter his/her position. In practice, though,

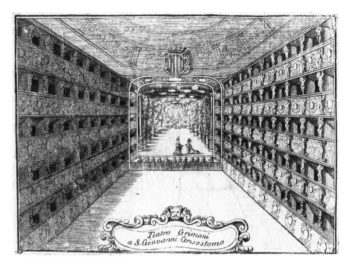

FIGURE 4.24 Vincenzo Maria Coronelli, Interior view of *Teatro Grimani a San Giovanni Grisostomo* (constructed 1678), Venice.

FIGURE 4.25 Left balconies and proscenium arch, *Teatro Vendramin di San Luca a San Salvatore* (now renamed *Teatro Goldoni*, 1720).

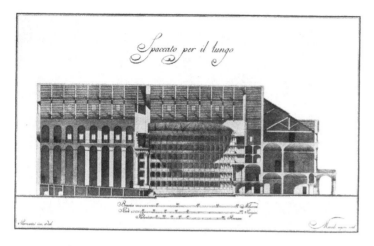

Spaccato per il lungo

FIGURE 4.26 Longitudinal section, *Teatro alla Scala*, Milan.

FIGURE 4.27 Drury Lane Theater, London, as it was from 1704–1809.

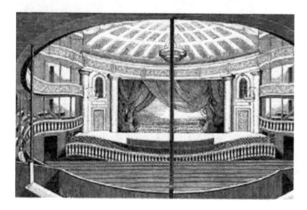

FIGURE 4.28 Park Theater, New York's second theater, as it was from 1798 to 1848.

the players tend to face one direction more than others, usually where the director sat in rehearsal.

The final theatrical venue is not really formal and could have existed at any time in history. A Found Space is any space that players choose to present a play, from an unused room to a structure adapted from its original purpose. Some years ago, I attended a small family performance. The children and their friends had developed a play on the Russian folk tale of *The Firebird*. They improvised a small theater in the attic, with a sheet for a curtain, household floodlights, and improvised special effects (none involving fire). It was very effective in its found space. At the opposite extreme are spaces developed from old buildings or ruins. One of the more spectacular is the Arena of Verona. For over a hundred years, the ancient Roman arena (rather like a small Colosseum) of Verona, Italy has been used for opera performances. Figure 4.31 shows a performance of Verdi's *Aida* in the arena. The grandeur and pageantry of the opera is reinforced and enhanced by the ancient and monumental setting.

It is important to emphasize one more time that Medium and Space are tied to one another, and that there is a remarkable variety of both. Cinema and video use almost every kind of space for production, but they are usually projected from one direction, often a theater proscenium. Spoken drama, like radio drama, may require certain equipment for production but can be appreciated wherever it can be heard. Puppetry does not even require visible human actors, just operators, and the many types of puppets offer many expressive possibilities—usually in a setting comparable to a proscenium stage. Live theater has greater immediacy and intimacy than other dramatic forms, as well as a great diversity of performance spaces, depending on the needs of the play. With these multiple media and venues, the dramatic art can permeate almost every aspect of our lives with whatever message it chooses to present, the seventh and last element of dramatic art.

7. MESSAGE

Dramatic Art is perhaps the most effective art form at conveying a message. The fact that drama presents its message in actual words brings it more directly to its audience than visual art, music or dance is able to do. Actors and actresses can portray situations and their consequences and even speak directly to the audience. Playwrights have often made powerful political and emotional statements with significant consequences, and the variety of messages possible is essentially infinite.

A Brief History of Drama

The length of theater examples hampers the inclusion in the book of as many of them as music or especially visual art. To make up for this, I include below a short history of dramatic art.

Formal theater began in Classical Athens. Hearing this, one tends to overlook how different Classical theater was from its modern descendent. Figure 4.32 is an ivory statuette of a tragic actor, as he appeared in Roman (or Greek) drama. He is fully robed and appears costumed as a woman, since women did not act. On his feet are a type of elevator shoes called buskins to raise him to increased stature and visibility in the enormous theaters of the time. On his face, he wears a mask of the character he portrays.

FIGURE 4.29 Opera House, Sydney, Australia, Jørn Utson, 1958–73.

FIGURE 4.30 Cockpit Theatre, Marylebone, London; an arena theater, or theater in the round.

Masks, all-male casts and buskins are physical differences in Greek theater, but there are others. Greek theater evolved from choral odes in honor of a god. Thespis of Athens was the first one to make the single soloist a character through impersonation. Aeschylus introduced a second character for dialog, and Sophocles added a third, permitting conflict.[8] Greek theater continued to give an important role to a chorus that played a crowd role. The texts are poetic, the dramas were sung, and there was instrumental music and dancing. The lack of these last two makes a complete reconstruction of Greek theater impossible, but that does not diminish the power of these plays. Beginning in 534 BCE, theater was so highly regarded

---

8   This development was recorded by Aristotle. Thespis lived in the sixth century BCE, Aeschylus, c. 525–455, Sophocles, c. 496–406. The third great tragic playwright was Euripides, c. 480–406, and the great comedy writer was Aristophanes, c. 446–386. These four (starting with Aeschylus) are the giants of Classical Greek drama.

FIGURE 4.31 Curtain call of Verdi's *Aida* presented at the Arena of Verona. The grandeur of the setting reinforces the opera's pageantry and spectacle.

that an annual competition began, each writer submitting three tragedies (called a Trilogy) and a short Satyr Play for comic relief. Full-length comedies were separate. Figure 4.33 shows the opening scene of *The Furies*, the concluding play of the only surviving complete trilogy, Aeschylus's *Oresteia*. Orestes grasps the navel stone of Delphi while consulting the god Apollo, who has put the pursuing Furies (foreground) to sleep. Two characters are in dialogue, while the Furies (when awake) are the chorus—simple but powerful, and the masks intensify the characterizations.

The masks are the most obvious difference between Greek theater and ours. They were of several styles depending on the nature of the play and the character. Tragedies used masks with expressions of anger, sorrow or horror, like that in Figure 4.34. Comedies used masks with a smile and often distorted features, like that in Figure 4.35. The two are opposite poles of theater; as such they were often portrayed together, as in Figure 4.36 and in the modern symbol of theater. Since every character wore a unique mask, the actor would prepare for his role by meditating on the mask, as in Figure 4.37, which shows the playwright and comic actor Menander meditating on the mask of a youth before a performance. Masks for a false maiden

FIGURE 4.32 Anonymous, Tragic Actor (1st century CE), painted ivory, Roman? Petit Palais, Paris.

FIGURE 4.33 The Opening of Aeschylus's Eumenides (The Furies).

FIGURE 4.34 Greek Tragedy Mask, Museum zu Allerheiligen, Schaffhausen, Germany.

FIGURE 4.35 Greek Comedy Mask, fourth-third century BCE, Ancient Agora Museum, Stoa of Attalus, Athens. Note the megaphone-like projections around the mouth for voice amplification.

Elements of Dramatic Art   69

FIGURE 4.36 Mosaic of Tragic and Comic Theatrical Masks (second century CE), height 76 cm, Capitoline Museum, Rome.

FIGURE 4.37 Menander Meditating on a Mask before Performance (first century BCE–first century CE), Roman marble high relief, 48 × 60 × 8 cm, Princeton University Art Museum, Princeton, NJ.

and an old man are on a table nearby. Menander was the leading writer of New Comedy, a more subtle style than the heavy and often vicious satire of Aristophanes. New Comedy was very similar to modern situation comedy, with standard settings and stock characters, like those in the figure.

FIGURE 4.38 Dioskourides of Samos, Scene from a Roman Comedy, Two Women Consulting a Witch (before 79 CE), mosaic from the Villa of Cicero, Pompeii, now in the National Archeological Museum, Naples.

The characters, settings and even plots of Greek new comedy were the inspiration for Roman comedy, whose best-known writers were Terence and Plautus. In addition to the characters above, there was usually a sly servant who controls and saves the situation, a shrewish wife and others as needed. These traditional stereotypes are not that unlike those found in the *commedia dell'arte* 1500 years later. Figure 4.38 shows a scene from Roman comedy in which two women consult a witch. Their masks are visible and clearly indicate the characters. Whether Greek, Roman or modern, one thing about theater has not changed, the organized chaos of preparation for a play, shown in Figure 4.39. This mosaic shows such preparation, probably for a tragic trilogy and satyr play. The two young men on the left are dressed in skins and chuckling; one wears a satyr mask while he adjusts the costume of a musician playing the double-barreled *aulos*, Dionysus's instrument. Behind, a dresser adjusts the back of the musician's robe. To the right, another dresser assists a young actor donning his robe, while an older man sits in front, lifting one of three tragic masks, two by his feet and one behind; he is wearing buskins. The older man may be the senior actor or the producer of the troupe. As in the minutes before a modern play, everyone is doing what he needs to do to prepare for the same moment—the play <u>will</u> start on time.

Theater declined in the Middle Ages. The church thought it sinful, and society was in disarray after the fall of Rome. There were occasional productions of the comedies of Plautus and Terence and probably some unwritten productions of which no trace survives. Beginning around 1000 CE, drama began to rise again—in the church. Out of the short biblical dialog at the tomb of Christ, below, Figure 4.40, grew a popular genre of drama.

Over the years, this expanded greatly. Next the principle was applied to Christmas, the characters being the shepherds and the (non-biblical) midwives of Mary. In the twelfth and thirteenth centuries, other plots arose: The Play of Herod (Christmas), the Play of Daniel (prophecy of Christ), and most popular of all, several plays of St. Nicholas, as well as some others. Most of these center around Christmas, and a few others around Easter. The Passion, preceding Easter, had been sung since the eighth century, and these were the two greatest feasts of the church year. Around 1150, Hildegard of Bingen wrote the first morality play, the *Ordo Virtutum* (Order of Virtues), sung in Latin.

In a morality play the characters are not people, but concepts, in this case virtues: Charity, Faith, Mercy, Patience, etc., as well as the devil and the tempted soul. In the fourteenth century, there appear over forty plays based on mythical miracles of the Virgin Mary. Liturgical Drama was sung in Latin and performed in the church. Over the centuries, the tales grew less

FIGURE 4.39 Actors Preparing for a Play (before 79 CE), mosaic from the House of the Tragic Poet, Pompeii, now in the National Archeological Museum, Naples.

Angel(s)—Quem quaeritis in sepulchro, O Cristicolae?	Angel(s)—Whom do you seek in the tomb, O followers of Christ?
3 Marys—Jesum Nazarenum crucifixum, O Caelicolae.	3 Marys—Jesus of Nazareth [who was] crucified, O heaven dwellers.
Angel(s)—Non est hic. Surrexit sicut praedixerat.	Angel(s)—He is not here. He has risen, as he had predicted.
Choir—Resurrexi ... (The Introit of the Easter Mass)	Choir—I have risen ... (The Introit of the Easter Mass)

FIGURE 4.40 The Dialog that Inspired Liturgical Drama, adapted from scripture.

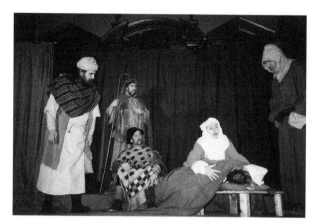

FIGURE 4.41 Scene from The Second Shepherds' Play, in which the shepherds discover the sheep.

FIGURE 4.42 A pageant vehicle with Christ bound before Pilate.

scriptural, the language vernacular, and the music abandoned except for incidental songs. By the fourteenth century, the plays include secular elements and are spoken in the vernacular. In the fifteenth century, the fully-developed Mystery Play appears. The Second Shepherds' Play, in Figure 4.41, begins with a humorous prologue in which shepherds seeking a stolen sheep find it dressed as a baby in the thief's house. After this jocular beginning, the play shifts to the real Christmas story. Such plays were not performed in church, but outdoors in the marketplace or on carts. (See Figure 4.42.)

Secular drama had also begun in the late thirteenth century. One of the best examples is the *Play of Robin and Marion* by Adam de la Halle, a short play in the vernacular with incidental songs.[9] By the sixteenth century secular theater was well developed throughout Europe. In Italy, Machiavelli, famed for *The Prince*, wrote two hilarious and racy comedies. *Commedia dell'arte* began, and traveling players proliferated. There were dramatic pageants with music at many courts, often for weddings, and in England there was the great flowering of Elizabethan drama that led to the works of William Shakespeare.

Shakespeare is traditionally regarded as the greatest playwright (perhaps the greatest author) in the English language. It is sad that the language has moved on, so that it takes a bit of effort for students (and actors) to appreciate his works easily. Like Greek drama, Shakespeare's plays are in poetry, in this case, English non-rhyming blank verse. He wrote in three genres: Tragedy, Comedy, and History. His tragedies, like Hamlet, Macbeth, and Romeo and Juliet, famous for their eloquence and intensity, have furnished many classic quotes.[10] His comedies are filled with comic situations, trickeries and often nobility and joy. One of the most comic situations is the Fairie Queen's infatuation with Bottom the weaver transformed into an ass in *A Midsummer Night's Dream*, shown in Figure 4.43. The third group of Shakespeare's plays, the histories, are somewhat less often performed but equally great. Most of them were propaganda

9   Yes, it is about Robin Hood and Maid Marion, but not the story we know. Robin and Marion are shepherds; the play depicts her and their friends as she escapes a knight's unwanted attentions.

10   "Something is rotten in the state of Denmark," "The lady doth protest too much," "To be or not to be, that is the question," *Hamlet;* "Double, double, toil and trouble. Fire burn and cauldron bubble," "Sleep that knits up the ravell'd sleave of care," "Something wicked this way comes," *Macbeth;* "What's in a name? That which we call a rose by any other name would smell as sweet," A pair of star-crossed lovers," "But, soft! What light through yonder window breaks?" *Romeo and Juliet,* and many, many more.

to expose the waywardness and evil of the previous Plantagenet kings (like *Richard III*), and to exalt the Tudor dynasty *(Henry VIII)*. Near the end of Shakespeare's career, new types of drama arose.

One seventeenth-century fashion was Royal Theater. Sometimes, as in Spain, royal patronage enhanced the stature of a great writer, in particular Pedro Calderón de la Barca (1600–1681), who as Spain's greatest dramatist also contributed to the development of Spanish musical theater. In England and France, kings, their families and the courtiers sometimes took part in the actual dramas, known in England as masques. One particular French performance had long-lasting significance (see Figure 4.44). In 1653, the *Ballet de la Nuit* (Ballet of the Night), a twelve-hour extravaganza, featured the young Louis, heir to the throne, as Apollo, who rose with the dawn near the work's end. When Louis (XIV) assumed power, he reinforced the Apollo persona by taking the name "Sun King" and emblazoning it on the gates of his palace of Versailles. It became a symbol of his absolute power, verging on deity.

During his reign, French drama turned in two directions. Tragedies by Pierre Racine (1639–1699) and Pierre Corneille (1606–1684) returned to the principles of Classical drama. Racine's works follow Aristotle's three dramatic unities with greater strictness than even Aristotle advocated. These are: Unity of Time—all action must take place in a short time span, preferably one day; Unity of Place—the action must occur in the same or nearby places; and Unity of Action—no sub-plots. Racine's best-known work is *Phèdre*, from the myth of the unrequited and cursed love of Phaedra, queen of Athens, for her stepson Hippolytus; they both die at the end. Phaedra's character is tormented and a wonderful role for a great actress, like Sarah Bernhardt, shown in Figure 4.45. But not only tragedy was written at this time. Comedy, sharp, satirical and therefore often condemned, was the specialty of Molière (1622–1673).[11] The ridiculousness of his characters usually expressed strong criticism of an institution—greed, marriage, science, rigidity of personality, poor education of women, aristocratic, moral and religious hypocrisy, and doctors of medicine. The last contributed the subject of his last play, *Le malade imaginaire* (The Hypochondriac), depicted in Figure 4.46. The play's first run was the occasion of a sad irony. Molière, who suffered from tuberculosis, had a coughing fit onstage. He completed the performance and died of pulmonary hemorrhage soon after.

As France groaned under Absolutism, England experienced rebellion and regicide as Parliament refused the Stuart kings authority like

FIGURE 4.43 Queen Titania and Bottom the Weaver, transformed into an ass, from Shakespeare's *A Midsummer Night's Dream*. Gaby Stenberg as Titania at Malmö, Sweden City Theatre, 1944.

FIGURE 4.44 *Dauphin* (heir apparent, later King) Louis XIV as Apollo in the *Ballet de la Nuit* (Ballet of the Night), 23 February 1653.

11   Stage name of Jean-Baptiste Poquelin.

FIGURE 4.45 Sarah Bernhardt as the title role in Racine's *Phèdre* (c. 1874), albumen silver photographic print, 15 × 11 cm, Getty Center, Los Angeles.

FIGURE 4.46 A scene from Molière's *Le malade imaginaire* (The Hypochondriac, or The Imaginary Invalid, 1673), engraving, 22 × 30 cm, Bibliothèque Nationale, Paris. Argan, the hypochondriac, examined by two quack doctors, is awaiting his injection (and not in the arm—the background servant holds the syringe).

FIGURE 4.47 Colley Cibber as Lord Foppington in *The Relapse*, by John Vanbrugh (c. 1700–25), engraving.

Louis'. After restoration of the monarchy, much of the country was severely and morally Protestant, but the court was racy. The king enjoyed the sexual explicitness found in Restoration Comedy, such as *The Relapse*, by John Vanbrugh, a sequel to a play by Colley Cibber (one of the time's most famous actors), called *Love's Last Shift*, or *Virtue Rewarded*, in which a virtuous wife disguises herself as a call-girl to seduce her lecherous husband, ten years absent in brothels. She succeeds in this "last shift"; he repents.

Popular in its first run, *Love's Last Shift* has failed the test of time and has been called a notorious tear-jerker, with flat characters and "four explicit acts of sex and rakishness with one of sententious [i.e. preachy] reform."[12] At the time, though, it had something for everyone, both sex and repentance, and was a great success. Cibber wrote a large secondary role for himself, Lord Novelty Fashion, whose name tells all. A few weeks later, Vanbrugh wrote the sequel, *The Relapse*, which takes the husband (under a different name) unapologetically back to debauchery. Vanbrugh included a parallel dandy role for Cibber, Lord Foppington, shown in Figure 4.47. Through all this, Shakespeare's works continued to be performed to acclaim and actors like David Garrick made their reputations through interpretations of the classic characters (see Figure 4.1).

---

12 Robert Hume, *The Development of English Drama in the Late Seventeenth Century* (Oxford: Clarendon Press, 1976).

After a dour Protestant replaced the Stuarts on the throne, sexual humor in the theater ceased, but one comic feature increased—a play on class differences and mannerisms that has been called the Comedy of Manners. Such plays rely on comical situations, wit and wordplay to achieve a success equal to, if different from Restoration bawdiness. One of the best-known examples is *The Rivals* (1775), by Richard Brinsley Sheridan (1751–1816). His character, Mrs. Malaprop, even gave her name to the kind of vocabular anarchy that permeates her lines—"He is the very pine-apple (pinnacle) of politeness!" or "Illiterate (obliterate) him from your memory." or "She's as headstrong as an allegory (alligator) on the banks of the Nile." Hilarity is achieved without the slightest offense to the delicate-minded.

Such single-minded decency remained a mark of English theater for more than a century. The great success enjoyed by Gilbert and Sullivan's operettas was based significantly on the fact that they resolved "never to let an offending word escape our characters…" unlike the raciness current on the London stage.[13] They succeeded in this for thirteen wonderful works that dominated the London musical stage for over a quarter century. Their success was based on the wit of Gilbert, Britain's greatest comic writer at the time, the talent of Sullivan, a composer of great gifts who could mimic any musical style, and an unerring sense of what institutions to satirize at any given time. These included the court, the Royal Navy, the House of Lords, fads in poetry, gothic novels, and any other social institution that fell into the net. The satire was both musical and verbal. *Iolanthe* (1881) is a confrontation between a flock of fairies and the House of Lords. The Lords are incompetent snobs, and the fairies win, led by their indomitable queen, a parody of Brünnhilde from Wagner's *Ring* cycle, as in Figure 4.48.

FIGURE 4.48 Alice Barnett as the Fairy Queen in *Iolanthe* by Gilbert and Sullivan (1881).

Contemporary with Gilbert and Sullivan were the plays of Oscar Wilde. Although most of his plays were clever comedies of manners, *Salome* (1893), a one-act elaboration of a biblical account, is filled with unnatural lust and bloodthirsty violence. Enraged by John the Baptist's condemnation of her divorce and remarriage, Herodias wishes his death. She convinces her daughter Salome to perform a risqué dance for her lecherous grandfather, Herod Antipas, Tetrarch of Galilee, who gives her the Baptist's head as a reward. This bloody work was Wilde's contribution to the literary movement of Decadence. In Strauss's hands, through the amplifying power of music, the opera moves even beyond the play to the horror of Expressionism. *Salome* is one of the works that bridges the gap between a nineteenth-century genre and its extreme Modernist offspring. Figure 4.49 shows a 1906–1907 opera production, with Salome about to claim her ghastly reward.

---

13   Harry How, quoting W. S. Gilbert, "Illustrated Interview No. IV," *Strand Magazine* 2 (1891); 330–341. Gilbert did actually write "damme" in one script and had the chorus crowd immediately object to the language. In one other, it is traditionally added off the cuff.

FIGURE 4.49 Alice Guszalewicz as Salomé claiming Jokanaan's severed head in Richard Strauss's opera (Cologne, 1906 or Leipzig, 1907).

FIGURE 4.50 Gertrude Elliott and Johnston Forbes-Robertson in George Bernard Shaw's *Caesar and Cleopatra*, (New York premier, 1906).

In the wake of these conflicting aesthetics rose George Bernard Shaw (1856–1950), often regarded as second only to Shakespeare. One of his first successes was *Caesar and Cleopatra* (1899–1906), which dramatizes their encounter (see Figure 4.50). Like many of Shaw's plays, it is neither a comedy nor a tragedy, although it may fall into the same category as Shakespeare's histories. Shaw's works are thoughtful, with deep philosophical implications, yet even when they express controversial views, the presentation is conventional and dignified.

In the twentieth century, live theater expanded to include alternative dramatic forms, like radio drama and cinema. These reflected the same artistic developments of live theater. They will not be treated separately in what follows, but they should be understood as offering expansion and enhancement of recent theatrical developments.

American theater in the early twentieth century tended to avoid extremes, although it began to move from comedies, pleasant operettas, vaudeville variety shows and reviews to drama with serious social commentary. One of the first breakthroughs in this process was *Showboat* (1927), a musical by Jerome Kern and Oscar Hammerstein that portrayed the lives of actors and crew on the boat from 1887 to 1927, including topics like unhappy love, interracial marriage and racial oppression with a mixed black and white cast. The show continues to stir controversy with each new production, even ninety years after its opening. A similarly controversial production was the opera *Porgy and Bess* by George Gershwin, based on a play by DuBose and Dorothy Heyward that portrays life in the African-American community of Catfish Row in Charleston, South Carolina (see Figure 4.51). Written for an all-black cast and with music inspired by spirituals and jazz, the show was a moderate success on Broadway, although the cutting or replacement of sung dialog in various revivals left some confusion about whether it was musical theater or opera. Performances at *La Scala* in 1955, the Houston Grand Opera in 1976 and finally at the Metropolitan Opera in 1985 have enshrined the work as an American operatic masterpiece.

FIGURE 4.51 George Gershwin's *Porgy and Bess* (1934) at New York's Harlem Theater (2009).

FIGURE 4.52 Scene from Rodgers & Hammerstein's *Oklahoma* (1943–1944), Theatre Guild production.

Of course, shows of sophisticated pleasantry still held their place in American theater, but the strain of social commentary begun in *Showboat* continued in *Oklahoma* by Hammerstein in collaboration with Richard Rodgers (see Figure 4.52). The show's plot about cowboys and farmers includes the death of a main character, revolutionary in Broadway musical theater in 1943. The show also incorporates serious dance, not just flashy production numbers, as part of the plot, the first Broadway choreography of Agnes DeMille. Contrary to predictions, the show was a smash. At 2,212 performances, it broke all previous records, won a Pulitzer Prize and has remained

FIGURE 4.53 The gang war Rumble concluding Act I of *West Side Story*, in which Tony stabs Bernardo after he stabs Riff. One scene includes a jazz dance that makes dance essential to plot development.

FIGURE 4.54 Vladimir and Estragon waiting beneath their dead tree in Samuel Beckett's *Waiting for Godot* (1953), produced at the Doon School, India.

a staple in the repertoire ever since. Social commentary and political criticism became important in the 1950s in works like Arthur Miller's *The Crucible*, which dramatized the Salem witch trials to denounce the paranoid Red Scare led by Senator Joseph McCarthy.

Social commentary mixed with realism and a classic plot in *West Side Story*, a four-way collaboration of Arthur Laurents, Steven Sondheim, Leonard Bernstein, and Jerome Robbins (see Figure 4.53). *West Side Story* derives its plot of Shakespeare's *Romeo and Juliet*, but with an urban ethnic gang war instead of a family feud. The dialog is contemporary slang, the music is alternately lyrical and jazzy and dance is integrated inextricably with the action. The work was a true collaboration that went through many stages of development over ten years and hit Broadway like an explosion. Walter Kerr, in one of the first reviews, wrote "The radioactive fallout from *West Side Story* must still be descending on Broadway this morning."[14] Among the innovations were the somber plot with two murders in the first act, the tough characters from society's underside and their slang, the jazzy contemporary musical score and the use of dance as an integral part of the drama. *West Side Story* left an indelible mark on American theater as a harbinger of things to come.

As American theater embraced the rough realities of its surroundings, European theater adopted the Existentialist concept that life is so complicated and purposeless and communication so futile that everything is essentially ridiculous. This is the premise behind Theater of the Absurd, that comes to life in plays by Jean Genet, Samuel Beckett, Eugène Ionesco, Edward Albee and many since. One of the first Absurdist plays was Becket's *Waiting for Godot*, shown in Figure 4.54. Two men arrive beneath a bare tree, which they assume is the place they are to meet Godot. Their aimless dialogue,

14   Walter Kerr, "Theater, 'West Side Story,'" *New York Herald Tribune* (27 September 1957.)

filled with digressions and a few recurring themes continues for two acts, interrupted by another pair of characters together and a boy who all enter and leave in each act, suggesting a kind of circular repetition. Godot never comes.

The superficial ridiculousness and the lack of direction in such Absurdist works were unprecedented in theater. They are a signpost of Postmodernism, which abandons specific aesthetic goals. And late twentieth-century drama fits this classification in many different ways, in works that may or may not have a plot, that may or may not have characters, that may use dialog, narrative or some other form of communication among human beings, machines or other substitutes, who may or may not involve or even require an audience in a work that may be classical, avant-garde or a mixture of both in style, that may contain music or dance or other supporting elements, or none at all. In short, in the Postmodern world, drama and theater have escaped their chains and are free to move in any direction creative artists can conceive.

Image Credits

Fig. 4.1: Copyright in the Public Domain.

Fig. 4.2A: Maurice Sand / Copyright in the Public Domain.

Fig. 4.2B: Maurice Sand / Copyright in the Public Domain.

Fig. 4.2C: Maurice Sand / Copyright in the Public Domain.

Fig. 4.3: Édouard Desplechin / Copyright in the Public Domain.

Fig. 4.4: Giacomo Torelli; Engraved by François Chauveau / Copyright in the Public Domain.

Fig. 4.5: Copyright in the Public Domain.

Fig. 4.6: Max Brückner / Copyright in the Public Domain.

Fig. 4.7A: Copyright in the Public Domain.

Fig. 4.7B: Copyright in the Public Domain.

Fig. 4.8: Copyright © 2007 by Nullcron / Wikimedia Commons, (CC BY-SA 3.0) at https://commons.wikimedia.org/wiki/File:Videowisconsinsoundstage.jpg.

Fig. 4.9: Copyright © 1983 by Nancy Wong, (CC BY-SA 3.0) at https://commons.wikimedia.org/wiki/File:Mike_Chin_filming_on_location.jpg.

Fig. 4.10: Mutual Broadcasting System / Copyright in the Public Domain.

Fig. 4.11A: Copyright © 2005 by Anah / Wikimedia Commons, (CC BY 2.0) at https://commons.wikimedia.org/wiki/File:Punch_and_Judy_Philadelphia.jpg.

Fig. 4.11B: Copyright © by Walter S. Wantman; Adapted by Gary Towne, (CC BY-SA 3.0) at https://commons.wikimedia.org/wiki/File:Bread_and_Puppet_Circus.jpg.

Fig. 4.12A: Copyright © 2009 by Jürgen Howalt, (CC BY-SA 3.0) at https://commons.wikimedia.org/wiki/File:TheaterFigurenMuseum_85.jpg.

Fig. 4.12B: Copyright © 2011 by Ji-Elle / Wikimedia Commons, (CC BY-SA 3.0) at https://commons.wikimedia.org/wiki/File:Opera_dei_Pupi-Lipari_(1).jpg.

Fig. 4.13: Cie. Coppelius / Copyright in the Public Domain.

Fig. 4.14: Copyright © 2006 by Parihav / Wikimedia Commons, (CC BY-SA 3.0) at https://en.wikipedia.org/wiki/File:Streetperformers.jpg.

Fig. 4.15A: Copyright © 2015 by Doc James / Wikimedia Commons, (CC BY-SA 4.0) at https://commons.wikimedia.org/wiki/File:TheatreofDionysus2015.jpg.

Fig. 4.15B: Copyright © 2008 by Night Flight / Wikimedia Commons, (CC BY-SA 3.0) at https://commons.wikimedia.org/wiki/File:Theatre_dionysos.gif.

Fig. 4.16: Copyright © 2013 by Ronnie Siegel, (CC BY 3.0) at https://commons.wikimedia.org/wiki/File:Epidaurus_Theater_04.jpg.

Fig. 4.17: Copyright © 2007 by Leonidtsvetkov / Wikimedia Commons, (CC BY-SA 2.5) at https://commons.wikimedia.org/wiki/File:Delphi_Composite.jpg.

Fig. 4.18: Copyright © 2010 by Franzfoto / Wikimedia Commons, (CC BY-SA 3.0) at https://commons.wikimedia.org/wiki/File:Sabratha_-_B%C3%BChnenhaus_des_Theaters_2._Jh..jpg.

Fig. 4.19: Copyright © 2007 by Culturespaces / Les Chorégies, (CC BY-SA 3.0) at https://commons.wikimedia.org/wiki/File:967_ORG2006.jpg.

Fig. 4.20: Pierre Patte / Copyright in the Public Domain.

Fig. 4.21A: Copyright © 2013 by Geobia / Wikimedia Commons, (CC BY-SA 4.0) at https://commons.wikimedia.org/wiki/File:3906VicenzaTeatroOlimpico.jpg.

CHAPTER 5

ELEMENTS OF DANCE

Dance is the final type of performing art or time art. As with the other art forms, the elements of dance are the basic structural components of works of dance. They are universal and comprehensive; that is, they can be used to describe any kind of dance from any culture known to man, and they cover all aspects of the dance. As before, not all of the elements will necessarily be required by every artwork.

Elements of Dance

The first element of dance is rhythm or time.

1. RHYTHM or TIME—the time structure of individual dance events, usually related to the musical accompaniment and its rhythm, but not identical. Music and dance rhythmic events may have different counts.
   • Structure—the organization of dance rhythm, by movement
   • Beat—a Rhythmic pulse of approximately uniform length
   • Tempo or Pacing—the speed of the piece

When the dance has a musical accompaniment, the two are related, but not all dance is accompanied, and even when it is, the rhythm of the dance is counted by the movements, not the musical beats. Musical beat—the rhythmic pulse—is still very important for the dancer, as is the tempo or speed, which determines the dance's pacing. A simple example of the difference between musical and dance rhythm is the Renaissance galliard in Figure 5.1.

The counts of the music and dance differ in the galliard because the dancer(s) have one group of movements that occupies two beats, so the dancers count five while the musicians count six. The movements on count four also determine the tempo of the dance. The dancers should land on their last stance on the music's sixth beat, so it is important that the music not be too slow. Gravity plays its part in determining dance speed. And bear in mind that movements require space, the second dance element.

2. SPACE—The use of space by the dancers; four components:
- Individual Movement—the bodily movements of an individual dancer
  - Footwork—steps, movements of a dancer's feet and legs
  - Gesture—in particular, hands and arms

Music Count	Dance Step	Action
1	1	**Left foot kick**—Left foot in the air (*Grève = pied en l'aire gauche*)
2	2	**Right foot kick**—Right foot in the air (*Grève droit*)
3	3	**Left foot kick**—Left foot in the air (*Grève gauche*)
4	4	**Raise right foot, jump up, switch foot positions**—Right foot in the air, large
5	—	jump, [reverse feet] (*Pied en l'aire droit, saut majeur, [renversez pieds]*)
6	5	**Land with left foot forward**—Left foot advanced (*Posture gauche*)
		Repeat pattern with opposite feet.
1	1	**Right foot kick**—Right foot in the air (*Grève droit*)
2	2	**Left foot kick**—Left foot in the air (*Grève gauche*)
3	3	**Right foot kick**—Right foot in the air (*Grève droit*)
4	4	**Raise left foot, jump up, switch foot positions**—Left foot in the air, large jump,
5	—	[reverse feet] (*Pied en l'aire gauche, saut majeur, [renversez pieds]*)
6	5	**Land—right foot forward**—Right foot advanced (*Posture droit*)

FIGURE 5.1 The Renaissance Galliard from Thoinot Arbeau (Jean Tabourot)—*Orchésographie* (1589) Rhythm & Steps. The jump on dance count 4 (music counts 4 and 5) determines the speed. The dancers need to jump and land on the beat.

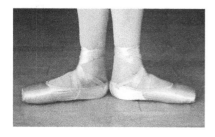

FIGURE 5.2A The Five Basic Stationary Positions in Ballet (1st Position).

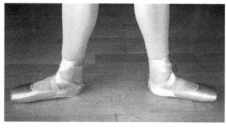

FIGURE 5.2B The Five Basic Stationary Positions in Ballet (2nd Position).

FIGURE 5.2C The Five Basic Stationary Positions in Ballet (3rd Position).

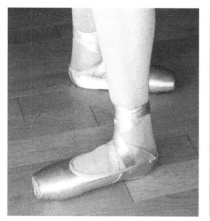

FIGURE 5.2D The Five Basic Stationary Positions in Ballet (4th Position—open).

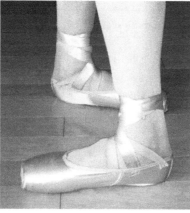

FIGURE 5.2E The Five Basic Stationary Positions in Ballet (4th Position—closed).

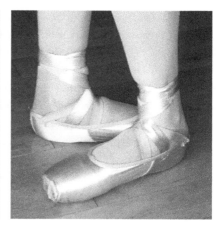

FIGURE 5.2F The Five Basic Stationary Positions in Ballet (5th Position).

- Special Movements—sophisticated movements that may involve more than one body part—head, neck, torso
  - Twirls, Leaps, Other Movements
  - Ballet Figures—*arabesques, pirouettes, jetés, cabrioles*, and more
- Choreography—of individual dancers' movements

Dance space in this context refers to a single dancer's personal use of space. There are four components, all interrelated: 1) the feet, 2) the arms, 3) other body parts, especially the head, and 4) the choreography that puts all these together.

Ballet has defined five positions for the feet and arms. The foot and arm positions are actually separate groups and they can be mixed. Figure 5.2 shows the positions of the feet. In first position, the heels are together and the arms hang in graceful curves at the side. Second position moves the feet apart and raises the arms at the sides to just below the shoulders. In third position, the heel of one foot moves in front of the arch of the rear foot and the hand on the rear foot's side moves down and over just in front of the waist. In fourth position, the front foot moves about a foot forward, the first moving hand reaches over the head in a graceful

FIGURE 5.3 Edgar Degas (1834–1917), *Grand Arabesque*, modeled 1885/90, cast posthumously, cast bronze, 42 × 57 × 14 cm, Los Angeles County Museum of Art.

FIGURE 5.4 Jiwee Kwen, A *pirouette*, from *La Bayadère*, at the Grand Prix de Lausanne, 2010.

curve, and the other hand takes its place centered in front of the waist. In open fourth position the two heels are aligned; in closed fourth, the heels line up with the opposite toes. In fifth position, the front foot moves back so that its heel is just ahead of the rear foot's toe, and both hands rise above the head.

These are just base positions. Dance, like any other art form, is creative. Rules are there to provide starting points for (in this case) the choreographer's creativity. Obviously, a dancer does not remain in a stationary position; there must be movement. Movement from one position to another is the simplest type, but there are many specialized movements in ballet as well, some of which are illustrated in the following figures.

Figure 5.3 is a sculpture by Edgar Degas that illustrates the *grande arabesque*, in which the dancer balances on one leg with one arm extended in front and the other arm and leg extended in back. Figure 5.4 illustrates a *pirouette*, in which the ballerina spins on one toe, with the opposite foot resting against the straight leg's knee. These two are commonly choreographed for women (ballerinas), as they embody grace. Some more athletic steps can be danced by either women or men. Figure 5.5 shows one of these more vigorous single dancer figures, the *grand jeté*, in which the dancer leaps from one foot to the other. It sounds simple, but, as the picture shows, with a high leap and full extension of the legs, it is spectacular. Another athletic figure, formerly reserved for men only, was the *cabriole* (Figure 5.6), in which the dancer leaps into the air and beats his legs together so they bounce off one another before he lands.

When you combine these movements and positions for a single dancer, it becomes clear how a dance develops from the interaction among them and the movement from one

FIGURE 5.5 Chenxin Liu, A *grand jeté*, from *Don Quixote*, music by Ludwig Minkus, choreography by Marius Petipa, at the Grand Prix de Lausanne, 2010.

FIGURE 5.6 Philip Handschin, A *cabriole*, in *Giselle*, music by Adolphe Adam, choreography by Marius Petipa, at the Grand Prix de Lausanne, 2010.

to another. This is the choreography of the individual dancer, but dance is more than one dancer moving in one spot. Dancers move, and they do so in patterns, the third element of dance.

3. PATTERN—the movement of one or more dancers through space
   - Floor Pattern—the geometric patterns on the floor created by dancers' movements, like (from square and other folk dancing): do-si-do (*dos-à-dos*), grand right and left
   - Stage Pattern—geometric design to be viewed from the side by an audience in front of a stage (mainly in performance dance): leaps, carries, and more

Pattern describes the geometry of the way dancers move among each other. These patterns are of two types: floor patterns and stage patterns. Floor patterns are older and are part of most dances, either social or performance. Stage patterns are of more recent development and reflect the performance need to interest portions of an audience that can only see the dancers from the side. Floor patterns are the patterns that dancers make as they move among each other in a geometry seen (or thought of) from above. Square dance or contra dance patterns are comparatively familiar examples of this. For persons not familiar with contra dance, rest easy—many of the patterns are the same for both, the only difference being that contra dances are danced in lines, unlike square dances. Figure 5.7 demonstrates some contra dance patterns, first those in which several couples move at once, then some with movement for two dancers and two couples.

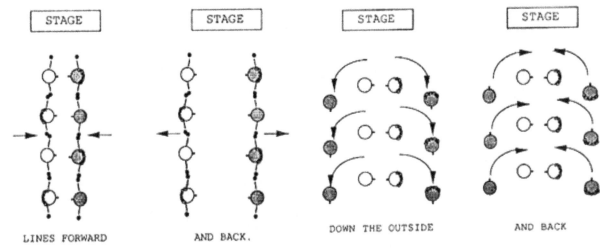

LINES FORWARD | AND BACK. | DOWN THE OUTSIDE | AND BACK

Long lines forward and back: Dancers take hands along the sides of the sets, and the two long lines walk four steps toward each other, and then four steps backwards to place.

Down the outside and back: This pattern is performed by the active couples, who turn away from the center of the set and walk down the outside of the set, and then turn and come back to place.

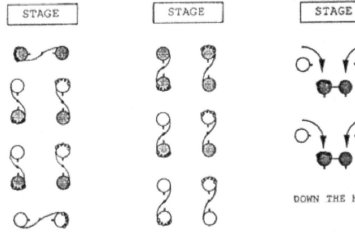

RIGHT WITH THE FIRST   AND LEFT WITH THE NEXT

DOWN THE HALL | TURN INDIVIDUALLY | OR AS A COUPLE | BACK UP THE HALL

Grand right and left: This pattern appears rarely in contra dance, and is from the square dance tradition. In a contra dance it moves around the circle that includes two sides of the set, joined at the ends. Dancers walk around the circle taking right hands and then left hands alternately with dancers as they pass.

Down the center and back: Active couples go down the center and back while the other dancers watch. The dancers may turn individually before returning up the hall, or they may turn as a couple. The caller will usually specify which way to turn, since this affects the dancers' positions for the next figure.

(Dark figures indicate active couples.
Curls on the heads indicate women.)

FIGURE 3.7 Simple Contra Dance Patterns.

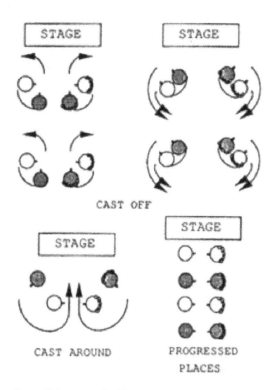

CAST OFF

CAST AROUND

PROGRESSED PLACES

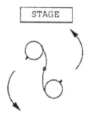

ALLEMANDE LEFT

Allemande left (right): Two dancers take left (right) hands and walk around one another, pulling slightly on one another's arms to facilitate the turn. The grip is a grip with the thumb pointing upward, which makes it possible to pull more effectively. "Once around" brings the dancers back to where they started.

Cast off (or around): The cast off is commonly used to accomplish the progression in a contra dance. Actives couples (usually returning from movement down the set) come up between the inactives and either take inside hands or put their nearest arms around these inactives, and turn with them, ending up below the inactives in the set. To cast *around* another couple, the actives merely turn to the outside of the set and walk out and around the inactives.

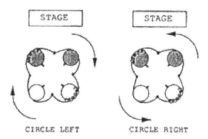

CIRCLE LEFT   CIRCLE RIGHT

Circle left (right): Four dancers (or six in triple formation) take hands in a circle and walk to the left (right) one full turn and back to place.

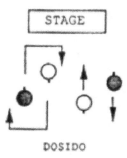

DOSIDO

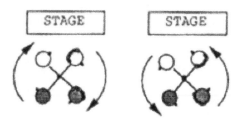

RIGHT HAND STAR   LEFT HAND STAR

Star: The star left (right) is performed by four dancers, who place their left (right) hands together in the center of their little circle and walk around counter-clockwise (clockwise).

Dosido: The basic dosido figure has two dancers pass right shoulders with one another, pass back to back, and back up passing left shoulders to return to place.

Adapted from Mary McNab Dart, *Contra Dance Choreography: A Reflection of Social Change* (New York: Garland Publishing, 1995): Appendix B.

FIGURE 5.7 Simple Contra Dance Patterns (*Continued*).

Be reassured that this extensive figure is not here to teach you contra dance (unless you want it to). It is here to demonstrate the variety of floor patterns that can be a part of even social dances. The first two groups are for dancers in two lines. *Forward and back* is self-explanatory, and *grand right and left* is familiar to anyone who has walked around a square dance trading hands with each person you meet. The next two figures show how active couples can move down the set (away from the band on stage) and back up, either outside or inside. When they reach the top again, they often *cast off*, which moves them down the set and the next couple up, so everyone gets a chance to be active. The next two figures are for two people: *do-si-do* (from the French meaning "back-to-back") is exactly that—two dancers facing each other move forward and pass back to back, returning to their places. In an *allemande*, the two dancers join the same arm and pull each other around in a circle. The last two patterns, for two couples, are simple: join hands and *circle left* or *right*, or all join the same hands and circle as a *star*.

Floor patterns are an important part of both social and performance dance. In performance dance, they are unique for each choreography, quite complex, and require a good memory on the part of each dancer.[1] With the development of more complex performance dance and larger theaters, more people were sitting where it was difficult to appreciate the floor patterns fully. However beautiful they were when viewed from above, it was inevitable that some patterns would just look like dancers passing each other back and forth when viewed from the side. This led to an increased emphasis on what I call *stage patterns*—movements designed to add interest when viewed horizontally. Jumps, gestures, and unusual steps had been a part of dance for centuries, but with the nineteenth-century development of ballet in large theaters, new steps and techniques appeared, and older ones were amplified. Dancing *en pointe* (on the tips of the toes) is an example of the first (see Figure 5.8). Primarily reserved for women, it gives their legs and steps greater extension and makes the movements appear more delicate. Vertical movements, which had also long been a part of dance, became more extreme. The *grand jeté* and the *cabriole* above are examples of this. In addition, to assist the ballerina in appearing more weightless in vertical movement, her male partner developed new ways to support, lift, and carry her; to make her *pirouettes* faster, her jumps higher, and her *jeté*s extend across the stage. Figure 5.9 shows the amazing carry in Act II of *Swan Lake*. This is an example of how the stage pattern amplified dance's third dimension in daring new ways. Some of these patterns involve various groupings of dancers.

FIGURE 5.8 Hinano Eto, An *attitude*, from *Don Quixote*, music by Ludwig Minkus, choreography by Marius Petipa, at the Grand Prix de Lausanne, 2010.

4. GROUPING—interaction of groups of dancers (including as a group a single dancer)
    *   Groups—Solo, Duet/Couple (*pas de deux*), Triplet, larger group (eight in square dance)
    *   Grip—by grasping each other, dancers can share weight, balance, and center of gravity; can add momentum to movement within a pattern; some examples:

1   Memory for movements is called kinesthetic memory. It is a learned skill. If you have difficulty with some unfamiliar dance, keep in mind that the ability to remember movement improves with time. It is not just memory; it is your body learning a new way to learn.

FIGURE 5.9 The carry in the *pas de deux* (Jean-Paul Andreani & Claire Motte) from Act II of *Swan Lake* at the Paris Opera, 1960.

FIGURE 5.10 The *corps de ballet* in a receding formation to accentuate the soloists in *Swan Lake*, music by Pyotr Ilych Tchaikovsky, choreography by Marius Petipa, Royal Swedish Opera Ballet, 2008.

FIGURE 5.11 *Pas de deux* (Grace & Christian) from *Don Quixote*, music by Ludwig Minkus, choreography by Marius Petipa, International Day of Dance, 2006.

- Folk Dance—swing, reel figure, grand right and left, and more
- Performance Dance—various inventive figures; one twentieth-century dance includes dancers gripping each other's shoulders with legs, like a totem pole.

Grouping is the fourth element of dance; many of the individual movements and patterns depend on it. The largest choreographed group is the *corps de ballet*, the ballet equivalent of a chorus. The dancers (usually twenty to thirty) move in ways that create beautiful geometric patterns and use poses and gestures to augment these. In addition, the *corps* often frames or accents the soloists, as in Figure 5.10. Dancers in the *corps* have less physical contact with each other, except as the dramatic action dictates; contact is common in smaller groups. When dancers form a group, it is more than just joining hands; it creates a physical link that influences the dance. In both social and performance dance, there are groupings of different sizes. (Since there is no other category for it, a solo dance will be considered a grouping.)

Groupings have different names. A couple in social dance is a *pas de deux* in ballet (see Figures 5.11, 5.12, and 5.13).[2] Larger groups

---

2   The *grand pas de deux* is a major part in any large ballet. It has five parts: the *entrée* (entrance), *adagio* (slow section), a solo for each dancer (variations), and a *coda* that uses parts of the other sections leading to a grand finale.

FIGURE 5.12 *Pas de deux* (Vadim Muntagirov & Alina Cojocaru), from *Le Corsaire*, music by Adolphe Adam, choreography by Marius Petipa, English National Ballet, 2013.

FIGURE 5.13 Lift in the Snow *pas de deux* (Daria L & Jeff), from *The Nutcracker*, music by Pyotr Ilych Tchaikovsky, choreography by Marius Petipa, 2010.

also take French names in ballet—*pas de trois, pas de quatre*, etc.—I will also refer to them in English as triplets/trios, quartets, etc. Figures 5.14 and 5.15 give examples of each of these—they are less common than the *pas de deux* and more difficult to choreograph without having the extra dancers seem extraneous. Both of these figures show moments added to the ballet *Paquita* by the composer Ludwig Minkus, in order to include a *pas de trois* and a *pas de quatre*. In Figure 5.14 (the *pas de trois*), the male dancer supports one ballerina in a "level" arabesque with a hand on her waist, while another ballerina behind holds his shoulders for balance in a half arabesque. Figure 5.15 shows the climax of the *pas de quatre*, which has become such a classic that is often danced without the whole ballet. All four dancers conclude in this striking pose, two ballerinas, one kneeling, and one standing, frame with outstretched arms the central couple in which the male dancer holds the lead ballerina on his shoulder. The dancers form a pyramid with outstretched arms in a starlike figure.

In addition to these three- and four-person figures, we have already seen some larger groups: the standard group of eight in square dance and the long lines of a longways set, such as is used for contra dances and reels. (For the record, in contra dances, those lines are divided into groups of two or three couples, depending on the dance, but that is beyond our needs for now.) From the discussion of patterns, it is obvious how groupings can make a dance more interesting and fun, but there is a very important additional aspect of a grouping—the *grip*.

FIGURE 5.14 Trio (*pas de trois*, Elsa Vil, Elizaveta Gerdt, Pierre Vladimirov), music by Ludwig Minkus added to the ballet *Paquita*, choreography by Marius Petipa, Ballet of the Mariinsky Theater, St. Petersburg, Russia, 1905.

FIGURE 5.15 Quartet (*pas de quatre*, Erin Joseph, Patricia Barker, Bathurel Bold, Kimberley Davey), music by Ludwig Minkus added to the ballet *Paquita*, choreography by Marius Petipa, Seattle, 2000.

A grip allows dancers to share a center of gravity, and their motion becomes relative to that point rather than just their own individual centers. This is just as true in social dance as in performance dance. In the *allemande* and the *grand right and left*, when both dancers pull firmly, it speeds their movement and propels them through the figure and into the next. The *circle*, the *reel*, and the *swing* all put dancers in grips that place the center of gravity in the middle of a circling figure. Assuming the dancers are all willing to give up their centers of gravity, the figures take on the feeling of a top, whirling energetically.[3] In performance dance, the same factors hold true, with the qualification that a dancer who cannot share a center of gravity will not last a day in a performance troupe. The grips also become much more varied in both their formation and their firmness. The grips in Figure 5.14 are light, and mainly for stability, but they move the center of gravity for all three dancers to the center. In the same way, the man assisting a ballerina in a pirouette maintains only the most delicate contact, if any, to help stabilize her spin without slowing it. In Figure 5.15, only the central couple actually share a center of gravity, but it requires considerable upper body strength in the man as well as in the woman's hips and back. A more unusual grip occurred in a modern dance I saw some years ago where the grip was between legs and shoulders in a totem pole-like connection among several dancers, in both horizontal and vertical positions. It was very unique, and the whole dance pivoted around that unusual grip. Of course, grip is for movement and movement requires energy.

5. ENERGY—the effort a dancer uses in the movement

    Force—the visible energy

    Concealed Energy—often used for grace (*pas de deux* in *Swan Lake*, Act 2)

Energy is the fifth element of dance; it revolves around the effort the dancer puts into the dance. It is not just effort in the sense of working hard. In ballet, effort involves both the actual exertion and the apparent exertion: force versus grace. Each is appropriate in different circumstances. In general, women's dancing should appear graceful and effortless almost all the time. Sometimes that is also true of men's dancing; at other times, the effort and exertion should show as symbols of strength and vigor. The figures above give various examples of this. It goes without saying that movements that do not involve lifting or carrying should show only a fluid grace, like

---

3   In the *reel* figure, the partners hook elbows and spin around one another, usually halfway, and then do the same thing with a dancer in the opposite line of the set, then back to the partner, then on to the next in line, all the way to the end of the set. In the *swing*, the couple is usually in waltz position, with one arm clasping the partner from behind and the other extended. Done right, the swing is exciting and fun, but if one partner starts on the wrong foot or refuses to lean into the movement, it is an awkward, stumbling, unpleasant struggle.

FIGURE 5.16 David Hallberg, A forward *cabriole*, in *The Sleeping Beauty*, music by Pyotr Ilych Tchaikovsky, choreography by Marius Petipa, Bolshoi Ballet, Moscow, 2010.

FIGURE 5.17 Nikolai Fadeyechev in a leap in *Swan Lake*, music by Pyotr Ilych Tchaikovsky, choreography by Marius Petipa, State Academic Bolshoi Theater of the USSR, Moscow, 1956.

Figures 5.8 and 5.11. Figure 5.12 shows some effort but no strain; the energy is channeled into a sense of bravura and showmanship in both dancers. On the other hand, the one-armed overhead carry in Figure 5.9, the lift in Figure 5.13, and the shoulder carry in Figure 5.14 obviously require great strength in the male partners—but it must never show. Their movements must appear as weightless as the ballerinas they are supporting. The opposite is true of movements that are deliberately flamboyant for both men and women, like the *grand jeté* and *cabriole* in Figures 5.5 and 5.6 and the leaps in Figures 5.16 and 5.17. The point of such movements is to display energy and strength. The balance between displayed and concealed energy is something the choreographer must always bear in mind.

6. CHOREOGRAPHY/COMPOSITION—the planning of all of the dancers' movements
    *   Formal—in performance dance, fully designed in advance; in social dance, follows a caller
    *   Informal—social dance without a caller; improvised performance dance
    *   Vocabulary—the repertoire of steps used in a particular type of dance; usually specific to period and place
    *   Style—the overall result of choreography with a given vocabulary

Choreography, the sixth element of dance, puts it all together: all the individual movements, all the patterns, all the groupings, the force appropriate to each, and, in some cases, the actual music to be used. Not all ballet or other dance has prescribed music, and in some cases, the choreographer may prefer something else to replace or supplement a particular movement in the score; for instance, Petipa had Ludwig Minkus compose additional music for *Paquita* (Figures 5.14 and 5.15). Persons taking on the role of choreographer for a ballet troupe must have the required knowledge and experience, usually from being dancers themselves. The choreographer creates a formal plan for the dance. This is especially important in a full-length *action ballet*. A two-hour evening's entertainment must be meticulously planned in advance. This is formal choreography. Some social dance is choreographed as well, although much more simply. The contra dance patterns in Figure 5.7 are mixed with others in different combinations in each named dance. The caller plans them formally so the patterns will work for the dancers.

Choreography can be informal as well. This is more common in social dance, especially since the 1960s, when it became possible for dancers to improvise any movements they wished on the dance floor, often or usually without contact with each other. Sometimes a folk-dance caller will improvise as well—it works particularly well in circle dances, where the caller can break the line and lead the string of dancers on a merry chase through any figure that comes to mind. Informal or improvised choreography is less common in performance dance, although it is not unheard of. Its principles are similar to those of theatrical improvisation: given a more or less detailed overall plan, dancers are free to express themselves with whatever figures strike them at the moment and respond to each other the same way.

Any dance style uses a particular vocabulary of movements that characterize and determine the style. Ballet has one of the largest such vocabularies, which has been convenient for so many illustrations in this chapter. Most of ballet's vocabulary comprises positions, steps, gestures, and interactions of dancers. The geometry of dance patterns is the choreographer's creative area. On the other hand, Figure 5.7 shows a number of standard patterns used in contra dance. Contra dance and other Western folk dances have a vocabulary that primarily prescribes patterns, and steps are largely left up to the performer. A third vocabulary that prescribes some steps and patterns is that of Renaissance dance, like the sixteenth-century galliard in Figure 5.1. That particular dance is mostly a vocabulary of steps, but they can be done in two patterns. The earliest such dances were danced with small steps by couples in procession. As the century wore on, the galliard grew more energetic and the processional pattern was a bit risky: dancers would separate, dance individually, and display their own special steps—the vocabulary grew.

Figure 5.18 shows some of these steps. At the beginning is the *reverence* (the courtesy movement that begins and ends each dance), in which the partners acknowledge one another. The next step is the *pied en l'air* ("foot in the air") or *grève*. The first is small for the processional version of the galliard. The *grève* is a higher kick used after the dancers separate. Next is the *posture*, which the dancer lands on for step five, beat six. Last is the *capriole*, one of the special steps added in the later galliard. It is also the ancestor of the ballet *cabriole* that appears in Figures 5.6 and 5.16. They look different because the ballet move is more highly developed, but the principle of moving the legs is the same in both.

7. DEPICTION—the portrayal of something specific in a dance
   • Mime Figures—isolated steps, movements, or patterns within a dance that are intended to portray something or someone
   • Action Ballet—full-length depiction of a story

The seventh element of dance is depiction. A dance doesn't *need* to depict anything. It exists in its own right to be appreciated for its movement or emotional expressiveness. But there are many dances that depict something small or large. In the social-dance context, many Renaissance branles (circle dances, mostly performed with hands joined) had a mime figure: in the horse branle, dancers stomp and turn like restless horses; in the pease branle, they hop like peas popping from a pod; the washerwoman shakes her finger and scolds; for reasons I don't understand, the official leaps sideways (perhaps it is political evasion). On the other extreme of depiction are dances that are full-length evening entertainments with plots. Most highly developed in the nineteenth century, these are called action ballets. Many composers wrote them, as the examples above show, but the three most famous are Tchaikovsky's *Swan Lake*, *Sleeping Beauty*, and *The Nutcracker*. These are the supreme examples of performance dance.

FIGURE 5.18A *Reverence.*

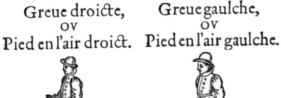

FIGURE 5.18B *Grève*, or Foot in the Air.

FIGURE 5.18C *Posture.*

FIGURE 5.18 Renaissance dance vocabulary—Four steps from Thoinot Arbeau's *Orchésographie* (Lengres: Jehan des preyz, 1589).

8. CONTEXT—the circumstances in which the art form takes place; more important for dance than any other art form
    -   Social Dance—participatory; still a very common social activity in America, typically on weekend nights, at weddings, holiday parties, or similar occasions
    -   Dance Performance—main involvement is as a member of an audience: an observer, as one would be at a musical concert or theater production

FIGURE 5.18D *Capriole.*

Dance has one element that the other art forms do not: context. Like drama or music, dance exists in a performance context—entertainment for an audience. Unlike the other arts, though, dance also exists as a social phenomenon. It is true that music lovers will sometimes get together for an evening of chamber music, and of course church choirs have a social component, but no other art provides occasions for large groups to assemble and socialize like Saturday night at a barn dance, a dance bar, or a charity ball. Dance is unique in being not only an art for observation but also an art for participation.

9. EXPRESSIVE CONTENT—what the dancer(s) are trying to say; may be a physical event or an emotional circumstance
   - Physical Event—may occur in either context
   - Emotional Expression—especially important in the performance context

As with the other art forms, the final element of dance is expressive content or message. Dance says something—even if it is as simple as "Let's boogie!" The first way dance can say something is at the concrete level with a physical action or event. The mime figures discussed above are the simplest example. Dances can also depict or commemorate events. *Sacket's Harbor* is an unusual contra dance named after an action in the War of 1812 at the northeast end of Lake Ontario. The event was a pair of battles. In the first, fought at the harbor mouth, American ships repulsed the British. In the second, the British landed and were defeated on land. (The naval base remained active until 1948.) The dance commemorates the naval battle. From the long contra dance lines, groups of three couples join hands and circle three-quarters around so each group is perpendicular to the set. The active couple dances down into the set (as into a harbor) then dances back and casts off. The full set of calls is in Figure 5.19.

FIGURE 5.19 Sacket's Harbor Calls & Steps.

Music Strain	Beats	Action
A	8	Long lines, forward and back. Active couple at top and every third couple first time through.
	8	Circle six left three-quarters, to lines of three across the set.
A (repeat)	8	Active couples down the center, turn. (can dance at a walk or sashay; the important thing is that the dancers don't change sides.)
	8	Dance back, cast off (this puts the active couple between the 2 inactives).
B	16	Turn contra (or country) corners. Be quick to be ready for the next call.
B (repeat)	8	Forward six and back.
	8	Circle six right three-quarters. This returns the set to two long lines.
The Harbor & Battle		Strain A repeat (down & back) defines the harbor. Strain B the first time (Contra Corners) is the battle.
	Unfamiliar Concept & Call	
The Progression		Casting off moves the active couple one place down the set. They remain active, though, until they reach the bottom (the end away from the music). Inactive couples that reach the top become active. A couple may need to wait out at the top or bottom if there are not couples to fill the figure.
Contra (Country) Corners		The active couple is between the two inactives. The active couple allemandes right with each other, then allemandes left with their right-hand opposite corners. Back in the center they allemande right with each other, then allemande left with the other corner and return to their places (with another allemande if there is time—there usually isn't in this dance).

Usually danced to "The Steamboat Quickstep." There is a tune named "Sacket's Harbor," but it is rarely used.

Expression of emotions in dance is especially important in action ballet, where it is critical to character development. Opposite extremes can be seen in the alternate endings of *Swan Lake*. The original ending was tragic: the evil magician triumphs and the lovers commit suicide. This did not appeal to everyone, so different choreographers have devised different happy endings: the couple rises together from the dead and the magician's spell is broken by their undying love; the prince duels with the unhappy magician, defeats him, the spell is broken, and the two lovers live happily ever after. There are others. The point here is not the substance of the endings but that the ballet, through its carefully controlled motion, can communicate sorrow, tragedy, and joy. Dance can express emotions.

FIGURE 5.20 Anonymous, Musicians and Dancers (ca. 1400 BCE), fresco, from Tomb of Nebamun, Thebes, Egypt, British Museum, London.

A Brief History of Dance

As with drama, the length of dance examples hampers the inclusion in the book of as many of them as music or, especially, visual art. To make up for this, I include a short history of dance below. Studying the history of dance begins with some frustration, because documentation of the actual dance steps began only in the fifteenth century. This means that for earlier periods, there are descriptions and pictures of dances, but we cannot reconstruct the steps. We begin with some assumptions. Aboriginal tribes in recent years have used dance in a wide variety of contexts: hunting reenactments, religious rites, preparation for battle, and social dances. This leads us to assume that our own prehistoric ancestors also enjoyed dance, perhaps in the same ways; beyond that, we cannot draw any specific conclusions.

From ancient and biblical times, we have pictures and descriptions. Some examples are included. Figure 5.20 is a scene of music and dancing from the Egyptian tomb of Nebamun, the custodian of grain for the pharaoh, ca. 1350 BCE. It shows a woman musician playing a double-barreled reed instrument while two other women dance. The musician sits with her legs curled on a low podium. The dancers both bend at the waist and appear to clap. The front dancer is performing some footwork. Beginning around the same time, the Bible mentions

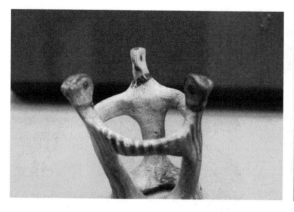

FIGURE 5.21 Anonymous, Three Dancers in a Ring (ca. 1300 BCE), terra-cotta (fired clay), British Museum, London.

FIGURE 5.22 Anonymous, Peleus with Dancing Nymphs before a Sacrificial Altar (ca. 560 BCE), polychrome black-figure cup, from Athens, Antiquities Museum, Munich, Germany.

FIGURE 5.23 Anonymous, Musician (Hermes?) Leading Three Dancers (the Graces?) in a Processional Dance Leading a Small Boy (ca. 500 BCE—Archaic), painted marble, Acropolis Museum, Athens.

dancing. There are at least four references to it as an activity and two metaphors.[4] Beyond the Bible, other sources mention dancing, so it was certainly widespread in the ancient world. Figure 5.21, a trio of women doing a circle dance, is one of the earliest sculptures of dancing from the earliest Greek culture. In Figure 5.22, an Athenian black-figure cup from about 560 BCE, shows Peleus (father of Achilles) behind dancing sea nymphs (Nereids) during a sacrificial burned offering. They are dancing in a processional line, slightly crouched with boldly swinging arms. From around fifty years later (Figure 5.23) comes a sculpture from the pre-Classical acropolis in Athens: a relief of the Three Graces, also dancing in a line behind a musician, who may be Hermes playing an *aulos*.

In Figure 5.24, a Hellenistic bronze statuette from around 200 BCE depicts a gracefully dancing woman in a flowing gown. From the same time or later, in a Roman house at Pompeii, comes a sprightly bronze statuette of a dancing faun (see Figure 5.25). He steps lightly on his toes as he gazes and gestures at the sky. These images and records tell us something about dance in ancient times, even if we would like to know more. First, people did

---

4   Exodus 15:20 and 32:19 record the Israelites dancing in celebration after crossing the Red Sea and later before the golden calf. In Judges 21:21–23, the women of Shiloh danced; in 2 Samuel 6:14, David danced before the Lord. Ecclesiastes 3:4 and Matthew 11:17 use the term poetically or metaphorically.

FIGURE 5.24 Anonymous, Woman Dancing (ca. 200 BCE—Hellenistic), bronze statuette, from Sicily, Museum at All Saints (Allerheiligen), Schaffhausen, Germany.

FIGURE 5.25 Anonymous, (Replica of) Dancing Faun (before 79 CE—Hellenistic or Roman), bronze statuette, House of the Faun, Pompeii, original in National Museum, Naples, Italy.

dance, and they did it for celebration, religious rituals, and entertainment. Dances for religious rituals were probably for groups. Celebratory dance could be solo or group, depending on the occasion. Dancing for entertainment seems to have been more often for one dancer or a small group. Group-dance formations included dancers facing one another, circles, line dances, and processions, and there was a wide variety of movements and steps for all groupings. A word of caution: these are generalizations from just a few examples of very different cultures over a span of nearly 1,500 years. They show a range of probabilities, but they do not exclude other modes of dance.

After the fall of the Roman Empire, the first few centuries of the Middle Ages were a period of social instability and political realignments. The rising power of the Christian church was also influential in prescribing morality, which excluded dance. From these times (early Romanesque period), there is little or no documentation of dance, although it probably still existed informally.[5] By the later Middle Ages (the Gothic period, 1100–1400), there are still no detailed descriptions

5   Figure 9.19 is an eleventh-century illumination of a dance condemned by Saint Radegunde.

FIGURE 5.26 Medieval Dance Types.

Name	Description
Danse	A social dance, with couples in procession.
Carole	A social dance, circle formation, a round dance.
Bal	A performance dance.
Saltarello	A dance with jumps or leaps. Latin–*saltus*, a jump; *saltare*, to dance.
Rota	Latin–a wheel or to turn around. Maybe a musical round, round dance or dance with refrain.
Estampie	The name of many surviving dance tunes. Most have repeated lines of unequal length with a refrain at the end.
Ballade, Rondeau, Virelai	The names of song types with refrains, associated with dancing. Italian–*ballare*, to dance; *virare*, to turn. French–*ronde*, a ring, around; *virer*, to turn.

FIGURE 5.27 Ambrogio Lorenzetti (1285–1348), *The Effects of Good Government in the City* (1338–39), fresco, Palazzo Pubblico (City Hall), Siena, Italy.

of steps, but some dance music survives, and writers began to give the names of dances with brief descriptions and occasional pictures. Figure 5.26 shows what is known.

The dance formations (circle, procession) are like those of the ancient period, and there remains a distinction between social and performance dance. In addition, there is now music; in particular, it often has repeated portions and refrains. The few pictures confirm the formations. Figure 5.27 is a detail from Ambrogio Lorenzetti's *Allegory of Good Government* in the city hall council chamber of Siena, Italy. It depicts a line of women dancing in an s-curve under the raised arms of two other women while a woman behind sings and plays a tambourine. The dance can be interpreted in two ways: either as a single-line procession or (more likely) the chain of a broken circle. The music is equally interesting. This is a dance song, with percussion to keep the beat. It is easy to imagine the singer singing the verse and the dancers joining in on the refrain as they danced.

It was not until the fifteenth century that dancing masters wrote down descriptions, which have survived, of the actual dance steps. The first dance-manual manuscripts appeared in the fifteenth century, written by dancing masters of noble courts.[6] Most of these sources are single-copy manuscripts; they include specific tunes, each with its own choreography of steps and patterns. In some cases, players needed to improvise beyond the music given, but the steps were fixed. The named dances are similar to the ones above, except that *balli* (Italian plural for the French *bal*) could be social dances, too. They were complex ones, though; these are court dances for the nobility, who had the leisure to spend time each day learning complex choreographies.

6   In Italy, they moved among the courts of Ferrara, Milan, Naples, Rome, Urbino, and Venice. Recent discoveries include dance books in Germany, Spain, and the Low Countries as well.

An important processional dance pair is the *basse danse* and *tourdion*—slow and fast, respectively. The *basse danse* could have different choreographies, but the *tourdion* is the early galliard described above. Figure 5.28 shows such a dance in progress. The costumes are typical mid-fifteenth-century court dress, and they reveal interesting features of the dance. The ladies wore trains. Not only did this risk having them stepped on, as in the picture, but it also excluded reverse steps (backing up) from the choreography.

In the sixteenth century, documentation of dance extended further down the social ladder. Arbeau's *Orchésographie*, published in 1589, was written by an elderly French priest who wanted to preserve the dances he enjoyed in his youth.[7] Arbeau goes beyond the court-dance books (which continued to appear) to teach less complex dances, suitable for middle-class merchants and businessmen who worked for a living. The book includes two prescribed groups of dances, a few single dances, and a large number of mimed branles.[8] The prescribed groups are 1) pavane and galliard, and 2) four branles: double branle, single branle, gay branle, and Burgundian branle. The pavane is slow and danced in procession—a slightly more complex version of what formal brides use today as the wedding march. The pavane's steps are step-half step, step-half step, then three steps and a half step (called two singles and a double). The steps can be done in any direction: forward, backward, or to the side. The galliard that follows is done as described above (Figure 5.1). Figure 5.29 shows a modern Estonian Renaissance dance revival group, Saltatriculi, performing what appears to be the beginning of a pavane. The gentlemen have stepped back with the near foot to acknowledge the lady, and most of the ladies are looking demurely downward—the *reverence* of Figure 5.18 (which could open any dance).

The branle is a circle dance, mostly performed with hands joined. The double branle is a double to the left, then two doubles to the right; the single branle is a double to the left, then one single to the right; the gay branle is four *pieds en l'air* (foot-in-the-airs) (see Figures 5.1 and 5.18), beginning with the right foot and alternating feet; the Burgundian branle is like a double branle but with a *pied en l'air* at the end of each double. The circle should always move

FIGURE 5.28 A *basse danse* of the fifteenth century.

FIGURE 5.29 Saltatriculi, an Estonian historical dance troupe performing a pavane for the annual Hanseatic Days Festival, Tartu, July 2012.

---

7   Possibly because of his religious profession, he published under a pseudonym, Thoinot Arbeau, which was an anagram on his real name, Jehan Tabourot. (I=J)

8   The remaining unique dances he lists are the Morris Dance, the Canary, the Spanish Pavane, and the Bouffons (or Buffens), a mock swordfight.

FIGURE 5.30 French School, "A Branle," detail from *A Ball at the Court of Henry III of France* (1551–1589), ca. 1580, Louvre, Paris.

FIGURE 5.31 Possibly Marcus Gheeraerts (1561/2–1636), (perhaps ironically entitled) *Queen Elizabeth I Dancing with Robert Dudley, Earl of Leicester* (c. 1580), Penshurst Place, Kent, England. Having a Dutch painter of the French Valois school, the painting's identification with Queen Elizabeth has been questioned.

left (clockwise); the other way is bad luck. The dances increase in vigor. Dancing the last two for any length of time is excellent aerobic exercise. Arbeau suggested that older folks might prefer to sit them out. For the twenty mimed or specialty branles, Arbeau makes no specific grouping except to say that they can be combined as the dancers wish; such a grouping he calls a *gavotte*.[9] One such *gavotte* that has been used in recent years is: 1) Horse Branle, 2) Pease Branle, 3) Aridan Branle, 4) Washerwoman Branle, and 5) Official Branle (with the tune now used for the Christmas carol "Ding, Dong, Merrily on High"). Figure 5.30 shows a round dance, probably a branle, at the court of Henry III of France, who held balls twice a week.

Dancing was very popular at royal and noble courts. When a courtier asked Queen Elizabeth I how she remained in such good health, she replied that she danced three galliards, using the man's steps, before breakfast. Figure 5.31 was long thought (perhaps erroneously) to show her doing one of the galliard's most vigorous variants, the *volta*. In the *volta*, the gentleman places his left hand in the small of the lady's back; his right hand grasps the base of her busk (the wedge-shaped stiffener in the front of her dress; the painting's hand placement is wrong—too low). Her right hand rests on his shoulder for stability while her left hand holds her skirts modestly down as he lifts her with his knee under her rump and spins them both around—*volta* means turn.

As dance instruction filtered down to the middle class, there was a broadening of dance repertoire and location. Figure 5.32 depicts a country dance in a French village, presumably to celebrate the wedding of the couple on the right (the lady has flowers in her hair). It is difficult to tell what the dance is. The poem underneath says branle. Since most of the visible men have their right feet in the air, it could be a gay or Burgundian branle. The art collection's cataloger calls it a gavotte, but that could indicate a collection of branles, as noted above, and the verse underneath refers to a branle. In any case, the circle is broken, so the dance line is snaking along to the accompaniment of two shawms under the tree on the left.

---

9   This terminology is confusing because he also uses the name "gavotte" for a specific dance that he places first in the group. It has the steps of a double branle. In later decades, the branles fell into disuse and the gavotte alone developed new steps.

While country dancing was popular in France and eventually attracted the nobility as well, it was in England that the greatest variety of country dances developed. John Playford's *English Dancing Master* went through eighteen complete editions and over a dozen partial editions and supplements between 1651 and 1728. The cover of the tenth edition gives a clear picture of the kinds of dances it describes (see Figure 5.33). Playford describes circle dances, square dances, and two types of dance for the longways set formation. The contra dance (Figures 5.7 and 5.19) is the more complex type, as every second or third couple is active, so the whole line of dancers is busier. The other dance type for longways sets is the reel, where only one couple is active at a time. Figure 5.34 shows the steps for one version of the Virginia Reel.[10] This is one of the best-known reels, and it includes the reel figure that gives the type its name: the head couple links right arms, goes half

FIGURE 5.32 Abraham Bosse (1602–1676), *Country Dance Performed by Villagers* (1633), engraving, 22 × 30 cm (Paris: Le Blond, 1633). A bride and groom lead a dance) from the church behind, as an old man on the right adjusts his glasses. A band of two shawms plays under the tree.

FIGURE 5.33 John Playford, *The [English] Dancing Master*, 10th ed. (London: John Playford, 1698), title page. One cupid and two musicians play violins as four couples prepare for a longways set dance. "English" was dropped from the title after the first edition.

---

10   It is also called Sir Roger de Coverley's Reel, after a country squire character in *The Spectator* by Joseph Addison (1711); in Scotland, it may be known as The Haymakers. Elsewhere it might be known as The Finishing Dance because it was traditional to end a ball with it. There is a tune named "Sir Roger de Coverley," but the dance is often performed with any suitable tune.

FIGURE 5.34 Virgina Reel (Sir Roger de Coverley's Reel).

Dancers	Action
Head L, Foot G	Forward & Back (or Take hands Right, Left or Both once around, or Dosido) in center of set. Return to place.
Head G, Foot L	Forward & Back (or Take hands Right, Left or Both once around, or Dosido) in center of set. Return to place. (The same as the first couple,)
Repeats *ad lib*	If desired, the above figure can be repeated by both couples as desired, each time with a different figure from the group listed above (Forward & Back, Take hands Right, Left or Both once around, or Dosido)
Head Couple	Do the reel figure down the set—Hook right arms (or hold right hands) with your partner until reaching the opposite line; hook left (or left hands) with the person you meet; go around him/her until you meet your partner. Right arms or hands with your partner to the next side person and so on to the end of the set.
Head Couple	Sashay (or chasse = sideslip holding both hands) back up the set.
Head Couple	Split at the top and go down the outside; other couples peel off and follow.
Head Couple	Form London Bridge(one or two hands) at the foot. Others pass under; head stays at bottom.
New Head Couple	Start over again.

Technically, the dance ends when every couple has been head once, but you can keep going as long as it's fun!

Reels are less fussy than contradances. Because only one couple at a time is active, and the size of the set is variable, there is not an exact count of measures for each figure. Instead, each figure is danced until it is completed and then the dancers begin the next.

Eight couples per set is best; one or two more will work. Head couple (top) is at the music end. Ladies' line is on the right facing up. G is for Gentleman. L is for Lady.

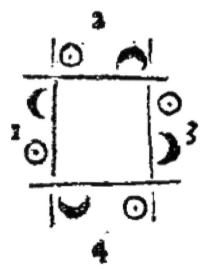

FIGURE 5.35 Square Dance diagram from Playford's *[English] Dancing Master.*

around, links left arms with someone in the opposite line, goes around them, meets their partner in the center, and continues thus down the set. It is called a reel because the figure depicts a reel or spool winding down the set (another example of a mime figure depiction), but not all reels have a reel in them! It is also a generic term for a longways set dance with one active couple.

The only country dance set remaining to be discussed is the most familiar: the square dance. Playford's diagram of the set is Figure 5.35. The crescents are men and the circles are ladies. Your partner is next to you on your side of the square (ladies on the right). Your corner is the person on the other side. The couple facing you is across. Head couples are those in line with the music (1 and 3); side couples are on the sides (2 and 4). These terms appear in the calls for square dances, many of which are the same figures already seen (e.g., allemande, circle, do-si-do, star). This raises the last point about Playford's book: it is a *call book*. It does not describe dances in as much detail as I have; it just gives tunes and the calls that go with them. Over the years' many editions, the Playfords (John and his son, Henry) and their successor, John Young, published around one thousand dances (counts vary), which required dozens of calls. It sounds like a lot, but considering that these calls served for all those dances, the vocabulary is fairly restrained. A final note is that Playford's dances are not really for country folk but are dances for society (which, in England, was heavily middle class), so these dances served a population similar to Arbeau's. They are also the ancestors of American folk dance, which has preserved the forms and many of the dances themselves.

In contrast to the broadening interest in dance across social classes in England, French aristocratic dance of the seventeenth century was the most complex social dance ever devised. This was partly due to Louis XIV, who himself was a superb dancer and who made dance his personal emblem from the time he portrayed Apollo as a youth (see Figure 4.44). Dance complexity was also affected by Louis's drawing all the nobility to Versailles where he could keep an eye on them; in their idleness, they had much time on their hands. Finally, dance complexity resulted from the desire of everyone at the court to be grander and more

FIGURE 5.36 Israel Silvestre (1621–1691), *La Fête "Les Plaisirs de l'Ile Enchantée"* (The Festival of the Enchanted Isle, 1664), detail of ballet from the comedy-ballet *La Princess d'Elide* (The Princess of Elis) for Louis XIV, engraving.

elegant than anywhere else. There were grand balls of such magnificence that pictures of them are too large to reduce in this book and see the details. Nearly every theatrical performance included dance to some degree. An example is Figure 5.36, the ballet from the *Princess of Elis*, performed for a festival called The Enchanted Isle in the gardens of Louis's court at Versailles. Dance grew so complex that the first detailed notation for dance was developed by Raoul Feuillet and Pierre Beauchamp; an example is shown in Figure 5.37, a rigadoon (Fr. *rigaudon*). Even in its complexity, this is a social dance for nonprofessionals. Contemporary professional dance became the basis of ballet.[11]

Acquiring a socially acceptable skill level in these dances required regular visits from a dancing master like the one in Figure 5.38. Elegantly clad, even to the extent of wearing a dress sword, the master is playing his miniature violin, called a *pochette* (from the pocket it could be carried in) or a "kit." He watches his pupil languidly while standing with the exactly correct and fashionable stance, feet turned at ninety degrees from one another, forty-five degrees from the direction of travel. This remained standard in social dance for a long time. Later ballet increased the turnout to 180 degrees, which is much more difficult and less natural. A poem printed under the picture reads, "This dancer has such a charming air that he is rigged out well for caresses. One can easily imagine that this master has plenty of mistresses."

In the eighteenth century, although French culture relaxed from the rigid discipline of Louis XIV's reign, dancing remained important on both the social and professional levels. Feuillet's notation system spread to instruct people in

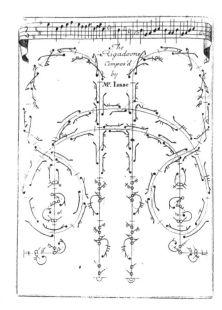

FIGURE 5.37 Rigadoon (Fr. *rigaudon*) by Mr. Isaac, using dance notation invented by Raoul Auger Feuillet and Pierre Beauchamp. From the translation of Feuillet's *Choréographies*, published as *Orchesography or the Art of Dancing ... an Exact and Just Translation from the French of Monsieur Feuillet*. By John Weaver, Dancing Master. 2nd ed. (London, ca. 1721).

---

11   Feuillet and Beauchamp's notation provided the means to record complex choreography. Beauchamp has also been credited with inventing the five ballet foot positions, but in fact they first appeared in Cesare Negri's *Le Grazie d'Amore* (1602).

FIGURE 5.38 A seventeenth-century dancing master playing the miniature violin he used in teaching, called a pochette or a "kit" (Paris: Bonnart, seventeenth century), New York Public Library.

FIGURE 5.39 Baroque dance, the final figure of the minuet—presenting both arms, with music above, Feuillet dance notation of steps below and dancers between. Plate from Kellom Tomlinson, *The Art of Dancing Explained* (London, 1735). Washington, DC, Library of Congress.

the still-complex steps of court dance; his system is again demonstrated in Figure 5.39, which shows the last of six pages of instructions for the minuet, the most popular dance of the time. For greater clarity, drawings of the dancers are superimposed on the notation for the steps of the dance. Balls remained major social occasions, and the dances developed a certain lightness and carefree attitude, as appears in Figure 5.40.

Ballet evolution also continued. One significant figure was the famous dancer La Camargo, pictured in Figure 5.41.[12] She was the first dancer to perform multiple *entrechats*, in which the dancer leaps upward and beats the legs together several times before landing. Famous for this technique, she shortened her skirts to calf length to display it, which was considered improper at the time. After her, the most revolutionary development in ballet was dancing *en pointe*, on the tips of the toes. The technique had been attempted as a stunt, with little grace, in the first decades of the nineteenth century. Marie Taglioni was the first ballerina to incorporate it as an integral part of dance and dramatic presentation in *La Sylphide* in 1831 (see Figure 5.42).

---

12   Full name Marie Anne de Cupis de Camargo.

FIGURE 5.40 Antoine-Jean Duclos (1742–1795), *Le bal paré* (The Dress Ball) (1773/4), hand-colored etching, Metropolitan Museum, New York. Notice the dancers' lightness of step and the perfect turnout of their feet.

FIGURE 5.41 Nicolas Lancret (1690–1743), detail from *La Camargo Dancing* (ca. 1730), National Gallery, Washington, DC. She and her partner rise to the balls of their feet for grace. In the background, a pipe and tabor one-man band provides the music.

While ballet was developing ever more advanced technique, social dance was also changing. The five basic dance positions were still taught in social dance at the beginning of the nineteenth century, as shown in Figure 5.43. The basic foot positions remained at a forty-five-degree turnout and were accompanied by a deliberate casualness of the upper body, even more than the dancing master in Figure 5.38. New dances also came into fashion. One of these was the quadrille, a rather formal version of the square dance. It had five sections, often in different meters or tempos.[13] Each couple had its own set of figures, and in the fifth section, they all danced together—not always perfectly, as shown in the caricature in Figure 5.44.

In the nineteenth century, formation dances remained popular. We know this from dance program cards that young ladies received for each ball. The dances were listed, with a line next to each. At the ball's beginning, a gentleman would circulate among the ladies and request particular dances; each lady would write his name down for one as an appointment. A late example of this, cleverly printed as a fan, is shown in Figure 5.45. By this time, couple dances were well on their way to supplanting formation dances. There are fourteen waltzes, three polkas, two lancers, and only one quadrille, but this was a gradual process, and formation dances of all sorts—squares, circles, and longways dances—appeared on dance cards well into the middle of the century. The waltz craze inspired the change. Developing out of a German country dance and popular on the continent in the late eighteenth century, the waltz arrived in England in 1813. It became popular immediately amid some disapproval of its close embrace,

FIGURE 5.42 Marie Taglioni dancing the title role in *La Sylphide*, (The Sylph, or Fairy, 1832), print.

13   In one popular version of the quadrille, called a Lancers, the figures could be more complex, and the fifth figure could include promenade-like movements for several dancers abreast in military fashion.

FIGURE 5.43 "The Five Positions of Dancing," from Thomas Wilson, *Analysis of Country Dancing*, 3d ed. (London: J. S. Dickson, 1811).

FIGURE 5.44 George Cruikshank (1792–1878), *Dos à Dos (do-si-do)—Accidents in Quadrille Dancing* (1817), engraving. (In later playful dances, this is called the "boomps-a-daisy.")

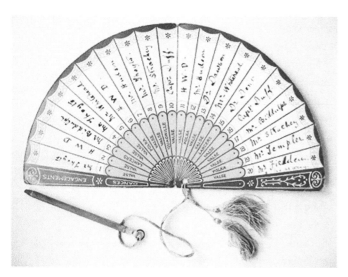

FIGURE 5.45 A dance engagement card in the form of a fan for a ball on January 11, 1887.

which some considered indecent. This shows clearly in Renoir's picture of an artist friend, Suzanne Valadon, dancing a waltz (see Figure 5.46).

The transition from the nineteenth century to the twentieth was momentous in all the arts. Visual art, music, and performance dance underwent earthshaking changes in their entire artistic languages. This was less obvious in dramatic art and social dance, but change did occur.

The rise of ragtime music inspired dances to go with it: the one-step, the two-step, the turkey trot, the fox-trot, and others, of which only the fox-trot has stood the test of time. These dances were popularized by the dance team of Vernon and Irene Castle, working with James Reese Europe, one of the first of a group of significant African American composers and the man whose 369th Regiment "Harlem Hellfighters" Band introduced ragtime and jazz to European audiences in the months following World War I. His "Castle House Rag," written for the couple, is pictured in Figure 5.47.

Jazz and jazz dance became all the rage in both Europe and the United States. They represented the first major unique American contributions to capture European fancies, marking a new era of respect for American arts. New jazz dances continued to develop over the next decades.

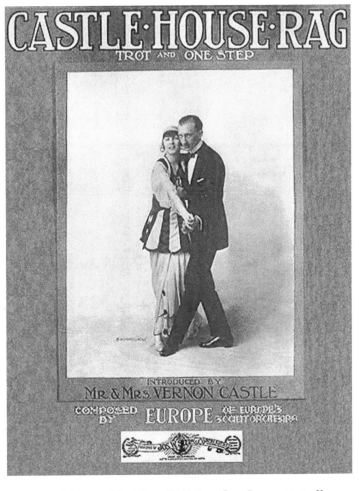

FIGURE 5.46 Pierre-Auguste Renoir (1841–1919), *Dance at Bougival* (1883/4), oil on canvas, 182 × 98 cm, Museum of Fine Arts, Boston.

FIGURE 5.47 Title page of "Castle House Rag" by James Reese Europe, picturing Vernon and Irene Castle, who introduced the dance (1914).

The best known was the Charleston, symbol of the flapper era in the 1920s. Figure 5.48 shows Josephine Baker performing the strangest move of the dance, which gives the appearance of the legs crossing back and forth.[14] Jazz dance's main competitors in the early twentieth century were South American and Caribbean dances like the tango, the rhumba, and the samba, joined by the mambo and the conga in the 1950s. Like jazz, these dances arose from a fusion of black and white culture. Ballroom dancing of all sorts was popularized by the smooth and elegant style of Fred Astaire, at first partnered with his sister Adele (Figure 5.49) and then most famously with Ginger Rogers.

Early twentieth-century performance dance experienced an aesthetic revolution similar to that in visual art and music. One dancer's influence stands out—Isadora Duncan. Born

---

14   Baker was an extraordinary woman who rose from abject poverty to become a celebrated performer at the *Folies Bergères* in Paris. Often discriminated against in the United States for her race, she became a French citizen and served the Free French cause as a spy in World War II. She was an outspoken supporter of the American civil rights movement.

FIGURE 5.48 Josephine Baker dancing the Charleston at the *Folies Bergères*, Paris, 1926.

FIGURE 5.49 Fred and Adele Astaire.

FIGURE 5.50 Isadora Duncan dancing at the Theater of Dionysus, Athens, 1903.

in San Francisco, she taught dance from an early age. Disillusioned with traditional dance and unappreciated in the United States, she opened dancing studios—first in London and then in Paris in 1902—and toured Europe with her new style. Figure 5.50 shows her dancing in Athens's theater of Dionysus in her trademark innovation of long, flowing dress. Instead of her customary bare feet, she wears sandals.[15] Soon after, choreographer Michel Fokine of the Ballets Russes abandoned traditional costuming but retained much traditional movement in Igor Stravinsky's first two commissioned ballets, *The Firebird* and *Petrushka*, in 1910 and 1911.[16] The following year, Vaslav Nijinsky, the company's lead dancer, choreographed *The Afternoon of a Faun* by Claude Debussy using completely nontraditional movements derived from Greek vase paintings and animal movements (see Figure 14.2 and discussion, pp. 387–390). The work was controversial because it defied audiences' expectations of dance, and the faun's very last movement was an erotic thrust of the hips. Only the faun and the lead nymph wore sandals; all other dancers were barefoot. In 1913's *Rite of Spring*, Stravinsky's violent music and Nijinsky's primitive choreography, which used stomping steps and other wild motions, caused a near riot at the premiere; dance would never be the same again (see Figure 14.39 and discussion, pp. 411–412).

15   This particular dress is Duncan's interpretation of the classical Greek woman's dress, the *chiton*.

16   Petrushka is the Russian version of Pulcinella or Mr. Punch, the *commedia dell'arte* puppet character.

FIGURE 5.52 Martha Graham and company in *Appalachian Spring*, composed by Aaron Copland for Martha Graham who dances the Bride.

FIGURE 5.51 Ruth St. Denis and Ted Shawn in an outdoor photo, in costume.

Following World War I, other dancers continued the innovations. Ted Shawn and Ruth St. Denis (Figure 5.51) were prominent not only as performers but also for beginning a tradition of dance that lasted at least three generations. One of their most prominent students was Martha Graham, who was one of the world's most famous dancers during her very long career. She inspired and commissioned dances from great composers. Probably the best known of these is *Appalachian Spring* by Aaron Copland, shown in Figure 5.52.[17] Graham's student Merce Cunningham continued her innovations with his own troupe, pictured in Figure 5.53. A contemporary who sought his own direction was Alvin Ailey, who founded the first interracial classical dance

FIGURE 5.53 Merce Cunningham Dance Company staging a Persepolis Event for the Shiraz Art Festival, Shiraz/Persepolis, Iran, 1972. Cunningham is on the right.

troupe. His most famous dance, *Revelations*, is pictured in Figure 5.54. Since their time, performance dance has continued to evolve in ways as varied as human anatomy will permit.

---

17   Copland was often amused by comments about the ballet. He had no program for the work, which he called *Ballet for Martha*. She devised the plot about a young farm couple. The title she chose, from a poem by Hart Crane, refers not to a season but to a water source in the Adirondack Mountains of New York.

FIGURE 5.54 Alvin Ailey's signature creation, *Revelations*, here performed at Miami's Adrienne Arsht Center for the Performing Arts in February 2011.

FIGURE 5.55 Competitive Ballroom Dance, 2011.

In social dance after World War II, jazz gave way to rock 'n' roll, as the world searched for new bearings. The jitterbug in the 1950s was followed by a series of short-lived novelty dances: the twist, the mashed potato, the frug, the pony, and others, after which social dance experienced the long-delayed identity crisis that had afflicted the other arts in the early 1900s. Physical contact between partners ceased, and standardized movement yielded to individualized self-expression, a situation that still prevails on dance floors today. There has been some reaction to this lack of structure, though, in developments that might be characterized as Postmodern: disco, country line dancing, the folk dance revival, and a rising interest in ballroom dance, both in mass media and in competition (see Figure 5.55). In the twenty-first century, dance is very much alive.

Image Credits

Fig. 5.2A: Copyright © 2014 by Richwales / Wikimedia Commons, (CC BY-SA 4.0) at https://commons.wikimedia.org/wiki/File:Ballet_feet_1st_position.png.

Fig. 5.2B: Copyright © 2014 by Richwales / Wikimedia Commons, (CC BY-SA 4.0) at https://commons.wikimedia.org/wiki/File:Ballet_feet_2nd_position.png.

Fig. 5.2C: Copyright © 2014 by Richwales / Wikimedia Commons, (CC BY-SA 4.0) at https://commons.wikimedia.org/wiki/File:Ballet_feet_3rd_position.png.

Fig. 5.2D: Copyright © 2014 by Richwales / Wikimedia Commons, (CC BY-SA 4.0) at https://commons.wikimedia.org/wiki/File:Ballet_feet_open_4th_position.png.

Fig. 5.2E: Copyright © 2014 by Richwales / Wikimedia Commons, (CC BY-SA 4.0) at https://commons.wikimedia.org/wiki/File:Ballet_feet_closed_4th_position.png.

Fig. 5.2F: Copyright © 2014 by Richwales / Wikimedia Commons, (CC BY-SA 4.0) at https://commons.wikimedia.org/wiki/File:Ballet_feet_5th_position.png.

Fig. 5.3: Copyright © 2012 by Edgar Degas; Photo by Museum Associates / Los Angeles County Museum of Art (LACMA). Reprinted with permission.

Fig. 5.4: Copyright © 2010 by Fanny Schertzer, (CC BY-SA 3.0) at https://commons.wikimedia.org/wiki/File:Jiwee_Kwen_-_La_Bayad%C3%A8re,_Ombres_2e_v._-_Prix_de_Lausanne_2010-2.jpg.

Fig. 5.5: Copyright © 2011 by Fanny Schertzer, (CC BY-SA 3.0) at https://commons.wikimedia.org/wiki/File:Chenxin_Liu_-_Don_Quichotte,_Kitri_-_Prix_de_Lausanne_2010-7_edit.jpg.

Fig. 5.6: Copyright © 2010 by Fanny Schertzer, (CC BY-SA 3.0) at https://commons.wikimedia.org/wiki/File:Philip_Hanschin_-_Giselle,_Prince_Albrecht_-_Prix_de_Lausanne_2010.jpg.

Fig. 5.7: Mary McNab Dart, "Appendix B," Contra Dance Choreography: A Reflection of Social Change. Copyright © 1995 by Taylor & Francis Group. Reprinted with permission.

Fig. 5.8: Copyright © 2010 by Fanny Schertzer, (CC BY-SA 3.0) at https://commons.wikimedia.org/wiki/File:Hinano_Eto_-_Don_Quichotte,_Kitri_-_Prix_de_Lausanne_2010-5.jpg.

Fig. 5.9: Copyright © 1960 by Christjeudi10 / Wikimedia Commons, (CC BY-SA 3.0) at https://commons.wikimedia.org/wiki/File:1960_Le_Lac_des_cygnes_-_Jean-Paul_Andreani_et_Claire_Motte_sur_la_scene_de_l%27Opera_de_Paris_-_Photo_3.jpg.

Fig. 5.10: Copyright © 2008 by Alexander Kenney / Kungliga Operan, (CC BY 3.0) at https://commons.wikimedia.org/wiki/File:Swan_Lake_prodution_2008_at_the_Royal_Swedish_Opera.jpg.

Fig. 5.11: Copyright © 2006 by Jeff / Wikimedia Commons, (CC BY-SA 2.0) at https://commons.wikimedia.org/wiki/File:Dq1.jpg.

Fig. 5.12: ASH / Copyright in the Public Domain.

Fig. 5.13: Copyright © 2010 by Jim Lamberson / Wikimedia Commons, (CC BY-SA 4.0) at https://commons.wikimedia.org/wiki/File:NutcrackerSnowPas.jpg.

Fig. 5.14: Copyright in the Public Domain.

Fig. 5.15: Copyright © 2000 by Angela Sterling.

Fig. 5.16: Copyright © 2010 by Tbonny / Wikimedia Commons, (CC BY 3.0) at https://commons.wikimedia.org/wiki/File:David_Hallberg.jpg.

CHAPTER 6

THE ARTS IN PREHISTORY, THE ANCIENT NEAR EAST, AND EGYPT

History, Prehistory, and Western Art

What makes something historic? The first things that come to mind are influential events, noteworthy achievements, famous people, and the like. Certainly these are all worthy of remembering, and that is the first criterion of history. But memory can be short, unclear, or distorted, so ultimately history depends on the written record. Without writing, historical events become legend, then myth. Without writing, history does not exist. Writing is essential for history. Events that occurred before the written record are termed prehistoric.

One consequence of this is that the borderline between prehistory and history varies from one region or culture to another. Writing in civilizations around the southeastern Mediterranean Sea seems to have begun toward the end of the fourth millennium BCE ("before the Common Era"; what was formerly known as BC, or "before Christ"). In some other parts of the world, preliterate cultures existed until the late twentieth century, and a few may still elude contemporary explorers. History for these people begins with their contact with advanced civilization. Even though the records are not their own, they will be recorded by those who made the contact. It will likely be spotty for some time, but that is the nature of all early history. Generally, people who have developed writing used it initially to record possessions, land allocations or ownership, lists of rulers, laws, and tales of the gods. More specific descriptions of people and events arose later. The arts, however, can bridge this gap and deepen our understanding of those who came before us.

As noted in Chapter 1, this book is primarily about Western art—the art of Western Europe and those cultures influenced by Europeans. Art from other parts of the world is called non-Western art. Obviously, Western art is by no means the only art, but since it is the art of those cultures from which ours arose, it makes sense for us to study our roots. In addition, Western European cultures have been preoccupied with history for at least five thousand years—one of the longest continuous historical traditions. This means that five thousand years of art are part of our cultural subconscious and are open to our appreciation and understanding. In fact, since we have a few prehistoric pieces of art from as long ago as 38,000 BCE, we might even say that our artistic tradition extends to a depth of forty thousand years. It can give us some glimpse into the culture and lives of our ancestors that far back, long before we have written historical records.

To make this more approachable, we divide art into standard time periods by style and the location of origin. These styles and their names vary somewhat from one art form to another, but in this book, we will use standard period names and dates derived from political, art, and music histories, according to which has the most general applicability.

Periods of History in Western Art

Period	Approximate Dates
Prehistoric	Before 3500 BCE
Ancient—Antiquity	3500 BCE–500 CE[1]
Middle Eastern	3500–550 BCE
Egyptian	3000–350 BCE
Classical Antiquity	500 BCE–500 CE
Classic Greek	500–325 BCE
Hellenistic Greek	325–30 BCE
Roman	500 BCE–500 CE
Medieval	500–1400 CE
Byzantine	300–1450 CE
Romanesque	500–1100 CE

(*Continued*)

Period	Approximate Dates
Gothic	1100–1400 CE
Renaissance	1400–1600 CE
Baroque	1600–1750 CE
Rococo	1725–1800 CE
Neoclassic	1750–1825 CE
(Long) Nineteenth Century—Romanticism, Nationalism, Realism	1789–1914 CE
Transition—Impressionism, Postimpressionism	1860–1910 CE
Twentieth Century—Many styles: Modernism, Postmodernism	1900–2000 CE

1   As previously noted, BCE stands for "before common era." Likewise, CE stands for "common era." The abbreviations ca. or c. mean *circa*, or "around" in Latin. They are used as shorthand equivalents. A serpentine hyphen (~) may also be used for the same meaning.

2   Rome first fell to barbarians in 410 CE, but the city was not definitively lost until 474 CE. 500 CE is a convenient and easily remembered boundary between classical antiquity and the Middle Ages.

Prehistoric Western Arts

Aside from bodily remains and tools, art objects are some of the earliest traces we have of prehistoric cultures. Without written records, we have little else upon which to base our understanding of these people. The earliest works of art we know of come from between 38,000 and 23,000 BCE, a period within the last Ice Age cycle (ca. 60,000 BCE–20,000 BCE). Figure 6.1 shows the extent to which ice covered land masses during much of this period. Of particular interest are the unglaciated areas of southern France, Swabia, Austria, Bohemia-Moravia and the open space between them (including much of the Danube flood plain). In these areas, some of the oldest known Western art has been found.

Some of the earliest known artworks include statuettes of women, called "Venuses" by the early discoverers. We do not actually know any facts about these objects beyond their physical description. Calling a statue "Venus" only reflects our theories about its possible symbolic representation of sexuality, fertility, fecundity, and abundance. There is

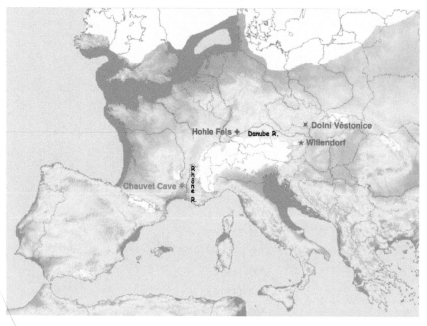

FIGURE 6.1 Europe in the Last Ice Age. Major prehistoric cultural artifact sites and adjoining rivers.

no relationship to later myths. More than two hundred of these "Venus" statuettes from all over Europe have been discovered, especially from sites in river valleys. These statuettes represent a span of about thirty thousand years (38,000–9000 BCE), six times as long as all of recorded history. They are not all from the same people, although later ones may have been made by the descendants of earlier artisans.

Although they arose over many millennia, these statuettes are stylized: the natural depiction of their features is adjusted to conform to a certain style. The stylization is apparent in several traits: prominent breasts, a broad pelvis with a protuberant (perhaps pregnant) abdomen, the clear depiction of the vulva, the absence of facial features (sometimes lacking the head

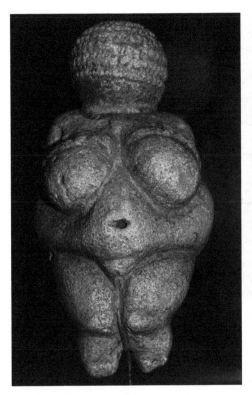

FIGURE 6.2 Anonymous, "Venus" of Willendorf, c. 28,000–25,000 BCE, oolitic limestone, 10.8 cm, Vienna, Natural History Museum.

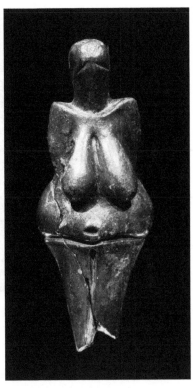

FIGURE 6.3 Anonymous, "Venus" of Dolní Věstonice, c. 29,000–25,000 BCE, terracotta (fired clay), Moravian Museum, Brno, Czech Republic (the oldest known piece of fired ceramic).

entirely), and pointed legs. The emphasis on primary and secondary sexual characteristics, along with the prominent abdomen, suggested to early scholars that these figures represent a fertility goddess or earth mother. These features, plus the images' nudity, gave rise to the name "Venus."

The best known of these figures, and one of the earliest discovered, is the Venus (or Woman) of Willendorf (Figure 6.2), found in 1908 near a village fifty-one kilometers southwest of Vienna, Austria and now in the Vienna Natural History Museum. Its estimated date is 28,000–25,000 BCE, and it shows clearly all of the features listed above.

A roughly contemporary "Venus" was discovered in the Moravian village of Dolní Věstonice (eighty kilometers northeast of Vienna, in the Czech Republic) in 1925 (see Figure 6.3). In addition to showing all of the features described above, this is the earliest example known of any fired ceramic, which indicates that artisans of that time were discovering how to alter naturally occurring substances with heat, a small first step toward metallurgy.

The oldest known "Venus" (Figure 6.4) was discovered in 2008 in a rock cave (*Hohle Fels*) just outside the village of Schelklingen, seventeen kilometers from the city of Ulm, Germany. Its estimated date is 40,000–35,000 BCE, the oldest known purely human representation. Like those above, it shows clearly the typical "Venus" characteristics, except that in this case the head is replaced by a small ring, perhaps for wearing the sculpture as an amulet.

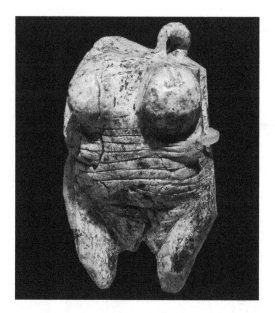

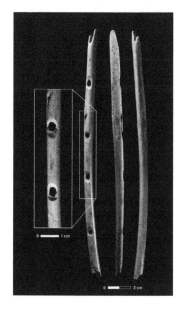

FIGURE 6.4 Anonymous, "Venus" of Hohle Fels (Schelklingen), c. 39,000–33,000 BCE, mammoth ivory, 6 cm, Schelklingen, Germany, not yet on exhibit.

FIGURE 6.5 Bone Flute, before 33,000 B.C.E, radius of a griffon vulture, 218 × 8 mm, discovered in Hohle Fels, 2008.

Hohle Fels and nearby caves are a particularly rich source of artifacts, including the oldest known sculpture (a part-human "lion person") and several bone flutes, one found less than a meter from this "Venus" statuette (see Figure 6.5). The sculptures, being solid, survived in fairly recognizable forms, but the flutes have very thin walls and are very fragile. They were reconstructed from hundreds of bits so small they would be swept away like crumbs on a breadboard. They were discovered because an archaeological team member recognized slight indentations on 31 of the "crumbs" as the edges of fingerholes. From this beginning, it was possible to fit the tiny pieces together as flutes. These instruments and the carvings show the unexpected sophistication of the culture that produced them—that it had had both sculpture and music.

All three of these statuettes, and many others, were found in or on the edge of the Danube River Basin. Since this was mostly ice-free during the last ice age, the river offered a route for east–west transmission of artistic and musical culture in Europe.

Works by many talented prehistoric painters of cave art have been discovered in Spain and France. More than 130 decorated caves have been found in the region. The first such cave discovered (in 1880) was at Altamira in northern Spain, but the southern French cave of Lascaux (discovered in 1940 and having more than two thousand figures) became the best known. For more than a decade after World War II, twelve hundred visitors a day viewed the paintings. Unfortunately, body heat, carbon dioxide, moisture, and other contaminants from visitors' respiration began to degrade the paintings. This degradation was first noticed in 1955; in 1963, the caves were closed to the public, and restoration, conservation, and preservation efforts have continued ever since. To preserve access to these priceless works without harming the originals, the most famous rooms are replicated in a visitors' center at the site.

The Lascaux cave paintings were created relatively late in the history of such art (ca. 15,000 BCE). In 1994, three cave explorers discovered a much older painted cave at Pont d'Arc in southeastern France. One of the explorers, Jean-Marie Chauvet, published an account of the cave two years later, and the cave is now known as the Chauvet-Pont d'Arc, or simply Chauvet, cave.

The Chauvet cave is in the middle of a cliff high above the Ardèche River near a striking natural bridge (the Pont d'Arc). The river is a tributary of the Rhône, 102 kilometers from the French Mediterranean coast. Migration via major river valleys, together with artistic and cultural traditions, could have reached from the upper Danube to the Rhône valley, as well as to other rivers (see Figure 6.1.). The paintings at Chauvet are the some of the best preserved and oldest European cave paintings, dating from ca. 33,000–28,000 BCE. Their preservation, and the cave's long freedom from human activity, resulted from a landslide that covered the original entrance. Since its discovery, the cave has been closed to all but selected scientific visitors in order to preserve the paintings from deterioration like that at Lascaux. To accommodate visitors, a full-size replica of nearly the entire decorated Chauvet cave opened in April 2015, and portions of the cave have also been replicated in other museums.

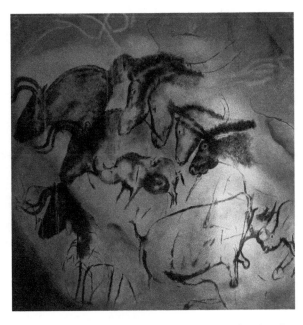

FIGURE 6.6 Horses, Rhinoceros, Aurochs (ancestor of cattle), replica of Chauvet cave paintings, c. 33,000–28,000 BCE, Brno, Czech Republic, Anthropos Museum.

Certain traits are common to most decorated caves: most depictions are of animals, with few, if any, depictions of complete humans, landscape, or vegetation. Three-dimensional roundness of the animals' images arises from two simple drawing techniques: varied use of lines (thin, thick, sharp, fuzzy, rounded, and angular) and careful shading of areas within outlines. Often the artists also used the contours of the base rock to further enhance the images' roundness. The colors are mostly earth colors, with little in the way of binder or fixative. In spite of these limitations, many cave paintings, especially those at Chauvet, are remarkably realistic—so realistic, in fact, that biologists were able to determine the absence of manes on extinct European male lions by the clearly depicted scrotum on a maneless cat.

Figure 6.6 shows a variety of animals. The three aurochs (the prehistoric ancestor of cattle) facing the same direction on the left appear to be part of a moving herd. The four horses, on the other hand, seem to depict different states of mind or activity levels of specific horses rather than a general group of animals. The central rhinoceros seems to be making a show of warning or threat, while the two lower ones are sparring or dueling. All of the animals and their situations are natural and intensely realistic; each one is completely unique and individual. This is accomplished with the simplest means listed above: line drawing, careful shading, and sensitive exploitation of the underlying rock's natural contours.

In Figure 6.7, we see a pride of lions moving together, prowling or strolling. Each head and face is unique and individual, even the stains of secretions from the eyes. The artistic

 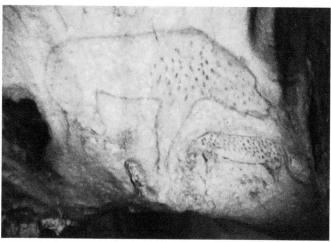

FIGURE 6.7 A Pride of Lions, replica of Chauvet cave paintings, c. 33,000–28,000 BCE, Brno, Czech Republic, Anthropos Museum.

FIGURE 6.8 Hyena or Cave Bear and Panther, c. 33,000–28,000 BCE, earth pigments on limestone, cave painting, Chauvet, France.

techniques are those already mentioned. Figures 6.6 and 6.7 are photographs from one of the replicas of the cave, since access to the originals is strictly controlled. One final figure, 6.8, was taken in the actual cave and gives an idea of the real conditions and difficulties the artist faced, including lighting and inconsistencies of rock shape, texture, and color. In light of these challenges, the realistic wary surveillance of the large hyena or cave bear further confirms ancient genius. The panther or leopard below it is the earliest known representation of this animal. Theories to explain these paintings abound: that they commemorate successful hunts; that they are artistic magic to invoke hunting success; that they are merely decorative; and so on, but we shall never know for sure.

The discussion above offers an extremely condensed summary of three different art forms from European prehistory. A more detailed and vivid discussion can be found in Werner Herzog's excellent documentary film *Cave of Forgotten Dreams*, which also includes music played on a replica of the Hohle Fels flute.[1] It is impossible to hear the actual music that the ancients played, but the flute's notes show that they used a scale similar to our own, simplified to five notes—pentatonic.

Before going further, there is one very important caution. The examples above are from a very broad geographical range (1450 km) and an even greater time span—8,000 to 12,000 years—that lasted twice the extent of all of recorded history and ended more than 20,000 years before that began. However inviting it would be to suppose that all prehistoric Europeans enjoyed these arts in the same way, the distances and times do not allow such generalization. Nevertheless, these surviving arts do contribute roundness and depth to our understanding of how these distant ancestors lived.

---

1   Werner Herzog, *Cave of Forgotten Dreams*, in collaboration with the French Ministry of Culture and Communication, Department of Cultural Heritage (Creative Differences Productions/History Films ICF9792, 2005). Wulf Hein, experimental archaeologist, plays the flute. Much of the preceding information appears there in greater detail.

Transition

Those distant prehistoric times are called Paleolithic or Old Stone Age (based on the simple rudimentary stone tools that were used at the time). Many advances occurred in the years between the prehistoric and historic eras: stone tools were refined, copper and bronze implements were developed, animals were domesticated, agriculture was born, and the beginnings of architecture emerged. Relics from much of this period survive—stone and metal tools and weapons, musical instruments, painting and sculpture, houses or living structures, towns and temples—but without written documentation. Real, in-depth information about the human condition and its interpretation in the arts was not available until the development of writing—and history.

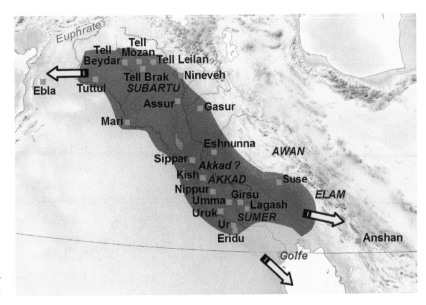

FIGURE 6.9 Mesopotamia—The land between the (Tigris & Euphrates) rivers (modern Iraq), ca. 2250 BCE, at the height of the Akkadian Empire. The Sumerian city of Ur is in the south. The Fertile Crescent adds the region down the coast of Syria, Lebanon, Israel & Palestine.

Mesopotamian and Middle Eastern Arts

Mesopotamia (from the Greek, meaning "between two rivers"), an ancient region nestled between the Tigris and Euphrates Rivers, forms the center of what is now Iraq. Adding to that the area from the northwest end of the upper river valleys and down the Mediterranean coast delineates the Fertile Crescent, one of the earliest cradles of Western civilization and history (see Figure 6.9).

Several successive civilizations in this region shared forms of government that expanded from individual city-states to territorial empires over a period of nearly five thousand years. These civilizations also shared many common artistic and cultural traits.

Settlement of Sumer, near the rivers' mouths, may have begun as early as 5500 BCE, but the history of the area awaited the development of cuneiform writing, around 3300 BCE. One important Sumerian city was Ur (of the Chaldees), mentioned in the Judeo-Christian Bible as the birthplace of Abraham. Around 2400 BCE, nearby cities of the Akkadians, a separate ethnic group, began to compete with the Sumerians and conquered them in 2270 BCE.[2] The resulting empire was short-lived and collapsed in 2154 BCE, followed by a period of anarchy and competition for regional dominance among Akkadian and Sumerian cities, as well as from barbarian invaders. This established a pattern

---

2   Sumerian was a language with no relationship to other known languages, although the Sumerians were the first to develop cuneiform writing (explained later). Akkadian was a Semitic language, related to modern Arabic and Hebrew. Both cultures are believed to have been widely bilingual.

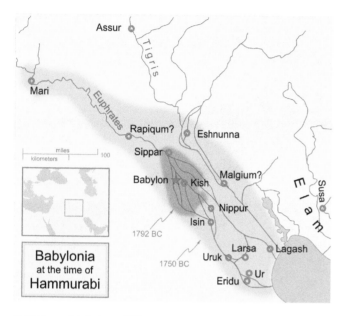

FIGURE 6.10 Babylonia, ca. 1750 BCE.

for the political control of the area: constant competition, warfare, and invasion. Various city-states, tribes, and cultures rose, fell, and sometimes rose again. The history of this region is not linear but rather more of a patchwork of frayed pieces. Nevertheless, although these groups spoke different languages, many of them were spoken concurrently and used the same cuneiform script, adapted from Sumerian, which continued as a ritual and literary language, rather like Latin in the modern era. This began in the earliest times, first with the coexistence of Sumerian with Akkadian and then Sumerian's retention even by the later Babylonians and Assyrians. Sumerian dominance experienced a resurgence for about a century around 2000 BCE before they were overrun by Semitic-speaking Amorite nomads who founded Babylon, which ruled an empire from ca. 1790 BCE to 1530 BCE (see Figure 6.10).

For the next nine centuries, regional dominance shifted among different invaders and several regional groups. Although tracking the shifts in regional political power during this period is difficult and confusing, many facets of culture remained relatively constant. Some of the competing powers are visible in Figure 6.11.

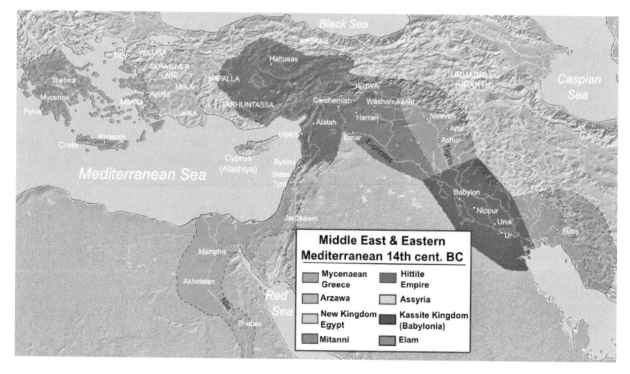

FIGURE 6.11 Political powers of the eastern Mediterranean and Middle East in the fourteenth century BCE.

One of these peoples, the Assyrians, achieved extensive dominance from 911–612 BCE, as seen in Figure 6.12.

After the Assyrians' fall and a resurgence of Babylon, power struggles and conquests continued in the region into later times—some would say even until the present day.

Although this history seems complex, its essential aspects are basic and simple: a series of states competing with, succeeding, and influencing one another for around three thousand years produced a rich artistic heritage that incorporated similar forms and common stylistic features. Artistic forms and features common to Mesopotamian civilizations include: cuneiform writing and the use of cylinder seals on clay tablets; a type of stylized depiction of humans that persisted even as it attained greater realism; mud-brick architecture that developed to a monumental level of grandeur; and the earliest written poetry and music.

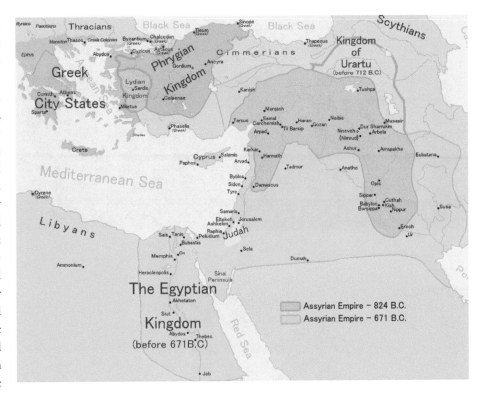

FIGURE 6.12 The late Assyrian Empire after conquest of Egypt.

The royal tombs of Ur (from ca. 2600 BCE) yielded a rich trove of artifacts, including some of the finest examples of Sumerian art. The Standard of Ur is the most elaborate example.

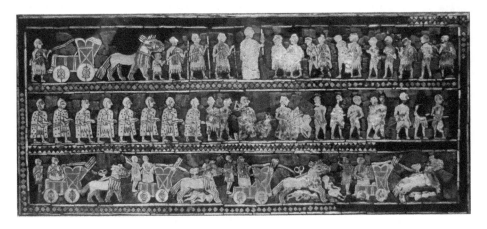

FIGURE 6.13 Anonymous, Standard of Ur, War Side, c. 26002 BCE, lapis lazuli, red limestone, mother-of-pearl, 50 × 22 cm at base, 22 cm high, London, British Museum.

FIGURE 6.14 Anonymous, Standard of Ur, Peace Side, c. 2600 BCE, lapis lazuli, red limestone, mother-of-pearl, 50 × 22 cm at base, 22 cm high, London, British Museum.

It is a rectangular box, narrower at the top, with detailed scenes on the four sides inlaid in mosaic technique using colored stones (lapis lazuli for blue, red limestone for red) and light gold-colored shell (mother-of-pearl) set in asphalt for glue. The scenes are in three horizontal registers (each with one long side and one end panel) and depict two subjects: war (or battle) and peace (or victory).

The war side (Figure 6.13) shows the king and his bodyguard receiving enemy prisoners at the top, an infantry battle in the middle, and chariot warfare at the bottom, with each four-wheeled chariot drawn by four donkeys. The related end panel may be an allegory of sacrifice for success in battle. The peace side (Figure 6.14) depicts a banquet with a singer accompanied by a lyre in the top register; the two lower registers show foodstuffs and possible spoils being carried in. The related end panel may be an allegory for plentiful game and other food.

The original wood has long since collapsed and decayed, but the excavator, Alexander Woolley, filled cavities in the excavation with plaster or wax and retrieved the mosaics in something like their original orientation, which permitted reconstruction. The actual purpose of the Standard is not known. Various theories have suggested it may have been used as a royal standard (the equivalent of a flag), a treasure chest, or the sound box of a musical instrument.[3]

Two different versions of one particularly beautiful sculpture were found in the royal tombs (Figure 6.15). Known as the Ram in a Thicket, it depicts a goat standing on its hind legs and resting its forelegs on the branches of a short tree. The branches end in delicate gold rosette flowers, and the statue rests on a finely inlaid base. The materials (gold, lapis, red limestone, and shell) are similar to those used in other objects from the tombs, with the addition of copper for the horns and silver for the belly. The illustration shows the ram in the British Museum. Its twin

FIGURE 6.15 Anonymous, Ram in a Thicket, c. 2600 BCE, lapis lazuli, gold, shell, oxidized copper & silver, height 45.7 cm, London, British Museum. (Standard of Ur visible in background).

---

3   I find the last proposal unlikely, since it is rather larger than the sound boxes of actual musical instruments found in the excavation. See Figure 6.25.

FIGURE 6.17 Cylinder Seal of Queen Puabi, c. 2600 BCE, lapis lazuli, 4.75 cm high × 2.5 cm diameter, London, British Museum.

in the University of Pennsylvania Museum is virtually identical, differing only in details.

Among the rich findings in these tombs were many headdresses (or crowns) and jewelry that belonged to Queen Puabi (she may rather have been a priestess; her title is ambiguous, see Figure 6.16) and her attendants. The headdress shown here has two rows of paper-thin gold leaves interspersed with narrow rows of lapis and carnelian beads, surmounted by three delicate gold flower rosettes (similar to those beside the ram, above). Beneath the gold leaves, possibly to shade the eyes, is a band of gold roundels set with lapis centers and interspersed with four more rows of narrow beads like those above. The jewelry includes a collar of alternating gold and lapis triangles above a row of carnelian and lapis beads, plus six varied necklaces of gold, carnelian, and lapis beads. The total effect is rich while remaining delicate and feminine. Whatever her station, Puabi was a very important figure.

Puabi's cylinder seal (for signing clay documents; see Figure 6.17) was also found near a gold pin that she may have used to attach the seal to her garments. The seal has two registers showing banqueters drinking next to a table with food. The figures are in the same style as those of the Standard (having rather squat proportions), and they follow the convention of showing the head and limbs in profile, with prominent eyes, and the torso full-front. Similar proportions occur in the portrait statue of Gudea (a later king), from the Sumerian resurgence shortly before 2000 BCE (Figure 6.18). The statue of the seated king has the same squat proportions and prominent eyes of the earlier works, although (since it is carved fully in the round) the head, limbs, and torso are depicted in their proper relationships.

Sargon, King of Akkad, led a powerful revolt against the Sumerians and established one of the first centrally governed, multiethnic empires. His empire ultimately reverted to local control (including the Sumerians) under his weaker successors; thus, his statue (Figure 6.19) stands between the works from the tombs of Ur and the statue of Gudea. Perhaps because of Sargon's different ethnicity, the style of this work varies from the Sumerian style. Although Sargon's head retains the prominent eyes characteristic of the Sumerian style and he wears a headdress similar

FIGURE 6.16 Anonymous, Crown & Jewels of Queen (or Priestess) Puabi (reconstruction), c. 2600 BCE, gold, lapis lazuli, carnelian, London, British Museum.

FIGURE 6.18 Anonymous, Statue of Gudea, Sumerian King of Lagash, c. 2120 BCE, diorite, height 46 cm, Paris, Louvre.

FIGURE 6.19 Anonymous, Head of Sargon, King of Akkad (or possibly his grandson), c. 2300 BCE, bronze, height 20.5 cm, Baghdad, National Museum of Iraq.

FIGURE 6.20 Cylinder seal depicting the worship of the sun god Shamash (on the left), accompanied by one of his scorpion-men servants, date uncertain, limestone, possibly Babylonian, size not available, Paris, Louvre.

FIGURE 6.21 Great Ziggurat of Ur, reconstruction on original base, c. 21st century BCE, mud brick, 64 × 45 m base, c. 30 m high.

FIGURE 6.22 Great Ziggurat of Ur, reconstruction.

to Gudea's, Sargon's facial features are more detailed and the shape of the face is more elongated. Sargon also wears a beard, which has remained a typical feature of Middle Eastern male grooming in later centuries. The more elongated proportions of this later style also appear in an undated Mesopotamian cylinder seal that depicts worship of the sun god Shamash (Figure 6.20). The figures on this seal retain the enlarged eyes and angular limbs found earlier—persistent traits in Mesopotamian art.

One of the most persistent architectural forms in Mesopotamia from Sumerian to Assyrian times was the ziggurat, a type of temple pyramid. The great Babylonian shrine of Etemenanki, ninety-one meters high, may have inspired the biblical story of the tower of Babel. The typical ziggurat form was a step pyramid of sun-dried brick with a main stair ramp in the front, usually with two side stairs that joined the main stair partway up. On top was an enclosed shrine; unfortunately, no remnant of any ziggurat shrine survives because of natural erosion, frequent wars, and the soft materials used in their construction. The ziggurat of Ur's base has been reconstructed, but without the shrine (Figures 6.21 and 6.22).

Mesopotamian cities were always walled. Their location in a plain that was fought over by many peoples made defensive measures essential, if often ineffective. At their greatest extent, the outer walls of Babylon were sixteen kilometers in length, twenty-five to thirty meters thick and the same height, and had 250 defensive towers. They were built by King Nebuchadnezzar, who also built the Ishtar Gate—the most beautiful known work of Babylonian architecture (see Figure 6.23)—and who supposedly built the Hanging Gardens (of which no trace has been found).

The Ishtar Gate was excavated by German archeologists in the early twentieth century and removed to Berlin, where the restored front portion is on display in the Pergamon Museum. The gate has two tiers; the back tier, higher and broader but of similar design, was too large for display and remains in storage. The gate's top edge has triangular defensive crenellations over a semicircular arch that caps a rectangular portal. The whole opening is eleven meters high, and the entire wall rises to fourteen meters. The facing is blue glazed-and-fired ceramic tile, with highlighting line patterns in yellow, black, and white tiles and rows of white and yellow rosette flowers. Large yellow beasts tread in rows along the structure's flat surfaces: aurochs bulls and fanciful (or fantastic) dragons on the gate itself and lions lining the walled approaches.

The use of fantastic beasts as symbolic gate guardians was also practiced by the Assyrians. Many examples survive, including the gate-flanking pairs of lamassus, winged bulls with human heads (often those of kings). They symbolize the zodiac, stars, or constellations, which were believed to encompass all life within them. Many of these pairs have been removed from their original locations and are displayed in the world's great museums. However one feels about the expropriation of archeological artifacts from their countries of origin, the recent barbaric destruction of several of these figures at their original sites by fanatical religious terrorists makes one thankful that some have been preserved. Photographs of those that were destroyed cannot have the full impact of viewing these majestic sculptures in person.

Figure 6.24 shows a pair of lamassus in New York's Metropolitan Museum. Because they are mounted to flank a portal within the museum's Near Eastern exhibit area, the viewer passing through experiences some of their original imposing effect. They guarded the gates of Nimrud, Assyria's capital, where their companions were hacked to bits and the ruins blown up by the modern barbarians. Carved during the reign of Ashurnasirpal II, the faces of the beasts may be his. They wear the then-universal Near Eastern beard, like Sargon (Figure 6.19), although their headdresses are taller and more elaborate than his. The lamas-

FIGURE 6.23 Ishtar Gate from Babylon, c. 575 BCE, glazed brick tile, Berlin, Pergamon Museum.

FIGURE 6.24 Pair of Gate Guardians (Lamassus), from Palace of Ashurnasirpal, Nimrud, c. 879 B.C.E., alabaster, New York, Metropolitan Museum.

sus also resemble Sargon in that they share the large eyes and stylized crescent eyebrows of long regional tradition. Notice one unique stylized convention that is just visible in the figure: these guardians have five legs. This does not reflect some bizarre mythical peculiarity; rather, it permits the side view to show the beast walking while giving it a firm stance when viewed from the front.

So far, our examples of Mesopotamian art have all been from the area of visual art: mosaic, sculpture, jewelry, and architecture. But other forms of artistic expression did exist. In music, Enheduanna, the daughter of Sargon of Akkad, was the earliest known poet and composer. The Sumerian royal tombs also held the earliest surviving stringed instruments, and

FIGURE 6.25 The Queen's Lyre and the Sliver Lyre from Ur, c. 2600 B.C.E., cedar wood, gold, lapis lazuli, shell & silver, British Museum, London, 44 cm high. The vertical post of the harp is between and behind them.

the earliest surviving work of Western music was found in an Amorite city (Ugarit, or Ras Shamra). The instruments of Ur included several lyres and a harp. The original forms of these instruments were again captured by Woolley in plaster casts that also preserved the locations of their decorations, which made reconstruction possible.

The lyres of the royal tombs were distributed among the Baghdad Museum (their lyre was destroyed in the looting of 2003), the British Museum, and the University of Pennsylvania, which participated in the dig. Figure 6.25 shows the Queen's lyre and the silver lyre in the British Museum. The vertical post of the harp is just visible behind them. All the lyres had a bovine head at one end—most of them the bull's head, usually bearded (in this case, with lapis lazuli) at one end. The silver lyre has a cow's head. Such heads seem to have been standard, as is visible on the lyre of the Standard of Ur (Figure 6.26).

Other typical features of these lyres include mythological scenes inlaid on the front column (usually in gold) and inlaid geometric patterns on the end posts and bordering the sound box. The number of strings (based on the number of surviving tuning rods) seems to have varied.

Although it dates from twelve hundred years after the lyres, the "Hymn to Nikkal" that survives on a tablet from Ugarit preserves music in the same ancient Middle Eastern tradition (see Figures 6.27 and 6.28).

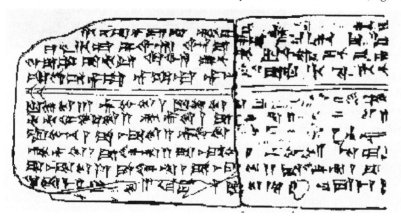

FIGURE 6.27 Anonymous, "Hymn to Nikkal," c. 1400 B.C.E., clay tablet h.6 from royal tombs of Ugarit (Ras Shamra).

Source	Background	Musical Features
1. A Hurrian Cult Song from Ancient Ugarit—transcribed by Anne Kilmer, sung by Richard Crocker, 1976.	The second try at deciphering the song; included two part and harmony, which no other work did for many centuries.	Rhythm - steady pulse, unmetered. Melody - some movement around repeated notes. Harmony - variety of consonant intervals. Texture - homophonic. Timbre - voice & reconstructed ancient lyre. Text Setting - syllabic. Form - 4 verses, all different, same repeated refrain, after each.
2. A Zaluzi to the Gods (Hurrian Hymn 6)—transcribed by Martin West (1994), sung by Gayle Newman, 1999.	This version discarded the idea of harmony and presents the song as a single melody.	Rhythm - steady pulse, unmetered. Melody - mostly repeated notes. Harmony - variety of consonant intervals. Texture - homophonic. Timbre - voice & reconstructed ancient lyre. Text Setting - syllabic. Form - several different verse, repeated refrain.
Comments	Nine people have tried to reconstruct this. Five are convincing to me.	
	Of these, 4 have many repeated notes, 3 have harmony.	
	The two above are the only two with recordings that did not add extraneous notes.	

1. "A Hurrian Cult Song from Ancient Ugarit," from Anne Draffkorn Kilmer, Richard L. Crocker and Robert R. Brown, *Sounds from Silence: Recent Discoveries in Ancient Near Eastern Music,* Bīt Enki Records BTNK 101, music in accompanying 26-page booklet.

sung by Richard Crocker. Licensed on YouTube at this time, as below.

https://www.youtube.com/watch?v=7ZatnTPhYWc

2. "A Zaluzi to the Gods (Hurrian Hymn 6)" (c. 1225 BCE), *Music of the Ancient Sumerians, Egyptians and Greeks,* Ensemble De Organographia. Pandourion Records PRCD1005, 1999, 2006, version, band 11. Music in Martin West, "The Babylonian Musical Notation and the Hurrian Melodic Texts," *Music & Letters* 75 (1994): 161–179.

sung by Gayle Neuman. Licensed on YouTube at this time, as below.

https://www.youtube.com/watch?v=czid8DT1t8c

Other Editions	Of the nine versions, four have two parts (voices), including Kilmer's. Four have one voice. West's falls in the middle—it is mostly monophonic, but in a few places, it doubles two notes an octave apart.
	4 versions, all with no repeated notes, I find unconvincing. Of the remaining, 4 have repeated notes, 3 1/2 have harmony
Kilmer (1974)	2 voices, steady pulse, melodic movement & repeated notes and refrain
Černý (1988)	2 voices, steady pulse, melody similar to Kilmer, but more repeated notes
West (1994)	1 voice except octaves, steady pulse, repeated notes, motives like Kilmer's
Dumbrill (1998)	1 voice, steady pulse through short motives, melodic, repeated ideas
Krispijn (2000)	2 voices, steady pulse, melodic movement & repeated notes and refrain
Wulstan (1971)	1 voice, steady pulse, melodic movement, notes left undetermined (-)
Duchesne-Guillemin (1977)	1 voice, very varied rhythm, melodic movement, no repeated units (-)
Vitale (1982)	1 voice, rhythmic variety, melodic movement, repeated phrases (-)
Monzo (2000)	2 voices, very varied rhythm, melodic movement, nothing repeated (-)

FIGURE 6.29 The Nile Valley Core of Ancient Egypt.

The cuneiform writing (used to record most languages of the region for millennia) here preserves an early form of musical notation; accompanying tablets explain the music theory that makes reconstruction and performance possible. Scholars have proposed several interpretations of the notation.[4] As of now, nine different versions have been proposed. The two presented here are to me the most compelling of which there are clear recordings, and they present a nice contrast. There are some differences, most obviously that the first version has harmony and a homophonic texture, while the second is a monophonic melody, and there are some differences in the melody as well. But the versions share several features: both have a steady, rhythmic pulse; their melodies are simple, with many repeated notes; and they also have multiple verses, although not always to the same music. Both are performed with voice and a replica of the Sumerian lyre.

This music rounds out our discussion of the arts of the ancient Near East, where remarkably consistent stylistic traditions developed over millennia under conquest and assimilation by many different ethnic groups. Comprehending these peoples' visual art, architecture, and music enhances appreciation of them as human beings.

Ancient Egyptian Arts

The culture of Egypt began slightly later and then flourished contemporaneously with its Middle Eastern neighbors for millennia. Centered on the Nile River that watered and fertilized its fields and offered some protection from invasion, Egypt enjoyed a history that was more continuous and less troubled by outside invaders than that of the Fertile Crescent. Over several generations, Egypt's pharaohs united the Nile valley past several cataracts upstream and at times extended their rule to the Red Sea shore, across the Sinai Peninsula, and even up the coast of the eastern Mediterranean. The river's annual flood provided new fertile soil and water for the year's crops; the resulting surplus of food freed labor for nonagricultural pursuits and made possible the development of a high culture. Figure 6.29 shows Egypt's Nile valley core.

---

4   The reason for the difficulty is that the musical symbols are for tuning strings on a lyre, and there is disagreement about how this reflects the notes.

Because Egypt suffered less competition among internal ethnic and territorial groups—as well as a lesser threat of external invasion—than Mesopotamia, an overview of Egyptian history is more linear. Discounting foreign conquerors, more than three hundred pharaohs ruled over thirty-one dynasties. These are consolidated into several distinct periods: the Early Dynastic Period that ended with the unification of Upper and Lower Egypt; the Three Kingdoms (Old, Middle, and New); three Intermediate Periods; and the Late, Persian, and Ptolemaic eras. See the table below.

Condensed History of Egypt

Historical Period	Dates
Early Dynastic Period	3100–2686 BCE
Old Kingdom	2686–2181 BCE
First Intermediate Period	2181–2055 BCE
Middle Kingdom	2055–1650 BCE
Second Intermediate Period	1650–1550 BCE
New Kingdom	1550–1069 BCE
Third Intermediate Period	1069–664 BCE
Late Period	664–332 BCE
Achaemenid (Persian) Egypt	525–332 BCE
Ptolemaic (Hellenistic Greek) Egypt	332–30 BCE

The Dynastic Period begins with the unification of Upper and Lower Egypt, whose capitals were Thebes and Memphis, respectively. The periods known as Kingdoms were times of relative stability. The Intermediate Periods, by contrast, were turbulent, with some disintegration of political control—sometimes including temporary conquest by an external foe. The last era, the Late Period, included some native Egyptian pharaohs and ended with conquests by the Persians, Alexander the Great, and the Romans.

Over three thousand years, Egypt's territorial holdings changed slowly. Although the core shown in Figure 6.29 was constant (albeit sometimes divided during turbulent times), Egypt's territory reached its maximum extent in the early New Kingdom (see Figure 6.30).

In keeping with the linear nature of Egyptian political history, Egypt's artistic traditions remained constant. Certain stylistic characteristics of Egyptian art persisted through most of its history: simplicity of form, durability, use of composite flat views in painting and sculpture, a fondness for monumental construction, and use of post-and-lintel construction in architecture.

Egyptian religion required preservation of the body after death. When people sought protection for their remains beyond simple burial, they initially built mastabas, rectangular shoe box–shaped buildings over underground burial shafts that might contain shrines for the decedent's veneration. Initially built of mud bricks and then later of stone, these shafts were

FIGURE 6.30 Ancient Egypt at its Maximum Territorial Extent (Fifteenth Century BCE).

FIGURE 6.31 Mastaba of Shepseskaf, 4th Dynasty, 25th century B.C.E. Pharaoh Shepseskaf was Menkaure's successor.

rectangular and varied in size, but they were often 12–15 meters wide, 40–60 meters long, and 8–10 meters in height (see Figure 6.31).

When even stone mastabas proved inadequate protection against grave robbers, Djoser, the first king of the Third Dynasty, commissioned the first pyramid, the Step Pyramid (Figure 6.32). This pyramid is composed of six nearly square mastabas of decreasing size piled on top of one another, perhaps conceived as a stairway to allow the pharaoh's soul to climb to heaven. The architect and engineer, Imhotep, who was also a priest and physician, has been described as the first genius; he was deified a few generations after his death.

This pyramid and its immediate successors are at Saqqara, across the river from Memphis, the capital of both the United Kingdom and Lower (downstream) Egypt. It was approximately seventy kilometers south of modern Cairo, which sits at the southern (upstream) tip of the Nile delta. The pyramid is one of the first monumental Egyptian constructions, and some consider it the earliest large-scale construction in cut stone. One indicator of Imhotep's genius was his ability to coordinate the quarrying, shaping, transport, and assembly of the stone to make construction possible—an achievement any civil engineer can appreciate, especially considering that it was done entirely with hand labor, the most rudimentary of simple machines (the ramp), and metal tools softer than the stone itself. A late image of Imhotep survives (see Figure 6.33).

Pyramid building increased until it culminated in the Fourth Dynasty with the construction of the pyramids of Giza, slightly downriver from Saqqara. The four great monuments here are well known: the Great Pyramid of Khufu (Cheops); the slightly smaller one of his son and successor Khafra (Chefren); the third, considerably smaller pyramid of Khafra's son and successor Menkaure (Mycerinus); and the Great Sphinx. A substantial city of smaller pyramids, mastabas, temples, and other ceremonial pits (e.g., for funeral barges) surrounds these ancient monuments (see Figure 6.34).

All these monuments are empty, having been looted at a time unknown; they were also stripped of most of their limestone facing, which lowered their heights. (See Figure 6.35.)

FIGURE 6.32 Imhotep, The Step Pyramid of Saqqara. 27th century B.C.E., cut stone, originally faced with white limestone, 62 m tall on a base of 109 × 125 m.

FIGURE 6.33 Anonymous, Statuette of Imhotep. Ptolemaic Egypt (332–30 B.C.E.), bronze, 13 cm high.

Khufu's pyramid was originally 230 meters square and 146 meters high. It is now eight meters lower. Khafra's pyramid is on a higher bedrock base, but is actually smaller than Khufu's: 215 meters square and originally 143 meters high. Some of the casing stones survive at the top. At 103 meters square by (originally) 65 meters high, Menkaure's pyramid is the smallest of the three large pyramids and is flanked by three partially finished small subsidiary pyramids. All three large pyramids originally had funerary temples next to them where reverence could be paid to the deceased. Each of these was reached by a causeway from a valley temple, where the Pharaohs' remains would have landed and begun their last trip from the Nile to their pyramid, visible on the plain of the Giza necropolis (City of the Dead).

The fourth colossal monument on the Giza plateau is the Great Sphinx. (See Figure 6.36.) It is the oldest known monumental sculpture as well as the largest carved from a single block—the bedrock of the plateau. The Sphinx is generally believed to have been produced during Khafra's reign; the statue rests behind the ruins of Khafra's valley temple and in front of his pyramid. The sculpture's face is thought to be his as well, although some plausible alternative theories have been advanced. The huge statue combines a man's head (wearing the pharaoh's *nemes* headdress) and the body of a crouching lion. The Sphinx is a symbol of power, mystery, and secrecy in many cultures—perhaps in ancient Egypt as well. Although mostly buried in sand for much of antiquity and into the twentieth century, the statue has suffered considerable deterioration.

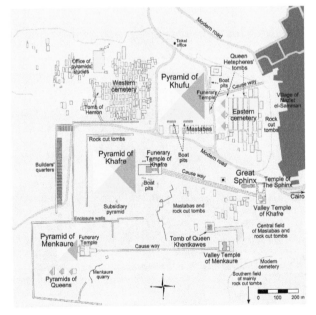

FIGURE 6.34 Giza Necropolis (City of the Dead).

FIGURE 6.35 The Pyramids of Giza. 25th century B.C.E., limestone. Menkaure's pyramid with its three subsidiaries is in the foreground. The next, Khafra's, appears deceptively taller than Khufu's behind it, because Khafra's is in front and its base is higher.

FIGURE 6.36 The Great Sphinx of Giza in front of Khafra's Pyramid, c. 2550 B.C.E., bedrock limestone, 73 × 19 m, 20 m high.

The nose broke off at an unknown time. The pharaonic false beard, a separate piece of stone, has largely disappeared, although a fragment is in the British Museum. The *nemes* headdress is missing below the level of the chin, and erosion has left horizontal grooves along the length of the upper body, perhaps due to the absence or loss of a masonry facing like the one that covers much of the lower body, paws, and tail.

Pyramid building declined after Giza and stopped at the end of the Old Kingdom, with a small resurgence in the Middle Kingdom. Although other monumental works continued throughout the Nile valley, countless smaller works of the highest quality were produced. One of these, a statue of Menkaure and his queen that resides in the Boston Museum of Fine Arts, is one of the finest and best-preserved examples of Egyptian sculpture. (See Figure 6.37.) The statue is less than life-size and unfinished, but the finished area's surface is nearly perfect. Traces of paint show that it was originally colored. The statue was found in the ruins of Menkaure's valley temple. The two figures are in a classic couple's pose. The outlines are firm and clear. Menkaure is dressed in the *nemes* headdress and kilt, standing with the left foot ahead but with weight evenly distributed. His hands are at his sides firmly grasping batons, and he wears a false beard. The proportions are lifelike. This is also true of the queen, who stands in a sheer, close-fitting, ankle-length shift through which her nipples and pubic triangle are visible; her hair is stylized and parted in the middle, with two cylindrical bunches falling to her breasts. Her left hand rests on the king's upper left arm, and her right arm is around his waist. Her left foot is also advanced. Stone left between carved areas of the figures may have been deliberate and helped preserve the statue in good condition.

Overall, the portrayal seems stylized, following established conventions for royal portraiture (note the pharaoh's exaggerated shins and knees), but also idealized, portraying the couple in the strongest and most favorable way—probably reflecting an Egyptian ideal of beauty as well as strength. The statue radiates power and leadership, especially on his part, while her pose expresses complete support. The sculpture may have been designed by outlining each face of the stone block and removing the excess, much as schoolchildren do when they make soap carvings. This design by composite flat views is one of the characteristic techniques of Egyptian visual art and is what produces the strong rectangularity of these figures. One can also see evidence of it in the Ptolemaic statue of Imhotep carved 2,200 years later (Figure 6.33), evidence of the extreme conservatism and durability of the Egyptian artistic style.

Although Egyptian art forms changed little through the millennia, their number and spread continued to expand. Politically, dynasties and pharaohs succeeded one another (with occasional intrusions by invaders and political turbulence within), but Egyptian culture remained largely static. One notable disruption was the reign of the heretic Akhenaten in the fourteenth century BCE, during the period of the New Kingdom. Egypt's priests acquired enormous wealth and power and often struggled against the pharaoh. This, along with personal religious enlightenment, may have been what moved the pharaoh to adopt a single new god, Aton. His successors rejected his ways, but during his short reign, artistic styles changed radically. Depictions of the pharaoh himself appear distorted, with exaggerated and elongated facial features and neck, and there are also depictions of him and his family in the midst of simple activities—a strong departure from stiff official poses like those of Menkaure and his queen.

On Akhenaten, the exaggerated features are unattractive, but applied more delicately to his queen, Nefertiti, they result in one of the most beautiful of all Egyptian sculptures (Figure 6.38). Her stylized features show some return to traditional Egyptian idealism, but her delicate face and long neck show the style of Akhenaten's reign at its best. The queen gazes forward, her right eye made of inset quartz with the pupil painted in black. The left eye is missing from its socket. The outer layer of stucco permitted very delicate modeling of the skin surface, including the nearly invisible wrinkles of a woman just past her youth. Her crown is a large inverted cone, similar to the bottom part of the red crown of Lower Egypt, and it originally bore the *uraeus* (a rearing cobra, the symbol of Lower Egypt) on

FIGURE 6.37 Menkaure and his Queen, 2548–2530 B.C.E, slate, originally painted, 140 cm high, Boston, Museum of Fine Arts.

FIGURE 6.38 Thutmose, Bust of Queen Nefertiti, 1345 B.C.E, limestone under painted stucco, 48 cm high, Berlin, Neues Museum.

FIGURE 6.39 Burial Mask of Tutankhamun, 1323 BCE, gold, lapis lazuli, quartz, obsidian, feldspar & colored glass, 54 × 15 cm, 10 kg, Cairo, Museum of Egyptian Antiquities.

the front. The serpent's head and forepart are broken off. The crown is also surrounded by the ancient type of diadem, a ribbon worn around the head to denote royalty. The diadem is decorated with colored geometric patterns, as is the collar on her shoulders and chest. Viewed from the front, the edge contours of the crown descend in straight lines and continue in the shape of her chin and the tendons of her neck, which gives visual unity and the crowning touch of refinement to this wonderful sculpture.

After the deaths of Akhenaten and Nefertiti, the throne passed to Tutankhamun, the son of the pharaoh and his sister or cousin. Egyptian royalty practiced incest (to keep the royal blood pure) without realizing the dangerous effects on their offspring. As a result, Tutankhamun was a sickly boy who reigned for only ten years and left no heirs. Genetic flaws arising from previous generations of incest left him with clubfoot, a cleft palate, various minor deformities, and probable susceptibility to many other conditions. He also suffered from severe malaria.

Tutankhamun left the greatest legacy of any pharaoh, since his burial is the only major pharaonic tomb to have survived substantially intact. Even this, the hidden burial site of a short-lived boy pharaoh whose family was denounced after his death, is overwhelmingly rich. The burial chamber contained four nested wooden shrines, all gilded and decorated. Inside the shrines was a granite sarcophagus in the shape of the mummy; three more nested sarcophagi (the outer two of gilded wood and the inner one of solid gold) shared the same shape. Within the gold coffin lay the boy king's mummy, with an elaborate inlaid solid gold mask over his head, shoulders, and upper chest. The tomb also contained 5,700 other objects to provide for the king in the afterlife. An additional cache of a dozen jars containing materials used in the embalming had been found earlier, where it had been reburied after a thwarted looting.

Tutankhamun's golden mask (Figure 6.39) is an astonishing work. Made of solid gold inlaid with various stones and colored glass, the mask fitted over the head, neck, and shoulders of the mummy, front and back. It depicts the pharaoh in the traditional striped *nemes* headdress with the vulture and cobra symbols of Upper and Lower Egypt mounted on the front. The face is delicately modeled with inlay around the eyes to represent the traditional kohl eyeliner. On the chin is the royal false beard, tightly braided, and the chest and shoulders are covered by a broad collar with thirteen circlets of different colored inlays: obsidian and quartz for the eyes; lapis lazuli for the eyeliner; colored glass for the *nemes* stripes; and lapis, glass, and feldspar for the cobra, vulture, and collar. The back has other decorations not visible in the figure. The style is almost a complete reversion to the Egyptian tradition that produced artifacts like Menkaure's image—rigid and imposing, unlike the delicacy of Nefertiti. Aside from its breathtaking artistic quality, the mask is quite a large example of gold sculpture. Artworks in precious metals can be short-lived due to the intrinsic value of the medium.

Akhenaten and Tutankhamen's dynasty, the eighteenth, began the New Kingdom at the summit of the Egyptian Empire (see Figure 6.30). During this time, successive pharaohs built the largest religious complex ever constructed in the Western world: the Sanctuary of Amun-Re at Karnak and its neighboring complex of Luxor. These are on the site of Thebes, the ancient capital of Upper Egypt (and of all Egypt during the early New Kingdom). In addition to these two enormous complexes on the Nile's east bank, many other temples and mortuary complexes exist, particularly on the west bank, which also holds the Theban necropolis and the valleys of tombs of the kings and queens.[5] As a political and religious center, Thebes acquired great power and wealth, which the priests retained even after the political capital moved.

The temple complex at Karnak centers on the great temple of Amun-Re. Worship of Amun-Re at Thebes supplanted the Memphis cult of Ptah and helped consolidate the power of the Theban kings in the Middle and New Kingdoms. Figure 6.40 shows the temple in its complex, but it is difficult

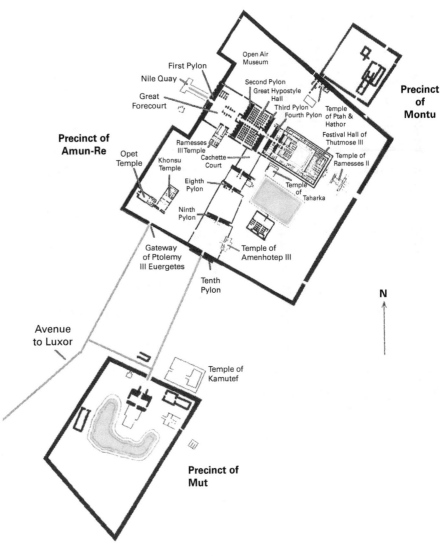

FIGURE 6.40 Map of Great Temple of Amun at Karnak.

to appreciate fully the temple's enormous size from the map alone. In addition, the design of Egyptian temples is different than what we are accustomed to seeing at ancient Greek religious sites. Examining the Temple of Khonsu in the lower left corner of the main precinct helps clarify these issues. Khonsu was the Egyptian god of the moon. His temple was completed by Pharaoh Nectanebo I (who reigned from 380–362 BCE), founder of the Thirtieth Dynasty (the last dynasty of native Egyptian pharaohs). In spite of its late date, this temple's design shows very clearly how Egyptian temples were constructed (see Figure 6.41).

As Egyptian temples developed, they acquired a design that led the visitor from an area of light (associated with the surrounding world) into increasing darkness, mystery,

5   A necropolis is a city of the dead; that is, of tombs.

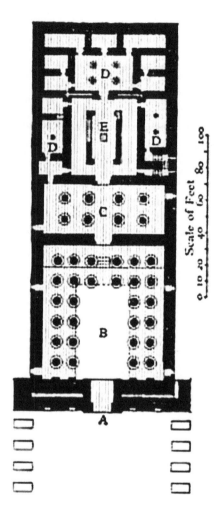

FIGURE 6.41 Plan of the Temple of Khonsu at Karnak. A. Pylon, B. Great Court, C. Hypostyle Hall (Hall of Columns), D. Priests' Rooms, E. Sanctuary.

FIGURE 6.42 Gate of Ptolemy III Euergetes and Pylon of Temple of Khonsu at Karnak, Body of a Sphinx in the Foreground, c. 235 B.C.E. (gate), c. 375 (pylon). Note scale of man beside gate.

and holiness. Passing through a unique Egyptian structure known as a pylon (A. in Figure 6.41), one first entered a peristyle (i.e., surrounded by columns) courtyard (B.) with shade around the edges. The next area was a hypostyle hall—roofed, filled with massive columns, and much darker (C.). The final room, which was probably restricted to priests, was the Holy of Holies (E.), the sanctuary of the god. Around this could be rooms for priestly use—to store treasure or equipment, or to prepare for ceremonies (D.). As one proceeded further into the temple, the floor rose and the roof lowered to increase the sense of entering a holy, magical, and secret place. Temples might have additional rooms, but this basic structure was nearly universal. This design was also adapted in simplified versions by the Israelites, first for the tabernacle and later for the two temples at Jerusalem. The Hebrews could have learned the basic principles in Egypt and brought the concepts with them.

The Khonsu temple is well preserved, and two of its structures are of particular interest. Figure 6.42 is an old tinted photograph of the Gate of Ptolemy III Euergetes that leads to the temple, with the temple's façade pylon behind.

I chose this photograph because it shows both structures with crystalline clarity, and there is a man standing next to the gate to show exactly how large it is. The gate was actually constructed after the rest of the temple—Ptolemy III Euergetes (a Greek) reigned from 246–222 BCE, well after the last native Egyptian pharaoh, but the gate is like any other built in previous millennia. Although the arch was widely used elsewhere by this time in history, here in Egypt the gate used the oldest and simplest structure for covering an opening in a wall—post-and-lintel. Two massive oblong posts support the lintel, or crosspiece, on top, and all parts are covered with traditional Egyptian reliefs that depict the interaction of the pharaoh and the gods. The gate clearly shows the extreme conservatism of Egyptian architecture, both in methods and in decoration, and its size is another reminder of the Egyptian fascination with massive structures.

The pylon behind is equally conservative—a traditional trapezoidal Egyptian temple façade such as had been built for centuries. The colossal size and massive weight of both the gate and the pylon combined with the gradual passage into darkness within the temple to overwhelm the visitor with grandeur, awe, and dread. Upon exiting the Khonsu temple and Ptolemy's gate, the visitor would see ahead the long processional avenue that leads all the way to the sister temple complex of Luxor, two and a half kilometers upstream (see Figure 6.43). In ancient times, this avenue, like many at other temples here and elsewhere, was entirely lined with sphinxes on both sides. The body of one is in the foreground of Figure 6.42.

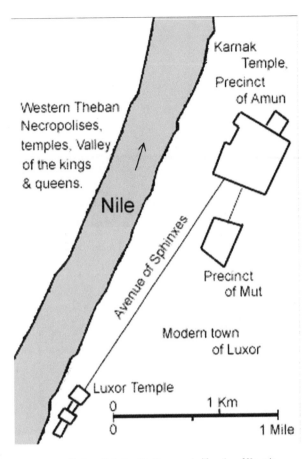

FIGURE 6.43 Thebes—Relationship Between the Temples of Karnak and Luxor.

Understanding the basic Egyptian temple design from Khonsu prepares us for the largest of all Egyptian temples, the Great Temple of Amun-Re. The plan (Figure 6.40) shows several noteworthy anomalies at a glance. Amun's temple is five times as long as Khonsu's. To Khonsu's one pylon, Amun has ten, aligned on two separate axes. Pylons 1 through 4 are labeled. Pylons 5, 6, and 7 are not numbered; 5 and 6 are the next two on the main temple axis after Pylon 4 (6 is quite small). The temple's second axis, at right angles to the main axis, contains the last four pylons. Number 7 is between the cachette court and Pylon 8. Pylons 8, 9, and 10 lead through courtyards to the avenue to the Temple of Mut. Amun's temple preserves the traditional structure but with complications: the second axis enters the temple between the hypostyle hall and the sanctuary to provide that connecting route with the second temple precinct of the goddess Mut. The sanctuary itself is preceded by a rabbit warren of ceremonial and storage rooms and is actually a courtyard, with the gods' images in the light—perhaps because Amun-Re was the sun god. The whole structure ends with another variation from the normal structure—a festival hall added by Thutmose III.

FIGURE 6.44 Karnak–Hypostyle Hall of the Temple of Amun-Re. Panorama of present appearance, fully excavated.

FIGURE 6.45 David Roberts & Louis Hahge, Karnak, lithograph. Hypostyle Hall of the Temple of Amun-Re as it appeared in 1838, before excavation.

In all this, the most breathtaking feature of the temple is the Great Hypostyle Hall, shown in Figures 6.44 and 6.45. The first figure shows the hall as it appears presently following excavation. The columns are enormous (ten meters in circumference) and the central rows are twenty-four meters high. There are 134 columns in sixteen rows. The outer rows have capitals shaped like stylized closed papyrus buds, while the two higher central rows are capped by open, spreading papyrus blossoms. Both are visible in the panorama of Figure 6.44.

The second figure shows the hall as it appeared in 1838, before excavation. The view is across the main axis, so the near column has the papyrus-bud capital. The next two, which flank the central aisle, are taller and have the open-flower capital. Note the colored decorations on the columns. Little of the paint now survives, but the lithograph gives a sense of how this temple and all Egyptian temples originally looked, garbed in vibrant exotic colors.

The richness of Egyptian heritage in sculpture and architecture is, alas, not paralleled in the performing arts. No notated music, plays, or dance instructions survive, and even visual representations of music are rather sparse, yet such activities were common and highly regarded. Our final figure (6.46, from the tomb of Nakht—an astronomer, scribe, and priest under the Eighteenth-Dynasty pharaoh Thutmose IV) shows three female musicians playing for a feast. Their skin color is darker than that of high-born ladies, which suggests that they were hired or servants. Behind them on a shelf are containers and bunches of grapes. From left to right, the three musicians are playing a double reed pipe, a long-necked lute with a very small resonating body almost under the player's arm, and a standing floor harp. All three musicians are wearing ornate circular collars, similar to those of Nefertiti and Tutankhamen. The two outer musicians are wearing sheer floor-length dresses (probably of linen; Egypt was famous for its monopoly on linen so fine that it was nearly transparent). The lutenist in the middle, who is wearing no more than enough to cover her pubic area, is also in front of the other two, and her reversed head, bent knee, and scanty costume suggest that she is dancing. All three women have the fashionable kohl-lined almond eyes of Egypt and many long small braids in their hair, held in place with hairbands. The cones just visible on their heads were probably a mixture of beeswax, animal fat, and perfume, which melted slowly and coated their bodies with scent.

The postures are characteristically Egyptian. Egyptian artists painted human figures similarly to artists of the Middle East by combining the view from two different flat planes. Heads, faces, and limbs are shown in profile, while the torso is viewed from the front. This posture, along with the almond

FIGURE 6.46 Anonymous, Musicians at a *Feast at the Home of Nakht*, 18th dynasty, portion of a tomb frieze in the necropolis on the west bank of the Nile across from Thebes.

eyes, make Egyptian painting instantly identifiable, especially since the painting style, like everything else Egyptian, changed very little over the millennia. Much Egyptian painting, like this one, was done as a decorative band or a frieze; in this case, it was for a tomb chamber. Yet, except for the legs and feet of two adjoining figures on the left, the composition is very self-contained. The loaded shelf delineates the section of the frieze with the musicians; the three players stand roughly symmetrically below it. Their size gives them prominence. There is no perspective of any kind; only overlap shows depth. Even so, the figures are lively and have a definite sense of movement. That such care was exercised on a work only to be seen by the dead is a clear indication of the depth of Egyptian belief. Certainly the strength of this faith was a factor in the stability and conservatism of Egyptian culture that produced such artistic masterpieces and monuments for such a long period of time.

Image Credits

CHAPTER 7

CLASSICAL AND HELLENISTIC GREEK ARTS

Prehistoric Greece

Classical Greek arts evolved along with the waves of modern humans who settled in early Greece starting around 6000 BCE. This New Stone Age (Neolithic) culture was the first of several waves of immigration (or invasion) into the Greek peninsula that resulted in Classical Greece as we know it. Early Bronze Age immigrants moved in on the earlier settlers around 3300 BCE. These people came both from the north and across the archipelago of islands in the Aegean Sea. Several related cultures arose: Cycladic in the islands, Minoan on and around the large island of Crete, and Helladic on the mainland. These cultures can be deemed historic only during the latter part of this period, since, for the earliest Bronze Age cultures, there are no written records; only archeological sites and art survive. All of these cultures produced unique art well worth study, but that is beyond the scope of this book.

The earliest version of the modern Greek language began to develop around 1600 BCE in what is known as the Mycenaean culture. The simplified map of ancient Greece in Figure 7.1 shows Greece at the end of this period.

The Mycenaean age is important because of its rich tradition of myth; many Greek myths appear to transmit a legendary version of history. These myths and legends (especially those surrounding the Trojan War) of the Mycenaean times have permeated Western art and thought ever since. The period of the legendary Greek kings, including Agamemnon of Mycenae, Menelaus of Sparta, Odysseus of Ithaca, and, across the Aegean, Priam of Troy, lasted from 1200–1100 BCE. The Trojan

War took place at the end of this period, shortly before another wave of destructive invasion by northerners (later known as Dorians) with iron weapons caused the Greek Dark Ages, which lasted until around 800 BCE. We will start with a brief summary of these seminal legendary stories.

In Greek mythology, the pantheon of gods as we know it was descended from several generations of supernatural beings, each of whom was defeated by his or her successors. The final battle was between the gods and the Titans (or giants) who preceded them. The triumphant Olympian gods included Zeus and Hera (the king and queen), Aphrodite (the goddess of erotic love), Athena (the goddess of wisdom), Ares (the god of war), Apollo (the god of the arts), and many others.

The fall of Troy, immortalized in Homer's *Iliad*, is the heart of ancient Greek legend. It begins with the wedding of Peleus, a mortal hero, and

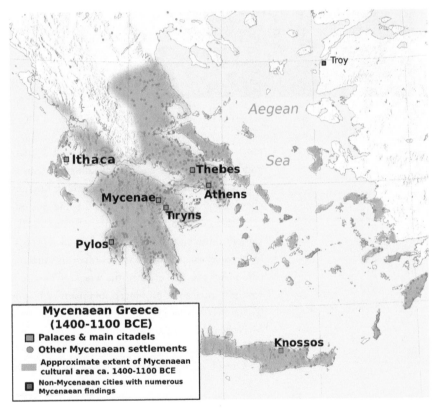

FIGURE 7.1 Greece at the end of the Bronze Age, Mycenaean culture dominant. Selected settlements at the time of the Trojan War. Note Troy at upper right.

Thetis, a sea nymph. Eris (goddess of strife) was jealous because she hadn't been invited to the wedding, so, out of spite, she threw a golden apple marked "To the fairest" at the feet of Aphrodite, Athena, and Hera. Peleus could not decide among them, so they asked Paris, Prince of Troy, for his judgment. All the goddesses offered Paris bribes for his favor: Hera offered worldly power; Athena offered great wisdom; and Aphrodite offered the world's most beautiful woman, Helen, who was the daughter of Zeus and the wife of Menelaus (the king of Sparta and brother of Agamemnon of Mycenae, the high king of the Greeks).

FIGURE 7.2 Archaic (Pre-Classical) Greek vase with the earliest known depiction of the Trojan horse. c. 670 BCE, height of jar (*pithos*) c. 1.5–2 m, Mykonos, Greece, Archeological Museum.

Aphrodite won; Paris abducted Helen, and Menelaus goaded Agamemnon into leading an armada of Greeks across the Aegean to recover her. The war lasted nine years, ending only when the wily hero Odysseus contrived a plan using the famous giant wooden horse, dedicated to Athena, in which he hid a Greek platoon. After leaving the horse outside Troy's fortress gates, the Greek army sailed out of sight, seemingly in surrender (see Figure 7.2). The horse was too large to fit through the largest Trojan gate, so the Trojans breached it, against the advice of the priest Laocoön, who cried, "Beware of Greeks bearing gifts!" In response to Laocoön's warning, Apollo sent two enormous serpents to kill the priest and his twin sons. After nightfall, the hidden Greeks climbed down and let in the rest of their army through the weakened walls, and Troy was sacked.

Of the hundreds of related myths, a few others are also relevant to the arts we will discuss. Apollo, protector of the nine muses (the goddesses of literature and music), killed the monster Python at Delphi, which became Apollo's greatest shrine. Priestesses there, breathing the fumes of the monster's decaying corpse while chewing laurel leaves, were renowned as the greatest seers in Greece.

Other tales concern Aphrodite, who had an affair with Ares, god of war. Their son, Cupid, combined their attributes ineffectively: he fired his father's arrows but with poor aim, and he inspired sexual passion that was often misdirected. Another son of Aphrodite was Priam's cousin Aeneas, who escaped the wreck of Troy to sail off and found Rome. Odysseus' return voyage to Ithaca was prolonged, and many of his adventures are recounted in Homer's *Odyssey* (encounters with a cyclops, cannibals, an enchantress, and others). Agamemnon's return to Mycenae was tragic, and his murder became a core inspiration for Greek theater, as described below.

Outside of the mythic tradition, early Greek chronology appears in the table below.

Chronology of Ancient Greece

Period	Approximate Dates
Neolithic	7000–3300 BCE
Bronze Age Cultures	
Minoan—Crete; Cycladic—islands; Helladic—mainland	3300–1100 BCE
Mycenaean (late Helladic, Heroic Age)	1600–1100 BCE

(*Continued*)

Greek Dark Ages—Iron Age (Dorian) conquest	1100–800 BCE	
Age of Homer, Proto-Geometric & Geometric pottery		
Archaic Period (distant colonization begins)	800–500 BCE	
Black-figure pottery, first Olympic Games—776 BCE		
Classical Period—Red-figure pottery, beginnings of theater	500–323 BCE	
Hellenistic Period (successors of Alexander the Great)	323–30 BCE	

This table shows more than artistic developments. It also shows the origins of the Greek tradition, as well as the names of some artistic styles we must pass over—many of them contemporary with, and influenced by, ancient Near Eastern and Egyptian art. These styles include much wonderful art and illustrate connecting pathways in the Western art tradition that led to the greatness of the art of Classical Greece.

Classical Greek Arts

The Classical period of Greece began around the time of the Persian wars, which began in 499 BCE and finished on mainland Greece shortly after 480 BCE but dragged on in the islands and Asia Minor until 451 BCE. To fight these wars, Athens had formed a defensive league of cities and islands that paid tribute to fund the Athenian navy and other forms of defense. Athens put a large excess of these funds to other uses, including building one of the most lavish temple complexes of any Greek city. In addition, Athens and her numerous allies came to be viewed as a threat by other Greek cities, so those cities formed a league, led by Sparta, to fight the Athenians. The Peloponnesian War (431–404 BCE) ended with Athens's defeat, but most Greek cities retained some degree of integrity and trade, even though they were considerably weakened (see Figure 7.3).

Greek weakness, sustained or worsened by continuing aggression between

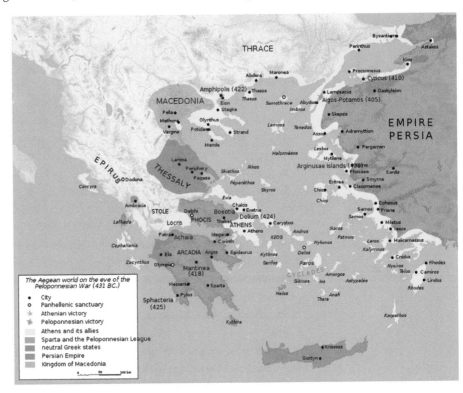

FIGURE 7.3 Mid-Classical Greece. The political alliances of the Peloponnesian War.

FIGURE 7.4 The Empire of Alexander the Great.

various cities, left Greece vulnerable. Philip II of Macedon, to the north, annexed the Greek cities one by one and completed his conquest by 338 BCE. He was assassinated two years later and succeeded by his son, Alexander the Great, whose vast campaigns over ten years subjugated all of Asia Minor, Egypt, and the East, from the Mediterranean Sea (through what is now Iraq, Afghanistan, and Iran) to the Indus River valley of northwestern India. Alexander died suddenly in Babylon during his return in 323 BCE. As a young prince, Alexander was tutored by Aristotle. This was a last link with the great period of Classical Greece, and Alexander's death marks the end of Classical Greek culture. Figure 7.4 shows the vast empire he conquered.

In the Classical period, the Greeks defeated the military forces of Persia (the largest empire in their world), invented dramatic arts and philosophy, and created some of the most beautiful and innovative art ever designed before destroying themselves through greed and city-state rivalry. Artistic developments in Classical Greece included increased realism in sculpture; new precision, clarity, and realism in painted pottery; the development of theater, philosophy, written history, and music theory; and refinement of architecture to a level previously unknown.

The Classical style of Greek art is best known from sculpture. While earlier Greek sculpture retained some of the stiffness of Egyptian works, Greek sculptors, beginning around 500 BCE, learned how to achieve a completely natural portrayal of the human body for the first time. They did this by two principal means: careful attention to proportions and relationships of all body parts, and designing the figures in natural poses, with particular attention to weight distribution and posture. They observed that a person standing at rest

FIGURE 7.5 Praxiteles, *Hermes with the Infant Dionysus*, c. 343 BCE (traditional date), Parian marble, height 2.1 m, Olympia, Greece, Archeological Museum.

FIGURE 7.6 Praxiteles, *Hermes with the Infant Dionysus*, reconstruction, engraving, 1895.

FIGURE 7.7 Polykleitos, *Doryphoros* (spear bearer), marble Roman copy of Greek bronze original, c. 440 BCE (original), 120–50 BCE (copy), height 2.1 m, Naples, Italy, National Archaeological Museum.

normally settles the body's weight over one leg, which remains vertical. The pelvis relaxes and tilts, leaving the other leg slightly bent. This posture, known as *contrapposto*, is one of the greatest discoveries in human portrayal. It is quite obvious in Praxiteles' *Hermes with the Infant Dionysus* (Figure 7.5).

Praxiteles was one of the greatest sculptors of the mid-fourth century BCE. This statue was found at its site described in the second century BCE, so it may well be a Praxiteles original. It shows the beautiful grace, perfect proportions, and natural stance of the greatest Classic Greek statuary, with the relaxed Hermes' missing arm holding something before the baby Dionysus. The drapes under the baby fall gracefully and naturally, as if pulled by gravity. The visible finish of the face and torso is smooth perfection (where it has not been damaged). The statue was originally painted or gilded. In one possible reconstruction, Hermes teases the infant god of wine with a bunch of grapes in the missing hand, as shown in Figure 7.6.

There is one characteristic of completely naturalistic sculpture that is uncommon in Classic Greek works: a sense of personal individuality in the facial expression; there is always some degree of distance and idealization. Perhaps this is because so many of these works depicted gods or goddesses, whose expression should be idealized rather than intimately human, but the idealization also appears in depictions of humans. One such example is the *Doryphoros* (spear bearer) of Polykleitos (see Figure 7.7).

FIGURE 7.8 Praxiteles, *Aphrodite of Cnidus*, marble Roman copy of Greek bronze original, 4th century BCE (original), marble, height c. 2 m, Rome, Palazzo Altemps. Head and limbs restored.

FIGURE 7.9 Praxiteles, *Aphrodite of Cnidus*, head, marble Roman copy of Greek bronze original, 4th century BCE (original), marble, Paris, Louvre. Named the Kaufmann head for its donors, this is the most refined surviving version of the statue's head and face.

Polykleitos designed this statue to illustrate his theory of perfect proportions of the human body; it became justly famous and was widely copied.[1] If possible, it shows an even more relaxed, natural posture than Praxiteles's *Hermes*, which was, in fact, one of Praxiteles's less famous works. Both works demonstrate the Greek ideal of the perfect male form. For the perfect female form, we return again to a work by Praxiteles, the *Aphrodite of Cnidus*, the first life-size statue of the nude female form (see Figure 7.8).

Like the *Doryphoros*, this *Aphrodite* (Venus) survives only in Roman copies, and the version shown is one of the most completely restored. The head and limbs are all restorations, but they agree with several other copies that preserve different parts, so the pose is close to accurate, and the face is close to one of the finest surviving copies of the head alone (see Figure 7.9). The female form of the statue is quite different from the two male forms above. The arms are less muscular, the hips are fuller, and the body curves are gentler, suggesting softness. The pose, with one hand modestly covering the pubic area, is known as the *Venus pudica*; it became a model for many later statues of the goddess, who was the Greek ideal of feminine beauty. As such, it is not surprising that the face shows a hint of the same idealization noted above, but it is risky to draw conclusions from a Renaissance restoration of a Roman copy of the Greek original.

Perhaps the best known of all Classical Greek sculptors was Phidias, who designed the sculpture program for the Parthenon, supervised its production, and executed the main statue (and possibly some of the other large ones) himself. This work was almost entirely architectural sculpture, so it requires definition of some architectural terms (shown in Figure 7.10). Greek temples are built with the post-and-lintel technique used by the Egyptians. This reflects a basic conservatism; the Greeks knew of the arch but used it rarely, mainly for internal passageways, tunnels, and other underground features.

---

1   One incomplete copy in the US of the *Doryphoros's* midportion is in the Minneapolis Institute of Arts.

The posts are the columns that completely surround a Greek temple. Each column has a capital that concentrates the weight of the lintel, or architrave. Above the architrave is a band of sculpture called a frieze. A Doric frieze, like the one on the Parthenon's exterior, is divided into individual panels (called metopes), which are separated by dividers called triglyphs (because they have three ridges). The Parthenon is unusually lavish because it has another frieze over the second row of columns on each end that flows onto the walls of the temple building. This inner frieze is Ionic in style—that is, it is continuous. Both friezes are richly adorned with sculpture, but the most elaborate sculpture program is set in the deep gables, called pediments. The most sumptuous statue of all was inside: the massive cult statue of the goddess Athena, called the *Athena Parthenos* and created entirely from gold and ivory.

The largest surviving sections of Parthenon sculpture come from the pediments (see Figure 7.11). The *Three Goddesses* from the east pediment make up one of the most elegant groups of figures from any time. The figures' grace is so great that, in spite of their damaged state, one is not immediately aware that their postures were dictated by the sculptures' placement near the pediment's shallow angle. The proportions are perfect, the postures are natural, and any potential for awkwardness is disguised by the almost liquid flow of their draperies. If not by Phidias himself, these figures were surely created by one of his most trusted associates. As a whole, the east pediment from which they came (over the temple's main entrance, but facing away from the Acropolis gateway) depicted the birth of Athena at the moment immediately after she burst, fully grown, from the head of Zeus. The central figures have been long missing, but drawings from 1674 permit a fairly complete restoration of the scene. Figure 7.12 presents one reconstruction of the east pediment.

The metopes of the Doric frieze functioned much like a cartoon strip or graphic novel, presenting a story or a group of related scenes. The Parthenon metopes presented four different allegories of the struggle between civilization and chaos: the Trojan War, the Amazon Invasion of Athens, the Battle of Gods and Giants (more on this later), and the conflict between the Lapiths and the centaurs. Figure 7.13 shows one of the south metopes; it depicts a vicious fight between a Lapith, representing human reason, and a centaur,

FIGURE 7.10 Parthenon of Athens, selected architectural features. Greek temples are surrounded by columns with capitals that support lintels topped with a band of sculpture called a frieze. The Doric frieze on the Parthenon's exterior is divided into individual panels called metopes. The Ionic frieze behind that is continuous. These are all positions for sculpture, as is the gable, or pediment.

FIGURE 7.11 *Three Goddesses* from the East Pediment of the Parthenon, marble, slightly over life size. London, British Museum. Possibly Hestia on the left, Aphrodite on the right reclining on the lap of her mother Dione in the center.

FIGURE 7.12 East Pediment of the Parthenon, reconstruction in the Parthenon Replica, Centennial Park, Nashville, TN. The central figures were already missing in 1674, so the reconstruction is somewhat conjectural, but these plaster casts used surviving portions of original sculptures wherever possible.

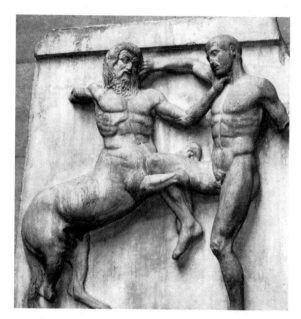

FIGURE 7.13 *Centaur Fighting Lapith.* A south metope of the Parthenon, marble, London, British Museum. The savage centaur chokes the Lapith man, who fends off his enemy with his knee and right hand.

representing chaotic savagery. This scene is depicted in high relief. Relief carving is a method of sculpture in which the figures project from, but remain part of, a wall. In low relief (*bas-relief*), no part of any figure projects beyond the wall. In high relief, such as this, portions of the carving project completely in front of the wall (in this case, both figures' arms and near legs).

In contrast to the allegorical content of the metopes, the continuous Ionic inner frieze depicted a regular festival event in Athens, the Panathenaic Procession. In the procession, a float in the shape of a ship was hauled through the city and up the Acropolis. As a sail, the ship bore a new garment (*peplos*) for the image of the goddess. The float was accompanied in the procession by representatives of all of Athens—men and women, young and old. It was the city's major religious event. The frieze procession begins at the southwest corner and proceeds in opposite directions, one across the west end and down the north side, the other down the south side. The two groups meet over the main east entrance, where young women prepare the *peplos* for presentation to the goddess. A considerable portion of the frieze survives; among the varied participants, roughly 40 percent are young men on horse-back or in chariots. Figure 7.14 shows an extremely active group of these youths. The section chosen is long enough to give some idea of the continuity of the frieze, and the figures show great variety. This jubilant, prancing, rambunctious group is another example of high relief.

The inclusion of an inner Ionic frieze (in addition to the outer Doric one) was unusual in a temple of the time. Even though all of the temple's other features were in the Doric style, the use of the more elaborate Ionic style for even part of the building added to the extravagance of the design. The three styles (orders) of Greek architecture are illustrated in Figure 7.15.

The Doric order, named for the tribes that overran Greece in its Dark Ages, is the simplest, most robust style. In addition to having the frieze divided into metopes, Doric columns are proportionately thicker than those of the other two orders: they have the simplest capitals on top, with just a spreading cushion to support the architrave, and (in Classic Greek Doric) no base on the columns, which just end at the floor. The later Roman Doric usually had simple bases on the columns.

In addition to its continuous frieze, the Ionic order (named for the Greek cities in Asia Minor) had more elaborate capitals with scrolls, called volutes, on either side of the column. Ionic columns were slimmer than Doric and always had bases.

The Corinthian order (named for the city of Corinth) was the most elaborate style, with a cluster of acanthus leaves spreading from the column top and bases, like the Ionic order. The Corinthian style is found most often in Roman architecture and somewhat in Hellenistic Greece. Only one Corinthian capital is known from a Greek temple of the Classical period, and that is in an isolated, rustic temple.[2]

FIGURE 7.14 *Riders in Procession* from the North Frieze of the Parthenon, marble, London, British Museum.

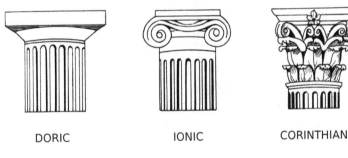

DORIC IONIC CORINTHIAN

FIGURE 7.15 The three orders of Greek architecture.

The columns point to another variation on standard Greek temple planning. The columns across a temple's front could vary in number, even sometimes including odd numbers (which could be problematic, since the center column stood before the door), but the most common arrangement was six columns (i.e., hexostyle; hexo = six, style = column). The Parthenon has eight (octostyle), as shown in Figure 7.16.

On each end of the temple, a second row of columns stood between the outer columns and the temple building proper. The sides continued only the outer row as a single colonnade. The building was otherwise typical in its construction, with two rooms, each with an entrance at the end. The smaller room was probably a treasury for holding precious offerings brought to the god or, in this case, goddess. The larger room was the god house, where the giant statue of the deity stood.

2 The temple of Apollo at Bassae. The location is so isolated that, on his second visit, the discoverer was murdered by bandits!

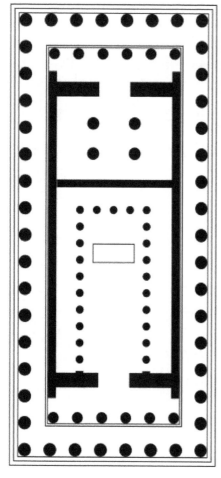

FIGURE 7.16 Plan of the Parthenon.

FIGURE 7.17 The Parthenon as it exists today, Iktinos and Kallikrates, c. 440 BCE.

The building was not designed for interior worship, however. The deity was believed to reside in some way (or to some degree) in the image, and the attendants were normally priests or the occasional individual worshipper with a special petition. Collective group worship took place outside, where animals were sacrificed and roasted on the altar; portions were reserved for the goddess and the worshippers.[3] The Parthenon, then, was designed to be appreciated mainly from the outside. It is a beautiful architectural sculpture whose beauty is best appreciated from some distance—it may invite one into the colonnade to view the frieze, but not to the dark and mysterious interior.

Figure 7.17 shows the Parthenon as it now stands. Figure 7.18a shows the same view, followed by a restoration (7.18b) of the missing portions and the original painting.[4] The building was much more colorful than is now obvious. Figure 7.19 shows the full-scale replica of the Parthenon in Nashville, Tennessee. Originally constructed of brick, wood, and plaster for the state centennial in 1897, the building proved so popular that it was rebuilt in concrete on the original foundation in the 1920s. Visiting this replica is as close as we can now get to experiencing the original.

Having viewed the Parthenon itself and its exterior sculpture, the moment has arrived to see its crowning glory. The Parthenon was noted for having one of only two colossal gold-and-ivory cult statues in Classical Greece. Its statue of *Athena Parthenos* (so-called because she was born directly from Zeus without a mother) was renowned throughout the ancient world. Not surprisingly, the original statue has not survived; the rich materials were too great a temptation

3   According to myth (and very conveniently for the Greeks), Prometheus tricked Zeus into taking the bones and fat for the gods' portion, while humans got the meat.

4   At the time of publication, an animated alternation of these two pictures could be found at https://commons. wikimedia.org/wiki/File:Parthenon_restoration.gif.

for later thieves. Reconstruction must be based on copies and replicas. The other colossal gold-and-ivory statue (also by Phidias), in the temple of Zeus at Olympia, was one of the Seven Wonders of the Ancient World. One small example of such a statue (not *Athena Parthenos*) was discovered at Delphi (see Figure 7.20).

Although the blackened ivory and eroded gold reveal just a shadow of the sculpture's original richness, it gives some idea of the extravagance represented by Phidias's enormous idol, six times larger than life-size. This statue has now been reproduced in the Nashville Parthenon (see Figure 7.21). The sculptor, Alan LeQuire, studied everything known about Phidias's sculpture, and LeQuire's *Athena Parthenos*, the largest indoor sculpture currently in existence, is probably as close to the original as it is possible to get. The standing goddess wears a breastplate (the *aegis*) adorned with the head of Medusa (the gorgon) to paralyze her enemies. On Athena's head is a battle helmet; its crest is a sphinx flanked by a griffin on each side. Over her floor-length tunic is a shorter *peplos*, cinched at the waist with serpents. A much larger snake rears under the round shield supporting her left hand, while her spear rests inside it against her left shoulder. Bracelets of snakes encircle both wrists, and her right hand supports a smaller statue of the goddess Nike (Victory).[5] Her hair flows in ringlets onto her shoulders, surrounding a face of austere, superhuman dignity. Except for the portions representing flesh (originally ivory), the interior of the shield, and the background of the base, the entire statue is gold—nowadays 3.9 kg of gold leaf one-third the thickness of tissue paper, but in the original, there were approximately 1100 kg of solid gold plates—a clever way of concealing much of the treasury of Athens.

In all its excellence and heavily researched authenticity, LeQuire's sculpture is the finest modern reconstruction of Phidias's original. Nevertheless, as

FIGURE 7.18A The current state of the Parthenon.

FIGURE 7.18B Reconstruction of the Parthenon as it originally appeared.

FIGURE 7.19 Parthenon Replica, Centennial Park, Nashville, TN, the east front of the original in Athens. The people standing on the steps give a sense of scale.

5   Some copies and reconstructions have a column under the right hand to support the extended arm and Nike. This would probably have been necessary in a stone statue, but LeQuire must have felt that the gold-and-ivory construction could have been stronger and/or light enough to eliminate the pillar.

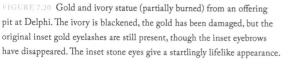FIGURE 7.20 Gold and ivory statue (partially burned) from an offering pit at Delphi. The ivory is blackened, the gold has been damaged, but the original inset gold eyelashes are still present, though the inset eyebrows have disappeared. The inset stone eyes give a startlingly lifelike appearance.

FIGURE 7.21 Phidias' *Athena Parthenos*, full-scale replica 1990, gilded 2002, gypsum and fiberglass on aluminum & steel armature, height 12.8 m, including base, Replica Parthenon, Centennial Park, Nashville, TN, by Alan LeQuire, b. 1955.

with all previous attempts to duplicate it, the spark of Phidias's genius, so renowned in the original, is difficult to discern. It is always difficult for an artist to recreate someone else's inspiration, but in this case, the variety of literary descriptions, coin portraits, vase paintings, and other sources that exist add many complications to the problem.

Figure 7.22 shows three different copies, made in Classical times, which demonstrate the difficulties in reconstructing Phidias's work. Figure 7.22a is a Roman copy, larger than life-size. Of the copies in existence, it has one of the finest faces and depicts the clothing and stance clearly, but the helmet is minimized and the figure lacks both arms (with whatever they held). Smaller copies also exist. Figure 7.22b, slightly less than one meter tall, is the most complete version of the original. It was found in Athens but is believed to be Roman. This was clearly LeQuire's primary source. Nevertheless, the face is uninspiring. Figure 7.22c, a second, even smaller and unfinished reproduction, is also in Athens. Although clearly of lower quality, it preserves some important historical details. The variations among these copies (and others) explain the difficulty encountered by any modern sculptor attempting to reproduce Phidias's masterpiece. We are fortunate to have as many survivors as we do, due in part to the obsession Roman collectors had with copying, buying, or looting Greek masterpieces, but also, no doubt, to pilgrims visiting Athena's shrine who wanted a souvenir to take home.

Phidias's original survived in some form until around 1000 CE, when its existence was recorded in Constantinople. The solid gold had long been replaced by gilt bronze, but the essential statue was still in existence—then it disappeared from reports. The Parthenon suffered as well. Quite possibly, the removal of the statues of Zeus and Athena from the east pediment coincided with the building's conversion to a Christian church in the Middle Ages. It was later converted to a mosque by the conquering Turks, but the building and most of its sculptures survived into the seventeenth century in reasonable condition for their age, as surviving sketches show. The calamity that reduced it to its present condition occurred on September 26, 1687: Turkish Athens was under siege by the Venetians, and a Venetian mortar shell detonated the powder magazine that was secreted in the Parthenon. The building was demolished, and some parts were completely and irrevocably destroyed (see Figure 7.23).

The Parthenon was the centerpiece of an entire complex of sacred sites and buildings on the Acropolis of Athens (see Figure 7.24). Most ancient Greek cities had an acropolis. The word means "city hill" or "high place." In prehistoric times, it might have been the site of the earliest settlement. During the time of the kings in the late Bronze Age, the acropolis was the site of the king's palace, which developed into a hilltop fortress for defense. After the Dorian invasions, as Greece stabilized, the acropolis retained its defensive function, but, because of its ancient and revered origins, it also became the city's main sacred place. These historic stages are visible for Athens on the plan in Figure 7.25. Figure 7.26 is a reconstructed model of Athens's Acropolis at its height around 400 BCE, with small figures that portray the Panathenaic procession from the Parthenon frieze.

FIGURE 7.22 Phidias' *Athena Parthenos*, c. 433 BCE, three early copies. L to R: 1) 1st-2nd-century CE Roman copy, marble, height 2.4 m, Paris, Louvre; 2) early 3rd-century CE copy, marble, height 94 cm, Athens, National Museum; 3) Probably 1st-century CE unfinished copy, marble, height 42 cm, Athens, National Museum.

FIGURE 7.23 Venetian destruction of the Parthenon, September 26, 1687, engraving by Francesco Fanelli, 1697.

FIGURE 7.24 The Acropolis of Athens. The two main buildings are the Erechtheum, left, and the Parthenon, right. The gap in the Parthenon's side is where the force of the 17th-century blast was greatest and reconstruction has been impossible.

FIGURE 7.25 The Acropolis of Athens, plan. Note the buildings of different historic periods and the dark outline that shows the defensive ramparts.

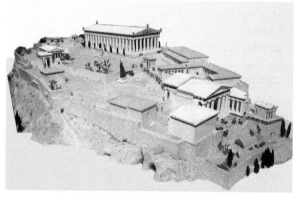

FIGURE 7.26 Scale model of the Acropolis of Athens in the Classical Period, Toronto, Royal Ontario Museum. The human figures portray the Panathenaic procession depicted in the Parthenon frieze.

Even sites without such compelling defensive needs usually had walls that defined the boundaries of the sacred compound. Such a site was the Temple of Apollo at Delphi, which housed the most famous oracle of the ancient world (see Figure 7.27). The temple was built where Apollo supposedly killed a giant serpent, Python, whose corpse produced fumes that issued from a crevice in the earth and put a priestess (e.g., Pythoness, Pythia, Sybil) into an oracular trance.[6] Kings, cities, and private individuals came from all over the known world to receive the oracle's prophecies. Their gifts were so abundant that a single room at the back of the temple (as at Athens) could not contain them all, so many cities built their own treasuries. In addition to the smaller gifts housed

---

6   Tradition records that the priestess chewed laurel leaves and sat on a tripod over the crevice to breath the fumes. After some controversy, recent work shows that Delphi sits on the junction of two faults in the earth's crust, and its underlying bituminous limestone can release volatile hydrocarbons under pressure. These compounds have been found in the waters of nearby sacred springs and in the ocean four kilometers away. The priestess may also have chewed similarly shaped leaves of a much more toxic plant in place of, or in addition to, the laurel. The tripod over the crevice was probably in the crypt (basement) near the back of the temple.

FIGURE 7.28 Model of the Sanctuary of Apollo, Delphi, State Antiquities Museum, Munich. This model shows the sanctuary's monuments and statues on its steep site.

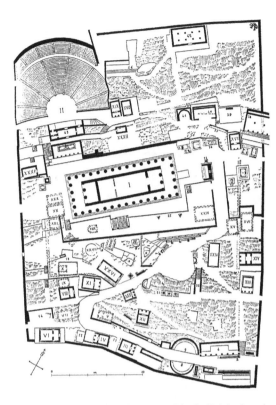

FIGURE 7.27 Site plan of the Sanctuary of Apollo, Delphi, from the original description of excavation, P. de la Coste-Messelière, 1936. Note the zig-zag sacred way flanked by cities' treasuries and many monuments. I-Temple of Apollo. XI-Treasury of Athens.

in the treasuries, donors offered statues and other monuments in profusion, as you can see in the model, Figure 7.28.

The ruins of Delphi did not survive even as well as those of Athens. Repeatedly toppled by earthquakes and rebuilt, the entire sanctuary was looted by the emperor Nero and then razed by Christians in the late fourth century CE to eliminate any residual pagan religious competition. Abandoned over the next centuries, a small village (which had to be completely transplanted when modern excavations began) arose on the site. In spite of this, reconstruction is possible, as the model shows, and ascending the sacred way to the remains of the temple can be an inspiring experience. Portions of columns have been re-erected on the temple's base (see Figure 7.29). Unlike the Parthenon, Apollo's temple was hexostyle.

The best-preserved structure at Delphi is the Athenian Treasury, built to commemorate the Battle of Marathon (490 BCE). It is a simple, elegant Doric structure with two columns in the façade (see Figure 7.30). Among its stones is one with two of the longest surviving examples of early Greek music, to be discussed below. One particularly fine votive statue (the *Charioteer of Delphi*, Figure 7.31) was also excavated.

This life-size statue was part of a larger group (including the chariot and its team of four or six horses and two grooms) that was dedicated by the ruler of a Greek colony on Sicily in thanks for having won the race at the Pythian (Delphic) Games of 478 or 474 BCE. It portrays the driver in a relatively calm stance during the victory round following the race—both feet flat, with only a slight asymmetry of weight distribution, arms forward (one still holding the reins, the other missing), expression calm, eyes focused, dressed in a customary long tunic

FIGURE 7.29 Delphi, remains of the Temple of Apollo with entrance ramp. The bases of all six façade columns can be seen. Four of them, plus two side columns have been more fully restored.

FIGURE 7.31 Anonymous, *The Charioteer of Delphi*, 478 or 474 BCE, possibly Athenian, commissioned by a Sicilian ruler, cast bronze, ceramic or onyx eyes, height 1.8 m, Archaeological Museum, Delphi.

FIGURE 7.30 Treasury of Athens, restored, Delphi. This small, elegant Doric building predates the Parthenon but is in much the same conservative, refined style.

hanging in long, straight pleats and belted above the waist, with thinner straps over the shoulders to prevent it from billowing in the wind. The refined calm and nearly even stance place this in the early Classical style. It is one of the best-preserved works of its kind. Ancient large-scale sculpture didn't fare well; limestone was reused or, like marble, was "burned" (roasted) to make lime for mortar; bronze like that used in this statue was melted down for reuse. This work survived because it had been buried by a rock fall in ancient times.

The work is a masterful example of lost-wax casting (see Chapter 2). It was cast in several parts that were welded together. Separate parts for the head's top and bottom permitted the insertion of the onyx or ceramic eyes that give the statue such a startling lifelike appearance. Eyelashes and lips are detailed in copper. On the head's bottom half, the hair is cast in the mold; on the top half, it is carved in the bronze to appear drenched with sweat from exertion.

The two halves are joined by a silver-inlaid headband. The charioteer is a crucial ingredient among the surviving artistic evidence for the Delphic pilgrimage center: the remnants of the sanctuary and temple, this votive offering, and the longest surviving example of ancient Greek music, carved on a stone from the Treasury of the Athenians (see Figure 7.32). Substantial portions of two hymns to Apollo appear on the stone. Figure 7.32 shows the first one, probably composed in 138 BCE, which is more commonly recorded and forms Figure 7.33.

The hymn is monophonic—having a single melodic line without harmony. The rhythm arises from the poetic meter and sounds odd to us because the count of beats is in groups of five. The melody sounds equally exotic, since it is based on the ancient Greek Phrygian and Hypophrygian modes rather than a modern scale. The performers may include accompaniment on a replica of a lyre, the instrument of Apollo, or other instrument.

Pictures of ancient Greek musical instruments survive mainly in vase paintings; almost the only painted images from the time are on pottery, which, even if broken, can be reassembled as long as the pieces are in one place. During the Classical era, Athenian potters discovered a technical innovation that enabled them to produce the most delicately decorated earthenware known at the time. In the sixth century BCE, the background of Athenian pottery was usually the red of the native clay or the white produced by painting on a slip of white kaolin clay. Figures appearing as black silhouettes were produced by a special firing process described below, but all the details had to be incised (scratched on) after the vessel cooled, leaving thin, white lines. This made it difficult for the vase painter to conceive of the drawing as a whole, since, until the firing was complete, he had only a black silhouette to work with, but skillful painters could still achieve remarkable results. Perhaps the finest example of black-figure technique is the drawing of Ajax and Achilles playing a board game at Troy (Figure 7.34). The needle-fine incision produces complex, lacelike patterns on the heroes' capes, and even the profile silhouettes reveal subtle character distinctions between the two.

To produce the color contrast, the Athenians used a special firing technique that incorporated a basic knowledge of chemistry. Attic clay contains iron. When heated in the presence of oxygen, the iron oxidizes to Iron (III), or ferric oxide, which is red. If the oxygen is removed, the fire will draw oxygen from the clay, leaving Iron II, III, or ferrous-ferric oxide, which is black. The Athenians had discovered that they could separate out the coarser, heavier clay particles. By using a slip of the finest clay, they could produce a coating that would fuse when heated a bit above the usual firing temperature. By mixing this with honey (for thickness) and some coloring agent, the potter could select the black areas with great finesse. After painting the design, he first fired the vase with plenty of oxygen to solidify the vessel. At this stage, all was red. Then he closed the vents and added green wood. This raised the temperature but sucked oxygen from the clay and turned the whole vessel black. But the fine slip-covered area

FIGURE 7.32 *First Delphic Hymn to Apollo*, original ancient notation, 128 BCE, carved on stone from the Treasury of Athens at Delphi. The musical notation is the intermittent line of small signs between the continuous lines of text.

First Delphic Hymn to Apollo

Summary of Text

From full translation in Thomas J. Mathiesen, *Apollo's Lyre: Greek Music and Music Theory in Antiquity and the Middle Ages* (Lincoln: University of Nebraska Press, 1999): 42–43.

O Muses, daughters of Zeus, fly from your home on Helicon to serenade your brother Phoebus Apollo, who sets out from Parnassus across Delphi to the Castalian Spring.

Behold Attica of great Athens, protected by Poseidon, sacrificing bullocks to Hephaestos with sweet Arabian incense, to the sounds of aulos and kithara.

All Athenian artists sing your glory beside this snow-crowned peak, Zeus's famed son, lyre-playing and of perfect oracles. Sing how you won the prophetic tripod from the monstrous Python and defeated the Gallic hordes …

Musical Features

Rhythm	Regular five-beat pattern derived from poetic meter.
Melody	Ancient Greek Phrygian & Hypophrygian modes. Phrases follow lines of text.
Texture	Monophonic
Text Setting	(if sung; see below)
Form	Through-composed—follows form of verse text
(Harmony	None)
Timbre	Varies according to the interpretation of the performing group

Performances—Interpretations

Musique de la Grèce antique (Atrium Musicæ de Madrid, Gregorio Paniagua, dir. Harmonia Mundi [France], 1979. HMA 1901015) Sung by men's chorus with lyre and deep drum.

Musiques de l'Antiquité Grecque: De la Pierre au son (Ensemble Kérylos, directed by Annie Bélis. K617 France, 1996. K617–069), not available to me at this time.

Music of the Ancient Greeks (De Organographia [Gayle Stuwe Neuman, Philip Neuman, and William Gavin]. Pandourion Records, 1997. PRDC 1001) Played on aulos and lyre only; not sung; fast tempo.

Music of Ancient Greece (OP and PO Orchestra, conducted by Christodoulos Halaris. Cultural Action—Emse, 2009. ASIN: B002E3L88E) Played with aulos and wire-strung (?) lyre over plucked drone.

Music of Ancient Greece & Music of Greek Antiquity (Petros Tabouris Ensemble. FM Records SA, 2011. ASIN: B004V7C8KI) Played on lyre and aulos (or modern oboe) with light small drum punctuation. Male vocal solo with some bending of pitch.

To the best of my knowledge, all of these recordings play the original melody. Their interpretations vary considerably, if not as much as Figure 6.28, Hymn to Nikkal.

fused, so when the potter allowed oxygen back in, the areas without the slip returned to red (or remained white, in the case of kaolin clay), and the fused areas remained black.

Around 520 BCE, painters began to change from painting black silhouettes and incising the details to using black for the backgrounds and painting the figures with delicate lines of red. This meant the entire figure could be drawn at one time, which made it much easier for the painter to draw realistically and with greater spatial effects. Examples of vase paintings also offer some glimpses into the performing arts.

FIGURE 7.34 Exekias, potter and painter, *Amphora* (wine storage jar) with Achilles and Ajax playing a board game, 540–530 BCE, black figure pottery, 61 cm, Vatican City, Vatican Museum.

FIGURE 7.35 Anonymous, White ground *kylix* (wine cup), with Apollo holding a lyre and pouring a libation, c. 480–460 BCE, diameter 18 cm, Delphi, Archaeological Museum.

Figure 7.35 shows the inside of a white ground wine cup, with the figure in red highlighted with black. The picture shows Apollo wearing a laurel wreath, pouring a libation of wine, and holding a lyre of the oldest type while a blackbird looks on. The lyre (the instrument of Apollo) uses a tortoise shell for a resonator. The strings are stretched over it to a crossbar supported by two wooden arms or horns that are inserted in the shell's leg holes. This is the original method of constructing a lyre. In Classical times, though, this was often replaced by the kithara, a larger, more sonorous concert instrument made entirely of wood. See Figure 7.36.

Figure 7.36 shows such a kithara being played by one of the muses (the nine patron goddesses of specific arts) under Apollo. The vase is a *lekythos*, a type of vase used to hold funeral libations of oil or wine; the painting in white-figure style depicts the lyre and its seven strings very clearly. In addition to lyres, the Greeks also had wind instruments, including the *aulos*, a double-reed pipe similar to the Egyptian one depicted in Figure 6.46. The *aulos* was sacred to Dionysus, the god of wine. Another instrument, the *syrinx*, has been named the panpipe for the god it was associated with (i.e., Pan, the god of, among other things, rustic music). Simple trumpets had military functions, and there was a variety of percussion instruments. The Greeks respected music. Both Plato and Aristotle wrote about its emotional effects and their cultural repercussions, and several writers developed extremely systematic music theory.

In addition to having music, the Greeks invented theater as we know it. Time-honored tradition attributes the innovation of having a soloist in a choral work impersonate a character—rather than merely singing about him—to Thespis in 534 BCE. Impersonation is the essential development that

FIGURE 7.36 Achilles Painter, White ground *lekythos* (funeral memorial vase), with a muse playing a *kithara*, c. 440–430 BCE, height 36 cm, State Antiquities Museum, Munich.

Classical and Hellenistic Greek Arts   165

differentiates acting from public speaking or reading aloud. Around 500 BCE, Aeschylus was credited with adding a second character and inventing dialogue. From these beginnings developed all of drama.

Many Greek religious festivals included performances of choral odes (like the "Hymn to Apollo," Figure 7.32 and Figure 7.33 above), sometimes as contests. With the development of drama, a dramatic competition developed in Athens for the festival of Dionysus. In this competition, three playwrights were each commissioned to write three tragedies and a satyr play to follow it.[7] These were performed on three consecutive days, and a prize was awarded for the best. The concept of the trilogy was invented by Aeschylus. Sophocles followed Aeschylus, added a third character (which enhanced conflict), and made other innovations. Euripides was the third great classical tragedian; he is renowned for the depth of his exploration of human nature and emotions. The works of these three playwrights have remained the epitome of ancient Greek tragedy ever since. A fourth classical writer, Aristophanes, was noted for writing comedy. Eleven of his plays survive.

Only one complete satyr play (by Euripides) survives, but we have thirty-two surviving tragedies, including the three plays of the only complete surviving trilogy, Aeschylus's *Oresteia*. All of these plays had conventions that differed substantially from what we are used to: they were played in enormous outdoor theaters seating thousands, and a chorus played the parts of crowds and performed an introductory prologue. All the performers were men, the lines were in verse, and much of the drama was sung, with dancing as well. All performers also wore masks that sometimes incorporated clever megaphones to enhance the reach of their voices in the vast theaters.

Aeschylus' *Oresteia* is one of the great monuments of world theater. In its first play, *Agamemnon*, the title character is murdered by his wife, Clytemnestra, because he had sacrificed their daughter (Iphigenia) in order to overcome contrary winds at the time of his departure for Troy. In the second play, *The Libation Bearers*, Agamemnon's son, Orestes, kills Clytemnestra (and her lover, Agamemnon's cousin Aegisthus) in revenge. The third play, *The Furies*, opens with Orestes seeking sanctuary from the avenging Furies and purification from Apollo at Delphi. After cleansing Orestes, Apollo sends him to Athens for trial by an Athenian jury. When the jury deadlocks, Athena's vote acquits Orestes. The Furies threaten revenge on Athens, but they are gradually calmed by Athena and invited to make Athens their home in a cave under a nearby hill.

In addition to its dramatic qualities, this story also explores the evolutionary currents of Greco-Roman polytheism. The Stone Age Greeks, like earlier prehistoric peoples, probably worshipped a fertility mother goddess (who later evolved into several goddesses symbolizing her various traits). Their society was matriarchal and did not recognize the need for intercourse in childbearing—conception was attributed to natural forces like wind or water. In this view, Agamemnon was only Clytemnestra's husband, but Orestes was her blood relative, so the Furies' role was to torment him, but not her, to death. Northern conquerors, however, recognized the male role in procreation. In the play, this is Apollo's defense of Orestes; Athena's respect for the male role influences her tiebreaking vote in his favor. The plot enshrines the clash between the ancient goddesses and the northerners' powerful new male gods. The fusion of the two groups of deities yielded the Olympian gods we are familiar with from the myths.

But Aeschylus explored several thematic levels. In addition to the conflict between old and new gods, the *Oresteia* explores hubris or excessive pride (Agamemnon's), the conflict of simultaneous love and hate (e.g., the murder of relatives), the replacement of the old vendetta/revenge system by justice through fair trial, the stabilization of society through legal institutions, the replacement of tribalism by the stable city-state,

---

7 The satyr play was a short work of bawdy rustic comedy within a tragic background, sometimes taking a standard myth and tossing in satyrs (coarse companions of Dionysus, god of wine) for effect. It provided comic relief from three hours of gloomy heavy tragedy. Full-length comedies were also part of the festival but in a separate contest.

FIGURE 7.37 Python, Scene from *The Furies* on a red figure krater (wine mixing pot), c. 330 BCE, London, British Museum. This work originated at Paestum, a Greek colony in southern Italy.

FIGURE 7.38 Orestes and Apollo, from Scene 1 of *The Furies*, directed by James Thomas.

and, finally, the conflict between order and chaos that we have already seen in the Parthenon sculptures.

The Furies complements the art forms we have studied, taking place in both of the sacred sites we have discussed. It also formed the subject for at least one vase painting in the red-figure style (Figure 7.37). The painting clearly shows the advance in spatial depiction developed in the red-figure style. Highly detailed and naturalistic figures of Athena (left), Orestes (center), and Apollo (right) stand in front of a sacred tripod. Orestes consults Athena, while Apollo glances at a fury or priestess standing on his left. A second Fury flies above, with the ghost of Clytemnestra in the upper left corner. Figure 7.38 shows the play's opening scene in one of two modern productions discussed in Figure 7.39.

At least two modern productions have attempted to capture as much of the original spirit of Aeschylus' work as possible. The first, Sir Peter Hall's *Oresteia* for the National Theater of Great Britain, was later performed in the Greek theater of Epidaurus (1981–82). Hall's production of *Eumenides (The Furies)*, the trilogy's third play, uses masks and augments its search for authenticity with an all-male cast and a translation by Tony Harrison that recreates the thumping, dactylic meter of Greek heroic verse. So little authentic ancient Greek theater music survives that it cannot be duplicated or imitated, but Harrison Birtwhistle has studied it, and his background score for Hall's production uses woodwinds and percussion to create an eerie evocation of the original's *aulos* player(s).

Macmillan Films offers a more recent production (2014), directed by James Thomas. This production also uses masks; it is available on DVD, and Figure 7.38 is a still photograph of Orestes and Apollo from the Macmillan production of *The Furies*. The Hall production seems not to have been reissued on DVD, but it is entirely available on YouTube at this printing. In both performances, the play's opening at Delphi with Apollo, Orestes, Clytemnaestra and the Furies, and the end, with Orestes' trial at Athens, are especially moving.

Hellenistic Greek Arts

Athens and Delphi have provided us with superb examples of the arts of Classical Greece, but artistic

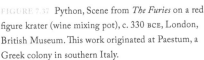

FIGURE 7.39 Aeschylus—The Furies (*Eumenides*).

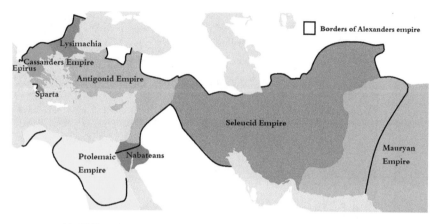

FIGURE 7.40 The Hellenistic kingdoms of Alexander the Great's successors ca. 300 BCE.

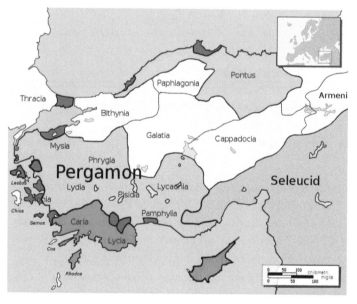

FIGURE 7.41 The Kingdom of Pergamon, 188 BCE.

development and evolution did not stop there. While artistic development is a continuum, certain changes occurred after the death of Alexander the Great that are characterized in the period name Hellenistic. His death was sudden and unexpected, and no effective provision had been made for the rule of his very new empire. As a result, it fell apart. For nearly fifty years, Alexander's generals and relatives fought for control of the whole empire. Boundaries were very fluid until 300 BCE, when they became fairly stable (as shown in Figure 7.40), although conflicts for dynastic control remained common until 275 BCE.

Perhaps because of the continuing political instability, the threat of war, the encounters with different cultures and beliefs, and the radical expansion of worldview, artistic style changed. This change is most obvious in the visual arts (especially sculpture), in which there were new intensity of emotion, more emotional situations, and greater emphasis on activity and motion. The new style is called Hellenistic because it derives from (or imitates) the Classical Greek (or Hellenic) style.

The decline of the city-states of mainland Greece was accompanied by a rise in the economic importance of more far-flung Greek communities, especially in Asia Minor–Ionian Greece. One of the most active artistic centers was the city of Pergamon. A clever governor of the city, managing to exploit the conflicts among Alexander's successors and achieve virtual independence, founded the Attalid dynasty by 282 BCE. The city was ruled by the family for 150 years until Attalus III bequeathed the country to Rome in his will in 133 BCE. Meanwhile, in the later third century, barbarian Gauls seized the opportunity provided by Greek disunity to invade Greece and Asia Minor. Pergamon played a decisive role in stopping them, which contributed to the city's importance and territorial growth (see Figure 7.41).

Well governed and stable, Pergamon became an important economic and cultural center. The Attalid kings worked to beautify it in much the same way as the Athenians had done three hundred years before. The Acropolis of Pergamon was beautiful and picturesquely situated high above the plain (see Figure 7.42). The most celebrated monument there was the Great Altar of Zeus, which can be seen slightly right of center on the Acropolis model.

The altar was built inside a courtyard, approached by a grand staircase flanked by two wings that projected from the altar enclosure. The whole structure was surrounded by an Ionic colonnade (see Figures 7.43 and 7.44). The dotted red line on the plan indicates the reconstructed portion of the altar enclosure. The entire building was transported to Berlin after excavation and installed in a specially constructed museum. The unique entrance area has been fully re-

FIGURE 7.42 The Acropolis of Pergamon, 2nd century BCE, Pergamon Museum, Berlin. Upper left—Arsenal, Palace and Temple of Trajan; Upper center—Library (two-storied) & Temple of Athena above theater; Center right—Great Altar of Zeus; Lower right—marketplace.

constructed, as seen in Figure 7.44. The remainder of the building is in storage except for the rest of the exterior frieze (which is mounted around the walls of the same room) and most of the interior frieze (on the walls of the next room). It is obvious at first sight that the architectural effect is completely different from that of the Parthenon. The Classical-style Parthenon is best seen at a distance and invites the viewer only so far in. The Great Altar of Zeus, with its massive staircase, summons the visitor to ascend between the wings and enter the sacred space. Whereas the Classical building exists in repose, the Hellenistic building calls for action, involvement, and participation.

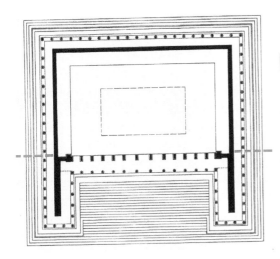

FIGURE 7.43 Great Altar of Zeus from Pergamon plan. The red line indicates the portion that has been reconstructed in the Berlin museum.

FIGURE 7.44 Great Altar of Zeus from Pergamon, restored entrance stairs (west side), 180–160 BCE, Pergamon Museum, Berlin.

FIGURE 7.45 Great Altar of Zeus, north wing, inner face. 180–160 BCE, marble, frieze height 2.3 m, Pergamon Museum, Berlin. Figures (sea gods), L to R: Nereus, Doris, titan, Oceanus, snake, more titans ascending stairs.

A parallel contrast exists in the sculpture of the two periods. Greek sculpture of the Classical style exists in repose, like the *Three Goddesses* (Figure 7.11). Even when action is depicted, as in the Parthenon metope (Figure 7.13) or frieze (Figure 7.14), the moment is frozen in time—the action is caught in the moment. The huge frieze on the Great Altar of Zeus (Figure 7.45) is a different matter. It depicts the battle of the gods and the giants, a favorite Greek theme. Their contorted, writhing, entwined figures seem about to leap or fall from the frieze and continue their battle in the surrounding space. They climb or kneel on the stairs themselves, as can be seen inside the left wing.

In antiquity, the main approach to the altar was from the east, and the visitor would walk around to the stairway on the west front. Among the first figures to greet the visitor were those of Zeus and Athena, the gods for whom the altar was constructed, symbolic of order (versus the chaos of the giants). Athena's battle with the titan (giant) Alkyoneus summarizes the theme of the whole altar (see Figure 7.46).

Athena, in the center, strides forward to seize the titan Alkyoneus by the hair. She is lifting him away from the earth mother, Gaia, from whom he receives his strength and immortality. As Alkyoneus stretches out his left leg out to remain in contact, Gaia reaches up from the earth to prevent Athena from lifting her son. Winged Nike (Victory) flies in to Athena's aid, and the titan is pinioned in the coils of a giant serpent. Even allowing for the damage the frieze has suffered, the sculpture's stylistic aura has clearly evolved a great deal since the Classical era. In place of the earlier refined repose, the altar frieze shows figures in agony and torment, in turbulent battle, and flying through the air. In their high relief, they seem about to escape from their backing. The occasion that inspired the altar is unclear; there are at least three possibilities. All of them involved battles, and any one of them could be symbolized by the struggle between order and chaos, so vividly and violently illustrated in the altar frieze.

Pergamon commemorated its history with sculpture. The city was one of the great artistic centers of the Hellenistic world, and its rulers consciously emulated Athens. Pergamon's first victory over the Gauls in 228 BCE was commemorated with bronze statues of the defeated enemies. Several of these survive in Roman marble copies. The finest is the *Dying Gaul* in Figure 7.47a. The Gaul, wounded on the lower right chest (not visible), has fallen to the ground, too weak to hold up his drooping head, and supports himself with great effort on his right arm, pressing his left arm against his right leg for additional support. He has fallen on his shield and sword (a later addition), and a trumpet lies beneath his left leg. His nudity accords with historical reports that Gauls went nude into battle, and other details of the head confirm the identity (see Figure 7.47b). Gauls wore gold collars (torcs) around their necks and mustaches, which were rather unique in the ancient world. They stiffened their hair with lime

FIGURE 7.46 Great Altar of Zeus from Pergamon, east side, 180–160 BCE, marble, frieze height 2.3 m, Pergamon Museum, Berlin. Figures, L to R: Alkyoneus, Athena, Gaia (below), Nike (above).

or chalk, similar to the current use of hair gel; the cemented locks were retained in the seventeenth-century restoration of the statue. Beyond these identifying characteristics, the face also depicts, with an inner intensity, the exhaustion of the warrior facing death.

FIGURE 7.47A *The Dying Gaul*, 230–220 BCE, 94 × 186 × 89 cm, marble Roman copy of (possibly) bronze original, Rome, Capitoline Museum.

FIGURE 7.47B *The Dying Gaul* (detail).

FIGURE 7.48A *The Winged Victory* (Nike) *of Samothrace*, 200–190 BCE, marble, height 2.44 m, Paris, Louvre. The Sculpture from the left on its original plinth

FIGURE 7.48B *The Winged Victory* (Nike) *of Samothrace*, as displayed in the Louvre.

A different aspect of the theme of battle or struggle that is common in much Hellenistic sculpture is the *Winged Victory* (Nike) *of Samothrace* (Samothraki), shown in Figures 7.48a & b. The statue, probably carved in 200–190 BCE, commemorates a naval battle, although which one of several among the incessantly warring Hellenistic kingdoms it depicts is unclear. The statue stood over a fountain above the theater that formed part of the Sanctuary of the Great Gods on Samothrace, an island in the north Aegean Sea. Discovered in 1863, the sculpture is mounted on its original plinth (base) in the form of a ship's prow. The statue alone is 2.44 m high, about 1.5 times life-size. It depicts the goddess of victory as she alights on the prow of a victorious ship. Her striding posture, gracefully windblown drapes, and outstretched wings (the right one is a reconstruction based on the original left one) convey motion, excitement, and triumph. The figure's proportions are ideal, and the modeling of her robe perfectly captures the wind pressing it against her body. The statue's placement in the Louvre (Figure 7.48b) is stunningly effective. Since its installation in 1884, the *Victory* has stood in the center of a central landing on the Daru Staircase. Approaching it from below, one feels that it is about to fly over one's head.

Along with the *Winged Victory*, probably the other best-known example of Hellenistic sculpture is *Laocoön and His Sons*, which depicts the Trojan priest attacked by snakes for prophesying against the Trojan horse (see Figure 7.49). Close to life-size, the incredible emotion depicted in the statue makes it seem much larger than life. Laocoön, in the center, is entwined with his two sons, being crushed by giant serpents. The son on the left is collapsing, dying or near death, presumably from snakebite. Laocoön, who is being bitten, is struggling futilely against the snakes. He writhes in agony, while the second son, in fear and pain, reaches toward him for aid while trying to free his own ankle from the snake's coils. The violence is expressed in the figures' twisted postures, incredible muscular exertion, the twisted coils of the snakes, and the agony of Laocoön's facial expression.[8]

FIGURE 7.49 Agesander, Athenodorus & Polydorus of Rhodes, *Laocoön and His Sons*, 60 BCE–79 CE, marble, height 2.1 m. Vatican City, Vatican Museums.

Whether this work is a Greek original or a copy is not clear, but it is fairly certain that it was in the gardens of the Roman emperor, where it was found in 1506. The work is in several pieces, and the figures have been tried in somewhat different positions and poses over the years. The current restoration dates from the 1980s. The group is also a clear example of one work's influence on another. Laocoön's pose is so close to that of Alkyoneus on the Great Altar of Zeus (see Figure 7.46) that the sculptor(s?) of the later work must have been familiar with the earlier one.

These are the greatest surviving examples of Hellenistic art and architecture, but the best-known ones from ancient times no longer survive. The Seven Wonders of the Ancient World, described by several Classical authors, included four Hellenistic works: the Lighthouse of Alexandria (at 125+ meters, the world's first skyscraper), the Colossus of Rhodes (a giant statue of the sun god holding a torch, rather like a naked male Statue of Liberty, thirty to forty meters high), and the Mausoleum of Halicarnassus (a monumental tomb, comparable in size to the Taj Mahal or the smaller pyramids) were all destroyed by earthquakes. The Temple of Artemis (Diana) at Ephesus (the Hellenistic one was the third) was destroyed in 268 CE by invading barbarian Goths.

To round out the picture of Hellenistic culture, we have the only complete example of ancient Greek music: the *Epitaph of Seikilos*. The four-line song is carved on a cylindrical marble tombstone found near the ancient city of Ephesus. In addition to a few dedicatory lines without music at the top, the bottom used to have the author-composer's name and

---

8   Charles Darwin observed that Laocoön's bulging eyebrows are anatomically impossible; nevertheless, their very extreme character adds great power to the work.

FIGURE 7.50A Tombstone of Seikilos, c. 100 BCE—100 CE, marble, height c. 38–40 cm, Copenhagen, National Museum of Denmark. a. The complete stone.

FIGURE 7.50B Tombstone *(Stele)* of Seikilos, b. the combined inscription from both sides.

some other data at the bottom, but the final syllable of this was ground off to level the stone so it could be used as a pedestal for the first modern owner's wife's flower pot. Figure 7.50a shows the whole extant stone. Figure 7.50b shows the two sides of the stone joined to show the entire inscription. Like the "Hymn to Apollo" from Delphi, the musical notation is the set of occasional smaller symbols written above the text, beginning at the sixth line.

There are a number of performances and reconstructions of this song available. (See Figure 7.51.) *Musique de la Grèce Antique* (Atrium Musicae de Madrid, dir. Gregorio Paniagua. Harmonia Mundi HMA1901015, 1979) has a performance on a reconstructed lyre with a female singer (perhaps inspired by the vase in Figure 7.36). *Music of the Ancient Greeks* (Ensemble De Organographia. Pandourion Records PRCD1001, 1995, 1997) has a purely instrumental performance with a drone on aulos, followed by one with female voice and lyre. There are several versions on the Internet; one on Wikipedia uses a male singer in a modern popular style.

Like other surviving examples of ancient Greek music, the "Epitaph of Seikilos" is monophonic, with a single melody and no harmony. The rhythm is, again, based on poetic meter mainly arranged around groups of six rhythmic pulses. The melody, on a different modal scale than the "Hymn to Apollo," sounds a little less strange to us, more like a modern major scale. The form is very simple: four short lines of music as required by the poetry. Since it is so short, the entire text is below, in the original Greek, a transliteration of the Greek, and an

FIGURE 7.51 "Epitaph of Seikilos," 1st Century CE.

Epitaph of Seikilos, 1st Century CE

Text

Greek	Transliteration	Translation
Οσον ζης φαινου,	Hoson dzes phainou,	While you live, be happy,
Μηδεν ολως συ λυπου.	Meden holos sy lypou.	Hold no grief at all.
Προς ολιγον εστι το ζην;	Pros oligon esti to dzen;	Life is short;
Το τελος ο χρονος απαιτει.	To telos ho chronos apaitei.	Time takes its toll.

Musical Features

Rhythm	Derived from poetic meter.
Melody	Ancient Greek Iastian mode. Phrases follow lines of text.
Texture	Monophonic
Text Setting	Mostly syllabic
Form	Through-composed in four lines. Some short motives repeat: End of first line with beginning of second line; ends of second and third lines.
(Harmony	None)
Timbre	Varies according to the interpretation of the performing group

Performances—Interpretations

Musique de la Grèce antique (Atrium Musicæ de Madrid, Gregorio Paniagua, dir. Harmonia Mundi [France], 1979. HMA 1901015) Played on lyre and sung as woman's solo.

Musiques de l'Antiquité Grecque: De la Pierre au son (Ensemble Kérylos, directed by Annie Bélis. K617 France, 1996. K617–069), not available to me at this time.

Music of the Ancient Greeks (De Organographia [Gayle Stuwe Neuman, Philip Neuman, and William Gavin]. Pandourion Records, 1997. PRDC 1001) Played first on on aulos with drone, then sung by woman with lyre.

Music of Ancient Greece (OP and PO Orchestra, conducted by Christodoulos Halaris. Cultural Action EMSE, 2009. ASIN: B002E3L88E) Played with flute and wire-strung (?) lyre. Male vocal solo in modern Greek style.

Music of Ancient Greece & Music of Greek Antiquity (Petros Tabouris Ensemble. FM Records SA, 2011. ASIN: B004V7C8KI) Woman's vocal solo with light percussion.

To the best of my knowledge, all of these recordings play the original melody. Their interpretations vary considerably.

English translation. Most of the text is set syllabically, one syllable per note. A good exercise would be to listen to it and mark those syllables with more than one note and how many each has.

When all the arts are taken together, the reconstruction of ancient Greek culture is quite full. Architecture, sculpture, painting, pottery, music, and drama make vital contributions and expand our sense of the humanity of the ancient Greeks far beyond the equally vital contributions of literature and political history. From the arts, we can sense the Greek soul.

Image Credits

Fig. 7.1: Copyright © 2005 by Alexikoua / Wikimedia Commons, Adapted by Gary Towne, (CC BY-SA 3.0) at https://commons.wikimedia.org/wiki/File:Path3959-83.png.

Fig. 7.2: Copyright in the Public Domain.

Fig. 7.3: Copyright © 2011 by Aeonx / Wikimedia Commons, (CC BY-SA 3.0) at https://commons.wikimedia.org/wiki/File:Map_Peloponnesian_War_431_BC-en.svg.

Fig. 7.4: Copyright © 2006 by Generic Mapping Tools, (CC BY-SA 3.0) at https://commons.wikimedia.org/wiki/File:MacedonEmpire.jpg.

Fig. 7.5: Copyright © 2005 by Praxiteles; Photo by Dennis Jarvis, (CC BY-SA 2.0) at https://commons.wikimedia.org/wiki/File:Hermes_Praxiteles.jpg.

Fig. 7.6: Praxiteles; Photo by Gustav Ebe / Copyright in the Public Domain.

Fig. 7.7: Copyright © 2014 by Polykleitos; Photo by Gautier Poupeau, (CC BY-SA 2.0) at https://commons.wikimedia.org/wiki/File:R%C3%A9plique_du_doryphore_de_Polycl%C3%A8te_(13668295194).jpg.

Fig. 7.8: Praxiteles; Photo by Marie-Lan Nguyen / Copyright in the Public Domain.

Fig. 7.9: Copyright © 2005 by Praxiteles; Photo by Eric Gaba (Sting / Wikimedia Commons), (CC BY-SA 2.5) at https://commons.wikimedia.org/wiki/File:Aphrodite_head_Kaufmann_Louvre.jpg.

Fig. 7.10: Copyright in the Public Domain.

Fig. 7.11: Copyright © 2009 by Yair Haklai, (CC BY-SA 3.0) at https://commons.wikimedia.org/wiki/File:Three_goddesses_Parthenon-British_Museum.jpg.

Fig. 7.12: Altairisfar / Wikimedia Commons / Copyright in the Public Domain.

Fig. 7.13: Copyright © 2005 by Adam Carr, (CC BY-SA 3.0) at https://commons.wikimedia.org/wiki/File:Ac_marbles.jpg.

Fig. 7.14: Copyright © 2009 by Yair Haklai, (CC BY-SA 3.0) at https://commons.wikimedia.org/wiki/File:Riders_in_the_procession-North_frieze-Parthenon-British_Museum.jpg.

Fig. 7.15: Pearson / Scott Foresman / Copyright in the Public Domain.

Fig. 7.16: Argento / Wikimedia Commons / Copyright in the Public Domain.

Fig. 7.17: Copyright © 1978 by Steve Swayne, (CC BY 2.0) at https://commons.wikimedia.org/wiki/File:The_Parthenon_in_Athens.jpg.

Fig. 7.18A: Copyright © 2011 by Jordi Payà, (CC BY-SA 2.0) at https://commons.wikimedia.org/wiki/File:Parthenon_restoration.gif.

Fig. 7.18B: Copyright © 2011 by Jordi Payà, (CC BY-SA 2.0) at https://commons.wikimedia.org/wiki/File:Parthenon_restoration.gif.

Fig. 7.19: Ryan Kaldari / Copyright in the Public Domain.

Fig. 7.20: Copyright © 2012 by Helen Simonsson, (CC BY-SA 3.0) at https://commons.wikimedia.org/wiki/File:Chryselephantine_Delphi_ver2.jpg.

Fig. 7.21: Copyright © 2002 by Alan LeQuire; Photo by Dean Dixon, (FAL 1.3) at https://commons.wikimedia.org/wiki/File:Athena_Parthenos_LeQuire.jpg. A copy of the full license can be found here: http://artlibre.org/licence/lal/en.

Fig. 7.22A: Phidias; Photo by Marie-Lan Nguyen / Copyright in the Public Domain.

Fig. 7.22B: Copyright © 2009 by Phidias; Photo by Ricardo André Frantz, (CC BY-SA 3.0) at https://commons.wikimedia.org/wiki/File:Athena_Varvakeion_-_MANA_-_Fidias.jpg .

CHAPTER 8

ROMAN AND BYZANTINE ARTS

Background

It may already be apparent that, even though we separate historical and artistic tradition by periods that reflect the cultures and their artistic styles, these cultures overlap. The conquest of a city in Mesopotamia was often not accompanied by its destruction, so many city-states continued to exist in close proximity to one another throughout the region. They rose, achieved dominance, fell, and sometimes rose again in a confusing web of political relationships while continuing to develop a fairly unified artistic and cultural tradition, even when speaking different languages.

The culture of ancient Egypt was much more unified, even with the breaks between dynasties, but in time, it, too, overlapped the Mesopotamian cultures, as well as Greek culture and others. Greek culture developed later, through several stages and in its own direction separate from Mesopotamia and Egypt, although some mutual influence occurred from time to time. The history of Greek culture overlaps the later parts of the history of Egypt and Mesopotamia, until Alexander the Great conquered both areas and Hellenistic Greek culture came to dominate them.

This set the stage for Rome. According to legend, Aeneas, cousin of Priam of Troy and supposedly descended from the goddess Venus, fled Troy's destruction, dallied with the queen of Carthage (a Phoenician settlement in North Africa), then sailed on to Italy, where he married the daughter of the king of the Latins. 430 years later, Aeneas's descendent Romulus, after killing his twin brother in a power struggle, became the first king of Rome. He was followed by six more kings; the traditional duration of these seven kings' reigns is 244 years, ending in 509 BCE with the founding of the Roman Republic.

The early history of Rome, then, overlaps with the cultures we have already studied: the founding of Rome in 753 BCE coincided with the period of Assyrian dominance in Mesopotamia and the end of the Dark Ages of Greece. The beginning of the Roman Republic in 509 BCE coincides with the high point of the Persian Empire in the Middle East, near the time that the Persian kings Darius and Xerxes invaded Greece just at the beginning of its Classical period. Meanwhile, the Romans were getting underway with their gradual domination of the western world.

The kings of Rome were elected for life and had unlimited absolute power in all things, with no means of recourse for the people. The seventh king finally abused his power to such a degree that he was driven out, and the Roman Republic was founded. Already, during the royal period, Rome, in fighting off its neighbors, had begun to expand its territory. This continued throughout the republic, often simultaneously with internal struggles, because the republic's governmental structure was developed over time by trial and error; it changed when an oppressed group became powerful enough to force that change. Development in this way left gaps in areas of governmental policy and control, which permitted civil strife, especially in the republic's last century. A second reason for Rome's internal difficulties was ineffective control of its military leaders, whose power grew with Rome's territorial expansion, shown in Figure 8.1.

Rome's expansion, while not exactly accidental, almost always occurred as a response to an attack on Rome or its allies. After repulsing the invaders, Rome assumed control of their territory. In 264–146 BCE, Rome conquered Carthage (the Punic Wars) and acquired southeastern Spain, the western Mediterranean islands, and the central part of the north African coast. Between 192 and 68 BCE, Rome conquered all of the Hellenistic kingdoms except Egypt, and two kingdoms were left to Rome in wills. During the same period, Rome defeated all other Italian states. In 58–50 BCE, Julius Caesar brought all of Gaul (roughly modern France) under Rome's control, and in 30 BCE, his nephew Octavian, in defeating Antony and Cleopatra, conquered Egypt.

During this time, enormous military growth and internal strife greatly stressed the republic. The assumption of power by Julius Caesar presaged its end. Caesar began to develop a more centralized governmental model based on republican structures, but he was assassinated by his conservative opposition. His nephew Octavian, adopted as Caesar's son, eliminated all of his enemies (the last of whom was Mark Antony in 30 BCE), and by 27 BCE, Octavian had consolidated his power. Although the republic continued in name, he assumed all of the powers of the various republican officials and thus became functionally a king, although this title was so hated in Rome that he used the titles Princeps (meaning first citizen) and Augustus (used as a name), and he was

KeyRoman Republic in 201 B.C.

Additions by 100 B.C.

EXPANSION OF ROME

about 2nd Century B.C.

N

SCALE OF MILES

0   100   200   300   400   500   600

FIGURE 8.1 The Growth of Roman Territory in the Second Century BCE.

also called Imperator (commander), which was the origin of the word *emperor*. Functionally, the Roman Republic had ended and the Roman Empire began. Augustus had founded the first Roman imperial dynasty (Julio-Claudians). By this time, the remainder of the African coast and Spain were also Roman, so the Roman Empire included the entire perimeter of the Mediterranean Sea. The empire continued to grow, achieving its maximum size in 116–117 CE. (See Figure 8.2.)

Roman Arts

The period of the late republic and early empire was one of the most fruitful for Roman art. Stimulated by contact with the Greeks and their own Etruscan predecessors, Roman artists and architects developed their own unique styles. In addition to what survives by means shared with other historical cultures, we are fortunate (as the inhabitants were not) to have two complete provincial Roman cities Pompeii and Herculaneum, that were buried by Mount Vesuvius's eruption in 79 CE. The bust from Pompeii in Figure 8.3 demonstrates clearly the difference between Greek and Roman artistic tastes.

FIGURE 8.2 The Roman Empire at its Greatest Size, 116–117 CE.

The bust of Lucius Caecilius Jucundus came from his Pompeiian house. In contrast with the stylized idealism of Greek sculpture, Caecilius Jucundus's bust shows the Roman desire for exact and true depiction—literally warts and all. Where Greek sculptors captured (as much as possible) perfection in what they depicted—even idealizing portraits of actual people—Romans wanted representations that were recognizable as the person being portrayed. In addition to the wart (or lipoma) on Jucundus's chin, the bust shows his oddly shaped protuberant ears, slightly bulbous nose, prominent cheekbones, receding hairline, and lined forehead, with an asymmetry in the frown lines that may be the result of an old injury. The eyes and facial expression are those of a strong, yet probably understanding, man. There is little, if any, idealism, but the bust is so realistic, it almost seems ready to speak.

Caecilius Jucundus lived from the last part of Augustus's reign through most of his dynastic successors. This was Rome's literary golden age, and the other arts were also at a high point. Slightly earlier than the bust is the finest surviving statue of the emperor Augustus (shown in Figure 8.4). This marble statue, perhaps copied from a bronze original dedicated for public display, was found in the excavations of his wife Livia's villa in Primaporta, a few miles outside Rome. The work borrows from both Greek and Roman traditions. It is clearly idealized (similar to Greek works), representing the emperor leading Rome onward in a striding version of the Classic Greek *contrapposto*, with right arm pointing upward as if leading or addressing troops. His left hand

FIGURE 8.3 *Bust of Lucius Caecilius Jucundus*, a Pompeiian Banker, bronze copy cast from original, which is from before 62 CE, bronze, height 35 cm, Archeological Museum, Naples, Italy; copy in Pushkin Museum, Moscow.

FIGURE 8.4 *Augustus of Primaporta*, marble, probably copy of bronze original, ca. 20 BCE–20 CE, height 2.03 m, Vatican Museums.

probably held a (missing) consular baton.[1] There are several symbolic elements: the armor and cloak of a general, the striding pose, and Cupid, sitting on a vase or rock at Augustus's feet and mirroring his arm gesture. The Julian family of Julius Caesar and Augustus's grandmother claimed descent from the goddess Venus through Aeneas; the presence of Cupid, as a cousin, emphasized the emperor's divine ancestry. The figure's face also preserves the emperor's youthful appearance for propaganda (no matter what his age was at the time), as do most of his many surviving statues.[2] Despite the Greek idealism in style and symbolism, the statue is clearly individual in the Roman tradition. The triangular face, clamshell-like ears and eyes deep-set under chiseled brows are clearly identifiable as Augustus's, no matter which statue one is viewing.

Augustus stabilized the empire after more than a century of strife. His reign was known for its "Augustan Peace." Symbolic of this is the *Ara Pacis*, or Altar of Peace (see Figure 8.5). Commissioned by the Senate in 13 BCE and dedicated four years later, the altar itself is inside a nearly square ornamental enclosure about eleven meters on a side and 3.7 meters high. Ten low steps lead to a nearly square opening 3.6 meters broad. Once inside this precinct, four more steps lead to the altar's base, with a further four steps leading to the table for animal sacrifice. The effect is not unlike that of the Great Altar of Zeus from Pergamon (Figs. 7.44–7.46), although the *Ara Pacis*'s proportions and confining walls invite the onlooker no further than the first flight of steps.

The altar's exterior decoration included an upper figured frieze, with a lower frieze of arabesque decoration (Figure 2.23); the stylized plant designs represent nature under control. On the front and back, flanking openings in the wall, were scenes from the mythic history of Rome (front, west), and two goddesses, possibly Roma and Mother Earth (back, east; see Figure 2.23). Like the Parthenon frieze, the two sides of the *Ara Pacis* frieze show a procession—in this case, moving toward the entrance on the west side. The north side included priests, the Senate, and the highest officials and their bodyguards, while the south shows four unique priests (*flamens*) and the imperial family (Figure 8.6). This last is so well preserved that it is possible to identify most of the figures as actual historical persons. No part of the frieze actually projects beyond the wall, so it is technically low (bas-) relief, but the sculptor has used different depths or levels of projection very skillfully to show figures in the depth of a crowd. Each side contains forty to fifty figures—every one unique in appearance, size, posture, and facial expression—all participating in stately movement toward the sacrificial gate on the west.

---

1   The consular or curule baton was a symbol of civil and military authority.

2   There are dozens of well-preserved statues of Augustus, as well as many others partially preserved or in deteriorated condition. One of these latter is in the Minneapolis Institute of Arts.

Citizens of lesser means who might not be able to afford a personal sculpture could still commission a painting of themselves. Such a painting is the portrait of Terentius Neo and his wife from Pompeii.[3] (Figure 8.7.) Neo was prosperous; not only could he afford a portrait, but he also wears the toga of a Roman citizen, and his wife wears a lovely crimson dress. Both he and his wife hold symbols of education and refinement: in his case, a scroll; in hers, a folding wax tablet and stylus for writing. He has a wispy beard, and she wears pearl earrings and a carefully parted hairstyle with a fringe of delicate ringlets. His skin is darker than hers, an artistic convention of the time. Both sitters gaze at the viewer with large, intense, almond-shaped eyes. The painting was on the wall of the atrium, the formal entrance hall of a Roman house, where it greeted visitors.[4] The style of this work is very similar to that of the contemporary mummy portrait in Figure 2.3. A century after Rome's conquest of Egypt, the Roman style had displaced the traditional Egyptian style of nearly three millennia.

Roman plane art had a much broader range of subjects and media than just painted portraits, though. Subjects could include mythology, religious rites, history, and natural scenes, and the medium of mosaic was also popular, especially for floors.[5] One such Roman mosaic may be a copy that provides the most complete example of ancient Greek painting (see Figure 8.8). The mosaic shows Alexander at the left on a rearing horse, spearing an enemy, while Darius, the highest figure on the right,

FIGURE 8.5 *Ara Pacis,* Main Entrance, marble, 13–9 BCE, 11.6 × 10.6 × h 3.7 m, reconstructed in its own museum, Rome.

FIGURE 8.6 *Ara Pacis,* South Frieze, showing Imperial Family.

3   This was long thought to be a portrait of Paquius Proculo, based on a graffito on the house's exterior. The new identification is based on an interior wall inscription.

4   The atrium, one of the oldest features of Roman domestic architecture, had a roof that sloped inward on all four sides to drain water into a central pool for household use. The mild climate permitted the open roof also to allow light and air into the house, which had few, if any, windows on its public thoroughfare for better privacy and security.

5   Mosaic is the art of making pictures by embedding tiny pieces of colored stone or glass in an adhesive bed, usually plaster or concrete. It will be discussed in greater detail later in the chapter.

FIGURE 8.7 *Portrait of Terentius Neo and His Wife*, fresco, ca. 55–79 CE, 58 × 50 cm, removed from wall, now in the Archeological Museum, Naples, Italy.

urges on his army from the back of his fleeing chariot amid a thicket of spears. The tumultuous action brilliantly captures the violent clash of armies in battle, with dying and fallen men beneath horses that gallop and die as well. The realism is striking, and, although there is no true perspective, the horse in front of Darius's chariot shows a masterful grasp of foreshortening, the art of drawing an object or figure from its end. Viewed from the tail, the entire horse is depicted as if seen in the act of trying to escape its downed rider.

Besides portraits and action scenes like battles, surviving Roman art includes numerous paintings of landscapes and garden scenes. The Romans embraced the natural life that surrounded them and vividly recreated it in wall paintings. The most extensive Roman garden painting covered the walls of a subterranean room in the same villa of the empress Livia at Primaporta where the statue of Augustus was discovered. Figure 8.9 shows a portion of this fresco. Every wall depicts a portion of the garden; most are centered on one tree flanked by smaller trees, with flowers and shrubs below, and abounding in flying and perching birds. The trees are all different: some deciduous, some conifers; some fruit-bearing, some not. Taller trees in the background add depth, while

FIGURE 8.8 The Alexander Mosaic depicting the Battle of Issus, in which Alexander the Great defeated Darius the Persian Emperor, mosaic, possible copy of third century BCE Hellenistic painting, 2.72 × 5.13 m, copy in the House of the Faun, Pompeii, original in the Archeological Museum, Naples.

FIGURE 8.9 Garden Room of Livia's Villa, Central Tree of One Wall, fresco, before 29 CE, c. 2.5 m, removed from wall, now in the National Roman Museum, Palazzo Massimo, Rome.

FIGURE 8.10 *Flora*, or *Primavera* (Flower as a name, or Spring), fresco, before 79 CE, 38 × 32 cm, originally in the Villa Arianna, Stabiae, removed from wall, now in the Archeological Museum, Naples.

many different flowers and shrubs beautify the ground level. Two low fences stand in front of the scene and behind the tree. All plants and birds are vivid and realistic, and all are identifiable.[6]

Some landscapes also included humans. One such (Figure 8.10) ranks with the most beautiful and graceful paintings of all time. Originally in a villa in Stabiae, near the edge of Vesuvius's ash deposit, the painting is now in the National Museum in Naples. A solitary woman, seen from behind, trips lightly through a meadow. She cradles a basket of white and yellow flowers in her left arm and delicately plucks one more bloom with her right hand as she passes. Her light brown hair is gathered at the back beneath a coronet or wreath, perhaps of the same flowers, and she wears a gold bracelet on her right wrist. Her loose, yellow, tunic-like dress has fallen off the right shoulder, and a light over-shawl hangs loosely from her arms. She moves delicately while a light breeze ruffles her skirts. The lack of perspective in the green background frames the elegant grace, simplicity, and refinement of this ethereal maiden. If no other Roman painting survived, we would know from this one that they had great artists.

---

6   Twenty-three varieties of plants and sixty-nine species of birds have been identified.

FIGURE 8.11 Reconstruction of the Roman garden in the House of the Vettii, Pompeii, in the Boboli Gardens, Florence, Italy.

FIGURE 8.12 Reconstruction of the Roman garden in the House of the Vettii, Pompeii, opposite end, on site, structure before 79 CE. Note the remnants of frescoes on the far wall.

The Romans appreciated the beauty of nature not only in paintings, but also in carefully designed environments both outside and inside their houses. Their approach to gardening is one that we can now reconstruct by analyzing the roots of plants buried by the volcano and comparing them with ancient pictures and descriptions. Many Roman houses augmented the basic arrangement around the atrium with a peristyle.[7] This area, open to the sky with a narrow, sheltered walkway around it, could lead to more rooms or a beautiful view, but it almost always provided a place where the residents could cultivate a garden, usually ornamented with a display of their prized sculptures and possibly a fountain. Figure 8.11 shows a reconstruction of such a garden from the House of the Vettii in Pompeii. Within a refined Doric peristyle, this modest (but not small) garden has engaging small statues around the periphery, with simple fountains filling rectangular basins on each end. Three doors at the far end lead to side rooms. (The entrance from the atrium is at the side.) Figure 8.12 shows the actual garden from the opposite end.

A central gravel walk divides the space, with rectangular beds at one end and semicircular ones surrounding a birdbath at the other. Each bed contains a row of flowers or shrubs of modest height on the periphery, with low herbs lining the paths. The Roman garden was a multisensual experience, with sculpture to delight the mind and the eye, plantings for the eye and nose and to brush the ankles, and fountains to contribute the babbling of water and cooling of the air. The original peristyle was also lined with frescoes, dimly visible in Figure 8.12. The wealthy owners decorated the house profusely in the latest style, although their taste was a bit risqué for a modern textbook.

Pompeii was buried early in the second dynasty of emperors (Flavians). Rebellion and execution removed the emperor Nero in 68 CE. His successors moved to obliterate from Rome the traces of his greatest excess—the grounds of his palatial Golden House, perhaps as large as a square kilometer, with a man-made lake and a 30–35-meter statue of Nero as the sun god. The statue, later called the Colossus because of its size, had its head replaced and was moved to

---

7 A surrounding colonnade (peri = around, style = columned)

a position beside the lake, where the second dynasty emperors had built a gigantic arena (which came to be called the Colosseum because of its proximity to the statue). Because it was built where the water table was high, the Colosseum was designed for mock sea battles as well as land-based gladiatorial combats and wild beast fights. Figure 8.13 shows the building's exterior, and Figure 8.14 shows the interior.

Roman construction differed from Greek masonry because the Romans generally used marble or other stone only for facing; the actual structure was of poured concrete. This permitted buildings of massive size, but it also means that many Roman ruins are unprepossessing because the stone facing was stripped away long ago for other construction. This is obvious in Figure 8.13. On the left, the arena's exterior survives in something close to its original appearance, while on the right, it has been stripped to its concrete core. The building is an ellipse, which we see from one end. At the top edge is an ornamental cornice, while below it are rectangular windows; above them is a row of projecting brackets to stabilize masts that supported a canvas awning to protect the spectators from the sun. Below this level are three stories of equally spaced apertures in the wall, each with a semicircular arch above a nearly square opening. Unlike Greek buildings, in which the arch appears only sparingly and mostly for passageways and underground cisterns, arches pervade Roman architecture. The semicircular arch

FIGURE 8.13 Colosseum (Flavian Amphitheater), 72–80 CE, Rome. Exterior.

FIGURE 8.14 Colosseum (Flavian Amphitheater), 72–80 CE. Interior, central walls probably constructed after 85 CE.

above a square is characteristic of most classic Roman architecture and helps to distinguish it from buildings of later periods. Except in aqueducts, doors, and vaults, Roman arches of the republic and early empire usually do not surmount a space higher than it is broad.

The Colosseum's arches penetrate the full depth of the surviving construction, as Figure 8.14 shows. A modern platform covers the near end for a better view of the structure and appreciation of its size as it originally stood. (Note the size of the people at the far end.) Beneath the slopes that once supported seats, the arches covered passageways for entrance and exit. Modern architects studied the Colosseum's provision for crowd access in designing the Harvard and Yale Bowls; these were the first comparably large arenas after the Colosseum, the largest of all Roman amphitheaters. The two-story walls in the central cavity were added some time after the original construction.

Only two mock sea battles are recorded here; the pit was drained and the central structures were probably added after the year 85 CE. The Colosseum's two stories housed an ingenious mechanism for storing and releasing the wild beasts. The animals were caged on the lower level.

The Pantheon, Emperor Hadrian, c. 126 CE, Rome. Exterior View.

A keeper in a protective niche opened the cage's gate, allowing the animal to run down a short corridor into an elevator. On the upper level, the elevator opened onto a ramp that led up to the arena's surface. Romans' insatiable appetite for these wild beast "hunts" consumed hundreds of thousands of animals over the centuries and contributed to the depletion, and possible extinction, of several species. Also popular were the mock battles already described, as well as gladiatorial combat—similar in appeal to modern boxing but with much more blood and greater threat of death.

The Colosseum is but one testimony to the Romans' technological genius, which continued on throughout the empire's history. Under its third dynasty (Antonines), the Roman Empire attained its maximum size, as shown in Figure 8.2. The emperor Hadrian, who ascended the throne in the year 117 CE, was not only a great ruler but an architectural genius. The best known of his works, and the best-preserved Roman building, is the Pantheon (Figure 8.15, not to be confused with the Greek Parthenon). Dedicated around the year 126 CE, it bears the inscription of the building it replaced, built by Augustus's greatest colleague, Marcus Agrippa.

The building comprises a simple domed cylinder fronted by a Corinthian portico three columns deep. Its simple form and dull exterior are deceptive. All of the original marble facing and decoration and the bronze roof were stripped off, as well as the pediment sculpture. Conversion to a church in 609 CE included the dumping of twenty-eight cartloads of early Christian bones beneath the altar. Despite this, the building retains its monumental dignity. The now-naked exterior reveals one of Hadrian's ingenious schemes. Behind and above the right-hand corner of the porch, the shape of a brick arch embedded in the wall is just barely visible. Two similar arches are visible just below it, and these features are repeated all around the building. The rotunda's interior has niches (cavities for statues that leave the wall thinner and unable to support the dome), so the brick relieving arches transfer the weight and stress to the thicker neighboring walls.

The niches are still visible, although they now house sculptures of Christian saints rather than "all the gods" that the building's name describes. There are places for fifteen statues, seven in large deep niches (now housing altars), and eight projecting pedimented porticos. Figure 8.16 shows the building's interior as painted by Giovanni

Giovanni Paolo Panini, *The Pantheon, Interior View*, oil on canvas, c. 1734 CE, 128 × 99 cm, Washington DC, National Gallery of Art.

Paolo Panini in the eighteenth century. A painting is the most effective way of depicting this space because of its unusual geometry.

The space is circular, exactly as high as its diameter (43.3 meters). The dome is a perfect hemisphere seated on a cylinder the height of its radius. The summit of the dome, an opening one-fifth of the diameter of the structure, provides the only light source besides the door. The dome remains the largest unreinforced concrete dome ever constructed. To achieve this, Hadrian used many strategies. The dome is coffered, with hollow squares that reduce its thickness between radial ribs. In addition, the dome's thickness decreases as it rises; this is easily visible by comparing its flattened exterior profile in Figure 8.15 with the interior hemisphere. Its concrete changes composition by including first stone, then pottery and, at the highest levels, lightweight volcanic stone. There are also more relieving arches concealed in the dome's concrete; the skylight removes all weight where it would be weakest, and its circle creates a 360-degree arch that resists the dome's compression, actually adding strength at what would otherwise be the weakest point.

FIGURE 8.17 Castel Sant'Angelo. Emperor Hadrian's tomb, converted to a defensive fort by the popes.

Another of Hadrian's monumental relics is his tomb (Figure 8.17), which was converted into a fortress in 401 CE and later named the Castel Sant'Angelo (Castle of the Holy Angel), from the legend of the apparition of the archangel Gabriel sheathing his sword as a sign of a plague's end in 590 CE; this was commemorated by statues atop the bastions in 1536 and 1753. The basic form of the tomb survives, but the battlements were added later, and scholars are unsure of the design of a small pavilion on top of the original tomb that was surrounded by a garden, grove, and perimeter of statues. The tomb is across the Tiber from ancient Rome, in part because tombs were not permitted within the city's sacred perimeter and probably also because the then-rural location enhanced the structure's visual drama. On the Vatican bank, it later became the pope's castle, fortress, and prison, with a fortified passageway connecting it to his palace next to St. Peter's Basilica.

FIGURE 8.18 The Via Appia (Appian Way), near the fourth milestone from the center of Rome. Originally built by Appius Claudius the Blind in 312 BCE.

While these buildings give ample evidence of Roman engineering excellence, the discussion would be incomplete without mention of their best-known achievements: roads (many portions survive, some still used), bridges (many still used), and aqueducts. Roads were among the Romans' earliest great engineering achievements. One of the first, the Via Appia (Appian Way) that connected Rome with the south was named after its builder, Appius Claudius the Blind, who constructed the first portion for military reasons in 312 BCE. The road still remains after 2,300 years (see Figure 8.18). Roman road construction was very durable (although quite labor intensive). A typical section shows the construction method (Figure 8.19). In a deep trench, on top of a packed base layer, were placed several layers of stone and cement

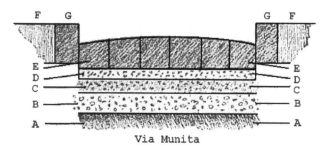

Via Munita

FIGURE 8.19 Cross-section of a *via munita* (a regular, or strong road). Layers (in 2–3-meter deep trench): A–packed base, earth with lime or sand foundation; B–fist-sized stones in clay or mortar; C–potsherds or coarse gravel in concrete; D–sand or ground potsherds for fine-grained cement; E–polygonal paving stones; F–optional sidewalk; G–curb. Sometimes a final top layer of ground lime.

FIGURE 8.20 Pons Fabricius, the Oldest Bridge in Rome, Lusius Fabricius (donor), volcanic stone, bricks and limestone, 62 BCE, 62 m long by 5.5 m wide, between Tiber Island and the center of Ancient Rome.

FIGURE 8.21 James (1813–1877) or Domenico (1854–1938) Anderson, *Claudian Aqueduct Arcade Ruins, behind the Via Appia Nuova* (New Appian Way), (aqueduct, 38–58 CE; road 1784), postcard, 1878.

of decreasing coarseness, with a layer of polygonal stone blocks on top. These would be turned over when worn. Sometimes a final layer of ground lime was added for a smooth surface. Ditches and a crowned road surface shed rain, and curbs were almost universal. The result was a road of essential utility and remarkable durability.

Roman roads tended to be built in straight sections, due to their surveying method. This meant that obstacles must be surmounted: cuts or tunnels through hills, fill in low spots, and bridges for rivers or chasms. The Pons Fabricius (Figure 8.20), in continuous use since its construction, is the only complete surviving Roman bridge in Rome, although there are many elsewhere. Its design is typical, with arch(es) shaped as portion(s) of a circle and a traveled surface that rises from the riverbanks to a higher central segment. The Pons Fabricius has two arches, but Roman bridges ranged from one arch to many, depending on the river's width.

A river's worth of water was what Rome's population of around a million needed. Between 312 BCE and 226 CE, eleven aqueducts were constructed to supply Rome with about one and one-eighth million cubic meters of water per day. Water from springs tapped in surrounding hills was carried in ground-level or underground channels until it arrived at the proper height to be conveyed across the city's surrounding plain. Since most of the conduit was masonry, the gradient had to be shallow and relatively constant, and it had to bring the water into the city at sufficient height to feed both hill and valley houses by gravity. The best-known remnants of the aqueducts are the long arcades that conveyed the water across the plain, as shown in Figure 8.21. This nineteenth-century photograph evokes what Rome's countryside looked like before the automobile. The eighteenth-century New Appian Way's dimensions were comparable with its antecedent. The aqueduct arcade, although broken, can be seen receding toward the distant hills.

The last new aqueduct was constructed during the fourth (Severan) dynasty. Within each dynasty,

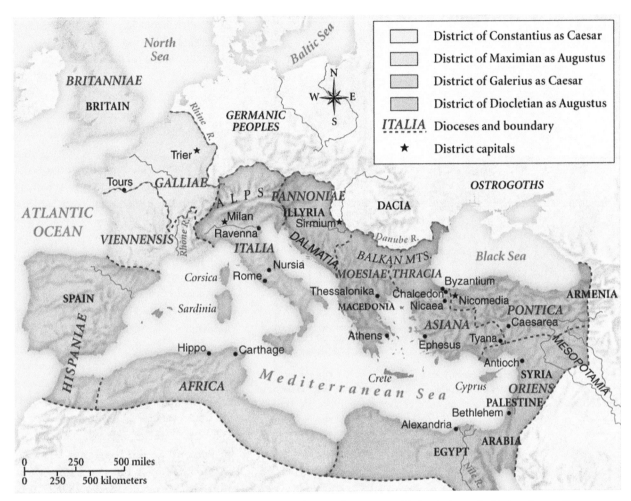

FIGURE 8.22 Division of the Roman Empire during the Tetrarchy, ca. 300 CE. Note the territories of the four leaders, each with three dioceses. The western capital became Milan, and the eastern one, Nicomedia (later Byzantium/Constantinople).

emperors generally succeeded a family member, but rarely by direct descent. Often, the emperor would adopt the person (usually a relative) who seemed most qualified for the post. Nevertheless, and inevitably, the quality of rulers declined within each dynasty until it was replaced in a coup. The four different dynasties between 27 BCE and 235 CE were separated by short periods of turbulence during which several people briefly claimed imperial authority. But the system's underlying weaknesses surfaced in 235 CE and led to a crisis of fifty years, during which there were twenty-six recognized emperors, of whom only about a dozen actually managed to retain power.

Beginning in 285 CE, the emperor Diocletian assumed autocratic power and greatly changed the Empire's administration to a structure called the Tetrarchy, which lasted for a few decades (see Figure 8.22). In the Tetrarchy, there were four rulers, two in the Latin-speaking west and two in the Greek-speaking east. Each half of the empire had one primary ruler (called the Augustus) and one secondary ruler (the Caesar). The empire was divided into twelve provinces, called dioceses, each ruler governed three. This greatly increased military responsiveness to increasing barbarian

FIGURE 8.23 Anonymous, *The Four Tetrarchs*, porphyry, height 130 cm, Venice, corner of San Marco facing the Doge's Palace.

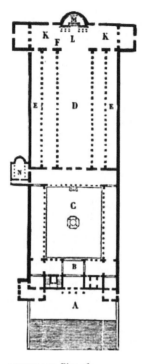

FIGURE 8.24 Plan of a Constantinian Basilica (Old Saint Peter's). C–Atrium with Peristyle; D–Nave; E–Aisles; K–Bema/Transept; L–Shrine; M–Apse; between C & D–Narthex.

FIGURE 8.25 Constantine's Basilica of Saint Peter, Cross Section from a Renaissance Fresco. The painting appears to be based on drawings that were made during demolition of Old St. Peter's.

incursions, but awarding military power to four simultaneous leaders was a sure recipe for internal strife, which bedeviled the empire until its fall.

One of the artistic remnants of the Tetrarchy is a sculpture, looted by the Venetians from Constantinople in 1204 CE during the fourth Crusade. *The Four Tetrarchs* (Figure 8.23), now surrounding a cornerstone of Venice's St. Mark's Basilica, depicts the four rulers embracing to convey their harmony and brotherhood. The difference between them and *Augustus of Primaporta* (Figure 8.4) is striking. The four rulers look the same, lacking individuality, except that two have beards (presumably the two Augustuses). They are dressed the same, in capes, body armor, and armored kilts, all with left hands on identical swords. Their faces are flat and expressionless, with exaggerated almond eyes in unfocused gaze; their proportions are short and blocky, with the visible left elbows at right angles. There is no *contrapposto*. All four figures stand with feet flat on the ground and weight evenly distributed. Despite what might seem a rudimentary style of depiction, this is clearly a work of high patronage. The stone porphyry was rare and reserved for the emperor, and, although the original location of the work is uncertain, it probably adorned a central square used for imperial ceremonies. The great stylistic divide between two sculptures of emperors (*Augustus* and the *Tetrarchs*), commissioned at the highest levels three centuries apart, demonstrates a dramatic change in art, culture, politics, and even the way in which humans were viewed. Diocletian's empire was not Augustus's, and the change was to continue.

Diocletian's administrative design soon succumbed to traditional Roman succession by violence. Constantine, elected as Augustus in 307 CE, eliminated his co-rulers and established a new dynasty. In 313 CE, with the Edict of Milan, he legalized all religions—notably Christianity, which had been sporadically persecuted. Within a century, this led to a remarkable transformation in the religious complexion of the empire and an entirely new architectural form: the Constantinian, or early Christian, basilica (see Figures 8.24–8.26).

The legalization of Christianity necessitated new premises for the religion, which had already attracted 10–15 percent of the population. Constantine's architects designed a new type of building derived from Roman law courts. Figure 8.24 shows the design of a typical Constantinian basilica, in this case St. Peter's; several such churches were constructed at this time at Rome's holy places. In front of the building itself was an atrium surrounded by a peristyle. Entry was through a transverse hall, or narthex, leading into the central nave, which had two aisles on either side. Crossing all five spaces at the

FIGURE 8.26 Giovanni Battista Piranesi (1720–1778), *Interior View of St. Paul's Outside the Walls*, before ceiling, 1748–1774, etching, 54.5 × 78.5 cm.

front was a bema, or raised area, which extended beyond the sides of the nave aisles to form a transept, a feature that increased in importance in later churches. Facing the central nave was a semicircular area known as an apse, in which officiating priests sat. St. Peter's had a shrine over the saint's reputed grave, under the altar in the center of the apse. The plan was designed to focus the worshippers' attention on the altar, since indoor worship was a substantial change from pagan sacrifices at open-air altars.

Perhaps to hasten construction of these churches, most of them did not have vaulted ceilings. Instead, the roof was supported by simple wood trusses, as seen in Figure 8.25, a cutaway view of the old St. Peter's. Several such churches of comparable size were built in Rome in the fourth and fifth centuries. All these churches had side aisles separated by columns under arches, by now surmounting spaces taller than their width. The naves were lined with colorful frescoes, and most had some sort of canopy over or around the altar or shrine. The church that survived longest without major alterations was St. Paul's Outside the Walls.[8] In the eighteenth century, it was still open to its wooden trusses and lined with ancient frescoes, as can be seen in Figure 8.26. This picture gives us an excellent idea of the appearance of the original Basilica of St. Peter.

In addition to his momentous religious changes, Constantine also moved the principal capital of the empire from Italy to the more defensible city of Byzantium at the outlet of the Black Sea; he renamed the city Constantinople after himself. His family dynasty and later emperors ruled from there, while the western empire experienced increasing pressures from surrounding German tribes. Finally, in 410 CE, Rome itself fell to the Goths, who maintained a nominal allegiance to imperial rule for a few decades. The last emperor, a mere boy, abdicated in 476 CE. A hoard of German tribes overran Europe, pushed and followed by the Huns,

---

8   St. Paul's Outside the Walls (*San Paolo fuori le mura*) was constructed over the grave of St. Paul.

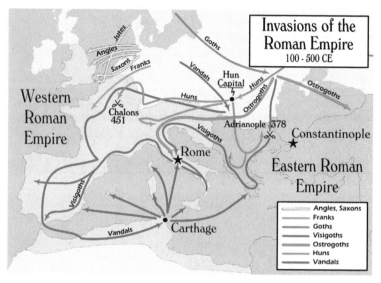

FIGURE 8.27 Barbarian Invasions of the Roman Empire 100–500 CE.

the most destructive of all, and the western empire was at an end (see Figure 8.27).

The eastern empire, however, continued until its final defeat by the Turks in 1453. It maintained toeholds in Italy and elsewhere in the west for some time, but the culture of the eastern (now sole) empire changed so much that we think of it differently from Rome and refer to it by its capital's original name—the Byzantine Empire. Meanwhile, what had been the western empire broke apart into several political units dominated by different barbarian tribes. The strife among these states, coupled with the destruction or neglect of much of the heritage of Classical Rome, resulted in a period of two to three centuries that some call the Dark Ages.

The darkness was held at bay, however, by the continuing traditions of government, learning, and art that emanated from Constantinople, and for many years, the Byzantine emperors fought to regain what they had lost. The most successful of these was the emperor Justinian I (the Great, 482–565 CE). He was the last emperor to speak Latin as his first language; he codified Roman law in a form that is still strongly influential today; and his general, Belisarius, recovered many western lands, including most of the North African provinces and a toehold on the Atlantic Ocean, as shown in Figure 8.28.

FIGURE 8.28 The Byzantine Empire at its Greatest Extent in 565 CE. Areas in green are Justinian's conquests.

Byzantine Arts

Among the lands recovered were several areas of Italy, including the city of Ravenna (at the north end of the Adriatic Sea), which had been the capital of the western empire since 402 CE, and continued so under the Goths. Ravenna is now famed for the mosaics in its churches; the Basilica of San Vitale is particularly important. It is the only church of Justinian's reign that survives intact, and it contains portraits of him and his empress, Theodora. Figure 8.29 shows the church's exterior.

San Vitale is brick, with two stories of arched windows beneath a third-story cupola. The view is from the altar end on the diagonal. The central apse with tall windows is between two lower apses, one of which is nearest the viewer. Note also the reinforcing ribs on the right. The one embedded in the wall is a simple buttress, while the one connected to it with arches is a type of flying buttress, a structure of great importance in Gothic architecture. Figure 8.30 shows the church's plan. Although this is a church of the rank of basilica, it does not have a basilican plan. It is octagonal, with a deeper apse for the altar. The cross section in Figure 8.31 shows the relationship of the levels and the plan. The central cupola is three stories high, supported by two stories of columns. Behind these colonnades are two levels of ambulatories, areas for walking or standing to attend the service. The upper one was reserved for women. Portions of this gallery can be seen on either side of the two-story extension for the altar, with its one-and-a-half-story, half-domed apse (Figure 8.32). The altar apse is especially renowned for the mosaics it contains.

We have already seen the mosaic technique used for a floor in Figure 8.8. Byzantine artists carried the technique much further and lined walls and ceilings of public buildings in this way, as at San Vitale (see Figure 8.32). Byzantine mosaics incorporate another innovation as well:

FIGURE 8.29 Julianus Argentarius, The Basilica of San Vitale, Ravenna, 526–547 CE, Exterior.

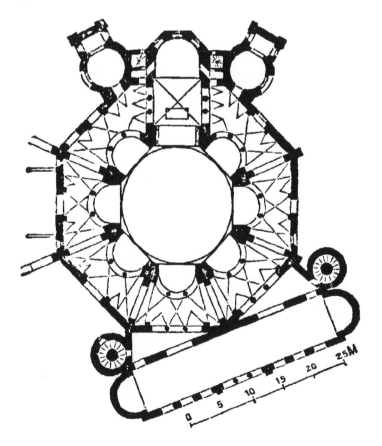

FIGURE 8.30 The Basilica of San Vitale, Ravenna, Plan.

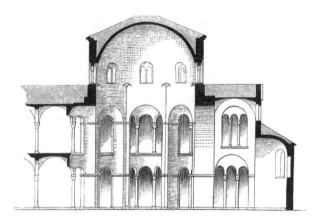

FIGURE 8.31 The Basilica of San Vitale, Ravenna, Cross Section.

the tiny tiles (*tesserae*) that comprise the picture are made of glass, colored in some cases and backed with gold leaf in others. All of the church's mosaics include substantial amounts of gold for its visual effect. The two most famous mosaics flank the altar near the end of the apse (see Figures 8.33a and b). The appearance of distortion at one end of each is caused by the beginning of the curvature of the apse at this point in the image. On the left is a picture of the emperor Justinian flanked by clergy and soldiers. Bishop Maximian, who dedicated the church, is labeled and carries a cross. On his left are two deacons carrying the Gospel book and an incense thurible. The figure between the bishop and Justinian is believed to be Julianus Argentarius, the banker who paid for the church. In addition to his crown, Justinian has a halo, symbol of the divine origin of his power; he carries a paten, the platter for the communion bread. On his right are two priests and the imperial Palatine Guard.

The mosaic to the right of the apse shows the empress Theodora and her attendants. She is haloed like Justinian and carries the chalice for the communion wine. Embroidered on the hem of her gown are the three kings bearing gifts, as she is. She wears a jeweled headdress, earrings, and collar, and she is richly dressed, as are her ladies-in-waiting. She is also accompanied by two priests. In both mosaics, the human proportions are slightly elongated and there is more emphasis on surface richness than depiction of depth (limited to overlap), despite some architectural background to Theodora. The men all have clearly individuated faces, as do some of the women. The lesser ladies-in-waiting all have very similar faces, and the postures are stiff, with all feet pointing outward, while the men's are slightly spread. The lifelike shading of all faces is quite skilled and subtle. This subtlety and the unusual tiles used for the rulers' jewels are visible in Figures 8.34a and b. Instead of glass, the round tiles are made of polished marble or mother-of-pearl for a distinctive sheen. Gold is abundant in the costumes and backgrounds. Figures 8.35a and b show the same details of Justinian and Theodora as the previous figure but in different lighting conditions. This reveals the glory of mosaic interiors. With every movement of the sun, every shift of cloud, every change of season, time of day, interior lighting, or even the viewer's own reflection or shadow, the images change. The figures float in a cloud of gold and brilliant colors for a glimpse of another world.

FIGURE 8.32 The Basilica of San Vitale, Ravenna, Interior.

Not far northeast of Ravenna is Venice, whose inhabitants fled the Huns to sandy islands in a lagoon; there, they built a village that became first a town and then a city republic that lasted twice as long as Rome's. Because of their location and trade, the Venetians adopted many features of Byzantine art.[9] This is most evident in the city's crown jewel, the Basilica of San Marco (Saint Mark, Figure 8.36). Constructed around 1100 CE, the building is in the form of a Greek cross (with all arms of equal length), although the altar arm is broader than the others. There is a central dome at the crossing, as well as a smaller dome on each arm. Every dome has an onion-shaped pinnacle and cross. The basilica's façade fills the head of Venice's largest open space, the Piazza San Marco, with a remarkable fusion of the Byzantine, Islamic, and Gothic influences that contributed to Venice's unique architectural style.

On the bottom level, five doors allow entrance into the church. They are all topped by semicircular arches in the Romano-Byzantine style. The tympanum—semicircular space—above each has a mosaic scene (some fairly recent, as the originals did not always survive). The two smaller, central flanking doors have three pointed Gothic windows inside a round arch below the mosaic, while the two outer doors have arches in which the curve reverses at the top to come to a point (a shape called an ogee). Immediately above the doors is a railed gallery over the narthex, in the center of which stand four ancient bronze horses. Behind the gallery is a large central window that fills its arch, with two smaller windows on either side, surmounted by more mosaics in the arch's tympana. Each of the five top arches is topped with an ogee.

The space between the central round arch and its ogee is dark blue with gold stars behind a gold winged lion with a book beneath its paw—the emblem of Saint Mark the Evangelist,

FIGURE 8.33A Anonymous, *Emperor Justinian in Procession, with Bishop Maximianus, Palatine Guards, Priests and Deacons*, 547 CE, mosaic, left side of apse, Basilica of San Vitale, Ravenna.

FIGURE 8.33B Anonymous, *Empress Theodora in Procession with Priests and Ladies-In-Waiting*, 547 CE, mosaic, right side of apse, Basilica of San Vitale, Ravenna.

9   As the greatest medieval seafarers, the Venetians controlled the spice and silk trade with the Orient through Islamic and Byzantine lands; they held many landfalls and some islands in the eastern Mediterranean. The Byzantines were both a trading partner and competitor, so, in 1204, the Doge of Venice, in return for transport, forced the fourth Crusade to lay siege to Constantinople. In the ensuing sack, the Venetians stole any precious objects they found, including *The Four Tetrarchs* (above) and the bronze horses and gold icon discussed below. The sack and subsequent decades of French rule sapped Byzantine power and began its decline.

FIGURE 8.34A Emperor Justinian, Mosaic Detail.

FIGURE 8.34B Empress Theodora, Mosaic Detail.

FIGURE 8.35A Emperor Justinian, Mosaic Detail in
Contrasting Light.

FIGURE 8.35B Empress Theodora, Mosaic Detail in Contrasting
Light.

Venice's patron saint.[10] Between and flanking the five ogee arches are Gothic pinnacles that house sculptures, which were added later. The four horses over the main door are noteworthy (see Figure 8.37). Those on the façade have been replaced by copies; the originals are now restored and placed inside for protection. Although their specific origin is unknown, they may have been the team of an emperor's chariot sculpture. The combination of all of these components makes San Marco's façade a sumptuous profusion of colors, forms, and styles of almost overwhelming richness.

FIGURE 8.36 Basilica of San Marco, façade, 1073–1117 CE; new outer domes and mosaics thirteenth century, Venice, formerly private chapel of the Doge (Duke).

The richness continues upon entering; all of the upper spaces of the basilica's interior are covered in mosaics on a gold ground, as seen in Figure 8.38. Byzantine artists began the work and taught the technique to Venetians, who took it over and continued until all of the ceilings and domes were covered. The process took some time, so not all of the work is in a pure Byzantine style, but the general effect is opulent. Figure 8.38 shows the mosaics of the central dome, looking past it to the dome and apse over the altar. In contrast with San Vitale, the predominance of golden surface at San Marco gives the effect of being submerged in a jewel box.

Gold attracted the Venetians in their looting of Byzantium. Objects they took are held in the basilica's treasury. Figure 8.39 is a golden

FIGURE 8.37 Classical Greek or Roman Horses from above the Main Entrance of San Marco, gilt bronze, fifth century BCE?, Basilica of San Marco, Venice.

10   In their aggressive trading style (verging on piracy), the Venetians heard in 828 of a plan for destruction of the bodily relics of St. Mark of Alexandria, the founder of the African Coptic church. They smuggled most of the body out of the city under a layer of cabbage and pork (which Muslim guards viewed as unclean) to deter a search. Upon reaching Venice, the body was lost until a miracle revealed its location near the time of the basilica's completion.

FIGURE 8.38 Interior of San Marco, twelfth century CE, Venice.

FIGURE 8.39 Byzantine gold Icon of the Archangel Michael, gold, enamel, glass and gems, tenth century CE, Treasury of San Marco, Venice.

Byzantine icon of Saint Michael the Archangel, flanked by enamel medallions of Saint Simon on the left and Christ on the right. The angel's person is entirely gold. His elliptical face has a long, thin nose, a small, pursed mouth, and large, oval eyes similar to those seen in mosaics. His hair, in stylized curls, supports a coronet of three precious stones. His right hand is raised in blessing, and his left hand bears a sceptre with a ruby at its tip. His sleeves and wings are also decorated in enamel, as are the geometric pattern of his halo, frame, and the small medallions bearing his name. Otherwise, all decoration is in precious stones or colored glass—on his cuffs and the collar, breast, and shoulder epaulettes of his imperial robe—and evenly spaced within his enamel halo. Gold icons like this were relatively rare and treasured, but the practice is an extension of the universal Byzantine practice of painted icons, which were, and remain, devotional aids for much of the history of eastern Christianity.

In proceeding from the Roman Republic to tenth-century Byzantium and Venice, this chapter has covered visual art, architecture, and the environmental art of gardening for a period of seventeen centuries. Other arts also existed, of course. Classical Roman culture disapproved of theater but also enjoyed it in a variety of forms, from rough and vulgar improvised farce, through situation comedies modeled on Greek New Comedy, to ancient Greek and occasionally more recent tragedies, in order of popularity. Theater production decreased but did not vanish with the advent of Christianity, but we have little surviving work. Of classical Roman music and dance, unfortunately, we have nothing except pictures, descriptions, and a small number of surviving or reconstructed musical instruments. Of these arts as well, Romans disapproved; they considered them decadent and foreign while still enjoying them. From Byzantium, religious chant survives in a continuous tradition, but it is difficult to separate modern performance practice from the chant that Justinian heard. Luckily, some of these arts reappeared and survived in the Medieval West. The barbarians destroyed much, but the desire and will to produce art outlived them as the regions of the West began to redefine themselves in ways that led to our modern world.

Image Credits

Fig. 8.1: United States Military Academy, Department of History / Copyright in the Public Domain.

Fig. 8.2: Copyright © 2008 by United Nations Development Programme, (CC BY-SA 3.0) at https://commons.wikimedia.org/wiki/File:Roman.gif.

Fig. 8.3: Copyright © 2007 by shakko / Wikimedia Commons, (CC BY-SA 3.0) at https://commons.wikimedia.org/wiki/File:Jucundus_pushkin.jpg.

Fig. 8.4: Copyright © 2007 by Till Niermann, (CC BY-SA 3.0) at https://commons.wikimedia.org/wiki/File:Statue-Augustus.jpg.

Fig. 8.5: Copyright © 2014 by Jose Antonio, (CC BY 4.0) at https://commons.wikimedia.org/wiki/File:Ara_Pacis_Roma.jpg.

Fig. 8.6: Copyright © 2006 by Sailko / Wikimedia Commons, (CC BY-SA 3.0) at https://commons.wikimedia.org/wiki/File:Ara_pacis_fregio_lato_ovest_1.jpg.

Fig. 8.7: Copyright in the Public Domain.

Fig. 8.8: Copyright © 2014 by Carole Raddato, (CC BY-SA 2.0) at https://commons.wikimedia.org/wiki/File:The_Alexander_Mosaic_depicting_the_Battle_of_Issus_between_Alexander_the_Great_%26_Darius_III_of_Persia,_from_the_House_of_the_Faun_in_Pompeii,_Naples_Archaeological_Museum_(15045954695).jpg?uselang=it.

Fig. 8.9: Copyright in the Public Domain.

Fig. 8.10: Copyright in the Public Domain.

Fig. 8.11: Mattes / Wikimedia Commons / Copyright in the Public Domain.

Fig. 8.12: Copyright © 2005 by Patricio Lorente, (CC BY-SA 2.5) at https://commons.wikimedia.org/wiki/File:Vettii2.jpg.

Fig. 8.13: Copyright © 2009 by xiquinhosilva / Flickr, (CC BY 2.0) at https://commons.wikimedia.org/wiki/File:10865_-_Rome_-_Colosseum_(3506623122).jpg.

Fig. 8.14: Copyright © 2012 by Danbu14 / Wikimedia Commons, (CC BY-SA 3.0) at https://commons.wikimedia.org/wiki/File:Binnenzijde_Colosseum.jpg.

Fig. 8.15: Copyright © 2009 by Keith Yahl, (CC BY-SA 4.0) at https://commons.wikimedia.org/wiki/File:Pantheon_Front.jpg.

Fig. 8.16: Giovanni Paolo Panini / Copyright in the Public Domain.

Fig. 8.17: Copyright © 2004 by Andreas Tille, (CC BY-SA 4.0) at https://commons.wikimedia.org/wiki/File:RomaCastelSantAngelo-2.jpg.

Fig. 8.18: Copyright © 2005 by Kleuske / Wikimedia Commons, (CC BY-SA 3.0) at https://commons.wikimedia.org/wiki/File:Via_appia.jpg.

Fig. 8.19: J. D. Redding / Copyright in the Public Domain.

Fig. 8.20: Copyright © 2008 by Matthias Kabel, (CC BY-SA 3.0) at https://commons.wikimedia.org/wiki/File:Pons_Fabricius.jpg.

Fig. 8.21: Copyright in the Public Domain.

Fig. 8.22: Copyright © 2008 by Coppermine Photo Gallery, (CC BY-SA 3.0) at https://commons.wikimedia.org/wiki/File:Tetrarchy_map3.jpg.

Fig. 8.23: Copyright © 2004 by Nino Barbieri, (CC BY-SA 3.0) at https://commons.wikimedia.org/wiki/File:Venice_%E2%80%93_The_Tetrarchs_03.jpg.

CHAPTER 9

ROMANESQUE AND GOTHIC ARTS

Background

The wreck of the Western Roman Empire following the barbarian invasions resulted in a calamitous disintegration of central political structure, the collapse of technological competence, and the obliteration of literary and artistic traditions. While certain barbarian groups, in particular the Goths in Italy, made some effort to prop up the political structures of Rome, most of Europe became a sea of competing and warring tribes as invasions from the north continued, conquerors strove to establish their own territories, and Roman Latin was corrupted by barbarian speech.[1]

From the unification provided by the Imperial Roman administration, European political leadership disintegrated into territories governed by regional kings of varying power—the earliest manifestations of the feudal system that defined European government for the next fifteen hundred years. The transformation was so catastrophic and complete that historians have long made a fundamental distinction between *ancient* (all Western history up to the fall of Rome) and *modern* (everything since). A convenient name for this first modern period of history that follows the Roman era is Romanesque, from the name for early medieval architecture that grew out of the Roman style. The history of the Romanesque era begins at the fall of Rome—476 CE is the usual specific date, but 500 CE is a reasonable approximation that is easier to remember—and continues until ca. 1100 CE.

---

1   The mixtures of Latin with barbarian tongues produced the modern Romance languages and dialects.

For around 250 years after the fall, there was minimal time or energy for producing or even preserving works in the fine arts. Much art and literature was lost, as well as widespread literacy; buildings and infrastructure like roads and aqueducts disintegrated without proper maintenance; and without communication, regions became isolated and remote. It is not without reason that the period from around 500 to ~750 CE is often called the Dark Ages. On the other hand, during this time, the ancestors of modern European states and their ruling structures emerged, and the growing influence of the Christian church provided some unity and stability. The new Western European countries remained aware of the Byzantine heirs of the Roman Empire, but they seemed irrelevantly remote for regular interaction.

In the fifth century, Germanic tribes from Europe's northwest coast and what is now Denmark invaded the British Isles. In the ninth and tenth centuries, after four centuries of relative stability, these Anglo-Saxon kingdoms were overrun by marauding Norsemen. These Vikings went on to pillage much of coastal Europe, including the Mediterranean, leaving lasting settlements in the Baltics, England, Iceland, Greenland, Sicily, and the Irish and French coasts (the name Normandy is derived from Northman). In the south, the Visigoths, who ruled much of the Iberian Peninsula (modern Spain and Portugal), lost most of it to the Muslim Moors after 711 CE. Inflamed with religious passion, Muhammad's followers had conquered the Middle East to India, the North African coast, southeastern Asia Minor, and most of Iberia in less than a century. Islam's sudden rise and rapid spread threatened the evolving Christian kingdoms of Europe, which were just achieving stability. The power that defended Europe against Muslim incursion evolved in what is now France.

In this land, the Merovingian kings rose even before the fall of Rome. The second king, Clovis, consolidated a large territory in what had been Gaul.[2] His successors, contentious and eager to overextend their domains, squandered and lost power. Control passed to the mayor of the palace—a kind of prime minister—named Pepin the Middle, who, with his son, Charles Martel (the Hammer), succeeded in reunifying the disintegrating realm. Charles also drove back the Moors at the Battle of Tours (Poitiers) in 732, halting Muslim advances in Europe. Charles's son, Pepin the Younger (sometimes mistranslated as Pepin the Short), forced the last Merovingian into a monastery and was himself named king by the pope. Pepin began territorial expansion, which was continued by his son, Charles the Great—Charlemagne (reigned 768–814 CE).

---

2   Clovis was also the first king of France to convert to Christianity, and Reims, the site of his baptism, remained the preferred coronation site for French kings and a powerful symbol of the realm.

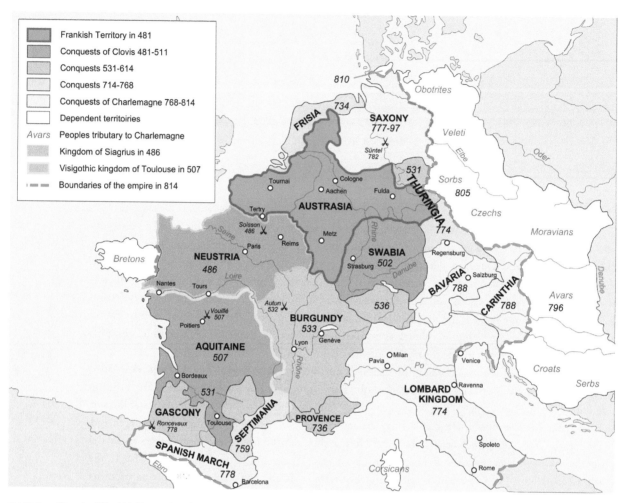

FIGURE 9.1 Growth of Frankish Empire from Clovis through Charlemagne, 481–814 CE. Childeric I (457–481 CE) was the first Frankish king.

Under Charlemagne, the empire expanded to control all of modern France except Brittany, most of modern Germany, Italy to south of Rome, and a small strip of northern Spain. He was crowned Holy Roman Emperor by the pope on December 25, 800 CE. The Holy Roman Empire lasted for a thousand years. Although Charles's realm was later divided among his sons, his strength and long rule fostered the development of culture, literature, and the arts by providing stability such as had been unknown in Europe for centuries. The invigoration of culture under Charles is often called the "Carolingian Renaissance." It began a movement in European culture that grew beyond the past to expand most art forms in new directions.

From the past, Romanesque architecture retained the Roman semicircular arch, but, as in Byzantine architecture, Romanesque arches usually surmount a space that is rather higher than it is wide. Romanesque church plans extend the apse and rudimentary transept of the early Christian basilica to form a true cruciform church. Romanesque sculpture has an ironical relationship with its predecessors: it shares the blocky stiffness and short-limbed proportions of the Byzantine *Four Tetrarchs*, but both styles seem to step backwards from the natural grace found in both Greek and Roman works of the Classical period. This may result from the Christian preference for the sacred story as the inspiration for artistic images over the natural and proportionate depiction of the human body. In music, the traditional Gregorian chant of the church was defined and prescribed around the time of Charlemagne, but the very rigidity of this mandate encouraged composers to explore new ways of augmenting the required chant, leading to the radical innovations of harmony and polyphony that set Western music apart from all others.

Charlemagne's palace chapel, now part of the Cathedral of Aachen in Germany, is a very elegant fusion of Byzantine and early Romanesque styles (see Figure 9.2). Having visited Ravenna personally three times, Charlemagne commissioned this chapel to be constructed in a style similar to San Vitale, as is clearly visible (Figure 9.2d, also Figures 8.29–8.32). A unique octagonal ribbed dome (Figure 9.2b) is supported by a three-tiered arcade of semicircular arches enclosing Corinthian columns, all of many colors of marble

FIGURE 9.2A Charlemagne's Palace (Palatine) Chapel (792–805), Interior, Cathedral of Aachen, Germany, Odo of Metz, architect.

FIGURE 9.2B Charlemagne's Palace (Palatine) Chapel (792–805), Exterior, Cathedral of Aachen, Germany, Odo of Metz, architect.

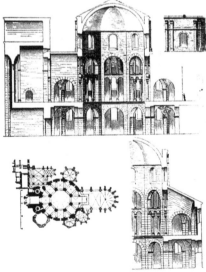

FIGURE 9.2C Cross section of Charlemagne's Palace Chapel, Cathedral of Aachen, Germany.

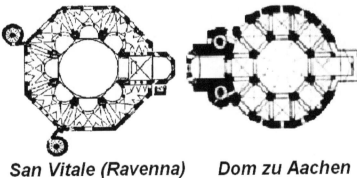

San Vitale (Ravenna)   Dom zu Aachen

FIGURE 9.2D San Vitale, Ravenna (left) and Charlemagne's Chapel, Aachen (right)— Comparison of Plans.

(Figures 9.2a and c). The mosaics above are recent; originally, the upper interior was frescoed. Charlemagne's throne is an important artifact in one of the bays at the base of the dome, and the shrine of his tomb is in the Gothic choir hall behind the altar.

The throne (Figure 9.3) is a simple stone chair, powerful in its rugged simplicity, made of rectangular stone plates bound with metal. The only curves are in the rounding of the back and the scooped-out areas for arms at the sides.

The shrine of Charlemagne (Figure 9.4a) is a gilded silver sarcophagus, elaborately decorated with enamels and jewels in the early Gothic style of around 1200, with inset sculptures of German kings on the sides and (ostensibly) Charlemagne himself at the end (Figure 9.4b). An earlier equestrian bronze statue of Charlemagne (or possibly his grandson, Charles the Bald) from the Cathedral of Metz is now in the Louvre (Figure 9.5). The Romanesque Louvre statue (which may be Charlemagne) is the closest we will get to an actual image of him, but the later Gothic sculpture on his sarcophagus does bear some resemblance to it.

Charlemagne's patronage of religion, education, learning, literature, and the arts is legendary. He used all of these as tools for the unification of his realm. His most important collaboration in all these areas was with the church. Bishops and monasteries shared many of Charlemagne's goals and aided

FIGURE 9.3 Charlemagne's Throne, Palatine Chapel, Aachen.

FIGURE 9.4A Sarcophagus Shrine of Charlemagne, silver & copper gilt, jewels, and enamel, 204 × 94 × 57 cm, 1215 CE, Aachen, Palatine Chapel.

FIGURE 9.4B Charlemagne and Two Bishops, silver and copper gilt, jewels and enamel, from Charlemagne's Sarcophagus, 1215 CE, Aachen, Palatine Chapel.

their attainment. Monasteries filled a crucial function, as a ready supply of educated scribes copied, and thus helped preserve, most of the literature that has come down to us from ancient times. Authors of the time also began to produce liturgical books, theological works, chronicles, and a modest amount of secular literature.

The Arts in the Romanesque Period

In addition to the reemergence of learning, the Romanesque period saw a significant innovation in church construction: the cruciform plan with a specific compass orientation (see Figure 9.6).

The main space in the early Christian basilica was the nave with side aisles. The apse at the altar end provided a focal point for worshippers, and there was a rudimentary transept in front of the apse that extended slightly beyond the width of the nave. In the Romanesque period, the area in front of the apse grew longer to form the chancel (or choir), with a walking space (called an ambulatory) around the chancel's sides. The transept, now pushed back toward the nave, was extended on both sides of the building, which took the form of a Latin cross—symbolic of Christ's crucifixion. In some churches, the axis of the choir is at a slight angle from the nave, similar to the way the head of Christ leans in paintings of the Crucifixion. The compass orientation of the church also gained new importance. The east end—of the dawn, symbolizing beginning, creation, and the Garden of Eden—became the altar end. The west end—of sunset and the main entrance—thus symbolizes ending and the Last Judgment. The symbolism is often reflected in the sculptural decoration.

At the Benedictine monastery of St. Gall in Switzerland, there survives a plan of Carolingian date for a monastery (Figure 9.7a). No known monastery matches the plan, so it seems that the plan is a template for the structures a monastery needs to function. As Figure 9.7 shows, a medieval monastery was a fully self-sufficient community. Centering on the church, there were: rooms for housing; a dining room; latrines and an infirmary for monks, the abbot, and guests; a schoolroom for the novices; a scriptorium and library; livestock barns, pens, and coops; medicinal herb and vegetable gardens; an orchard, fields, and pastures (outside the walls); food-processing spaces—a mill, bakery, brewery, and kitchen; craft shops (carpenter, cobbler, cooper, smiths, etc.); and a cemetery for the end of life. Once a young man had entered the monastery, there

FIGURE 9.5 Equestrian Statue of Charlemagne, bronze, 25 cm high, ninth century, Paris, Louvre.

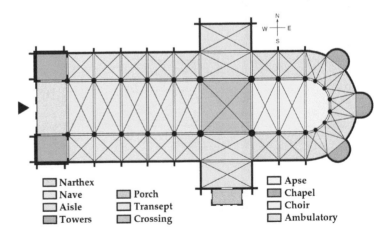

Narthex
Nave
Aisle
Towers
Porch
Transept
Crossing
Apse
Chapel
Choir
Ambulatory

FIGURE 9.6 Medieval Cruciform Cathedral Plan.

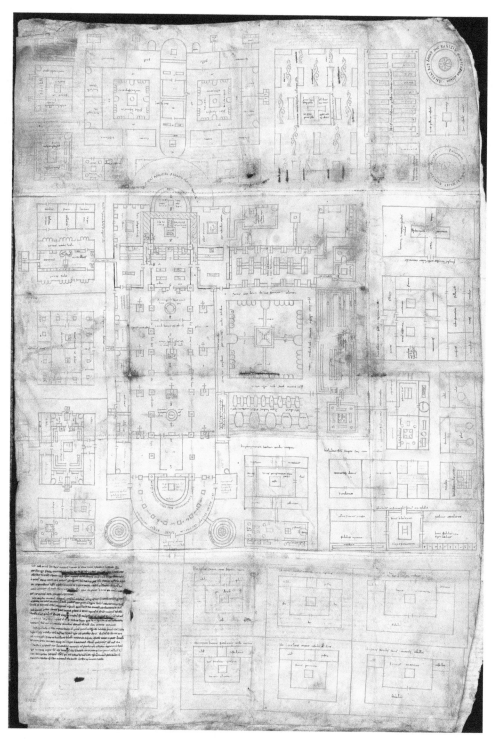

FIGURE 9.7A Idealized plan of a medieval monastery. a. original plan, St. Gall, Switzerland, Monastery Library MS 1092, early ninth century.

was no need ever to leave. Figure 9.7c is an artist's conception of what the plan's monastery would have looked like in real life: a small town, self-contained and self-sufficient.

That the plan is an accurate representation of building plans is shown by the Abbey of Maria Laach, eighty-five kilometers from Aachen in Germany. Although the abbey church was built around 1100 CE—250 years after the plan was drafted—the church, with its round towers, west porch (called a paradise), and transept, could have been constructed from the plan. Figures 9.8 and 9.9 show a side view and the west end. Figure 9.10 shows the interior (furnishings, mosaics, and other decorations are later). The typical Romanesque semicircular arch over a rectangular space (Figure 9.11) is visible in the nave vaults, the windows, and the doors. Maria Laach Abbey church is one of the most beautiful Romanesque buildings in Germany.

Romanesque architecture was not all sacred. Castles became increasingly common as the numbers of feuding nobles increased, and they were used especially by the Normans to dominate their Anglo-Saxon and British subjects. The typical castle of the Romanesque period was known as motte-and-bailey, the motte being a small, often artificial hill with a keep on top, and the bailey being the open space or courtyard surrounding it inside the defensive wall. Within the courtyard was a large tower, the *donjon* (from which we get the word *dungeon*), or keep, which provided living space for the lord and his retainers. A clear example is the Château (castle) de Gisors in northern France (Figure 9.12), although castles of this type could be much larger. The ribs built into the walls of the keep and the outer defensive wall are

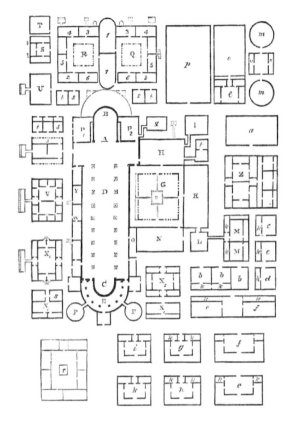

FIGURE 9.7B Idealized plan of a medieval monastery from St. Gall MS 1092. b. modern key.

A–D–church; E–narthex (paradise); F–towers; G–K–monks' quarters; L–O–food preparation; P–scriptorium & sacristy; Q–novice quarters; R–U–infirmary; V,W–school; X,Y–visitors; Z–craft shops; a–d grain preparation; e–i–livestock; k–servants; l–gardener; m–fowl; o,p–garden & orchard/cemetery; q–sacred stores; r–unknown; s–kitchens; t-v–latrines, bath

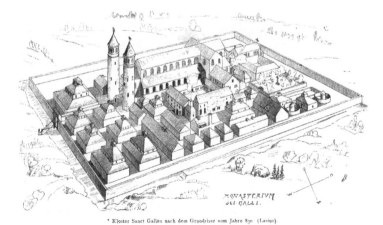

FIGURE 9.7C Reconstruction of a medieval monastery from plan in St. Gall MS 1092. c. reconstruction view.

FIGURE 9.8 Maria Laach Abbey from the northwest, Germany, eleventh century.

ordinary (or simple) buttresses, a common reinforcement in Romanesque stone architecture of any height, including churches as well as castles.

With the greatly reduced trade of the Middle Ages, both castles and monasteries needed to be as completely self-sufficient as possible. In addition to retaining skilled craftsmen, it also meant growing as much as possible for foodstuffs and medicines. Although no actual medieval gardens survive, it has been possible to reconstruct some based on descriptions, pictures, and sometimes local records. The largest-scale cultivation was grain for bread, beer, and livestock fodder. The next need was for fruits and vegetables for the table. Every castle, monastic community, and private house of any size had a kitchen garden and usually one or more fruit trees. The gardens differed from the ancient Roman ones in being more functional than decorative, but they were usually laid out with an eye for beauty as well as practicality. Grain fields could be at

FIGURE 9.9 Maria Laach Abbey, West End.

FIGURE 9.10 Maria Laach Abbey Interior. Note the architectural proportions, and arches (Romanesque). Mosaics, furnishings and other decorations are later.

some distance, since grain was harvested once a season and stored. Vegetable gardens needed to be near the kitchen, and the orchards were usually nearby as well for convenience. Figure 9.13 shows the reconstructed garden and orchard of the former Abbey of the Holy Trinity in Thiron-Gardais, France, about thirty-five kilometers southwest of Chartres.

Planted on the south side of the church for winter warmth, in the back are rows of fruit trees. Between them and the vegetable garden is a hedge, in front of which are large beds of vegetables (more efficient than rows), with paths between. Among the vegetables visible are cabbages, nasturtiums, onions, and squash (a New World plant, but possibly grown here in the seventeenth and eighteenth centuries). Pole frames in the background appear to be for beans just sprouting. There are other flowers, too, which, in the Middle Ages, might have been grown for the church altar (some for medicines as well).

The smallest garden was usually for medicinal plants and herbs for flavoring. Until after 1900, most medicines were derived from plants. In the Middle Ages, gardeners grew all of the native remedies they could, but they also grew those that had been carried back from the East after the Crusades. Some of these species were more delicate or accustomed to different growing conditions than those that prevailed in Europe. One solution to this problem was to sow them in raised beds, which warmed the soil earlier in the spring and stimulated summer growth as well as draining excess moisture. The reconstructed herb garden at the Castle of LaRoche-Jagu in Brittany has particularly elegant beds. They are raised about thirty centimeters above the surrounding ground and held up by low fences of wattle—thin branches or dried vines woven like wicker—a common construction material of the time. The beds contain a variety of low herbs as well as some flowers that were used medicinally in the

FIGURE 9.11 Cross-section of a Romanesque church. Note semi-circular arches over rectangular spaces higher than wide, with a higher nave flanked by lower side-aisles.

FIGURE 9.12 Château de Gisors. The keep, with an apron wall, stands on top of the hill, or motte, which is surrounded by an open space within walls (not visible), called a bailey.

FIGURE 9.13 Vegetable garden and orchard, former Abbey of the Holy Trinity, Thiron-Gardais, Eure-et-Loire (former County of Perche), France.

Romanesque and Gothic Arts **215**

FIGURE 9.14 Medicinal herb garden, Château (Castle) de la Roche-Jagu, Brittany, France. In addition to small herbs, medicinal properties were attributed to many plants we grow as flowers today.

Middle Ages. The habit of agricultural self-sufficiency was deeply ingrained and remained strong throughout the Middle Ages, even as travel increased.

The Romanesque style in sculpture as well as architecture spread throughout Europe. Some particularly fine examples are churches along one of the great pilgrimage routes—the Way of Saint James. Tradition holds that, after preaching in Spain, Saint James the Greater returned to the Holy Land, where he was beheaded. Pious followers brought his remains back to Spain, and since the ninth century CE, their resting place has been one of the greatest pilgrimage sites in Europe. A fan of routes through France and beyond converges just south of the Pyrenees to cross a thin strip of northern Spain held by Christians after the Moorish conquest. Santiago (Saint James in Spanish) de Compostela is in the northwest corner of the country, only thirty kilometers from the sea; the symbol of the pilgrimage is a scallop shell (see Figure 9.15).

A pilgrim from southern France would begin the pilgrimage at Arles, where the ancient church of St. Trophime has a west-end portal (1180–1190) with a very fine Last Judgment scene as well as sculptures that indicate the church's relationship to the Way of Saint James (see Figure 9.16). The tympanum (semicircular space over the doors) holds a scene from the Book of Revelation, Chapter 4. Christ the King, seated in a *mandorla* (almond-shaped halo) and holding

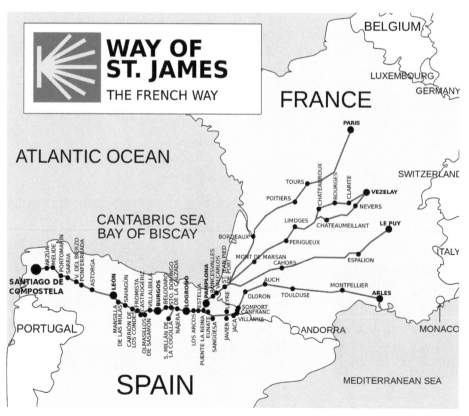

FIGURE 9.15 Pilgrimage routes to Santiago de Compostela in the Middle Ages.

the book of seven seals in his left hand, raises his right hand in judgment. Surrounding him are the symbols of the four evangelists: Matthew (angel), Mark (winged lion), Luke (winged bull), and John (eagle). Above them in the arch is the choir of angels, three in the middle blowing trumpets. The center section of the frieze below holds the twelve apostles, each with a book. On the left (Christ's right) end of the frieze is a procession of the blessed, facing Christ. On Christ's left, the damned are being led away in chains over a bed of flames. The smaller frieze below contains scenes from the early life of Christ. Below that is a row of large statues. On our left, St. Bartholomew, St. James the Greater, and St. Trophime; facing inward, four other apostles; and on the right side, a curious representation of the martyrdom of St. Stephen, then St. James the Less and St. Philip. Some of the lions, snakes, and perhaps other beasts at the bottom appear to be chewing on the damned. The façade appears simple and straightforward at first but contains a rich assortment of different scenes and tales. The judgment scene expresses the traditional symbolism of the west end of the church, while the statues of both Saints James confirm the church's importance in the pilgrimage route.

Another pilgrim, perhaps from northern or western France, would follow a different route that begins in Paris and continues south through Tours and Poitiers. In Poitiers, our pilgrim would encounter the church of Notre Dame la Grande (Our Great Lady, or St. Mary Major, consecrated 1086). This is perhaps the most richly decorated of all surviving Romanesque façades, but much of the sculpture is damaged. The central door has a wooden tympanum with the Blessed Virgin in a *mandorla* as Queen of Heaven,

FIGURE 9.16 West portal of the church of St. Trophime, Arles, France, begun 12th century. A Last Judgment scene surmounts a small frieze of the early life of Christ and a row of larger statues of saints.

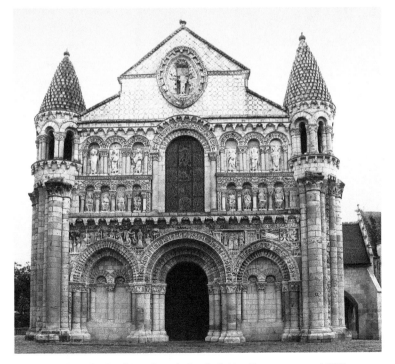

FIGURE 9.17 West façade of Notre Dame la Grande, Poitiers, France, consecrated 1086.

FIGURE 9.18 Crucifixion Window, Cathedral of St. Pierre, Poitiers, France.

surrounded by angels. The door and the two blind side portals are surmounted by several concentric decorative sculpture bands. Over and between them are scenes from the Old Testament (left), New Testament (right), and several prophets in the middle. Two rows of large sculptures above contain bishops, apostles, and other saints, each in its own decorated niche. The peak of the gable holds a *mandorla* of Christ surrounded by the symbols of the four evangelists—the Last Judgment again. The richness of the façade makes the damage to the sculpture more regrettable. It is not the result of weather or natural forces: in 1562, fanatical Protestants chopped the heads off most of the figures, which they regarded as idolatrous. It is hard to understand how they felt it more evil to leave the works untouched than to make the symbolic gesture of beheading Christ in his *mandorla,* but reason is not the strong suit of religious fanatics in any era.

In both of these churches, the sculpture is classically Romanesque in style. The proportions of the figures are not quite right, and the figures themselves are a bit squat and stocky. There is very little individualism among the various figures; if the large figures did not have their names carved on their shields, we could not tell them apart. The Bible stories are relatively easy to understand because of their scenes, but their figures are individualized only by costume and activity. Romanesque sculpture like these examples is heavily influenced by both the decreasing realism already apparent in late Roman sculpture (like *The Four Tetrarchs*) and the ambivalence of the church toward representation of the human body. Although not as rabidly iconoclastic as later Protestants, the medieval church did not value the visual arts for beautiful depiction of the human body but rather as a vehicle for communicating the sacred stories to an illiterate populace. There was no inclination or sense of obligation to strive for anatomical perfection, as long as the story was correctly told.

While in Poitiers, the pilgrim might also visit the cathedral of Saint Peter and see the wonderful Crucifixion window (one of the oldest surviving examples of stained glass). This window has three main bands. The middle band depicts the crucifixion of Christ. On the left are his mother (Mary) and the soldier who stabbed him in the side to see if he still lived.[3] On the right are the man who gave Christ vinegar on a sponge to drink and St. John the apostle. Above the Crucifixion is a scene of the apostles gazing upward at the ascension of Christ, who appears above in a *mandorla* flanked by adoring angels. The bottom scene is St. Peter, crucified upside down as he requested because he felt unworthy to be in the same position as Christ. Smaller scenes related to martyrdom surround

3   Pious tradition holds that the soldier's name was Longinus and that his lance point is in Saint Peter's Basilica in Rome.

the saint. As with the sculpture, the portrayal of figures and their stories are quite clear, but bodily proportions are distorted and postures are exaggerated.

Our two pilgrims would meet south of the Pyrenees and travel westward to Compostela. Their final destination, the great basilica, is another (and quite large) Romanesque church (see Figure 9.19). This is still apparent on the interior, although the façade has been heavily decorated since the eighteenth century in the most exuberant Spanish Baroque style. In addition to the typical Romanesque round arches, two unusual features are visible. The four U-shaped structures projecting toward each other in the middle distance are trumpet pipes on the two organs on either side of the nave. Such royal trumpets are a unique trait of Spanish organs. The rope behind the organs is another matter.

For at least the last seven hundred years (and quite possibly longer), the pilgrim arriving at a great feast-day mass would encounter a special phenomenon. Practically all Catholic churches use incense on important occasions. Since the eleventh century, Santiago de Compostela has used one of the world's largest censers (or thuribles), the *botafumeiro*. At the offertory of the mass, the *botafumeiro* is attached to a rope suspended from a pulley that is level with the tops of the walls in the center of the crossing, just where the vaults begin. (See Figure 9.20.) One man starts it swinging, and eight men pulling on ropes increase the swing until the thurible is swinging across the transept to where the rope is nearly horizontal, producing huge clouds of the fragrant smoke of frankincense. Cynics have suggested that this served to cover up the aroma of pilgrims who had traveled for weeks without a bath, but the use of incense in worship is far older than Christianity, and it has been an important adjunct of Christian worship at least since the emperor Constantine. As the incense begins to burn out, the censer is allowed to slow, then removed, and the mass proceeds. One might regard this spectacle as a unique instance of fragrance as a fine art.[4]

FIGURE 9.19 Basilica of Santiago de Compostela, Spain. Interior of nave facing altar. Note the organ trumpet pipes in the middle ground and the rope for the censer (*botafumeiro*) suspended from the crossing.

The largest amount of Romanesque painting that survives is in the form of manuscript illumination. The images vary widely in sophistication but often provide insights into the life of their times. One provides a very early medieval image of dancing. *The Life of Saint Radegund*

---

4   The *botafumeiro* has been replaced several times. The current one was made in 1851. There are exciting videos of the ceremony listed under "*botafumeiro*" on YouTube. Before a sailor's knot became the standard way to attach the censer, a hook was used, and the censer sometimes flew off. The most notable example of this was in 1499, when it flew out the transept window during the visit of Princess Catherine of Aragon on her way to marry the future king of England. Perhaps she should have regarded it as an omen.

FIGURE 9.20 *Botafumeiro* (censer) of Santiago de Compostela, viewed across the transept. The assistant on the left is starting the censer's swing. The eight *tiraboleiros* who swing it is are on the right.

FIGURE 9.21 *The Dance of Saint Radegund*, from *La vie de Sainte Radegonde* Poitier, France, Municipal Library, MS 250 (eleventh century).

records the saint's life with numerous illustrations.[5] The saint, a German princess, became one of several wives of the Merovingian king Clotaire, son of Clovis. The marriage was for political reasons, and she remained childless. She escaped to Poitiers and founded a convent, of which she was a severe abbess. On the occasion illustrated, she reproved a nun who was watching people sing and dance for taking pleasure in secular activities (see Figure 9.21). In the painting, the figures depict women shown in the typical rudimentary style of Romanesque drawing. The figures' faces are clear, but their eyes are rather larger than natural, and their gazes—even that of the right-hand figure, whose head is turned toward the group's center—are always toward the front. The proportions are relatively accurate, but the figures are a bit squat, as we have seen in Romanesque sculpture. The women wear tunics with decorated hems and hoods that drape in patterns that are as much geometric as the result of gravity. The figures are holding hands in a line dance, and all three right feet are extended with toes pointed in dance steps.

Another eleventh-century book from the western Way of Saint James is a commentary on the Book of Revelation from the Abbey of Saint Sever (on another of the Compostela pilgrimage routes). It contains a fascinating map (called a *mappa mundi*) that illustrates the medieval view of world geography (see Figure 9.22). The map is oriented at ninety degrees from our usual perspective. East is at the top, and north is at the left. Leaving the map in that position, one center of the world, more or less, is Jerusalem—the large castle in Judea to the right of a globular peninsula extending into the Mediterranean Sea (dark greenish-blue). Above it is the Jordan River, the Sea (Lake) of Galilee, and the Dead Sea, with Asia above and beyond. Arabia is to their right, with Egypt, Libya, and Africa below. In the far east (top center) is the square Garden of Eden with Adam, Eve, and the serpent climbing a tree. Far to its left is Albania, separated by mountains from Asia Minor (modern Turkey), and Achaia (Greece), a peninsula divided from Asia by the multi-dumbbell-shaped watercourse that must include the Black Sea, Bosporus, and Hellespont. Below that is Italy (with Rome in the center), separated from the rest of Europe by the arch of saw-toothed Alps. Spain is below (west), separated by the Pyrenees from Gaul (France) to its left (north), with various regions of northern and central Europe above left. The presumably flat world is surrounded by ocean. The British Isles are the green sausages in the ocean to the

5   *La vie de Sainte Radegonde* (eleventh century) is Manuscript 250 in the Municipal Library of Poitiers, France.

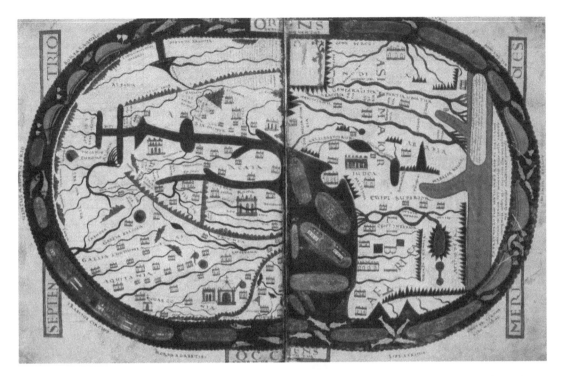

FIGURE 9.22 World Map (*mappa mundi*), from The Apocalypse of Saint-Sever, Paris, Bibliothèque Nationale, MS lat. 8878, folios 45v-46r, eleventh century.

lower left. This (to us) astonishing world view resulted from the medieval desire to place Christ, and thus Jerusalem and Rome, at the center of all.

But not all Romanesque two-dimensional art was sacred. One of the largest works of the period is historical in nature. The Bayeux Tapestry tells the story of the Norman Conquest of England in 1066 CE (see Figure 9.23). Vikings conquered the region in the ninth century, adopted the Gallic French language, and intermarried, forming the Duchy of Normandy. William, the Norman duke, claimed the English throne after the death of the childless Edward the Confessor. The dispute and William's invasion appear in

FIGURE 9.23 Bayeux Tapestry, Scenes 32 and 33, men staring at Halley's Comet, and King Harold (soon vanquished) at Westminster, with ghostly ships beneath, wool yarn on linen, whole tapestry 68.3 meters × 50 cm, Bayeux Tapestry Museum, Bayeux, France, ca. 1070 CE.

this remarkable work of textile art. Technically an embroidery rather than a tapestry, the work is 68.3 meters long and 50 centimeters high, with explanatory captions in Latin.[6] One of the most famous scenes is that showing Halley's Comet, which appeared in 1066.

---

6   Technically, the image in a tapestry is woven in the cloth, while embroidery is sewn onto it.

The first half of the tapestry shows the negotiations about Edward's successor. The second half shows the battle caused by Harold's breaking his alleged oath to support William for the throne. The comet scene is near the center. The tapestry's main band shows a crowd of men pointing and marveling at the comet (labeled *stella*, meaning star) in the top band over the next scene, which shows Harold being told the news in his palace. The lower band contains an uncolored band of ghostly ships, as if the comet is an evil portent that foretells the invasion. The story is paramount, so, again, the figures show some distortion: this time, they are elongated and their postures are contorted. The faces gaze in the right directions, but chins are nearly nonexistent, which confuses the separation between head and the neck. The clothing is clear, but, except for the draping of the king's robe, the folds show little influence of gravity. The architecture and king's throne are stylized rather than natural, but they tell the story clearly. For all of this, the colors are remarkably bright for a work nearly a thousand years old, and the tapestry has survived nearly intact, lacking only a couple of scenes at the end that probably depicted William's coronation.

The reigns of Pepin and Charlemagne were very significant for the art of music. As they wished to enlist the church in the unification of their realm, they sought to standardize worship and its music throughout their dominions. The various regions of Europe had all developed their own forms of worship and its music, just as they developed different Latinate languages and had different governments. With the pope's collaboration, over several decades, the monarchs acquired the ceremonies and music of Rome and did their best to impose them throughout the kingdom. Since this involved teaching some ten thousand pieces of music to singers who already had a memorized repertory of similar size of the chants of their own region, it was inevitable that the two repertories should become somewhat mixed. The result, which came to be known as Gregorian chant, has been the standard chant of the Roman Catholic Church ever since.

An example of this chant is the *Kyrie cunctipotens genitor*, Figure 9.24. The *Kyrie* is sung near the beginning of every mass. It has nine lines of music. The first three originally had Latin texts invoking God the Father; all but the Greek words for "Lord have mercy" (*Kyrie eleison*) have been removed. This leaves many notes over the syllable "-e-," a long melisma. Similarly, the second group of three lines has a melisma on the words "Christ have mercy" (*Christe eleison*) for God the Son, and the third group ("Lord have mercy" again), invokes God the Holy Spirit. The music is monophonic, with no harmony and just one melody alone, which uses a scale from a medieval mode. The melody

FIGURE 9.24A *Kyrie cunctipotens genitor* Gregorian chant (c. 800 CE) Musical Form

Text	Translation	Melody Line
Kyrie eleison	Lord, have mercy	A
Kyrie eleison	Lord, have mercy	A
Kyrie eleison	Lord, have mercy	A
Christe eleison	Christ, have mercy	B
Christe eleison	Christ, have mercy	B
Christe eleison	Christ, have mercy	B
Kyrie eleison	Lord, have mercy	C
Kyrie eleison	Lord, have mercy	C
Kyrie eleison	Lord, have mercy	C'

Line C' is slightly different from C; its first part is repeated to give a greater sense of ending.

Recordings of this vary little, so there is little reason to prefer one over another. The work also appears in some widely-used anthologies.

is a mixture of stepwise motion with some small skips; the first three lines share a melody, and the second three share a different one, although the two melodies have the same ending. The third melody (for lines seven and eight) is more elaborate, has more obvious skips, and ends on a higher note than the first two. Line nine uses a variant of this melody that has the first portion repeated to signal the approaching end. In performance, the first eight lines are often sung in alternation by the two sides of the choir, who faced one another in a medieval church; the ninth line may be performed by the two sides together.

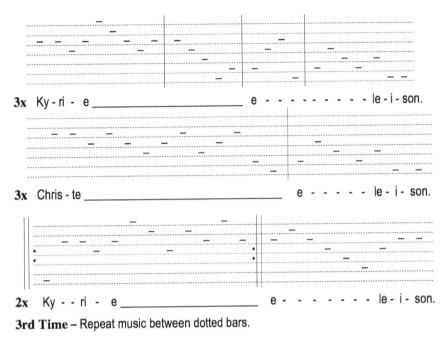

FIGURE 9.24B *Kyrie cunctipotens genitor*—Music—Phrases and melodic contour unmetered, monophonic Gregorian chant (ca. 800 CE), melismatic text setting.

The imposition of Gregorian chant involved certain restrictions on composition of church music. When one liturgy and its chants were required throughout the realm, it limited the ability of composers to express themselves musically. Creative personalities resist restriction, so composers sought new ways to write church music that functioned along with the required Gregorian chant. In addition to inserting words or music within or between existing chants, composers began to take a step that led to the fundamental difference between Western music and the music of the rest of the world. They added notes above or below the chant and began the uniquely Western practice of harmony. The earliest book that describes this does not contain full pieces, just short examples to demonstrate the process. Two of these are in Figures 9.25 and 9.26.[7]

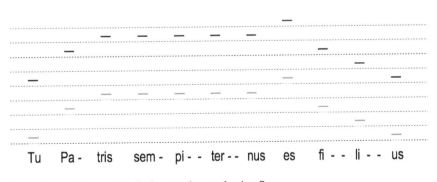

Translation: Thou of the Father art the everlasting Son.

FIGURE 9.25 *Tu patris sempiternus es filius*—Parallel Organum, harmonized entirely in perfect consonances (fifths), with a very simple homophonic texture.

7 Recordings of these works exist in several music history text anthologies.

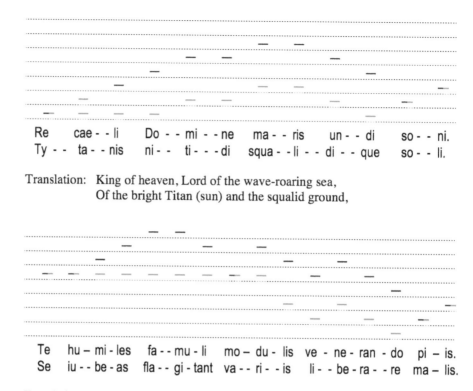

Re cae - - li Do - - mi - - ne ma - - ris un - - di so - ni.
Ty - - ta - - nis ni - - ti - - - di squa - - li - - di - - que so - - li.

Translation: King of heaven, Lord of the wave-roaring sea,
Of the bright Titan (sun) and the squalid ground,

Te hu – mi - les fa - - mu - li mo - du - lis ve - ne - ran - do pi – is.
Se iu - - be - as fla - - gi - tant va - - ri - - is li - - be - ra - - re ma – lis.

Translation: Thee humble servants with pious rhythms must venerate,
Begging that thou wouldst ordain to liberate them from various evils.

FIGURE 9.26 *Rex caeli, Domine*—Modified Parallel Organum—Lines start together, then move apart and move in parallel fourths, with a very simple homophonic texture.

The first example, *Tu patris sempiternus* (Figures 9.25), demonstrates what is known as *parallel organum*. The original chant is in the top line. A second line of music is added below that exactly parallels the chant. The second example, *Rex caeli undique*, shows a related process, *modified parallel* or *oblique organum*. The original chant is still on top, but the added line (voice) is not exactly parallel all the time. The two voices start on the same note, but the lower added voice stays in place as the original chant rises until the two voices are a certain distance apart, then they move in parallel motion until a midpoint or the end, when they reverse the process and come back together. These two examples show the evolution of harmony—the idea that music could have two or more pitches at the same time. In both examples, especially the second, the top melody is more important than the other, so the texture is melody and accompaniment, or *homophony*. The development of musical harmony is one of the most important contributions of the Romanesque era.

The Gothic Period

It is church architecture that manifests the most dramatic development of the Gothic period, which was in general a period of momentous developments in many spheres of life: international awareness, regional politics, religion, and human health. The Crusades began in 1095. The Byzantine emperor had requested military assistance to repel the Turks. Pope Urban II promoted this strongly and offered absolution of all sins for those who would endeavor to free Palestine from control of the Turks, who had restricted or denied pilgrimages to Christians, who had been on peaceable terms with earlier Muslim rulers. It was also an opportunity to send contentious European fighting men away and attempt to pacify what had been a very turbulent century. Europeans of all ages and social classes responded in astonishing numbers and with unexpected zeal but little or no concept of morality or even, in some cases, geography. Jerusalem and the coasts of the northeastern corner of the Mediterranean Sea did indeed come into the hands of Western Christians for nearly two hundred years, and Mediterranean trade was restored. Europeans also came into contact with the much wealthier and more sophisticated cultures of Muslim lands as well as the Byzantine Empire, both of which influenced intellectual and artistic developments thereafter.[8]

From a moral standpoint, though, the Crusades were disastrous. In spite of giving lip service to the ideals of chivalry, Crusaders massacred Jews in Europe and elsewhere and attacked and looted many lands they passed through, not always understanding that those they attacked were not the intended enemies. In 1204, the doge of Venice blackmailed the French army to sack Constantinople and eliminate a trade rival. This and several decades of occupation so weakened the Byzantine Empire that it finally fell to the Turks in 1453. Theologically, the Crusades also provided a precedent for the association of military force with religious endeavors, which led to later abuses of the feudal system and the Inquisition. The most lasting and damaging result, though, was a climate of smoldering mistrust and outbreaks of hostility between the peoples of the Middle East and Europeans, which have lasted even until the present day. Nevertheless, an unforeseen European consequence of the Crusades was the first document leading toward popular government.

While King Richard the Lionhearted was on crusade, his brother John was viceroy in England. Upon Richard's death, John took the throne. As viceroy and king, John was despised for his cruelty, exorbitant taxation, and military ineptitude. He lost 75 percent or more of English territories in southern France, which, at the beginning of Richard's reign, had actually exceeded the lands of the French king. This fiasco earned him the name "John Lackland." In 1215, the English barons forced King John to sign the *Magna Carta* (Great Charter), which promised swift justice and protection from illegal imprisonment and certain forms of taxation unless confirmed by a council of barons, who monitored compliance. Although the *Magna Carta* did nothing for the welfare of commoners, the document was a landmark in the control of royal power by a council drawn from lower ranks.

One of John's military debacles was the loss of Château (Castle) Gaillard in Normandy. The castle was designed and begun by Richard in 1196 to replace the Château de Gisors (Figure 9.12) thirty kilometers away, which had fallen to the French in 1193. Richard followed a new design of concentric fortifications, first developed in the Holy Land. In place of the single court of the old motte-and-bailey,

---

8   Western musicians acquired several new musical instruments based on eastern models: the shawm, ancestor of the oboe; the nakers, ancestor of the tympani; the lute; and others. Western literature developed new genres based on romance and chivalry.

concentric fortifications had several rings of walls, each higher than the one surrounding it. The strongest and highest was the *donjon* keep, retained from the older-style castle. Château Gaillard was virtually complete in 1198 but fell to the French only six years later. Figure 9.27 shows the plan of the castle and a reconstruction of the 1204 siege in which it fell. The fortress's concentric rings of walls with a moat between and its placement high on a hill should have rendered it impregnable, had it not been for an unguarded latrine chute and inadequate food stores.

In part because communities provided some protection from military adventures and a haven from cruelties of noble overlords, towns and cities exerted an increasingly important role in the Gothic period. Larger collections of citizens could resist encroaching barons, obtain royal charters, and become centers for trade. Craft guilds made technological development profitable, and universities stimulated intellectual development. The first universities took over education from cathedral schools, which were unable to keep up with demand. Universities

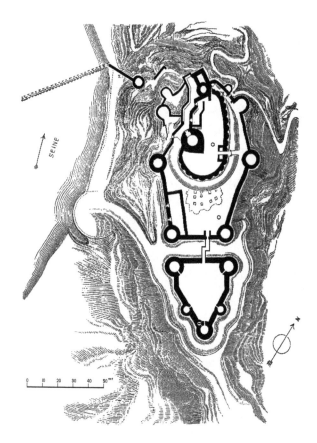

FIGURE 9.27A Chateau Gaillard, Plan, designed by Richard the Lion-hearted, ca. 1196–98, overlooking the Seine river at Les Andelys, Normandy, France. A concentrically fortified castle. The outer bailey is a separate island at the bottom, connected by a bridge with the middle bailey, in which a moat surrounds the inner bailey, on whose far side is the donjon keep, the final defense.

FIGURE 9.27B Siege of Château Gaillard by the French in 1204.

were separate institutions arising from communities of scholars and students. Inheriting intellectual leadership from rural monasteries, universities in towns opened the doors of education to a larger and more mobile population.[9]

The basic university curriculum centered on the seven liberal arts. The *trivium* included the essential literary studies: Latin grammar, logic (for determining truth), and rhetoric (for persuading others of the truth logic demonstrated). The *quadrivium* included the mathematical–scientific studies: arithmetic, geometry, astronomy (what we would call astrology), and music (to understand by ratios how motions of the stars influenced human activity). This last explained the interactions of Ptolemy's Earth-centered universe.

With the earth at the center, the heavenly bodies were believed to revolve in invisible crystal spheres: the sun, moon, Mercury, Venus, Mars, Jupiter, and Saturn, encircled by the stars in the firmament. The rubbing of the spheres was understood to produce musical tones beyond human perception that influenced human activities with their vibrations. Medieval scholars explained these relationships through the ratios of musical intervals. Beyond the seven liberal arts, the universities' higher studies included three leading to the doctorate: theology, medicine, and law (canon and civil). Growing intellectualism also had a revolutionary effect on literature as well.

Although Latin was the language of education and the church, vernacular works rose in importance. In the twelfth and thirteenth centuries, noble poets (called *troubadours* and *trouvères*) wrote thousands of poems and songs of courtly love in Provençal and old French, but Dante's *Divine Comedy* (ca. 1300) was the greatest revolution. In this one epic poem, which describes hell, purgatory, and heaven, Dante sums up medieval cosmology while establishing the modern Italian language; it is the first major work in a modern vernacular tongue—so modern that Italian junior high school students read Dante more easily than American university students read Chaucer's *Canterbury Tales*, written seventy years later. Both works show the first stirrings of modern language literature, which also began to arise in other languages as well.

The rise in intellectual, cultural, and technological activity spurred by the growth of towns was enhanced by the winding down of the Crusades, which had sapped a great deal of the political and creative energy of Europe for most of the two centuries before 1300. In addition, the fourteenth century brought serious challenges and catastrophes at home to replace those of foreign adventures.

One such event was the Hundred Years' War (1337–1453), in which the Norman English successors of William the Conqueror laid claim to the kingdom of France. After more than a century of sporadic warfare that involved most of the countries of Europe at one time or another, the English lost all the rest of their extensive holdings on the continent except the city of Calais, but both sides were significantly weakened, and England descended into civil war for the next thirty years.[10] The century's greatest catastrophe began in 1347, when rats, migrating from a drought in central Asia, entered Turkey, bearing fleas that carried what may have been a new and virulently mutated strain of bubonic plague. From Asia Minor and the Byzantine Empire, the plague spread on trading ships to southern Europe, thence throughout Europe for the next five years. The only communities spared were those that lived in near-total isolation.

---

[9]The first three universities were in Bologna (1088), Paris (teaching began in the eleventh century, institution recognized in 1150), and Oxford (begun in 1096, recognized in 1167). By 1300, there were four more universities each in Italy and France, one more in England, two in Spain, and one in Portugal.

[10]The long conflict also caused significant changes to warfare, including decreasing reliance on mounted knights in favor of infantry and improvement of gunpowder weapons.

By 1353, the Black Death had killed 30–50 percent of Europe's population, resulting in a profound economic depression.

The third momentous event of the fourteenth century was the removal of the pope from Rome to France. Precipitated by the election of a French pope who refused to move to Rome, the period 1305–1377 of the papal court in Avignon acquired the nickname "Babylonian Captivity," after the forced exile of the ancient Israelites. The papal court returned to Rome in 1377, but a new Italian pope quickly alienated the French cardinals, who elected an antipope. The subsequent period of two popes, known as the Great Schism, lasted until 1417. These two episodes weakened papal influence on secular politics, and the schism, with two popes claiming divine ordination, greatly discredited the pope in religious matters. The bipolar medieval world of secular rulers versus the pope and church was disintegrating.

FIGURE 9.28 Abbey Church of Saint-Denis, Ambulatory, 1140–1144. Pointed arches, with ribbed vaults leading to clustered columns, concentrate weight of vault and permit more window space.

The Arts in the Gothic Period

Nevertheless, the most visible artistic transformation of the Gothic era was in church design. A new fervor in devotion to the Blessed Virgin Mary and other saints resulted in the construction of many new cathedrals and abbey churches, with the greatest number dedicated to Mary. These enormous architectural projects also provided work for generations of a town's craftsmen, attracted pilgrimage and trade, and raised the town's prestige. The new architectural style began at the Abbey of Saint Denis, outside Paris. Saint Denis was one of France's patron saints, and his church became the burial place of almost all of France's kings for eight hundred years. In 1135, to accommodate increasing numbers of pilgrims in a church that was old and becoming unsafe, Abbot Suger undertook reconstruction. After work on the west front, Suger began the choir in 1140. His stated goal was a choir "suffused with light," which was not possible in the Romanesque style, with its thick walls and small windows. Most of the work completed under Suger's direction has been replaced, but the ambulatory of his choir remains intact and shows some of the structural modifications that his architects employed (see Figure 9.28).

The ceiling is supported by ribbed vaults in pointed arches, which transmit more of the weight directly downward and less outward than semicircular arches. The weight of the vaults themselves is transferred to ribs

FIGURE 9.29 Cross section of a Gothic church (Woodcut of Reims Cathedral).

FIGURE 9.30 Cathedral of Notre Dame, Paris, East End. Flying buttresses rise above the ambulatory with "flyers" bridging the gap to the main wall at two levels.

that concentrate the force and transmit it downwards to single and clustered columns. By concentrating the weight of the upper areas, more wall space is free to devote to windows, which allows much more light in the church. These developments provide better illumination of relatively low spaces, but to achieve the same effect on the much higher parts of the church, one definitive development was needed: the flying buttress.

Figure 9.29 is a cross section of a Gothic church. The side aisles have a structure not unlike that of Suger's ambulatory, but in order for the upper parts of the nave wall to have more window space, they need more support than ordinary buttresses can provide. The solution is the flying buttress. The ordinary buttress that supports the aisle (and ambulatory) walls is extended straight upward and connected by masonry arches to the nave wall at two points higher up. This is effective because the ribbed vaulting we have already seen concentrates the forces on those areas of the wall that the buttresses support. The two bridges (or flyers) from the buttress pier connect with the wall at two critical spots. The upper one takes the outward force from the roof beams and lead roof. The lower one connects with the point at which the vault arches exert their greatest outward pressure. (The lowest portion of the arch presses mainly downwards.) By concentrating the force at limited points in the wall and then transferring it to buttress piers that stand away from the wall, much more wall space can be opened into windows, and much more light enters the church.

One of the first completely new churches to employ this technique was the Cathedral of Notre Dame in Paris. The exterior of the choir in Figure 9.30 shows this very clearly. The bases of the piers support the walls of the ambulatory, while the upper flyers support the walls and roof of the apse. The figure shows clearly how much window space the new design made available. In the bottom and top stories, nearly two-thirds of the wall space is window. Even considering the lesser window capacity of the middle story and aisle roof, Gothic engineering

FIGURE 9.31 Cathedral of Notre Dame, Paris, West End Façade, freshly cleaned.

FIGURE 9.32 Cathedral of Notre Dame, Paris, Tympanum of Central Portal, thirteenth century, The Last Judgment.

opened nearly half of the entire wall for magnificent depictions of sacred subjects in stained glass.

Unlike many Gothic cathedrals, Notre Dame of Paris was completed with few interruptions between 1163 and 1345. Designed in the new Gothic style, the west façade (Figure 9.31) especially shows the builders' conception. Three portals beneath Gothic pointed arches provide entrance to the church. Above them, a row of niches contains 3.5-meter statues of twenty-eight kings of Judea who preceded Christ. Their heads are replacements for originals decapitated during the French Revolution. Above these sculptures is a gallery centered on statues of the Blessed Virgin flanked by angels under an enormous rose window, with double Gothic portals on each side under the two symmetrical towers. The next level links the towers with a row of elaborate empty arcades that also disguise the top of the west gable. Above this rise the towers, each with a pair of Gothic arches to permit the cathedral bells to ring clearly.

The three portals, from the left, depict the Blessed Virgin, the Last Judgment, and Saint Anne. The Last Judgment is simpler but more detailed than that of Saint Trophime (see Figure 9.32). Bands of angels and blessed souls form the portals' arches. The tympanum shows Christ seated in judgment, enthroned by two angels holding symbols of the passion: the veil and nails, the lance, and the cross. They are flanked by the Virgin and a kneeling Saint John. Christ's throne rests on the heavenly Jerusalem, beneath which are the archangel Michael holding scales to weigh souls and two devils trying to tip them. To the left (Christ's right) is a row of blessed souls facing Christ; on the opposite side, more devils lead the damned away in chains. The bottom level shows the dead rising from their graves, summoned by trumpeting angels. Only the top level is original, but the lower levels were restored according to early drawings.

The sculptural decoration of a Gothic church like Notre Dame can be overwhelming. At times, the sacred purpose retreats behind secular humor. This is true of the gargoyles and chimeras in Figure 9.33.

The grotesque beasts projecting from the lower level of the corner and below the gallery rails are true gargoyles that served as medieval waterspouts. The statues above, leaning over the railings' corners, are chimeras, nineteenth-century additions in medieval style.

Whole books have been devoted to the construction and decoration of Notre Dame, but we cannot leave without seeing one of the most famous surviving original windows, the rose window of the north transept (see Figure 9.34). Gothic designers developed ingenious patterns of stone ribs to support much larger expanses of colored glass and its lead junctions than were previously possible. Rose windows are the crowning result. Notre Dame's north rose holds the Virgin and Child at the center, surrounded by medallions. The first circle contains fifteen prophets and Pharaoh's prophetic dream. The second circle contains Abraham, Moses, Joshua, and judges and kings of Israel and Judah. The third circle contains the remaining kings and high priests, while the two lower corners contain episodes concerning defeat of the antichrist. The overall theme is that the Virgin's bearing of Christ brings the link that connects all of his predecessors with the ultimate fate of

FIGURE 9.33 Cathedral of Notre Dame, Paris, Gargoyles and Chimeras, medieval and nineteenth century.

FIGURE 9.34 Cathedral of Notre Dame, Paris, Rose Window of North Transept, thirteenth century, restored.

FIGURE 9.35 *La Sainte Chapelle* (Holy Chapel), chapel of the royal palace, Paris, constructed by Louis IX (Saint Louis).

humankind. The medallions are ornamented with geometric patterns, many of them in triple (trefoil) design symbolizing the Trinity. The design is filled with rich, vibrant colors, with blue predominating among many shades of red, green, lavender, yellow, and brown.

In addition to Notre Dame, Paris also holds the most concentrated collection of medieval stained glass anywhere—the *Sainte Chapelle* (Holy Chapel) constructed in the royal palace by Louis IX (Saint Louis) to hold his collection of holy relics.[11] Although a few portions have been removed to museums, most of the chapel's glass remains in its original location and state. The effect of so much glass with minimal stone structure is breathtaking, as Figure 9.35 shows.

The most elaborate Gothic cathedral is Our Lady (*Notre Dame*) of Reims (Figure 9.36a). Depending on whether one counts only freestanding statues or every architectural figure, there are between 2,300 and 5,000 sculptures on Reims Cathedral. The reason is partly historical. As noted earlier in the chapter, France's first Christian king, Clovis, was baptized at Reims. From 1031 on, five-sixths of France's kings were crowned at Reims, even after the Revolution during one brief period when the monarchy was restored. The church's ceremonial importance demanded an edifice of great richness. The west façade is similar to that of Notre Dame of Paris but looks like the whole design has been stretched upward and loaded with additional decoration.

As at Paris, there are rows of twice-life-sized statues flanking three portals that have further rows of figures arching over them. Unlike Paris, all three *tympana* of Reims have rose windows to replace the usual sculpture: simple four-petal roses on the sides, with a complete sixteen-ray rose in the center. The sculpture is raised to the elaborate pinnacles above the portals. The left pinnacle depicts the Crucifixion; the right, Christ in Glory. The central pinnacle's sculpture is another deviation from the usual: instead of the Last Judgment, the scene is the coronation of the Virgin as Queen of Heaven, as seen in Figure 9.36b. At the next level above, narrow open arcades in the towers flank the major west rose, nearly twice the diameter of the *tympanum* rose below. The

---

11 Relics are bodies, body parts, or items associated with saints that had attracted increasing veneration from the early church through the Middle Ages. One of Louis's main relics in the Sainte Chapelle was the supposed Crown of Thorns (one of several) from Christ's passion. There are fewer relics in the Americas because Christianity did not originate here, but in addition to the remains of American saints, some European relics have been imported; for instance, the church of Saint John's Abbey, Collegeville, Minnesota (the largest Benedictine Abbey in the Western Hemisphere) houses the earthly remains of Saint Peregrine, an early Christian martyr.

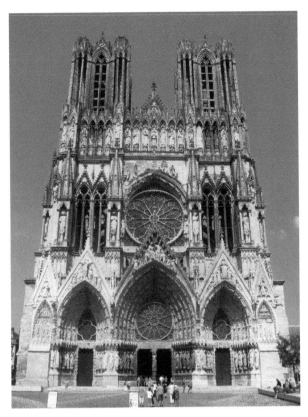

FIGURE 9.36A Cathedral of Notre Dame, Reims, West Façade, fourteenth century, restored.

FIGURE 9.36B *The Coronation of the Blessed Virgin*, Cathedral of Notre Dame, Reims, pinnacle of west façade central portal, fourteenth century, restored.

gallery of kings (these of France) has been moved from its lower position in Paris to the next level above the rose, where the central section covers most of the gable. The central figure is King Clovis, being baptized.

The three-meter statues flanking the west doors are a mixture of patriarchs, prophets, and kings of Israel among apostles and medieval saints. Only the central portal has identifiable scenes, all about episodes in the life of the Virgin around the birth of Christ. On the left, Joseph and Mary face Simeon, the aged priest who blessed the infant Jesus in the temple. A servant stands to his right. The central statue between the doors is the Blessed Virgin holding the infant, while on the right are two scenes preceding the birth of Christ (see Figure 9.37a). The first is the Annunciation of the angel to Mary that she would bear a child; to the right, Mary appears again in the Visitation with Elizabeth, who faces her.[12] All of these statues show great individuality, much more than most Romanesque sculptures, although these Gothic works still do not exactly correspond with actual human proportions—the heads are a bit too small.

Despite the slight disproportion common in medieval sculpture, these Gothic works show much more variety of posture and drapery than their earlier counterparts, and especially more variety of emotion. In the Annunciation is one of the best-known Gothic sculptures, the

12 In the Bible, the episodes are found in Luke 2:22–35, Luke 1:26–35, and Luke 1:39–45.

FIGURE 9.37A Cathedral of Notre Dame, Reims, right door jamb statues, 13th century. From left: *The Annunciation by the (Laughing) Angel Gabriel to the Virgin Mary,* and *The Visitation of Mary and Elizabeth.*

FIGURE 9.37B *Laughing Angel,* Cathedral of Notre Dame, Reims, thirteenth century.

Laughing Angel (see Figure 9.37b). This angel is so happy with his errand that his teeth actually show in his smile. Something new has entered sculpture; the artist felt free to show a degree of emotional expression rarely seen since Classical Antiquity. A Smiling Angel also flanks the left portal, although it does not seem to have any narrative significance. Lining the arches of the porticos are two hundred smaller figures.

Much of the sculpture shows evidence of damage, but we are lucky to have all that survives. In World War I, the cathedral was heavily bombarded by German troops more than once, even after the fire following the first attack (Figure 9.38). This may have been due to the church's significance as a symbol of French history. During the fire, the lead roof melted, draining through the gargoyle downspouts and burning down the bishop's palace. Some hardened as it cooled, as can be seen in Figure 9.39.

Reims cathedral was also the site of one of the great monuments of medieval music, the Mass of Our Lady (*Messe de Nostre Dame*) by Guillaume de Machaut (1300–1377). Machaut was a well-educated man and cleric from the region of Reims who became secretary to John of Luxembourg and Bohemia and served other nobles after the king's death until ca. 1340. Machaut then returned to Reims and took a position at the cathedral

FIGURE 9.38 Cathedral of Notre Dame, Reims, burning following the bombardment of World War I. Between 1914 and 1918, the cathedral received 42 direct shell hits before the fire and 245 shots after it.

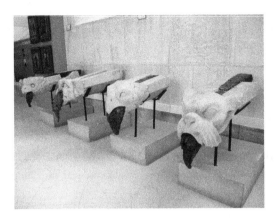

FIGURE 9.39 Cathedral of Notre Dame, Reims, original gargoyles filled with lead that melted from the roof sheathing during the bombardment and fire of World War I. Reims, Palais du Tau. This figure shows graphically the use of the gargoyles as rainspouts and gives a clear sense of their actual size.

FIGURE 9.40 Guillaume de Machaut (1300–1377), "*Kyrie*" from *Messe de Nostre Dame*, (after 1360)—*alternatim*—polyphony and Gregorian chant. Machaut's mass, the first conceived as a whole, was sung in Reims cathedral.

Text	Translation	Music
Kyrie eleison	Lord, have mercy	A—Elaborate non-imitative polyphony, chant hidden within
Kyrie eleison	Lord, have mercy	A—Gregorian chant *Kyrie cunctipotens genitor*
Kyrie eleison	Lord, have mercy	A—Elaborate non-imitative polyphony, chant within
Christe eleison	Christ, have mercy	B—Gregorian chant
Christe eleison	Christ, have mercy	B—Elaborate non-imitative polyphony, chant within
Christe eleison	Christ, have mercy	B—Gregorian chant
Kyrie eleison	Lord, have mercy	C—Elaborate non-imitative polyphony, chant within
Kyrie eleison	Lord, have mercy	C—Gregorian chant
Kyrie eleison	Lord, have mercy	C'—Elaborate non-imitative polyphony, chant within

Machaut based his polyphony on the *Kyrie cunctipotens genitor*, to be sung in alternation with the chant, therefore called *alternatim*.

until his own death. Machaut was one of the greatest poets and composers of his age and is the only medieval composer of whom we have all his works. The "*Kyrie*" movement from the mass (Figure 9.40) is based on the same chant, *Kyrie cunctipotens genitor*, as in Figure 9.24. The original chant is nearly impossible to hear, though, as it is buried within intricate polyphony in four voices that swirl around one another with great complexity. Polyphony is used for the odd-numbered verses of the nine-line chant. The even-numbered verses are sung in the original chant. This alternation of polyphony with chant is called *alternatim* performance.

Another art form popular in north French cathedrals was liturgical drama. It originally developed out of a three-line dialogue—based on the Bible scene at the tomb of Christ—that was used to introduce the first chant of Easter mass. Over years, more lines were added to this dialogue, a similar play was written for Christmas, and soon, plays were written on other subjects. Popular ones included the legend of Saint Nicholas, those of other saints, and *The Play of Daniel*. (See Figure 9.41.) A particularly elaborate version of the play fully set to music appears in a manuscript from the cathedral of Beauvais, a city north of Paris, nearer than Reims.

Not all medieval religious art was monumental. The finest surviving examples of Gothic painting are in manuscripts (some of them small) for personal use. The *Book of Hours of Jeanne d'Évreux* (Figure 9.42) is such a book. The book, only 9.2 × 6.2 cm, was a gift from the king of France to his queen for her private devotions. It contains simplified versions of daily prayer services. As befits a queen's book, it is highly decorated and made of the richest materials. The

Act 1—*The Play of Daniel*, written ca. 1230, tells the story of the prophet Daniel in the lions' den. Since it ends with a prophecy of the birth of Christ, it is a Christmas play. The plot begins as King Belshazzar of Babylon, feasting using vessels looted from the Jewish temple, sees mysterious words appear on the wall. After his wise men fail to read them, the queen proposes fetching Daniel the Israelite, who says they foretell doom, conquest, and death for Belshazzar. Belshazzar is murdered.

Act 2—The new king, Darius the Persian, takes the throne. Darius honors Daniel, but jealous councilors convince the king to forbid worship of any god except himself. They report Daniel's violation, and he is thrown to the lions, from which he is protected by an angel, who also brings a farmer, Habakkuk, to Daniel with food. Darius inquires about Daniel, then opens the lions' den and finds Daniel alive, so he throws the evil councilors to the lions. Daniel prophesies the messiah's birth, and the angel proclaims it.

Notes—The music of the original play is monophonic, with just one melody line and without notated rhythm. Most modern performances, however, have added rhythms in some places to fit the meter of the poetry and drones or organum for harmonic color. Some kind of minimal set can be used to provide concealed entrance doors or a lions' den, but the most necessary scenery is a stage prop—a throne for the kings. Some stage movement from behind or from side to side is possible, and the main aisle of the church is wonderful for processions: for entrances of the Queen, King Darius, and the Angel, to search for Daniel, or other movement. Good movement, colorful costuming, strong acting, and clear, tuneful singing bring *The Play of Daniel* to life as an elaborate Latin medieval opera.

FIGURE 9.41 *The Play of Daniel*—Liturgical Drama, Beauvais Cathedral, Beauvais, France, ca. 1230.

FIGURE 9.42 The beginning of the *Book of Hours of Jeanne d'Évreux* (Queen of France), New York, Metropolitan Museum of Art, The Cloisters collection, cat. 54.1.2, pen, ink, and tempera on uterine vellum. 9.2 × 6.2 cm, 1324–1328.

vellum on which it was copied was the finest available (made from the uterine membrane of a pregnant ewe), and the illuminations are very finely drawn and detailed. The main scene on the left-hand page is the Arrest of Christ (compare with Figures 2.1 and 10.3). In the center, Judas kisses Christ; on the right stand the priests, their soldiers, and servants, one of whom has seized Christ's robe; on the left are the apostles, with Peter cutting off the high priest's servant's ear. The introduction is below in red letters.[13]

On the right is the scene of the Annunciation. The angel Gabriel kneels and presents Mary with a scroll reading *Ave Maria* ("Hail Mary"). They are in a small house, with an angel choir above and the dove of the Holy Spirit descending through a trap door. On either side are angel musicians playing string instruments, and below is the first line of prayer, "Oh Lord, open thou my lips," from Psalm 51, verse 15. A royal figure—probably King David—kneels within the initial letter "D" holding a book. But not all the pictures are sacred. For the queen's amusement, the lower half of the left page shows a mock tournament, with the contestants riding a lion or bear and a goat and spearing a quintain, a moving target that spun around and hit the knight with a sandbag or bucket of water. The lower right page seems to show two women competing for the attention of a man while another man tries to drag one of the women away—a scene that was probably familiar at court; or perhaps they are playing a game like tag. The figures are very precisely drawn; the proportions are accurate, but some of the postures are awkward or stiff, and many heads have an enlarged cranium. Still, the amount of detail is truly astonishing; the book fits in the palm of one hand, and eyeglasses were only just being developed. This new precision in drawing exceeds anything that survives from classic antiquity.

Between the Fall of Rome (in 476) and 1400, Europe underwent a remarkable transformation that is clearly evident in the arts. Visual art moves from realistic to symbolic portrayal, and music becomes Christian. Theater all but disappears until it resurfaces as sacred drama. Of dance we know virtually nothing. But, approaching 1400, visual art becomes more realistic and expressive; architecture becomes monumental and ornate to a degree unknown before. Music develops polyphony and new and more precise notation. Theater rises from oblivion, and music—if not the steps—for dance comes to be recorded. The Middle Ages have arrived at their culmination; soon, people will begin to look further back than the immediate past; they will rediscover ancient Greece and Rome. Their astonishment at what they see will inspire them to emulation, and the Renaissance will arrive.

---

13   The introduction reads, "Here begin the Hours of the Blessed Virgin according to the rite of the Preachers (Dominican friars)."

Image Credits

Fig. 9.1: Copyright © 2007 by Sémhur / Wikimedia Commons, (CC BY-SA 3.0) at https://commons.wikimedia.org/wiki/File:Frankish_Empire_481_to_814-en.svg.

Fig. 9.2A: Copyright © 2014 by Velvet / Wikimedia Commons, (CC BY-SA 3.0) at https://commons.wikimedia.org/wiki/File:Aix_dom_int_vue_cote.jpg.

Fig. 9.2B: Copyright © 2014 by CaS2000 / Wikimedia Commons, (CC BY-SA 3.0) at https://commons.wikimedia.org/wiki/File:Aachener_Dom_Pfalzkapelle_vom_M%C3%BCnsterplatz_2014.jpg.

Fig. 9.2C: Georg Dehio / Copyright in the Public Domain.

Fig. 9.2D: Matthias Holländer / Copyright in the Public Domain.

Fig. 9.3: Copyright © 2013 by Torsten Maue, (CC BY-SA 2.0) at https://commons.wikimedia.org/wiki/File:Thron_Karls_des_Gro%C3%9Fen_-_Flickr_-_tm-md_%281%29.jpg.

Fig. 9.4A: ACBahn / Wikimedia Commons / Copyright in the Public Domain.

Fig. 9.4B: Copyright © 2011 by Beckstet / Wikimedia Commons, (CC BY-SA 3.0) at https://commons.wikimedia.org/wiki/File:Aachen_Pfalzkapelle_SchreinKarl4.jpg.

Fig. 9.5: Copyright © 2014 by Marie-Lan Nguyen, (CC BY 2.5) at https://commons.wikimedia.org/wiki/File:Charlemagne_Louvre_OA8260_n1.jpg.

Fig. 9.6: Copyright © 2010 by Ttaylor / Wikimedia Commons; Adapted by Gary Towne, (CC BY-SA 3.0) at https://commons.wikimedia.org/wiki/File:Cathedral_schematic_plan_en_vectorial.svg.

Fig. 9.7A: Copyright in the Public Domain.

Fig. 9.7B: Copyright in the Public Domain.

Fig. 9.7C: J. Rudolf Rahn / Copyright in the Public Domain.

Fig. 9.8: Copyright © 2004 by Donar Reiskoffer, (CC BY-SA 3.0) at https://commons.wikimedia.org/wiki/File:Maria_Laach_Abbey.jpg.

Fig. 9.9: Copyright © 2006 by Nikanos / Wikimedia Commons, (CC BY-SA 2.5) at https://commons.wikimedia.org/wiki/File:Maria_Laach_02.jpg.

Fig. 9.10: Copyright © 2006 by 567411xy / Wikimedia Commons, (CC BY-SA 3.0) at https://commons.wikimedia.org/wiki/File:Maria_Laach_Abbey_01.jpg.

Fig. 9.11: Eugène Viollet-le-Duc / Copyright in the Public Domain.

Fig. 9.12: Copyright © 2006 by Nitot / Wikimedia Commons, (CC BY-SA 3.0) at https://commons.wikimedia.org/wiki/File:Chateau-de-Gisors.jpg.

Fig. 9.13: Copyright © 2013 by Patrick Giraud, (CC BY-SA 3.0) at https://commons.wikimedia.org/wiki/File:France_Centre_Eure-et-Loir_Thiron-Gardais_15.jpg.

Fig. 9.14: Copyright © 2006 by Patrick Giraud, (CC BY-SA 3.0) at https://commons.wikimedia.org/wiki/File:France_Cotes_d_Armor_Roche_Jagu_jardin_04.jpg.

Fig. 9.15: Copyright © 2014 by Vivaelcelta / Wikimedia Commons; Adapted by Gary Towne, (CC BY-SA 3.0) at https://commons.wikimedia.org/wiki/File:French_Ways_of_St._James.svg.

Fig. 9.16: Copyright © 2012 by Finoskov / Wikimedia Commons, (CC BY-SA 3.0) at https://commons.wikimedia.org/wiki/File:Arles,ancienne_cath%C3%A9drale_St_Trophime,portail_roman1190.jpg.

Fig. 9.17: Gibert Bochenek / Copyright in the Public Domain.

Fig. 9.18: Copyright © 2009 by Paul M.R. Maeyaert, (CC BY-SA 3.0) at https://commons.wikimedia.org/wiki/File:Poitiers,_Cath%C3%A9drale_Saint-Pierre_-PM_34985_lighter.jpg.

CHAPTER 10

THE ARTS
IN THE
RENAISSANCE

Background

The boundaries of all historical periods are fluid, and there is overlap, sometimes more obvious than others. In looking at the Renaissance, it is important to be aware of this, for different features arise at different times, some as early as 1300. Chapter 9 described the major events of the fourteenth century, especially as they summed up the Middle Ages. But the same time period also encompassed early developments that led to the Renaissance. Scholars began studying the great authors of Classical Antiquity, at first in Latin and later in Greek, which attracted more study in Western Europe. The most prominent figure was Petrarch, still today regarded as Italy's greatest lyric poet. He was the first person to conceive the idea that the time between the fall of Rome and his own present was an "Age of Darkness." This evolved into the concept that the current centuries were a time of rebirth (*renaissance* in French) of the glories of ancient Greece and Rome; thus, the intervening centuries became the time between, or the Middle Ages (*media aeva* in Latin—the root of the word "medieval"). The Renaissance was the first historical period to name itself.

Study of the ancient authors had several important consequences. In government, people became more aware of the variety of ancient forms—from democracy to republic to empire—as well as more conscious of the pitfalls of them all. The recovery of the ancients' works often involved deciphering texts that were garbled or in disagreement, so scholars developed processes of linguistic analysis and critical thinking. The ancient works also exposed the corruption that the Latin language had suffered over the previous thousand years and enabled Renaissance writers to recover the purity of classical Latin. Finally, the ancient authors also presented a worldview centered on human beings, their works, and their strivings—vastly different from the medieval worldview focused on the afterlife through Christian salvation. From study of the ancient texts arose the philosophy of *humanism*, which combined 1) the ancient focus on human existence with 2) a moral concern to which both ancient and Christian ethics contributed and 3) a search for truth through observation, evidence, and analysis. Humanistic studies amended the medieval *trivium* to a five-part curriculum of grammar, rhetoric, poetry, moral philosophy, and history.

Transition in the Arts

In addition to the changes in literature, scholarship, and philosophy, the fourteenth century also saw changes in the visual arts as naturalistic portrayal of the human form and its surroundings began to supersede stylized medieval representations. This transition is especially clear in comparing the works of Cimabue (ca. 1240–1302) and Giotto (1266/7–1337). Both were famous painters from Tuscany, the region around the city of Florence. Cimabue was the greatest Florentine painter of his generation and learned his art from Byzantine painters hired to decorate a family chapel in Florence. One day, when he was traveling through the hills around Florence, he came across a shepherd boy who was scratching an amazingly lifelike picture of a sheep on a rock, so Cimabue took the boy, Giotto, as his apprentice. Similar Madonnas by both of them in Florence's Uffizi gallery show the evolution between their styles.

Both paintings are very large and were painted as center panels for altarpieces. They show the Blessed Virgin, enthroned and holding the Christ child on her lap, surrounded by angels and saints. This particular pose is known as a *Maestà* (majesty). Cimabue's *Santa Trinità Madonna* (Figure 10.1) shows the Byzantine derivation of its style: the painting's background and halos are gold, the poses of the figures are stylized, and the figures' images are somewhat flat in appearance. The throne is a collection of geometric shapes, and there was very little effort to show depth except for the slight convergence of its sides to show their interiors. In the center, the enthroned Virgin holds the (adult-appearing) infant Jesus on her lap and gestures toward him, indicating that she has brought salvation through him to the world. On either side is a row of four angels in stylized poses with gold halos. The only effect used to show depth is overlap, and the angels' heads appear to be stacked equidistantly. Under the throne are four male figures (left to right): Jeremiah, Abraham, King David,

and Isaiah. Their facial expressions are the most varied and natural in the work. The angels, Virgin, and child have similar fixed stylized expressions; all hands are simplified, without finger joints. All of the draperies fall naturally in response to gravity, but those of the Virgin have stylized, somewhat geometric highlights in gold.

In contrast with Cimabue's Madonna, Giotto's *Ognissanti Madonna* (Figure 10.2), from only 25–30 years later, is much more natural. Background and halos are still gold, and the throne still shows only rudimentary depth through convergence of the sides, but in many ways the illusion of depth is more convincing. The throne has a canopy, an interior background, and decorated openings on the canopy's sides that reveal figures behind. Two angels kneel on either side of somewhat convincing steps and gaze adoringly at the Virgin, as do three more angels on either side of the throne. Behind these figures is a row of six unidentified saints. The central figures are the only ones facing the viewer. The six saints are in three-quarter views, and the angels are in profile. The bottom angels hold gifts for the Virgin: on left and right, a crown and a little chest; below, vases of lilies (for purity) and roses (the flower of Mary). Instead of stacking, the background and side figures overlap one another in a much more convincing way than Cimabue's, and their facial expressions are more natural and varied. The drape of their robes is natural, without gold highlights but with occasional gold borders. The only slight detriments are the adult appearance of the child and some difficulties with the figures' gaze, which is common in Giotto's work as we find it today. The difference between Cimabue's and Giotto's Madonnas shows a clear transition from medieval to Renaissance artistic principles.

Giotto's best-preserved large-scale program is the frescoed interior of the Scrovegni (or Arena) Chapel in Padua. Constructed by a wealthy Paduan banker either as a family chapel or to atone for the sin of usury (i.e., lending with interest, which was

FIGURE 10.3 Giotto, *The Kiss of Judas (Arrest of Christ)*, c. 1305, fresco, Scrovegni (Arena) Chapel, Padua, Italy.

forbidden by the church), the chapel is relatively small (21 × 8.5 meters, 12.5 meters high) but has a richly decorated interior entirely covered with frescoes. The frescoes are in three narrative bands, each with twelve scenes. The top band is the life of the Blessed Virgin and her parents. The middle band is the life of Christ, and the bottom band is the Passion of Christ. Below that are allegorical figures of the virtues and vices. The ceiling is deep blue with gold stars and symbolic heavenly bodies. The west end is the Last Judgment, and the east end includes scenes of the Annunciation, Visitation, and Christ in Glory. The scene of the *Kiss of Judas (Arrest of Christ)* is from the Passion story (see Figure 10.3).

The painting depicts all of the elements of the Bible story: the crowd of priests, soldiers, and servants with lanterns, torches, and weapons surround Judas, who is betraying Jesus with a kiss while St. Peter, on the left, cuts off the high priest's servant's ear. The composition is similar to that in Figure 9.42, but the style is very different. Giotto's colors are much more vivid; his figures' poses and proportions are more natural, as are their facial expressions. Giotto conveys activity, while the earlier work is static. Barely visible lines along figures' outlines reveal separate days' work, and the blotchy dark blue of the background shows the result of pigment applied to dry plaster, unlike the vivid colors of the robes that were applied wet. (The blue pigment—azurite, copper (II) carbonate—reacts with wet plaster and must be applied after it dries.) This work shows the natural quality of movement, posture, and expression that will characterize Renaissance painting, yet it still preserves the figures' medieval gold halos—clearly a demonstration of artistic style in transition.

FIGURE 10.4 Giovanni Pisano, *Nativity*, marble, 84 × 102 cm, Pistoia, Italy, Church of Sant'Andrea, Pulpit (c. 1301).

A sculptural example of the same transition appears in the *Nativity* panel of Giovanni Pisano's pulpit in the Church of Sant'Andrea in Pistoia, a small city near Florence (see Figure 10.4). Giovanni's surname refers to his origins in the city of Pisa, as does his father's (Nicola Pisano). Giovanni's Pistoia pulpit is the last of three carved by the father and son and is the most advanced in style. The hexagonal pulpit, elevated on columns, bears five scenes from the life of Christ, the sixth side being open for the steps. The composition of Giovanni's *Nativity* panel is modeled on the same scene as in his father's pulpits, but the figures' postures and facial expressions are more natural. Since sculpture was much more costly than painting, panels like this often compress several story episodes into one scene, as this does. The story begins on the left with the Annunciation of the angel Gabriel to Mary that she is to bear a child of the Holy Spirit, who descends as a dove. To the right, the Virgin is reclining next to the manger holding her newborn son; a donkey and ox look on. In the lower right corner is a flock of sheep. Shepherds, one carrying a lamb, climb the right side; the top one listens to angels above calling them to Bethlehem while also singing over the manger. On the lower left is an episode absent from the Bible story: Joseph, bemused, looks on as two handmaids bathe the baby.

The naturalism of the figures, their postures, and their facial expressions are clearly something new—a foreshadowing of an artistic style to come—but there is one medieval feature: some figures are larger than others, not from their position in space but to show their theological importance. This is a survival of the medieval emphasis on the sacred story over realistic portrayal. The largest figures are in the Annunciation, the moment God became man, and the next largest are the Virgin and child at the birth. All the others are somewhat smaller and similar in size; they are secondary parts of the story. Like Giotto's painting, this pulpit shows a new naturalistic artistic style, influenced by ancient Greek and Roman works. The new style matured as that of the Renaissance, but the development was slowed by the many catastrophic events of the fourteenth century described in Chapter 9. The next significant evolution of visual art took place in the fifteenth century, and Florence was where it came to life.

Italy in the fifteenth century was a mosaic of small and large states of different sizes and different forms of government (see Figure 10.5). The largest of these was the kingdom of Naples, which, with Sicily, was from time to time controlled by Spain. Other monarchies included the duchies of Milan, Modena and Ferrara, and Savoy and the marquisates of Mantova, Monferrat(o) and Saluzzo. All of these were nominally fiefdoms of the Holy Roman Emperor, but, in practice, they were independent. There were four large republics (Florence, Genoa, Siena, and Venice),

FIGURE 10.5 Italy in the fifteenth century, showing the patchwork of small independent states. D. = Duchy, M. = Marquisate, Rep. = Republic. Modena & Ferrara were a single Duchy, under the Este family.

FIGURE 10.6 Filippo Brunelleschi (1377–1446), Cupola /Dome (1436), Cathedral of Santa Maria del Fiore (Saint Mary of the Flower), Florence. The dome's uncommon gothic style complements the rest of the cathedral building. The galleries to decorate the drum were never completed after Michelangelo sneered at the design.

and the middle of the peninsula was the papal state, where the pope was the secular monarch. All these political units were competitive, minor disputes and wars were incessant, and dynastic marriages further confused territorial claims. All of this provided a highly stimulating environment that bore its fruit in many developments of the Renaissance.

The most significant European event of the fifteenth century was the fall of Constantinople to the Turks in 1453. This demise of the last Byzantine remnant of the Roman Empire caused a large migration to Italy of refugee Greek scholars with their libraries, which greatly stimulated the evolution of Renaissance humanism and other scholarship. The Turks also imposed high taxes on the spice and silk trade from the Orient, which led the Portuguese to discover the sea route to the Orient around Africa and the Spanish to seek a similar route to the west, leading to the colonization of America—the Age of Discovery. The invention in 1454 of moveable type and the printing press by Johannes Gutenberg led to the diffusion of many more books at much lower prices than hand-copied manuscripts, but the greatest engineering accomplishment of the century was Brunelleschi's dome for the Cathedral of Florence in 1436 (see Figure 10.6).

Renaissance Arts in Florence

The church was begun in 1296 from a design by Arnolfo di Cambio. Work was sporadic for the next sixty years and stopped completely in 1348 due to the Black Death. Work was resumed the next year under Francesco Talenti, who also enlarged the plan, which made the dome design even more challenging. In 1418, Filippo Brunelleschi won the design competition for the dome, which took eighteen years to complete. He had to cope with several intimidating problems: lifting stone, brick and other materials fifty meters just to reach construction level; construction of the dome without interior scaffolding; and structural soundness with minimum weight. 1) His hoisting machine designs were not surpassed until the Industrial Revolution; 2) he used herringbone brickwork to reinforce and connect each level of the dome with the next and with its own level's ribs; and 3) he built a hollow double dome bound with stone, iron, and wood chains. The result was the first monumental dome since ancient Rome, and it remains, with the Pantheon and Michelangelo's dome for St. Peter's, one of the three largest masonry domes ever constructed.[1]

---

1   First place varies, depending on who measures the dome and where the measurement is taken. All three domes are between forty-two and forty-five meters in diameter.

FIGURE 10.7 Arnolfo di Cambio & Francesco Talenti, Cathedral of Santa Maria del Fiore. An example of Italian gothic architecture.

FIGURE 10.8 Cathedral of Notre Dame, Reims, France. An example of French gothic architecture.

Brunelleschi's dome is a stylistic compromise. Although the dome is a Renaissance concept and construction, Brunelleschi had to match the Gothic style of the cathedral (Figure 10.7). The church's interior shows the characteristic pointed arches and cross-ribbed vaults of the Gothic style. Italian Gothic uses these features with more restraint than the exuberant French Gothic style of Reims cathedral (Figure 10.8), which was constructed around the same time. In contrast to his Gothic dome, Brunelleschi's greatest monument as a Renaissance architect is the Basilica of San Lorenzo, the parish church of the Medici family.

In contrast with the pointed arches and vertical emphasis of the two Gothic cathedrals above, San Lorenzo (Figure 10.9) is purely Classical in its inspiration. Round Roman-style columns with Corinthian capitals divide the higher nave from the lower side aisles. The opening for the transept is flanked by square pilasters (pillars with flattened faces partly embedded in the wall), and every opening is surmounted by a Roman-style semicircular arch. The ratio of the column height to the whole arched space, the ratio of the arched space to the height of the nave, and the ratio of the nave's width to its height all approximate the Golden Section (1.618 to 1.0, to be discussed below), a proportion discovered in Classical Antiquity that seems most perfect to the eye.

A few years before his major architectural projects, Brunelleschi had discovered linear perspective. He demonstrated it with a small hole in the center of a painting of the

FIGURE 10.9 Filippo Brunelleschi, Basilica of San Lorenzo (Saint Laurence), Florence. One of the great examples of the new style of renaissance architecture.

Florence baptistery. A viewer who looked at the painting in a mirror through a hole in the back found the actual baptistery indistinguishable from the painting when the mirror was removed. Brunelleschi's friend, Leon Battista Alberti (1404–1472), later published the principles behind perspective in his *Della pittura* (1434–5).

Alberti's book is extremely detailed because it describes something no one had attempted scientifically before: how to draw three-dimensional depth realistically on a flat, two-dimensional space. The basic concept is that of the vanishing point, which is on the horizon line—a line that represents the level of the viewer's eye. Lines (black rays in Figure 10.10) from this point to the two-dimensional picture's ground baseline diverge, but they represent parallel lines or sides in the three-dimensional space. To relate the dimensions in side width to those in depth, the artist draws lines (green) from the imaginary viewer's eye to where the vanishing point's rays meet the baseline. The points where these sight lines cross a vertical line indicate the levels of horizontals (red) that define a square seen in perspective. A cross-check is that diagonal lines (lower right) will cross the corners of diagonally adjacent squares. These lines, too, converge in another vanishing point; in fact, Alberti also described using the diagonal crossings as another way of determining the placement of the horizontal lines. This is Alberti's basic method; he goes on to show how to apply perspective to objects with height and irregular shapes.[2]

Alberti's description of the linear perspective technique was groundbreaking; it was adopted by many painters and established a scientific basis for visual representation. One of the early artists to adopt this technique was Fra Angelico (ca. 1395–1455), a Dominican friar in Florence. He was a very prolific painter, and numerous works of his adorn his Convent of San Marco in Florence. His *Annunciation* of 1451–52 (Figure 10.11) is a fine demonstration of several traits of Renaissance painting: linear perspective, realistic portrayal, balance *and* symmetry,

---

2   Cecil Grayson, in his edition and translation of Leon Battista Alberti, *On Painting and On Sculpture* (London: Phaidon, 1972), 57, 112–113 n, partly republished as *idem, On Painting*, trans. Cecil Grayson, introduction and notes by Martin Kemp (London: Penguin, 1991), 56–58, describes this process, which is clarified in only a few Latin manuscripts of the text, one with annotations in Alberti's hand. Another edition of Alberti's work is a translation by Rocco Sinisgalli (Cambridge: Cambridge University Press, 2013). See also Frederick Hartt, *History of Italian Renaissance Art*, 3rd ed. (New York: Harry Abrams, 1987), 230.

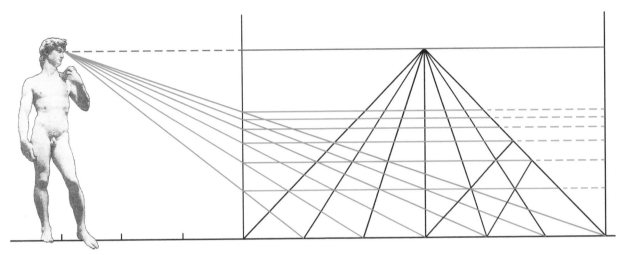

FIGURE 10.10 Linear Perspective as described by Leon Battista Alberti (1404–1472). 1. On the horizon line (blue, at eye level), place the vanishing point in the center and draw rays (black) from it to the ground line, at equal intervals—here, 1/3 of the distance from horizon to ground. These define an object's sides. 2. Draw lines from the eye to where these rays meet the ground (green). The points where these sight lines cross a vertical line indicate the levels of horizontals (red) that define the proportions of a square. 3. When this is correct, diagonal lines (lower right) will cross the corners of diagonally adjacent squares.

variety, vivid colors, and symbolism. Above and below the scene are Bible-verse captions that explain the event.[3]

In the foreground, an angel in flowing pink robes with gold trim and polychrome (multicolored) wings kneels on his right leg with left hand raised as if to instruct. Facing him on the other side is the Virgin Mary in a blue robe with brown lining and a pink shift. She kneels on both knees with her hands folded across her breast and bears an expression of dismay. In front of her is a low wooden bench or stool. Instead of circles of gold, the halos are depicted from the side as thin lines. The rich colors give the two figures comparable visual weight; even the shapes are similar, as Mary's stool occupies a space like that of the angel's raised knee. She is also slightly taller, which compensates for the bulk of the angel's wings. The two figures are balanced visually but not the same—they show variety of pose, color, and facial expression.

The background, though, is near perfectly symmetrical, with matching colonnades on either side leading to a wall with a central doorway. On top of the wall and colonnades are symmetrical potted plants, and behind the wall are

FIGURE 10.11 Fra Angelico (c. 1395–1455), *Annunciation* (1451–52), tempera on wood, 38 × 37 cm, National Museum of San Marco, Florence, Italy. The work shows the difference between balance (foreground) and symmetry (middle and background), with true linear perspective, as well as symbolism.

3   Top: "Behold, a virgin shall conceive and bear a son and shall call his name Emmanuel" (Isaiah 7:14). Bottom: "Behold you shall conceive in your womb and bear a son, and you will call his name Jesus" (Luke 1:31). Although now displayed in Fra Angelico's monastery, the work is one panel of a series of thirty-five on the life of Christ, from prophecy to the Last Judgment, painted for the communion silver cabinet of the Basilica of the Annunciation in Florence.

symmetrical trees. Two more potted plants on low stools appear through the door in what appears to be a fenced corridor leading to a door or gate in a high wall, revealing what may be a fountain. Above, between two tall conifers, descends the dove of the Holy Spirit. The linear perspective of the flanking colonnades points to the fountain (?) in the center of the distant gate. This is the entrance to a walled secret garden (Latin: *hortus conclusus*), symbolic of purity and associated with the Virgin Mary; such a garden also symbolizes the womb. Above it the Holy Spirit descends, and the gate is open. The painting symbolizes the exact moment of conception.

Another sacred work from a few years later, by a pupil of Fra Angelico's, is Benozzo Gozzoli's (ca. 1421–97) *Procession of the Magi–3, the Youngest King.* (See Figure 10.12.) This fresco is in a small chapel in the Medici palazzo in Florence—the first family chapel ever constructed. The chapel's decorations depict the journey of the Magi to Bethlehem to worship the Christ child. The walls show crowded, richly dressed and outfitted processions, all of which contain portraits of historical figures. The goal of the procession is the chancel painting, Filippo Lippi's *Adoration of the Christ Child* (also called *Madonna of the Forest*). The remaining walls were designed or painted by Gozzoli. The chancel side walls show adoring angels; flanking the chancel in the main space are shepherds in poses of meditation. The head of the procession places the oldest king on the left-hand wall. The middle king is on the rear entrance wall; portions of this wall were lost during remodeling of the palace by the Riccardi

FIGURE 10.12 Benozzo Gozzoli (c. 1421–1497), *Procession of the Magi—The Youngest King* (1459–61), fresco, 405 × 516 cm, Palazzo Medici-Riccardi, Florence.

family, and some areas were repainted by later artists. The right-hand wall shows the *Procession of the Youngest King*, the most familiar part of the work and the last part of the procession.

Descending from a castle (one of the Medici's) on a typical Tuscan hill, the procession winds down on the left through a rocky and forested landscape as it approaches the viewer and then crosses the foreground from left to right. The young king is center right, in white and gold garments, his sword and gift of myrrh held up by pages riding on the right. Behind him, a small hunting party chases uphill. Following the king is a crowded procession with many famous people. The king himself may be an idealized portrait envisioning the future adult Lorenzo de' Medici (who was only ten at the time of the painting). Following him on a white horse is the current family leader, Piero the Gouty, next to whom is the family founder, Cosimo I, on a mule. This front row is completed with portraits of two noble allies, Galeazzo Maria Sforza, soon to be Duke of Milan, and Sigismondo Pandolfo Malatesta, Lord of Rimini (right to left). Two rows behind them, the central face under a trapezoidal red beret is a self-portrait of Gozzoli, identified by his name on the hat brim. Directly in front of him are the two Medici sons at their current ages: Giuliano (six), partly hidden by Lorenzo (ten), the eldest son, identifiable by his unusual saddle nose.

Surrounding these historical figures and throughout the remaining walls' paintings are many others, including the next-to-last Byzantine emperor (who visited Florence in 1439), more Medici family members, and their retainers. But identifiable people comprise only about a tenth of the faces in the works, which overflow with a rich variety of individuals, most of whom were probably portraits as well. The painting's composition is bilateral, the left side showing the serpentine procession, the right side showing the rocky hill with the hunt. They are divided by a slender tree in the middle and unified by the procession crossing the foreground. The costumes are rich and brightly colored and provide a vehicle for Gozzoli to show his skill at portraying the textures of animals, rich fabrics, precious metals, and jewels, as well as people. After the wet-painted fresco dried, Gozzoli added touches of glossy lacquer and gold leaf to glimmer in the dim candlelight. In addition to these details, Gozzoli demonstrates his mastery of depth in the foreshortening of horses on the left. Rigorous linear perspective is absent, since there are no man-made straight lines in most of the painting, but figures' sizes are roughly proportionate to their distance. Several motives inspire the work: a record of historical figures, religious devotion (especially that of the family members portrayed), ostentation, and patronage—tangible evidence of the Medici generosity toward the arts and letters.

The Adoration of the Magi was a popular theme in contemporary Florence. A related work (1475/76) by Sandro Botticelli was motivated by flattery as well as ostentation. (See Figure 10.13.) Commissioned for his family chapel by a Medici hanger-on (a lesser Florentine banker of dubious ethics), the work is thickly populated by Medici family members. In front of a background row of colossal Roman columns, a rustic ruin of crumbling stone walls and a wood-beamed roof shelters the Holy Family. Mary, in front of a resting Saint Joseph, holds the infant Jesus, before whom the aged Cosimo de' Medici kneels and touches the babe's feet. There is disagreement about the identities of the other figures. It is probably Piero in the foreground, in the scarlet cape; Giuliano kneels to his right, with Giovanni standing behind in the red-striped black cape. The saddle nose identifies Lorenzo standing at the far left in front of his horse. Two figures on the right return the viewer's gaze. The blond man in the foreground may be Botticelli, while the white-haired man in the middle of the last row is the shifty banker patron who ordered the work.

The painting's composition is innovative and ingenious. The Magi and retainers are grouped around the Holy Family instead of moving forward in a line. Piero's red cape, the greatest visual weight in the work, forms an arrowhead pointing at the Christ child. Following the figures' gazes leads the viewer into, then back and forth

FIGURE 10.13 Sandro Botticelli (1445–1510), *Adoration of the Magi* (1475/6), tempera on wood, 111 × 134 cm, Uffizi, Florence.

across, the painting, finally coming to rest on the Christ child. The colors are brilliant and the drawing precise and detailed—even the backdrop, which, however, does not conform strictly to the rules of perspective. But that slip can be overlooked among the rich details of this entrancing sacred work.

In addition to his sacred commissions, Botticelli also painted one of the most controversial secular paintings of the time, *The Birth of Venus* (Figure 10.14). The work's origin is not known, although a Medici family member may have commissioned it. In the center, Venus stands on the lip of a scallop shell as she arrives at the shore. She is nude but modest, in the *Venus pudica* posture, with right hand covering her breasts and left hand holding a flowing tress of hair over her pubic triangle. She stands in exaggerated *contrapposto*, with left leg bent and weight on the right. On the left, two flying allegorical figures waft Venus to shore with their flower-bearing breath. They are Zephyrus, the west wind, who carries Aura, the gentle breeze. On the right, Flora, goddess of spring, brings a robe for the goddess, in front of a grove. In addition to the flying winds, there are other dreamlike, almost surreal qualities to the work. Venus is standing in a position tilted enough to defy gravity, on the edge of a shell that would certainly spill her if she had weight. The ripples in the sea are almost unreal, and the grove is geometric in its perfection.

The painting seems to show a vision or dream of Venus's birth, appropriate for a myth. At least three places claimed her: two Greek islands, Kythera and Cyprus, and the

FIGURE 10.14 Sandro Botticelli (1445–1510), *The Birth of Venus* (1486), tempera on wood, 278 × 172 cm, Uffizi, Florence.

Italian location of Portovenere. Her painted figure is modeled on the ancient Venus statues that were being discovered at that time, like the *Aphrodite of Cnidus* (Figure 7.8). Another possible model, very like Botticelli's figure, is known as the *Venus de' Medici* (Figure 10.15). When the family acquired the statue is unknown; it is not recorded until an inventory of 1638, but a miniature copy had appeared in 1559. It is likely that Botticelli was aware of it and used it for a model, although he had to guess at the position of the arms, which were only restored later by a seventeenth-century sculptor. For the face, Botticelli may have used the most beautiful woman in Florence, Simonetta Vespucci, who had died ten years before and supposedly came from Portovenere. But the painting's meaning goes beyond the obvious. Although controversial because it represented a nude pagan goddess, the painting's Venus might have symbolized divine love, which was also associated with the Virgin Mary. Such a combination would have fit the Neoplatonic philosophy of the day, which tried to amalgamate pagan and Christian beliefs.

A more conventional type of secular painting was the portrait, and Leonardo da Vinci was one of its greatest masters. His portrait of *Ginevra de' Benci* (Figure 10.16) is the only work of his displayed in the Western Hemisphere.[4] Ginevra, daughter of a wealthy Florentine family, was sixteen when she sat for the painting, which may have commemorated her marriage. She sits before two juniper trees, one of which fills the left background; the other frames her face. Its Italian name, *ginepro*, is a pun on hers. The right background shows a placid pool in a misty twilight, with lacy brown trees in the foreground fading to blue hills, trees, and village church steeples in the background. The painting is in excellent condition for its five-and-a-half-century age, with only a few hairline cracks in the surface of Ginevra's upper chest, although it stops just below the top of her bodice; arms and hands may have been trimmed off long ago.

Ginevra bears a calm, solemn expression. Her complexion is fashionably white, her hair a dark blond. Her eyes are brown, and her lips and cheeks are a delicate pink. She wears a sheer cream-colored shift with one tiny gold button under a rich brown dress with a gold border on its square collar and gold grommets for the blue lacings of the bodice. Around her neck is a deep brown stole, possibly velvet. The precision of Leonardo's drawing shows especially in the juniper needles, her eyelids, the delicate halo of curls that frame her face, and the filmy delicacy of her shift, barely visible on her skin. Leonardo also employed a characteristic technique of his in the portrait: *sfumato*. In the general sense, this is the use of blurred outlines rather than crisp, dark lines. The result is actually more natural than outline drawing, as anyone knows who has blown up a digital photograph to find outlines very difficult to see among the thousands of pixels in fine gradations of color and value. *Sfumato* serves two functions in Ginevra's portrait: it shows the delicate contours of her lower eyelids, cheeks, and neck, as well as a certain atmospheric haze that complements the bluish aerial perspective of the background scene.[5]

Leonardo and Alberti both described aerial perspective, the third method for showing depth in painting. In overlap (the oldest and simplest), an object or figure in front covers

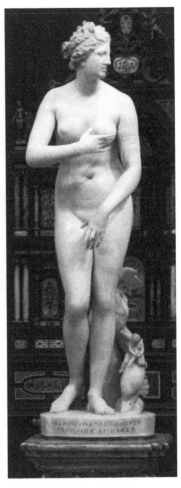

FIGURE 10.15 Cleomenes (?), *Aphrodite (Venus de' Medici)*, Roman copy (original ca. 200 BCE), marble, 155 cm, Uffizi, Florence.

---

4   I was truly torn between including this work or the *Mona Lisa*, possibly the most famous painting of all time. I chose *Ginevra* for several reasons: the work is in the United States and therefore more accessible to American students; it is also in better condition than the *Mona Lisa*, and it demonstrates Leonardo's meticulous precision and care. The painting's journey is also a romantic tale. Owned by the Prince of Liechtenstein, a tiny country once part of the Austro-Hungarian Empire, the prince requested permission from the WW II Nazi government to remove household items (including the painting) from his palace in Vienna to his castle in the principality. Some years after the war, in financial difficulties, he sold the painting to the National Gallery in Washington, DC.

5   As his style developed, *sfumato* became one of Leonardo's signature techniques. Indeed, the *Mona Lisa*, thirty years later, uses almost no crisp outlines for the features.

FIGURE 10.16 Leonardo da Vinci (1452–1519), *Ginevra de' Benci* (1474), oil on wood, 38 × 37 cm, National Gallery of Art, Washington, DC.

FIGURE 10.17 Donatello (1388–1466), *David* (ca. 1430), cast bronze, 158 cm, Bargello Museum, Florence.

part of one behind. In linear perspective (described above), the objects' or figures' sizes are regulated proportionally to their distances from the viewer. (Foreshortening, the depiction of an elongated object from its end, is a related concept.) Aerial perspective in painting uses color to recreate the effect of the atmosphere on distant things. Light near the blue-purple end of the visible spectrum has shorter and therefore higher-energy wavelengths than those at the red-orange end of the spectrum. In traveling through the atmosphere, the less energetic wavelengths are lost, so the farther away an object is, the more blue or violet is its color. The loss of color contrast also makes details less visible. A particularly striking example is to drive west across the Great Plains until one sees the distant Rocky Mountains rising blue from the horizon. The sky is blue partly for the same reason, although atmospheric scattering also plays a role in sky color. Light bouncing off mist droplets can produce blurring of outlines, and dust or fumes can shift the color toward red or brown, as in sunsets and smoggy conditions.

The new, free naturalism of the Renaissance also arose in sculpture. Donatello's bronze *David* (Figure 10.17) was the first freestanding male nude since antiquity. Its background and date are uncertain, although it may have been commissioned by Cosimo de' Medici for the courtyard of his new *palazzo*. David stands in a pronounced *contrapposto*, with his weight on the right leg and the left leg bent at nearly ninety degrees, since the foot rests on the helmet on Goliath's severed head. The left hand rests on his hip, while the large sword in his right hand touches the ground. David gazes pensively downward, his long locks spreading over his shoulders. His only clothing is a brimmed hat or helmet with a laurel garland (a symbol of victory) and knee-length boots with open toes. His right foot rests on one wing of Goliath's helmet, while the other wing brushes David's leg up to his knee. The work is beautifully and naturally fluid in its shape and posture, but close inspection suggests that Donatello was not able to study human anatomy through dissection. A short list of the slight inaccuracies includes an overly smooth border of the ribs at the abdomen, insufficient definition of the bands of abdominal muscle, unclear modeling of the thigh and forearm muscles, and elbows a trifle too sharp and angular. The statue's overall grace and beauty surmount these minor problems, though, in a work that revolutionized sculpture in its time.

Other artists also created statues of David during Donatello's lifetime and after. The symbolism of a small figure of righteousness triumphing over an evil giant was especially vital in Florence, a small republic surrounded by powerful monarchies. The next renowned *David* is that of Michelangelo Buonarroti (Figure 10.18). Originally commissioned to stand atop a buttress of the Florence cathedral, its great size and weight were impossible to raise thirty-five meters safely, so it was erected before the Florence city hall (*palazzo vecchio*) as a symbol of Florence's independence. Whereas Donatello portrayed David after his victory, Michelangelo chose the boy's moment of preparation. David stands at rest, in *contrapposto*, weight on the right leg, with the left leg lightly extended forwards and to the side. David's right arm hangs down, holding the stone(s), while his left arm is bent at the elbow to grasp the sling over his shoulder with which he will make the fatal

FIGURE 10.18 Michelangelo Buonarroti (1488–1566), *David* (1501–1504), marble, 5.17 m, Accademia Museum, Florence.

throw. He looks to the left intently, taking his opponent's measure. All anatomical details—bony prominences, muscles, tendons, even the veins on the dependent right hand—are precise and accurate, perhaps even slightly exaggerated, as Michelangelo often did. This accuracy results from Michelangelo's having been able to dissect the bodies of executed criminals, permitted by Pope Sixtus IV and his successors.

Renaissance Arts in Rome

While Florence is usually regarded as the cradle of the Renaissance, Rome, the center of the pope's power and wealth, quickly assumed an equal or greater importance in artistic development. A major reason was the popes' decision to replace Constantine's Basilica of Saint Peter. To understand this, background is important.

The Roman emperor Nero first martyred Christians, blaming them for the burning of Rome. Many of these killings took place in a circus (U-shaped stadium) built by Emperor Caligula on the Vatican side of the Tiber. Saint Peter, the first bishop of Rome, was crucified upside down in that circus and buried in a cemetery beside it (Figure 10.19). The walled city

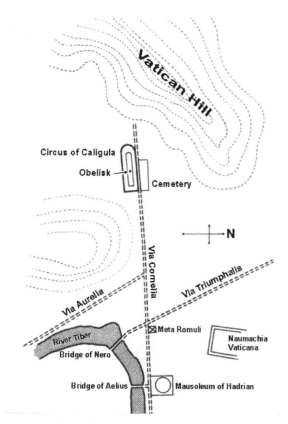

Plan of the Vatican side of the Tiber River in the second century CE showing Hadrian's tomb and the circus of Caligula (later of Nero), with the cemetery beside it.

Tombs lining the road leaving the Roman city of Pompeii.

Tomb of the emperor Hadrian (76–138 CE, crowned 117), across the Tiber from the ancient city. Originally crowned with an artificial hill and grove of trees, the tomb was converted into a defensive castle by medieval popes.

of Rome proper was on the left bank of the Tiber (the figure's lower left corner). The right bank was a developing suburban area with housing, a temple, a boat basin for naval spectacles (*naumachia*), a fortified hill (left) and the circus, which stood between the two hills. Next to the circus was a cemetery, partly for victims of the circus "games," but also for burial of ordinary Romans, since, in ancient Roman cities, burial of the deceased was forbidden within the city walls. All tombs were erected outside them (Figure 10.20). The largest of these tombs was built by the emperor Hadrian in 127 CE, shown at the bottom of Figure 10.19. In the Middle Ages, it was converted into the pope's fortress, the Castel Sant' Angelo (Figure 10.21).

The Castel Sant' Angelo (Mausoleum of Hadrian) is a landmark on the Vatican side of the Tiber, directly east of the position of the ancient circus and cemetery associated with St. Peter. Figure 10.22a reconstructs the positions of the circus and cemetery as demolition began in the fourth century, The central spine contained an obelisk looted from Egypt by the emperor Caligula, the only construction left untouched for centuries. A large public building flanked the circus, next to the cemetery of small streets lined with tombs. A temple stood on the hill behind. Christians revered the spots where St. Peter was martyred and buried and preserved the memory of them. When Christianity became legal in 313 CE, they built a church over the grave (323–350) and preserved the obelisk near the site of the saint's crucifixion. Figure 10.22b reconstructs the completed church a few years later, with remnants of the circus and cemetery, and the

FIGURE 10.22A A reconstruction of the demolition of the Circus of Caligula/Nero and neighboring structures, ca. 318 CE. Note the cemetery's rows of tombs uphill from the circus.

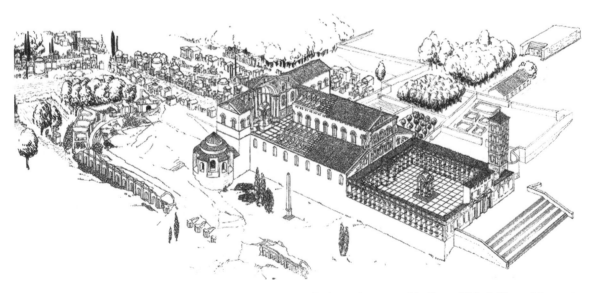

FIGURE 10.22B A reconstruction of the completion of the original St. Peter's Basilica, with remnants of the Circus of Caligula/Nero and the cemetery, after 350 CE. The new church is on top of some tombs.

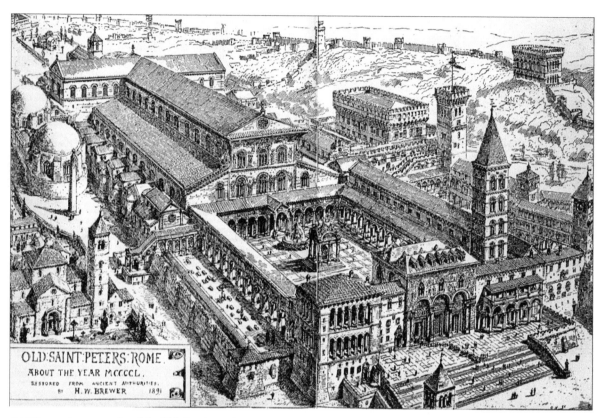

FIGURE 10.23 A reconstruction of the old St. Peter's in 1450.

foundations of the destroyed temple behind. At this time, the pope lived in the city proper, so there was as yet no palace adjoining the church.

During the "Babylonian Captivity" (see Chapter 9) and the Great Schism, St. Peter's was neglected. When the popes returned to Rome, they found the church deteriorating badly. By the 1450s, Leon Battista Alberti recorded that one wall was six feet from vertical and verging on collapse. Pope Nicholas V began repairs but also commissioned a plan for a new building and demolished part of the Colosseum for its stone. Foundations for a new larger choir and transept were completed to enlarge the altar end of the old church, but after the pope's death, work was abandoned and resumed only under Pope Julius II in 1505. Actual construction resumed in 1506 under Donato Bramante (architect 1506–14), who designed a completely new domed Greek cross (arms of equal length) and began the dome piers. Following Bramante's death in 1514, a long series of architects continued construction. Figure 10.24 is a list of the most important architects of St. Peter's.

A visiting Dutch artist in the 1530s recorded the construction's disruption. Figure 10.25 shows the new church's hub at the crossing, viewed through the right transept end with the apse on its right. On the left is the remnant of the old church (with the cross over the entrance); in front of that, the building with battlements is the Sistine Chapel. Everything is surrounded by piles of dirt. Figure 10.26 shows a view down the nave of the old Saint Peter's toward the new construction. Bramante's enormous arches dwarf the older church. The

1506–1514	Donato Bramante began piers of dome.	Began dome piers, apse & transept vaults; Greek cross plan
1514–1516	Giuliano Sangallo briefly; he had worked on the church in the 1470s.	
1514–1520	Fra Giocondo da Verona & Raffaello Sanzio (Raphael)	Designed a Latin cross plan
1520–1536	Baldassare Peruzzi	
1536–1546	Antonio da Sangallo, Giuliano's nephew, promoted, after working on the church since 1513.	Strengthened cracking dome piers; returned to Greek cross
1547–1564	Michelangelo Buonarroti	Restored, simplified and strengthened Bramante's Greek cross plan. Completed dome drum
1564–1573	Jacopo Barozzi	
(1586)	(Domenico Fontana, Assistant Architect)	Moved obelisk to front piazza
1573–1602	Giacomo della Porta	Completed small domes between transept & nave and main dome (1590)
1605–1606		Demolition of last remnant of old St. Peter's
1607–1629	Carlo Maderno	Completed nave in Latin cross to cover entire area of old church, façade (1615), rebuilt steps (1617), rehung doors (1619)—church complete!

Finishing Touches

1626	Dedication of church—176 years after first conception, 120 years after Bramante's beginning
1624–1633	Interior furnishings by Gian Lorenzo Bernini—Baldacchino over altar, Chair of Peter and Gloria in apse
1612/14, 1667	Fountains flanking obelisk in piazza—first on the right by Maderno, that on the left by Bernini
1657–1670s	Piazza colonnade completed to Bernini's design

FIGURE 10.25 Maarten van Heemskerck (1498–1547), St. Peter's Basilica under construction (1536), pen and ink on paper, Gemäldegalerie, Berlin. The view is from the right transept of the new construction, with the remaining nave of Old St. Peter's on the left and part of the Sistine Chapel in front of it.

FIGURE 10.26 Maarten van Heemskerck, St. Peter's, nave under construction (1536), pen and ink on paper, 22 × 27 cm, Gemäldegalerie, Berlin. The remnant of Old St. Peter's is in the foreground with the elevated organ cabinet on the right. Behind the gap in the walls is the new construction, with Bramante's vaults towering above a temple-like structure that protected the saint's grave.

temple-like building was built to house and protect St. Peter's grave; the cabinet on stilts on the right is the old organ.

Over the many years of construction, the church's design changed with nearly every architect, as each tried to make his own mark on the church while satisfying the current pope. For comparison, the most significant plans are in Figure 10.27.

Over the decades, the design went through several revisions, influenced by considerations of aesthetics, structural soundness, and theological worries about holy ground. Bramante's Greek cross was briefly superseded by Raphael's Latin cross plan (longer nave) that was never begun. The dome piers needed reinforcement in ensuing decades, then Michelangelo took over until his own death in 1564; he continued the Greek cross plan and completed the drum of the dome, which he had entirely redesigned. In addition to the plan changes, the exterior design also went through several modifications (see Figures 10.28 and 10.29).

Bramante's plan (Figure 10.27a) and his exterior design, shown on Caradosso's medal (Figure 10.28a), are rather fussy, with many small cavities and repeated domes and pediments. His main dome (Figure 10.28b) is higher than that of the Pantheon (Figure 8.15) and busy but still a bit squat. Sangallo's profile (10.29a) is busy, with its many levels of colonnades, even on the dome; the dome's lantern is broader and somewhat bulbous. In contrast, Michelangelo's plan (10.27c) and profile (10.29b) are simpler and elegant in their genius. In the plan, the thicker piers and wall give greater underpinning to the dome and vaults' enormous weights, and elimination of minor apses and cavities achieves a refined simplicity of a cross enfolded in a square. Similarly, on the exterior profile, Michelangelo brings elegance with a device invented by Alberti (see above, perspective)—the colossal order. A colossal order uses very tall columns to frame two (usually) stories defined by smaller columns. This device unifies Michelangelo's design and uses the progression of column size to mediate between the gigantic church and human scale. Michelangelo also elevates Bramante's

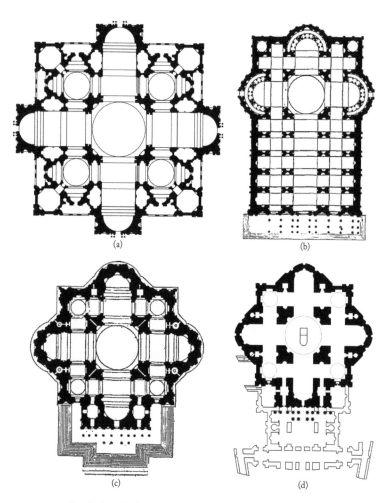

(a)

(b)

(c)

(d)

FIGURE 10.27 Plan Designs for St. Peter's Basilica a. Bramante's Greek cross, 1506; b. Raphael's Latin cross, 1516; c. Michelangelo's Greek cross, 1547; d. Maderno's Latin cross superimposed on Michelangelo's design, 1615. Michelangelo simplified Bramante's design and used thicker, stronger walls and piers. Maderno followed Michelangelo's design up to the point where he lengthened the nave.

FIGURE 10.28A Caradosso (Cristoforo Foppa, 1445–ca. 1527), medal celebrating Bramante's beginning the new St. Peter's (1506), gold.

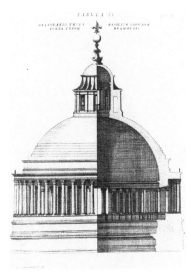

FIGURE 10.28B Bramante's design for St. Peter's dome (1506).

FIGURE 10.29A Sangallo's design for St. Peter's Basilica, from the entrance.

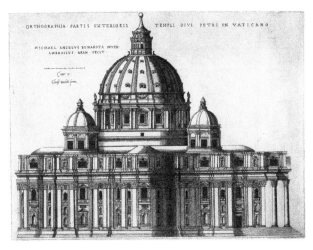

FIGURE 10.29B Michelangelo's design for St. Peter's Basilica, from the side.

dome design and simplifies Sangallo's. In the final construction, the dome's height is increased even higher by having an oval profile instead of a sphere. The altar end of the church (Figure 10.30) shows the part of the actual building constructed to Michelangelo's designs.

A critical refinement provides the finishing touch. The "Golden Section" proportion governs the relationships of many of the building's components, especially the relation between the colossal order and the total height. The proportion is an ancient one that has

FIGURE 10.30 St. Peter's Basilica from the apse end, showing the part completed according to Michelangelo's design.

been found or designed in several of the fine arts as well as in the natural sciences and mathematics. It seems to define the most perfect, most appealing relationship among the parts of a work. As shown in Figure 10.31, the Golden Section is the proportion that divides a straight line into two parts, such that the proportion of the larger division to the whole line equals the proportion of the smaller division to the larger one: a / (a + b) = b / a; that is, 1:1.618 or 0.618:1 (slightly less than two-thirds). The appeal of this relationship cannot be explained—even the number is irrational, but works of art designed with this ratio seem the most perfect from the human point of view. We have already seen hints of it in Brunelleschi's Basilica of San Lorenzo in Florence (Figure 10.9), and it is quite obvious in the façade of St. Peter's, as designed by Carlo Maderno (Figure 10.32). The columns and pilasters (rectangular column-like projections built into the wall) of the façade's colossal order are in exact proportion to its height by the ratio of the Golden Section.

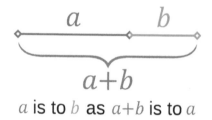

a is to *b* as *a+b* is to *a*

FIGURE 10.31 The Golden Section or Golden Ratio—1.618 to 1.0 (or 1.0 to 0.618).

Appointed in 1602, Maderno demolished the last remnants of the old St. Peter's and completed the new church on a Latin cross plan in 1615 (Figure 10.27d). In 1617, the steps were completed, and in 1619, the doors were re-hung. Attempts to place matching bell towers on either side were thwarted by inadequate foundations, and in 1626, the church was dedicated. The 175-year project was complete. By this time, art had entered a new stylistic period, the Baroque, so discussion of the church's furnishings and extensions await the next chapter. It is near miraculous that such a series of architects over such an extended time should have produced an enormous building of such visual harmony and beauty, in addition to its being the largest church in Christendom. The magnitude and complexity of the project demonstrate the enormous artistic and technological advances made in the Renaissance, although funding the enormous cost played a role in the Protestant Reformation.[6]

Why, then, the prodigious effort? There is a tradition of more than 1,700 years that the bones of St. Peter rest beneath the basilica's high altar. Under the floor of St. Peter's today

---

6   When the pope allowed an indulgence for forgiveness of sins to large contributors, it was interpreted by many in the north to be a required payment for absolution. Repugnant to Martin Luther and many others, the practice aroused tremendous opposition and, ultimately, religious division and war; the Catholic Church responded in midcentury with reforms at the Council of Trent, leading to the Counter-Reformation.

there are two levels: the modern crypt, or grotto, and below that, the ancient cemetery or necropolis. Constantine's fourth-century church was built to place the altar directly over a site that was revered as the last resting place of St. Peter, who had been crucified in the adjacent circus, near the obelisk in its center. Every high altar since has been built over that same place. Around 1940, excavations found a red wall in the holy spot with remnants of a small shrine (*aedicula*). Nearby was a *graffito* that said "πετροσ ενι" ("*petros en i*"—"Peter is within"). (See Figure 10.33.) Under the *aedicula* in the red wall, near the inscription, were found the bones of a robust man who died in his sixties about 1,950 years ago. The inscriptions and other evidence support the traditional belief that the basilica's high altar is directly over St. Peter's grave. Hence the enormous efforts over two thousand years to protect, hallow, and venerate this place.

But St. Peter's was just the most obvious of many creations of genius in sixteenth-century Rome. Next to the work in progress, Pope Sixtus IV commissioned a new private chapel for (and ultimately named after) himself. It was built on

FIGURE 10.32 The main entrance to St. Peter's, with Maderno's façade, with the top of Michelangelo's large dome. In the foreground is the ancient obelisk.

the dimensions of the Temple of Solomon (41 × 14 m) and decorated by the greatest artists of the time. Figure 10.34 shows its appearance in 1480. The most famous picture of this initial design is Perugino's *Christ Giving St. Peter the Keys of Heaven*, noted for its balanced foreground and middle ground with the nearly symmetrical background, the meticulous perspective, and the vivid colors (Figure 10.35). The picture depicts Christ's metaphorical words to Peter: "I will give you the keys of Paradise …" (Matthew 16:19). Perugino's painting and the chapel that it adorned were two of the most significant artistic productions in fifteenth-century Rome's last decades, but that was about to change. A few years later, a French cardinal commissioned a tomb statue from Michelangelo, who brought it to Rome in 1499.

The *Pietà* (Figure 10.36) was the work that brought Michelangelo fame. It depicts the Blessed Virgin Mary supporting the dead Christ in her lap after his removal from the cross. Christ lies supine, with his head to Mary's right and his knees bent over hers on the left. A young Mary gazes down in sorrowful peace while gesturing with her left hand (although the precise position may be an eighteenth-century alteration). Christ is naked except for a drape over his pelvis, and Mary is heavily robed. The drapes over her knees fall fluidly, while those over her chest are slightly rumpled by the body's position. The white Carrara marble

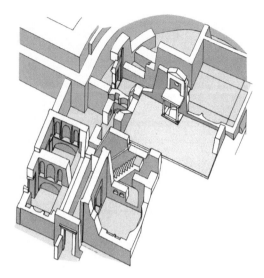

FIGURE 10.33 Reconstruction of the area around the tomb of St. Peter. Red = aedicula and Red Wall; Blue = Pre-Constantinian tombs; Green = The apse of the old St. Peter's basilica.

FIGURE 10.34 Reconstruction of the appearance of the Sistine Chapel in the 1480s (nineteenth-century engraving). The starry ceiling was used in many contemporary churches. The bands of paintings include painted draperies on the bottom, scenes of Christ's life on the right (visible), Moses's life on the left, and Popes' portraits between the windows. The small balcony was for singers. The screen was later moved back to the near side of the singers' gallery.

FIGURE 10.35 Perugino (Pietro Vannucci, c. 1446–1523), *Christ Giving St. Peter the Keys of Heaven* (1481–82), fresco, 3.35 × 5.5 m, Sistine Chapel, Vatican City.

FIGURE 10.36 MIchelangelo, *Pietà* (1499), Carrara marble, 174 × 195 cm, St. Peter's Basilica, Vatican City.

is beautifully finished in a high polish. The work adorned the cardinal's tomb until it was moved to its present location in St. Peter's in the eighteenth century. Michelangelo's genius was recognized by Cardinal Giuliano della Rovere (nephew of Pope Sixtus), who later became Pope Julius II (see discussion of Figure 1.7).

Julius engaged Michelangelo to build for him the largest tomb of any pope, but it was modified repeatedly over the decades, as shown in Figures 10.37 and 10.38. Initially planned as a monstrous freestanding structure with more than forty statues, the tomb was subject to numerous delays and funding problems. A dispute over it (between Michelangelo and the pope), the pope's death, and disputes with the pope's heirs prolonged its construction and led to much reduction in size. The final tomb (Figure 10.38) is against a wall and includes just seven full figures—only one by Michelangelo—and is not even in St. Peter's. Nevertheless, Michelangelo considered the central statue of Moses his most lifelike and supposedly cried, "Now speak," striking it with his hammer and leaving a scar visible on the knee. The original bottom level included prisoners in various degrees of bondage, symbolizing escape from the slavery of sin. Two of these were completed and are now in the Louvre in Paris. Other incomplete ones are in the Accademia Gallery in Florence, where they line the colonnade leading to Michelangelo's *David*.

The unfinished slaves vividly reveal Michelangelo's philosophy of artistic creation. He believed that he did not carve a statue in the stone; rather, he freed or liberated a form

FIGURE 10.37A Michelangelo, Tomb of Julius II, 1505 project. This figure shows only the end view of the planned huge free-standing structure with over forty statues.

FIGURE 10.37B Michelangelo, Tomb of Julius II, 1513 project. This and later revisions placed the tomb against a wall and kept reducing the number of statues.

FIGURE 10.37C Michelangelo, Tomb of Julius II, 1516 project.

FIGURE 10.37D Michelangelo, Tomb of Julius II, 1531 project.

that already existed. This concept is closely related to the Neoplatonic philosophy, developed in his time, which argued that abstract perfect forms underlay all visible reality. Michelangelo's working method reflects this concept. He carved freehand, starting from the front and working around to the back, as if the figure were gradually emerging from a pool of water. All of these concepts are visible in *Young Slave* (Figure 10.39). The torso arches slightly as the figure seems about to stretch its arms and pull its legs free, its left hand pulling away from the stone still imprisoning its head. Behind this clear anatomy is rough stone, from which the figure seems to emerge as it awakens.

FIGURE 10.38 Michelangelo, Tomb of Julius II as completed (1545), Church of San Pietro in Vincoli (St. Peter in Chains), Rome. The central Moses is by Michelangelo, and Leah and Rachel, flanking him, are by his apprentice, Raffaello da Montelupo (c. 1504–c. 1567).

FIGURE 10.39 Michelangelo, *Young Slave*, for the Tomb of Julius II, Accademia Gallery, Florence.

According to Giorgio Vasari (perhaps the first art historian), Bramante and Raphael, jealous of Michelangelo's tomb commission, convinced the pope it would be bad luck to have his tomb built during his lifetime and that Michelangelo's time would be better spent on the Sistine Chapel ceiling in the Vatican Palace. They assumed that Michelangelo, primarily a sculptor, would have great difficulty in completing a painting of such scale—Michelangelo finished, in only four years, one of the greatest works of art in the world! The ceiling contains more than three hundred figures in a complex program, seen in Figures 10.40 and 10.41.

The pope originally wanted paintings of the twelve apostles. We may be thankful that Michelangelo convinced him otherwise. The central story is that of Creation and early biblical history. These nine panels are in green on the diagram. In the corners (corner spandrels, or pendentives) are four Old Testament stories related to the salvation of the Jewish people. Over the windows in triangular spandrels and semicircular lunettes (not on the diagram) are the ancestors of Christ from the beginning of the New Testament.[7] Between them are alternating figures of Old Testament prophets and the famous pagan sibyls, or oracles. The mingling of these two groups is part of Michelangelo's Neoplatonist mixture of Christian and pagan virtues.

---

7   The Gospels of Matthew, Chapter 1 and Luke, Chapter 3.

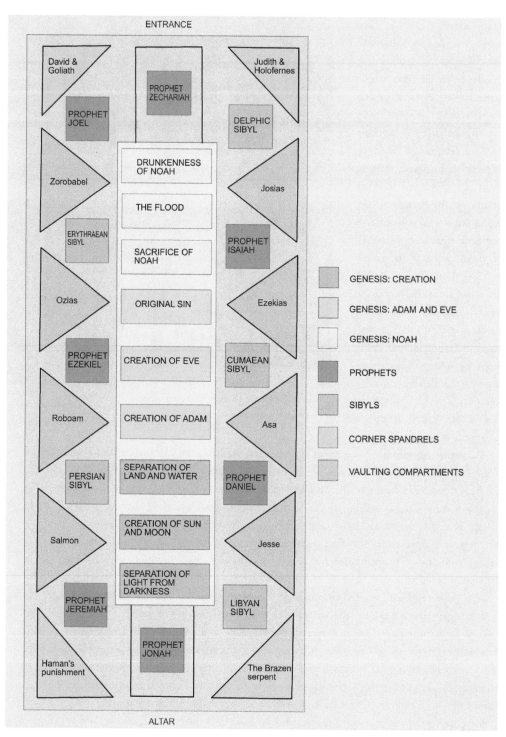

ENTRANCE

David & Goliath

PROPHET JOEL

Zorobabel

ERYTHRAEAN SIBYL

Ozias

PROPHET EZEKIEL

Roboam

PERSIAN SIBYL

Salmon

PROPHET JEREMIAH

Haman's punishment

PROPHET ZECHARIAH

DRUNKENNESS OF NOAH

THE FLOOD

SACRIFICE OF NOAH

ORIGINAL SIN

CREATION OF EVE

CREATION OF ADAM

SEPARATION OF LAND AND WATER

CREATION OF SUN AND MOON

SEPARATION OF LIGHT FROM DARKNESS

PROPHET JONAH

Judith & Holofernes

DELPHIC SIBYL

Josias

PROPHET ISAIAH

Ezekias

CUMAEAN SIBYL

Asa

PROPHET DANIEL

Jesse

LIBYAN SIBYL

The Brazen serpent

GENESIS: CREATION

GENESIS: ADAM AND EVE

GENESIS: NOAH

PROPHETS

SIBYLS

CORNER SPANDRELS

VAULTING COMPARTMENTS

ALTAR

FIGURE 10.40 Michelangelo, Diagram of the Sistine Ceiling Frescoes. This diagram and the view of the ceiling that follows show all of the central portion but not the lunettes on the walls around the windows.

Obviously, there is no room here to discuss the entire ceiling. A few representative examples must suffice. Michelangelo presents many more family members of Christ's ancestors than are listed in the Bible; many of them are not clearly identified. The lunette in Figure 10.42 shows Zadok the priest and his father, Azor. The awkward shape of the lunettes means that most of the figures in them are back to back, as these are. The coloring of the robes is significant; it demonstrates a Renaissance technique called *cangiante*, of which Michelangelo was the great master. Where a particular color could not be made light or dark enough for shading, another color was used. Zadok's robes (on the left) use lavender and salmon shading, while Azor's use lavender and yellow.

Cangiante is also significant in the robes of two persons encountered in previous chapters, the Delphic Sybil (Chapter 7, and Figure 10.43) and the prophet Daniel (Chapter 9, and Figure 10.44). The Sybil's inner gown and the robe on Daniel's right knee use yellow and green; Daniel's underrobe uses lavender and red. All of the figures mentioned have poses twisted to some degree, especially Daniel. Others on the ceiling are even more extreme. This twisting is one of the ways in which Michelangelo's work began to move beyond the Renaissance style toward its successor. The transitional style is called Mannerism and includes exaggeration and transformation of Renaissance characteristics, like twisted or stylized poses, distorted proportions, diagonal composition, and an increased sense of motion.

The last two are evident in the most famous of the Sistine ceiling scenes, *The Creation of Adam* (Figure 10.45). Adam reclines on a green hillside, his left arm extended to God the Father, who flies toward him enveloped in billowing maroon draperies and supported by a throng of wingless angels. God reaches toward Adam with his right hand to

FIGURE 10.41 Michelangelo, Sistine Ceiling Frescoes (1508–1512), 41 × 14 m, Vatican City.

FIGURE 10.42 Michelangelo, Lunette of Azor and Zadok, Sistine Ceiling Frescoes (1508–1512, 41 × 14 m) Vatican City.

The Arts in the Renaissance   269

Michelangelo, *Delphic Sybil*, Sistine Ceiling.

Michelangelo, *Prophet Daniel*, Sistine Ceiling.

convey the invisible spark of life, finger to finger. The figures' poses and coloring are conservative, fully in keeping with High Renaissance style, but the crowd of angels with the billowing draperies and the sense of flying they convey, plus the strong diagonal of the hillside, which divides the mortal and immortal parts of the picture, are features that move beyond the Renaissance to a new level of expression—that of Mannerism, the precursor of the Baroque.

The Sistine Chapel ceiling had a profound influence on Raphael, who changed his own painting style as a result. Before Michelangelo's ceiling, Raphael had painted one of his most significant works, *The School of Athens* (Figure 10.46). Commissioned to redecorate four rooms in the papal apartments, Raphael gave each room a unique theme. That of the *Stanza della Segnatura* (originally the pope's library, later housing the *Segnatura*, the church supreme court) was the contrast of Christian and pagan virtue. Two walls were Christian in subject, and two were pagan. *The School of Athens* is the greatest of the latter. It shows all of the most famous philosophers of history, beginning with Socrates.

Socrates, however, left no writings, so he is relegated to a side position. In the central focus are Plato, his student, and Aristotle, who followed Plato. Plato, whose philosophy revolved around ideal forms, gestures upward; Aristotle, who wrote about concrete matters, gestures down. There are many portraits of Raphael's contemporaries among the ancients, including several discussed in this chapter. Plato is Leonardo da Vinci; Aristotle, Giuliano da Sangallo; Plotinus (top row, fourth from right) is Donatello; bending down in the foreground, in rust-colored robe and holding calipers, is Bramante, representing Euclid or Pythagoras; across from him, leaning grumpily on a stone block and writing, is Michelangelo as Heraclitus; Raphael appears twice, once second from the far-right middle row as Apelles and again in full-figure white as himself, second behind

FIGURE 10.45 Michelangelo, *The Creation of Adam*, Sistine Ceiling.

FIGURE 10.46 Raffaello Sanzio (Raphael, 1483–1520), *The School of Athens* (1505), fresco, Papal Palace (Vatican Museum).

The Arts in the Renaissance   271

Michelangelo. Other figures hold an identity only from antiquity: eighth on Plato's right, in khaki, is Socrates; sprawled on the steps below Aristotle is Diogenes the Cynic, remembered for telling Alexander the Great to get out of his sun.

Some consider this Raphael's great masterpiece. It certainly demonstrates the classic Renaissance style: balance and variety—the groups of figures on either side are of nearly the same size (some exactly so), yet every figure is in a unique pose. The two large statues in background niches balance each other and show more Classical influence: they are Apollo and Athena. The rest of the background is beautifully symmetrical and in perfect linear perspective, with the focal point between the heads of Plato and Aristotle, and (like Leonardo's *Last Supper*, Figure 2.2) surrounds them with a halo of natural light. Finally, in the background structure, we recognize the vaults of Bramante's St. Peter's (Figure 10.26).

After this explosion of painting by Michelangelo and Raphael was a period of relative calm; the artists turned to other projects, and Raphael died. In 1536, though, the pope hired Michelangelo to complete the work on the Sistine Chapel with the *Last Judgment* over the altar. This may seem an odd place for such a work. In the Middle Ages, the altar was at the east end of the church and symbolized dawn and creation, while the west-end entrance symbolized sunset and the Day of Judgment. St. Peter's was built before this tradition developed, so its altar is in the west end, and the Sistine Chapel faces the same way. Michelangelo's ceiling follows the tradition of beginning Creation above the altar and working toward the back as the story proceeds in time. Nevertheless, he felt quite comfortable painting the *Last Judgment* on the west wall, even if over the altar (see Figure 10.47).

The work is monumental. The wall's windows, visible in Figure 10.34, were covered and the whole wall was frescoed. The composition is conservative: it is organized vertically and horizontally, with little emphasis on diagonals, and groups of figures show both balance and variety. In these respects, the painting is Renaissance in style. Most other aspects of the painting are Manneristic: the violent pose of Christ the Judge in the upper center, the dead rising on his right, and the damned, horrified and falling down to torment, on his left. The top level under the ceiling arches holds symbols of Christ's Passion, the cross, the crown of thorns, and the whipping column. Below these is a horde of saints. The next plane down has the dead rising through the air on the left, angels blowing the last trumpets in the center, and the damned falling on the right. On the bottom, graves open on the left; devils lurk underground; Charon, the mythical ferryman of Hades, whacks at the damned with his oar to drive them from his boat; and damned souls cower and flee on the right. In the bottom right corner, Minos, judge of the damned, wears ass's ears, as in the myth. He is wound around with a snake that chews on his genitals. All of the figures are in motion, and there is a subliminal symbolism in the background. If one views the painting squinting or otherwise out of focus, the areas of blue sky leap out as the cavities of a skull, the symbol of death.

There is space to identify only a few figures, mostly among the saints in heaven. The most complete figure on the left is St. John the Baptist; next, to the right, is St. Andrew with his cross, then the Blessed Virgin and Christ in judgment. Proceeding right, St. Peter holds keys, and on the edge, Simon of Cyrene carries a cross. Many saints carry the instruments of their martyrdoms. Below Simon is Saint Sebastian, holding arrows; moving left again, we encounter St. Catherine with her wheel, and above her, St. Blaise with iron carding combs. Next to him, Dismas, the good thief, holds his cross, and Simon the Zealot holds a saw. Seated on

FIGURE 10.47 Michelangelo, *Last Judgment*, Sistine Chapel Altar Wall, fresco, (1536–1541), 13.7 × 12.2 m, Vatican City.

clouds in the middle are St. Bartholomew holding his skin (Michelangelo's self-portrait) and St. Lawrence holding his grill. One final figure remains to be identified. Biagio da Cesena, the pope's master of ceremonies, said the nude figures were disgraceful in a sacred place and that the painting was suited for a bathhouse. The figure of Minos, with asses' ears, is his portrait. Responding to Cesena's complaint, the pope replied that hell was outside his jurisdiction, so Michelangelo's revenge has survived through the centuries. Regrettably, prudery triumphed. Pope Paul IV had Daniele da Volterra paint draperies over the genitals, which earned him the scornful title *Braghettone*, "Britches-painter." Some of these have been removed in restoration.

Renaissance Music and Dance

Few places or periods in history have had the concentration of artistic genius that flourished in Renaissance Italy (which perhaps justifies the length of this chapter), and the genius permeated the arts: music, theater, and dance. Beginning in the fifteenth century, France and the Low Countries adopted a new musical style they learned from English musicians during the Hundred Years' War. Churches in these northern countries established large choir schools in excess of their own needs and exported musicians trained in the new style throughout Europe. They supplied the greatest singers and composers of the day, and many of them performed in the Sistine Chapel. A chapel at this time was more than a building. It was also the staff—as in a school today. The Sistine Chapel, for centuries, employed the world's most famous choir, made up entirely of priests—adult men, with a very large proportion of the world's greatest composers among them. They were famous for their skill and for performing always without accompaniment.

FIGURE 10.48 Josquin Des Prez (c. 1450–1521) *Ave Maria … Virgo Serena* (polyphonic sacred motet, 4 voices, c. 1485).

Latin Text	Translation	Musical Texture
Ave Maria gratia plena, Dominus tecum, virgo serena.	Hail Mary, full of grace, the Lord is with thee, fair virgin.	Through imitation.
Ave cujus <u>conceptio</u>, solemni plena gaudio coelestia, terrestria, mundum replens laetitia.	Hail to thee, whose <u>conception</u>, full of solemn rejoicing, fills heaven and earth with new happiness.	Paired imitation followed by through imitation.
Ave, cuius <u>nativitas</u> nostra fuit solemnitas, ut Lucifer, lux oriens, verum solem praeveniens.	Hail to thee, whose <u>birth</u> brought our festival, as Lucifer, the light of the east, came before the true sun (son=Christ).	Paired imitation followed by through imitation.
Ave, pia humilitas, sine vero fecunditas, cuius <u>annuntiatio</u> nostra fuit salvatio.	Hail, pious humility, fruitful without a man, whose <u>annunciation</u> brought our salvation.	Paired imitation, then single duet.
Ave, vera virginitas, immaculata castitas, cuius <u>purificatio</u> nostra fuit purgatio.	Hail, true virginity, immaculate chastity, whose <u>purification</u> cleansed us.	Nearly homophonic.
Ave, praeclara omnibus angelicus virtutibus, cuius fuit <u>assumptio</u> nostra glorificatio.	Hail to thee, shining with all angelic virtues, whose <u>assumption</u> made our glorification.	Paired imitation three times.
Mater Dei, memento mei. Amen	O Mother of God, remember me. Amen.	Long, slow notes in homophony; ends on perfect consonance.

The text begins with the the usual Hail Mary prayer, then adds verses praising each of the miraculous events of her life (underlined): Conception, Birth, Annunciation, Purification and Assumption.

The rhythm is regular; the melody uses a standard scale, the harmony is consonant in triads; the texture mixes imitative polyphony with homophony. The timbre is voices; the overall form is through-composed.

The most famous of the Sistine singers was Josquin Desprez (1450–1521), who sang in the chapel from 1489 to 1495. His *Ave Maria, Virgo Serena* (Figure 10.48) demonstrates what made Josquin's work special in his own time. He was one of the first composers to master the art of through-imitation, using imitation which involves all of the voice parts of a texture. For variety, Josquin also uses paired imitation (in which pairs of voices imitate one another) as well as homophony. *Ave Maria, Virgo Serena* contains all of these textures in a sparkling display of polyphonic genius. The work is a wonderful example of the kind of music produced by the Sistine Chapel at this time of artistic ferment.

Florence also nurtured a crucial musical development. While northern musicians explored polyphony and complex innovations, Italian musicians and composers pursued the relationship between the music and the words. Joining this preoccupation with the advanced musical techniques, composers in Italy developed the *madrigal,* the first musical form to express its text's meaning throughout the work and the most significant advance in secular music in the Renaissance. The novelty of text depiction gained such popularity that both northerners and Italian composers wrote many madrigal books for over a century. Jacob Arcadelt (ca. 1507–1568), a northerner, was one of the first composers of the Italian madrigal; he was active in Florence for some time. His work *Il bianco e dolce cigno* (Figure 10.49) uses many musical elements to depict a torrid love tryst.

FIGURE 10.49 Jacob Arcadelt (c. 1507–1568) *Il bianco e dolce cigno* (Italian madrigal, 4 voices).

English Translation	Italian Text	Key Words	Musical Depiction
The white and sweet swan	Il bianco e dolce cigno	*bianco* (white)	Texture—no bass, clear sound
Dies singing. And I	Cantando more. Et io,	*more* (dies)	Melody—falls off
Weeping, arrive at	piangendo, giung' al	*piangendo* (weeping)	Harmony—strange, Eb chord
the end of my life.	fin del viver mio	*fin del viver mio* (end of my life)	Melody—first time, descends
Strange and varied fate,	Stran' e diversa sorte,	*stran' e diversa* (strange and varied)	Texture—one voice offset
That he dies unconsoled,	Ch'ei more sconsolato,	*more sconsolato* (dies unconsoled)	Melody—very narrow range
And I die happy.	Et io moro beato.	*moro beato* (die happy)	Melody—lightly ornamented, more range
A death that in the dying,	Morte che nel morire	*morire* (death)	Harmony—strange, Bb chord
Fills me with joy.	M'empie di gioia	*M'empie di gioia* (fills me with joy)	Harmony—tightly filled major chords, like a barrel of sweets
If in dying I feel no other pain,	Se nel morir altro dolor non sento,	*morir* (death)	Harmony—strange, Bb again
With a thousand deaths a day	Di mille mort' il di	*mille mort' il di* (a thousand deaths a day)	Texture—imitative polyphony
I would be happy.	Sarei contento.	*contento* (happy)	Form—14 repetitions!

The madrigal was the first musical form to depict the text's meaning throughout by "painting" the meaning of specific words or phrases. Any of the musical elements could be used for this—in this case Melody, Harmony, Texture and Form. The rhythm is regular; the timbre is voices; the overall form is through-composed.

The madrigal builds on the legend that a swan only sang at its death, and it uses the common metaphor comparing death with sexual climax. The musical phrases follow the sentences, not the artificial poetic line structure, but there is text (or word) painting on almost every line of poetry. The first text/word painting uses just the top voices, without the bass, for a clear "white" sound to depict the swan. Then comes a falling melody on "*morte*" ("dying") and a chord (E-flat) outside the key on "*piangendo*" ("weeping"). After beginning with homophony, the texture changes to polyphony at "*stran' e diversa sorte*" ("strange and varied fate"). The swan's sad death ("*ei more sconsolato*") has few notes close together, like last gasps. But the lover's death gets a happy, delicately ornamented melody of a slightly wider range on the word "*beato*" ("happy" or "blessed").

The next two lines describe the paradox of death filled with pleasure. Death ("*morte/morire*") again receives an unusual harmony (B-flat) before the music descends to low chords with notes closely spaced—like a jug or barrel packed full of something sweet—for the words "*M'empie di gioia tutt'e di desire*" ("fills me with joy and desire"). In the final two lines, death ("*morir*") again receives the B-flat unusual harmony, then the texture shows the joyful vigor of love with imitative polyphony on "*mille mort' il dì*" ("a thousand deaths a day"), in which a lilting motive is repeated fourteen times as the voices wind among themselves like lovers entwined.

Theater and dance also revived at this time. Niccolò Machiavelli, best known for his political writing, wrote two delightful (and racy) comedies, *La Clizia*, adapted from a play by Plautus, and *La Mandragola* (The Mandrake Root), an original. The Renaissance is also the earliest period in history from which we can actually reconstruct the dances; no earlier choreographies exist. In the fifteenth century, the first manuscript dance manuals appeared. They were written by a few dancing masters for noble courts in Ferrara, Florence, Milan, Naples, and Venice. Because the nobility had time to spare and money for instruction, the dances are complex, with a large vocabulary of steps. They included the *basse danse* and *tourdion*, processional social dances, as well as the *ballo*, a performance dance, and the *saltarello*, a leaping dance. This manuscript tradition continued into the sixteenth century, but in 1589 appeared the first dance print, *Orchésographie*, by Thoinot Arbeau, a French priest who felt obliged to hide his real name, Jehan Tabourot, in an anagram.

Arbeau's book was intended for broad circulation (unlike the single-copy manuscripts), so its dances are simpler, more suited to upper-middle-class merchants, who had less time on their hands. Arbeau's dances (Figure 10.50) include the *pavane* and *galliard* (slow and fast processional dances descended from the *basse danse* and *tourdion*) as well as a standard group of *branles* (circle dances): double branle, single branle, gay branle, and Burgundian branle. He also includes around twenty mimed branles that include movements depicting something: the horse branle—stamp foot and turn like a restless horse; the pease branle—hop like peas from a pod; the Aridan branle, for which I can discern no obvious depiction but is unique nonetheless; the washerwoman branle—wag finger as if scolding; and the official branle, with leaping double sidesteps (although why an official would do that, I don't know—perhaps it mocks political evasiveness)—the tune

The Pavane and Galliard are done in procession, ladies on the gentlemen's right.

A dance (especially the Pavane) should at least begin (and sometimes end) with a Reverence: The gentleman steps back with his right foot, doffs his hat with his left hand, bends his knees slightly and acknowledges the lady, then returns to the dance position. She merely remains in place, bends her knees slightly and looks demurely downward. This can be done on a count of 4, the partners joining hands on the last count.

Pavane	Drum pattern is 1 long + 2 shorts per long beat. 1 step per pattern (= beat)		
Music Count	**Dance Step**		**Action**
1	1	Left Foot Forward	This is a Single.
2	2	Right Foot Together	
3	1	Right Foot Forward	Another Single.
4	2	Left Foot Together	
1	1	Left Foot Forward	This is a Double.
2	2	Right Foot Forward	
3	3	Left Foot Forward	
4	4	Right Foot Together	

Repeat pattern (2 singles & a double) beginning with opposite foot.

Stepping may be done in any direction: forward, backward, or to the side. An interesting variation is for the gentleman to step backwards while the lady advances. In one 4-beat pattern, this will turn the couple 180 degrees. If couples arrive in two lines facing each other, the two lines may also approach and retreat.

	Galliard		
Music Count	**Dance Step**	**Action**	
1	1	Left foot in the air	
2	2	Right foot in the air	
3	3	Left foot in the air	
4	4	Right foot in the air, jump, reverse feet.	
5	—		
6	5	Land with left foot forward	

Repeat pattern beginning with opposite foot.

Foot may be raised in the air in any direction: forward as above, to the back = *ruade*, or to the side = *rue de vache*. This last is ungainly, therefore uncommon. Skilled dancers may also try crossing one foot in front of the other when raised, or a little capriole in the air on beats 4 & 5 (see Chapter 4).

FIGURE 10.50A The Pavane and Galliard from Thoinot Arbeau (Jean Tabourot)—*Orchésographie* (1589).

for this has been adapted as the Christmas carol "Ding, Dong, Merrily on High." There are also other single dances—the allemande, the canary, the *courante*, the morris dance and the Spanish *pavane*, as well as one performance dance, the *bouffons* or buffens, a choreographed sword fight. The two standard dance sets are described in detail in Figures 10.50a and b. Figure 10.50c is a summary of distinctive features of some mimed branles.

Branles are done in a circle, ladies and gentlemen alternating, holding hands.

Double Branle — One step per beat

Music Count	Dance Step	Action	
1	1	Left Foot Left	
2	2	Right Foot Approaches (but does not touch)	This is a Double to the Left.
1	3	Left Foot Left	
2	4	Right Foot Together	
1	1	Right Foot Right	
2	2	Left Foot Approaches	This is a Double to the Right.
1	3	Right Foot Right	
2	4	Left Foot Together	

Repeat pattern (doubles left & right).

Steps left should be a little larger so the circle revolves clockwise (for good luck).

Single (Simple) Branle — One step per beat

Music Count	Dance Step	Action	
1	1	Left Foot Left	
2	2	Right Foot Approaches	This is a Double to the Left.
1	3	Left Foot Left	
2	4	Right Foot Together	
1	1	Right Foot Right	This is a Single to the Right.
2	2	Left Foot Together	

Repeat pattern (doubles left, singles right).

Gay Branle — Fast count of 6

Music Count	Dance Step	Action	
1	1	Right foot in the air	
2	2	Left foot in the air	
3	3	Right foot in the air	This is one pattern.
4	4	Left foot in the air	
5	—	Hold Position	
6	—		

Repeat pattern (always moving slightly to the left).

Burgundian Branle — One step per beat

Music Count	Dance Step	Action	
1	1	Left Foot Left	
2	2	Right Foot Approaches	Burgundian Double Left.
1	3	Left Foot Left	
2	4	Right foot in the air	
1	1	Right Foot Right	
2	2	Left Foot Approaches	Burgundian Double Right.
1	3	Right Foot Right	
2	4	Left foot in the air	

Repeat pattern (Burgundian doubles left & right—basically a Double Branle with a kick). Again, steps left should be a little larger so the circle revolves clockwise. The leader may break the line in any of these dances and lead the dance anywhere in a serpentine fashion.

FIGURE 10.50B Branles: The Standard Set from Thoinot Arbeau (Jean Tabourot)—*Orchésographie* (1589).

All Branles in Circle Formation

Horse Branle

Distinctive Feature—Men, then Women stamp feet and turn, like a horse in a stall.

Pease Branle

Distinctive Feature—Men, women jump once, then each 3 times, like peas popping from pod.

Aridan Branle

Distinctive Feature—Irregular meter; groups of 2, 3, 4 & 6 beats.

Washerwoman Branle

Distinctive Feature—Men shake fingers at women standing hands on hips; this is reversed, all clap.

Official Branle

Distinctive Feature—Leaping doubles, mostly to the left, then man turns and lifts partner into the air.

FIGURE 10.50C Features of Some Mimed Branles from Thoinot Arbeau (Jean Tabourot)—*Orchésographie* (1589).

In all the arts, dance, theater, music, and magnificent visual art and architecture, the Renaissance was a formative period for modern culture, a turning point from the Middle Ages, and a reintegration of knowledge from the ancient world. The arts express the period's deepest conceptions and feelings and give us insight into its people's highest hopes and deepest thoughts—their very souls.

Image Credits

Fig. 10.1: Cimabue / Copyright in the Public Domain.

Fig. 10.2: Giotto di Bondone / Copyright in the Public Domain.

Fig. 10.3: Giotto di Bondone / Copyright in the Public Domain.

Fig. 10.4: Giovanni Pisano; Photo by Mattis / Wikimedia Commons / Copyright in the Public Domain.

Fig. 10.5: F l a n k e r / Wikimedia Commons; Adapted by Ultimate Destiny / Wikimedia Commons / Copyright in the Public Domain.

Fig. 10.6: Copyright © 2015 by Fczarnowski / Wikimedia Commons, (CC BY-SA 4.0) at https://commons. wikimedia.org/wiki/File:Florence_duomo_fc10.jpg.

Fig. 10.7: Copyright © 2009 by DearEdward / Wikimedia Commons, (CC BY 2.0) at https://commons. wikimedia.org/wiki/File:Florence_Cathedral_%283702727172%29.jpg.

Fig. 10.8: Copyright © 2009 by Ra Boe / Wikimedia Commons, (CC BY-SA 3.0) at https://commons. wikimedia.org/wiki/File:Reims_2008_-Nave_of_Notre-Dame_de_Reims-_by-RaBoe_01.jpg.

Fig. 10.9: Copyright © 2004 by Stefan Bauer, (CC BY-SA 2.5) at https://commons.wikimedia.org/wiki/ File:Einblick_LH2_San_Lorenzo_Florenz.jpg.

Fig. 10.10: Copyright © 2008 by Photo by Jörg Bittner Unna; Adapted by Gary Towne, (CC BY-SA 2.5) at https://commons.wikimedia.org/wiki/File:%27David%27_by_Michelangelo_JBU0001.jpg.

Fig. 10.11: Fra Angelico / Copyright in the Public Domain.

Fig. 10.12: Benozzo Gozzoli / Copyright in the Public Domain.

Fig. 10.13: Sandro Botticelli / Copyright in the Public Domain.

Fig. 10.14: Sandro Botticelli / Copyright in the Public Domain.

Fig. 10.15: Copyright © 2016 by Wai Laam Lo, (CC BY-SA 3.0) at https://commons.wikimedia.org/wiki/ File:Venus_de_Medici.png.

Fig. 10.16: Leonardo da Vinci / Copyright in the Public Domain.

Fig. 10.17: Copyright © 2010 by Patrick A. Rodgers, (CC BY-SA 2.0) at https://commons.wikimedia.org/ wiki/File:Donatello_-_David_-_Floren%C3%A7a.jpg.

Fig. 10.18: Copyright © 2008 by Jörg Bittner Unna, (CC BY-SA 3.0) at https://commons.wikimedia.org/ wiki/File:%27David%27_by_Michelangelo_JBU0001.jpg.

Fig. 10.19: Source: http://stpetersbasilica.info/Plans/vatican-area.jpg.

Fig. 10.20: Thomas George Tucker / Copyright in the Public Domain.

Fig. 10.21: Copyright © 2004 by Andreas Tille, (CC BY-SA 4.0) at https://commons.wikimedia.org/wiki/ File:RomaCastelSantAngelo-2.jpg.

Fig. 10.22A: Source: http://stpetersbasilica.info/Plans/vatican-area.jpg.

Fig. 10.22B: Source: http://stpetersbasilica.info/Plans/vatican-area.jpg.

Fig. 10.23: H.W. Brewer / Copyright in the Public Domain.

Fig. 10.25: Maarten van Heemskerck / Copyright in the Public Domain.

Fig. 10.26: Maarten van Heemskerck / Copyright in the Public Domain.

Fig. 10.27A: Copyright in the Public Domain.

Fig. 10.27B: Léon Palustre / Copyright in the Public Domain.

Fig. 10.27C: Léon Palustre / Copyright in the Public Domain.

CHAPTER 11

THE ARTS IN THE BAROQUE PERIOD (1600–1750)

Background

The word *baroque* derives from the Portuguese word *barroco*, which describes a large, irregularly shaped pearl. The word expresses additional concepts as well: intensity, grandiosity, exaggeration, ornamentation, excess, and sometimes deformity. The term was invented to disparage an eighteenth-century opera, but it soon lost its negative connotation and was applied to the artistic developments of the previous century, which the word's implications describe well. Interestingly, many contemporary political and cultural developments share these same traits.

Politically, the late seventeenth and early eighteenth centuries were characterized by expansion of the wars of religion that had resulted from the Protestant Reformation and the Catholic Counter-Reformation of the previous century. Chief among these was the Thirty Years' War, which ended by delineating Protestant and Catholic regions among the states of continental Europe. Several countries were convulsed: Germany-Austria, divided between south and north; France, through a reversion to persecution of a large Protestant population by a Catholic king; England, where Catholic Stuart kings clashed with a Puritan and Anglican Parliament; and the Low Countries, where a heavily, but not exclusively, Protestant population wearied of Spanish domination and expelled the government of the "Most Catholic Monarch." An external religious threat was that of the Ottoman Turks, who controlled much of Eastern Europe and were only finally repulsed in 1683 at the walls of Vienna.

The seventeenth century saw great expansion of European colonization worldwide, especially in North America, where the English, French, Dutch, and smaller groups all established colonies, following the previous centuries' South and Central American leads of Spain and Portugal. These great changes naturally brought disturbance. Regional dynastic and religious wars in Europe were complicated by involvement of their colonies and affiliated Native Americans. The great influx of New World gold and silver in the decades around 1600 led first to continent-wide inflation, followed by recession as the imports dwindled. At the same time, the economic center of Europe moved northward, from Italy and Spain to the aggressive maritime powers of Holland and England, well positioned to embrace worldwide trade.

Intellectually, Renaissance insights and development of critical and evaluative thinking lit the fuse for an explosion of learning and the beginnings of modern science. Figure 11.1 lists some of the greatest scholars of the age and their accomplishments.

Seventeenth-century society was one of great contrasts. Throughout Europe, a middle class was rising in prosperity, with economic (and sometimes political) power. This was especially true in the Netherlands, where wealthy middle-class (usually Protestant) merchants exercised great influence. It was also true in England, where the middle class controlled Parliament and sought limitation of royal power. When Charles I (Stuart, a Catholic) refused such limitations, he was deposed and eventually beheaded. Similar intransigence led to the exile of his son, James II, later in the century. Aside from their Catholicism, these kings' principal error was their persistent emulation of Louis XIV of France, who described himself as the Sun King and created the model for absolute monarchy with his pronouncement, "*L'État, c'est moi!*" ("The state, it is I!"). Struggles between monarchs and people set the stage for devastating conflict in the future. Of course, religion played an important part, as it did in the fine arts.

The several Christian religious groups all had different attitudes toward the arts. The Catholic Church had always avidly supported the visual arts and music—even, to a certain extent, drama—and it tolerated dance in a secular context. Most Protestants developed skepticism or downright opposition to the visual arts based on the Second Commandment,

Francis Bacon..	Scientific Method
Galileo Galilei, Johannes Kepler	Astronomy
Robert Hooke, Antonie van Leeuwenhoek	Biology
Jean-Baptiste Colbert, Thomas Hobbes, John Locke	Economics, Political Philosophy
René Descartes, Pierre Fermat, Gottfried Leibniz, Blaise Pascal	Mathematics
Francesco Redi, William Harvey	Medicine
Baruch Spinoza	Philosophy
Robert Boyle, Christiaan Huygens, Isaac Newton	Physics

FIGURE 11.1 Great seventeenth-century thinkers and their work.

FIGURE 11.2 Andrea Palladio (1508–1580), Church of San Giorgio Maggiore (1566–1575), brick with white marble façade, Venice.

although Anglicans tolerated some religious imagery (through their residual vestiges of Catholic practice) as well as theater and dance in secular contexts. Lutherans and Anglicans both embraced music, as long as it was in the vernacular, but Calvinists despised all the arts. They permitted no visual art, theater, or dance and allowed only monophonic singing of psalms without instruments. At first, Anabaptists followed the Calvinists' lead. An interesting quirk developed in the Netherlands, where Calvinism was very strong but there were still numerous Catholics. The mixed society had to be officially tolerant of all (Christian) religions, although Calvinists destroyed and prohibited religious art. For both groups, however, secular portraits, landscapes, still lifes, and interior genre scenes proliferated.

Visual art in the Baroque extended the developments of sixteenth-century Mannerism, but to a greater extreme. Strong emotion, turbulent activity, and supernatural symbolism, as seen in Michelangelo's *Last Judgment*, became common. Strong contrast of light and shade known as *chiaroscuro*, initially used in the Renaissance, became characteristic of the Baroque style. Diagonal lines and asymmetry became common in painting composition, and twisted or awkward poses pervaded both painting and sculpture. Artists sought to trick the eye (*trompe l'oeil*) to make the depicted space seem an extension of reality. And in contrast to these powerful developments, genre painting of interior or domestic scenes and many types of still lifes became popular. Architects molded the shapes of buildings with curves, protrusions, and cavities, often in vividly colored marble and covered with rich arabesques in gilt bronze. Louis XIV's palace and gardens at Versailles became the models for monarchs throughout Europe. All visual art forms participated in rich development and substantial patronage.

Transition and Italian Baroque Arts

An interesting view of transition and contrast between the Renaissance and Baroque can be found at the Church of San Giorgio in Venice. (See Figure 11.2.) Designed by the great Venetian Renaissance architect Andrea Palladio, the church sits on a low island half a kilometer from the main city. Only two or three meters above the water, from a distance it seems to rise miraculously out of the sea. The façade is a pristine example of Renaissance reinterpretation of classical temple design, which Palladio has adapted ingeniously to the needs of a Christian church. The problem is the side aisles, which are lower than the central nave. A classical temple front that covered the nave and both aisles would be both disproportionate and nonfunctional, with false fronts above the lower aisles. Palladio solved the problem by embedding one temple façade in another.

The lower façade covers the aisles; its pediment is supported by Corinthian pilasters, but it is broken in the center to accommodate a second higher temple front that covers the nave. To preserve correct proportions, the central section's column bases are raised from ground level by the smaller unit of the Golden Section. The result is elegant visual harmony in Renaissance style.

In contrast to the serene Renaissance classicism of the façade, the altar inside is flanked by two large Baroque paintings by Tintoretto, done in the last year of his life. (See Figure 11.3.) The best known is his *Last Supper*. The contrast with Leonardo's depiction (Figure 2.2) could not be more dramatic. Tintoretto's work reveals the power of the Baroque as it emerges from Mannerism: diagonal composition (the table slashes across the scene) and intense *chiaroscuro*, with deep shadows and sparkling light emitted by the halos of Christ, the apostles, and the flickering lamp, which also emits filmy angelic spirits. The central figures in ancient garb are serene as they receive the sacrament from the hands of Christ, but the surrounding servants (who are not biblical) are dressed like the artist's contemporaries and are moving around in pursuit of their duties, which appear to include a servant girl's passing clams—forbidden by Jewish dietary law. The inclusion of the modern servants, Venetian seafood, and the diagonal of the table (such that it seems in the church an extension of the altar) all express the theological concept that Christ's actions were not limited to the past but cross time and space to include the eternal present.[1]

In spite of this wonderful foretaste in Venice, the origin of the Baroque properly belongs in Rome and in the hands of one of its greatest artists, Gian Lorenzo Bernini. Bernini's largest works are his furnishings for St. Peter's Basilica and the colonnade for its piazza. The first of these is his *baldacchino* over the main altar. (See Figure 11.4.) Smaller such canopies appear over altars and shrines in other churches and cloth canopies carried over sacred objects in processions. Bernini's huge columns rest on marble bases the height of the altar. They tower over it to support an elaborate canopy of *trompe l'oeil* cloth and four large

FIGURE 11.3 Tintoretto (Jacopo Comin, 1518–1594), *The Last Supper* (1594), oil on canvas, 3.6 × 5.7 m, San Giorgio, Venice.

FIGURE 11.4 Gian Lorenzo Bernini (1598–1680), Baldachino (1623–34), gilt bronze, 20 m high, St. Peter's Basilica, Vatican City. Behind the baldachino on the right is a false balcony with the ancient Solomonic columns that provided models for Bernini. On the left in the apse are Bernini's *Gloria* and *Throne of Saint Peter*.

---

1   This theology is also expressed in the traditional nativity scenes of Mediterranean Europe, in which the basic scriptural characters are surrounded by scenes of everyday village life, sometimes animated.

FIGURE 11.5 Giovanni Paolo Pannini (1692–1765), *The Interior of St. Peter's in Rome* (c. 1755), oil on canvas, 75 × 100 cm, Hermitage Museum, St. Petersburg, Russia. Note how the baldacchino in the distance mediates between human scale, so small in relation to the heights of the vault and dome.

ogee-curved decorative ribs, with angel sculptures atop each column. The columns are Solomonic—with spiral twists. Bernini took the model from similar columns, donated by Emperor Constantine and supposedly from the temple in Jerusalem, that screened the saint's shrine in the old St. Peter's and were reused in *trompe l'oeil* balconies on the new church's dome piers, visible behind the altar. Bernini's columns are decorated with bees from the pope's Barberini family crest. Stories abound about the source of the massive amount of bronze needed. Romans said it was stripped from the Pantheon roof.[2] The pope said it came from Venice and the Pantheon bronze went into a cannon. Another account says that some even came from the ribs of St. Peters' dome itself. Whatever the source, the *baldacchino* is a work of genius that provides a focal point to moderate between the enormous church and human scale. Its success is visible in Giovanni Paolo Pannini's painting of the church in Figure 11.5.

Bernini's remaining interior furnishings are the *Throne of Saint Peter* and the *Gloria* behind it that fill the apse behind the altar (see Figure 11.7). Created between 1647 and 1653, these unique structures serve a dual purpose. They provide a final focal point behind the altar at the end of the church, and the *Throne* houses a holy relic: a chair that is supposedly the bishop's chair of St. Peter himself (see Figure 11.6). This chair was given to the pope in 875 by Emperor Charles the Bald. It is rarely out of Bernini's reliquary, but it has been studied at least twice in modern times. In 1863, it was concluded that the protective outer frame of oak was medieval but that the inner chair remnants of acacia (visible in the chair's back) were older, possibly from the first century. More recent study between 1968 and 1974 suggests that no part of the chair is older than the sixth century. Whether or not it served St. Peter himself, it certainly served many of his successors.

Bernini's chair is much larger than human scale. Its four curved legs are supported by the four great Doctors of the Church: Saints Ambrose, Augustine, Athanasius, and John

2   About the Pantheon's roof, scoffing Romans, long disillusioned about popes, said, *"Quod non fecerunt barbari, fecerunt Barberini"* ("What the barbarians didn't do (strip the Pantheon), the Barberini [the pope's family] did").

FIGURE 11.6 Relic of St. Peter's Chair (probably sixth to eighth century, possibly earlier), acacia chair encased in later oak covering.

FIGURE 11.7 Gian Lorenzo Bernini, *Throne of Saint Peter*, and *Gloria* (1647–53), gilt bronze, St. Peter's Basilica.

Chrysostom. Their statues are twice life size. All of them are posed with swirling flourishes of drapery, and the two front figures (the western Doctors—Ambrose and Augustine) wear tall miters. The figures and the throne itself are dark bronze with gilt bronze decoration. Cherubs atop the throne support a crown. Above and behind the chair is a fantastic gilded sunburst known as the *Gloria*. In its center is a window—made not of stained glass but of thinly sliced alabaster—that shows the dove of the Holy Spirit emanating rays of golden light. These light rays lead outward onto rays of gilt bronze behind a boiling throng of golden angels. Below them, billowing gold clouds descend behind the throne. The complete sculptural combination fills the apse from the floor to the top of the walls. The golden fantasy exalts the relic of the apostle and draws the eye from the church's entrance two hundred meters away.

The culmination of Bernini's work on St. Peter's came several years later with the design of the Piazza San Pietro (St. Peter's Piazza) in front of the basilica's entrance. The project's beginnings go back to 1586, when Domenico Fontana was assistant architect (Figure 10.24). The obelisk, imported for the center of Emperor Caligula's circus, stood near the place where St. Peter is believed to have been crucified.[3] For that reason, it was left alone when the circus was

---

3 According to tradition, St. Peter requested to be crucified upside down, as he felt himself unworthy to be crucified in the same position as Christ (see Figure 9.18, lower panel).

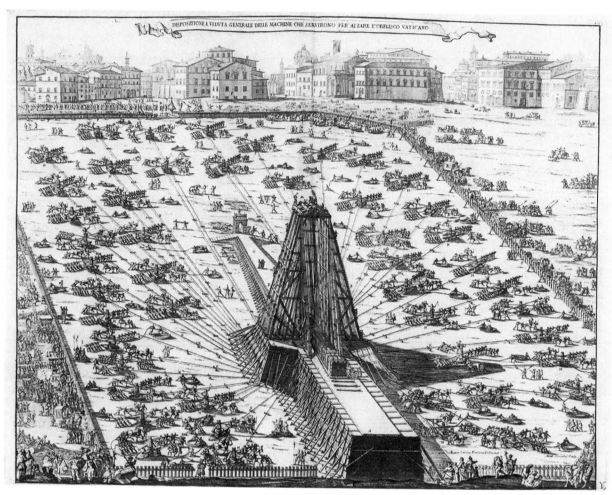

FIGURE 11.8 Raising the Vatican obelisk after moving it from beside St. Peter's to the center of St. Peter's Piazza (Domenico Fontana, 1586).

demolished, and it remained as a monument beside the old St. Peter's Basilica (see Figures 10.22 and 10.23). Fontana moved it at the pope's request to the center of what was to be the piazza in front of the church. It was a tremendous undertaking—the obelisk is the second largest in Rome (25.5 m, 41 m counting base and pinnacle) and the only one that has not tumbled at least once. Figure 11.8 shows its raising and gives some idea of the size of the task. Figure 11.9 shows its position in the center of Bernini's elliptical piazza, between fountains on either side.

Bernini's piazza is in two sections: one elliptical, and one trapezoidal that connects the ellipse and the church. The trapezoidal piazza seems odd at first glance. Its narrow end is toward the ellipse, and it grows wider as it approaches the church; this is a carefully calculated design that creates false perspectives through architectural *trompe l'oeil*. From either direction, the straight walls appear parallel. Looking from the piazza end, their disguised broadening makes the church seem closer, the façade more human in scale, and the church as welcoming—the piazza embracing the observer "like the maternal arms of Mother Church," in Bernini's words. Piranesi's etching in Figure 11.10 demonstrates this. From the other direction, the church steps, with unperceived narrowing of the trapezoid's walls, make the outside world appear more distant and Christendom greater. The deliberate use of false perspective is concealed in apparent simplicity to support theological illusion. This is Baroque architecture at its most sophisticated.

The outer elliptical piazza also shows hidden ingenuity. The piazza centers on the obelisk, with large fountains on either side. But the ellipse's geometrical foci are not at the fountains. They are marked by circles in the pavement roughly halfway between each fountain and the obelisk. To the observer standing at a focus, the elaborate forest of columns, four deep, becomes a single row as each group of four falls into alignment, perhaps symbolic of the Christian faith's clarity rising from worldly confusion. The columns themselves are Tuscan Doric (columns without fluting), and above each column and pilaster of the piazza's arms is a saint's statue—140 in all. The piazza and the basilica together are one of the world's greatest monuments of architecture.

Bernini was as influential a sculptor as an architect. Cardinal Scipione Borghese commissioned sculpture from the teenage Bernini to decorate the family villa in the northern part of Rome. The best known of these works is *David* (Figure 11.11). It depicts the hero at the very moment of casting the stone to defeat Goliath. David is twisted to the right, his feet in a broad stance. At his feet are a harp (he is recorded as a musician and composer of the Book of Psalms) and remnants of armor. His left hand holds the sling's loop; his right hand pulls back the pouch with the stone that he is about to throw. Behind and beneath him is the cuirass (torso part) of the armor, and a sash hanging from his right shoulder holds the pouch for sling stones. A drape hanging from his waistband conceals most of his genitals. He gazes fiercely at Goliath and almost makes the viewer duck. The extreme twisting pose and the gaze's emotional intensity define the Baroque style of Bernini's *David* and clearly distinguish it from the repose seen in the Renaissance *David*s of Donatello and Michelangelo (Figures 10.17 and 10.18).

A later celebrated work of Bernini that combines sculpture with architecture is the Cornaro family chapel in the Roman church of Santa Maria della Vittoria, the only church Maderno designed and completed in his lifetime. Bernini's work adorns the shallow left transept. The chapel (Figure 11.12) is designed like an opera staging. On either side are balconies with statues of the donor, Cardinal Federico Cornaro, a Cornaro

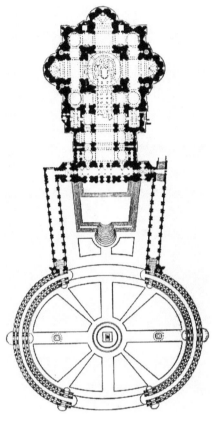

FIGURE 11.9 St. Peter's Piazza, plan.

FIGURE 11.10 Giovanni Battista Piranesi (1720–1778), *St. Peter's Basilica and Piazza* (1748/74). Egyptian obelisk, date unknown, from Caligula's Circus–center foreground; fountains–right by Maderno (1612/14, left by Bernini (1667); colonnade (1656–67) by Bernini, Piranesi captures accurately the effect of Bernini's false perspective.

The Arts in the Baroque Period (1600–1750) 289

FIGURE 11.11 Bernini, *David* (1623–24), marble, 170 cm, Galleria Borghese, Rome.

FIGURE 11.12 Bernini, Cornaro Chapel (1647–52), Santa Maria della Vittoria, Rome.

Venetian doge, and other famous family members. They observe and discuss the scene taking place in a small stage-like pavilion over the altar. This pavilion is an elegant demonstration of the Baroque sculpted wall. Projecting from the side panels are two portions of a Corinthian colonnade under pediment sections in concave curves. Immediately after the second column on each side, the pediment breaks back by the column's depth. The central pediment then continues in a convex curve that forms the proscenium lintel for the scene within. In white marble, St. Theresa of Avila reclines on a cloud in voluptuous ecstasy before a smiling angel who aims the arrow of divine love at her heart (see Figure 11.13). Behind them, gilt bronze rays shower divine light from above through the pavilion's open top. At least eight different colors and textures of marble adorn this opulent construction, which embodies the intense emotion of Counter-Reformation Catholicism.

Bernini set the style and tone of the Baroque to be soon adopted by others. One of these was Fra Andrea Pozzo of the new Jesuit order, called to adorn the new church honoring the order's founder, St. Ignatius of Loyola. Pozzo's great work is the church's ceiling, *The Triumph of St Ignatius* (see Figure 11.14). The ceiling is the ultimate in the *trompe l'oeil* technique. It fills the entire ceiling of the nave, which is illuminated by seven windows—six set in dormers at the sides and one at the rear of the church (the top of the figure). At the other end is an arch to connect with a planned dome.[4] Viewed from the center of the nave, there seems to be no ceiling; columns extend the real architecture into an apparent opening at the top. The sky is filled with lavender clouds, on one of which sits the blue-robed saint as he rises into heaven. Above his head greeting him is Christ, carrying the cross. In the heavens, in the gaps between painted columns, sitting on the painted architecture, and even extending down between the real windows, are swirling angels, cherubs, and many other figures, most dressed in windblown

---

4   When conflict with the donors terminated construction, the dome was unfinished. Pozzo painted an enormous *trompe l'oeil* dome on canvas to substitute. Unfortunately, his canvas has not survived like his frescoes. It was destroyed in 1891 but has been replaced.

FIGURE 11.13 Bernini, *Ecstasy of St. Theresa*, Cornaro Chapel (1647–52), marble, life-size, Santa Maria della Vittoria, Rome.

FIGURE 11.14 Fra Andrea Pozzo, S.J. (1642–1709), *The Triumph of St. Ignatius* (after 1685). fresco, approx. 26 × 17m , Church of Sant' Ignazio, Rome.

drapery. The corners are allegories representing the Jesuits' missionary work in the four corners of the earth. The work creates a virtual reality that erases the boundaries between the real architecture of the church and the ideal world of the saints in heaven.

Blurring the boundaries of reality and enhancing the artistic expression of dramatic and historical events was also a fundamental rationale for the development of opera. Opera was first devised for weddings at north Italian courts, initially with plots about Greek myths and later about great historical events. Opera creates a grand spectacle that includes all the arts: great composers, musical performers, and dancers presented grand theater, with poetic texts by great poets and ennobled by sets and costumes designed by great artists. Like Baroque visual art, opera stretched the borders of reality, as characters from mythology sang their speeches and expressed emotions with elaborate song and dance. Expressing all this required a new musical style: recitative. Recitative presents dialogue in simple, unadorned melodies over a light accompaniment, usually what is called *basso continuo*. In *basso continuo*, the only instruments are those that play the bass line and simple chords above it. It is a musical background or environment that enhances the text above it but leaves the words clear and understandable.

At moments of great emotion, one or more characters may burst into a more traditional melodic song called an aria; briefer emotions may burst through the recitative as moments of more elaborate melody known as arioso.

Like the Baroque style in art and architecture, opera and its new creation, recitative over *basso continuo*, took Europe by storm. Every European nation developed its own style of opera or musical theater in its own language, although Italian opera, the original, was often performed side by side with the local style. Opera even penetrated Rome in spite of its condemnation by the church for plots involving illicit love affairs, pagan gods, and violence. Nevertheless, because of these, it was completely banned during Lent. But the music itself could not be suppressed. For this penitential season, a related new form arose: oratorio. Oratorio is opera with a biblical or other sacred plot, performed in a sacred space instead of a theater, without sets, costumes, or dramatic action. The greatest Roman oratorio composer was Giacomo Carissimi; his most famous work is *Jephte*, from the Old Testament story. (See Figure 11.15.) A general of Gilead, Jephthah swears that, if

FIGURE 11.15 Giacomo Carissimi (1605–1674), *Jephte* (Jephtha, 1648) Oratorio, final scene.

Only text is given. It is easier to follow than timings.

The story of Jephthah from the Old Testament. In order to win a battle, Jephtha promised God to sacrifice to him whatever first greeted him on his return. After his victory, when he entered his yard, his daughter ran to his arms.

The oratorio's final scene contains her lament to her woman friends, with echo effects and a grand final chorus. The daughter's solos are in a recitative style. The echos are in an ornamented recitative style called arioso (aria-like). Recitative was the new musical style developed for opera for presenting dialog and other dramatic content.

Jephte—Final Scene		Jephtha—Final Scene	
Filia—	Plorate colles, dolete montes, et in afflictione cordis mei ululate!	Daughter—	Weep & grieve hills & mountains; in my heart's pain—Wail!
Echo—	Ululate!	Echo—	Wail!
Filia—	Ecce moriar virgo et non potero morte mea meis filiis consolari, ingemiscite silvae, fontes et flumina, in interitu virginis lachrimate!	Daughter—	I shall die a virgin, unable to see my children. Lament, forests, springs & rivers, for a virgin's death—Weep!
Echo—	Lachrimate!	Echo—	Weep!
Filia—	Heu me dolentem in laetitia populi, in victoria Israel et gloria patris mei, ego, sine filiis virgo, ego filia unigenita moriar et non vivam. Exhorrescite rupes, obstupescite colles, valles et cavernae in sonitu horribili resonate!	Daughter—	Woe is me, sorrowful in the people's joy at Israel's victory and my father's glory. I, a childless virgin & only daughter, shall die, not live. Tremble & be dazed, crags, hills, valleys & caves. With the horrible sound—Resound!
Echo—	Resonate!	Echo—	Resound!
Filia—	Plorate filii Israel, plorate virginitatem meam, et Jephte filiam unigenitam in carmine dolore lamentamini."	Daughter—	Weep, children of Israel, for my virginity; for Jephtha's only daughter, in songs of sorrow—Lament!
Chorus—	Plorate filii Israel, plorate omnes virgines, et filiam Jephte unigenitam in carmine doloris lamentamini.	Chorus—	Weep, children & virgins of Israel; for Jephtha's only daughter, in songs of sorrow—Lament!

Musical Elements in the Work
Rhythm—regular, but flexible; Melody—minor scale, very expressive, follows voice's emphasis; Harmony—minor, mainly triads, some dissonance; Texture—homophonic, except chorus, which—polyphonic at the end. Timbre—voice(s) and continuo (bass plus chords); Text Setting—syllabic; Form—refrain structure with through-composed melody.

he defeats the Ammonites, he will sacrifice the first thing to greet him on return. It is his daughter.

In the final scene, Jephthah's daughter has gone into the hills to prepare for her fate. She laments in an extended recitative, broken by increasingly elaborate wails in arioso. Each wail is echoed by the hills in duet. This occurs three times. Her final lament is answered by the whole chorus, which calls on all Israel to lament the fate of Jephthah's daughter. The text is in Latin, and the simple but expressive music enhances its power. The rising emotions of the daughter and her echoes culminate in a grand final chorus. The chorus begins in homophony to express the unanimity of lamentation; in the second section (which is repeated), on the words "*in carmine doloris*" ("in songs of sorrow"), the texture changes to imitative polyphony, as one voice after another repeats the short sorrowful descending melody. It is as if the entire crowd has broken down and each individual weeps alone in one of the most moving moments in all music. New and dramatic music like this echoes the new and dramatic art and architecture in attempting to bring reality into closer contact with a spiritual realm of the sacred or ideal.

French Baroque Arts

As the world's most famous artist, Bernini was in demand outside Italy. Invited to France to design the major façade of the Louvre palace (which was ultimately rejected), he took the time while there to carve a bust of the young king, Louis XIV. The bust (Figure 11.16), now in the Palace of Versailles, shows the king's head and shoulders rising from a swirling fantasy of drapery. Above armored shoulders and a lace frontlet surrounded by elaborate curling locks that descend to his chest, the king gazes up and to his right. His gaze suggests the new vision of France that he was creating for the future, while his raised chin and set jaw show his pride and determination to hold absolute power—which he did, becoming the model of the absolute monarch. This is very clear in his most famous portrait, by Hyacinthe Rigaud (Figure 11.17).

Rigaud painted Louis in his coronation regalia for the fortieth anniversary of his personal assumption of power.[5] The portrait was intended as a gift for Louis's grandson, Philip V of Spain, but it appealed so much to Louis that he kept it and had a copy sent to Philip. The pride evident in Bernini's bust has become fully developed haughtiness that combines with all the royal trappings to express the king's majesty and power. Beneath his flowing black wig, Louis stands in three-quarters view in a rich purple velvet coronation robe that flows from his shoulder across the floor and furniture behind him. It is embroidered with gold *fleur-de-lys* (stylized lilies or irises), the symbol of royal France, and lined with ermine. His weight rests on his right leg, and his left turns out at a perfect fashionable ninety-degree angle. His gold shoes have elevated red heels, red bows, and diamond buckles, and he wears silver trunks, diamond garters, and light blue hose.

---

5   Louis became king on his father's death when he was nearly five, but his mother, as regent, and her chief minister, Cardinal Mazarin, controlled France until Mazarin died, and Louis personally assumed power at the age of twenty-three. When he died days short of his seventy-seventh birthday, he had established the longest reign of any European monarch before or since.

FIGURE 11.16 Gian Lorenzo Bernini, *Louis XIV* (1665), marble, 105 cm high, Palace of Versailles, France.

FIGURE 11.17 Hyacinthe Rigaud (1659–1743), *Louis XIV, King of France in Coronation Robes* (1702), oil on canvas, 3.13 × 2.05 m, Apollo Salon, Palace of Versailles.

Louis' youthful legs have aroused comment, but they are significant. Louis developed his royal image through dance from his youth, when he portrayed Apollo as Sun God in a ballet (see Figure 4.44). He later adopted the image of *le roi soleil*, the Sun King, with a sunburst as his emblem and Apollo as his alter ego. Within his vast artistic patronage, dance was supremely important: he personally took part in balls and ballets; the latter permeated all performing arts at his court. It is hardly surprising that, even at sixty-three, he should want his legs to appear shapely. The king's left hand rests on his hip above the Sword of Charlemagne. He wears a lace frontlet (as in Bernini's bust) and the collar of the Order of the Holy Spirit around his neck. He rests his right hand on the butt of the royal scepter of Henry IV, pointing downward to rest on a velvet pillow that bears the royal crown and a second scepter, the Hand of Justice, behind which is a column on whose base is the goddess of justice with her scales. Behind the king is the throne under a rich scarlet canopy with gold borders and tassels; he stands on a cloth of gold carpet, and behind him a palatial corridor fades in the background. The portrait became a classic and defined the style of royal portraits for more than a century, both in France and beyond.

Louis embodied the absolute monarch whose word was law, a model for other European rulers that was ultimately fatal to feudal power in Europe.[6] He built himself the grandest palace in Europe at Versailles, eighteen kilometers southeast of Paris (see Figure 11.18). It was originally a hunting lodge for Louis XIII, but Louis XIV and his successors enlarged the palace and its gardens enormously. Like Louis's absolute monarchy, Versailles became a model. The king's and queen's apartments occupied the central block, surrounded by numerous rooms for royal functions. The north wing (left in the figure) housed the royal chapel and later the opera house. Hundreds of remaining rooms lodged all of Louis' noble courtiers. The grandest space is the Hall of Mirrors (Figure 11.19) in the center overlooking the gardens. The seventeen windows on the garden side face matching mirrors on the opposite wall that enlarge and further brighten the room. The mirrors and windows are grouped in threes with single ones at each end. Between the mirror groups are sculpture niches lined in colored marble. Pilasters of a different marble and with gilded capitals bearing symbols of France

---

6   As early as 1579, Théodore de Bèze wrote, "... the power of the ruler is delegated by the people and continues only with their consent."

divide the niches, mirrors, and windows. Elaborate tables and cushioned ottomans line the inner wall; gilded cornices crown the walls, and gilded frames on the vaulted ceiling enclose frescoes that glorify Louis' deeds. Magnificent crystal chandeliers and gilded statue candelabra provide illumination. The room is a great monument of French Baroque architecture, still used for historic events—the treaty ending World War I was signed here.

Beyond the Hall of Mirrors are the gardens. The aerial view in Figure 11.18 shows a portion of those closest to the palace. Gravel avenues divide and flank two long ornate pools. On either side are four side gardens with hedges, flower beds, paths, pools, and fountains in formal geometric designs. There were as many as twenty of these in the historic plans. Beyond them are hidden gardens, groves, woods, grottos, and smaller palaces for royal use. But the greatest feature is the central perspective in Figure 11.20. Just beyond the two long pools visible in the aerial view is the Fountain of Latona. Latona/Leto was the mother of Apollo and Artemis/Diana. When certain peasants refused her a drink from their pond, she turned them into frogs. In the fountain, Leto and her children are on the center pedestal, surrounded by gilded frogs, turtles, and peasants in various stages of transformation, all spouting jets of water. Beyond the fountain, a wide gravel walk divides to flank a lawn, known as the green carpet or royal avenue, at the end of which is the Fountain of Apollo (only the vertical jets are visible). Apollo in his chariot (as the sun god), rises from the sea amid gushing torrents, surrounded by dolphins and tritons (mythological mermen) blowing shell trumpets (see Figure 11.21). Beyond the fountain is the central stem of the Grand Canal, a cross-shaped artificial lake large enough to float small ships. (Rowboats are barely visible as tiny dots in the first photograph.) The final green lawn rises to a seemingly endless view, symbolizing Louis as monarch of all he surveys.[7]

FIGURE 11.18 Palace and City of Versailles, aerial view. Converging avenues in the background lead to the great courtyards at the palace entrance; the gardens begin in the foreground.

FIGURE 11.19 Palace of Versailles, Hall of Mirrors (1684), 73 × 10.5 m, 12.3 m high.

---

7   The gardens' water supply has always been a problem. At the time, the fountains required more water than the city of Paris. To augment the existing system of windmills, horse-powered pumps, and thirty pools and reservoirs, Louis constructed one of the age's greatest mechanical marvels, the waterwheel-powered *Machine de Marly*, to pump water from the Seine River 1.4 km in distance and 162 m vertically to an aqueduct and reservoirs 6.4 km long. The system was one-way, and the Grand Canal served as a reservoir and catch basin. Even this was insufficient, and gardeners whistled to signal the king's location so fountains could be turned on or off. Nowadays, the system recycles water but still cannot run continually.

FIGURE 11.20 Palace of Versailles, Center Gardens, front to back: Fountain of Latona, Green Carpet/Royal Avenue, Fountain of Apollo, Grand Canal, Endless Vista.

FIGURE 11.21 Pierre-Denis Martin (1663–1742), *Louis XIV at the Basin of Apollo in the Gardens of Versailles* (also the Grand Canal and Endless Vista, 1713).

Louis supported all the arts. Among the less common ones was the textile art of tapestry. In the most general sense, tapestries are pictures produced on cloth. A very significant early one is the Bayeux Tapestry (Figure 9.21), although, strictly speaking, the Bayeux Tapestry is not tapestry but embroidery, since the images are sewn onto a white cloth. Technically, images in tapestry are woven directly as part of the cloth itself. Unfortunately, this complex and difficult process has often left transitory results, as many of the dyes used in centuries past have turned out to be fugitive—the colors have faded, leaving large works mere ghosts of their original beauty. Fortunately, a few have survived the test of time better than most. One of these is Figure 11.22, *Visit of Louis XIV at the Gobelins Workshop*. The king had rented space for tapestry weavers from the Gobelins, a family of dyers, since 1602. In 1660, the workshop was enlarged to produce upholstery and furniture, as well as tapestries, for the rising Palace of Versailles. The artistic director was Charles LeBrun, perhaps Louis's most famous court painter.

Figure 11.22 is his design. The detailed and realistic image is bordered with ornamental fruit and flower garlands twisted around a column. The large work is a wall hanging. In the picture, the king and his ministers stand at the left; the king gestures toward the whirl of activity his visit has prompted. Workers and assistants bring samples of the workshop's production for royal approval. From left to right: a worker turns to remove a tipping carved pedestal from a pile of tapestries; three other workers move large, ornate carved stone or ceramic objects, while two behind them hold an elaborate vase in front of a large painting; in the center, a worker lifts an intricately carved painted table. To the right, workers lift furniture, a silver tray, and a rolled tapestry. Standing on a chest, another worker unveils more creative wonders. In the background is a hanging tapestry of a battle scene. This tapestry of Louis's visit is very

FIGURE 11.22 Charles Lebrun (1619–1690, designer), *Visit of Louis XIV at the Gobelins Workshop* (1667), tapestry, 3.7 × 5.8 m, Palace of Versailles.

well preserved. Although some colors have faded, it shows the high artistic level that tapestry could achieve while also illustrating Louis's avid patronage of the arts.

Louis provided rich support for the performing arts as symbols of his majesty. He supported the creation of new and unique genres of musical theater. The royal composer, Jean-Baptiste Lully, created a unique French musical drama that mingled dance and instrumental music with song. These grand works were hours in length, beginning with an extended prologue in praise of the king. Often generically referred to as French Baroque opera or ballet, the productions went by a variety of names, depending on the proportion of dance to singing and the nature of the plot. These productions were lavish. Figure 5.36 showed the production of a *Comédie-Ballet* by Molière, *La princess d'Élide* (*The Princess of Elis*) in an elaborate theater in the Versailles palace gardens that was temporary—built only for a few days' festival.

Figure 11.23 shows a production staged in the marble court of the palace. As one approaches the palace from the front (the top of the picture in Figure 11.18), the marble court is the last and smallest of the spaces, flanked by the royal apartments on both sides. A stage was built to raise the level of the court, which is already five steps up from the preceding one. Boxes were constructed on either side for the orchestra accompanying Lully's opera *Alceste* as just one part of several days' celebration in July, 1674. As the figure shows, the audience sat in the next courtyard out. Indoor performances could be even more extravagant. Figure 11.24 is the stage set for the last act of Lully's last opera, a *tragédie lyrique*, *Armide*, in 1676. In the finale, Armide, sitting on the boat, is rejected by Renaud (standing) who is about to depart with his military companions on the beach. Armide is so devastated that she has called demons to destroy her palace. The scene has the boat and beach in the

Premiere Journée.

Alceste, Tragédie en musique, orné d'entrées de Ballet, representée à Versailles dans la
cour de marbre du Chasteau éclairé depuis le haut jusqu'en bas d'vne infinité de lumieres.

Dies primus.

Alcestes Tragœdia, perpetuo cantu et variis Saltationibus decorata, in marmoreo
Palatij Versaliarum cauædio, vndequaque, facibus accensis illuminati, acta.

FIGURE 11.23 Jean Le Pautre (1618–1682), Presentation of *Alceste* (4 July 1674), opera by Jean-Baptiste Lully, in the Marble Court of the Palace of Versailles, engraving.

foreground, while in the background, demons, one riding a dragon, descend in flames and tear the palace apart in full view—quite a show, especially considering the stage machinery involved. Fortunately for us, within these grand spectacles, Lully hid a few small musical jewels.

Lully's productions were so successful because he devised music suited to the French language, and he developed musical forms that communicated the drama with improved continuity. One of the new musical forms was the French *ouverture*, an opening instrumental work to signal the king's arrival and quiet the audience. The *ouverture* to Lully's *Atys* (a *tragédie lyrique* performed in 1676, 1678, and 1682) is an elegant and compact example (see Figure 11.25). The form has three parts. The opening section is slow to moderate in tempo (speed), with a distinctive rhythm that might be described as "lurching along." In musical terms, it is a "dotted rhythm," since dots following alternate written notes hold them longer, followed by a short note or notes. This first section is usually homophonic and is followed by a middle section that is faster and in imitative polyphony. Following this is a concluding section

FIGURE 11.24 Jean Bérain (1640–1711), Set Design for Act V of *Armide* (1686) by Jean-Baptiste Lully.

In addition to inventing French opera and ballet, Jean-Baptiste Lully singlehandedly devised the musical style and forms they required. One of these was the instrumental work that opened a stage performance, called an *ouverture* from the French word *ouvert*, meaning open. (in English we say overture.) Lully designed these works according to a standard form, ABA'. This ouverture to his fourth opera (or *tragédie lyrique*) is a small, jewel-like example of the form, lasting barely a minute and a half. The form is below.

A Tempo—Slow to moderate; Rhythm—"jerky" or "lurching," technically a "dotted" rhythm, since the effect comes from notes prolonged by dots in the music. This combined with the melody and harmony in the minor, the homophonic texture and the rich orchestral timbre give the piece a dignity (some might say pomposity) worthy of the great Louis XIV, monarch of all he surveyed.

B Tempo—Fast, with smooth rhythms and a polyphonic texture. The opening melody can be clearly heard in imitation at the beginning, before it gets too busy. Still in a minor key, the energy of this section contrasts strongly with the A section. It lasts about half as long.

A' Tempo—Slow to moderate, with the same musical ideas as the opening A. This section is very brief, barely ten seconds in length.

This work is a wonderful example because it shows the demonstrates the classic French *ouverture* in an example brief enough for anyone to grasp. Not all of Lully's ouvertures are this short. None of them are long; this is just one of the shortest. Most of them do demonstrate a very characteristic French sound, as this one does. It is the sound of the oboes playing the melody with the violins, which affects the whole orchestral color.

FIGURE 11.25 Jean-Baptiste Lully (1632–1687), *Ouverture* to *Atys* (1676), orchestra of strings and woodwinds.

of dotted rhythm similar to the opening, although often shorter. The musical form, then, is **A-B-A'**, or slow (dotted)—fast (imitative)—slow (dotted). Such a French *ouverture* expressed the majesty, even pomposity, of Louis, the absolute monarch.

Baroque Painting in the Low Countries

In stark contrast with the monolithic magnificence of France stood the Netherlands. Inherited by Charles V of Spain in 1506, the Low Countries did not favor their new overlords. Language, culture, and Spanish taxation divided the peoples, as did religion after the Reformation. Spain also coveted Dutch wealth from trade, especially after New World revenues began to decline. By the mid-sixteenth century, increasing tensions ignited rebellion, which lasted until 1648. Religion was an ongoing problem. From the beginning, fanatical Calvinists stormed and desecrated churches (see Figure 11.26), but the presence of a significant Catholic population meant that the Netherlands practiced more religious toleration than many other countries. In visual art, both religious and secular production continued, and the long local tradition of superb painting flourished as never before.

FIGURE 11.26 Dirck van Delen (1604/5–1671), *Iconoclasts in a Church* (1630), oil on panel, 50 × 67 cm, Rijksmuseum, Amsterdam. Protestants tumble and break religious sculpture in a church. In the middleground, they are piling paintings and gilded statues to burn, although they have not yet destroyed the crucifixion painting on the left. They have whitewashed the nave in the background and are pulling down the crucifix on the rood screen; a mob with hammers and crowbars runs across the middleground.

Peter Paul Rubens painted *The Assumption of the Virgin* as the high altarpiece of the Antwerp Cathedral in 1626. The painting depicts an event not recorded in the Bible but having a pious tradition going back at least to the fourth century CE. According to this, when Mary neared death, the twelve apostles were miraculously transported to her bedside; she fell asleep and was raised bodily into heaven without death. This is accepted dogma in the Catholic and Orthodox traditions. Protestant traditions vary in their attitudes. Rubens depicts the scene (Figure 11.27) with the Virgin rising in a swirl into the blue sky, supported by cherubs; other angels carry her crown as she gazes devoutly toward heaven. Below, a crowd of people surrounds the bed or bier, those on the right staring uncomprehendingly downward, while those on the left, including some women, watch adoringly her rise into the sky. *Chiaroscuro* contrasts the light of life on the left and the dark of death on the right. The dividing line, a major factor in the composition, is a series of scallops (in Figure 11.27a) extending from

FIGURE 11.27A Peter Paul Rubens (1577–1640), *Assumption of the Virgin* (1626), oil on panel, 490 × 325 cm, Cathedral of Our Lady, Antwerp, Belgium. Note the small differences between the (possibly) preparatory version in Figure 27b and this final altarpiece in Figure 27a.

FIGURE 11.27B Workshop (?) of Peter Paul Rubens, *Assumption of the Virgin* (mid 1620s), oil on panel, 125 × 94 cm, National Gallery of Art, Washington, DC.

upper right down to the left. This changes somewhat between the very large finished version and what may have been a preliminary study or later copy, now in the Washington National Gallery (11.27b). The dividing line of the Washington study's composition is straighter and more diagonal; the figures are essentially the same, but the upper part is less cramped, since the top is rectangular rather than circular, and there is a tomb on the right that is absent in the final version. To me, the smaller study has more spontaneous facial expressions and poses as well. Either version illustrates important features of the Baroque: nonhorizontal composition, strong *chiaroscuro*, a sense of turbulent motion, and a mystical vision.

Sacred art was part of the larger category of history painting and was an important portion of the output of many Dutch artists, including Rembrandt. Portrait painting was another important category. Even Calvinists who deplored religious imagery seemed to loosen their scruples when it came to memorializing themselves. Rembrandt's portraits delve into his sitters' depths. In addition to his portraits of others, Rembrandt also did nearly one hundred self-portraits (that survive). They document the human soul, its growth, and its aging as no other artist has done. Figure 11.28 presents a selection including examples from all three of the media he favored: etching, drawing, and painting. These reveal his own physical and psychological development as well as that of his style. Figure 11.28a is an etching from the artist's

FIGURE 11.28A Rembrandt van Rijn (1606–1669), Self-Portrait, Staring (1630), etching on paper, 5 × 4.5 cm, Rijksmuseum, Amsterdam.

FIGURE 11.28B Rembrandt, Self-Portrait (1637), red chalk on paper, 13 × 12 cm, National Gallery, Washington.

FIGURE 11.28C Rembrandt, Self-Portrait (1650), oil on canvas, 92 × 76 cm, Widener Collection, National Gallery, Washington.

FIGURE 11.28D Rembrandt, Self-Portrait at the Age of 63 (1669), oil on canvas, 80 × 70 cm, National Gallery, Washington.

twenty-fourth year. In some works from this time, he used himself as a convenient model for experimenting with various facial expressions and emotions, as he does here; he stares with wide eyes and pursed lips, as if with surprise and consternation (and perhaps a bit of youthful whimsy).

The medium is etching, which Rembrandt employed for most of his career. In etching, the artist covers a metal plate with a thin layer of wax. (S)he then scratches off the wax with a needle or stylus in the areas where (s)he wants lines and dips the plate in acid, which "bites" into the bare metal, creating cavities. The acid and wax are removed and the plate is inked and wiped, then pressed on paper, which takes up the ink left in the etched lines. Etching is very effective for recording casual impulses; the technique and artistic control are similar to drawing, and the tools are simple. For self-portraits, etching offers an interesting twist. In Rembrandt's time, self-portraits had to be done with a mirror, which meant that the drawn image was reversed left to right. If a self-portrait is etched, this reversed image is on the plate, so when the plate is turned over for printing, the image is reversed a second time, leaving the artist/subject's face in its true orientation. Etched images' spontaneity and this re-reversal in the process make it the truest hand medium for self-portrayal (without photography, of course).

Drawing is equally spontaneous but, in one respect, less forgiving. A mistaken line in etching can be corrected imperceptibly before the acid wash merely by smoothing on fresh wax. In drawing, however, erasure is almost never complete. In Rembrandt's time, the common drawing media were charcoal, chalk, pen and ink, and sticks of metallic lead. Graphite pencils were rare and costly. Figure 11.28b is a chalk self-portrait of Rembrandt at the age of thirty-one, when he was enjoying his first successes. Youthful whimsy is replaced with the sober image of a confident, well-dressed young professional. The drawing is self-assured—not a line is missing, wasted, or out of place. Next, Figure 11.28c shows the artist when he was forty-four, at the height of his career. The work is a good example of the precise style that fueled his prosperity, which shows in his dress: a velvet or suede beret over a patterned skullcap, a Baroque pearl earring, a rich doublet with slit sleeves over a yellow silk tunic, and under those, a fine layered linen shirt.

Every article of clothing has a border, most embroidered, some with gold thread and perhaps jewels on the doublet. The face is clearly drawn, with delicate shading and smooth, nearly invisible brushstrokes. It glows in light, while the rest of the portrait is in shadow. The clothing, especially the outer garments, is a bit rougher, with visible brushstrokes and a bit of *impasto* (thick, pasty paint).

Impasto becomes more pronounced and brushwork rougher and more visible in Rembrandt's late style (Figure 11.28d). Rembrandt had lived well, but he suffered financial reverses late in life. Simultaneously, his painting acquired new depth; he had always showed great empathy for his subjects, but his last self-portraits are especially profound. Figure 11.28d was painted in the last year of his

FIGURE 11.29 Frans Hals (1582/3–1666), *The Women Regents of the Old Men's Home in Haarlem* (1664), oil on canvas, 170 × 249 cm, Franz Hals Museum, Haarlem, Netherlands.

life. The old man gazes at us with moist eyes behind pouched lower lids. His wrinkled skin shows the lentigo (liver spots) of age. As in the other pictures, he wears a beret. His grizzled hair flows over his ears down to his neck. He wears a maroon robe with modest borders and perhaps a brass button. The face is bathed in light, with a certain resignation in his expression; the rest of the figure is in darkness. Such *chiaroscuro* is characteristic of Rembrandt's portrait style from the middle of his career on. The other distinctive quality of his last works, though, arises from the thicker paint on all parts of a portrait, which still almost miraculously contains fine detail, the placement of the very obvious brushstrokes is so precise. As in this work, Rembrandt's depiction of personal depth has hardly ever been matched. Intense individuality pervades even his largest work, a group portrait.

Membership in a military company, guild, or charitable board of trustees was an honor that members wanted recorded for posterity. Such groups often commissioned group portraits, usually at the members' own expense. Typically, these groups are portrayed in a line or around a table, as in Frans Hals's *Women Regents of the Old Men's Home* (Figure 11.29). The portrait shows the four women (of nine total) members of the almshouse board around a table—three seated, one standing (center)—and a maid. A landscape painting hangs behind them. The women are conservatively dressed, with long black dresses, wide white collars, and starched cuffs. All wear close-fitting white or black bonnets that almost completely conceal their hair; facial expressions are serious but highly individual and not unkind.[8] Hand positions are all unique; the lady on the left holds one hand palm up, perhaps symbolizing offering. The standing woman holds a tablet and gloves or a brown cloth; in front of her is a large book (perhaps she was board secretary). The maid brings a note to someone, perhaps the stander or the

8 Pictures like this demonstrate the millenium-old tradition of women in Western society concealing their hair with a wide variety of bonnets, caps, hats, kerchiefs, and other head coverings. Indeed, until the Second Vatican Council (1962–1965), Catholic women were required to cover their heads in church—many nuns still do, and the custom was also observed by most older Protestant women (as it still is by the British Royal Family). It was memorialized in Irving Berlin's song, "Easter Parade": "I could write a sonnet/About your Easter bonnet …" This history of dress exposes the foolish misconceptions and prejudice behind recent controversy over Muslim women's headscarves.

rightmost lady, whose right hand on hip suggests authority. Individuality shows through the board's professional unity. The painting also shows one of Hals's signature techniques: clearly visible brushstrokes. They show in the sheer wrap on the standing lady's shoulders and in several women's pink cheeks. Less obvious in the dark areas, this trait pervades this painting and virtually all of Hals's works, to which it gives great vitality. Hals was one of the first painters to leave brushstrokes unconcealed. A generation older than Rembrandt, Hals may have influenced the younger artist's stylistic change in this direction. Yet

FIGURE 11.30 Rembrandt, *The Militia Company of Frans Banninck Cocq and Willem van Ruytenburch (The Night Watch)*, 1642, oil on canvas, 3.8 × 4.54 m, Rijksmuseum, Amsterdam.

this fashion was short-lived, and Hals's work languished in obscurity until revived by the French Impressionists.

Notwithstanding the adventurous painting technique, Hals's *Women Regents* is quite conservative in composition, in contrast to Rembrandt's great *Militia Company of Frans Banninck Cocq and Willem van Ruytenburch*, long known as *The Night Watch* because centuries of grime darkened it so (see Figure 11.30). In this work, Rembrandt relieved the tedium of placing the group members in a line by showing the musketeer company spilling out of a gate on its way to maneuvers.[9] The sense of action is vivid and immediate. Two leaders (Cocq in black, Ruytenburch in yellow) stride forward from the gates. Behind them, three musketeers are in various stages of loading their weapons; a man bent over carries on his back a helmet with a sprig of oak leaves. In a gap between him and the red-clothed musketeer runs a little girl in a yellow dress, holding a pewter goblet, with a dagger, a dead chicken, and a pistol at her belt. Other background figures brandish the company's banner, pikes, lances, and guns. A helmeted boy on the left carries a powder horn, and a stray dog barks at a drummer on the right. There is no standard uniform, and the whole picture is one of semiorganized chaos. Even though there are no smiles, the atmosphere is one of festive excitement, which suggests that the company is going to maneuvers rather than battle. Virtually every face can be

9   Technically arquebusiers, but both terms are used for several types of firearms in this period.

identified, and nearly every figure has symbolic meaning—just a few: Cocq was Protestant and Ruytenburch Catholic. Their union symbolizes Dutch unity against Spain. The helmet with oak leaves, chicken claws, and pistol symbolize musketeers, and the goblet the girl holds is the company's cup. Yellow symbolizes victory. The work ingeniously combines the genres of group portraiture and history painting with spirited activity and pervasive symbolism; it shows Rembrandt's great mastery as well as his effortless use of Baroque characteristics of action, asymmetry, and *chiaroscuro*.

In addition to the prodigious numbers of single portraits, group portraits, and historical and sacred paintings, Dutch painters also popularized other genres; think of them as those parts of paintings relegated to subsidiary areas in earlier works, now painted as items of interest in their own right. These include scenes of everyday life (genre scenes), often indoors, as well as various types of still lifes and landscapes. One artist who painted mainly genre scenes was Judith Leyster. Leyster was a contemporary and acquaintance of Frans Hals. Her style is so much like his that most of her work was falsely attributed to him until her existence was rediscovered in 1893. The largest proportion of her work is made up of genre paintings, generally of happy scenes (often involving drinking) and scenes with music. She did a few portraits and still lifes but only one known biblical painting. *Young Flute Player* (Figure 11.31) is a sensitive portrait of a boy playing a transverse flute. He is obviously from a musical family; there are a violin and a recorder hanging behind him. His face is in the light as he looks up as if to ask, "Is this right?" Despite the broken chair he is sitting in, he is clearly from a family of some means. He wears a brown coat of a luxurious thick fabric, a millstone ruff around his neck, and a red velvet beret. His picture is detailed, precise, and sensitive, one of Leyster's finest works. This may have been one of the last works of her period of greatest activity. Only four paintings are known from the years after she married in 1636—a hazard for women professionals of that era.

Such was not the case for another genre painter, Jan Vermeer, although despite his gender, his output was also small. Vermeer painted some of the finest indoor scenes known, with meticulous attention to details and usually some veiled symbolism. His paintings usually show one or two figures indoors, illuminated by a window and often engaged in some activity related to the symbolism, with other symbolic elements in the background. *Woman Holding a Balance* (Figure 11.32) is a very fine typical example. A solitary woman, possibly pregnant, stands on the right at a simple wooden

FIGURE 11.31 Judith Leyster (1609–1660), *Young Flute Player* (1635), oil on canvas, 73 × 62 cm, National Museum, Stockholm.

FIGURE 11.32 Jan Vermeer (1632–1675), *Woman Holding a Balance* (ca. 1664), oil on canvas, 40 × 36 cm, National Gallery, Washington.

The Arts in the Baroque Period (1600–1750)   305

table before a window, gazing thoughtfully at a delicate set of empty scales in her right hand; her left hand rests on the table. On the table is an open jewel box with gold and pearl necklaces hanging out. Other necklaces and piles of coins lie on the table in front of a yellow ribbon and another smaller open box. At the table's back, in front of the boxes and precious objects, is a pile of luxurious cloth of true ultramarine blue. Above, on the wall, is a mirror; the window behind is covered by a mustard-yellow curtain. On the back wall, window light and shadow play in *chiaroscuro* next to a painting of the Last Judgment hanging behind the woman. She wears a rough linen headscarf and a white chemise, over which is a dark blue jacket of heavy fabric with fur cuffs and edging. Her simple skirt is brown. She has a delicate complexion, and her facial features are drawn in delicate *sfumato* rather than sharp outlines. The woman may be Vermeer's wife, Catharina.

The precision of the work, the sense of stillness, the use of a costly pigment, and the symbolic content are typical of Vermeer's work. Several interpretations have been advanced. I find the most plausible that this painting depicts the contrasts among transitory worldly wealth on the table, vanity conveyed by the mirror, and the passing of all things in the judgment scene. The woman meditates on these things and possibly that, even when her own life ends, life may continue in her unborn child. Still lifes with such a spiritual message were popular and occupied a genre all to themselves, called *vanitas* still lifes. Here the message is conveyed in a genre scene. One final aspect of Vermeer's technique deserves comment: he had little or no training and left no preliminary sketches; he may have used a *camera obscura* or *camera lucida* to produce his paintings. These devices project an image on a flat surface, where it can be traced or painted. The evidence is the precision of his drawing, especially in the modulation of light and shade, which is finer and more delicate than the unaided eye can achieve. Whatever the method, Vermeer's few works are some of the finest genre scenes known.

Related to genre scenes in their portrayal of everyday objects were different kinds of still lifes, also quite popular. Figure 11.33, a still life by Clara Peeters, actually combines two different varieties. The best-known type of still life depicts food, often fruit, on a table. Seventeenth-century Dutch people were very fond of flowers, though, and painted many flower still lifes. Peeters's work, known simply as *Table*, combines the two types. The simple wood table has a tempting display of fruit and treats on the right, with a beautiful bouquet on the left. From right to left, there is a silver platter of filled pretzels, some tidbits made of nuts and sugar, a fig, two dates, and an almond.

FIGURE 11.33 Clara Peeters (1580s-1641/61), *Table* (Still Life, 1611), oil on panel, 52 × 73 cm, Prado, Madrid.

Other pretzels, molded and iced, lie on the table. A white scalloped porcelain dish holds figs, dates, almonds, and more of the tidbits. In front of the plate, almost in the center, is an elaborate chased-gold goblet; its matching lid supports the figure of a knight with a shield and spear.[10] Behind the silver plate is a pear-shaped pewter teapot (?) with a handle, tankard lid, and long, straight covered spout. Behind the spout is a fluted conical goblet of rosé wine. Its base is delicately gilded. An ornate porcelain vase with handles holds a mixed bouquet, which fills the left part of the painting with buttercup, columbine, daffodil, iris, narcissus, peonies, periwinkles, roses, tulips, and other blooms, as well as their leaves, sprigs of rosemary, and other greenery. The bouquet has overflowed; four flowers lie on the table.

Flowers, food, and containers are meticulously realistic; one is tempted to reach out for a snack or sniff the flowers. The detail extends to the containers; every elaborate design is depicted with care. Veins, ridges, and serrations on the flowers and leaves are precise, and reflections in shiny surfaces reveal hidden aspects of the scene. A woman (presumably Peeters) with a broad lace collar and headpiece appears no less than five times in the surface of the teapot/tankard (once upside down) as well as thrice in the medallions on the gold goblet. The teapot/tankard and its lid also reflect a small-paned window. In the still life, the painter displayed her talent for depiction of an incredible variety of surfaces and textures, here perfectly conveyed (see Figures 10.12 and 10.13 for similar attainments). It is possible that there is some symbolism as well—perhaps of the transitory nature of life through the ephemeral reflections, the fallen flowers, and the plate of half-eaten pastries. Symbolic or not, the still life reveals Peeters as a commanding artistic talent.

The final popular genre is the landscape. Painted by the majority of Dutch painters, these scenes brought a bit of the outside world into cramped, narrow Dutch houses. Like the still life, the landscape also comes in several varieties. We have seen a Dutch seascape by Aelbert Cuyp (Figure 1.1) and a later mountain landscape by Albert Bierstadt (Figure 1.2). Another important Dutch landscape painter was Jacob van Ruysdael. His *View of Grainfields with a Distant Town* (Figure 11.34)

FIGURE 11.34 Jacob van Ruisdael (1628–1682), *View of Grainfields with a Distant Town* (ca. 1670), oil on canvas, 51 × 65 cm, Los Angeles County Museum of Art.

10   This cup appears in other paintings by Peeters.

The Arts in the Baroque Period (1600–1750)   307

demonstrates his work. Ruysdael painted exceptionally fine skies. These are particularly important in Dutch landscapes because the Low Countries are generally quite flat; paintings of the region generally have low horizon lines, and the sky occupies the majority of the painted surface.

In *Grainfields with a Distant Town*, a medium-blue sky is mostly obscured on the left by billowing cumulus clouds realistically shaped by subtle shading. A small flock of birds flies from left to right. Below the clouds, a low hill with trees raises the horizon on that side. There are gullies around its base and a shepherd with sheep on the grassy hilltop. The clouds shadow parts of the hill as well as most of the foreground, where a single log bridges a small stream lined with gnarled shrubs. From the bridge's far end, a man with a pole walks toward the partly mown wheat field in a ray of sunlight, which is the brightest spot in the painting. His two dogs play along the front mown edge, while further down, a farmer binds harvested wheat in sheaves. At the end of the row of sheaves, a church tower, windmill, and village cottages rise in the distance on the low horizon. The level of detail in vegetation, persons, landscape, and clouds is carefully adjusted for distance. The axis of the bridge and that of the front edge of the uncut wheat, if extended, cross at a vanishing point on the horizon just below the church steeple. Inconspicuous, off-center vanishing points like this were a favorite device of Ruysdael's. This one conceals the disciplined organization behind the painting's imbalance while reinforcing the overall natural effect. Ruysdael uses the Baroque effects of asymmetry, light, and shade to give a picture of humans' place in a broad and only partially tamed world.

Baroque Arts in Germany

The final region to visit in our circular tour of the international Baroque is Germany. In the eighteenth century, prince-bishops of Würzburg, in Catholic southern Germany, built what is sometimes regarded as the finest example of Baroque architecture in the German-speaking lands. In some respects, the palace is Versailles in miniature. Two rooms stand out: the chapel and the imperial hall. The chapel (Figure 11.35) is a confection of multicolored marbles; Tuscan and Solomonic columns; gilded Corinthian capitals, arabesques, and sunbursts; *trompe l'oeil* ceiling frescoes; and sculptures of saints and angels that stand on pedestals supporting the pulpit and perching on cornices, canopies, and other furnishings. The decoration is almost unbelievably rich, perhaps to convey the impression of heaven itself. The imperial hall (Figure 11.36) is similar.

The imperial hall again uses multicolored marbles and gilded capitals, arabesques, and

FIGURE 11.35 Balthasar Neumann (1687–1753), Palace Chapel (1743), Prince Bishop's Residence, Würzburg, Germany.

drapery frames for frescoes and mirrors.[11] The columns here are Corinthian; crystal chandeliers are much more ornate, and windows admit more light. Portraits hang on the walls where there is room, and elaborate frescoes adorn the ceiling. These were painted by Giovanni Battista Tiepolo (1696–1770), perhaps the greatest Venetian artist of the time. The end panels depict episodes from the history of the Würzburg diocese; the one in Figure 11.36 shows the (medieval) bishop of Würzburg marrying Emperor Frederick Barbarossa and Beatrix of Burgundy. The ceiling center (not visible) depicts in *trompe l'oeil* Beatrix striving toward Frederick, who is accompanied by the bishop. Additional *trompe l'oeil* figures move around the cornice between the window levels and even overlap it and the window frames. The windows themselves overlook the garden.

FIGURE 11.36 Balthasar Neumann, Kaisersaal (Imperial Hall), 1742, Würzburg Residence.

Like Versailles's Hall of Mirrors, the imperial hall occupies the center of the eastern garden front of the palace. From its balcony, one sees the view in Figure 11.37. Out of the figure on the sides are geometric beds, as at Versailles. Some of this geometry is visible in the central circular walks, potted trees, and fountain, although the original garden design filled in what are now lawns with more elaborate floral designs and beds. The arcaded hedges on either side are a bit of the old that survives. Like Louis, the prince-bishop (who was secular ruler of the territory of Würzburg) wanted a central view suggesting large domains, but the designer faced a serious problem in the city walls directly behind the palace grounds. His ingenious solution was to

FIGURE 11.37 View of East Garden as it now appears, Würzburg Residence.

have a series of elevated terraces and stairways that rise to wall height in the center as the formal geometric gardens yield to informal gardens and groves in the English style on the sides.[12] Beyond the walls, which are crowned with a formal balustrade (rail), the informal

---

11 The colored "marble" of the columns is actually an imitation in stucco (plaster), which was also used for the gilded arabesques and other decorations.

12 The English style was invented by Lancelot "Capability" Brown, whose nickname arose from telling his noble clients that their grounds had great capability for improvement. Sometimes described as England's greatest gardener, his approach was to design natural-appearing views of groves, meadows, pools, streams, and sometimes follies that framed and enhanced the palaces and important constructions of the estate. These designs swept Baroque formality aside and formed a theoretical core for freer modern landscape design.

FIGURE 11.38 George Bähr (1666–1738), Frauenkirche (Church of Our Lady), 1726–43, exterior, sandstone, 96 m high, Dresden, Germany.

FIGURE 11.39 Ruins of the Dresden Frauenkirche in front of the City Hall Tower after World War II firebombing, Dresden, Germany.

grove continues, as if a grand forest. The result is a grand vista that moves from formal design to a natural informality in the distance.

To the north, across the boundary between Protestant and Catholic areas of the German-speaking lands, lay the Duchy of Saxony, whose capital city is/was Dresden. Saxony was in a peculiar position: although its people were Protestant, the duke was an elector of the Holy Roman Emperor and at times King of Poland; the Ducal family changed sides but was Catholic in the eighteenth century. Dresden's major church was the Frauenkirche—the Church of Our Lady, dedicated to the Virgin Mary but Protestant (Figure 11.38). This huge church is ninety-six meters high. Its dome, an engineering feat comparable to St. Peter's in Rome, is nicknamed the Stone Bell. For more than two hundred years, it was (and is again) the defining feature of Dresden's skyline. Remarkably strong, it survived several bombardments until American and English firebombing in World War II raised the internal temperature to over 1000° C and the stone literally exploded. The rubble lay mostly untouched for forty-five years (see Figure 11.39). Since the reunification of Germany, however, it has been completely reconstructed, using original stone wherever possible (the black spots and, just visible on the far left, one of two complete walls). In front of the church is a statue/monument of Martin Luther.

The church's exterior is an elegant Baroque that could be Roman in its majesty and use of the sculpted wall, highlighted by shadows in Figure 11.38. Corinthian pilasters support broken pediments on the long walls, and the corners are crowned with (relatively) small towers topped with decorative finials. As part of these finials are square, onion-shaped cupolas with inset round faces. A similar unembellished cupola crowns the central dome. Such onion cupolas—square, polygonal, or round—are a characteristic feature of Baroque architecture in German-speaking countries, whether Catholic or Protestant.

The Protestantism of this church is especially evident in the interior (Figure 11.40). The building is square, and instead of a long nave with worshippers facing a distant altar, the seating is arranged in arcs that face the chancel, in which the altar is elevated but well behind the prominent pulpit, the true focus. Behind the altar is a relief plaque that survived the bombing; it bears a Latin inscription and two figures holding symbols of the Christian faith. Above that is a relief of Christ on the

Mount of Olives. Statues of saints (Paul and Philip), Moses, and Aaron flank the scene under garlands of wheat and grapes, symbolizing the sacrament of communion. The eye of God surmounts it all, concealed in clouds with gilded cherubs and sunrays. Above that is the reconstructed organ, with about half of the instrument's stops designed to replicate the original Silbermann organ, inaugurated by J.S. Bach in 1736. Additional pipes and a manual keyboard have been added to make the instrument better suited to play more recent compositions as well, but the visible casework reproduces the original. The interior décor has many of the features of the Würzburg chapel—faux-colored marble and gilded arabesques—but much more restrained, with few pictorial frescoes and no sculptures beyond those above the altar.

FIGURE 11.40 George Bähr, Frauenkirche restored interior, Dresden.

Congregational seating rises above the floor in a windowed gallery and three more balconies that surround the sides away from the altar. The Frauenkirche is a magnificent example of Baroque architecture in the service of the Protestant faith.

As mentioned above, J.S. Bach, who some consider the greatest composer of all time, played an inaugural recital on the Frauenkirche's new Silbermann organ in 1736. Bach traveled very little during his lifetime and spent over half of it in Saxony, the last twenty-seven years in Leipzig, 102 km west of Dresden. During this time he offered several tributes to the Duke of Saxony, who awarded Bach the honorary title of Royal Saxon Court Composer. Among his offerings, in 1733, as a memorial to a recently deceased duke, he sent two sections of a Latin mass, the *Kyrie* and the *Gloria*, each subdivided into several movements. Bach later expanded this and finished all five sections of the complete mass in 1749. Although he gave it no overall title, it is known as the Mass in B Minor, and it is perhaps the greatest setting of mass music ever written, although it is so long as to be generally impractical for actual worship.

Whether even part of the work was performed in Dresden in Bach's lifetime is an open question. It was not performed (complete) publicly until 1828 and not in the United States until 1900. Figure 11.41 includes the first four movements of the *Gloria* section (movements 4 through 7 of the complete work). These are two choral movements with orchestra in rather different styles, followed by a solo aria for soprano; I included one more chorus to give the example a grand close. The opening chorus, "*Gloria in excelsis Deo*," is for a five-part choir with a full orchestra of trumpets and kettledrums, flutes, oboes, and bassoon, and a full string section, from violins to double bass. This first chorus alternates brief, short sections for certain sections of the orchestra and chorus with large homophonic sections. Some of the smaller sections have a little imitative polyphony. The chorus begins with an introduction for full orchestra, followed

FIGURE 11.41 Johann Sebastian Bach (1685–1750), Mass in B Minor (1733–49).

Movements—4. *Gloria*, 5. *Et in terra pax*, 6. *Laudamus te*
7. *Gratias agimus tibi*

Historical note—Bach composed the first two parts (Kyrie & Gloria) of the B-Minor Mass, as a gift to the Duke-Elector of Saxony, Augustus III, when Bach visited Dresden in 1733. This music may have been performed in Dresden during that visit. The rest of the mass was not completed until 1747 for a similar gift. There are no records of its performance as a whole before 1828.

The B-Minor Mass is the largest, grandest setting of the texts of the Mass ever written. Five texts occur in virtually every mass: the *Kyrie* (like Machaut's), the *Gloria* (four of its parts here), the *Credo*, the *Sanctus*, and the *Agnus Dei* (not included here). Each text is divided into several musical movements, to express the mood of particular texts. Bach's B-Minor Mass has 30 musical movements; the Gloria alone has nine. The work as a whole is too long to be practical for a religious service. However, the first two (1533) parts were used by both Protestants and Catholics in Bach's time

Latin	English
4 Gloria in excelsis Deo	**Glory to God in the highest**
Big, fast, jubilant. Chorus and orchestra in concerto style—a single instrument or small group of them alternates with whole orchestra. In this case, the trumpets and the voices are two groups that alternate with the whole. Often the choir begins with two voices in imitation followed by everyone (the *tutti*). The groups alternate and the whole texture grows until a sudden change leads into—	
5 Et in terra pax hominibus bonae voluntatis.	**And on earth peace to men of good will.**
Peaceful. Chorus and orchestra in fugue style. One voice enters at a time singing a lilting melody, followed by the orchestra playing it. Then there is a true fugue-style entry, with every voice coming in singing the theme until all voices have entered; then the chorus performs this theme together, with the orchestra gradually entering. The process is repeated. After this modified repetition, a final fugal entry brings in voices and instruments piecemeal until the trumpet signals the end.	
6 Laudamus te, benedicimus te, adoramus te, glorificamus te.	**We praise thee, we bless thee, we adore thee, we glorify thee.**
Joyful. Soprano solo with violin and orchestra strings—Aria in ABA form. Introduction in major key—The violin plays the melodic theme, punctuated by continuo and strings to introduce the A Section. The soprano echoes the violin theme, and they twine around each other in counterpoint, adding and imitating new melodies for each bit of text. The B section changes to a minor key, using similar melodies and techniques. The A section in the major key returns, without the introduction. The ABA form was typical of opera arias in Bach's time.	
7 Gratias agimus tibi propter magnam gloriam tuam.	**We give thanks to thee because of thy great glory.**
Rising joy. Fugal stretto style—each voice enters on the melody beforer the previous one finishes. This happens several times, each time growing louder on the rising melody to express the idea of thanks, then there is a fugal entry on a new more complicated melody that expresses the idea of great glory This, too, grows until a final trumpet entry leads the chorus to a close.	

by imitative entries for two voices interrupted by the full choir and orchestra. Alternation of large and small sections like this is a hallmark of the *concerto* style, which was a musical innovation of the Baroque period. This pattern is repeated with variations several times before a final orchestra and choir section makes a grand closure of the first chorus.

The second chorus, "*Et in terra pax hominibus bonae voluntatis*," begins with slow entries of individual voice parts in imitative polyphony, without trumpets and drums—a much-subdued instrumentation. Again, individual sections of a few parts (sometimes just instruments) alternate with the full ensemble until a final, longer instrumental section in a minor key leads into a series of entries of individual voice parts that builds until all have entered. After these entrances, the orchestra again alternates with the choir, at first homophonically. Then sections similar to the beginning occur again, and the alternation becomes more complex: the ensemble and orchestral volume increase, the trumpets and drums return, and the chorus arrives at a majestic close.

The third movement, "*Laudamus te, adoramus te, benedicimus te, glorificamus te,*" is for solo soprano and violin with occasional strings and *basso continuo*. This movement's form and style are modeled on the typical opera aria of the time. Typical opera arias followed a ternary A-B-A form and had elaborate melodies. This aria does too, with a few small changes of Bach's. The melody for this aria is complex, with several different musical ideas shared by the voice and violin in elaborate and delicate polyphony, often mixed in different orders and with the remaining strings. The same text and melodies are used in both sections but in different ways and keys. The A section begins with a solo violin introduction that leads to the soprano's entrance. The entire section, twenty-nine measures long, uses all the melodic ideas in a major key. The B section, of twenty measures, uses similar melodies in a different order and in a minor key, with less participation of other strings, leaving the solo voice and violin more exposed. The final A section is shortened, as in the similar form of the Lully *ouverture*. The final section is once again in the major key, but it rearranges the melodic ideas to fit in a mere twelve measures. The solo aria leads into the example's final chorus, "*Gratias agimus tibi propter magnam gloriam tuam,*" a double fugue with two melodic ideas—one in long sustained notes, the other contrasting in short, faster notes. They are combined in elaborate polyphony in many different ways. The movement begins with the chorus, the softer parts of the orchestra, and *basso continuo*, then gradually builds, with the addition of trumpets and drums, to a majestic closure for yet another demonstration of the Baroque magnificence of the music of J.S. Bach.

The wonderful complexity and ornamentation of Bach's music (and the expressiveness of Carissimi's and Lully's) add perfect musical counterparts to the powerful sculpture of Bernini; the rich paintings of Venice, France, and the Netherlands; and the elaborate architecture of Rome, Versailles, Würzburg, and Dresden (and the elegant gardens that accompanied them). The arts of this period express the complexity of the era—in politics, in religion, in social evolution, in scientific development, in literature, and in philosophy. The era of the Baroque, conceived in the seventeenth century and culminating in the eighteenth, was the grand finale of millennia of cultural development about to undergo revolutionary change in the subsequent era.

Image Credits

Fig. 11.3: Tintoretto / Copyright in the Public Domain.

Fig. 11.4: Jebulon / Wikimedia Commons / Copyright in the Public Domain.

Fig. 11.5: Giovanni Paolo Panini / Copyright in the Public Domain.

Fig. 11.6: Francis Bond / Copyright in the Public Domain.

Fig. 11.7: Copyright © 2005 by Dnalor 01 / Wikimedia Commons, (CC BY-SA 3.0) at https://commons. wikimedia.org/wiki/File:Rom,_Vatikan,_Petersdom,_Cathedra_Petri_(Bernini)_4.jpg.

Fig. 11.8: Niccola Zabaglia / Copyright in the Public Domain.

Fig. 11.9: Encyclopædia Britannica / Copyright in the Public Domain.

Fig. 11.10: Giovanni Battista Piranesi / Copyright in the Public Domain.

Fig. 11.11: Copyright © 2014 by Sailko / Wikimedia Commons, (CC BY-SA 3.0) at https://commons. wikimedia.org/wiki/File:Museo_borghese,_sala_del_sole,_g.l._bernini,_david,_1623-24,_03.jpg. org/wiki/File:Museo_borghese,_sala_del_sole,_g.l._bernini,_david,_1623-24,_03.jpg.

Fig. 11.12: Copyright © 2006 by Nina Aldin Thune, (CC BY-SA 2.5) at https://commons.wikimedia.org/wiki/ File:Santa_Maria_della_Vittoria_-_1.jpg.

Fig. 11.13: Copyright © 2015 by Joaquim Alves Gaspar, (CC BY-SA 4.0) at https://commons.wikimedia.org/ wiki/File:Ecstasy_of_Saint_Teresa_September_2015-2a.jpg.

Fig. 11.14: Copyright © 2009 by Bruce McAdam, (CC BY-SA 2.0) at https://commons.wikimedia.org/wiki/ File:Andrea_Pozzo_-_Apoteose_de_Santo_Inacio.jpg.

Fig. 11.16: Gian Lorenzo Bernini; Photo copyright © 2011 by Melberg / Wikimedia Commons, (CC BY-SA 3.0) at https://commons.wikimedia.org/wiki/File:Ch%C3%A2teau_de_Versailles,_salon_de_Diane,_buste_de_ Louis_XIV,_Bernin_%281665%29_03_black_bg.jpg.

Fig. 11.17: Hyacinthe Rigaud / Copyright in the Public Domain.

Fig. 11.18: Copyright © 2013 by ToucanWings / Wikimedia Commons, (CC BY-SA 3.0) at https:// commons.wikimedia.org/wiki/File:Vue_a%C3%A9rienne_du_domaine_de_Versailles_par_ ToucanWings_-_Creative_Commons_By_Sa_3.0_-_073.jpg.

Fig. 11.19: Copyright © 2011 by Myrabella / Wikimedia Commons, (CC BY-SA 3.0) at https://commons. wikimedia.org/wiki/File:Chateau_Versailles_Galerie_des_Glaces.jpg.

Fig. 11.20: Copyright © 2010 by Moyan Brenn, (CC BY 2.0) at https://commons.wikimedia.org/wiki/ File:Versailles_perspective_of_the_famous_grand_canal,_2010.jpg.

Fig. 11.21: Copyright in the Public Domain.

Fig. 11.22: Charles Le Brun / Copyright in the Public Domain.

Fig. 11.23: Jean Le Pautre / Copyright in the Public Domain.

Fig. 11.24: Jean Bérain / Copyright in the Public Domain.

Fig. 11.26: Dirck van Delen / Copyright in the Public Domain.

Fig. 11.27A: Peter Paul Rubens / Copyright in the Public Domain.

Fig. 11.27B: Peter Paul Rubens / Copyright in the Public Domain.

Fig. 11.28A: Rembrandt / Copyright in the Public Domain.

Fig. 11.28B: Rembrandt / Copyright in the Public Domain.

Fig. 11.28C: Rembrandt / Copyright in the Public Domain.

Fig. 11.28D: Rembrandt / Copyright in the Public Domain.

CHAPTER 12

THE ARTS IN THE EIGHTEENTH CENTURY (1700–1800)

Background

As we approach the present, the speed of historical development speeds up. Increased population, more (if not better) transportation, increased exchange of ideas, and increased political and religious ferment brought accelerating change. Yet older ideas did not immediately disappear, and the result is overlap and often conflict among opposing concepts, ideas, and ideals. This is true in all areas of human endeavor. In the eighteenth century, the simultaneous existence of different social and artistic visions led to the coexistence in the arts of several stylistic periods at the same time. The eighteenth century saw the last stage of the high Baroque, its devolution to the Rococo, and the reaction to it in the Neoclassic—all at the same time.

The causes for this surge in analysis and inspiration are multiple: 1) greater contact with other cultures around the world; 2) increasing awareness and resentment of a stratified social structure that burdened the lower classes; 3) disgust with wars of religion and the dogmas behind them; and 4) expansion and organization of the scientific advances of the 1700s.

Contact with other cultures brought awareness that the European, Christian way of life was not the only one. Even if it were superior, curiosity arose about the state of human existence before and outside it: the condition of "natural man"—prepolitical, preeconomic—what were the conditions of his/her life?[1] In the natural state,

---

1   I use the term "natural man" because this is the traditional term for discussing humankind in this context, and I don't want to confuse the discussion with terms like natural human, natural people, natural

humans are equal; therefore, all humans have certain rights that cannot be taken from them (unalienable): life, liberty, and property. People found serious disparities between these rights and Europe's feudal social class structure: life and liberty were threatened by arbitrary imprisonment, torture, and execution, often for no more than speaking one's mind. Government by a few oppressed the many. Property was threatened by confiscation and heavy taxation at levels of perhaps twice or more than in the United States today.

Concern about these disparities and study of historical governments led to important new concepts: 1) that government requires the consent of the people governed; 2) that uniformity of government and law requires a written constitution; 3) that this constitution must separate powers to protect against abuse of power by a leader or group; 4) that laws should be uniformly applied, without regard to social class or influence; 5) that legal proceedings must have absolute safeguards—abolition of torture, due process for all, and presumption of innocence until proven guilty; 6) that those governed must have freedoms of thought, speech, and assembly for public commentary; and 7) that religion must have no role in government.

In contrast to this revolutionary vision for society, European politics and international relations stumbled much as they had—at least for the first three-quarters of the century. There were European wars based on royal family politics—who should succeed to the Spanish and Austrian thrones, should Protestant Hanoverians or Catholic Stuarts rule England; others were based on territory—Russia and Sweden, the southern Netherlands, America, and other colonies (see Figure 12.1). Some European countries had achieved the status of unified nation-states, but Germany and Italy were still fragmented, and Scandinavia and Eastern Europe were dominated by large states that overrode natural ethnic and linguistic boundaries. Religious persecution still drove emigration of many dissenting Christian groups: Anabaptists, Calvinists, Catholics, Methodists, Moravian Brethren, Quakers, Shakers, and others. Yet some sects fostered growth: Methodists sought to revitalize Anglicanism and inspired the Great Awakening; the Catholic Church expanded its missionary efforts worldwide, including Asia and the California missions.

In addition to political and religious turbulence, technological advances produced a flurry of new inventions: accurate clocks, bifocal lenses, new musical instruments (e.g., the clarinet and piano), hot-air and hydrogen balloons, the lightning rod, spinning and weaving machines, the steam engine and boat, the thermometer, the thresher, and smallpox vaccination. The scientific and scholarly revolution of the previous century continued and grew. Some of those who made great discoveries are listed in Figure 12.2.

persons, and the like. In addition, for better or worse, society and the arts between 1600 and 1800 (as they were earlier and later) were overwhelmingly male dominated, which gives some applicability, however unjust, to the term. Outside of this exception, I try to use only gender-neutral or inclusive terms for generalities.

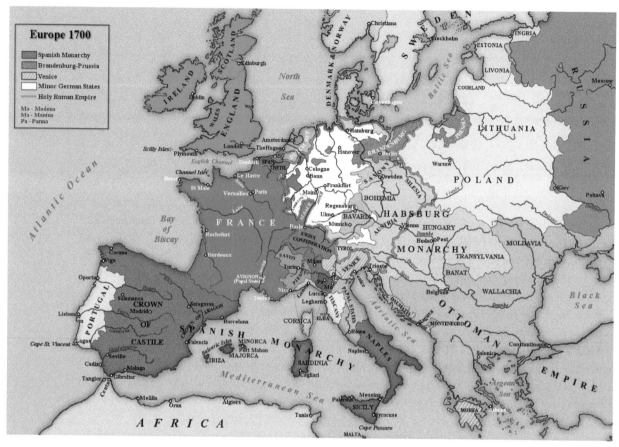

FIGURE 12.1 Europe, 1700–1714. France, Spain, Portugal, Great Britain and Switzerland approximate their modern boundaries. Germany and Italy are divided. Northern and Eastern Europe have units that overrode ethnic or linguistic boundaries.

Frederick William Herschel	Astronomy
Henry Cavendish, Antoine Lavoisier, Joseph Priestley	Chemistry
Cesare Beccaria	Criminology
Joseph Banks, Georges Buffon, Carl Linnaeus	Biology, Natural History
Robert Malthus, Adam Smith	Economics
Captain James Cook	Exploration
Benjamin Franklin, James Watt	Inventors
Carl Friedrich Gauss, Leonhard Euler, Pierre Fermat	Mathematics
Edward Jenner	Medicine
Denis Diderot, Immanuel Kant, Voltaire	Philosophy
Daniel Bernoulli, Anders Celsius, Daniel Gabriel Fahrenheit, Benjamin Franklin, Alessandro Volta	Physics
Jeremy Bentham, Charles-Louis Montesquieu, Thomas Paine, Jean-Jacques Rousseau, Mary Wollstonecraft	Political Science

FIGURE 12.2 Great eighteenth-century thinkers and their work.

Such an explosion of information and ideas led to groundbreaking innovations and required new ways to share them. Summaries of knowledge multiplied: dictionaries, histories, technical manuals, and encyclopedias. A few examples include: the first encyclopedia, compiled by Denis Diderot; the first *Encyclopedia Britannica*; Edward Gibbon's *Decline and Fall of the Roman Empire*; Samuel Johnson's *Dictionary of the English Language*; Jean-Jacques Rousseau's *Dictionary of Music*; histories of music by Charles Burney and John Hawkins; and method books for piano, violin, and flute by Carl Philipp

Emanuel Bach, Leopold Mozart, and Johann Joachim Quantz. Scientific and scholarly societies and journals appeared.

The explosion of information and analysis of new scientific and political concepts, along with the effort to increase, codify, and spread knowledge, is known as the Age of Reason or the Enlightenment. This time in history is the root of the modern world, as government, education, science, writing, and the arts took a new direction, based not on religion and the exercise of arbitrary power by a few but on rational thought, debate, and decision by representatives of the people governed.

Such a bubbling cauldron of ideas and developments had to overflow, and it did by the end of the century in two formative revolutions. The American Revolution arose from peaceful differences in 1765, when colonists demanded representation in Parliament before paying taxes to Great Britain for British protection and governance of North America. The simmering dispute grew violent in the 1770s, and in 1776, the United States of America published the Declaration of Independence, and war ensued. After the war's 1783 conclusion, representatives wrote the United States Constitution and the Bill of Rights between 1787 and 1789. These three founding documents of American democracy were the first to embody the ideals of government and society that were developed in the Age of Reason.

The American Revolution's success seeded social and political ferment throughout Europe. The first monarchy to fall was the *ancien régime* of France. After the death of Louis XIV, French kings and queens had continued in luxury, power, and privilege despite war and famine. Prices rose, lower-class taxes reached 70 percent or higher, and the country was essentially bankrupt. The dam burst in 1789. A National Constituent Assembly replaced the old Estates-General, which favored the nobility and clergy; partisans stormed the Bastille, a Paris medieval prison that symbolized monarchy, and the Assembly published the Declaration of the Rights of Man and of the Citizen, largely written by Thomas Jefferson (then in Paris) and the Marquis de Lafayette (who had been a general in the American Revolution). The declaration was a noble one and remains a fundamental document in the history of human rights. Unfortunately, extremist forces were too strong. After a brief period of constitutional government, the Reign of Terror occurred from 1793–1795, followed by another constitution, until a *coup d'état* in 1799 made Napoléon Bonaparte first consul.

Rococo Art

It is not hard to see, in this ferment of culture, ideas, and politics, why there were at least three different artistic styles in the eighteenth century. The pace of creative development accelerated with everything else. We have discussed the first style, the Baroque, which started in the previous century and continued into the eighteenth. The second style—an offshoot, moderation, or dilution of the Baroque beginning shortly after 1700—is called the Rococo or Galante style. The third style, the Neoclassic, rejected the Baroque and returned again for inspiration to works of the classical Greeks and Romans, starting in the eighteenth century and continuing after 1800.

The French Royal Academy of Painting and Sculpture was established under Louis XIV. Although disputes arose between advocates of drawing and color, the Academy was unified in its hierarchy of paintings' worth: 1) history painting (which also included allegorical, literary, mythical, and religious subjects); 2) genre painting; 3) portraiture; 4) still life; and 5) landscape. Each new member had to submit a painting. Antoine Watteau's *Pilgrimage to Cythera* (Figure 12.3), submitted in 1717, fit none of the established categories, so a new category was invented: *fêtes galantes* (elegant festivals), which described the frivolous pastimes of the royal court. The painting's final version here (1721) is a slightly embellished version of the original; the main differences

FIGURE 12.3 Antoine Watteau (1684–1721), *Pilgrimage to Cythera* (1721 embellishment of original of 1717), oil on canvas, 129 × 194 cm, Charlottenburg Palace, Berlin.

are more cupids, a more prominent statue of Venus, and the rosy haze around the boat. The painting(s) depict couples in various stages of intimate encounters. Beginning on the right, under a statue of Venus (the goddess of erotic love), a couple reclines and embraces on the grass. Behind and to their left are two seated couples. Moving left, we find a couple rising from the grass and another ambling toward the boat while turning to look wistfully at those remaining. Surrounding the boat, a small crowd prepares to board, and throughout the work, cupids cuddle the lovers, play tag, and fly around like bumblebees.[2] Venus's statue crowns a small hill under an ancient tree whose every leaf shows, while a rosy haze surrounds the ornate boat.

The frivolity and sensuousness of Watteau's *Pilgrimage* inaugurated a new artistic style: the Rococo. Works in this style have many of the characteristics of Baroque works but to a lesser degree—diluted. There is contrast between light and dark, but it is more modulated and less abrupt; composition retains some diagonal organization and imbalance but may also include vertical, horizontal, and balanced components; there is gentle movement, as the couples amble, and their poses are fashionable and relaxed; there is emotion, but it is sentimental and pleasant, not powerful. Echoes of the style also penetrated other genres like portraiture.

François Boucher's portrait of *Madame de Pompadour* (Figure 12.4) demonstrates how the Rococo style changed portraiture. Madame de Pompadour was King Louis XV's chief mistress. Although merely a well-educated commoner, she attracted the king's interest. Their physical intimacy ended after five years, but she retained honor and influence due to her creativity, intelligence, skillful diplomacy, wit, and friendship with the queen. As a patroness of the arts and letters, she supported François Boucher to become First Painter of the King. Boucher's portrait of Pompadour, one of several, shows Rococo effects in portraiture. She stands in a relaxed pose, leaning slightly on the pedestal of a statue of Cupid cuddling Venus (a bit like Watteau's). Her gown is an elaborate, low-cut salmon-colored silk decorated with bows, flounces, and floral embroidery. In her right hand is a closed fan; beneath it are a rose bush, a garden bench, and a little dog gazing at her. Two roses tumble to the ground, and the whole scene takes place in a garden bower, with leaves of the shrubbery depicted in detail. Her face is oval, with prominent, intelligent eyes and a delicate mouth. There are some symbolic elements in the work. Venus and Cupid express her place in the king's affections; the dog represents her fidelity to their relationship; and the fallen blossoms may be a delicate reference to her position as mistress.

---

2   Cupid, son of Venus and Mars, was a single figure in Greco-Roman mythology, but even then, such figures appeared in art in multiples, under a variety of names, representing spirits inspiring, or an atmosphere of love and passion. Suppressed in the Middle Ages, they reappeared in Renaissance and subsequent art.

FIGURE 12.4 François Boucher (1703–1770), *Madame de Pompadour* (1759), oil on canvas, 91 × 68 cm, Wallace Collection, London.

FIGURE 12.5 (Marie-Louise) Élisabeth Vigée-LeBrun (1755–1842), *Marie Antoinette with a Rose* (1783), oil on canvas, 113 × 87 cm, Palace of Versailles.

The frivolity of the Rococo style symbolized the monarchy until its fall. The last queen was Marie Antoinette, whose favorite painter was Élisabeth Vigée-Lebrun. Her 1783 portrait of the queen (Figure 12.5) shares features with Boucher's work. The queen stands before a rose bush in a wooded space, with foliage again depicted in some detail. She is dressed lavishly in a lace- and bow-trimmed, low-cut blue silk gown with a simple two-strand pearl necklace. Her grey hair is in a bouffant coiffure with large ringlets falling behind. Ostrich plumes adorn her grey silk hat, and her left hand holds a rose. It is an elegant royal portrait. The dress is somewhat simpler than Pompadour's. The new queen, Marie Antoinette, enjoyed role playing as a peasant shepherdess, had a play farmhouse constructed on palace grounds, and made simpler gowns fashionable.

Artistic styles from Versailles continued to influence the rest of Europe. Just outside Dresden, in the town of Meissen, porcelain clay was discovered and a royal factory founded. The most famous modeler of Meissen (Dresden) porcelain was Johann Joachim Kändler, best known for his figurines, like those in Figure 12.6. The figures in *Lady and Cavalier Dancing* are a model of the elegance of eighteenth-century society. They gaze at each other with polite friendship. Their posture is erect but nonchalant as they touch hands in the dance. The gentleman's feet are turned out at exactly the fashionable angle—ninety degrees from each other, forty-five degrees from the direction of movement. Hers are undoubtedly the same under her

FIGURE 12.6 Johann Joachim Kändler, *Lady and Cavalier Dancing* (1744), Meissen Hard Porcelain, Porcelain Museum, Meissen, Germany.

FIGURE 12.7 Johann Joachim Kändler (1706–75), *Commedia dell' arte* Figures (1740, c. 1744, c. 1735), Meissen Hard Porcelain, Birmingham Museum of Art, Birmingham, Alabama. From left: Arlecchino, Columbina & Arlecchino, Pantalone.

modest but rich flowered gown with a voluminous skirt spread by crinolines, hoops, and hip panniers. His elegant yellow frock coat with gold buttons matches his knee breeches; underneath he wears a gold embroidered white waistcoat and, of course, a sword, with a scarlet sash completing the ensemble. The couple represents the utmost in courtly deportment, meticulously depicted in porcelain.

Meissen artists portrayed figures in all activities, from dance and courtly portraits to mining and other occupations, always with perfect finish and meticulously detailed painting. Some of their favorite and most-repeated figures are those of stock theater characters from the *commedia dell' arte*, the improvised Italian comedy that dates back to the Renaissance and, in the eighteenth century, formed the basis for plays by Carlo Goldoni and others as well as for comic opera plots (see Figure 12.7). Harlequin (Arlecchino), in his costume of colored patches, appears twice. Columbine (Columbina), with whom he dances in the center group, is his girlfriend. Both of them are tricky comic servants who delight in outwitting their master, often the miserly old man, Pantaloon (Pantalone), on the right. These delicately modeled and painted humorous figurines reflect the lighthearted playfulness and whimsy of the Rococo.

A particularly fine example of such humor is Kändler's white porcelain bust of "Baron Schmiedel," court jester to Augustus III, King of Poland and Elector of Saxony (see Figure 12.8). The jester, whose real name was Johann Gottfried Tuscheer, attended the king at all times, cracking jokes, making witty conversation, or playing tricks with mice (of which he was supposed to be morbidly afraid).[3] He was well rewarded with titles like Postmaster General. The bust is finely modeled and very lifelike. Head turned to the right, Schmiedel wears a tricorne hat with a bow, a ruffled shirt, and a formal jacket with molded buttons. A medallion with the king's portrait hangs around his neck; a barely visible badge on his left chest bears the royal crest under a chain with a posthorn, the symbol of his honorary

3   Eva Czernis-Ryl, "*Baron Schmiedel* by Johann Joachim Kändler, 1739," Powerhouse Museum, online catalog, consulted June 11, 2016, describes another copy, now in Australia; it lacks one mouse.

title. He wears a generous upturned mustache and a wig and is riddled with mice—four of them: one on his hat, one nuzzling him from his shoulder, one peering out of his jacket, and one dangling from his mouth!

In architecture, we have already seen some anticipation of the Rococo in the gilded arabesques of the chapel and Imperial Hall in Würzburg (Figures 11.35 and 11.36). The Rococo is, indeed, often called the Late Baroque. The origin of the name is not clear—it may be a combination of *barocco*, the Italian word for baroque, and *rocaille*, a type of ornament using seashells and pebbles. A remnant of the latter appears today in the scallop shell sometimes carved in fine furniture. Typically, the style involves ornamentation in delicate (often asymmetrical) curves and may use marine motifs. Figure 12.9, from the antechamber to the Imperial Hall of Würzburg, is an example of such a motif. This room, called the White Room, is a deliberate contrast from the brilliant formality of the Imperial Hall. Decorated in light grey, there are elaborate white stucco designs on the walls and ceiling in Rococo style. The figure shows a small portion—a goddess (perhaps Athena or Diana) holding a spear sits among elaborate arabesques, among which two cupids gambol. The asymmetry is pronounced but not unpleasant. The designs do not actually imitate shells, but they do have a marine quality: the curves are shell-like, and the finer details resemble a seahorse's ridged back or the joints of a crayfish or lobster. The overall effect is one that preserves the rich embellishment of the Baroque, but with lighthearted delicacy.

FIGURE 12.8 Johann Joachim Kändler, *Bust of Baron Schmiedel (Johann Gottfried Tuscheer)*, 1739, Meissen Hard Porcelain, Porcelain Museum, Meissen, Germany.

Neoclassic Art

Especially when older styles overlap, there is potential for conflict between opposing concepts and ideals. This is not the case between the Baroque and the Rococo, but the Neoclassical style represents a deliberate repudiation of, and reaction to, both the Baroque and Rococo. In place of elaborate and complex ornamentation surrounding figures in motion, Neoclassic art emphasizes simplicity, symmetry, and clear organization modeled on the current perception of Classic Greek art. It could have great power but rarely any sense of motion, even when movement was depicted. The image is like a "moment frozen in time."[4] The movement was heavily academic. History painting reigned supreme: subjects from mythology

FIGURE 12.9 Antonio Bossi (seventeenth c.–1764), Rocaille design (1744–45), stucco, White Hall, Würzburg Residence.

---

4   I am indebted to my colleague, Dr. Dorothy Keyser, for this elegant turn of phrase.

FIGURE 12.10 Jacques-Louis David (1748–1825), *The Oath of the Horatii* (1784–5), oil on canvas, 330 × 167 cm, Louvre, Paris.

or ancient history were obligatory. Even for contemporary occurrences, the Academy's attitude was that the event should be idealized—depicted *as it should have been* rather than as it was. If contemporary individuals appeared, they should be dressed in ancient garb. It could be controversial to paint the portrait of a nobleman *not* dressed in a toga!

Jacques-Louis David was the leading painter of the Neoclassical style. In the 1780s, his severe style moved away from the Rococo, as seen in *The Oath of the Horatii* of 1784, Figure 12.10. The work depicts an episode from legendary Roman history. To decide a dispute between their two cities, two families—the Horatii for Rome and the Curiatii for Rome's enemies—had agreed that their sons would fight to the death to avoid a full battle. Here, the three Horatii brothers, standing with widespread feet, raise their right arms to swear their oath on the swords raised by their father, Horatius. The foremost son will survive and avenge his brothers by killing all three Curatii. The mourning women include, on the far right, a Horatius, who weeps for her Curiatius fiancé as well as her brother. Beside her, a reclining Curiatius, married to one of the Horatii, weeps for her husband and her brother. Her two children stand behind with their nurse.

The strongly colored figures overlap in a foreground plane before a background divided into three Roman-style arches on Doric columns. The brothers' poses' straight lines echo those of the columns, while the women's curves reflect those of the arches.[5] The composition is centered on the hand holding the raised sword. The brothers' and father's arms point toward it, as does the father's back leg and a line connecting the sisters' faces. That is also the vanishing point of the pavement and the masonry of the side walls. The arches divide the painting into three thematic zones: the brothers swearing the oath, Horatius holding the swords, and the weeping women. The painting is filled with powerful emotions frozen in time. It expresses a theme of loyalty to the state over the family, a theme that was to fuel the flames of revolution in five years. The work came to be regarded as an ideal model for the Neoclassical style.

Instead of legendary history, David's *Death of Socrates*, Figure 12.11, depicts a documented historical event described by Plato: Socrates's condemnation to death by poison for (allegedly) denying the gods and corrupting the youth of Athens. The charge was false, and Socrates could have substituted exile, but he chose to make his death a final lesson and teach his students the triumph of the soul over death. His shackles lying on the floor, Socrates sits on his bed with one leg raised, the other on a stepstool. His left arm is raised in a gesture, while his right arm reaches for the goblet of hemlock held by an unidentified mourner with his back turned.

---

5   "Jacques-Louis David: *The Oath of the Horatii.*" *Smarthistory.* Khan Academy, consulted June 10, 2016.

A smoking lamp on a stand behind the scene symbolizes the life about to be extinguished. On the right, Socrates's student Crito sits gripping his teacher's thigh, while others listen and mourn. Seated at the bed's foot is Plato, and behind him, sobbing against the exit arch's wall, is the student Apollodorus. Socrates's wife Xanthippe raises a hand in farewell as she follows two men up the stairs in the background.

David takes liberties with the scene. David shows fewer attendants than are recorded and includes two who were not present: Apollodorus (who, like Xanthippe, was sent away for excessive grief) and Plato, who is also depicted as much older than his age at the time. He is there only as the recorder of the event, which may be why he faces out of the scene. Socrates's face is also younger than his age of seventy, but it does seem to be modeled on a surviving bust. Socrates, the executioner, and the cup are bathed in light, while the rest fade into shadow. As in *The Oath* above, most of the figures form a plane in the foreground. The heads on the right, the executioner's head and shoulders, and Xanthippe's and Apollodorus's heads define lines that all meet at the cup, the painting's focal point. The vanishing point of the pavement lines is the exit passageway's center, which suggests that it symbolizes Socrates's passage out of life. *The Death of Socrates* was painted three years after *The Oath*, on a commission by two advocates of reform. It appeared shortly after the attempt to move toward government by assembly failed, and the painting's stark walls must have evoked the cells of political prisoners. Its theme of strength and self-control in the face of adversity was also timely. Thomas

FIGURE 12.11 Jacques-Louis David, *The Death of Socrates* (1787), oil on canvas, 130 × 196 cm, Metropolitan Museum, New York.

FIGURE 12.12 Angelica Kauffman (1742–1807), *The Judgment of Paris* (c. 1781), oil on canvas, 80 × 101 cm, Art Museum of Ponce, Perto Rico.

Jefferson admired it immensely, and it became another icon of the Neoclassic style.

In addition to paintings of actual or legendary history, Neoclassicism also applauded depictions of myth. Angelica Kauffman's *Judgment of Paris*, Figure 12.12, depicts the fateful moment that caused the Trojan War.[6] Paris, Prince of Troy, was asked to award a golden apple

---

6   The Trojan War is one of the great themes in Western legendary history, and it reappears pervasively throughout Western art. Other episodes appear in Figures 7.2 and 7.49, as well as in many other artworks throughout history.

inscribed "To the fairest" to one of three goddesses: Athena (of wisdom), Hera (queen of the gods), and Venus (of beauty and sexual love). Each bribed him: Athena with wisdom and skill in war, Hera with worldly power and wealth, and Venus with the world's most beautiful woman—Helen, wife of King Menelaus of Sparta. Venus won and, on Helen's abduction, the Greeks attacked Troy. From right to left, Athena points accusingly at Paris, Hera raises her hand as if to stop him, and Venus slinks toward him in the center of the painting, exposing her thigh and lifting a drape from her breasts while gazing seductively into his eyes. Cupid hides under her skirt, his discarded quiver, having done its job, lying in front, while Paris, mesmerized, returns Venus's alluring gaze and drops the apple into her outstretched hand. The background is a rocky grotto behind Paris, a tree trunk behind Venus, and a distant landscape behind the other two goddesses.

Portraiture also adopted the Neoclassic style. In general, strict Neoclassic portraits of women are more convincing than those of men because gowns in the ancient style became all the rage. Their lighter, free-flowing fabrics and high waistlines offered a great deal more comfort and freedom of movement than the heavily decorated, multilayered gowns that preceded them. Thus, a woman portrayed in a Neoclassic gown was dressed at the height of fashion, while this was most untrue of a man in a toga. In her portraits of ladies of high standing,

FIGURE 12.13 Élisabeth Vigée-LeBrun, *Emma, Lady Hamilton as a Bacchante* (c. 1790), oil on canvas, 132 × 106 cm, Lady Lever Art Gallery, Liverpool.

Élisabeth Vigée-Lebrun was quick to adopt the new style, as is seen in her portrait of Emma Hamilton, a clever woman with no formal education who managed to raise herself quite high through her beauty, quick mind, social skills, and romantic alliances (see Figure 12.13). At the time of the painting, she had married an elderly widower, Sir William Hamilton, from whom she received her title and surname. Shortly before, she had developed a unique entertainment, called "attitudes" (a mime-like cross between posing, dancing, and theater) in which she impersonated historical and mythical figures. Vigée-Lebrun was charmed by these, and her portrait captures the essence of one: *Lady Hamilton as Bacchante*. Bacchantes were priestesses of Bacchus (god of wine) who accompanied him in drunken revels (and more) through the woods. They were described as singing and dancing wildly while accompanying themselves on pipes, drums, and tambourines.

In her Bacchante role, the portrait catches Emma in a moment of running or dancing from right to left, gazing back at the viewer and holding and playing a tambourine high in her hands. Mount Vesuvius smolders in the background. Emma is a beautiful woman with a riveting gaze; her arms are slender and beautifully shaped, and her long brown tresses flow below her waist behind. She wears a red ribbon around her head, and a gold sash cinches her simple purple sleeveless gown just below her breasts. Her figure fills the picture from lower right to upper left. The depiction of her movement conforms to the frozen moment of Neoclassic style. The vital moment is arrested in midglance. This momentary pause, Emma's classical gown, her flowing hair and Bacchic activity, and the background's Italian volcano all express the Neoclassicism of this work.

As noted, attempts to portray men in Neoclassical garb were bound to be less successful than depictions of women. Even David, the grand master of Neoclassicism, had his lesser moments. As a partisan of the revolution, in 1794 he took it upon himself to design appropriate dress for the legislator of the new republic. The incongruous result (Figure 12.14) is a peculiar combination of current and ancient. The man wears a red hat (similar to those still worn by some French civic societies) with a plume of wheat, on top of what looks like the edge of a blue Phrygian cap, the mark of an ancient freeman or an eighteenth-century French republican. His blue cape, with a republican motto, "*Peuple Français—Égalité, Liberté*" ("People of France—Equality, Liberty"), is gathered over his right shoulder in ancient style. Underneath, he wears a Greek-style tunic, but with long sleeves and a modern collar. The tunic is bound at the waist with blue and red sashes with gold fringe. On his legs and feet, he wears green late-medieval hose and boots. His outstretched right hand holds a paper with the words "*Rapport sur les costumes français*" ("Report on French dress"). The peculiar hodgepodge of ancient, medieval, and eighteenth century is quite impractical, and it is hard to imagine anyone wearing it seriously.

David's synthesis of old and new was a bit more successful in his sketch for a coronation portrait of Napoléon as emperor (where practicality was no concern—see Figure 12.15). The work is partly modeled on the famous portrait of Louis XIV in Figure 11.17, especially in the design and fall of the robe—both robes are rich velvet with ermine linings and collars and have long trains that fall out of the portrait on the right. There the similarity ends. Louis's portrait is described earlier. Napoléon's pose is a broad stance, facing slightly to his right. His robe is reddish purple (the color of royalty) with embroidered gold bees, copied from some found in the tombs of France's first kings. Beneath it, he wears a white silk tunic with gold embroidery and fringe over similar shoes. On his head is a golden laurel wreath in ancient imperial style. Around his neck is the collar of the new republican medal, the Legion of Honor. His right hand holds the long Imperial Scepter. His left arm rests on his hip holding the Hand of Justice. Behind him is the ornate gold throne, and over him are rich, dark blue drapes with gold fringe supported on gold columns decorated with sphinxes. The ancient

FIGURE 12.14 Jacques-Louis David, *Design for Costume of Legislator of the Republic* (1794), hand-colored etching, Library of Congress, Washington, DC.

FIGURE 12.15 Jacques-Louis David, *Portrait of Napoléon in Imperial Costume* (1805), oil sketch on panel, 50 × 58 cm, Palace of Fine Arts, Lille, France.

The Arts in the Eighteenth Century (1700–1800)   327

FIGURE 12.16 Jean Auguste Dominique Ingres (1780–1867), *Napoléon I on the Imperial Throne* (1806), oil on canvas, 260 × 163 cm, Musée de l'Armée, Paris.

elements of tunic, crown, and scepter meld fairly well with the more recent ones, but the sketch was, nevertheless, rejected by Napoléon.

Jean-August Dominique Ingres, a student of David's, attempted a portrait of Napoléon in virtually the same costume the following year (Figure 12.16). Ingres seats the emperor on the throne; his right hand holds the scepter of Charlemagne instead of the imperial one, and the background is stark and dark. This work disturbed the public because of its revival of Charlemagne's imperial heritage (a relic of the deposed kings) and the starkness of the background. Even David did not approve. It is nevertheless a wonderful example of Ingres's remarkable talent, expressed in several ways: the precision and detail of his drawing, the delicate *sfumato* modeling of the face and folds of robe and fur, and, overall, the magnificent use of color. It is worth noting, too, that no matter what Napoléon himself thought of the work, Ingres brilliantly captures in his face the coldness, the determination, and the power that fueled his rise. The work validates Ingres's reputation as one of the greatest portraitists of the Neoclassic period.

Neoclassicism had widespread influence, even across the Atlantic Ocean. By the mid-eighteenth century, North America was beginning to produce artists of talent and promise but with limited educational opportunities and market for their work. One of the first great American artists was Benjamin West. He was largely self-taught in all respects, but Americans of greater prosperity recognized his genius, and, after he studied with an immigrant English painter, West's patrons provided education—first in Pennsylvania, then Italy, and finally London, where he ended up spending the rest of his life, becoming the second president of the Royal Academy and London's leading artist until his death. West had a natural affinity for the Neoclassical style, which imbued most of his works. But he was not afraid to innovate, and his painting of *The Death of General Wolfe* (Figure 12.17) exemplifies this. Although advised to depict the event in a Greek or Roman setting, Wolfe chose contemporary dress and an imaginative but current interpretation of the scene.

The work depicts the death of the British general James Wolfe at the Battle of the Plains of Abraham in 1759. This battle was for control of Quebec City and was decisive in determining the fate of North America.[7] Quebec City is on a high promontory that juts out from the north shore of the St. Lawrence River next to a small tributary. Wolfe landed a small squad in darkness about six kilometers upstream to climb a precipitous bank and secure a road for the main force. The two armies finally met before the city at 10:00 a.m. The fight was intense but brief, lasting only about fifteen minutes. General Wolfe was killed just as the French began to retreat. The French general, Marquis de Montcalm, died the next day. The engagement was so brief that Wolfe's officers were all occupied with the battle, and only four of those depicted were even present on the battlefield. Although avoiding ludicrous togas, West nonetheless

---

7   It has been said the Battle of the Plains of Abraham determined that the language of what is now the United States would be English and not French.

painted a memorial icon rather than a historically accurate painting.

In the background, blue sky appears above a church tower on the left as the wind blows the dark clouds of battle to the right. Two of a group of officers and allies gesture toward an approaching runner who brings news of victory, waving his hat and carrying a French flag. Behind him, troops move left. The group includes four British officers (one a Scot) and one wood trooper in green (all standing), along with a crouching Native American.[8] All of them stare at the dying general, who is the focus of the central group, surrounded by two kneeling officers on the left, two standing behind with the flag, and the doctor kneeling on the right. Two more soldiers pray on the right in front of a crowd of soldiers who seem disengaged from battle, and the river with ships is behind. The central group is slightly right of center and is triangular in shape. The figures around Wolfe are grouped like those in images of Christ removed from the cross.[9] Wolfe's face, slightly right of center, is the bright focus of the painting, his eyes rolling upward toward the side of victory. The artist uses the rightward deflection of the center scene, the flag, and the visual weight of the dark cloud to balance the greater number of figures on the left. The work presents the moment of Wolfe's death, frozen in time, as an eternal monument.

West's work has remained a monument of history painting and was influential in artists' discarding of classical dress. It elevated his reputation as one of the foremost history painters of his time. He was robbed of such success with his *American Commissioners of the Preliminary Peace Agreement with Great Britain* or *The Treaty of Paris* in 1783 (Figure 12.18).

FIGURE 12.17 Benjamin West (1738–1820), *The Death of General Wolfe* (1770), oil on canvas, 151 × 213 cm, Royal Ontario Museum, Toronto.

FIGURE 12.18 Benjamin West, *American Commissioners of the Preliminary Peace Agreement with Great Britain or Treaty of Paris* (1783–84), oil on canvas, 72 × 92 cm, Winterthur Museum, Delaware. L–R—John Jay, John Adams, Benjamin Franklin, Henry Laurens, and William Temple Franklin (Benjamin Franklin's grandson). No British representative would sit for the artist.

---

8   Supposedly, the artifacts and clothing West used for the Native American are not only authentic, they are still preserved in the British Museum.

9   Bryan Zygmont, "Benjamin West's *The Death of General Wolfe*." *Smarthistory*. Khan Academy, consulted June 9, 2016.

FIGURE 12.19 John Singleton Copley (1738–1815), *Portrait of Paul Revere* (1768), oil on canvas, 89 × 72 cm, Museum of Fine Arts, Boston.

This incomplete oil sketch was to be part of a series about the American Revolution. It portrays the American negotiators—John Jay, John Adams, and Benjamin Franklin—with Henry Laurens and William Temple Franklin (Benjamin Franklin's grandson). David Hartley, the British representative, refused to sit, possibly on the orders of superiors still embittered by America's victory. The surviving work is a memorial of petty spite, even though, as an expatriate from the colonies, West was especially appropriate for the job. He had intended to return to America after his study abroad, but he was so successful in London that he never did. Nevertheless, he remained a close friend of Benjamin Franklin and many others, and he was instrumental in teaching the next wave of American art students.

One such student was John Singleton Copley. He was born in Boston in the same year as West, and Copley's widowed mother remarried when he was ten. His stepfather was an engraver, and a neighbor's family was also artistic; they must have helped Copley polish a great natural genius. He was painting portraits professionally at the age of nineteen, and sketches from the next year show great precision. A portrait of his stepbrother, Henry Pelham, was entered in competition in London in 1766 and brought praise from Benjamin West, who had then been there for three years.[10] Copley finally sailed for Europe in 1774; his wife joined him in London a year later, one month after the battles of Lexington and Concord. Like West, the Copleys never returned. Having delayed his emigration longer than West, Copley painted some of his finest works on American shores. One of the most renowned is his *Portrait of Paul Revere* (Figure 12.19).

Revere was a second-generation Boston silversmith later famed as a revolutionary patriot. After the French and Indian War, a recession aggravated by the tax acts of 1765 and 1767 hurt Revere's business, although it must have improved somewhat for him to commission his portrait in 1768. Lit from his right, Revere leans on his right elbow on a polished table that reflects his clothing. He rests his chin on his hand and gazes piercingly at the viewer. The left hand, holding a teapot, rests on a round cushion. His clothing is informal—a vest or waistcoat of dark turquoise and an open shirt—but too fine to be work clothing. He wears no wig; his brown hair covers his ears. The teapot is finished but not yet engraved; the engraving tools lie on the table. The teapot is perhaps provocative, since tea was the taxed commodity that tipped the balance toward revolution. Revere was a member of the Sons of Liberty insurgent group, and Copley's family was Loyalist—he was engaged to the daughter of the merchant whose tea would later be dumped in the Boston Tea Party. Despite their opposing politics, Revere's portrait is a wonderful example of Copley's talent. His depiction of surfaces, textures, reflections, and the details of clothing is precise, and the line and shading in the face and hands is delicate and expressive. The result is a portrait of great perception and depth.

---

10   Four years later, in 1770, Henry Pelham engraved a picture of the infamous Boston Massacre that was pirated by Paul Revere.

Not all American artists who worked or studied in England remained there. Charles Willson Peale attempted several crafts before settling on painting. He studied with Copley in America, then in England with Benjamin West, before returning to the colonies. He was an American patriot and was bankrupted by Loyalists for his membership in the Sons of Liberty. He fought in the Revolution and painted many portraits of important Americans, notably George Washington. In addition to painting, Peale pursued many different fields and established America's first museum. He married three times and named most of his children after his favorite painters. *The Staircase Group* (Figure 12.20) portrays two of them in an ingenious *trompe l'oeil tour de force.*

The painting shows his sons on what appears to be a staircase that rises from a doorway and

FIGURE 12.20 Charles Willson Peale (1741–1827), *The Staircase Group*—Portrait of Raphaelle Peale and Titian Ramsay Peale (1795), oil on canvas, 226 × 100 cm, Philadelphia Museum of Art.

FIGURE 12.21 Gilbert Stuart (1755–1828), *George Washington* (*Lansdowne Portrait*) (1796) oil on canvas, 2.44 × 1.52 m, National Portrait Gallery, Washington, DC.

turns sharp left with wedge-shaped corner steps. Raphaelle stands at the top, peering around the doorframe, while Titian's right foot is on what is actually the second step; with his left, he steps to the next.[11] He holds a palette and brushes in his left hand and a walking staff in the right. Both young men wear knee breeches, waistcoats, and swallowtail coats. They look out at the viewer as if noticing his/her presence for the first time. The painting is remarkably realistic, but it is even more so when viewed in the environment for which it was painted, which has been duplicated in the Philadelphia Museum of Art. The work was/is mounted in a doorframe with a step projecting from it at the bottom, one step below the lowest in the figure (which is cropped). Peale painted it for his own museum and also, perhaps, to confirm his reputation as the best artist in the United States. He succeeded. The image is absolutely realistic. It is said that when George

11   Raphaelle was born in 1774; Titian Ramsay Peale I was born in 1770; therefore, they were ages twenty-one and twenty-five, respectively, at the painting's date of 1795. But they look younger, so perhaps the work was based on sketches from a few years earlier. One source erroneously places Raphaelle as the lower figure, assuming that the upper one is his brother, Titian Ramsay Peale II, born in 1799, one year after his namesake's untimely death. Obviously, the picture's date precludes that. Genius though he may have been, Charles Willson Peale could not see the future.

Washington visited, he tipped his hat at the two young men. It is a truly remarkably example of *trompe l'oeil* painting.

Perhaps the most famous portrait from the early United States is Gilbert Stuart's portrait of George Washington (Figure 12.21). This original was commissioned by a US Senator and presented to the British prime minister, who was instrumental in securing peace with Britain; it was purchased in 2001 for the US National Portrait Gallery. Of several copies Stuart painted, the one in the White House East Room was cut from its frame, under the direction of First Lady Dolley Madison, to save it from British arson during the War of 1812. The work is a revered artifact of American history. Stuart, born in 1755, found work as a painter difficult during the Revolution and went to Britain (his second time) to study with West, as others had before him. Returning in 1793, he settled first in Philadelphia, then New York and Boston. Following in Peale's footsteps, Stuart is known for more than one thousand portraits of the new republic's founding fathers.

The *Lansdowne Portrait* (the original) carries a powerful message. Washington is dressed in a black frock coat with lace ruffs at the chest and sleeves and simple black buckled shoes. He looks to his right into the distance with a firm gaze and determined chin.[12] His white hair (or wig) is brushed to the back. He stands before a carved gilded chair that has elements of the new flag on the back and dark red upholstery. In front of it, his left hand holds a ceremonial sword, point down to symbolize peace while maintaining military authority. Behind him, two Doric columns symbolizing strength stand before a rainbow that represents the great future of the republic. To his right (the viewer's left), partly opened red drapes with gold tassels reveal a clearing stormy sky, symbolic of the concluded Revolution. In front of that, his right hand gestures toward a table showing emblems of his office, pen and paper symbolizing law, and an inkwell with his coat of arms. A quill holder in the shape of a dog symbolizes loyalty. Books on and below the table refer to Washington's roles as commander in chief and president of the Constitutional Convention, as well as records of the young government. The table leg is carved as *fasces*, the ancient Roman symbol of authority, surmounted by American eagles. Washington's portrait is a symbol of his leadership, in both war and peace, of the trail-blazing new republic based on the Enlightenment's rational, classical ideals.

Beyond such symbol-laden portraits, history painting (which the academies considered the highest type of art) was very important for recording the milestone events and creating the unique identity of the young United States. Perhaps the best known of these works is John Trumbull's *Declaration of Independence* (Figures 12.22a and b).[13] Trumbull was another American who served in the Revolution and later studied with Benjamin West. He also served as a diplomat in the 1790s and was later a leader in American fine arts institutions. His history paintings are especially valuable because, whenever he could, he painted the subjects and locations from life. This is true of *The Declaration of Independence*; in addition to painting as many men from life as he could, Trumbull omitted those of whom he could find no likeness. He also included five men who participated in the debate or served as secretaries but did not sign, and he included everyone he could, even though the Continental Congress membership changed during the writing and the men were never all in the room at the same time. Nevertheless, the painting is the most accurate depiction of the event we have and has become an icon of the origin of the United States.

The painting depicts the five-man drafting committee presenting the document to the assembly. In Neoclassic tradition, it freezes the moment. The five—John Adams, Roger Sherman, Robert Livingston,

---

12   The somewhat stiff appearance of the chin, in contrast with other portraits of Washington, was caused by a new set of ill-fitting false teeth.

13   The full-size work, as noted, is in the US Capitol. A smaller version is in the art gallery of Yale University, to whom Trumbull sold many paintings (including portraits and other historical works) in exchange for an annuity as he approached old age.

FIGURE 12.22A John Trumbull (1756–1843), *The Declaration of Independence* (1819), oil on canvas, 3.7 × 5.5 m, U.S. Capitol, Washington, DC.

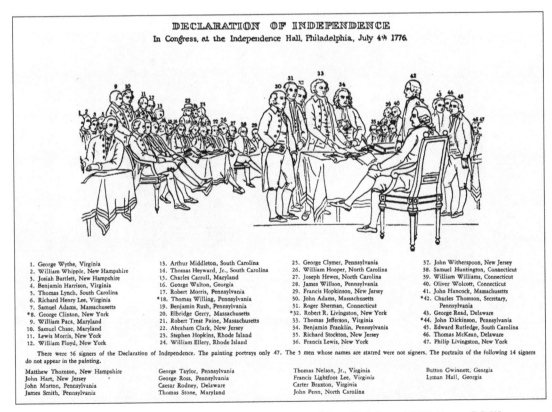

DECLARATION OF INDEPENDENCE
In Congress, at the Independence Hall, Philadelphia, July 4ᵗʰ 1776.

1. George Wythe, Virginia
2. William Whipple, New Hampshire
3. Josiah Bartlett, New Hampshire
4. Benjamin Harrison, Virginia
5. Thomas Lynch, South Carolina
6. Richard Henry Lee, Virginia
7. Samuel Adams, Massachusetts
*8. George Clinton, New York
9. William Paca, Maryland
10. Samuel Chase, Maryland
11. Lewis Morris, New York
12. William Floyd, New York

13. Arthur Middleton, South Carolina
14. Thomas Heyward, Jr., South Carolina
15. Charles Carroll, Maryland
16. George Walton, Georgia
17. Robert Morris, Pennsylvania
*18. Thomas Willing, Pennsylvania
19. Benjamin Rush, Pennsylvania
20. Elbridge Gerry, Massachusetts
21. Robert Treat Paine, Massachusetts
22. Abraham Clark, New Jersey
23. Stephen Hopkins, Rhode Island
24. William Ellery, Rhode Island

25. George Clymer, Pennsylvania
26. William Hooper, North Carolina
27. Joseph Hewes, North Carolina
28. James Wilson, Pennsylvania
29. Francis Hopkinson, New Jersey
30. John Adams, Massachusetts
31. Roger Sherman, Connecticut
*32. Robert R. Livingston, New York
33. Thomas Jefferson, Virginia
34. Benjamin Franklin, Pennsylvania
35. Richard Stockton, New Jersey
36. Francis Lewis, New York

37. John Witherspoon, New Jersey
38. Samuel Huntington, Connecticut
39. William Williams, Connecticut
40. Oliver Wolcott, Connecticut
41. John Hancock, Massachusetts
*42. Charles Thomson, Secretary,
        Pennsylvania
43. George Read, Delaware
*44. John Dickinson, Pennsylvania
45. Edward Rutledge, South Carolina
46. Thomas McKean, Delaware
47. Philip Livingston, New York

There were 56 signers of the Declaration of Independence. The painting portrays only 47. The 5 men whose names are starred were not signers. The portraits of the following 14 signers do not appear in the painting.

Matthew Thornton, New Hampshire
John Hart, New Jersey
John Morton, Pennsylvania
James Smith, Pennsylvania

George Taylor, Pennsylvania
George Ross, Pennsylvania
Caesar Rodney, Delaware
Thomas Stone, Maryland

Thomas Nelson, Jr., Virginia
Francis Lightfoot Lee, Virginia
Carter Braxton, Virginia
John Penn, North Carolina

Button Gwinnett, Georgia
Lyman Hall, Georgia

FIGURE 12.22B Key to Trumbull's *Declaration of Independence*; Art of the United States Capitol, page 133, Washington, DC: US Government Printing Office, 1978.

Thomas Jefferson, and Benjamin Franklin—present the document to Charles Thomson (secretary) and John Hancock, the seated president. Most of the remaining delegates sit and stand to the left, with a few to the right behind Thomson and Hancock. They are in the assembly room of Independence Hall in Philadelphia. Two windows on each side wall have elegant, dark red drapes, and a classical design borders the ceiling. On the back wall are four crossed flags surmounted by gilded trumpets and a drum. The top two flags are those of the colonial province of Pennsylvania—the British union flag in the upper canton of a red field. The lower two I cannot identify: the left one is similar to the ones above, but the field is gold; the right flag has St. George's cross in the gold field's canton. Two exit doors flank the flags. The perspective's vanishing point is just below a medallion on the left-hand flagpoles (above the head of North Carolina's Joseph Hewes). The same point measured from the painting's right side falls just between Jefferson and Franklin, two of the document's critical writers. The two points' mirror placement expresses the writers' roles as representatives of the whole assembly.

Just as Neoclassical painting provides vital insights into the character and history of the eighteenth century, so also does the sculpture. One of the most famous statues of the period is Canova's *Pauline Borghese as Triumphant Venus* (Figure 12.23). The sitter was Napoléon's sister, who married Prince Camillo Borghese upon the death of her first husband. She was a passionate and egotistical woman, given to love affairs and eccentric habits: her huge African slaves carried her to her bath, and she used her ladies-in-waiting as footstools. These eccentricities

FIGURE 12.23 Antonio Canova (1757–1822), *Pauline (Bonaparte) Borghese as Triumphant Venus* (1805–8) marble and gilt bronze, 160 × 192 cm, Galleria Borghese, Rome.

support two anecdotes about the sculpture. First, although her husband commissioned a sculpture of the chaste goddess Diana, Pauline insisted on the notorious Venus. Also, when asked if she objected to posing unclothed, she replied, "Why should I? There's a little stove in the studio that keeps me warm." Whatever the motivations and undercurrents, Canova's sculpture is elegant in its repose, with a bit of amusing *trompe l'oeil.*

Everything in the sculpture except the gilt is stone. "Venus" reclines on a daybed with luxurious gilt-fringed hangings and a tightly stuffed mattress and pillows; a drape covers her pelvis and thighs. The daybed has gilt ornaments and a dolphin head at the headboard angle. The draping and wrinkles in the hangings, pillow, and mattress are completely convincing—they look like satin; veining in the mattress marble even looks like a stain, although that may not be deliberate: Canova did deliberately use a veined lavender marble for the bedframe. It is not absolutely like wood—the grains are different—but Canova's intent is clear. Venus herself reclines in the bend of the bed. Her legs extend along it, left knee slightly bent. Her upper body rests against the pillows piled on the head of the bed, and her right elbow is atop the pillows with her arm supporting her head, which looks down at the apple she holds in her left arm. Her hair is put up in a style reminiscent of ancient Rome, and she is naked except for the drape on her midsection and a bracelet on her right arm. Her skin, polished to a glow to rival that of Michelangelo's *Pietà* (Figure 10.36) is soft and alluring; her pose is casually sensuous. She is reveling in her moment of triumph.

FIGURE 12.24 Jean-Antoine Houdon (1741–1828), *George Washington* (1785–1792), Carrara marble, life-size, State Capitol, Richmond, VA.

Another great sculpture in the modernized approach to the Neoclassic style is the statue of George Washington by Jean-Antoine Houdon, perhaps the greatest Neoclassic sculptor in France (see Figure 12.24). On the recommendations of Jefferson and Franklin, who were then in Paris, the Virginia General Assembly commissioned the work from Houdon in 1784. He actually sailed to America and stayed for three months at Washington's Mount Vernon estate, taking measurements and making sketches and a life mask. On returning to Paris, he made at least one plaster bust; he completed the statue in 1791/92, and it arrived in 1796. It is considered one of the most true-to-life depictions of Washington.

Washington stands in classic *contrapposto*, with left knee slightly bent, left foot slightly forward and at a ninety-degree angle to the right. His right hand rests on a walking stick with a tassel. His left arm rests on a chest-high bundle of rods, the ancient Roman *fasces*. His cape rests on top, his sword hangs at the side, and a plow rests behind. He wears his military uniform but is bareheaded, with his natural hair rather than a wig. As in the Stuart portrait, he gazes forward, as if envisioning the republic's future. Washington himself requested the portrayal in clothing of his time rather than a toga.[14] Other elements are symbolic of his dual roles as president:

---

14   Statues of Washington in classical dress include those by Giuseppe Ceracchi (1795, from life), in the Metropolitan Museum in New York City and Horatio Greenough (1832), in the National Museum of American History, Washington, DC.

FIGURE 12.25 Thomas Jefferson (1743–1826), Monticello (1768–1810), west front, near Charlottesville, Virginia.

FIGURE 12.26 Thomas Jefferson, Rotunda (1822–1826), University of Virginia, Charlottesville.

civilian—the cane and plow; military—the uniform, cape, and sword; and overall authority—the *fasces*. When it was commissioned, Washington had not yet served in the Constitutional Convention. When it was delivered, he was in his last year as president. The work is an outstanding example of Neoclassic statuary memorializing our first president at his peak.[15]

The third president, Thomas Jefferson, was noted for his own artistic flair and ingenuity, particularly in Neoclassic architecture. Among several buildings he designed are his own residence, Monticello, and the Rotunda at the University of Virginia. Monticello (Figure 12.25) is the main house of Jefferson's plantation, which he designed by himself. What we see now is actually the second design. After his years in France (1784–89), Jefferson removed the original second floor and east front. The later design dates from 1796 to 1809 and is elegant and ingenious in many ways. What appears in the west front of Figure 12.25 to be mainly a one-story house actually has a two-story-high rooms in the central section, with two visible stories on the east face of the wings, plus a third-story room under the dome. There are cellars and below-grade wings for services, for a total of forty-three rooms. Both entrances, east (main) and west (Figure 12.25), have Doric porticos. The two-story central rooms are the east entrance hall, used as a museum and gallery, and the west parlor/music room. Other two-story west-side rooms include Jefferson's suite and the dining room. The understated upper stories give the design a simple elegance, enhanced by the use of the Golden Section in the portico columns' proportions (see Figure 10.31).

Monticello has many unique design features that express Jefferson's genius. To save floor space, beds were built into the walls. Jefferson's was open on both sides—to his bedroom and study. There were five indoor privies in stairwells, service passages, and the master suite. Three dumbwaiters brought bottles and food from cellars connected with the kitchen in a wing. Service wings at basement level are barely visible from the main grounds. One held carriages,

---

15   More than twenty-five cast copies of Houdon's statue have been made. There is one in the base of the Washington Monument. Some others in public spaces around the country include the National Heritage Museum, Lexington, MA; Washington Square, Philadelphia, PA; National Historical Park, Valley Forge, PA; Jefferson Memorial Park, Pittsburgh, PA; State Capitols, Raleigh, NC and Columbia, SC; Lafayette Park, St. Louis, MO; Fair Oaks Park, Minneapolis, MN; and Civic Center Plaza, Los Angeles, CA.

horses, and the washhouse; the other contained food preparation facilities and servants' quarters. The whole ensemble is a large, elegant house in a refined and deceptively simple Neoclassical style.

Jefferson's other famous building is the Rotunda at the University of Virginia (Figure 12.26). It is the centerpiece of Jefferson's "Academical Village." Leading down from the Rotunda was a long lawn flanked by ten pavilions for classrooms and professors' residences. Behind them were gardens and one-story student rooms in "ranges." All were designed in Neoclassic style, and each row was connected with arcades. The Rotunda at the lawn's head is a one-half-scale model of the Pantheon (Figures 8.15 and 8.16) on the outside, but the interior is not a single space; it has three floors for classrooms and assembly halls. The third-floor dome room was the original location of the university library. Here again, Jefferson took a hallowed classical design and modified it to serve practical uses. In some ways, this is a distinctive trait of American Neoclassicism.

FIGURE 12.27 William Williams, *A View of the 1781 Iron Bridge of Thomas Pritchard (1723–1777) in Coalbrookdale, Shropshire, England* (1780).

The final architectural example is back across the Atlantic in England and reveals the first large-scale use of structural iron.[16] Abraham Darby III (1750–91) was the third generation to run the family iron- and brass-smelting business in Coalbrookdale, Shropshire, England. The furnace and foundry location was determined by the sources of high-quality coal and iron ore, but the Severn River Gorge impeded road transport. Architect Thomas Pritchard suggested iron to bridge the gorge (see Figure 12.27). As the largest early all-iron construction, many design features were experimental. In place of heavy rectangular trusses with triangular bracing, Pritchard's design borrows the arch from stone bridges. Each of the five ribs that carry the road has three delicate cross-braced concentric arches. The inner arch is complete; the others end at the roadway deck. At either end are rectangular frames capped with ogee arches (see discussion of Figure 8.37). Between the frames and the semicircular arches are large iron rings. The rings and the rectangle provide support between that part of the roadway supported by the arches and the masonry abutments on either bank. The roadway has delicate iron railings, and the whole design is understated and elegant. The bridge's beauty is best seen in William Williams's 1780 painting. The painting is not absolutely accurate. It omits a small iron span over a towpath on one side, but it shows the perfect circle the bridge's arch makes with its reflection, a subtle touch of grace and refinement.

16   There had been one attempt (never finished) to build an iron bridge in France, and a footbridge was built in Yorkshire, England, but Darby's was the first full-scale iron road bridge.

Pritchard's bridge combines Neoclassical elegance with a delicate tracery made possible only by the use of structural iron. It combines old and new—Ancient Rome and the Industrial Revolution to come.

Music of the (Neo) Classic Period

In the visual arts, we must speak of the Neoclassic with regard to eighteenth-century works because they were inspired by and modeled on the many great surviving works of classical antiquity. That is not true of music. Figure 7.51 presents the only complete example of ancient Greek music, and it is only four lines long. Figure 7.33 is the longest example, about two-thirds of a hymn to Apollo. Only about fifteen surviving examples are long enough to merit recording. The remaining dozens are mere fragments. The term for this tiny repertoire is Ancient Greek music. The term Classic (without the Neo) is used for eighteenth-century music.

The Classic period in music is the time when many musical conventions arose that we still observe today: public concerts, symphony orchestras, chamber music, and the musical forms used for the works performed. By the eighteenth century, a prosperous middle class had become a visible component of society, especially in England. Their numbers, combined with the aristocracy, created a demand and an audience for public concerts. These concerts would often have a much more varied program than we expect today, including perhaps some songs, some small-ensemble chamber music, a concerto for soloist with orchestra, and a symphony for orchestra alone. The orchestra as we know it became more standardized at this time. It is an ensemble made up mainly of string instruments—the violin family. To add different tone colors, groups of two to four of each type of wind instruments may be included. The symphony as a type of musical work for orchestra arose and became very popular in the eighteenth century. More than ten thousand symphonies from the period survive.

Partly because of the rise of these new music patrons (many of whom lacked unlimited leisure) and partly because this public favored artistic structures based on reason and proportion, a new musical style developed that was based on simple melodies over distinctive accompaniments in clear phrase structures, usually based on multiples of two. The new style rejected the polyphonic complexity of Baroque music, but since composers, like other creative artists, always seek to create something interesting, they replaced complexity in the element of texture with new and varied approaches to the element of form. This is the time when most of the standard musical forms still in use today developed. Figure 12.28 diagrams these common forms. The musical examples that follow will explain them.

These forms describe single pieces of music, which were usually combined in groups in instrumental music. The four main forms of instrumental music are symphony, concerto, chamber music (most often string quartet), and sonata. Each of these included a standard set of separate pieces known as movements (because they had different movements or speeds). The two standard arrangements are in Figure 12.29.

Juxtaposed like this, it is obvious that the two forms' outlines are nearly identical. The only difference is that the symphony and chamber music include a dance movement that is absent in the concerto or sonata. Always bear in mind, though, that these structures were subject to change according to the composers' whims. Music is a creative art governed by malleable principles, not strict laws.

Beyond this new interest in the element of musical form, music of the Classic period embraced several other features. The accompaniments to the simple melodies could have many styles: a second musical line; chords played at once or broken into notes in sweeps or repeated patterns. And the melody did not have to be on top; it could be in the middle or on the bottom, with the accompaniment swirling around or above it. Sometimes the composer would add notes or ornaments to the melody as well. Even so, as long as a single melody stands out against a different accompaniment, the texture is called "homophonic."

<u>Basic Forms</u>
Variation Form—A A' A'' A''', etc., the instrumental equivalent of a strophic song, which sets verses of different texts to the same music.
Binary Form—||: A :||: B :|| = AA BB, can be instrumental or vocal.
Ternary Form—A B A, can be instrumental or vocal, sometimes used in opera arias.
Rondo—A B A C A D A, etc.—like expanded ternary form, mostly instrumental.

<u>Through-composed Form</u>—The single standard one.
Sonata-Allegro Form—Through-composed, combines Binary and Ternary.

<u>Exposition</u>—Two themes (melodies, ideas) in different keys.
Theme 1—Tonic (main key).
Transition—modulates to new key.
Theme 2—Dominant (new key—can also be Relative Major if main key is minor).
Closing—remains in new key.

<u>Development</u>—Composer "plays with" Themes 1 and 2—breaks them into small units, may repeat themes or units, change keys, mix themes together, even introduce new themes or ideas. Anything goes.

<u>Recapitulation</u>—Two themes—the same ones, but *this time in the same key.*
Theme 1—Tonic (main key).
Transition—leads to *same key,* can remain there or modulate and come back.
Theme 2—Tonic (main key).
Closing—remains in main key.

<u>Coda</u> (optional, means tail)—a short section often added to enhance the final ending.

FIGURE 12.29 Movements of multimovement forms.

Four-movement forms—Symphony, Chamber Music	Three-movement forms—Concerto, Sonata
1. Sonata-Allegro Form—fast or grand	1. Sonata-Allegro Form—fast or grand
2. Slow—often binary or ternary	2. Slow—often binary or ternary
3. Minuet and Trio (later Scherzo)	----------
4. Fast, often Rondo, but variable	3. Fast, often Rondo, but variable

In addition to varied accompaniments and the new forms, composers also sought to add interest through the element of timbre, especially instrumentation (see Chapter 3). Instruments enter and fall out of the texture in less predictable ways than they did in earlier music. In addition, new instruments appeared. The most durable of these are the clarinet and piano. The clarinet added a new timbre in instrumental music, and the piano revolutionized keyboard music because it was the first keyboard instrument whose player could control loudness by the force of touch alone.

The first signs of the emerging Classic style appeared in Italy, but it developed and spread rapidly throughout Europe. Hundreds of composers adopted it, but the two who came to the fore were both Austrian: Wolfgang Amadeus Mozart and Franz Joseph Haydn. Both traveled, although at opposite ends of their lives. Mozart was a child prodigy whose father took him (with his musical older sister) on several tours of Europe, including Italy, France, England, and various German principalities. His *Air and Variations* (see Figure 12.30) on the French tune,

FIGURE 12.30 Wolfgang Amadeus Mozart (1756–1791), *Twelve Variations on "Ah, vous dirai-je, Maman,"* (1781/2), pianoforte.

Air (basic tune)—Simple, two-voice, homophonic, melody on top.

Var. 1—Fast notes ornamenting melody on top, slow notes and chords underneath.

Var. 2—Melody and chords on top, fast notes on bottom.

Var. 3—Triplets and arpeggios (sweeping broken chords) on top, chords on bottom.

Var. 4—Melody and chords on top, triplets and arpeggios on bottom.

Var. 5—Single notes and two-note groups trading between top and bottom.

Var. 6—Melody with chords mostly on top, fast notes close together on bottom; reversed in middle, with melody above bottom chords, then returns to original style.

Var. 7—Fast scales on top, longer notes and chords on bottom.

Var. 8—Minor key, three parts, slower, bit of imitative polyphony at beginning of each section.

Var. 9—Back to major key, very short notes, imitative polyphony again, still slower.

Var. 10—Longer notes, first in melody, then bass, alternating with faster three-note groups; left hand crosses over right when melody is the highest.

Var. 11—Slow, begins with a little bit of imitation, later melody nicely ornamented.

Var. 12—Finale, fast, triple meter, begins with melody ornamented over a very fast bass, then both hands play fast before the opening section returns with a *coda* (tail) at the end.

"*Ah, vous dirai-je, maman,*" is a wonderful example of both his ingenuity and the variations form (see Figure 12.28). Figure 3.11 gives a short summary. A more detailed description is in Figure 12.30.

This simple tune provided Mozart with a wonderful opportunity to show his ingenuity. The original tune (or air) is in binary form (Figure 12.28) and is set in very simple, two-voice homophony. After this, Mozart composed two pairs of variations. In Variations 1 and 2, he uses fast notes: on top in Variation 1 and on the bottom in Variation 2. Variations 3 and 4 use the same exchange, but the fast notes are in triplets (three-note groups) and often sweep upwards or downwards in what is known as an *arpeggio* because it is harp-like.[17] Variation 5 exchanges small groups of notes between top and bottom. Variation 6 uses fast neighbor notes in the accompaniment: first below, then above, then below again. Variation 7 uses rapid scales on top over longer notes and chords. Variation 8 is the only variation in the minor key, and each section is introduced with a little bit of imitative polyphony—the different harmonies arise from the interaction of the melodic lines. Variation 9 returns to the major key, but it, too, begins each section with imitative polyphony. Variation 10 requires that the player cross the left hand over to play part of the melody above a constant right-hand figure. Variation 11 is the first with a tempo marking, *adagio*, for slow. It begins with another bit of imitation and then adds delicate ornaments, some rather elaborate, to the melody. Variation 12 is marked *allegro* (fast), and is in triple meter. At its ending, there is a short *coda* to close the piece.

Mozart started composing when he was very young, and he died at the age of thirty-five, just as he was nearing regular employment in Vienna. Haydn was born before Mozart; they became good friends and dedicated music to one another, but Mozart died young, while Haydn had a long and productive life, mostly under one patron, Prince Nickolaus Esterházy. As a member of the prince's household, he was not allowed to travel. Only on the prince's death could Haydn accept invitations to London, where he enjoyed much renown. For these visits, he composed his last twelve symphonies, including Symphony no. 100 in G Major—the *Military Symphony*.

17   *Arpa* is Italian for harp.

FIGURE 12.33 Franz Joseph Haydn (1732–1809), Symphony no. 100 (*Military Symphony*), (1793/4), string and wind orchestra with Turkish instruments. (*Nudel* is short for *Nudelschrift* [noodle-writing] in German, a term for musical busywork, usually in the accompaniment.).

Movement 1—Sonata-Allegro form, with slow Introduction and *Coda*.

Section	Description	Timing
Introduction—*Adagio*, slow—begins soft, grows louder as orchestra enters.		c. 1 min. 30 sec.
Exposition (of Sonata Form)—*Allegro*, fast.		
Theme 1—main key (G), four-note idea, rises then returns; flutes, then strings, then all.		25–30 seconds
Transition—changes key, a bit of Theme 1 in the minor; mostly busy work (*Nudelschrift*), ends in new major key (D).		40–45 seconds
Theme 2—new key (D), neighbor-note idea over busy repeated notes.		c. 15 seconds
Closing—stays in new key, lots of *Nudel*, then downward scale and end. (Most performances repeat the exposition as directed to make sure the listeners remember the themes.)		c. 15 seconds
Development—begins and spends most time with Theme 2, breaks it into small bits, modulates to many different keys, brings Theme 1 in briefly near the end of the section.		c. 1 min. 15 sec.
Recapitulation		
Theme 1—main key (G); flutes, then all.		15–20 seconds
Transition—changes key for a moment only, then returns; very short.		7–10 seconds
Theme 2—main key (D), short appearance; short key change, then back to main key.		20–25 seconds
Closing—main key, *Nudel*, then ornamented downward scales.		c. 20 seconds
Coda—Lots of *Nudel*, one downward scale, then strong ending.		c. 15 seconds

Movement 2—Modified Ternary Form—*Allegretto* (not too fast or slow)—A B A' *Coda*

One theme only throughout; related key of C instead of G, uses Turkish instruments.

	Timing
A Section, major key—introduces theme, first in strings, then winds.	c. 1min. 30 sec.
B Section, minor key—suddenly loud, uses Turkish instruments for the first time—cymbals and bass drum especially obvious. This section gave the symphony its name.	55–60 seconds
A Section, major key again—brief excursion into minor; Turkish instruments continue, then ends quietly.	c. 1min. 35 sec.
Coda—begins with trumpet fanfare, drum roll, then loud chords in minor, then alternating soft and loud, ending with another fanfare.	50–55 seconds

Movement 3—Minuet and Trio—ternary meter

Haydn alters this from the usual, which is normally two binary forms tacked together.

	Timing
Minuet (*not* binary)—A ‖: B-A :‖ = A B A B A	
A Section—thumpy question–answer theme—first loud, then soft.	15–20 seconds
B—A Section—opens with theme of descending two-note groups, then becomes soft, brings back thumpy theme to end.	c. 45 seconds
B—A Section—then repeated exactly.	c. 45 seconds
Trio—This *is* a standard binary form—‖: C :‖: D :‖ = CC DD	c. 10 seconds each time
C Section—short, fluttery theme in flutes and strings.	
D Section—fluttery moment, then loud section, then fluttery again.	c. 20 seconds each time

Da Capo—Normally one returns to the Minuet, but without repeats. In this case, since the Minuet form is unusual, the choice to repeat or not depends on the conductor's preference.

Movement 4—Combined Form—Sonata-Rondo—*Presto* (very fast)

This is not as complicated as it sounds. It is basically a rondo with the themes arranged in such an order that it fits the definition of sonata form too. This one also moves like the wind, so fast that I will not try to indicate the sections. Instead, I give the timing of the main rondo theme so you can identify it. Then listen to the whole movement and hear how *many* times it comes back, usually even in the same key.

A Theme, major key—very fast, strings, first a repeated note, leaps up on a broken chord, repeats top note, then comes down, first as a question, then as an answer.	c. 7 seconds!

The whole movement lasts about five minutes, and you will hear this theme many times, like the rondo form in Figure 12.28.

The Arts in the Eighteenth Century (1700–1800)   341

Haydn's Symphony no. 100 is an excellent example of a typical Classical symphony. It has the usual large orchestra of the Classical period: strings, winds in pairs (flutes, oboes, clarinets, bassoons, trumpets, and horns), and tympani (kettledrums). For the second "military" movement and afterwards, it also adds instruments from Turkish military bands (a current fad at the time): triangle, cymbals, and bass drum. The movement structure is diagrammed in Figure 12.31. As you can see, it includes examples of all of the forms in Figure 12.28 that have not already been discussed. Figure 12.31 gives about as clear a description of Haydn's Symphony no. 100 as is possible without using musical notation or going into excruciating detail, so I will not review the whole work again in prose here. I'll just add a few observations.

Haydn was essentially a cheerful person with a good sense of humor, and this comes out in his music, so allow yourself to be a bit less than serious in listening to this piece.[18] After writing ninety-nine (actually more) symphonies, it is not surprising that Haydn might want to change things a little. What is surprising in this work is that he changed so little. Some of his favorite musical jokes were sudden changes from soft to loud or vice versa, sudden interjections of a theme or part of it where it wasn't expected, modulations to wildly distant keys, sudden drum strokes, and other sudden changes of instrumentation. If you look for them, you can find all of these effects in this symphony. One special feature of this work is the use of Turkish (or Janissary) instruments. Janissaries were a crack regiment of the Ottoman sultan's army, with their own special uniforms and music. Supposedly, when the Turks were repulsed from the walls of Vienna in 1683, their bands left instruments on the field that excited the interest of European musicians. Much of the percussion section of our orchestra comes down from such Turkish instruments: tympani (kettledrums), bass drum, cymbals, and triangle, as well as other less common jingly instruments.

Although the Turks continued to menace Europe for another 140 years, they never came that close to the center again. Perhaps the decline of the threat spurred interest in their music's exotic sound. Many composers wrote Janissary works, and even some pianos had Janissary pedals that could imitate the bass drum and cymbals. It is the sudden entrance of these instruments in the second movement's B section that inspired one reviewer's comment that the second movement evoked the "hellish roar of war increas[ing] to a climax of horrid sublimity!" This remark gave the work its "Military" nickname.[19]

It is perhaps not inappropriate to wind up the discussion of the eighteenth century with a military-themed work. In this century, there were many wars—some of great significance. In addition, world trade blossomed, the organization and codification of knowledge expanded, new artistic styles vied for recognition, technological innovation accelerated, scholarship and reason assaulted feudal tyranny, and entirely new forms of governments arose. It was prophetic that the British army surrendered to American rebels to the tune "The World Turned Upside Down." Perhaps they and their contemporaries thought that they had endured all the change that was to come. If so, it was a vain hope. Looking backwards, we can see that the developments of the eighteenth century were but a prelude to the increasing clamor and wild, tempestuous, and by turns, thrilling and monstrous developments of the nineteenth century to come.

---

18   Mozart's temperament was much the same. They both liked jokes.

19   H.C. Robbins Landon, *Haydn: Chronicle and Works.* 5 vols. (Bloomington: Indiana University Press, 1980), 3:247.

Image Credits

Fig. 12.1: Rebel Redcoat / Wikimedia Commons / Copyright in the Public Domain.

Fig. 12.3: Jean-Antoine Watteau / Copyright in the Public Domain.

Fig. 12.4: François Boucher / Copyright in the Public Domain.

Fig. 12.5: Louise Élisabeth Vigée Le Brun / Copyright in the Public Domain.

Fig. 12.6: Johann Joachim Kändler; Photo by Ingersoll / Wikimedia Commons / Copyright in the Public Domain.

Fig. 12.7: Johann Joachim Kändler; Photo copyright © 2012 by Sean Pathasema / Birmingham Museum of Art, (CC BY 3.0) at https://commons.wikimedia.org/wiki/File:MeissenGroup-JohannKaendler-BMA.jpg.

Fig. 12.8: Johann Joachim Kändler; Photo by Ingersoll / Wikimedia Commons / Copyright in the Public Domain.

Fig. 12.9: Antonio Bossi / Copyright in the Public Domain.

Fig. 12.10: Jacques-Louis David / Copyright in the Public Domain.

Fig. 12.11: Jacques-Louis David / Copyright in the Public Domain.

Fig. 12.12: Angelica Kauffman / Copyright in the Public Domain.

Fig. 12.13: Louise Élisabeth Vigée Le Brun / Copyright in the Public Domain.

Fig. 12.14: Jacques-Louis David / Copyright in the Public Domain.

Fig. 12.15: Jacques-Louis David / Copyright in the Public Domain.

Fig. 12.16: Jean Auguste Dominique Ingres / Copyright in the Public Domain.

Fig. 12.17: Benjamin West / Copyright in the Public Domain.

Fig. 12.18: Benjamin West / Copyright in the Public Domain.

Fig. 12.19: John Singleton Copley / Copyright in the Public Domain.

Fig. 12.20: Charles Willson Peale / Copyright in the Public Domain.

Fig. 12.21: Gilbert Stuart / Copyright in the Public Domain.

Fig. 12.22A: John Trumbull / Copyright in the Public Domain.

Fig. 12.22B: U.S. Government Printing Office / Copyright in the Public Domain.

Fig. 12.23: Copyright © 2014 by Antonio Canova, (CC BY-SA 3.0) at https://commons.wikimedia.org/wiki/File:Venus_Victrix_(Canova)_01.jpg.

Fig. 12.24: Copyright © 2010 by AlbertHerring / Wikimedia Commons, (CC BY 3.0) at https://commons.wikimedia.org/wiki/File:Virginia_State_Capitol_complex_-_Houdon%27s_Washington,_seen_from_the_front.jpg.

Fig. 12.25: Copyright © 2010 by YF12s / Wikimedia Commons, (CC BY-SA 3.0) at https://commons.wikimedia.org/wiki/File:Monticello_2010-10-29.jpg.

Fig. 12.26: Aaron Josephson / Copyright in the Public Domain.

Fig. 12.27: William Williams / Copyright in the Public Domain.

CHAPTER 13

THE ARTS
IN THE
NINETEENTH
CENTURY

Background

The events of the eighteenth century set the stage for the spread of radical change in the nineteenth. The French Revolution of 1789 released forces that Europe struggled to deal with, leaving unaddressed ills to fester and ultimately leading to World War I in 1914.

The American Revolution presaged the changes in Europe, but the real catalyst was the revolution in France. America was half a world away, and its struggle ended in peace. The French Revolution occurred in the center of Europe's greatest power and included mob rule, bloodthirsty violence, and an orgy of sanctioned murder. The execution of the king in 1793 provoked European monarchies to unite against France (a coalition renewed several times), which forced France and Napoléon Bonaparte, its greatest general, into war.

If Napoléon responded to the full extent of his formidable abilities, what else could be expected? After his first campaigns, beginning in 1797, he led a *coup d'état* that made him first consul in 1799. By 1811, he had defeated or co-opted all of the royal governments of Europe except Sweden and Russia (England being technically not part of Europe, and the Ottoman Turks controlling southeastern Europe). Napoléon's failure to conquer Russia was the beginning of his downfall. Defeated and exiled in 1814, he escaped and returned briefly to power before his final exile in 1815.

Aside from his astonishing military successes, Napoléon limited the church's power, emancipated

Jews and Protestants, reformed education, stabilized the metric system, and introduced a complete revision of law that has persisted throughout most of Europe. He was also a despot, a ferocious general, and a plunderer. By spreading the power of revolutionary France, he shook European governments and society to their roots and kindled popular revolutionary movements, especially in Germany and Italy, which led to their unification as well as the fall of the Holy Roman Empire. As a side effect, the young United States was also dragged back into war.

The Louisiana Purchase of 1803 was concluded by the United States and Napoléon, who wished to cut his losses in colonial struggles and concentrate on European enemies—especially Britain, the coalition's most tenacious power. Britain plotted with Midwestern native tribes to divide eastern states from the immense new territory and hijacked American ships and sailors, which forced the United States to declare war in 1812. Britain also blockaded American ports to cut off trade with France and attacked the US mainland, burning Washington. Napoléon's defeat ended both the American and European wars.

Meanwhile, however, Britain abolished its slave trade in 1807 and began to attack slave-carrying ships of other nations. In the United States, opposition to slavery had existed in some areas since the 1600s. In 1808, the United States abolished slave importation but allowed enslavement to continue in the South. Americans founded the colony of Liberia in 1821 as a homeland to which freeborn African Americans could return. These were the first stirrings of the abolition movement, and slavery became the main issue in American politics, leading to the Civil War (1861–65), which ended legal US slavery.

Inspired partly by US independence and empowered by European turmoil, South and Central America won their independence from Portugal and Spain. In other less developed regions, however, European nations consolidated and expanded colonial holdings. The United States expanded through treaty, conquest, and purchase to its present continental boundaries. The Spanish-American War in 1898 also brought a few overseas colonies, most of which have been freed. These sudden expansions of political power were enabled by remarkable technological and scientific advances in the nineteenth century. Figure 13.1 lists the most important of these.

Rapid political and technological changes often raised unprecedented issues or conflicted with previous ideas and practices. This affected the arts no less than other areas. New styles developed and contended with traditional approaches. Neoclassicism remained influential, but new styles like Romanticism, Nationalism, and Realism—alone and together—reflected societies' new directions.

Agriculture	Phosphate Fertilizer, Steel Plow, Mechanical Reaper, Improved Crop Rotation
Biology	Cell Theory, Environmental Awareness, Genetics, Theory of Evolution
Chemistry	Chemical Dyes, Organic Chemistry, Periodic Table of the Elements
Communications	Telegraph, Morse Code, Telephone, Radio, Mechanical Typesetting, Photography, Film Camera, Photoengraving, Stock Ticker, Phonograph, Stop-Action Photography, Motion Pictures
Electricity	Electrical Battery, Electric Generator and Motor, Electric Light, Electrical Utilities, Alternating Current
Engineering	Iron Truss Bridge, Suspension Bridge, Transportation Tunnels, Safety Elevator
Household Convenience	Indoor Plumbing, Cast Iron Stove, Washing Machine and Wringer, Sewing Machine, Safety Razor, Zipper, Ballpoint Pen
Industry	Mass Production, Mass Steel Production, Steam Shovel, Aluminum Smelting
Medicine	Aspirin, General Anesthesia, Germ Theory, Rabies Vaccination, Pasteurization, Microscopic Anatomy, X-Ray
Music	Cast Iron Piano Frame, Saxophone, Chromatic Instruments
Physics	Absolute Zero, Asteroid Belt, Radioactivity
Sanitation	Faucet, Flush Toilets, Sewage Treatment
Textiles	Cotton Gin, Power Loom, Aniline Dyes
Transportation	Steamboat and Ship, Steam Locomotive, Railroad Sleeping Car, Air Brake, Internal Combustion Engine, Airship, Automobile, Pneumatic Tire, Bicycle
Warfare	Breech-Loading Rifles and Artillery, Machine Gun, Torpedo, Naval Mine, Submarine, Dreadnought Battleship

Romanticism in the Arts

The first of these new styles was Romanticism. In the visual arts, several features distinguish it from Neoclassicism. Romantics rejected the rational order, proportion, and ancient Greek inspiration of the Neoclassical style and rebelled against its restrictions.[1] They sought more intense emotion and free expression of feelings, with a sense of mystery, fantasy, horror, the supernatural, and other irrational or exotic subjects, especially from the Middle Ages or folk tradition. There was a new fascination with nature, which elevated it from the naturally beautiful to the supernaturally sublime—a new concept that expressed boundless, overwhelming awe and grandeur. Romanticism as an artistic movement carries emotional range far beyond mere love affairs. The greatest creative artists were even alleged to have supernatural inspiration—to be "geniuses."[2]

Perhaps the most striking example of the "genius" phenomenon is Ludwig van Beethoven. He became the leading composer in Vienna following Haydn and Mozart. He never married and maintained a gruff demeanor. His musical innovations included extremes of tempo (speed)

---

1   This progression from order to turbulence occurs three times in the history of visual art. It appears first in the evolution from the Classical Greek style to the Hellenistic. It recurs in the transformation of the Renaissance style to that of the Baroque and again in the present case, from the Neoclassic to the Romantic.

2   The term "genius" implied that the artist had some sort of tutelary deity or spirit that worked through him/her to produce works that were not just beautiful but sublime.

FIGURE 13.2 Ludwig van Beethoven (1770–1827), Piano Sonata No. 8 in C Minor, *"Pathétique,"* Op. 13 (1798–9), Movement 1, *Grave–Allegro di molto e con brio*, piano sonata.

Performances of this work vary in speed. Timings below are based on a total duration of 7:15 without repeats.

Timing (approximate)	Music	
0:00–1:35	**Slow Introduction**	Dotted rhythms with strong dynamic contrasts: loud first chord; what follows is softer. An ornamental flourish leads to repeated chords that grow in strength until a second flourish leads to the very fast main section.
1:35–1:50	**Exposition—First Theme**	Fast, "rocket" upwards—C minor.
1:55–2:10	**Transition**	Sustained notes, rapid movements down twice; three rapid ascents, slow descent, slow trill—C minor to E-flat minor.
2:10–2:45	**Second Theme**	Smaller rise, one skip plus steps up, followed by trills downward. With repeats, changes to E-flat major, more usual key for this section.
2:45–3:25	**Closing**	Repeated notes then rise, busy accompaniment, twice; rapid descent twice, short reminder of first theme, 8 strong chords—E-flat major, last chords modulate back to opening.
3:25–6:50 with Intro; to 4:35 without.	**Exposition Repeated (sometimes)**	Variants—Some performers go back to the Introduction; others to the fast section; yet others omit the repeat. Timing omits any repeat; add difference in Development if repeated.
3:25–4:50	**Development**	Slow introduction theme, then transition theme, ends with long downward flourish—modulation to several keys.
4:50–5:00	**Recapitulation—First Theme**	Fast, "rocket" upwards—C minor, cut off after second rise.
5:00–5:15	**Transition**	Chords from end of first theme; original transition material omitted. Short—moves away, then back to C minor.
5:15–5:45	**Second Theme**	Small rise, skip plus steps, downward trills—C minor
5:45–6:25	**Closing**	Repeated notes, rise, busy accompaniment, rapid descents, short reminder of first theme, 6 strong chords—C minor.
6:25–7:15	**Coda**	Short fragment of slow introduction theme, then first theme, then crashing chords to end—C minor.

and dynamics (volume), as well as enhancements of form, instrumentation, and harmony. His works' emotionalism electrified contemporary audiences, and the semidivine reverence he received lasted well into the next century. The cult of Beethoven was a major factor in the substitution of music for religion in an increasingly secular Germany. Even Beethoven's early works show emotional power. Piano Sonata no. 8 was named the *"Pathétique"* by its publisher for its grand and tragic pathos. This is especially clear in the first movement, which is a straightforward sonata form with slow introduction, like many of the symphonies of Joseph Haydn, with whom Beethoven studied (see Figure 13.2).

The sonata is in C Minor, the key contributing to its ominous quality. It begins with a slow introduction in dotted rhythms (see discussion of Figure 11.22). There are strong dynamic contrasts: the first chord is quite loud, and what follows it is very soft, building through an ornamental flourish to repeated chords that grow in strength until a second flourish leads to the

FIGURE 13.3 Gerhard von Kügelgen (1772–1820), *Portrait of Johann Wolfgang von Goethe* (1808/9), oil on canvas, 72 × 64 cm, University Library, Tartu, Estonia.

FIGURE 13.4 Gerhard von Kügelgen (1772–1820), *Portrait of Caspar David Friedrich* (1810–20), oil on canvas, 54 × 42 cm, Kunsthalle, Hamburg.

very fast main section. The first theme leaps upward in a gesture called a "rocket." This is followed by a transition that modulates to the relative major key for the second theme. The closing modulates to a chord that may lead back to the opening for the repeat of the exposition; a different chord leads onward into the development. The development itself is brief (it mushrooms dramatically in Beethoven's later works), and the recapitulation functions in an almost textbook manner. This movement is conservative in musical form, but its dramatic contrasts of themes, tempos, and dynamics show very clearly the direction in which Beethoven led Romantic music.

Even before Beethoven, early expressions of the Romantic spirit arose in Germany, like the play *Faust*, by Johann Wolfgang von Goethe, in which Faust sells his soul to the devil for knowledge and power. Goethe's work was a major stimulus of the Romantic movement. His personal character was transitional—a Romantic author, he was also a lawyer, statesman, and scientist in the classical model. This is apparent in his portrait by Gerhard von Kügelgen, an early German Romantic painter (Figure 13.3). The portrait is very traditional and fits the Neoclassical model. It shows Goethe's upper torso and head against a dark background, only slightly lightened for contrast around the figure, but with a volcano on the right edge. Goethe wears a dark blue overcoat with an honorific emblem on the right breast, partly concealed by a maroon sash wrapped around his shoulders. His waistcoat is scarlet and his shirt open, with a ruffled frontlet and neckband. His brown eyes gaze solemnly at the viewer, his high forehead is brightly lit, and his brown hair is swept back. The volcano may symbolize his explosive literary influence and the prominent forehead his great intellect. For such a seminal figure in Romanticism, the portrait is very conservative, perhaps reflecting his official rather than literary pursuits.

The opposite is true of Kügelgen's portrait of his contemporary, friend, and sometime student, Caspar David Friedrich, perhaps the greatest German Romantic painter (Figure 13.4). Friedrich's portrait, perhaps painted within a year of Goethe's, is radically different—the perfect Romantic portrait. Against an olive-green background that deepens, fades, and contains a few mysterious wisps of mist, Friedrich stares at the viewer with penetrating intensity. His cape and topcoat are nearly the same shade as the background and almost seem to emerge from it. He wears a brighter green waistcoat, a ruff, and a collar similar to but simpler than Goethe's. Above this, emerging from the cape's high collar, is a face of riveting concentration. Reddish-gold hair is combed forward and cascades into rich sideburns. On the brightly lit face, chin and cheekbones are flushed pink; the full lips are red, and the prominent nose carries the bright highlight of the furrowed brow. The portrait reflects the same mystery and power that is found in Friedrich's own paintings, which capture all of the Romantic mystery and fascination with the medieval and supernatural.

In his early years, Friedrich worked mostly in drawing, etching, and watercolor. From the beginning, he was fascinated by landscapes, and this interest remained dominant in his works.

He gained a reputation after winning a prize in 1805. *The Abbey in the Oak Wood* (Figure 13.5) is from this early period. The painting shows a small procession of monks carrying a coffin through the door of a ruined Gothic church, of which a wall is all that remains. They have passed an open grave in a decrepit cemetery filled with gnarled, leafless trees and toppling tombstones. It is late twilight, so the ground is shrouded in darkness; the arch of the sky is deep purple with a tiny crescent new moon, where a band of light brightens at the horizon. The atmosphere is gloomy and mysteriously spiritual, raising questions:

FIGURE 13.5 Caspar David Friedrich (1774–1840), *Abbey in the Oak Wood* (1809/10), oil on canvas, 171 × 110 cm, Old National Gallery, Berlin.

Why are they entering a ruined church? What does the open grave mean? Why are two tiny lights (visible in larger reproductions) flanking the cross in the church's portal? What do the light horizon and the new moon mean—resurrection? The fascination with light, mystery, and landscape remain constant in Friedrich's work—with one other unique feature: human figures almost always face away from the viewer—but not all his works are quite as dark as this one.

Wanderer above the Sea of Fog, (Figure 13.6) painted ten years after *The Abbey*, is Friedrich's best-known work. It shows a man with red-blonde hair wearing a frock coat and resting on a walking stick in the right hand, left foot stepping upward on a jagged rock formation. He looks out over more rocks through a shallow valley to two larger peaks, the right one having distinctive vertical sides. Between the man and the valley are wisps of fog that conceal all other landscape features and continue into the background in less detail, eventually yielding to a light-blue sky with a few fluffy clouds. The mood is pensive instead of gloomy, and the work shows many of Friedrich's characteristics: the significant landscape, its mystery, the virtuosic depiction of light and atmosphere, and the figure turned away. Is it the artist? The hair is suggestive, but we are not to know.

The same kind of mystery and emphasis on the supernatural is found in Franz Schubert's song "*Erlkönig*" ("The Goblin King," Figure 13.7). Based on Goethe's poem of the same name, it demonstrates the Romantic fascination with horror, mystery, and the supernatural. The poem is strophic, as the example shows, but the dialogue and music do not follow the verse structure, having as many as three speakers in one four-line verse. The singer must

FIGURE 13.6 Caspar David Friedrich, *Wanderer above the Sea of Fog* (1818), oil on canvas, 98 × 74 cm, Kunsthalle, Hamburg.

FIGURE 13.7 Franz Schubert (1797–1828), *Erlkönig* (The Goblin King, 1815–21), Op. 1, D. 328, Lied (Song), piano and voice.

Only text is given. It is easier to follow than timings.

Erlkönig Music by Franz Schubert		The Goblin King Poem by Johann Wolfgang von Goethe
Wer reitet so spät durch Nacht und Wind? Es ist der Vater mit seinem Kind; Er hat den Knaben wohl in dem Arm, Er faßt ihn sicher, er hält ihn warm.	N	—Who rides so late through night and wind? It is the father with his child He has the boy fast in his arm, He holds him safely, he keeps him warm.
"Mein Sohn, was birgst du so bang dein Gesicht?" "Siehst, Vater, du den Erlkönig nicht? Den Erlenkönig mit Kron und Schweif?" "Mein Sohn, es ist ein Nebelstreif.	F S F	—"My son, why do you hide your face in fear?" —"Father, do you not see the goblin king? The goblin king with crown and cape?" —"My son, it's just a whisp of fog."
Du liebes Kind, komm, geh mit mir! Gar schöne Spiele spiel' ich mit dir; Manch' bunte Blumen sind an dem Strand, Meine Mutter hat manch gülden Gewand."	GK	—"You dear child, come with me! I will play beautiful games with you; There are many pretty flowers on the shore My mother has many golden garments."
"Mein Vater, mein Vater, und hörest du nicht, Was Erlenkönig mir leise verspricht?" "Sei ruhig, bleibe ruhig, mein Kind; In dürren Blättern säuselt der Wind."	S F	—"My father, my father, don't you hear, What the goblin king softly promises me?" —"Be calm, stay calm, my child; Withered leaves are rustling in the wind."
"Willst, feiner Knabe, du mit mir gehn? Meine Töchter sollen dich warten schön; Meine Töchter führen den nächtlichen Reihn, Und wiegen und tanzen und singen dich ein."	GK	—"Do you, fine boy, want to go with me? My daughters should be pleased to wait on you; My daughters will lead the nightly dance, And will rock, dance and sing to you."
"Mein Vater, mein Vater, und siehst du nicht dort Erlkönigs Töchter am düstern Ort?" "Mein Sohn, mein Sohn, ich seh' es genau: Es scheinen die alten Weiden so grau."	S F	—"My father, my father! Don't you see there Goblin king's daughters in the shadowed place?" —"My son, my son, I see it clearly: Old grey willows shimmer there."
Ich liebe dich, mich reizt deine schöne Gestalt; Und bist du nicht willig, so brauch' ich Gewalt." "Mein Vater, mein Vater, jetzt faßt er mich an! Erlkönig hat mir ein Leids getan!"	GK S	—"I love you, your beautiful form entices me; But if you're not willing, I will need force." —"My father, my father, he's grabbing me now! The goblin king has done me an injury!"
Dem Vater grauset's, er reitet geschwind Er hält in Armen das ächzende Kind Erreicht den Hof mit Müh' und Not In seinen Armen das Kind war tot.	N	—The father shakes with fear; he gallops headlong, He holds in his arms the moaning child, He reaches home with toil and trial. In his arms, the child was dead.
A powerful, mysterious and tragic tale of the supernatural	N F S GK	—Narrator—Full vocal range —Father—Low vocal range —Son—High vocal range —Goblin King—Mid vocal range

convey four characters: the narrator, the father, the son, and the Goblin King. There are pounding repeated notes in the pianist's right hand, with a repeated short figure in the left hand—a quick scalar ascent followed by two jumps downward to the starting note. This musical idea depicts a galloping horse and persists through the entire song. The narrator, who uses the singer's full vocal range, tells the story. The father (in a low vocal range) tries to reassure the son as they ride through the woods. The son (high range) keeps having terrifying visions of the Goblin King, who is enticing him. The Goblin King (midrange and very smooth) tries to lure the child away and finally takes him by force. When they arrive home, the child is dead. All the emotion and mystery of natural and supernatural forces in folklore are present in the song.

FIGURE 13.8 Moritz von Schwind (1804–1871), *Erlkönig* (The Goblin King) (c. 1830), painting for illustration of Goethe's works, Galerie Belvedere, Vienna. Original painting on exhibit in Vienna; also reproduced on a postcard in 1917.

The song and poem have also inspired visual art. Moritz von Schwind was a close friend of Schubert's who regularly attended his home musicales. His painting of the *Erlkönig* (Figure 13.8) is one of the earliest. The twilit sky behind a forest is deep purple with one yellow streak from the setting sun. The middle-ground trees are wildly windblown, and in the foreground is a large misshapen stump. Riding on a wildly galloping white horse toward the left border is a man in brown, hunched over the horse's neck and tightly holding a small boy in light blue. Running on the air from behind the stump and reaching to grab the child is an eerie, bearded old man in windblown white robes (*Erlkönig*). Reaching around from the stump's right side are three young women in blue and pink robes, also floating (*Erlkönig*'s daughters). Behind them, holding the song's golden robe, is his mother. The scene captures the poem and song's frenzied horror.

Another very Romantic story is told in the ballet *Swan Lake* (Figure 13.9). Composed in 1875–76, it is the first of Tchaikovsky's three great full-length action ballets. The origin of the plot is not clear. It contains elements of folk tales from Russia and Germany, together with some plot devices common to many fairy stories—the enchanted princess who is free only at night, the lovesick prince who tries to save her, and the evil magician, all described in the figure. The first performance in Moscow was not successful. Its 1895 revival in St. Petersburg, with revised music and new choreography by Marius Petipa and Lev Ivanov, has become the absolute standard for this work. It is the classic example of ballet—especially Act II—and it includes virtually all of the art's most beautiful features. In Act I, Prince Siegfried receives a crossbow as a birthday present. Noteworthy features of this act include masculine characterization through the jester's striking athletic leaps. The prince's tutor is made to look aged and foolish by always dancing with flat feet. Men and women dance together to celebrate the birthday. In Act II, Siegfried happens on the lake of swans. When they become women, the *corps de ballet* dances as a large group, then the prince and Odette, the swan princess, fall in love and dance a *pas de deux* (duet in ballet) with solos for each and beautiful lifts in which the prince extends Odette's leaps by carrying her across the stage—another traditional way in which ballet distinguishes gender roles, as is the use of toe-dancing (*en pointe*) by women. After the extended duet, there are dances of different types for small groups of dancers, followed by a finale for all. The *corps*

FIGURE 13.9 Pyotr Ilyich Tchaikovsky (1840–1893), *Swan Lake* (1875–76), action ballet with full orchestra. Plot Summary.

Performances of this work vary in speed. Due to its length, timings are detailed only for Act I, Scene 2.

Timing (approximate) 3:15	Section Overture	Dance
24:00 (whole scene)	**Act I—Park near Prince Siegfried's Castle**	Prince Siegfried's birthday, general rejoicing. Jester opens with athletic leaping dance. Tutor enters dancing flat-footed. Prince Siegfried enters, dances with several partners as others dance, Tutor brings book from Queen listing prospective brides for Prince, who is not amused. Jester gets Tutor drunk; Queen enters attended, gives Siegfried crossbow as present. Party continues into evening—solo and group dances.
0:00–2:50	**Act II—Lake of the Swans**	Siegfried solo, swans enter on backdrop; Rothbart enters, solo.
2:50–4:30		Siegfried discovered by Rothbart. Single swan enters on backdrop. Siegfried aims, lowers bow as swan enters as Odette.
4:30–7:30		Odette solo; Siegfried pursues, she evades, quivers with fright then accompanies him–duet. Rothbart enters, drives her off.
7:30–11:30		*Corps de ballet* (swans), dance in geometric patterns. Siegfried searches, cannot find Odette. *Corps* forms lane for her. She enters, dances briefly with Siegfried, exits; he follows.
11:30–14:20		*Corps de ballet* dances as group, in quartets and duet.
14:20–23:10		Siegfried enters, seaches for Odette. She enters, falls in love. They do extended duet (*pas de deux*)—very classic—she displays grace, dancing *en pointe* (toes); he assists, supports, lifts, carries—very strenuous for both, but must seem effortless. *Corps de ballet* moves to frame & compliment their dance.
23:10–24:50		Dance of the cygnets (swan chicks)—A quartet with a bit of humorous relief, arms linked, cross-legged steps.
24:50–26:20		Second quartet dances more individually to a waltz.
26:20–28:40		Siegfried and Odette enter; she dances a final solo, he observes, they exit.
28:40–33:00		*Corps de ballet* dances as whole, in quartets. Odette enters for short solo with pirouettes (twirls). Corps dances finale. Siegfried and Odette enter for a final brief duet; he swears to be true. Rothbart enters and summons Odette; swans exit.
32:30 (whole scene)	**Act III—Ballroom in Siegfried's Palace**	Princesses presented for Siegfried to choose; he refuses. Baron Rothbart brings daughter Odile, disguised as Odette. National dances of Hungary, Spain, Naples & Poland. Siegfried pledges for Odile to become his wife. Odette appears depairing behind scene. Siegfried realizes deception, dashes to lake.
23:00 (whole scene)	**Act IV—Lake of the Swans**	Swan maidens comfort Odette. Siegfried arrives, begs for and receives forgiveness. Rothbart threatens Odette. Alternate endings: 1) Lover's leap into lake to die together, Rothbart's power is broken; couple ascends to heaven together. 2) Sigfriend defeats Rothbart; he dies. Couple lives happily ever after. 3) Several other variants on these.

de ballet departs, and Rothbart, the evil magician, drives Siegfried off. The remaining acts conclude the plot as described in the example. *Swan Lake* defines the Romantic style in dance: the magical plot, the love affair, the use of folk or fairy stories, and magical stage effects. It is a great monument of Romantic dance and music.

Another painter who evokes many of the Romantic emotions is Karl Friedrich Schinkel. Figure 13.10, *Gothic Church on a Crag by the Sea*, is typical of his paintings, which often contain a Gothic church in a beautiful landscape with glowing light and small human figures dwarfed by the scene. A darkening blue sky, striated with thin clouds, is the backdrop for forested hills on the left, with a magnificent Gothic church high on a crag near the center of the middle ground. The sunset behind the church gives it a light pink, glowing halo. Below the church, two jetties of a small harbor extend into the sea, with ships in

FIGURE 13.10 Karl Friedrich Schinkel (1781–1841), *Gothic Church on a Crag by the Sea* (1815), oil on canvas, 72 × 98 cm, Old National Gallery, Berlin.

the distance. Moving across the foreground from left to right, we see a lush grove. A house nestles below the church on the near shore of a small bay. A rustic road leads from the center to the right. Cresting a rise leading down to the sea is a nobleman's carriage surrounded by his retainers. On their right, the land rises to a monument and gnarled trees. Schinkel's work has much the same character as Friedrich's—for example, having human figures secondary to the landscape—but Schinkel's work seems more approachable to the viewer than Friedrich's. Perhaps Schinkel thought this a deficiency, for after seeing Friedrich's *Wanderer in the Sea of Fog*, Schinkel gave up painting and concentrated solely on architecture.

Schinkel was already a successful architect and stage designer in both Neo-Gothic and Neoclassical style. Not long after his disillusionment, he designed the first Neo-Gothic church in Germany, which initiated a surge in Gothic design throughout Europe and North America for decades to come. Figures 13.11a and b show this church. The Friedrichswerder church is a block from the Spree River in central Berlin. It is part of the city's complex of art museums, most of which are on the adjacent island. At this time (2016), the church and its exhibits are closed because of structural damage from nearby construction four years ago, but photographs show Schinkel's achievement. The exterior in Figure 13.11a shows a very austere Gothic façade. This is less decorated than medieval Gothic (common in the revival style), although the absence of statuary is explained by this being a Protestant church. Nevertheless, the forms are there—pointed arches over doors and windows, with triple rosettes at the peak of each main window. The building is not tall enough to require flying buttresses, but it has simple buttresses along the sides, each of which is topped with a pinnacle. Not visible in the exterior photograph is the semicircular apse at the altar end—very typically Gothic.

The interior, shown in Figure 13.11b, is much more like earlier Gothic. Clustered pillars stretch up to pointed vaulting with beautiful tracery of secondary ribs. Along the windows' baseline is a shallow balcony, similar to that in earlier Gothic style. Below the balconies are side aisles

FIGURE 13.11A Karl Friedrich Schinkel, Friedrichswerder Church (1824–31), Exterior, Berlin.

FIGURE 13.12 Jacques-Louis David (1748–1825), *Napoléon Crossing the Alps*, first version (1800), oil on canvas, 2.6 × 2.2 m, Château de Malmaison, Reuil-Malmaison, France.

FIGURE 13.11B Karl Friedrich Schinkel, Friedrichswerder Church, Interior, Berlin.

behind pointed arches. The figure shows the church as it was before 2012, filled with sculpture presently in storage. Other Protestant features include the prominence of the pulpit about halfway down the left side and the deemphasized altar in the apse. Still, it is clear why the church's beauty spurred the renewal of the Gothic style as part of the manifestation of Romanticism.

The Romantic style appeared in its earliest, purest form in Germany, partly because of the influences described above and probably also because Germany was somewhat stable during this period. France, as we have seen, was in turmoil. Art production did not cease there, but Romantic features tended to be applied to concrete events of the time rather than the dreamy or spooky fantasy found in Germany. This is very evident in Jacques-Louis David's *Napoléon Crossing the Alps* (Figure 13.12).

David's painting is something out of two worlds. It has the neoclassical immediacy of his earlier works—the moment frozen in time. But the frozen moment is in the midst of driving activity: the rearing horse, Napoléon's right hand gesturing onward, and the artillery column plodding along behind. The composition is dramatic. The mountain slopes and rearing horse form one diagonal, while Napoléon's body forms a crossing one. The line of the clouds, his bicorn hat, and the horse's head form a third that intersects the mountains at their peak. All is caught up in a powerful wind that sweeps the tail, mane, and cape onward and upward. In a historical allusion, the foreground rocks carry the names "Bonaparte," "Hannibal," and "Carolus Magnus" (Charlemagne). The sense of action is very Romantic but also very direct, in contrast to the German style. It shows clearly the use of Romantic emotional appeal as a nationalistic propaganda vehicle—a development with serious consequences.

FIGURE 13.13 Francisco Goya (1746–1828), *The Third of May, 1808* (1814) oil on canvas, 2.7 × 3.5 m, Prado, Madrid.

The problem, of course, is that nations don't agree, and conflicting nationalisms cause violence. Napoléon tried to install his brother on the Spanish throne, beginning in 1807. On May 2, 1808, citizens blocked the removal of the royal family's last members from Madrid and were fired upon by French troops, who led a cavalry charge and provoked rioting throughout the city. Retaliating viciously, the French captured hundreds of the poorly armed civilians and executed them the following day in revenge for French blood spilled. This is the brutal side of Napoleonic glory. Goya's masterpiece in Figure 13.13, *The Third of May, 1808*, illustrates this.

Soldiers and their victims face each other across the painting. On the right, the soldiers, wearing shako hats, backpacks, knee-length coats, and sabers, are dark and sinister. A lantern on the ground lights them from the front, and the slight glow of predawn reveals buildings in the distance. The soldiers' muskets and bayonets extend the line of their heads toward the victims as they lean forward for the next shot. In the foreground, corpses lie in their own blood. Behind them, a friar prays, and the condemned approach death with various responses: grimacing in horror, hiding a face, clenching a fist. The most dramatic victim suggests martyrdom: staring directly at his adversaries, hands raised as if in crucifixion, with a hole in the right palm as if from a nail. His white shirt is the brightest spot in the painting. Behind him and the bayonets, the next victims await their deaths in fear. The painting is deliberately violent and horrifying. It dramatizes the act's evil to express the power of Spanish revulsion toward the French. In a way, all three of the artistic styles of the early eighteenth century appear in this work: Romantic emotion, Nationalism, and the grittiness of Realism.

Not all French Romantic art was realistic or nationalistic, though. *The Barque of Dante* (Figure 13.14) by Eugène Delacroix depicts a scene from early in Dante's *Inferno*. Guided

FIGURE 13.14 Eugène Delacroix (1798–1863), *The Barque of Dante* (1822), oil on canvas, 1.9 × 2.5 m, Louvre, Paris.

FIGURE 13.15 Eugène Delacroix, *July 28: Liberty Leading the People* (1830), oil on canvas, 2.6 × 3.2 m, Louvre, Paris.

by the poet Virgil, Dante stands in the ferry crossing the river Styx (or in this case, its tributary, Acheron) into hell. The boat passes from dark shores on the right toward the fires of hell on the left. The ferryman, Charon (or Phlegyas) rows from the stern, bent over so his face is hidden.[3] Virgil, wearing a laurel wreath, raises his left hand to shield his head with his brown robe. His right hand clasps Dante's in reassurance. Dante, on Virgil's right in a green robe and red cowl, recoils from the approaching shore. His left hand gropes for Virgil, and his right is raised protectively. Figures of the damned surround the boat. One supine man is corpse-white. To his right, another tries to clamber aboard while kicking a deathly white woman who grasps the boat unconsciously. Before her, two men wrestle to force each other under. On the left, a monstrous man with devilish eyes and pointed nose gnaws at the prow, while a powerful man with red eyes tries to crawl over the rear gunwale. The scene arises from a literary classic, but the sense of turbulence and horror is purely Romantic, and Delacroix has taken liberties to intensify the work. The poem actually does not describe this moment, for Dante had fainted. Still, the image is very powerful. When first exhibited in 1822, it paved the way for French Romanticism.

Delacroix did not shrink from placing Romanticism in the service of nationalism when it served his purpose. The imagery of Figure 13.15 is a bit paradoxical. Following Napoleon's defeat, the monarchy of the House of Bourbon was reinstated. The second king of this line proved so resistant to constitutional monarchy that he was replaced in the July Revolution of 1830 by a distant cousin, who assumed the title "King of the French" instead of "King of France." This is the event Delacroix commemorates. From our perspective, it is difficult to see why replacing one monarch with another is a move in the direction of popular government, but Delacroix found the sentiment useful.

Liberty Leading the People is filled with Romantic action and turbulence. It shows a crowd of civilian revolutionaries, led by a bare-breasted woman symbolizing Liberty. On her left is a young boy brandishing pistols. The background is filled with the smoke of battle, except on the right, where the steeples of Notre Dame rise behind urban blocks. The left middle ground

---

3 The confusion of names is traditional. The Styx had five tributaries that met in a swamp. The Acheron was one tributary, and the swamp was called by either name. Although Charon was traditionally the ferryman of hell, Phlegyas sometimes received the assignment, here perhaps because Charon tried to block Dante's living soul from entering. Since Dante depicts Charon with fiery eyes, the background figure grabbing at the boat's gunwale may be him.

holds a crowd brandishing weapons. In the foreground, on the far left, a youth stumbles over a fallen stone barricade. Behind him, a man with a pistol in his belt brandishes a saber. He is led by a gentleman in a top hat with a musket, in front of whom a wounded partisan strains toward Lady Liberty. On the bottom margin, a fallen partisan in a white shirt lies dead. Liberty, in the center, strides forward waving the *tricolour* (the French republican flag) while carrying a musket with bayonet in her left hand. Her yellow dress, fallen from her shoulder, exposes her breast, and she wears a red-brown Phrygian cap, the ancient symbol of a free person. The boy on her left steps forward toward two fallen soldiers. Barely noticeable, the *tricolour* also flies from Notre Dame, symbolizing that the battle Liberty leads is won. The picture is another demonstration of powerful Romantic imagery in service of nationalistic violence—a great nineteenth-century ethical failure. For the rest of the century, France continued to simmer in conflict, with numerous changes of government—from monarchy to republic to empire, and on and on.

Once Napoléon was dealt with, Britain was able to enjoy some degree of relative peace, although it was troubled by internal controversies and wars of colonial suppression. English taste ran strongly toward landscape painting, and the upper classes commissioned paintings of their grand country residences. Such a painting is *Wivenhoe Park, Essex*, by John Constable, one of England's greatest painters (see Figure 13.16). This wonderful painting has, however, its own paradoxes. The commissioning family was not nobility but distinguished military commoners; the house is not that old, having been built only in 1759; and the landscape, although clearly inspired by those of Capability Brown, is not.

Even so, the work depicts an ideal English landscape. In the foreground, a rolling meadow slopes down to a large pond; left of that, a rail fence confines a pasture with black-and-white cows. In the pond, two men in a rowboat set a fishing net; to their left swim two swans; further

FIGURE 13.16 John Constable (1776–1837), *Wivenhoe Park, Essex* (1816), oil on canvas, 56 × 101 cm, National Gallery of Art, Washington, DC.

left swim two ducks trailing seven ducklings; and yet further left, the stream issues from a low dam or weir that supports a drive. Behind the weir is a shaded pool with a grotto folly. Two ladies in a donkey cart have just crossed the bridge, and behind them groves of old and newly planted trees and another rail fence define a boundary. This extends upward past the water and other groves and trees until the brick mansion can be seen peeping around a mature grove by the pool's edge. On the pool's back bank are a brown-and-white cow, a flock of geese, and children playing in front of a distant cottage. The sky is that of a beautiful summer day, with puffy clouds below cerulean blue. The scene is one of pastoral perfection that any Englishman might dream of. Such was Constable's style.

FIGURE 13.17 Aelbert Cuyp (1620–1691), *The Maas at Dordrecht*, c. 1650, oil on canvas, 115 × 170 cm, National Gallery, Washington.

FIGURE 13.18 Joseph Mallord William Turner (1775–1851), *Dort or Dordrecht: The Dort Packet-Boat from Rotterdam Becalmed* (1818), oil on canvas, 1.8 × 2.6 m, Yale Center for British Art, New Haven, CT.

The second great English Romantic landscape painter began his career in much the same realistic, detail-filled style. Joseph Mallord William Turner began painting early. Born in 1775, he was selling his work by the age of eleven. He soon began studying and exhibiting at the Royal Academy, and in 1802, he went on an extended trip to Europe. Turner was financially secure, which enabled him to develop his own style without market-driven constraints imposed by fashion. Turner's work provides a dramatic example of this evolution. Aelbert Cuyp's *The Maas at Dordrecht* (Figures 1.1 and 13.17) was in the Netherlands until at least 1804. Between then and 1814, it was acquired by an English baronet. Either in Holland or England, it was seen and sketched by Turner, who painted Figure 13.18, *The Dort Packet-Boat from Rotterdam Becalmed*, in 1818. The similarities are unmistakable. Both depict a party boarding or disembarking a tubby ship of a type that was old-fashioned even in Turner's day. Both scenes are at Dordrecht, and the same church tower appears in both, although at opposite sides of the paintings. Some of the subsidiary ships are similar as well, as are even the clouds. Turner was by no means a copyist, but he appreciated a great painting, and at the time, his style echoed Cuyp's precision. In later years, light and atmospheric effects superseded detail as Turner's great preoccupation.

From Figure 13.18 (*The Dort Packet-Boat* of 1818) to Figure 13.19 (*Wreckers, Coast of Northumberland, with a Steamboat Assisting a Ship off Shore* of 1833–34), there is a distinct change in style and technique. The later brushstrokes are heavier, leaving blobs of paint in places (*impasto*). Many details are visible, but often only by suggestion rather than precision. The light and clouds swirl vividly—brightly around the castle and cliffs behind the foreground salvage crew (wreckers) and darkly around the background steamboat towing the sailing ship off the rocks. In this work, Turner's personal stylistic development is well underway. And he continued further, as seen in Figure 13.20, *Snow Storm: Steamboat off a Harbor's Mouth* (ca. 1842). Turner recorded on the back of the painting that he was himself in this storm, and there is a story that he had himself tied to the mast for four hours to experience it.

Turner painted *Snow Storm* at the age of sixty-seven. It is a remarkable work. The innovations seen in Figure 13.19 permeate the painting. The black shadow of the steamboat is barely discernible from the semicircle of its paddlewheel, its mast, and the plume of orange-brown smoke from its funnel. Behind it, a few grey geometric shapes suggest a town. A bright area behind the boat may be a break in the clouds, with the boat's shadow extending toward the viewer. Aside from these, the air, water, waves, and spume merge into great, nearly abstract swirls of color, some with an almost silken texture. This is Turner at his most intensely personal. Some describe the style as a precursor of Impressionism (see Chapter 14), but this is a potential fallacy. Turner died in 1851, and the first works with even a trace of Impressionist style did not appear until more than a decade later; the term itself does not appear for twenty-one years. While Turner's work (and Delacroix's) did indeed influence the later Impressionists, the two earlier artists were just expressing their individuality; they had no idea of what was to come.[4]

FIGURE 13.19 J. M. W. Turner, *Wreckers, Coast of Northumberland, with a Steamboat Assisting a Ship off Shore* (1833/34), oil on canvas, 90 × 121 cm, Yale Center for British Art.

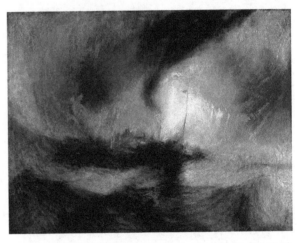

FIGURE 13.20 J. M. W. Turner, *Snow Storm: Steamboat off a Harbor's Mouth* (ca. 1842), oil on canvas, 91 × 122 cm, Tate Gallery, London.

Romanticism to Realism

A final example of English art that is realistic and has an almost antinationalist tone is Figure 13.21, *Remnants of an Army*, by Elizabeth Thompson, Lady Butler. Thompson-Butler's knighted husband was an Irish general in the English army. They spent many years in foreign service, and she specialized in history paintings, especially of England's colonial wars. Her husband's Irish background aroused their concern about colonialism. She painted battles as thrilling but with added emphasis on the common soldier's heroism. Occasionally, her deeper feelings crept out, as shown in the figure. It depicts the return of the only European survivor of the 1842 retreat from Kabul, in which more than sixteen thousand British and Indian soldiers and their camp followers were massacred by Afghan tribesmen (a situation which resonates even today).

---

4   Turner's interest was in more than depiction of light and atmosphere; his ultimate goal was to convey a spiritual quality in his work.

FIGURE 13.21 Elizabeth Thompson, Lady Butler (1846–1933), *Remnants of an Army* (1879), oil on canvas, 1.32 × 2.34 m, Tate Gallery, London.

The painting depicts Assistant Surgeon William Brydon careening in his saddle on a staggering, exhausted bay horse. He is about to turn the corner into the walled city of Jalalabad, from which riders gallop for support. The solitary surgeon is slightly right of center, facing left before a bare desert landscape with the low city on his right, in line with the background's purple mountains. The mountains fade into the distance behind a marshy pool under a nearly cloudless sky. Except for the mountains, the color palette is entirely desert colors: brown, red, and yellow, with bits of dusty green. The mood is one of despair and exhaustion, and the painting's message is a tribute to Brydon's heroism. Thompson's painting is an indictment of colonialism in a powerful realistic documentation of diplomatic and military blunders only two months before England repeated them. The blindness of nationalism overcame all rational and ethical opposition.

The United States had its own bloodbath in the American Civil War, fought to abolish slavery and preserve, rather than extend, the nation. Pictorial documentation of this was largely limited to newspaper engravings and photography—only the third war to be so documented. Contemporary painters, however, had developed an almost hypnotic fascination with the beauty of American landscape. This beginning is especially clear in the works of the Hudson River School, whose most famous painting is *Kindred Spirits* by Asher Durand (Figure 13.22). Durand painted this for William Cullen Bryant (the gentleman on the left) as a memorial to their mutual friend, the painter Thomas Cole (standing on the right), who had died the previous year. The cascade is Kaaterskill Falls, in its proper place in Kaaterskill Clove, a gorge in the Catskill Mountains west of the lower Hudson River. The rocky ledges in the foreground are also in the gorge, but they are in a different location; Durand has moved them for a more striking composition.

FIGURE 13.22 Asher B. Durand (1796–1886), *Kindred Spirits* (1849), oil on canvas, 117 × 92 cm, Crystal Bridges Museum of American Art, Bentonville, AR.

The work depicts Bryant and Cole in formal dress, standing in sunlight on a rocky prominence above a brook and facing a higher precipice on the other bank. The immediate foreground frames them with gracefully arched deciduous trees on the bank, and conifers grow from the riverbed opposite. Every leaf is clearly painted, forming a lacework in front of the beautiful mountainous landscape that fades into the mist behind. Cole is pointing out to Bryant the beautiful waterfalls farther up the gorge. The sunlight and misty atmosphere make the light an important contributor to the scene—a feature called *luminism* that became very characteristic of American landscapes at this time. The magical light accentuates the landscape's poetic beauty and imparts to its Realism a Romantic intensity.

FIGURE 13.23 George Caleb Bingham (1811–1879), *Fur Traders Descending the Missouri* (c. 1845), oil on canvas, 74 × 93 cm, Metropolitan Museum of Art, New York.

Nor was this Romantic Realism confined to the East. Around the same time, George Caleb Bingham painted *Fur Traders Descending the Missouri*, a scene from the American West (see Figure 13.23). Bingham originally named this *French Fur Trader and Half-Breed Son*, but the exhibitor thought it controversial because of the term "half-breed," which described the common-law marriages between traders and Native American women. We might be equally squeamish about its possible interpretation as ethnic prejudice, except for the fact that the original title is early documentation of a fascinating historical development: the widespread practice of such marriages in previous centuries has resulted in a new and unique ethnic group, the *Métis* or *Michif*, found today throughout the Northern Plains and Rocky Mountains. The different ethnicities are clearly visible in the contrast between the grizzled, suspicious trader and his calm, handsome son.

The scene occurs before a sky twice as luminous as Durand's, the setting sun on the left imparting a pink glow to the mist dividing the foreground from wooded islands and the riverbank far behind. The calm river shines like glass, except where protruding snags ruffle the surface. Most of the painting's width is filled with a dugout canoe floating low in the water. On the right, paddling in the stern, is the pipe-smoking trader, wearing a loose striped shirt and a version of the Phrygian (or freeman's) cap with a tuft on top, similar to winter hats still worn in the Northern Plains today. In front of him is a large covered bundle, presumably of furs, on which are a recently shot duck, a red sash, and a red wampum bag. The boy, resting across the bundle toward his father, leans on his elbow over the gun with which he shot the duck. He wears a loose blue striped shirt with red pants and gazes calmly toward the viewer. Two small bundles are at his feet near the boat's bow, on which sits a tethered bear cub; above the cub, a flock of geese is barely visible in the distant sky. The painting's luminous beauty creates an almost magical, romantic atmosphere to fascinate, hypnotize, and ensnare Eastern viewers who had never seen the Great American West.

FIGURE 13.24 Albert Bierstadt (1830–1902), *The Rocky Mountains, Lander's Peak*, 1863, oil on canvas, 1.87 × 3.07 m, Metropolitan Museum of Art, New York.

A similar goal motivated Albert Bierstadt nearly twenty years later when he painted *The Rocky Mountains, Lander's Peak* (Figures 1.3 and 13.24).[5] Bierstadt, born in Germany, came to the United States with his parents at the age of one and began to paint as a child. He returned to Germany for four years in his twenties to study art. When he returned to the United States, he painted scenes of the northeastern United States and adopted the style of the Hudson River School, in particular luminism. Two trips to the West in 1859 and 1863 provided sketches for many years of painting. The magnificent large-scale landscapes arising from these, in particular those of the Yosemite Valley, captured the public imagination and were influential in the establishment of the National Park System. In 1865, he sold *Rocky Mountains, Lander's Peak* for $25,000.

At 1.87 × 3.07 meters, *Lander's Peak* fills a wall with a highly detailed scene of breathtaking beauty. A wide meadow in the foreground hosts a Native American encampment of around one hundred people of all ages, with horses, dogs, and eight teepees. There is a grove on the left, and behind the meadow is a mountain lake filled by a waterfall cascading down golden crags in the middle ground. The background is filled with craggy, glaciated peaks, the tallest of which (Lander's Peak) rises to a sharp point above the wispy clouds that drift from right to left. The grand size permits an extraordinary amount of detail. Viewed on a wall, it brings the viewer right into a scene such as (s)he has never before experienced. The work's luminous beauty makes the highly detailed Realistic landscape also a Romantic masterpiece.

After the Civil War, the same economic boom that fueled the gilded age of millionaires created a market for other types of painting, including portraits, imaginary landscapes, and seascapes, as well as opulent architecture. James Abbott MacNeill Whistler was an important painter and innovator whose portraits attracted widespread notice. Born in the United States, Whistler traveled with his family to Europe, and then England, beginning when he was eight. Returning after his father's death, he spent his educational years

FIGURE 13.25 James Abbott MacNeill Whistler (1834–1903), *Arrangement in Grey and Black No. 1*, or *The Artist's Mother* (1871), oil on canvas, 1.44 x 1.62 m, Musée d'Orsay, Paris.

5   Note that the painting's date (1863) is actually in the middle of the Civil War. The artistic value of such works was deeply appreciated. It also served as a subtle reminder of the wide-open spaces threatened by the country's disunion.

in this country. At the age of twenty-one, he decided to become an artist and went to study in Paris. His developing personal style included an emphasis on line over color and a theory associating art with music so that he gave his works musical names: arrangement, nocturne, symphony, etc. Whistler's most famous work is *Arrangement in Grey and Black No. 1*, or *The Artist's Mother* (Figure 13.25).

The painting is a study in shades of grey and black, although it is not completely monochromatic. The face and hands are flesh-colored, and there is yellow in the footstool, the rug, and the drapery. Anna Whistler sits in a simple wooden chair facing left, her figure occupying about 50 percent of the painting's width, somewhat right of center. A dark flowered drape hangs on the left, and a landscape hangs on the grey wall. Mother Whistler's dress is completely black. There is white lace on her cuffs, the high collar, and the sashes of her bonnet, which hang down in front of her shoulders. Her face is gentle but firm, and her hands rest demurely in her lap, holding a lace handkerchief. Her feet rest on a small footstool. Contrasting with the deep black of her figure is the dark grey of the drape; the wall is a lighter grey, and the landscape's matting is a very light grey, nearly white. The composition is based on the placement of large areas of solid grey shades in an arrangement that is pleasing and interesting. At this, Whistler has succeeded. The work is one of a very small number that have risen to near-universal recognition. Its success in parodies shows its familiarity, and it has become a symbol of motherhood, even commemorating that on a postage stamp.

FIGURE 13.26A James A. M. Whistler, the Peacock Room, north end (1876–7), 4.22 m (height) × 6.13 × 10.26 m, Freer Gallery of Art, Washington, DC.

The artist's devotion to his mother might suggest that he lived quietly—not true. After she moved in with him, her reserved piety tempered his lifestyle and helped him find patrons. He had been living riotously in Paris until she arrived, and he had a difficult and prickly personality tempered by witty humor—he drew mermaids and sea serpents in maps he prepared for the Coast Guard. His impulsiveness influenced his largest work, the Peacock Room, designed for a wealthy Englishman and later sold to Charles Freer, who incorporated it as a permanent installation in his DC art gallery (see Figures 13.26a and b). Asked to complete the room after the original designer had fallen ill, Whistler received permission to make small changes to

FIGURE 13.26B James A. M. Whistler, the Peacock Room, south end.

complement his painting over the fireplace. He then ran riot and completely revised the decoration, painting over historic Renaissance wall hangings in the process. The original designer was shocked and collapsed, dying insane three years later. The patron quarreled violently with Whistler, who commemorated that by painting fighting peacocks on the end wall.

The room is perfectly intact and is a work of genius. Its color scheme is a deep green with gold highlights, in the fashionable Orientalized style. Delicate gold shelves for the patron's Chinese porcelain collection line three walls and the spaces on the fourth wall between three louvered window shades. The window shades and the south-end wall are filled with elaborate paintings of peacocks in gold leaf. Other gold designs adorn the wainscoting, the spaces between the shelves, the ceiling filigree, and the unusual egg-shaped lights. The shades of green vary, from speckled blue-green porphyry on the fireplace to a dark emerald green around the windows. The coloring is entirely Whistler's. From the original design survive the shelving, a hutch on the south end, the fireplace and, ironically, Whistler's *Rose and Silver: The Princess from the Land of Porcelain* above it. The room is one of Whistler's most inspired creations; its Oriental style can be considered an outgrowth of Romanticism, and the *Princess* is Realistic, if exotic. The room attests to the artist's genius for innovation, which in other works sometimes yielded almost abstract results.

An American artist of much more concrete tastes was Thomas Eakins, whose work shows the appeal Realism had for Americans, who were in an optimistic mood following the Civil War. *Max Schmitt in a Single Scull* (Figure 13.27a) shows one of the era's great athletes. Competitive rowing was the first intercollegiate sport and was all the rage in the late nineteenth century. Rowing clubs sprang up all over the country; those on the Schuylkill River of Eakins's painting are still very active. Eakins's commitment to Realism is confirmed by a picture of the same place nearly 150 years later (Figure 13.27b), which shows replacement bridges at the same location and angle, trees on the far bank matured, and even a rowing team (many of which passed during the photo session). The skyscrapers of modern downtown Philadelphia disfigure the background.

In Eakins's work, save for a few roofs behind the bridgehead, there is no distant construction. The leafless trees and clear blue sky suggest the season of autumn, as does the brown vegetation on both riverbanks. The time of day is around 4:00 p.m., based on the shadow of the far bank that camouflages a low boathouse. A house

FIGURE 13.27A Thomas Eakins (1844–1916), *Max Schmnitt in a Single Scull* (1871), oil on canvas, 83 × 118 cm, Metropolitan Museum, New York.

FIGURE 13.27B Location of Eakins's Max Schmitt Painting—May, 2015.

stands on the bank's top. The corner of a stone building appears above a marshy area in front of the near bank's grove. Wherever needed, figures and objects are clearly reflected in the placid water, which also reflects the deep blue of the sky. In the foreground, Schmitt rests, partially turned to the front; ripples show that his boat has been approaching the viewer diagonally from right to left. Parallel ripples lead to a boat that has just passed and is rowed by the painter. Three other sculls and a steam launch appear in the background. Crisscrossing diagonals beginning with Schmitt's ripples lead the eye back through several intersections to the thin line of clouds. They link the foreground, background, and sky and draw the viewer into the scene, which Eakins depicts with crystalline clarity and realism.

His interest in Realism also led to experiments with the improving medium of photography, which he began after exposure to the work of Eadweard Muybridge, the inventor of stop-action photography. After inventing a camera that could place several successive images on a single negative, Eakins used it to study human motion. Figure 13.28 is one of his studies. In it, a bearded man in trunks pole-vaults from right to left. Eakins's method is especially appropriate to this image, since it shows the successive images with the pole radiating from the same fulcrum, which helps to unify the motion better than images side by side. Eakins's photography shows the analytical side of his work, all of which is clear, documentary, and realistic. This is not always the case for another great American Realist whose works often involve the viewer in an emotional context.

Winslow Homer's *Breezing Up* (Figure 13.29) shows a man and three boys sailing a sloop off the Massachusetts coast (the stern's lettering shows that they hail from Gloucester). The boat travels from the center of the painting toward the left, heeled over in a stiff breeze on a sunny day with puffy clouds in the sky. The bellied-out sail, the thirty-degree heel, and the rudder's bubbling turbulence indicate a bracing speed over the lightly choppy waves. A two-masted schooner travels the same way in the background, and a third sail is barely visible on the horizon. The man sits in the stern of the cockpit, left hand on the rudder and right on the sheet (sail rope). One boy sits casually on the upside of the stern deck; his younger brother sits on the upper gunwale with his feet in the cockpit, and the third reclines precariously on the foredeck with his feet hanging over the edge. All three boys are leaning against the heel, and

FIGURE 13.28 Thomas Eakins, *Man Pole-Vaulting* (ca. 1885), stop-action photography using special camera of Eakins's invention.

FIGURE 13.29 Winslow Homer (1836–1910), *Breezing Up* (1873–6), oil on canvas, 62 × 97 cm, National Gallery, Washington.

FIGURE 13.30 Winslow Homer, *The Gulf Stream* (1899), oil on canvas, 72 × 123 cm, Metropolitan Museum, New York.

the whole sunburned crew is basking in the glow of an invigorating day in the sun on the sea.

Later in life, Homer's works developed a darker mood. This is obvious in *The Gulf Stream* (Figure 13.30). The boat is in almost the same position, but it is smaller, more at the mercy of larger waves in a rising sea. The boat, hailing from Key West, is heavily damaged—lacking bowsprit, mast, and rudder—and it plunges in the Gulf Stream's deep blue waters, circled by sharks. A black man lies helplessly across the deck; red stains on the hull and in the water suggest that a companion has recently fallen victim to the sharks. Diagonals that lead the eye are very clear in this work's composition, from the top edge of the dark foreground wave, back across the lighter blue edge to the waterspout on the horizon, and finally across that to the ship too distant to help. The work powerfully radiates desolation and despair. Homer took great care with this work. Parts appear in sketches as early as 1885; even after exhibiting it in 1900, he continued to tweak it. Some consider it the artist's greatest work.

The most fashionable portrait painter of the time was another American expatriate, John Singer Sargent, born to American parents who had stopped in Florence. He spent most of his life in Europe, but he also visited the Middle East as well as cities and picturesque spots in the United States. Sargent is best known for his elegant portraits of society ladies. *Margaret Stuyvesant Rutherford White (Mrs. Henry White)* (Figure 13.31) is one. Margaret Rutherford had a distinguished pedigree; daughter of a US Senator from New Jersey she married Henry White, who became US Ambassador to Austria, then England.

In Sargent's portrait, she stands before an elegant chaise longue in front of floor-length drapes. The drapes and frame of the chaise are gold and its cushions a dark salmon. They highlight the statuesque figure of Mrs. White, who stands in the foreground. Customarily, Sargent slightly elongated the women in his portraits to add dignity. It is very successful in this case. Her dark hair elegantly piled, the subject gazes directly at the viewer, her elliptical face crowning a gracefully long neck encircled by a single strand of pearls. Her right hand holds a fan at her side, and the left holds a small decorated container. The portrait's opulence comes from her dress, an elaborate design in white (pun?) silk with white tulle at the neck, the tips of the sleeves, and an overskirt. A lace-trimmed train descends from the left hip, curves behind, and ends at her right in front of the chaise. Sargent's portrait expresses the dignity and position of this beautiful woman.

FIGURE 13.31 John Singer Sargent (1856–1925), *Margaret Stuyvesant Rutherford White* (Mrs. Henry White) (1883), Oil on canvas, 2.25 × 1.44 m, Corcoran Collection, National Gallery, Washington, DC.

The travels of American diplomats, artists, and others between Europe and North America reflect increased conveniences, comfort, and safety in the age of steamships and railroads, as well as a desire to raise American arts to a stature equal to those of Europe—something that Whistler and Sargent were among the first to achieve. The same aspirations also affected musicians. Several musicians from the Northeast studied in Europe and brought a new sophistication to American music on their return. Many of them were instrumental in developing music studies at America's oldest and most distinguished universities—mostly in New England, and thus called 'The Second New England School.'

The first of these was John Knowles Paine, originally from Maine, who studied in Germany and returned to become the first organist and music professor at Harvard. A brief work that shows his sophisticated skill as well as his sense of humor is the *Fuga Giocosa*, or "Jolly Fugue" (Figure 13.32). A description of what Realism means in musical terms is elusive at best, but this work can perhaps be considered Realist because it borrows the tune of an American baseball song—not the well-known "Take Me Out to the Ballgame," but one whose words are forgotten yet whose tune is still known: "Over the Wall Is Out, Boys." The short opening motive sets the first five words with a melody that revolves around three adjacent notes, then leaps up an octave on the word "boys" to depict the flying ball. Paine turns this into a fugue, a sophisticated form of imitative polyphony of which Bach was the great master. The work is quite short—less than two minutes. Its rollicking feel comes from the popular tune and its major key.

The exposition presents the theme four times, building the number of voices with each entrance. Then there is an episode in which Paine modulates to the minor before returning to the major and modulating beyond until he stops short on a dissonant diminished chord at the work's halfway point. After this, he develops the theme in different ways: fragmentation, using only the first part; sequence, with a scalar motive repeated at descending pitch levels broken

FIGURE 13.32 John Knowles Paine (1839–1906), *Fuga giocosa* (Jolly Fugue, 1900) Fugue for Piano.

Performances vary in speed. Timings below are based on a total duration of 1:45.

Timing (approximate)	Section	Music
0:00–0:19	**Exposition**	Voices enter on the same theme (melody) and pile up on one another until the total number of voices is reached—the only rule of a fugue.
0:19–26	**Transition**	Parts move in parallel scales upward, modulates—new key.
0:26–0:35	**Episode 1**	Theme enters several times in a minor key.
0:35–0:44	**Transition**	Rising scales, this time mainly in bass, modulates again.
0:44–0:59	**Episode 2**	Theme in major key, then modulates, rises to heavy chord.
0:59–1:05	**Episode 3**	Theme in stretto (piled up, not waiting for theme to finish before next one enters), very brief, moves into—
1:05–1:14	**Transition**	Parallel scales, rising to theme once in high range, pause.
1:14–1:18	**Episode 4**	Theme fragmented, only first four notes used going lower.
1:18–1:36	**Transition**	Rising scales to high chord, theme briefly inverted, then parallel scales down, two sweeps upward.
1:36–1:45	**Conclusion**	Partial theme repeated descending. Grand concluding upward flourish.

FIGURE 13.33 John Singer Sargent, *Frederick Law Olmsted* (1895), oil on canvas, 2.5 × 1.4 m, Biltmore Estate, Asheville, NC.

briefly by a soft pause, followed by repetition at one pitch (*ostinato*), then falling thirds, a rocketing upward flourish, and a *stretto*, in which the theme enters in one voice after another (like the exposition, but squeezed together), and ending with a grand, rising flourish. A great deal happens in this very short work, with great sophistication. Part of the humor arises from whimsically using this trifling tune for a textbook example of how to develop a fugue theme.

Like Whistler, Sargent, and Paine, many Americans traveled to Europe in this age of improved travel, and Sargent often painted their portraits, always trying to convey the subject's individual character. One such subject was Frederick Law Olmsted, America's greatest landscape architect, who visited English gardens but then became a writer before joining the winning proposal for the design of Central Park. Other works include the Vanderbilts' North Carolina Biltmore estate and many other parks and gardens. Sargent's portrait of Olmsted at Biltmore shows the elderly designer walking with a cane through rhododendron-filled woods (Figure 13.33). He is wearing a brown topcoat over a grey-green suit and a black cravat. Olmsted gazes ahead over a grey beard, his hair forming a fringe around his central baldness. The portrait of Olmsted contrasts strongly with Mrs. White's. The subjects are of opposite genders. She stands with dignity indoors; he walks in the woods. Her garments are white; his earthy green and brown. She gazes at the viewer; he looks toward the distance. Sargent's portraits use such details to convey subjects' individualism while preserving their dignity.

And in spite of the cane and his age, Olmsted's portrait dignifies America's greatest landscape architect. Unlike many artists whose talents grow with time, Olmsted's first work, Central Park, is one of his best. The map in Figure 13.34 reveals at once the influence of Capability Brown's English landscaping style on Olmsted. Drives, walks, and bridle paths meander among a glade, a lake, a meadow, a pond, a promontory, groves, and rambles. Dispersed among these features are constructions and grounds dedicated to the many communities and tastes of a large city: a ball ground, children's playhouse, boathouse, concert area, music pavilion, snack bar, the Metropolitan Art Museum, and even a folly, the Belvedere Castle. The paths and drives curving among groves, copses, and open spaces give many areas of relative privacy that still preserve enough visibility for safety. The park originally incorporated two reservoirs of the New York water system. Both are now decommissioned, and the smaller rectangular one has been mostly filled in to make a great lawn with eight baseball diamonds.

The baseball diamonds are clearly visible in the two aerial views shown. The first (Figure 13.35) is photographed on a late summer day from the top of Rockefeller Center, south of the park. Most of the park's area appears to be woodland, which emphasizes its value as a natural oasis in the midst of a great city. Certain large features are also visible: the south baseball diamond, the meadow and lake on the lower left, the natural-shaped reservoir at the top, and a bit of the Metropolitan Museum above the building on the right. The listed south-end

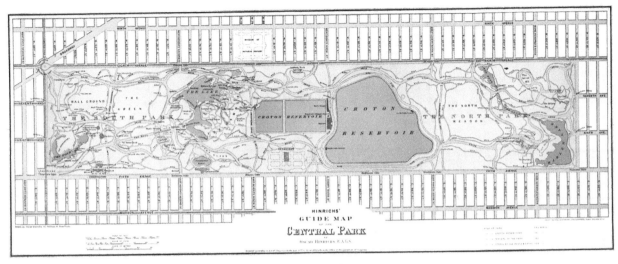

FIGURE 13.34 Frederick Law Olmsted (1822–1903), Map of Central Park from the 1870s.

features and a few more (the pond and ornamental water) are visible on the aerial photograph in Figure 13.36. This second picture shows more ground because the picture was taken on February 12, 2005, to document the installation of *The Gates* by Christo Yavacheff and Jeanne-Claude (see also Figure 2.15).

Figure 13.36 also shows the Turtle Pond—the last remnant of the south end of the rectangular reservoir, which was redesigned in 1998 with

FIGURE 13.35 Central Park from the south (top of Rockefeller Center).

banks so irregular that no two places offer the same view (see Figure 13.37). Although the design is not Olmsted's, it captures his plan's spirit with great fidelity (and it is the easiest spot in the park to get a picture that minimizes urban intrusion). The pond's artificial ledges and marshy areas host many species of turtles and other reptiles, and the surrounding groves shelter many different birds. The pond also makes admirable use of Belvedere Castle, the large folly at the former reservoir's southwest corner. Designed by Olmsted's collaborators (Calvert Vaux and Jacob Wray Mould) with no particular purpose, it housed New York's station of the National Weather Service for many years until that was automated; the tower still supports the wind equipment. The lower stories now house nature exhibits. The castle crowns the park's second-highest point and provides a focus for the beautiful and tranquil Turtle Pond.

FIGURE 13.36 Central Park with Christo & Jeanne-Claude's Gates, February 12, 2005

FIGURE 13.37 Central Park, Turtle Pond (1998), with Belvedere Castle (1865), Calvert Vaux and Jacob Wray Mould.

Photography

For all the care exercised by Realist painters, production of an image still required time. Capturing the details of an actual single moment awaited the invention of photography. Reliable methods of producing a black-and-white photographic image became commercially available around 1840. Photography quickly became popular for portraits and documentation of a wide variety of scenes and occurrences because it achieved something that artists and painters had only approached: instantaneous capture of an image at a single moment in time. This advantage could not be exploited fully for several decades. Long exposure times, blurring of movement, distortion of certain colors, limitation to black-and-white, a cumbersome development process, and lack of efficient methods for mass reproduction meant that photographs continued to be produced in single or small numbers of copies for several decades. During the American Civil War (1861–65), a newspaper might include a single still photograph, but action pictures were done with engravings. Artists on the scene would sketch the battle in progress and send the sketches by express train to New York, where engravers would produce the woodcut or copperplate for the next issue.[6]

Harper's Weekly was one of the most important papers of the time, and it had a national circulation. Figure 13.38 shows such a sketch by Alfred Waud, one of *Harper's* staff artists, of the Union Army pursuing retreating Confederates from Yorktown, VA in May, 1862. Figure 13.39 shows a woodcut engraving of the same pursuit published by *Harper's* two weeks later from a sketch by Winslow Homer (then also on staff). The excitement and action that is so immediate in Waud's sketch is also clear in Homer's engraving, but the photography of the time could not record it, so photographic images were posed or still. Figure 13.40 shows Mathew Brady's posed image of a flying artillery unit from the same campaign.[7]

---

6   "Express" is a relative concept. Trains of the era moved at 15–25 mph (25–40 kph). The sketches went to New York because the two important national newspapers of the day, *Harper's Weekly* and *Leslie's Illustrated Weekly*, were based there.

7   Called flying artillery because it moved faster—the soldiers rode their own horses rather than weighing down the wagons.

FIGURE 13.38 Alfred R. Waud (1828–1891), *Pursuit of the Rebels from Yorktown, VA, Sunday Morning (May 4, 1862)*, pencil and Chinese white on tan paper, 24 × 34 cm, Library of Congress, Washington, DC.

FIGURE 13.39 Winslow Homer (1836–1910), *The Union Cavalry and Artillery Starting in Pursuit of the Rebels up the Yorktown Turnpike (1862)*, wood engraving, Harper's Weekly VI (May 17, 1862), 308.

FIGURE 13.40 Mathew Brady (ca. 1823–1896), *Flying Artillery in the Attempt on Richmond, June, 1862*, black-and-white photograph from H. Elson, The Civil War Through the Camera, Springfield, MA: Patriot Pub. Co., 1912.

FIGURE 13.41 Mathew Brady (ca. 1823–1896), *Professor Lowe's Military Balloon Intrepid Near Gaines Mill, Virginia* (June 1, 1862), black-and-white photograph, albumen print from stereoscope slide.

Photographs also document the technology of the time. In the upper left corner of the engraving (Figure 13.39) is a reconnaissance balloon. Figure 13.41 shows (probably the same) balloon's preparation at the campaign's end.[8] The sketches and engravings depict action thrillingly, but they lack precision.

---

8   This was the first major campaign of the war, as both sides took a year to mobilize. Known as the Peninsula Campaign, the Union moved up the Virginia Peninsula between the James and York Rivers and aimed at Richmond (the Confederate capital), where they were finally repulsed. Mathew Brady was the most famous Civil War photographer. Thousands of his images survive. Balloon reconnaissance was important in this campaign, but political conflicts led to its abandonment a year later. The boxy wagons hold gas generators to inflate the balloon. Photography also made this and contemporary wars much more immediate to civilians, as there were now many wrenching pictures of fallen soldiers on battlefields.

The photographs captured every detail at single moments but could not capture things in motion. And none of these image types used color, so they are solemn, even gloomy, and somewhat detached from vivid reality. Thus, photography did not immediately threaten hand-produced art, in particular painting, because drawings and paintings could capture action, atmosphere, color, and mood in ways that photographs could not. And even as photography took its place in art, painters were seeking new directions.

Three factors influenced the development of transitional styles. Photography was naturally an important one. Romanticism provided a second through its search for individual expression and rejection of traditional models. The third grew in importance as the century moved toward its end—a sense that traditional modes of artistic expression were being exhausted, that new paths were needed. But the new styles did not assume their rightful place without controversy.

Impressionism

By the mid-nineteenth century, objections to the Academy's selection process were gathering force. Even after the development of the Romantic movement, the Academy of Fine Arts (*Académie des Beaux-Arts*) in Paris maintained a stranglehold on artistic taste. Painters who trained at the Academy, painters who exhibited at Academy "salons," and painters who won Academy competitions were virtually guaranteed success. As noted previously, the Academy enforced a rigid hierarchy of genres, with history painting (and by extension, mythology and religion) at the top and portrait, still life, and landscape after. In the academic style, drawing took precedence over color, images of imaginary ideals over realistic portrayal, and depictions based on reasoning over natural appearance.

Realists objected to the idealized style and often artificial subjects of academic painting and preferred depiction of reality, however mundane or disagreeable. The emerging Impressionists objected to the artificially smooth or slick finish of academic paintings that were done in the studio from sketches. They advocated, for the first time, painting the finished work outdoors (*en pleine aire*) exactly as the scene appeared, without artificial manipulation of composition, perspective, atmosphere, or mood. But Paris's main yearly art exhibit, the Paris Salon, was tightly controlled by the Academy. Judges of the salon were often very conservative and rejected nonconforming works. In order to have such work shown, the artist had to mount a private exhibition, but the limited audiences for such exhibits were much less beneficial to the artists. Finally, in 1863, the number of rejected paintings was so large that Emperor Napoléon III created a second official salon for artists turned away—the *Salon des Refusés*. This marked the beginnings of the *avant-garde* and the decline of the academic style.[9]

Figure 13.42, Édouard Manet's *Le Déjeuner sur l'herbe* (*Luncheon on the Grass*) was the most controversial work at the 1863 *Salon des Refusés*. It combines Realism with Classical forms and a hint of Impressionism to come. The painting shows a nude woman seated on the ground with two clothed men in an island grove, while a second, clothed woman bathes in the stream behind. A spilled picnic basket rests on the nude's clothing in the left foreground. She gazes directly at the viewer while the men converse. In this and other works, Manet portrayed scenes realistically—as he saw them. The setting is believed to be an island in the Seine near his family property; the figures were Manet's relatives. The classical influence shows in the poses of the foreground figures and the central triangle they make in the composition. On the other hand, the

---

9   *Avant-garde* is a bit difficult to translate in this context. Its literal meaning is "vanguard," the soldiers that lead an army into battle. The artistic meaning makes that a metaphor for those artists who are ahead of the pack—who are defining a new artistic direction.

technique is modern, moving toward the Impressionist movement—the background foliage is rough with visible brushstrokes. The foreground figures' finish is also rougher than was usual, although they are drawn with precise detail. Public recognition of Impressionism took another decade.

After later *Salons des Refusés* were denied, a group of artists whose works had been suppressed for a decade formed a society to mount their own exhibit in 1874. A caustic critic took the name of Monet's *Impression, Sunrise* (Figure 13.43) and applied it to the whole style. The painting depicts the view from Monet's hotel room in Le Havre, northern France's principal port, shortly after dawn. In the foreground, a standing figure guides a small boat in charcoal hue over tranquil waves depicted with large horizontal brushstrokes. In a diagonal line behind it are two other small boats of decreasing clarity and bluer hue. Behind the center boat is a three-masted sailing ship that defines the middle ground of factory chimneys, steamboat stacks, docks, and cranes, depicted in broadly drawn royal-blue silhouettes. In the center, a ship channel leads back to a harbor basin. Over all, a brilliant orange sun glows just above the horizon, reflected in the water beneath and tinting the atmosphere above.[10] The indistinct middle and backgrounds capture the effect of smog—smoke plus fog—air pollution. This capture of a momentary impression with rapid brushstrokes in bright colors defines Impressionist painting. So does the nontraditional compositional geometry, in which an off-center triangle linking the three small boats, the channel, and the sun with its reflection carries the eye into the depth of the painting. In the end, Monet's title, *Impression*, is very appropriate for the works of this revolutionary artistic circle.[11]

Another important Impressionist was Edgar Degas (although he preferred to be called a Realist). He was particularly skilled at portraying movement, especially in his favorite subjects, horse-race scenes and ballet dancers. Figure 2.10 (*The Little Dancer*, already discussed)

FIGURE 13.42 Édouard Manet (1832–1883), *Le Déjeuner sur l'herbe (Luncheon on the Grass)* (1863) oil on canvas, 2.08 × 2.64 m, Musée d'Orsay, Paris.

FIGURE 13.43 Claude Monet (1840–1926), *Impression, soleil levant (Impression, Sunrise)* (1872), oil on canvas, 48 × 63 cm, Musée Marmottan Monet, Paris.

10   Juxtaposition of a primary color with its complement directly across the color wheel (see Chapter 2) produces a vibrant effect: red against green, yellow against purple, or, as here, orange against blue.

11   Recent meteorological research by a Texas State University physicist, places the painting on 13 November 1872, between 7:30 and 7:40 am, which shows how precisely Impressionist painting can capture a moment. See Donald W. Olson, "Dating Impression, Sunrise," in *Monet's Impression Sunrise: The Biography of a Painting*, Exhibition Catalog, Musée Marmottan Monet, 18 September 2014–18 January 2015.

FIGURE 13.44 Edgar Degas (1834–1917), *The Rehearsal Onstage* (c. 1874), pastel over brush-and-ink drawing on wove paper, mounted on bristol board and canvas, 53 × 72 cm, Metropolitan Museum, New York.

is an example of his sculpture in wax. Figure 13.44, *The Rehearsal Onstage*, is a vivid example of his work that includes figures in many different attitudes. Viewed from downstage right, the scroll of a string bass stands before two ballerinas stretching as they await their entrances, one holding her wrist behind her back and the other with an extended arm gripping a scene flat. Behind the flat, three other dancers wait: one is adjusting her slipper; a second, almost hidden, looks across the stage; and a third stretches and yawns. In front of her, the director or choreographer steps forward with arms raised to give direction, and a sixth ballerina dashes forward while adjusting her shoulder strap. In the middle ground, two groups of two dancers in a diagonal line perform various dance figures, while in the far corner before the proscenium boxes are two male observers, one sitting back-to-front in a chair and the other leaning backwards. Behind all is the nearly complete scenery.

The activity and variety in this work almost overshadow the special visual effects made possible by its unique medium: pastel (colored chalk) over brushed ink. No single technique is used for the basic drawing. Ink outlines show on the string bass, the leftmost dancer's arm, and the scenery framework. Ink is also used for features and drawing of the men's dark suits, including elbow wrinkles on the director's. Feathery pastel strokes convey beautifully the delicacy of the ballerinas' tutus, but pastels used very differently—almost in a scrawl—cover the unfinished scenery. As with Monet's *Impression*, the composition uses an asymmetrical triangle to carry the eye into the scene. The heads of the foremost dancer and the director lead the eye back to the yawner, where that line intersects another drawn along the distant scenery's base. Another line connects the two leftmost dancers with the yawner and the most distant dancers. The geometry is well concealed, and the scene appears to naturally capture the mood and all the participants' attitudes in a ballet rehearsal.

Figure 13.45, Mary Cassatt's *Mother and Child before a Pool*, shows some of the earliest influence of French Impressionism on an American artist, a student of Degas. Cassatt, the daughter of wealthy Pennsylvania bankers, traveled as a child and then studied in Paris for four years (briefly with Eakins's teacher). She traveled briefly to America and then returned to Paris, where she studied with Edgar Degas. She mastered many different media, including etching, pastels, and watercolor. Aside from its excellence, her work is especially interesting because she often combines the American taste for Realistic depiction with elements of Impressionism, and sometimes with a unique combination of media.

This is true of *Mother and Child before a Pool*. To begin with, the mixed medium is interesting. On handmade (laid) paper, Cassatt began with a dry-point print, which she overlaid with watercolors. Her use of dry point is very sparing, though; it never shows intrusive, sharp lines but merely provides a skeleton to help define the watercolor. The Realistic foreground shows a lovely mother, with her dark hair in a chignon, in an informal white blouse and yellow dress. Her right hand supports a child with beautiful blonde ringlets, at whom she gazes lovingly while drying her after the child had played in the pond behind. The figures are delicately detailed, with meticulous shading and attention to realistic facial expression. The background is completely opposite. Here Cassatt used the Impressionistic properties of watercolor to great effect. Very few outlines define the trees, the shoreline, the gravel path, and the sky. Shading is produced by puddling water in different densities of color until they merge to produce the indistinctness of the Impressionist style. Impressionism like that in Cassatt's background was the beginning of transition to a new era in visual art.

Three factors influenced the development of transitional styles. The first is rooted in Romanticism, a search for individual expression and rejection of traditional models. The second arose from the first—a sense that traditional modes of artistic expression were being exhausted, that new paths were needed. The third reason arises from technological development—particularly for visual arts, the development of photography.

A third great Impressionist painter was Pierre-Auguste Renoir. *By the Water* or *Near the Lake* (Figure 13.46) is a brilliant

FIGURE 13.45 Mary Cassatt (1844–1926), *Mother and Child before a Pool* (1898), dry point and aquatint on laid paper, 32 × 43 cm, Brooklyn Museum, New York.

FIGURE 13.46 Pierre-August Renoir (1841–1919), *By the Water*, or *Near the Lake* (c. 1880), oil on canvas, 46 × 55 cm, Art Institute of Chicago.

example of both his personal style and of Impressionism overall. On the left, a mustached man in a straw boater hat relaxes, leaning against a simply decorated wooden railing and holding a cigarette. A young girl in light blue with a flowered hat, holding something in both hands, moves toward him from the right, as if to show him her prize. Above them, foliage offers shade in maroon, purple, and blue. Rising behind the man is a tree that droops tendrils down to the railing between the figures and behind the girl. In the background, a lake with two boats stretches from the right in a parabolic curve. Two couples stroll along the bank, one near, one far. Behind the lake is a grove or forest in light green and blue with hints of pink that echo the lake and the shade. The colors and the way they are used are vibrant and happy.

All brushstrokes are vague and fuzzy, with different values and hues overlaid on one another throughout the painting. This makes everything in the painting shimmer as if from the light sparkling on the leaves and reflected from the lake. Renoir creates different textures by using roughly parallel brushstrokes for fabric, water, and the lake's bank and footpath; short diagonal ones for the straw hat; short arched ones for leaves; and a relatively smooth surface for flesh. The composition has at least two levels: in the foreground, the line of shade, the drooping tendrils or vines, and the horizontal railing frame the man and the girl. In the background, the parallel lines of shading foliage and distant forest on top converge slowly from left to right, reversing the curve of the lake. A second near-parallel concentric curve links the right end of the railing, the girl's face, the footpath, the man's face, a tree branch, and the shade. These lines draw the eye across the painting from left to right, then deeper into the background. Renoir has depicted the spirit of delight in a summer's day with scintillating light.

The use of light to communicate mood was a great interest of the Impressionist painters—no one more than Claude Monet. Monet painted hundreds of works in several series that explored changes of light and mood on the same subject: Rouen Cathedral (more than thirty between 1892 and 1895); haystacks (more than twenty-five, 1888–91); water lilies (more than 250, ca. 1895–1926); poplar trees; the Japanese bridge in his garden; and more. Figure 13.47 shows two of three Rouen Cathedral paintings in the National Gallery. In these works, Monet capitalized on the nineteenth-century revival of interest in Gothic architecture. The church's orientation places this traditional west façade slightly north of true west, which gives more interesting shadows than if the façade were completely bathed in light. Figure 13.47a shows the cathedral in sunlight, probably around 4:00 p.m. Bright cream and sand colors cover the areas in direct sunlight with lavender shading to an orange-brown for the shadows. Three small, indistinct figures in the bottom left give scale to the church.

Figure 13.47b shows the same view in shade, probably before 8:00 a.m. The sand-colored highlights appear only on the south sides of the tower and nave. All else is in lavender shadow, deepening through a darker purple to brown. Neither painting shows the complete façade. Monet shows all but the cross atop the central façade and enough width to include part of both towers on the sides. Only a small area of sky appears. The composition is dominated by the cathedral façade, which is also interesting because it is asymmetrical: the two towers are different. Monet chose to emphasize the left (north, older) tower, possibly because its simpler profile and larger openings were better suited to Monet's emphasis on large shapes rather than Gothic details, of which there are many. Like Reims Cathedral (Figure 9.36a), Rouen's façade is elaborately decorated, with arched and pinnacled niches for multiple rows of statues. None of this detail shows—just the basic large arch and pinnacle shapes. Instead, Monet sprinkles tiny dabs of contrasting color on larger shaded areas to create the illusion of detail. He also uses a prominent *impasto* to emulate the dark crevices of obscured ornament and sculpture. Comparing these and Monet's many other Rouen paintings makes clear how the Impressionists captured changing atmosphere and mood with colorful paintings done quickly, on-site (*en pleine aire*). Figure 13.47a, *Sunlight*, also uses a developing technique where adjacent small dots of contrasting colors are left to be resolved by the eye, similar to Renoir in *By the Water*.

FIGURE 13.47A Claude Monet, *Rouen Cathedral, West Façade, Sunlight* (1892), oil on canvas, 100 × 65 cm, National Gallery, Washington.

FIGURE 13.47B Claude Monet, Rouen *Cathedral, West Façade, (Shade)*, (1894), oil on canvas, ca. 100 × 65 cm, National Gallery, Washington.

Postimpressionism

The first painter to adopt this concept for an entire painting was Georges Seurat, who invented a technique called *pointillisme*. Figure 13.48, *A Sunday Afternoon on the Island of La Grande Jatte*, is his most famous work. This very large painting took Seurat two years to paint because it is entirely done with tiny dots of different paint colors placed side by side. The artist was inspired by the work of Ogden Rood, an American whose color theories had been published in French only three years earlier. Rood noted that adjacent small dots of different colors would blend at a distance to form a different color and would be more vibrant than a single color, especially if complementary colors were used. *La Grand Jatte* is perhaps the ultimate demonstration of this.

A long wooded island in the Seine River is filled with people amusing themselves on a summer day. Most of them sit on the grass in the shade or under parasols, but an elegant

FIGURE 13.48 Georges Seurat (1859–1891), *A Sunday Afternoon on the Island of La Grande Jatte* (1884–87), oil on canvas, 2.08 × 3.08 m, Art Institute of Chicago.

FIGURE 13.49 Georges Seurat, *Les Poseuses (the Models)* (1887–77), oil on canvas, 2 × 2.5 m, Barnes Foundation, Philadelphia.

couple stands on the right with a little dog and monkey on leashes. Another dog sniffs behind a reclining man on the left smoking a pipe, while on his right, a woman embroiders and a top-hatted gentleman gazes at the river. A woman on the shore is fishing. In the middle ground, a man plays the trumpet and a little girl skips. The shoreline and an avenue of trees behind the dignified couple establish the asymmetrical linear perspective, reinforced by the distant sandy riverbank. The river itself carries sailboats, steam launches, a boating party, and a rowing team. Two other interesting features are the narrow red-and-blue outline Seurat added in the painting's last stage, along with the fact that it is hung in a white frame—very unusual for its time. Seurat made this preference known in another *pointillistic* painting—*Les Poseuses (The Models)* (Figure 13.49)—in which three nude models pose in a classic triangle in front of *La Grande Jatte* in its white frame on the wall behind.

For all of its complexity, *La Grande Jatte* is static. On the land, the little foreground dog and the middle-ground skipping girl are the only moving figures. On the water, the smoke drifting from the launches, along with the rowing team, suggest motion, but at a frozen moment. In addition, everything in the painting is somewhat lacking in detail (even in the elegant couple in front), and it is especially noticeable in the trees' leaves and in the eyes of the lady and her small child in the middle ground. This results from the *pointillistic* technique, which, however, does produce a painting that shimmers with great beauty. In order to paint with such small points of color, Seurat had to draw the painting thoroughly in advance, then move in and paint the dots very close to the canvas. This prevented his seeing the overall view as he was applying the paint, and he could not respond as a traditional painter would, applying the color from arm's length while viewing his subject. The technique is also a reversal of the method of the Impressionists, even though it arises from a similar approach to color theory. Rather than capture a moment's fleeting mood on-site, the *pointilliste* labors in the studio for months or years. Seurat's result is a static view, firmly based on outlines, shapes, and the geometry of perspective. While it still portrays a scene with depth, there is a new emphasis on the two-dimensional surface design, which becomes increasingly prominent in subsequent painters' works. This new style was initially called Neo-Impressionism; we now know it as Postimpressionism.

The Postimpressionist emphasis on the painting's flat surface took a different guise in the works of Paul Cézanne. *Chestnut Trees at Jas de Bouffan* (Figure 13.50) shows a view behind his family's country manor and farm in southern France. The house is in Aix-en-Provence, about fifteen kilometers north of the Mediterranean coast at Marseilles. The property's axis faces north, with the farm behind the house on the southeast side, bordering a road. Cezanne's work looks eastward across a noble *allée* of chestnut trees, with the last farm buildings to the left and a a low wall extending from them across the painting that hides a road. In the background is another farm on a hill to the right, while near the center, blued by distance, is Mont Sainte-Victoire, due east of the estate and a favorite subject of Cézanne's throughout his life. The shadows reveal the time of day as late morning, approaching noon.

FIGURE 13.50 Paul Cézanne (1839–1906). *Chestnut Trees at Jas de Bouffan* (1880/1891), oil on canvas, 71 × 90 cm, Minneapolis Institute of Arts.

The pattern of the trees is deceptively simple—larger branches form a lacelike pattern, highlighted by lines of snow on their tops. The pattern is delicate as it stands but is not blurred by the smaller twigs that naturally occur. The emphasis on large shapes and the painting on-site come from the Impressionist tradition, as does the asymmetry. The dirt path between the two rows of trees is visible. Two vanishing points are well outside the left edge of the painting. One arises from the lines of the roofs and mountain as they meet the line of the wall. The other joins the wall line with that of the dirt path. There are two points because the wall is not parallel to the path, although this is not obvious in the painting. It is in the tree lace that the Neo-Impressionist flat pattern is most obvious, and in the foreground is another flat pattern very characteristic of Cézanne's work throughout his life: bricklike brushstrokes, almost like a tiled floor. In his later works, such brushwork covers more of each painting and is a basic identifying characteristic of Cézanne's style. Although it is more restrained here, this work clearly shows Cézanne's Postimpressionist orientation.

Vincent van Gogh (1853–1890), *The Starry Night* (1889), oil on canvas, 73 × 92 cm, Museum of Modern Art, New York.

The creation of patterns to enrich the flat dimensions of a scene is especially obvious in the last works of Vincent van Gogh. Van Gogh was a thoughtful child raised unhappily in a strict Calvinist household. He was interested in art from an early age. By the age of twenty-seven, his behavior was at times erratic and came in time to be recognized as major mental illness. He was hospitalized intermittently during the last nineteen months of his life until he committed suicide at age thirty-seven. It is unclear what condition Van Gogh suffered from in modern terms, but it seems clear from his last works that he experienced auras. An aura is caused by unusual neuron behavior in the brain and can be associated with many organic as well as mental illnesses. For instance, they can be a symptom of migraine headaches. Auras can arise from any one of the five senses, although visual disturbances are the most common. Van Gogh's auras were apparently visual, resulting in texture lines on surfaces and halos or rings of dashed lines around points of light. This is very obvious in *The Starry Night* (Figure 13.51), his most famous work.

Starry Night depicts a village beside a forest beneath rising hills and mountains. On the left, cypress trees rise dramatically in the foreground; all is enveloped in a star- and moon-filled sky. This sounds pleasant in an ordinary way, but the reality is exciting. Eighty to ninety percent of the painting is blue, a color painters had traditionally used sparingly.[12] The mountain mists, the moon, and the stars and their halos are yellow, as are the lights in the village windows. The cypresses are a dark, nearly black green with brown highlights, while other highlights are olive green and, on two roofs, rust. Outlines are heavy, and the brushwork's texture is amazing. The foreground cypresses rise like dark flames on the left side of the work; bushes near them and trees in the distance use inverted crescents to outline their foliage. The lines of the village structures follow their builders' shapes. The hills and mountains' brushstrokes flow down their slopes like rushing torrents. These earthly things comprise less than one-half of the painting; the rest is sky—a living sky. Above the mountains, flowing lines depict a mist; above that, the sky is filled with visual vibration that arises from the stars and moon, which are outlined in hazy concentric halos. Flowing in from the left, a cloud swirls in spirals in the painting's center. The two-dimensional design and textured brushstrokes dominate the painting.

A friend of Van Gogh's with a distinctly different approach to Postimpressionist work was Paul Gauguin. Gauguin spent his first years in France and Peru. In early adulthood, he was a married businessman who painted on the side, but in 1884, he began to paint full-time,

---

12   Joshua Reynolds said, in the eighteenth century, "Let the light be cold (blue or green, ed.), and the surrounding colour warm … and it will be out of the power of art … to make a picture splendid and harmonious."

and his marriage foundered, although it did not end decisively for another decade. He began to travel in 1890, making two trips to Tahiti, where he took up residence before moving to the Marquesas Islands for his last years. *Mahana no atua (The Day of the God)* (Figure 13.52) was painted in Paris just after his first visit to Tahiti; it shows the strong influence of Polynesian culture, classical composition, and Gauguin's unique use of color.

The work shows a ceremony honoring a pagan idol in the top center. In the foreground, three nude women rest on a pink

FIGURE 13.52 Paul Gauguin (1848–1903), *Mahana no atua (The Day of the God)* (1894), oil on canvas, 66 × 87 cm, Art Institute of Chicago.

beach; two on either side are curled up to sleep, and a central one sits modestly with her feet in a pool filled with multicolored abstract shapes: a lily pad and possibly reflections or ripples. The women make a low triangle that points up at the idol adorned with a palm canopy. On the left, two women in white muumuus carry a platter of food beneath some gnarled trees, and a boy plays a flute. On the right, a man rests pensively and two women in orange dance. Another person stands behind the low dune, and in the background a sinuous line of golden beach leads to a rocky headland, with a rider on horseback showing the scale. A brilliant blue sky arches over the distant rocks and crashing breakers in the background. Outlines are crisp, but what is revolutionary is Gauguin's use of solid blocks of color that still create a convincing, deep aerial perspective, even with only minimal shading. The blue of distant rocks is completely effective without haziness or mist. Gauguin's robust blocks of color show another way to express the Postimpressionist vision that elevates the surface design to a level of importance that competes with the scene portrayed.

From Neoclassicism to Romanticism and Realism to Impressionism, nineteenth-century arts show the beginnings of the revolutionary changes that were to appear in the years to follow. This has been most obvious in painting, where clear Neoclassical rationality competed with Romantic fantasy and hardcore Realism gave way to shimmering Impressionism. Some of this was evident in the performing arts as well (for instance, in the Romanticism of Schubert's song and Tchaikovsky's ballet). But it is misleading to think of this development as lurching from one style to another, which survey text like this unfortunately suggests by showing mainly isolated examples without a continuous progression. To be sure, some works, like Monet's *Impression, Sunrise*, are startling innovations. But, as the works of Turner show, progressive development is often a linear process. And both processes continued in the next century—the new competing aggressively with tenacious tradition. In this, the arts reflected the progress of political and technological development.

Old political concepts like monarchy battled with new revivals like republicanism, while European nations continued territorial competitions that reached back to the Middle Ages. And as if what they did had no consequences, engineers, inventors, industrialists, and scientists discovered new things, invented new technologies, and, most perilously, created devastating killing machines. A stew of discoveries, inventions, and scientific advances—some beneficial, others dangerous—was Pandora's box, waiting for irresponsible politicians with childish rivalries and demands to release the good and evil it contained.

Image Credits

Fig. 13.3: Gerhard von Kügelgen / Copyright in the Public Domain.

Fig. 13.4: Gerhard von Kügelgen / Copyright in the Public Domain.

Fig. 13.5: Caspar David Friedrich / Copyright in the Public Domain.

Fig. 13.6: Caspar David Friedrich / Copyright in the Public Domain.

Fig. 13.8: Moritz von Schwind / Copyright in the Public Domain.

Fig. 13.10: Karl Friedrich Schinkel / Copyright in the Public Domain.

Fig. 13.11A: Copyright © 2005 by Manfred Brückels, (CC BY-SA 3.0) at https://commons.wikimedia.org/wiki/File:Berlin_Friedrichswerdersche_Kirche_a.jpg.

Fig. 13.11B: Copyright © 2010 by Manfred Brückels, (CC BY-SA 3.0) at https://commons.wikimedia.org/wiki/File:Friedrichswerdersche_Kirche_Innenraum.jpg.

Fig. 13.12: Jacques-Louis David / Copyright in the Public Domain.

Fig. 13.13: Francisco Goya / Copyright in the Public Domain.

Fig. 13.14: Eugène Delacroix / Copyright in the Public Domain.

Fig. 13.15: Eugène Delacroix / Copyright in the Public Domain.

Fig. 13.16: John Constable / Copyright in the Public Domain.

Fig. 13.17: Aelbert Cuyp / Copyright in the Public Domain.

Fig. 13.18: J. M. W. Turner / Copyright in the Public Domain.

Fig. 13.19: J. M. W. Turner / Copyright in the Public Domain.

Fig. 13.20: J. M. W. Turner / Copyright in the Public Domain.

Fig. 13.21: Elizabeth Thompson / Copyright in the Public Domain.

Fig. 13.22: Asher Brown Durand / Copyright in the Public Domain.

Fig. 13.23: George Caleb Bingham / Copyright in the Public Domain.

Fig. 13.24: Albert Bierstadt / Copyright in the Public Domain.

Fig. 13.25: J. A. M. Whistler / Copyright in the Public Domain.

Fig. 13.26A: J. A. M. Whistler; Photo copyright © 2014 by Smithsonian's Freer and Sackler Galleries, (CC BY-SA 2.0) at https://commons.wikimedia.org/wiki/File:The_Peacock_Room.jpg.

Fig. 13.26B: J. A. M. Whistler; Photo copyright © 2000 by Smithsonian's Freer and Sackler Galleries, (CC BY-SA 2.0) at https://commons.wikimedia.org/wiki/File:The_Peacock_Room_%282%29.jpg.

Fig. 13.27A: Thomas Eakins / Copyright in the Public Domain.

Fig. 13.28: Thomas Eakins / Copyright in the Public Domain.

Fig. 13.29: Winslow Homer / Copyright in the Public Domain.

Fig. 13.30: Winslow Homer / Copyright in the Public Domain.

Fig. 13.31: John Singer Sargent / Copyright in the Public Domain.

Fig. 13.33: John Singer Sargent / Copyright in the Public Domain.

Fig. 13.34: Frederick Law Olmsted; Adapted by Matt Wade / Copyright in the Public Domain.

Fig. 13.35: Copyright © 2008 by Martin St-Amant, (CC BY-SA 3.0) at https://commons.wikimedia.org/wiki/File:26_-_New_York_-_Octobre_2008.jpg.

Fig. 13.36: Copyright © 2005 by Ellen Murphy, (CC BY-SA 3.0) at https://commons.wikimedia.org/wiki/File:CentralParkWithGatesFrom2000feet.jpg.

CHAPTER 14

THE ARTS IN TRANSITION AND THE TWENTIETH CENTURY

Entering the Twentieth Century—Background

Blundering into the twentieth century, nations' political trends and technological development continued on their earlier courses, with bombastic nationalism, exploitive colonialism, and a fascination with engines of destruction—the fatal combination that led to World War I. European states, with their mixture of feudalism and increasingly republican governments, played and tottered on the brink of disaster from 1900 to 1914. While the upper classes reveled in spectacles like ballet, opera, country-house parties, safaris, grand tours, and similar luxuries, the lower classes remained mired in the poverty of industrial cities and rural squalor. Industries ground out increasingly powerful weapons; generals itched to try them out, and governments signed interlocking alliances—just in case. Some artistic creators began to seek new directions, while others continued to build on tradition. A transitional work that draws the old and new centuries together, creates a link between Impressionism and Postimpressionism, and combines multiple art forms is the 1911 choreography of Claude Debussy's *L'Après-midi d'un faune* (*The Afternoon of a Faun*).

While Cézanne, Gauguin, Seurat, and Van Gogh are the best-remembered Postimpressionists, other practitioners of the style broadened its scope through multimedia collaborations. Figure 14.1 is the stage set by Léon Bakst for the Ballets Russes production of *The Afternoon of a Faun*, choreographed to the work of the same name by Claude Debussy. Debussy's music (based on a poem by the Symbolist poet Stephan Mallarmé) describes a faun awakening from a nap to sensual encounters with nymphs in the woods.[1] Debussy's 1894 orchestral work (Figure 14.2) depicts the poem in music without words. An opening flute solo symbolizing the faun descends and then moves back up in a chromatic scale—a sequence of half steps. This theme recurs in the flute and other instruments throughout the piece. The orchestra enters and the texture builds. There are several musical episodes that may represent the faun pursuing or fantasizing about nymphs until the sound grows to a throbbing texture that suggests the oppressive heat of midafternoon or intense passion, after which the music (and presumably the faun) return to the initial sleepy lethargy.

Debussy's music is usually called Impressionistic. To the modern ear, it evokes moods and images similar to a work like Renoir's *By the Water* (Figure 13.46). The composer, however,

FIGURE 14.1 Léon Bakst (1866–1924), Backdrop for Debussy's *Afternoon of a Faun* (1911).

disliked this term. He thought of his music as Symbolist, like the literary movement led by Mallarmé. Actually, the two movements are closely related. From our perspective, the main feature of both is the creation of moods, feelings, impressions, and images through delicate allusion and symbolism. Debussy's music does this by using new approaches to the musical elements: Rhythm is mostly flexible and free. Debussy's melodies often replace traditional scales with those that do not pull toward goals. He does the same with harmony, using pleasant chords (sometimes mildly dissonant) that never pull in a particular direction but seem to drift along. Texture varies according to the desired mood, and timbre changes delicately, using the instruments of the orchestra like brushstrokes on canvas. The form, too, follows the desired mood with a mixture of musical ideas that is carefully planned (but never seems so) and does not follow any standard form. The work is a masterpiece of refinement.

Eighteen years after Debussy's work, Vaslav Nijinsky, the lead dancer of the Ballets Russes (Russian Ballet) in Paris, choreographed it in a breathtaking new style (see again Figure 14.2). Bakst's stunning scenic design (Figure 14.1) was just the beginning. This is Postimpressionism at its most powerful. The scene is a wooded glade with a waterfall and pool on the right and a rocky outcropping rising on the left. More rocks lead up a steep slope

---

1   The faun (half man and half goat), is a symbol of unbridled eroticism from Greek mythology, associated with the rustic god Pan and often depicted playing the syrinx (panpipes), a multibarreled, organ-like flute.

FIGURE 14.2 Claude Debussy, *Prélude à l'après-midi d'un faune* (Prelude to the Afternoon of a Faun) (music 1894, ballet 1911), Action ballet with full orchestra.

Performances of this work vary in speed. Timings below are based on a total duration of 12:15.

Timing (approximate)	Music	Dance
0:00–1:50	Flute solo; other woodwinds enter, horns, harp; strings flutter behind.	Faun lies on rocks playing flute, rises turns around, stretches, sits up, plays flute again (oboe in orchestra).
1:50–2:20	Full chord, oboe melody.	Faun kneels, picks up grapes, raises them, eats (twice), stretches, poses.
2:20–3:20	Opening theme in flute expanded with string accompaniment.	Three nymphs enter, followed by three more, all in Greek vase poses. One nymph poses solo.
3:20–3:50	Opening them in flute with harp, then speeds up, different flute melody with strings, then slows.	Lead nymph enters; faun watches her cross stage. Other nymphs dance delicately. Lead nymph displays, then drops sheer scarf. Other nymphs pose.
3:50–4:50	Clarinet enters, new whole-tone melody, trades with flute. Strings enter, activity increases.	Nymphs exchange places, pose. Lead nymph displays scarf, poses. Faun stands, backs down from rock as nymphs move. Lead nymph poses. Faun approaches nymphs carrying scarfs across, then off stage. He accosts single nymph, laughs wildly; she flees; lead nymph remains. Faun follows, looks after group.
4:50–5:50	Music slows, flute enters, mingles melody with other woodwinds.	Lead nymph poses, displays scarf. Faun turns to her; they meet.
5:50–6:25	Oboe melody over low chords, mainly in strings	He touches her shoulders, she kneels. He poses, raises legs in high steps, springs past her, turns and kneels.
6:25–7:30	Throbbing texture of harp, repeated woodwind notes, long-note melody in strings becomes more active.	He rises, she kneels, bends backward with scarf. He nears, arms outstretched; she evades him. They cross stage, repeat in opposite direction. He embraces her; they move together. She drops scarf. They lock arms; she kneels, rises and exits.
7:30–8:00	Violin and oboe solos.	Faun rises, moves away, raises arm in lament, turns back, moves to center, raises arms in longing.
8:00–8:30	Harp enters, then flute solo, strings rippling. Oboe "laughs."	Faun looks gleeful, turns to scarf, kneels, picks it up, laughs holding it. Three nymphs enter, glare, exit. He moves away.
8:30–9:15	Oboe on original flute theme; english horn "laughs"; clarinet ripples.	He gazes at scarf, moves slowly acros stage, raises it, laughs again. Nymphs return; one shakes arms in reprimand; they exit.
9:15–11:00	Flute enters on original theme with strings, then with violin solo	Faun steps slowly across stage holding scarf to his chest, climbs back onto rock, lays scarf on rock, gazes at it.
11:00–11:35	Oboe, then long string chords.	He raises scarf, blows kiss, caresses it, raises it as offering.
11:35–12:15	Horn and low string melodies; then flute & chords to end	He kisses scarf, lays it on the rock, lies on top of it, thrusts pelvis, raises head in ecstasy, then releases.

to turf in blues and greens. Overhanging this is the foliage of a wildly colored wood that seems to incorporate several seasons: the greens of spring and summer with the golds and browns of fall. The colors occur in crisply outlined shapes that delineate a landscape that recedes in a series of virtual planes. Only the rocky slope and front flat surface are actually used in the dancing.

The ballet was very controversial. Nijinsky moved completely away from the traditional movements and positions of ballet. His nymphs moved barefoot in patterns he developed from ancient Greek vases he studied in the Louvre, and the faun, which he danced himself, moved on toes with bent knees, like an animal. As much as possible, he incorporated animallike movements throughout. Bakst's costumes reflect this. Figures 14.3a and b show a) Bakst's program cover picture of Nijinsky and b) a cartoon that accompanied a scathing newspaper review. They show the faun's mottled leotard and tights, with the animal position of the legs, the pointed ears, and the wig arranged to look like horns. The cartoon also shows the faun's tail and the nymphs' poses behind. Bakst's picture places the faun holding grapes and surrounded by a swirling scarf, while the cartoon emphasizes angular arm positions. One image is positive and sensual, while the other tries to be critical, but in fact, they are more similar than different, and both show the revolutionary choreography, just from differing points of view.

Figures 14.4a, b, and c are actual photographs of the production taken in 1912. Figure a shows the faun laughing wildly with intense desire. In Figure b, his arms are interlocked with the lead nymph. The nymph's ancient costume and angular posture are intertwined with the animal intensity of the faun; she cannot resist him until he frightens her away. Figure c is at the end of the ballet, when he mounts the sloping rock to caress and lie on a scarf the nymph dropped in her flight. The still pictures show how different this dance is from classical ballet, and moving pictures confirm it. In the 1980s, the shorthand of Nijinsky's original choreography was deciphered. Since then, several companies have performed and recorded it with wonderful success.

Very recently, several short film clips of the original dance have been discovered. They are an astonishing legacy, since Diaghilev, the Ballets Russes manager, forbade filming of his productions because the movie technology of the time could not capture his company's fluid perfection. The clips are very short, but they will be invaluable for future reconstructions; they show Nijinsky moving with animallike smoothness and confirm his position as the greatest male dancer of the twentieth century. *The Afternoon of a Faun* and the following year's production of Stravinsky's *Rite of Spring*, again with revolutionary choreography by Nijinsky, were complete breaks with dance's traditions. In this way, these were artistic stirrings before the storm, and the storm of controversy that surrounded both productions was almost a harbinger of the political tragedy to come.[2]

FIGURE 14.3A Léon Bakst, Program Cover Depicting Vaslav Nijinsky for Debussy's *Afternoon of a Faun*, Paris, France.

FIGURE 14.3B Daniel de Losques (1880–1915), Cartoon of Vaslav Nijinsky in *Afternoon of a Faun*, *Le Figaro*, 30 May 1912, Paris, France.

---

2   *The Rite of Spring* will be discussed among the musical examples at the end of the chapter.

FIGURE 14.4A Vaslav Nijinsky in *Afternoon of a Faun*, photograph, 1912.

FIGURE 14.4B Baron Adolph de Meyer, Nymph and Faun Entwined, in *Afternoon of a Faun* (1912) photograph from *La Prélude a l'après-midi d'un faune* (Paris: Paul Iribe, 1914).

FIGURE 14.4C Baron de Meyer, Faun Caressing Scarf, in *Afternoon of a Faun*, photograph, 1912, from 1914 Iribe book.

The assassination of the Archduke of Austria by a Serbian rebel in 1914 pulled the trigger that set off a chain reaction among the alliances. Within two months, all the major powers of Europe and their colonies around the world were at war, centering on a four-year entrenched stalemate that all but destroyed northern France and Belgium.[3] In the east, overflowing violence and a withdrawn, incompetent Russian czar fostered a revolution and the first Communist state. Following the war (which the United States entered near its end), punitive war reparations inflicted on Germany, coupled with widespread financial manipulation and inflation, led to a worldwide depression. Desperate conditions and the Russian example gave Communism an unprecedented attractiveness to much of Europe. Fear of this (and of Russia) bred ultra-conservative reactions and the rise of Fascism in Italy, Falangism in Spain, and Nazism in Germany—vicious military dictatorships that ultimately ignited World War II, an even more inclusive and devastating war that culminated in two uses of the atomic bomb.

---

3   See Figures 9.35 a and b, with the discussion of the burning of Reims cathedral.

The arts both reflected and embodied this turmoil. In some ways, they advanced ahead of political developments. Even before World War I, creators in all the fine arts had sensed a need for drastic change. We have already seen the beginning of this in the move away from detailed depiction in visual art, the abandonment of directional force in music, and the replacement of traditional choreography with powerful new movement. In dramatic forms, cinema and theater both moved from mere entertainment toward more thoughtful plot development and ultimately toward more pointed social commentary; of all the arts, drama is best suited for this, as it is the most direct in its communication.

Since 1900, revolutions in education, scientific development, and communication, along with a population explosion, have produced a rate of change so rapid that it is not possible to make chronological distinctions between artistic styles or periods. At any given time, many styles are in fashion, and artists themselves adopt, change, and mix styles. Many different artistic styles can be discerned, but the closest a chronology can come to describing them is a Modernist movement for the earlier part of the century and a Postmodernist one since, with considerable overlap.

FIGURE 14.5 Vassily Kandinsky (1866–1944), *Der blaue Reiter (The Blue Rider)* (1903), oil on canvas, 52 × 55 cm, Stiftung Sammlung E.G. Bührle, Zurich, Switzerland.

Modernism in Art

Modernism developed gradually out of nineteenth-century movements that were ready to explode with innovation in the first years of the twentieth. Manifestations of Modernism include 1) disillusionment—the sense that old forms, patterns, methods and styles are exhausted and no longer function effectively; 2) experimentation—the drive to find new ways of doing things and means of expression that respond powerfully to the current moment or anticipate the future; and 3) sensationalism—the desire to surprise, excite, shock, and demand attention for the new with its striking, jarring, or even offensive character. Such things appear in virtually every art form in the twentieth century, especially at its beginning.

Wassily Kandinsky was one of the first to experiment with completely abstract art, which slowly attracted increasing numbers of followers. In 1896, at the age of thirty, he abandoned law for art school, where he easily produced traditional representative art. Over the next decade, his interest in color gradually overcame his interest in precise depiction. An early example of this is Figure 14.5, *Der blaue Reiter (The Blue Rider)* from 1903. The painting is Impressionist. Its texture is a rough *impasto* with indistinct outlines and large blocks of color, like Gauguin's, and highlighted by tiny dabs of contrasting colors, similar to Monet's (see Figures 13.52 and 13.47a). Beneath a blue-green sky with white clouds, a blue mountain background shows behind a grove of autumn birch trees with orange-brown leaves and white trunks. A rocky green meadow descends to a purple pool. Just up the hill from the pool, a rider in a blue cape gallops on a white horse from right to left. He appears to hold something in his arms, perhaps

Vassily Kandinsky (1866–1944), *Improvisation 27, The Garden of Love II* (1912), oil on canvas, 47 × 55 cm, Metropolitan Museum, New York.

Henri Rousseau (1844–1910), *The Hungry Lion Attacking an Antelope* (1905), 2 × 3 m, oil on canvas, Beyeler Foundation, Riehen, Switzerland.

a child. Some have seen the horse's gait as unnatural, but it is perhaps more profitable to see everything in the painting as stylized—adopting an assigned style rather than a natural appearance. The painting also calls to mind Schubert's and Von Schwind's *Erlkönig* works, with which Kandinsky was probably familiar (see Figure 13.7 and Figure 13.8). He loved music; he saw colors when hearing it and spoke of visual art with musical metaphors.

The Blue Rider of 1903 offered just a hint of the direction in which Kandinsky was going. By 1909, he had formed a society of the most advanced artists in Munich (where he lived), and two years later, he led another group that advocated even more experimental ideas to secede from the first one. The new group took the name "The Blue Rider." By this time, Kandinsky had turned from representative art to complete abstraction, which he probably invented. Figure 14.6, *Improvisation 27, Garden of Love II*, shows how revolutionary his work had become. The canvas is filled with nonrepresentative, irregular areas of many colors and sizes. Most lines and borders are curved, but some are straight with angular intersections. Contrasting colored highlights appear in some places. Although no specific depiction is intended, some may see a yellow artist's palette in the center, red lips in the lower right, and other things. The object is to arouse an individualized psychological response. It is up to the viewer to interpret the work for him/herself. In any case, the whole is colorful and appealing. Significantly, this painting was part of the first exhibition of modern art in the United States: the New York Armory Show of 1913, which brought modern art from Europe (especially Paris), attracted much attention, and set the course of art in the United States.

Kandinsky's abstraction integrated the experimental and sensational approaches to Modernism, but during his earlier developmental period (when he was still working from a representative style), his style was closer to those of his contemporaries. Henri Rousseau was one of these. The 1905 Autumn Salon in Paris moved decisively in new directions, as shown by Rousseau's *The Hungry Lion Throws Itself on the Antelope* (Figure 14.7). The painting is very characteristic of Rousseau's work. A jungle of many types of vegetation, all with large smooth leaves, conceals or reveals animals that are often sinister. In this case, the lion of the title is chewing on the neck of the antelope it has already wounded on its flank and thigh, and the victim collapses under the lion's weight. But there are others. A leopard in shadow looks on from a tree branch on the right. An owl is perched before a huge orange sun that is rising or setting among the trees, and an unusual bird with something red dangling from its beak rests in the crotch of the tree above the lion's tail. Various patterns of light hint at other beasts hidden in the rich foliage. The beasts in this work (*fauves* in French) even contributed to the name for a new style: Fauvism. The irony is that this work is not itself Fauvist but might best be classified as Primitivist.

Henri Matisse's *Woman with a Hat* (Figure 14.8) was also presented at the salon; it is typical of the Fauvist style that appeared in many works there, and it was hung near Rousseau's in a room that centered on a Renaissance sculpture. An influential critic described the bizarre conjunction as "*Donatello chez les fauves*" ("Donatello among the beasts"), and the name stuck. Unlike Rousseau's painting, Matisse's portrait is the embodiment of Fauvism. Wild, sometimes irrational blotches of color are thickly applied. Outlines can be thick or nonexistent. The woman gazing at the viewer wears a wide, bowl-like hat in vivid blue that seems to overflow with a variety of feathers, flowers, and other adornments in red, green, lavender, and yellow, all carelessly defined. The woman herself has auburn hair, and her green face has pink and cream highlights and rust-colored eyebrows. She holds a flowered fan opened to cover her chest, and she appears to wear green-and-pink gloves as she rests her hand on a green cane. Her skirt is green, with a salmon-colored pouch or ornament hanging from her belt. The background has irregular splotches of nearly all the colors that appear elsewhere in the painting. Despite the exotic coloring, we might very well recognize this woman in person, and the total effect is lovely if one abandons usual color expectations.

FIGURE 14.8 Henri Matisse (1869–1954), *Woman with a Hat* (1905), oil on canvas, 80 × 60 cm, San Francisco Museum of Modern Art.

Unusual color assignment was not confined to Matisse. Figure 14.9 is *The Old Guitarist* by Pablo Picasso, perhaps the greatest artist of the twentieth century. At the time this was painted, Picasso's closest friend had committed suicide. He himself was struggling for success and was very poor. His depression shows in the blue color of most of his works from that time, which is therefore called his "Blue Period." The old guitarist is a haggard blind man who sits cross-legged against a wall. He holds his guitar nearly vertical, resting the body on his lap. His head falls forward, as if he cannot hold it up, and his bony right hand seems barely able to pluck the strings. The painting is monochromatic in shades of blue, except for the dull brown guitar and a few yellow highlights on the old man's flesh. Only muscles, bones, and tendons show three dimensions; all else is flat. The guitarist must play to survive; the painting may symbolize the struggle the arts face in the world.

Not long after he emerged from poverty, Picasso began to experiment with new approaches to the geometry of painting. In Figure 14.10, we can actually see this change in process. *Les demoiselles d'Avignon* (*The Ladies of Avignon*) is a picture of five nude prostitutes from the Avinyó red-light district of Barcelona. The three central figures face the viewer directly, while the two outer ones stand

FIGURE 14.9 Pablo Picasso (1881–1973), *The Old Guitarist* (1903–4), oil on panel, 123 × 82 cm, Art Institute of Chicago.

The Arts in Transition and the Twentieth Century   393

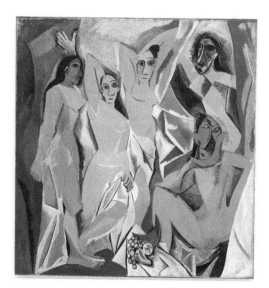

FIGURE 14.10 Pablo Picasso, *Les demoiselles d'Avignon (The Ladies of Avignon)* (1907), oil on canvas, 2.4 × 2.3 m, Museum of Modern Art, New York.

FIGURE 14.11 Pablo Picasso, *Girl with a Mandolin (Fanny Tellier)* (1910), oil on canvas, 100 × 74 cm, Museum of Modern Art, New York.

at angles. Their skin is in various shades of pink, for the most part, and the background is a geometric fantasy in rust on the left, blue on the right, and white on the lower right and center front, where a small still life of fruit sits. There is no modesty among the sitters, and changes from one figure to the next show the evolution of Cubism.

None of the women is truly realistic, but the second woman from the left is the most natural. Her body is nearly all curves except for her elbows and right armpit. To her left (our right) stands a woman with pointed breasts and pointed elbows. The leftmost woman preserves a fairly natural shape and stance but with almost entirely straight lines and angles. Her head is unlike the first two. With brown skin and long dark hair, she resembles one of Gauguin's Polynesian portraits. On the far right, what is visible of the fourth woman's body is entirely angular, mostly in diamond shapes. Her face is dark and carved like an African mask. In front of her, the fifth woman faces the viewer with her legs spread. Although there are curves in her body, they define shapes that do not correspond to anatomy. Her face, although rose-colored, distorts even the mask shape. From one figure to the next, there is a decrease in natural body contour and an increase in angular geometric shapes. The background is even more nonrepresentational. Cubism is making its entrance.

In Figure 14.11, *Girl with a Mandolin (Fanny Tellier)*, it has completely arrived. The subject should imply some visual relationship to *The Old Guitarist*, but implication is all it is. Fanny Tellier does hold a plucked string instrument (similar to the guitar in the other work), but everything in the painting is reduced to angular shapes. Even parts with curves, like one breast and the mandolin body, are connected to straight lines at angles. The painting is dichromatic in bronze and steely blue-grey. Only these two colors appear, although each occurs in several values of light or dark. Fanny stands with her body facing the viewer while she looks down at her left hand on the fingerboard of the mandolin. Her right hand plucks the strings. Reduction to geometric forms in this way is called Analytic Cubism, because the artist analyzes the image, takes it apart, and reassembles its geometry. Soon after this work, Picasso was recognized as Cubism's inventor. This painting was also included in the New York Armory Show of 1913.

The best-known painting at that show takes Analytic Cubism one step further by adding stop-motion. Marcel Duchamp's *Nude Descending a Staircase, No. 2* (Figure 14.12) not only reduces the figure to angular shapes; it also superimposes these shapes on top of each other to show the movements of head, legs, and torso in a descending figure, not unlike the stop-action photography of Muybridge and

Eakins that developed into motion picture technique (see Figure 13.28). Duchamp's painting is nearly monochromatic, with all shapes defined in values from brown through tan to golden and sand-colored. Most of the shapes are outlined in black, some with adjacent white highlights. For the most part, the shapes are angular and made of straight lines, although some curves are used for the pelvis and the back of the neck. The staircase is dark brown divided into superimposed shapes of different shades. The background is similar but darker. This was one of the most controversial works at the Armory Show.

Duchamp did not confine himself to either one style or a completely serious style. He invented a style called Anti-Art, which evolved into Dada. In Europe, Dadaists rebelled against bourgeois (middle-class, everyday) and capitalist expectations and styles, which some said had caused World War I. In New York, to which Duchamp had immigrated in 1915, Dada was less cynical and more humorous. In 1917, he mounted the most famous of his "ready-mades," in which he made art from common manufactured objects. For these, Duchamp invented the name "*objet trouvée*" ("found object"). Duchamp's most famous readymade is *Fountain* (Figure 14.13).[4] *Fountain* is a urinal turned over, with its wall mounting used as a base and signed "R. Mutt 1917." The work was rejected for exhibition but was photographed and then lost. Duchamp commissioned copies of it in 1960, one of which is in Figure 14.13.

FIGURE 14.12 Marcel Duchamp, (1887–1968) *Nude Descending a Staircase, No. 2* (1912), oil on canvas, 147 × 89 cm, Philadelphia Museum of Art.

Cubism was used by different artists in many ways. Marc Chagall used cubist forms in combination with natural depiction and bright colors reminiscent of Fauvism. Very long-lived, he was raised in a Russian Jewish village. His heritage remained very important to him throughout his life and inspired many works, especially in his early career. *I and the Village* (Figure 14.14) compresses several village scenes in a geometric framework with bright, pure colors. A mainly red circle in the lower center of the frame pulls several images together. On the right is the green profile of a man in a decorated peasant's cap, with a cross hanging on beads around his neck. The circle defines his jowl line. At the base of the circle is a wedge shape whose peak is at the center. Within it a milkweed plant releases its seeds. To its left, the circle cuts a red-and-white ball before arriving at another wedge (this one white) that is a cow's muzzle. The rest of the cow's head completes the wedge in the upper left corner of the picture. It is divided into more geometric shapes in red, white, and blue. Beneath its eye, which gazes at the man, a small woman milks another cow. On the upper edge, between the cow and the man, stands the village, small houses arranged in a row with an Orthodox church. Hanging upside down from the ground line, another woman plays the fiddle. Walking toward her, right side up, is a man carrying a scythe. The painting catalogs village life in a cheerful context of loving memory.

FIGURE 14.13 Marcel Duchamp, *Fountain*, (1917, [replica]), glazed porcelain, Philadelphia Museum of Art.

4   Duchamp wrote that a friend had sent him the piece to be made into art—probably the Baroness Elsa von Freytag-Loringhoven (born Else Hildegarde Plötz), who liked off-color humor.

FIGURE 14.15 Pablo Picasso, *Three Musicians* (1921), oil on canvas, 2.04 × 1.88 m, Philadelphia Museum of Art.

FIGURE 14.14 Marc Chagall (1887–1985), *I and the Village* (1911), oil on canvas, 1.9 × 1.5 m, Museum of Modern Art, New York.

Around 1920, Cubism started in a new direction, with Synthetic Cubism reversing the approach of Analytic Cubism. Instead of separating an image into various geometric components, the artist now built up an image from prepared geometric shapes, as could be (and sometimes was) done in a collage. In 1921, Picasso painted two nonidentical works named *Three Musicians*. Figure 14.15 shows the one in Philadelphia. It contains three masked figures built of mostly angular shapes. On the left is Harlequin, from the *commedia dell'arte* (see Figures 4.2 & 12.7), identified by his red and yellow diamond-patched costume. He wears a bicorn hat and plays the violin. Next to him, also from the *commedia*, is Pierrot, dressed in white and playing a recorder. On the right, a monk holds an accordion. The three figures may show the poets Max Jacob (as the monk) and Guillaume Apollinaire (as Pierrot)—close friends of Picasso—with the artist himself as Harlequin, a guise he sometimes used during this period.

Cubist principles remained strong in Picasso's work throughout his life, although his style changed, chameleon-like, over the years.[5] Figure 14.16, *Girl before a Mirror*, shows this evolution. It is probably a portrait of his current mistress, Marie-Thérèse Walter. Her image is split. Her blond-haired, white-haloed face shows a natural profile, overlapping a second view gazing forward with yellow skin and a red blotch.[6] There is no neck; instead, a black-and-white triangle descends to her torso, where a red-and-black-striped drape covers the top of her lavender breasts. A green-and-black-striped robe veils the back part of her body, while

---

5   A composer who shared this pattern of changing styles throughout his life was Picasso's friend, Igor Stravinsky.

6   The double face from two perspectives appears in so many of Picasso's works from these years that it is almost a trademark.

her lavender abdomen protrudes from the front. Her right arm reaches to the side of a mirror that distorts her reflection, in which her face becomes purple and red, with less distinct details and an orange streak. The red-and-green-striped fabrics remain the same, but her breasts tilt and her belly is in front view. Nearly all shapes have heavy black outlines. The double image has been interpreted several ways. The split face may show her in day and night. The contrast between the first image and the mirrored one may indicate youth and old age, life and death, or a self-conscious awareness of the girl's own flaws. The diamond-patterned wallpaper recalls Harlequin, Picasso's alter ego.[7]

Not many years later, the Spanish Republican government commissioned from Picasso a large painting for the Spanish display at the 1937 Paris International Exposition (World's Fair). In nearly a year of civil war, the leftist coalition Republican Party had sought aid from France and the Soviet Union. Franco's rightist Nationalists sought aid from Germany. On April 26, 1937, Hitler, at Goering's urging and Franco's request, sent the Condor Air Legion to try out Goering's new tactics by bombing Guernica, a small town in the Basque area of northern Spain. The German commander offhandedly reported that the bombing continued for two and a half hours and that most of the citizens were out of town, so only a few were killed. Other correspondents reported that the men were away fighting, leaving only women and children, who were in the center of town for market day and could not escape. Those reports also said that the bombing continued for three and a quarter hours (first with 1,000-pound high-explosive bombs and then with more than 3,000 incendiary bombs) and that fighter planes swooped low to strafe and massacre civilians fleeing in the fields. Through all this, the town's only military factory was left untouched. The raid's sole purpose was intimidation through mass murder. The result appears in Figure 14.17. The attack was one of the most infamous atrocities of war.

Four days later, after reading the newspaper account of the tragedy, Picasso abandoned the painting he had planned and, in one month, completed *Guernica* (Figure 14.18). The painting is basically monochromatic, although inconsistent lighting over its great size can make some areas look light brown or yellow. On the left, a bull with a two-perspective head stands behind a woman wailing for the dead child in her arms. In front of them lie a man's severed arm and head. To their right, a light bulb

FIGURE 14.16 Pablo Picasso, *Girl before a Mirror* (1932), oil on canvas, 1.6 × 1.3 m, Museum of Modern Art, New York.

FIGURE 14.17 Destroyed buildings in the ruins of Guernica after the attack of the German air squadron "Legion Condor" (May, 1937), archival photograph, German Federal Archives (Bundesarchiv), Koblenz, Germany.

---

7   Much of this interpretation comes from the Museum of Modern Art, http://www.moma.org/collection/works/78311.

FIGURE 14.18 Pablo Picasso, *Guernica* (1937), oil on canvas, 3.5 × 7.8 m, Museo Reina Sofia, Madrid.

FIGURE 14.19 Pablo Picasso, *Chicago Picasso Sculpture* (un-named), COR-TEN™ steel, 15.2 m tall, Daley Plaza, Chicago.

forms the center of an evil eye that radiates sharp light rays. Beneath, a screaming horse with a gaping wound stands over various broken objects, including a severed arm with a broken sword, from which a flower sprouts. Moving upward from the flower are the horse's splayed foreleg, a woman running from the right dragging a severed leg, and a ghostly head and lamp-bearing hand streaming in from a window. In the upper right, flames erupt from a building, while a trapped woman screams amid more flames that trap her below. Sharp-angled shapes appear in the background and on the figures. The horror of the atrocity is clear. Picasso evaded interpretation of the work, except to say that the bull represents brutality and darkness (i.e., Fascism/Falangism) and the screaming horse represented the people of Guernica. It is notable, too, that all of the living figures are women in agony. Many other reinforcing symbols can also be found. Picasso, exiled in Nazi-occupied Paris, was asked by a Nazi SS officer, "Did you do that?" He responded, "No, you did."

One of Picasso's last works, and his largest, was a sculpture for the city of Chicago (see Figure 14.19, *The Chicago Picasso*). Then-mayor Daley, although no connoisseur, wanted a great artwork for the city and accepted his advisors' recommendation of Picasso. A city architect requested the work with a poem; Picasso replied that he never accepted commissions but that the Chicago sculpture would be the second of two projects for great gangster cities (the other being Marseilles, France). He refused payment and made it a gift for Chicago's people. After two years, he submitted a one-meter model; when this was approved, a 3.5-meter mock-up was made to guide the final production by a subsidiary of U.S. Steel in Gary, Indiana (the foundry city on Chicago's outskirts).[8] The work is made of COR-TEN™ steel, an alloy for which oxidation produces a protective patina rather than rust that flakes off. The sculpture weighs 147 metric tons and was paid for by three charitable foundations.

No one can say what the work depicts; Picasso refused to. It has a long face (mainly a nose with close-set eyes) supported by a flat post with a profile like a turned chair leg. From the back of the head and extending nearly to the ground are two arched plates (like wings or ponytails) that are connected to the front post with rods like ladder rungs. The whole rests on a sloped plate that is bent sharply up at the back in a curved shape to support the bottom points of the wings. Possible human inspirations (with ponytails) have included Lydia Corbett (a nineteen-year-old model who spurned Picasso's advances) or the actress Brigitte Bardot. Other suggestions have included an aardvark, an Afghan hound, a baboon, and the Egyptian god Anubis. Mike Royko, the *Chicago Sun-Times* columnist famous for his straight talk and barbed humor, said, "[It] looks like some giant insect that is about to eat a smaller, weaker insect.... Everybody said it had the spirit of Chicago. And from thousands of miles away, accidentally or on purpose, Picasso captured it.... Its eyes are like the eyes of every slum owner who made a buck off the small and weak. And of every building inspector who took a wad from a slum owner to make it all possible.... Picasso has never been here, they say. [But] you'd think he's been riding the L all his life."[9] Since its unveiling, the work has become a treasured emblem of the city. People and films use it as a backdrop, a Christmas fair occurs at its foot, and children slide down the base. It is ironic that barely a year after its dedication, Chicago and Mayor Daley became infamous for their violent police response to protesters at the 1968 Democratic National Convention.

Picasso was perhaps the greatest artist of the twentieth century and merits more than this brief review of his evolving style, but other great artists also evolved during the epoch's overwhelming rate of change. Piet Mondrian began by painting in a naturalistic or impressionistic style, but around the age of forty, this began to change. By 1911, he was experimenting with his own style of Cubism, shown in Figure 14.20, *The Gray Tree*. The work does not abandon natural forms to the extent that Picasso's contemporary ones do, but its geometric qualities are very prominent. The broad, spreading tree is depicted with curved intersecting black lines, a little like a stylized horizontal version

FIGURE 14.20 Piet Mondrian (1872–1944), *The Gray Tree* (1911), oil on canvas, 80 × 109 cm, Gemeentemuseum, Den Haag, Netherlands.

FIGURE 14.21 Piet Mondrian, *Composition II in Red, Blue and Yellow* (1930), oil on canvas, 46 × 46 cm, Kunsthaus, Zürich, Switzerland.

8   This process of using models of increasing size for monumental sculpture is similar to that used for the Statue of Liberty, although that is three times as tall.

9   Mike Royko, "Picasso and the Cultural Rebirth of Chicago," *Chicago Sun-Times*, August 16, 1967.

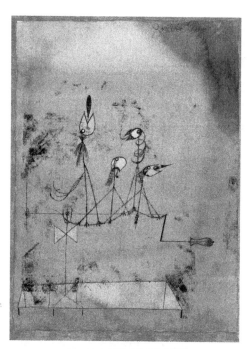

FIGURE 14.22 Paul Klee (1879–1940), *Die Zwitscher-Maschine (The Twittering Machine)* (1922), watercolor & ink, oil transfer on paper with gouache and ink borders on cardboard, 64 × 48 cm, Museum of Modern Art, New York.

of Cézanne's *Chestnut Trees* (Figure 13.50). Between and below the branches, the spaces are filled with a heavily textured gray applied in broad rectangles, horizontal on the ground and following the curves of the branches above. The shape of the brushstrokes, too, recalls those of Cézanne. The work is a graceful, if austere, stylization of a natural form.

Mondrian's later works are perhaps more severe than any other artist's. Except for a time in the Netherlands during World War I, Mondrian spent most of his creative life in Paris, emigrating first to London and then to New York near the end of his life to escape Fascism and Nazism. The style he developed in his more mature later years is the ultimate combination of abstraction with Cubism, and his works from this period are instantly identifiable. Figure 14.21, *Composition II in Red, Blue, and Yellow*, is one of the best-known examples. Thick black lines divide the canvas into several rectangular sections. The longest lengths, placed at about three-quarters of the distance from the top and right borders, place a large red square in the upper right. A nearly square blue rectangle opposes it from the lower left. The remaining narrow spaces are divided: that on the upper left at a point slightly higher than half its height by a thicker black line; that on the bottom by a line about one-tenth of the work's width from the corner to yield a vertical rectangle further divided in half by a wider line that doesn't quite reach the edge. The small rectangle in the lower right corner is yellow. The brilliant primary colors seem luxurious in a work that is otherwise so restrained and strict; they reveal the cheerful side of a compulsive personality.

Cheerfulness tempered with humor is the distinguishing trait of another style of this period. Surrealism has some roots in Dada (like making artistic jokes), but Surrealism goes farther by distorting or reinventing reality. Paul Klee's *Twittering Machine (Die Zwitscher-Maschine)* in Figure 14.22 is not only Surrealistic; it is an early example of Conceptual Art. Given the name of a concept (twittering machine), Klee has invented its surreal image. He produced a deceptively simple image with a complex process, beginning with watercolor and ink and followed by oil transfer on paper with gouache (tempera) and ink borders. The original paper and the blue-gray border's brushstrokes are clearly visible. Within that, the original paper backing presents an image of thin ink lines and smudges over a background of pink, lavender, blue, and gray blended together on a constantly changing surface by washing the colored areas with water. The line drawing over them presents one of the weirdest simple machines ever conceived.

Conceived is the key word, for every element of the imaginary concept ("twittering machine") is present. "Twittering" is obvious; it requires birds. Amid random ink smudges, four stylized bird heads point their open mouths at the four edges of the painting. From each beak issues a different shape—presumably the twitters. Bodies and wings are superfluous, but three of the birds have crests of a sort, and the outer birds have straggly tails. They stand on or are tethered to a curved string wrapped around a horizontal line. The machine part of the concept begins with the crank on the end of that line. In 1922, clockwork phonographs used such a crank. The other sound machine is the radio, which Klee knew from military experience and his presence in Germany for the first German radio music broadcast. The two triangles on the upright support constitute a bowtie antenna. That same support connects with a flimsy, four-legged stand that seems suspended in a rectangular hole projecting above the table or floor. The whole is difficult to describe precisely, but the twittering machine concept is very clear, as is the painting's surreal quality.

Salvador Dalí is for many the personification of Surrealism, and *The Persistence of Memory* (Figure 14.23) is his most famous work. Under a sky fading from blue to gold (as just after sunset) is a golden picture of Cape Creus on Spain's Mediterranean coast, twenty-five kilometers south of France. In front of that is a beach changing from gold at the shore to a deep brown as it falls under a mountain's shadow. The left middle ground has a flat, water-colored, table-like surface. In front of that stands a brown box, on which stands a dead tree with a floppy pocket watch drooped over its limb. A second similar watch with a fly on it hangs over the box's edge, and the gold back of a third watch rests in front with ants approximating a clock face. To the right in the painting's center is a bizarre object with long human eyelashes, a nose, perhaps a sand-covered tongue, and a slug-like body that seems to fade into the background. A fourth floppy watch rests on its back. The entire painting has the quality of the partial images that arise in dreams. The floppy watches symbolize the impermanence of time, and the ants represent decay. The cape and mountain shadow represent Dali's memories of his native Catalonia—fond memories that persisted through fleeting time.[10] Painted in Spain, this work was first exhibited in New York, where it is now in the Museum of Modern Art.

An American artist who painted realistic images (but with a spiritual quality that approaches Surrealism) was Georgia O'Keefe. Born in the Midwest, O'Keefe lived in several places before settling in New York. In 1929, she discovered Taos, New Mexico and its landscape. After spending part of each of the next twenty years there, she finally moved to Abiquiú, New Mexico in 1949 and stayed for the rest of her life. As her style matured, she first created delicately colored and shaded abstract and realistic images derived from flowers and plants seen at very close range, a subject to which she often returned. Many of her New Mexico works, like Figure 14.24, *Cow's Skull with Calico Roses*, use local objects with symbolic meaning. This work is a still life. A sun-bleached cow's skull hangs in the gap between two severely weathered boards; it is decorated with two white cloth flowers. The work is another monochrome, except for the skull's less-weathered

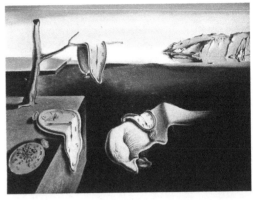

FIGURE 14.23 Salvador Dalí (1904–1989), *La persistencia de la memoria (The Persistence of Memory)* (1931) oil on canvas, 24 × 33 cm, Museum of Modern Art, New York.

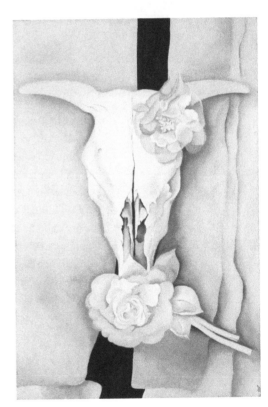

FIGURE 14.24 Georgia O'Keefe (1887–1986), *Cow's Skull with Calico Roses* (1931), oil on canvas, 91 × 61 cm, Art Institute of Chicago.

---

10   This work has become so famous that it needs to be said that only in this work and its successor did Dalí actually paint floppy watches, although he did use them in a few later prints and sculptures. His works include a much broader and brilliant variety of images.

FIGURE 14.25 Grant Wood (1891–1942), *American Gothic*
(1930), oil on beaverboard, 78 × 65 cm, Art Institute of Chicago.

nasal cavities. Again, we feel the passing of time, symbolized by the bleached skull and weathered boards. The two cloth roses confirm the skull's motif of the impermanence of life; such flowers are often used in Native American cemeteries. O'Keefe's delicate shading is minimal—just enough to bring out the three dimensions while retaining a spiritual, otherworldly quality.

The prominence of New Mexico in so many of O'Keefe's later works makes her something of a representative of the region; certainly her presence is well remembered there. In the 1930s, artists in several parts of the country began to create works with a deliberate regional flavor; this movement became known as Regionalism. The most celebrated of these artists was Grant Wood, who memorialized Iowa. Figure 14.25, *American Gothic*, is universally known. The background is a house in Eldon, Iowa in the Carpenter Gothic style, with vertical-slat siding and a pointed arched window under the gable. All shades are drawn, and there are potted plants on the porch. On the right is a red barn, and all is backed by groves of trees. The distinctive foreground figures are portraits of Wood's sister and his dentist. She is standing on his right—a woman's proper place, according to Victorian etiquette. She is also looking toward him from slightly behind. She wears a brown calico apron tunic with rickrack border over a black dress with a high collar and cameo brooch. Her blond hair is parted in the middle; her eyes are blue and her expression solemn. The equally sober man is older and balding, with round wire-rimmed glasses. He wears a black jacket over bib overalls and a white shirt, pinstriped in green, with a collar button but no collar. He holds a pitchfork, tines up, in his right hand.

Wood himself said that these are the kind of people he imagined would live in that house. There may also be some symbolism in what appears to be a very matter-of-fact image: the dark clothing and the drawn window shades signify mourning, but for whom is unclear. Of more immediate significance are the ways in which Wood uses visual echoes to unify the painting and give it its power. The peak of the woman's hairline echoes the window's pointed arch and the slope of her shoulders matches the gable. The arch of the man's forehead is repeated upside down in the pitchfork curves, and the pinstripes of his shirt echo the slat siding on the house and barn. The result is a tightly unified picture of a sturdy farm family like those who are America's strength.

The Later Twentieth Century

In spite of the worldwide depression, the 1930s were a very fruitful time for the arts. World War II changed that. That war was so all-encompassing that production of new artworks slowed to a crawl. After the end of the war, society and the world had changed so much that artists found themselves adopting widely varying responses to unprecedented situations, as did politicians, governments, and people of all kinds, professions, and nationalities. Since that war, nuclear weapons have been universally feared, especially because of the spread of their technology such that arsenals now include thousands of them. The rise of Communist powers Russia and China resulted in a long standoff between them and the West (Europe and America) called the Cold War. This spawned regional spinoffs, notably in Korea and Vietnam, but there has not been a third world war, for which we must be thankful. Fear of these regimes also provoked the rise of paranoid political movements like McCarthyism in the United States. Even after the downfall of Russian Communism, philosophical gulfs, race, religion, anti-colonialism, and other causes have ignited tensions in many parts of the world. Nevertheless, efforts to reduce nuclear weaponry continue, and human rights, ecology, population control, financial inequality, pollution, and climate change are attracting ever greater concern.

On the positive side, after the war, the United States' Marshall Plan injected money into devastated economies (friend and foe alike), made friends for the United States, and helped free resources from war production. Living standards rose. Awareness of wartime genocide and the rising American civil rights movement spotlighted the need for universal human equality. And technology continued to drive forward. The peaceful use of nuclear power generation spread, for better or worse, but the world began to become wary of nuclear dangers. A ban on atmospheric nuclear tests was the first sign of this, and later in the century, the process of nuclear disarmament began. Air travel replaced railroads and ocean liners for long-distance travel; technological leaps placed men on the moon, and satellites proliferated—for communication, navigation, and, of course, spying. Computers, developed in the 1940s, shrank from facilities that filled a room to handheld devices with much greater power, and the Internet facilitated a revolution in communication. Unfortunately, human thirst for violence rose again as paranoia, greed, race, religion, and other forces spawned new regional wars, persecution, and genocide that continue to this day. From the twentieth century to the present remains a challenging time.

The arts have continued to mirror and express the times, but new movements have not replaced the old. They have developed side by side, mingled, and multiplied. One of the most striking exponents of a Modernistic style was Jackson Pollock. Born in Wyoming and educated in Arizona and California, Pollock eventually settled in New York, where his style took the decisive turn to Abstract Expressionism that brought him fame.

Beginning in the early 1940s, Pollock used a technique called drip painting. He used liquid paint: thinned house paint, industrial paint, or alkyd enamel that he dripped, flung, poured, or squirted onto large flat canvases. Figure 14.26, *Number 1, 1950 (Lavender Mist)*, is one of his most beautiful works. The work does not actually contain any lavender color; rather, it uses black, white, olive, pumpkin, salmon, silver (aluminum), and steel blue in color conjunctions that seem to draw lavender out of nowhere. The work shows

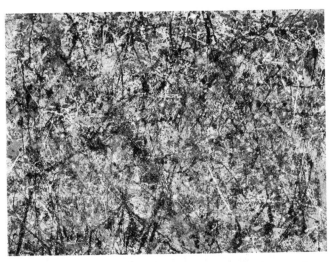

FIGURE 14.26 Jackson Pollock (1912–1956), *Lavender Mist* (1950), oil, enamel and aluminum on canvas, 2.2 × 3 m, National Gallery, Washington, listed as not on display but recently hung in the National Portrait Gallery.

Pollock's technique perfectly. There are irregular spots of solid color that vary in size—mainly in grey-blue, salmon, and black, with just a few in olive. Over these, long drizzles of black and white flow in every direction, interspersed with small starlike drips. The dense network has been compared to the natural mathematical pattern of a fractal, which can arise from random constructions like Pollock's. As with any abstract painting, seeking images is futile. The way to appreciate the work is to gaze at it and let the colors and patterns saturate the visual field. Allow the mind to wander, the eyes to stray, and the details of the work to select themselves. In repeated viewings, the features never look the same or rise to the same prominence. A psychological impression may or may not develop, but the work's dynamic response confirms its greatness.

Postmodernism

In the face of extreme Modernism like Pollock's, it was natural that some artists would decide that the style was exhausted, much as Modernism's predecessors had abandoned Realism fifty years earlier. A new variety of styles developed, but unlike the earlier revolution, the creed of Postmodernism abandoned the idea of chronological development: all styles, of whatever epoch or newly invented, may be used or combined as the artist sees fit. This step away from Modernist principles may also have arisen from the growing awareness that Modernist thought had included pseudoscience like eugenics (which led to forced abortion, sterilization, involuntary euthanasia, and genocide) as well as the premise that technological development should proceed without pause or ethical restraint, which led to the use of poison gas, biological warfare, and the atomic bomb—the first real threats to all human existence.

In any case, the 1950s saw the development of new styles of art that sometimes swung dramatically away from Modernistic abstraction. One of the first of these was Pop Art, whose most renowned practitioner was Andy Warhol. In an echo of Dada, Pop Art elevated everyday objects to the realm of high art. Unlike Dada, though, Pop Art often—even usually—takes or imitates commercial art for its subject. Commercial artists design products and packaging to attract consumer purchases. Until this point, commercial art and design had been a way for aspiring artists to support themselves while seeking recognition. Warhol enlarged and enshrined these designs—after all, packaging that remained unchanged for decades must have artistic merit beyond mere brand recognition. The year 1962 saw the creation of two of his most famous works. The first, a collection of paintings of Campbell's Soup cans (named by the flavors displayed) remained an inspiration for many years and led to a second set of similar paintings, sculptures of various sizes, and other derivative works. The second was a painting of Coca-Cola bottles that began a similar series. Warhol had personal attractions to both products. He reported eating Campbell's Soup for lunch for twenty years, and he saw Coca-Cola as a commercial symbol of democratic equality: "The president drinks Coca-Cola, Liz Taylor drinks Coca-Cola, and just think, you can drink Coca-Cola, too. A Coke is a Coke and no amount of money can get you a better Coke than the one the bum on the corner is drinking. All the Cokes are the same and all the Cokes are good. Liz Taylor knows it, the president knows it, the bum knows it, and you know it."

Figure 14.27, *Green Coca-Cola Bottles*, is the first of the *Coca-Cola* series, as well as being Warhol's first use of a silk-screen printing method he had developed. It is believed that he used silk-screen printing for the colored portions and printed the black bottle shapes with a wood block because the bottle outlines are identical, there are individual variations in their placement and image intensity, and, in the second line, the fifth bottle from the left is offset from its color. The work celebrates the unique beauty of Coca-Cola's trademarked bottle, its color, and the logo. By lining them up to overflow the canvas, it expresses their universality. Although the composition is flat, the bottle shapes suggest a certain depth that makes the spaces in between retreat so there are two planes, or one plane plus infinity. The composition also represents a grid of repeated images, a format that Warhol used for many of his works. In *Green Coca-Cola Bottles*, he used realism to elevate an everyday object to the status of high art and to lead the evolution into Postmodernism.

Another nearly simultaneous Postmodern movement was Op Art. One aspect of Op Art is the production of optical illusion; in this way, it is a distant descendant of *trompe l'oeil* painting, although Op Art does not necessarily trick the eye with representations of recognizable things. Another technique of Op Art is to juxtapose shapes and colors in such a way as to give a sense of vibration or movement. A third approach evolved from *pointillisme*, using small dots of color to produce the illusion of three-dimensional shapes on the canvas. One of the pioneers of Op Art was Bridget Riley; her first New York show was in 1964. Included in the exhibit was Figure 14.28, *Movement in Squares*. A black-and-white checkerboard pattern begins at the left edge. Beginning with the fifth column, the squares begin to narrow into rectangles of progressively decreasing width. This process continues to a point at a distance roughly equal to the Golden Section, where the rectangles begin to widen again until they reach the right edge of the work just before they would again become squares. The effect is a precisely controlled optical illusion. The point of the narrowest rectangles appears to be a fold from which the two sides rise to a flat plane in smooth curves. The alternation of black and white also gives the work a slight optical vibration, which gives life to this vivid Postmodern work.

The whimsical aspect of Dada also arose again in Postmodernism, notably in the work of Claes Oldenburg and his wife, Coosje van Bruggen, whose most famous work is Figure 14.29, *Spoonbridge and Cherry*, in the Minneapolis Sculpture Garden of the Walker Art Center in Minneapolis, MN. *Spoonbridge* is a fountain in the shape of a giant (sixteen meters) spoon with an exaggerated curve to the handle and the bowl bent sharply up. On the tip of the bowl, defying gravity, is a huge cherry, stem up. During the warm months, the stem top

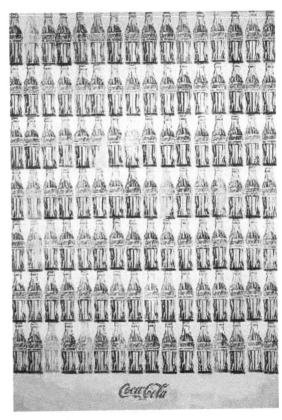

FIGURE 14.27 Andy Warhol (1928–1987), *Green Coca-Cola Bottles* (1962), oil on canvas, 2.1 × 1.45 m, Whitney Museum of American Art, New York.

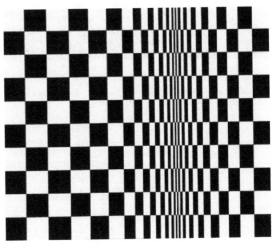

FIGURE 14.28 Bridget Riley (b. 1931), *Movement in Squares* (1961), tempera on hardboard, dimensions and location not available.

FIGURE 14.29 Claes Oldenburg (b.1929) & Coosje van Bruggen (1942–2009), *Spoonbridge and Cherry* (1988), stainless steel and aluminum, polyurethane paint, 9 × 15.7 × 4.1 m, Walker Art Center Minneapolis Sculpture Garden, Minneapolis, MN

FIGURE 14.30 Ralph Goings (b. 1928), *Ralph's Diner* (1981–82), partial photograph; full dimension, medium and location of work not available.

sprays a fine mist to make the cherry glisten, while a thin sheet of water issues from its base and flows down the bowl to spill into the surrounding pool. As the focal point of a long *allée* of linden trees for sculpture display, the fountain attracts the eye of every visitor and has become the garden's symbol. Its huge size and lighthearted parody are typical of the work of Van Bruggen and Oldenburg, who have installed giant replicas of a typewriter eraser, a rubber stamp, an electrical plug, garden tools, a hose, binoculars, and the list goes on. Oldenburg's funny bone has a long tradition. In 1967, he proposed an "antimonument" for the Thames River to commemorate its pollution and obstruct shipping: two giant toilet ball floats attached to London bridges.

But parody was not the only guise in which representative art revived. It also returned in Photorealism, which brings ordinary settings and objects to a kind of enhanced reality. Photorealists often work from photographs, and initially they were criticized for it, but their work shows that they often elevate the depiction to a kind of hyperreality that goes beyond any image the camera can achieve. An example of this is Ralph Goings's *Ralph's Diner* (Figure 14.30). Goings has been an eminent practitioner of the style, and his work radiates perfection. *Ralph's Diner* looks at the gleaming counter of a country diner from its end, with two waitresses conversing behind the counter and a customer seated at the far end, gazing out the window at the parking lot and low hills with farms, pastures, and woods beyond. The edge of a row of booths is visible on the left. Everything is perfect—too perfect. The shining reflections in the countertop and the tiling on the bar and floor, the gleam of the stainless steel on the kitchen door, the counter's and stools' edges and ceiling, the smooth glow of the leather stool tops—are all beyond credibility. This diner is immaculate to an almost unearthly degree, and no photograph could have shown it. Goings has taken what the photograph showed and exalted it. Such hyperrealism is common in Photorealistic work.

Another pioneering Photorealist, Audrey Flack, changed courses in the middle of a very illustrious career. After beginning with Abstraction, she moved into Realism and Photorealism and became the first Photorealist painter represented in the New York Museum of Modern Art. After a celebrated career in that field, she began to find it limiting and has since moved into sculpture. Figure 14.31, *Daphne*, was acquired by the University of North Dakota Art Collections during a significant residency by the artist a few years ago. *Daphne* is a monumental head of the nymph Daphne from Greek myth. When pursued by the lustful god Apollo, she pleaded to her river god father and Mother Earth for help and was transformed into a laurel tree. Laurel leaves were used thereafter to crown victors at the games of Delphi and were chewed by Apollo's prophetess there (see Chapter 7, Figures 7.27, 7.28, and 7.31).

Flack's statue presents Daphne at the moment of transformation. She gasps, wide-eyed, as the magic unfolds. Her shoulders and chest are already growing bark. Gnarled branches descend from her hair as small ones grow from her brow, and fruit and flowers grow from her temples. From a cord binding her brow rise three ammunition cartridges—anachronistic for the myth but Flack's symbols for the triumph of nature over violence as Daphne bursts with life, promising future bounty. In this work, far from abandoning Realism, Flack has magnified it, partly through the statue's monumental size and partly through its spiritual symbolism. Here again, Postmodernism strives in new directions beyond Modernistic doctrines.

Abstract spirituality combines with a plethora of traditional techniques in the work of Art West (the professional name of Alan Heuer), who follows in the New Mexico tradition of Georgia O'Keefe and the Taos School. In *The Long Road to Santa Fe* (Figure 14.32), he follows the age-old tradition of building a work from images collected (like the Photorealists), in this case from photographs taken around New Mexico. The church is San Miguel Mission in Santa Fe, the oldest church in the continental United States, always restored around its original adobe. Feeling that its modern setting was anachronistic, the artist made it rural: along the road between Española and Santa Fe, with a backdrop of the Santa Fe Mountains as seen from Los Alamos. The cowboy was photographed walking through Santa Fe Plaza.

In keeping with the freedom of Postmodernism, the work shows a heritage of other styles and techniques. The bright colors and purple shadows recall Van Gogh and Gauguin, and their purity, Chagall. The use of small highlights of contrasting colors on the hillside is similar to that of Renoir and Seurat. The texture of the adobe is very deftly captured with a delicate impasto like Monet's. The artist supplements these inherited techniques with some very personal characteristics. Most evident in the clouds is a stylized method of shading through minimally blended rings or areas of solid color that nevertheless achieve realistic roundness. The same can be seen in the sand hills toward which the road leads. Despite

FIGURE 14.31 Audrey Flack (b. 1931), *Daphne* (1996), cast and painted polyurethane with tree branches, 1.8 m high, UND Art Collections, displayed in the Education Building, University of North Dakota, Grand Forks, ND.

FIGURE 14.32 Art West / Alan Heuer (b. 1959), *The Long Road to Santa Fe* (2016), oil on canvas, 76 × 76 cm, private collection.

FIGURE 14.33 Robert Smithson (1938–1973), *Spiral Jetty* (1970), installation of basalt, mud, salt crystals & water, 460 m long, Great Salt Lake, Utah

its sometimes Impressionistic shaping, some of the vegetation is also identifiable by its color, the tall blue Russian olive behind the mission, and the yellow-topped chamisa in front—all high-desert or prairie plants that flourish there in spring, when soil moisture persists to nourish the growth. The pensive cowboy faces a long walk, but it is through a rich, warm, and inspiring land. This truly contemporary painting is a Postmodern visionary landscape.

Landscape exists outside of painting, of course, and the late twentieth century found ways (other than gardens) to enrich it through artistic installations. One such work is Robert Smithson's *Spiral Jetty* (Figures 14.33 and 2.14). This monumental installation is 460 meters long and built of large blocks of basalt and mud. It originally projected into the Great Salt Lake about twenty-two kilometers southwest of Promontory, where the first transcontinental railroad was completed. Water and salt crystals contributed to its medium, which varied with the height of the lake. Unfortunately, recent drought and the drawing of excessive water from the lake's inflowing rivers leave the spiral half a kilometer from the water, although its blocks and shape remain well defined. It is the fate of such installations to be subject to the vagaries of nature, and some are intentionally designed for a brief life.

Such has been the case with the works of Christo Yavacheff and his late wife, Jeanne-Claude. Their works have involved installations of an imposing scale designed for lifespans of only days or weeks. These include using polymer fabrics to wrap several major buildings and geographic features, constructing a forty-kilometer fence over California hills, and simultaneously installing three thousand giant umbrellas in California and Japan. Most recently, Christo installed floating paths over three kilometers of Lake Iseo in northern Italy. Some of the projects have had unfortunate consequences, but one very successful one was *The Gates*, installed in New York's Central Park (see Figures 2.15, 13.36, and 14.34a and b). For three weeks in February 2005, they installed more than 7,500 orange steel frames, with matching fabric suspended from them, along the pathways of Central Park. Reactions were very positive—for three weeks the installation splashed color over the byways of a drab, gray city in its drabbest, grayest month.

More permanent environmental modifications fall in the realm of architecture. Frank Lloyd Wright's Kaufman House (Fallingwater) in Bear Run, Pennsylvania is a brilliant example of Modernist architecture (see Figure 14.35). Commissioned to replace a modest group of summer cabins below the little brook's falls, Wright designed a daring project above them that actually incorporated the stream, using a masonry core of local stone that supported multiple terraces, cantilevered out over the falls, for entertainment.[11] There are guest bedrooms (one with a spring

11   A cantilever is an architectural structure that is supported at one end only. It typically requires special bracing for support.

FIGURE 14.34A Christo Yavacheff (b. 1935) and Jeanne-Claude (1935–2009), *The Gates*, February 2005, Installation of steel, vinyl and fabric, 7,503 gates, Central Park, New York City

FIGURE 14.34B Central Park with Christo & Jeanne-Claude's *Gates*, February 12, 2005.

that trickles down inside before flowing out) and access to a plunge pool in the stream from the living room. The result is a house integrated with the landscape to a degree unattained by any other building. It is, of course, absolutely Modernist in its design.

The remaining two buildings (one large and one small) are Postmodernist. As in painting, the Postmodernist aesthetic permits incorporation of features from any design style—new or old, Western or non-Western—as the architect sees fit. The first building is Figure 14.36, the Sony/AT&T Tower by Philip Johnson and John Burgee, three and a half blocks southeast of Central Park. Completed just as AT&T was broken up under antitrust law, the building was sold to the Sony Corporation, which has sold it again; it is currently vacant—a sad fate for the first Postmodern skyscraper. Certain design features—the Neoclassical broken pediment top, light-pink granite sheathing, and a seven-story arched entrance (not visible)—give the building a special refinement and a unique skyline profile but were ridiculed by

FIGURE 14.35 Frank Lloyd Wright (1867–1959), Fallingwater (Kaufmann House) (1935), Bear Run, Stewart Township, PA.

The Arts in Transition and the Twentieth Century

some architects, even though the pediment at least is entirely functional, concealing air handling and other utilities. Although these features have not been imitated, they have inspired similar aesthetic designs in other new high-rise buildings.

Postmodernism has spread to smaller centers as well. After East Grand Forks, Minnesota was devastated by a 1997 flood that forced its (and its sister city's) complete evacuation, the city hired William Schoen Associates, a local firm, to design a new city hall. The result, completed in 2001, is dignified and elegant (see Figure 14.37). The plain brick walls and the extensive use of glass are very obviously contemporary, but the shapes are pure Roman, either Classical or Baroque. A curved central Doric colonnade projects toward the street; it is flanked on either side by niches in reverse curves that lead to long wings on either side with their own rows of columns. Above the central hall rises a second story capped with a Roman-style dome and a delicate pinnacle. What crowns the classical symmetry with amazing effect are the floor-to-ceiling glass walls spanning the entire façade (except the niches) and comprising the dome drum. Supported by a colonnade only on the dome's back and sides, from the front it appears to float in the air. The classical elements contribute the dignity appropriate for a governmental edifice, while the glass walls imply transparent and good government. In this building, this small city has gained an architectural jewel.

Historical events close to one's own time can be difficult to analyze or classify. In the arts, it means that some branches of the fine arts may seem to lack styles found in others or to have unique styles of their own. For instance, in Figure 13.32, it required a stretch to find a musical work that might be classified as Realist. This even more true for specific twentieth-century styles, although the general classifications of Modernist and Postmodernist do hold true for music at least.

The musical elements of Modernism are parallel in a way to those of visual art. Passing beyond the transitional style of Debussy's Impressionism, composers experimented with greater divergence from traditional methods of composition. Figure 14.38 shows the changes in musical elements adopted in the turn to Modernism.

A profound turning point for both music and dance was Igor Stravinsky's *Rite of Spring*, choreographed by Nijinsky for the

FIGURE 14.36 Philip Johnson (1906–2005) and John Burgee (b. 1933), Sony Tower, formerly AT&T Building (1981–84), 550 Madison Avenue, New York.

FIGURE 14.37 William Schoen Associates, City Hall (2001), 600 Demers Avenue, East Grand Forks, MN.

Rhythm	Irregular meters replace standard, regular ones.
Melody	Nontraditional scales replace traditional ones.
	Melodies may become angular and jagged or otherwise lose expected shape.
Harmony	Abandonment of traditional harmony, often dissonance for its own sake.
	Polytonality—Playing two or more keys simultaneously.
	Atonality—Replacement of traditional tonal harmony with nontraditional dissonance, often extreme.
Texture	Some works tend toward very complex polyphony.
Timbre	Unusual instrumental combinations; experimental and electronic instruments.
Text Setting	May be traditional, or voice may be used as an instrument—with only sounds instead of text.
Form	May adapt traditional forms with the elements above.
	May also use completely new, experimental forms.
	May use chance (dice, card shuffling, etc.) to determine form.

FIGURE 14.38 Elements of Modernism in music.

Ballets Russes. The composer employed the most drastic of the elements described above, and Nijinsky's choreography was equally revolutionary. At the opening (May 29, 1913), the audience was so shocked and some persons so disruptive that a riot nearly ensued; the uproar was so great that Nijinsky had to shout the rhythm count to the dancers from the wings. The performance was a landmark in the evolution of music. The entire ballet is short: only about one-half hour in total length, with each act lasting about fifteen minutes. Act I is summarized in Figure 14.39. It presents a series of primitive rituals, several ritual dances by young people, a prophecy by a 300-year-old woman, the blessing of the earth by an ancient sage, and a final, frenzied "Dance of the Earth." Act II depicts mysterious rites of the young girls, who select the "Chosen One." She is blessed by the ancestors and becomes the sacrifice, dancing herself to death.

The music used an orchestra of one hundred, counting the conductor (very large for a stage work), and much of the music was very percussive, using different groups of instruments playing huge dissonant block chords in pounding irregular rhythms. Softer sections sometimes use melodies, the best-known being the opening bassoon solo, played at the instrument's extreme high range. That tune in particular (and, it has been discovered, others) derive from Lithuanian folk songs. The movement of Modernism in music, as in visual art, includes several styles. *The Rite of Spring's* is Primitivism. Traces of this in visual art include Rousseau's works and Picasso's use of a Polynesian profile and African masks in *Les demoiselles d'Avignon* (Figure 14.10).

In *The Rite of Spring*, as in *The Afternoon of a Faun*, Stravinsky broke completely with traditional harmony, and Nijinsky broke completely with traditional ballet movement. The dancing involved crouching, jumping, shuffling, stomping, and wild, frenzied movement. The set design and costuming were more conservative than in *Afternoon*, though. They were designed by a folklore expert who had worked closely with Stravinsky. The set is an open meadow before a pool, with mountains in the background. From our perspective, the costumes seem like an odd combination of Native American dresses for the women, with primitive versions of the robes of Russian noblemen. Still, given the designer's expertise, they must have some authenticity. The entire spectacle is an explosive twentieth-century evocation of an imaginary primitive rite.

Not all Modernist music is so overwhelming, although it is a challenge to find examples that are not alienating to inexperienced listeners. One such work is Figure 14.40, *The Unanswered*

Performances of this work vary in speed. Due to its length, timings are detailed only for Act I.

Timing (approximate)	Music	Section & Dance
	ACT I	
0:00–2:55	Famous high bassoon solo opens & closes; chirping woodwinds between.	**Overture-Introduction**—No dance.
2:55–4:55	Strong irregular rhythmic pattern for young men. Bassoon melody for old woman.	**Auguries (Prophecies) of Spring**—Young men in two tribes dance, jumping, leaping, stomping; 300-year-old woman dances around, casts sticks for prophecy. Men observe, acknowledge, stalk around thinking. Old woman leaves; company kneels.
4:55–6:05	More melodic, woodwinds first, then brass, then more insistent accompaniment more twittering in winds.	**Dance of the Young Girls**—Young women enter–one tribe–other kneeling on stage. Dancers lean, sway, strut in crouch, twirl, attract men's attention. Men's tribes join in; two groups move back and forth across stage. Women stop.
6:05–7:30	Loud brass chord, timpani, then squawking woodwinds, sporadic drumbeats.	**Ritual of Abduction**—Men jump, chase women Women and men exchange tribes; all dance in couples that separate, then two men choose two women and conclude.
7:30–11:15	Clarinet and piccolo melody, then ponderous low chords with winds. Drums thunder, whole orchestra melody, then homophonic brass melody.	*Khovorod*-**Spring Round Dances**—Three more elaborately-dressed women enter, dance first with three women from each group. Then whole company dances; they divide into tribal groups of men and women. Women's groups form small circles that revolve; men make bows. Then women bow, men appeal to sky.
11:15–13:00	Music fast, chaotic, then slows; then loud with drums and dissonant chords, melody moves among different instrument groups.	**Ritual of the Rival Tribes**—Mock battle between tribes of men, various figures, then running processions of all. Then whole troupe divides into tribes that face off in various ways. Whole group jumps then freezes.
13:00–14:10	Drumbeat begins, music slows—then pause—then slow softer music.	**Procession of the Oldest and Wisest One, Kissing the Earth**—Old man (Sage) enters with aides. Group dances in welcome, forms circle around Sage. Sage lies on earth to kiss/bless it.
14:10–15:00	Music chaotic with loud irregular brass chords, ends with loud single chords	**Dance of the Earth**—Frenzied, with jumps, running in circles around Sage, then crowd in and throw hands into the air to end.

ACT II

Introduction

Mystic Circles of Young Girls—One falls out. Selected by Fate, she becomes the Chosen One.

Glorification of the Chosen One—Girls dance in honor of the Chosen One.

Invocation of the Ancestors—Girls dance to summon the Ancestors.

Ritual of the Ancestors—The Ancesters prepare the Chosen One.

Sacrificial Dance—The Chosen One dances to death, is offered up by company.

Performances of this work vary widely in speed. Timings below are based on a total duration of 4:30.

Timing (approximate)	Music	
0:00–1:15	**Opening—The Silence of the Druids**	Strings—Very slow, sustained chords, continue throughout.
1:15–1:25	**Question 1**	Trumpet—Angular melody, seems inconclusive, unfinished.
1:25–1:45	**Answer 1**	Woodwinds—Slow, top descends, rises to high note at end.
1:45–1:55	**Question 2**	Trumpet—Angular melody again.
1:55–2:15	**Answer 2**	Woodwinds—Slow, twice as long, top descends slowly.
2:15–2:25	**Question 3**	Trumpet—Angular melody again.
2:25–2:45	**Answer 3**	Woodwinds—Still descending, but a little more movement.
2:45–2:55	**Question 4**	Trumpet—Angular melody again.
2:55–3:15	**Answer 4**	Woodwinds—Faster, angular, low to high twice, ends high
3:15–3:25	**Question 5**	Trumpet—Angular melody again.
3:25–3:40	**Answer 5**	Woodwinds—Move separately, top angry trill, short, high squawk at end; low grumbling chord through next question.
3:40–3:45	**Question 6**	Trumpet—Angular melody again.
3:45–4:15	**Answer 6**	Woodwinds—Faster, agitated, ends frustrated, high, shrill.
4:15	**Question 7**	Trumpet—Angular melody again.
To End	**Conclusion**	Strings—Slow, sustained chords continue, fade at end.

Question, by Charles Ives, written in 1908 and revised in the 1930s, but not performed until 1946 due to Ives's unusual life. He grew up in Danbury, Connecticut, where his father, the town bandmaster, taught Charles in an unusual, even foresighted way. When he had learned a piano piece, Charles was encouraged to play the two hands simultaneously in different keys. In this way, he came to enjoy polytonality and employed it in many of his works. Ives heard all the music of a small New England town—band concerts in the park, church music and hymns, folksongs and fiddle tunes—and he used them all in his compositions. He attended Yale University, where he studied with Horatio Parker, Yale's composer of the Second New England School (see Figure 13.32). On graduation, Ives entered the insurance business; he virtually invented the concept of estate planning and became quite wealthy. He composed music as a hobby until 1927, retired soon after, and spent the rest of his life revising his works, supervising their performance, and supporting new music. Ives was one of the twentieth century's most original composers.

The Unanswered Question is written for an unusual combination of instruments: four woodwinds (flutes preferred), trumpet, and strings. The strings play "The Silence of the Druids" in traditional chords of extremely long notes that change very slowly. Over this, the trumpet plays—in a different key or no key at all—a very angular melody that seems unfinished (the Question). The woodwinds attempt to answer this with dissonant responses, getting audibly more agitated and frustrated as each attempt fails. After six failures, they give up; the trumpet's seventh and last question remains unanswered as the strings fade into silence. Rhythm, melody, harmony, texture, and timbre are all Modernist. The form bears some resemblance to a Classical rondo (ABACADA, etc.), but there is a slight element of chance in it. Ives wrote the entrances of the trumpet and woodwinds above the strings in a traditional way, but the string notes are so long that the entering instruments seem to come in at random. All of this is very easy to hear. *The Unanswered Question* is an unusually transparent example of Modernist music.

A composer whose style became the epitome of American music in the twentieth century was Aaron Copland. Like artists and composers before him, he went to Paris to study—in his case, with a young teacher of genius, Nadia Boulanger, who ended up teaching many of Copland's generation of American composers. He experimented with several styles at different times in his life, but he is best remembered for his works of the 1940s, which can be described as Neoclassical. Neoclassicism in music is quite different from the style of the same name in visual art. In art, Neoclassic works are those that revive the style of ancient Greece and Rome, beginning in the eighteenth century. Recall that in music, the same time period is called just Classical, because so very little music of the ancients survives. So the term Neoclassicism in music refers to music of the twentieth century that avoids the extremes of Modernist music. Neoclassical music is more tuneful, less dissonant, and often more regular in its rhythm. The orchestration may still be experimental, though, and the form is often free to respond to the music's needs—unbound to tradition. Texture in Neoclassical music is as variable as in any period.

In 1942, in solidarity with the war effort, the Cincinnati Orchestra commissioned eighteen fanfares to open its concerts. Aaron Copland's *Fanfare for the Common Man* (Figure 14.41) was the most unorthodox and is the only one that remains in the repertoire. It is written for the brass section of the orchestra, with tam-tam (what most people mistakenly call a gong), timpani, and bass drum. The fanfare begins with slow timpani strokes punctuated by the tam-tam—a pattern that is repeated. The trumpets then play the fanfare theme in unison.

FIGURE 14.41 Aaron Copland (1900–1990), *Fanfare for the Common Man* (1942), trumpets, horns, trombones, tuba, tam-tam (gong), timpani, bass drum.

Performances of this work vary in speed. Timings below are based on a total duration of 3:30.

Timing (approximate)	Instrumentation	Music
0:00–0:25	**Timpani & tam-tam**	Slow beats: 1 then 2 with tam-tam intersperse–repeated.
0:25–0:55	**Trumpets**	All play one melody (unison) gestures leap up, around, down.
0:55–1:00	**Timpani & tam-tam**	Pattern above repeated once.
1:00–1:35	**Trumpets & horns**	Melody in trumpets expanded; horns play countermelody, many perfect consonances, timpani/tam-tam play 2 beats in middle.
1:35–1:50	**Timpani & tam-tam**	Pattern above repeated twice.
1:50–2:35	**Trombones, then trumpets, horns & all**	Melody & countermelody in trombones, echoed by trumpets with countermelody in horns, then fuller harmony on new closing phrase; regular percussion punctuation.
2:35–3:05	**All**	Similar to above, more frequent echoes, fuller texture.
3:05–End	**All**	New phrase extension—Coda—leads to large final chords.

Performances of this work vary in speed. Timings below are based on a total duration of 1:40. Each note has a unique timbre according to the way the strings have been prepaired.

Section	Timing (approximate)	Structure	Music
A	0:00–0:22	2 units of 9 = 18 measures	Left hand—steady pattern of faster notes. Right hand—eight note group with stumble on 2nd note played three times, then altered twice, followed by long held notes of irregular length.
A	0:22–0:44	2 units of 9 = 18 measures	
B	0:44–1:12	2½ units of 9 = 22 ½ measures	Left-hand pattern falters while right hand plays longer notes of irregular length then interjects chords, Both hands play faster notes in short groups, then end with long notes alone.
B	1:12–1:40	2½ units of 9 = 22 ½ measures	

The percussion motive returns once, followed by the fanfare in the trumpets accompanied by a countermelody in the horns. At this point, we get a taste of Copland's harmonic style. Chord progressions are not standard, but he aims for mainly consonant harmonies, in this case usually perfect consonances. The percussion pattern returns twice. The third time, the fanfare returns in echoes, first in the trombones, then the trumpets and horns. It opens to a new closing phrase in full harmony of a kind typical of Copland—mainly consonant with just a touch of dissonance. A varied version of this last section returns, with more frequent echoes and a fuller texture, then continues on to a new phrase extension that becomes the coda, ending in large, full chords. *Fanfare for the Common Man* is a staple of American concert music and a model example of the Neoclassical style.

A puzzling work, by a puzzling contemporary of Copland, is the Sonata V for Prepared Piano by John Cage (Figure 14.42). Cage composed like no one else. When he decided to compose, he went to UCLA and USC to study for two years with Arnold Schoenberg (one of the great modernists and teachers of early twentieth-century Vienna), who fled the Nazis to the United States. The two men's approaches to composition were diametrically opposite. Schoenberg asserted that harmony was indispensable for writing music. Cage claimed no feeling for it but went on to invent entirely new musical approaches based on timbre, aleatoric techniques, innovative uses of instruments, and electroacoustic music. Between them, Schoenberg and Cage were two of the greatest musical innovators of the twentieth century.

Although Cage had been very active and respected as a composer through the 1930s and '40s, his works for prepared piano were the first products of his genius to attract attention from the startled general public. Cage had developed an interest in percussion ensemble music, but when he and his partner, dancer Merce Cunningham, were to present a dance performance in a hall too small for the ensemble and the dancers, Cage invented the prepared piano. By carefully inserting various objects (screws, bolts, nails, plastic, etc.) between piano strings at specific measured points and placing materials (paper, felt, etc.) over or under the strings, the prepared piano gives every note on the keyboard a different timbre—some completely without pitch—to make a whole percussion ensemble controlled by one player.

Sonata V is one of a group of twenty short pieces for prepared piano. All are in simple binary or ternary forms, but their proportions are determined by mathematical process rather than classical symmetry. This sonata's first section comprises two units of nine, while the second is two and a half such units—a far cry from the two-, four-, and eight-unit sections of the Classic period. Within each section, the phrase length varies, sometimes unpredictably. The A section has a steady pattern of faster notes in the left hand. The right hand plays a pattern of eight notes with a "stumble" three times, then twice more with increasing alterations. The remainder of the section places three long notes of unequal length over the left-hand pattern. Since the piece is binary, the section is repeated. The B section begins with the same left-hand pattern, but under long notes and with pauses. After this, the pattern appears four more times, with interruptions leading to a section where both hands play faster notes, then end with long notes alone, and this section, too, is repeated. The work's innovation makes it clearly Modernist and experimental. The good humor and touch of whimsy may also link it to Surrealism in the visual arts.

In addition to classical concert music, the American musical world developed a rich variety of popular styles and song, going as far back as the early nineteenth century. This movement gained momentum in the twentieth century with the inventions of blues, jazz, and rock styles, to name a few. Several composers have integrated popular and classical styles, from George Gershwin in the 1920s and '30s (*Rhapsody in Blue*) through Gunther Schuller in the 1950s and '60s (*Third-Stream Jazz*), to a variety of later mingled styles. One group from the 1970s that stands out is the trio Emerson, Lake, and Palmer (ELP). Their hallmark was to take a classical work (in some cases one of several movements) and use it as a basis for jazz–rock improvisation. One of their most enduring hits is *Fanfare for the Common Man* (Figure 14.43).

ELP's three members were Keith Emerson (keyboards), Greg Lake (guitar), and Carl Palmer (drums). For the *Fanfare*, they added a four-man trumpet section and Palmer opened on timpani. Their arrangement begins with the unison trumpet motive, followed by the three-note drum motive played by all three band members, with Palmer on timpani; he then improvises a short riff before moving to the drum set, where he sets up a rock beat. Emerson, after trading short riffs with Lake, plays Copland's extended theme on keyboard. The band

FIGURE 14.43 Emerson, Lake & Palmer, *Fanfare for the Common Man* (after Aaron Copland, 1977), trumpets, electric keyboards, electric guitar, timpani, drum set.

The band's performances of this work included improvisation and vary in timing.		
Timings are included for the beginning only, until the band's rock fantasia takes off.		

Timing (approximate)	Instrumentation	Music
0:00–0:35	**Trumpets**	All play Copland's melody (unison) gestures leap up, around, down.
0:35–0:45	**ELP**	Enter on motive of three loud repeated bass notes.
0:45–1:00	**Timpani**	Takes off on improvised riff; drummer (Carl Palmer) moves to drum set.
1:00–1:35	**ELP, especially keyboards**	Led in by drum set rhythm; band starts rock beat, short drum set riff, theme enters on keyboard (Keith Emerson), trades riffs with guitar (Greg Lake), thenplays all of Copland's extended theme.
1:35–2:55	**ELP**	Varied repeat of the section above, with increasing departure from Copland theme.
2:55-End	**ELP, Keyboard lead**	Keyboards take the lead on rock/jazz fantasia until end.

FIGURE 14.44 Terry Riley (b. 1935), *In C* (1964), assorted instruments, evolving form.

Performances of this work vary in speed and length. Recordings vary from 16 to 76, average 44 minutes.	
Notes in motives described as scale degrees (1-8+) of C Major Scale. S=Short, M=Medium, L=Long.	
	Gesture
0	Repeated high C to establish pulse for group—plays throughout.
1	Repeated S note 3 (E) with 1 (C) ornament
2–7	Other notes of C major chord,with added ornamental notes: S 3 + 4, S 3–4–5, L 8 (=1), S 1
8	L 5 + 4
9–10	S 7, 5
11–13	S 4, 5, 7
14	L 8, 7, 5, raised 4
15	S 5
16–17	S 5, 7, 8
18	S 3, raised 4
19	M 12 (=5)
20	S 3, raised 4, 5
21	L raised 4
22–26	S, repeated notes, 4, raised 4, 5, 6, 7
27	S 3, raised 4, 5
28	S 3, raised 4
29	L 3, 5, 8
30	L 8 (=C)
31–32	S 4, 5, 7
33–34	S 4, 5
35	Very Long Phrase—S 4 ,5, 7, lowered 7, L 12, S 13, 12, 14, 10, 12, L raised 11, 10, 11
36–41	S 4, 5, 7, 8
42	L 8, 7, 6, 8
43–44	S 11, 10, 8
45	M 9, 5
46–47	S 11, 10, 8
48	L 5, 4
49–53	S 4, 5, lowered 7

repeats this with increasing departures from Copland's theme until Emerson leads off on a wild rock/jazz fantasia until the end. The work's mixture of styles, including reference to a past masterpiece, makes it musical Postmodernism.

The final musical work to be discussed is very clearly Postmodernist. It is one of the first works composed in the Minimalist style. *In C* by Terry Riley (Figure 14.44), like many minimalist works, can be performed by any number of players for any length of time. In general, Minimalist works have motives that slowly change or evolve so that the sound color gradually changes. They are best appreciated in the same way one looks at a work of Abstract Impressionism—sit back and let the music wash over, letting the instrumental colors and melodic patterns flow as they will. Allow the mind to wander and the details of the work to select themselves. Repeated hearings are always different and may or may not create psychological impressions. *In C* has fifty-three separate motives, most of them short notes, some longer. Performers are to establish a pulse (beat) then play the motives in order as many times as they wish but trying to stay within two or three motives of one another in the order given. The work takes its name from the fact that most of the notes are part of a C Major triad (1, 3, and 5 on the figure). Non-chord tones add dissonance. The first one introduced is 4, then 7, then altered 4, altered 7, and 14 (=6). The gradual addition of dissonant notes at varying speeds is what creates the work's flowing beauty.

Moving from the thoroughly prescribed works of Debussy and Stravinsky to the experimental work of Cage and the evolutionary work of Riley shows the tremendous change in twentieth-century music. It is parallel in some ways to the equally extreme changes in other arts during the same period. They all reflect the history, culture, and lives of the time, as the arts will always continue to do.

Image Credits

Fig. 14.1: Léon Bakst / Copyright in the Public Domain.

Fig. 14.3A: Léon Bakst / Copyright in the Public Domain.

Fig. 14.3B: Daniel de Losques / Copyright in the Public Domain.

Fig. 14.4A: Copyright in the Public Domain.

Fig. 14.4B: Adolph de Meyer / Copyright in the Public Domain.

Fig. 14.4C: Adolph de Meyer / Copyright in the Public Domain.

Fig. 14.5: Wassily Kandinsky / Copyright in the Public Domain.

Fig. 14.6: Wassily Kandinsky / Copyright in the Public Domain.

Fig. 14.7: Henri Rousseau / Copyright in the Public Domain.

Fig. 14.8: Henri Matisse / Copyright in the Public Domain.

Fig. 14.9: Pablo Picasso / Copyright in the Public Domain.

Fig. 14.10: Pablo Picasso / Copyright in the Public Domain.

Fig. 14.11: Pablo Picasso / Copyright in the Public Domain.

Fig. 14.12: Marcel Duchamp / Copyright in the Public Domain.

Fig. 14.13: Copyright © 2009 by JasonParis / Flickr, (CC BY 2.0) at https://commons.wikimedia.org/wiki/
File:Philadelphia,_PA_%283623831113%29.jpg.

Fig. 14.14: Marc Chagall / Copyright in the Public Domain.

Fig. 14.15: Pablo Picasso / Copyright in the Public Domain.

Fig. 14.16: Copyright © 1932 by Pablo Picasso.

Fig. 14.17: Copyright © 1937 by Bundesarchiv, Bild 183-H25224, (CC BY-SA 3.0 DE) at https://commons.
wikimedia.org/wiki/File:Bundesarchiv_Bild_183-H25224,_Guernica,_Ruinen.jpg.

Fig. 14.18: Copyright © 1937 by Pablo Picasso.

Fig. 14.19: Pablo Picasso; Photo copyright © 2004 by J. Crocker. Reprinted with permission.

Fig. 14.20: Piet Mondrian / Copyright in the Public Domain.

Fig. 14.21: Piet Mondrian / Copyright in the Public Domain.

Fig. 14.22: Paul Klee / Copyright in the Public Domain.

Fig. 14.23: Copyright © 1931 by Salvador Dali.

Fig. 14.24: Copyright © 1931 by Georgia O'Keefe.

Fig. 14.25: Grant Wood / Copyright in the Public Domain.

Fig. 14.26: Copyright © 1950 by Jackson Pollock.

Fig. 14.27: Copyright © 1962 by Andy Warhol.

Fig. 14.28: Copyright © 1961 by Bridget Riley.

Fig. 14.29: Copyright © by Claes Oldenburg and Coosje van Bruggen.

Fig. 14.30: Copyright © 1982 by Ralph Goings.

Fig. 14.31: Copyright © 1996 by Audrey Flack; Photo by University of North Dakota Art Collections.

Fig. 14.32: Copyright © 2016 by Art West.

Fig. 14.33: Robert Smithson; Photo copyright © 2005 by Soren Harward, (CC BY-SA 2.0) at http://
en.wikipedia.org/wiki/File:Spiral-jetty-from-rozel-point.png.

Fig. 14.34A: Christo and Jeanne-Claude; Photo copyright © 2005 by Morris Pearl, (CC BY-SA 3.0) at
http://en.wikipedia.org/wiki/File:The_Gates.jpg.

CPSIA information can be obtained
at www.ICGtesting.com
Printed in the USA
LVHW01s2112210817
545834LV00004B/59/P

9 781516 511099